Ordnance Survey

STREET ATLAS
Oxfordshire

Contents

III *Key to map symbols*
IV *Key to map pages*
VI *Administrative and post code boundaries*
1 *Street maps*
261 *Index of street names*

GW00640669

PHILIP'S

First edition published 1992
Fourth edition published 1994
First colour edition published 1998
Reprinted 1999 by

Ordnance Survey® and George Philip Ltd, a division of
Romsey Road   Octopus Publishing Group Ltd
Maybush   2-4 Heron Quays
Southampton   London
SO16 4GU   E14 4JP

ISBN 0-540-07512-4 (hardback)
ISBN 0-540-07513-2 (spiral)

To the best of the Publishers' knowledge, the information in this atlas was
correct at the time of going to press. No responsibility can be accepted
for any errors or their consequences.

The representation in this atlas of a road, track or path is no evidence
of the existence of a right of way.

**The mapping between pages 1 and 260 (inclusive) in this atlas is
derived from Ordnance Survey® OSCAR® and Land-Line® data,
and Landranger® mapping.**

Ordnance Survey, OSCAR, Land-Line and Landranger are registered trade
marks of Ordnance Survey, the national mapping agency of Great Britain.

Printed and bound in Spain by Cayfosa

Digital Data

The exceptionally high-quality mapping
found in this book is available as digital
data in TIFF format, which is easily
convertible to other bit-mapped (raster)
image formats.

The index is also available in digital form
as a standard database table. It contains
all the details found in the printed index
together with the National Grid reference
for the map square in which each entry
is named and feature codes for places
of interest in eight categories such as
education and health.

For further information and to discuss
your requirements, please contact
Philip's on 0171 531 8440 or
george.philip@philips-maps.co.uk

Motorway (with junction number)

Primary route (dual carriageway and single)

A road (dual carriageway and single)

B road (dual carriageway and single)

Minor road (dual carriageway and single)

Other minor road

Road under construction

Pedestrianised area

Railway

Tramway, miniature railway

Rural track, private road or narrow road in urban area

Gate or obstruction to traffic (restrictions may not apply at all times or to all vehicles)

Path, bridleway, byway open to all traffic, road used as a public path

The representation in this atlas of a road, track or path is no evidence of the existence of a right of way

179

Adjoining page indicators

106

Acad	**Academy**	Mon	**Monument**
Cemy	**Cemetery**	Mus	**Museum**
C Ctr	**Civic Centre**	Obsy	**Observatory**
CH	**Club House**	Pal	**Royal Palace**
Coll	**College**	PH	**Public House**
Ent	**Enterprise**	Recn Gd	**Recreation Ground**
Ex H	**Exhibition Hall**	Resr	**Reservoir**
Ind Est	**Industrial Estate**	Ret Pk	**Retail Park**
Inst	**Institute**	Sch	**School**
Ct	**Law Court**	Sh Ctr	**Shopping Centre**
L Ctr	**Leisure Centre**	Sta	**Station**
LC	**Level Crossing**	TH	**Town Hall/House**
Liby	**Library**	Trad Est	**Trading Estate**
Mkt	**Market**	Univ	**University**
Meml	**Memorial**	YH	**Youth Hostel**

■ The dark grey border on the inside edge of some pages indicates that the mapping does not continue onto the adjacent page

■ The small numbers around the edges of the maps identify the 1 kilometre National Grid lines

British Rail station

Underground station

D **Docklands Light Railway station**

Private railway station

Bus, coach station

Ambulance station

Coastguard station

Fire station

Police station

Accident and Emergency entrance to hospital

H **Hospital**

+ **Church, place of worship**

i **Information centre** (open all year)

P **Parking**

PO **Post Office**

Sch **Important buildings, schools, colleges, universities and hospitals**

County and unitary authority boundaries

River Medway **Water name**

Stream

River or canal (minor and major)

Water

Tidal water

Woods

Houses

House **Non-Roman antiquity**

VILLA **Roman antiquity**

The scale of the maps is 5.52 cm to 1 km
(3½ inches to 1 mile)

0		¼		½		¾		1 mile
0	250m		500m		750m	1 kilometre		

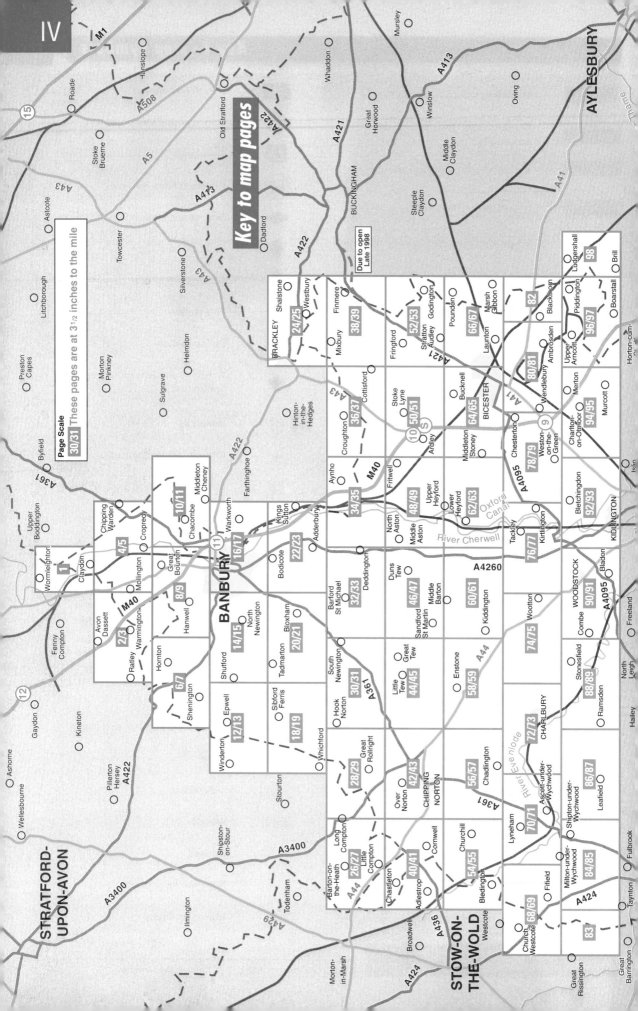

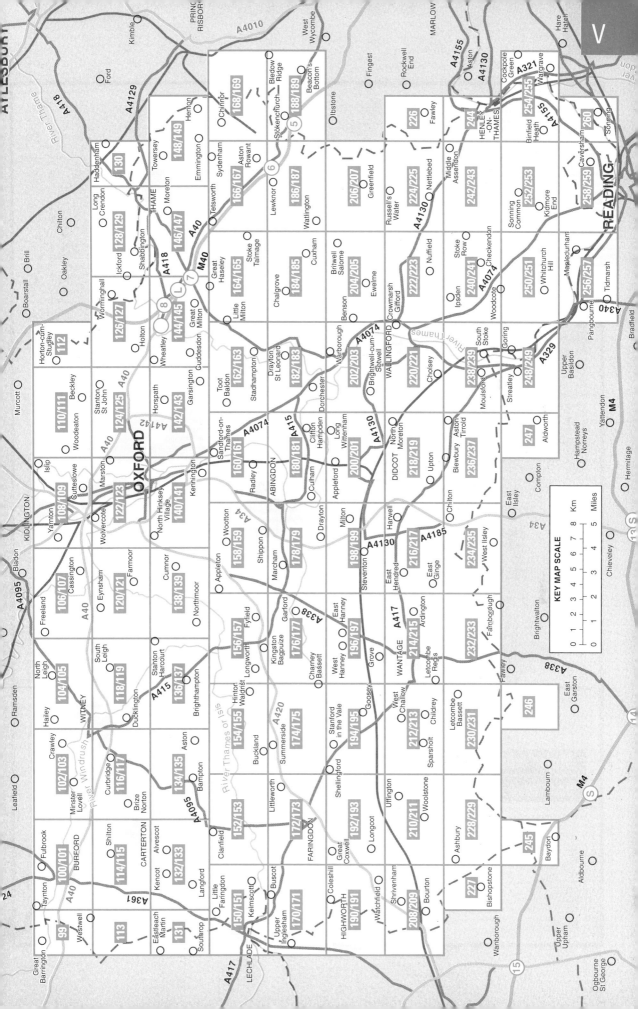

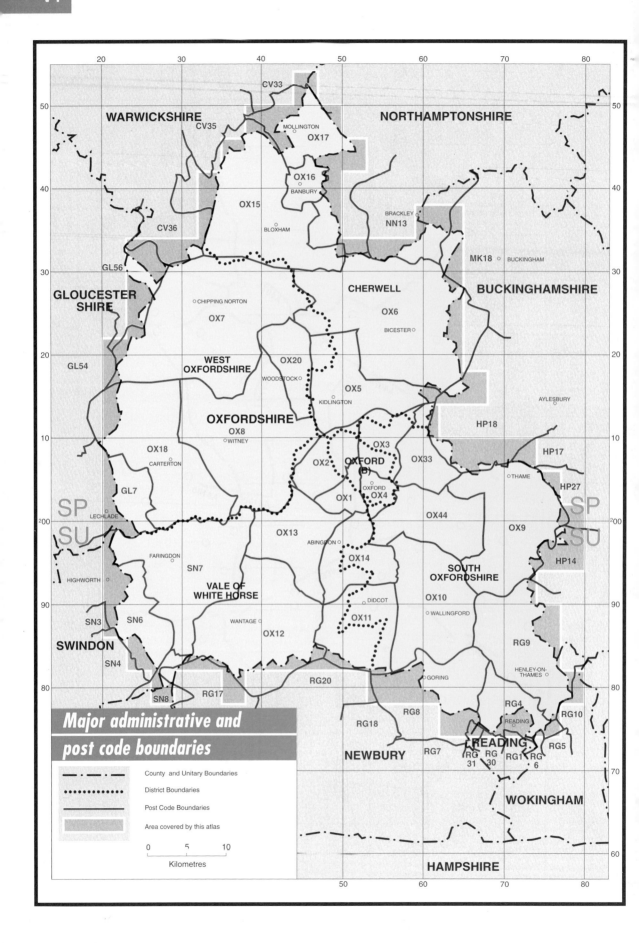

WARWICKSHIRE

CV33

CV35

MOLLINGTON

OX17

NORTHAMPTONSHIRE

OX16
BANBURY

OX15

BRACKLEY
NN13

CV36

BLOXHAM

GL56

MK18   BUCKINGHAM

GLOUCESTER
SHIRE

CHIPPING NORTON

CHERWELL

BUCKINGHAMSHIRE

OX7

OX6

BICESTER

GL54

WEST
OXFORDSHIRE

OX20

WOODSTOCK

HP18

AYLESBURY

OX5
KIDLINGTON

HP17

OXFORDSHIRE
OX8
WITNEY

OX3

THAME

OX18
CARTERTON

OX2

OXFORD
(B)
OXFORD

OX33

HP27

GL7

OX4

OX1

HP14

SP
SU

LECHLADE

OX44

OX9

SP
SU

OX13

ABINGDON

SOUTH
OXFORDSHIRE

FARINGDON

SN7

OX14

HP14

HIGHWORTH

VALE OF
WHITE HORSE

DIDCOT

OX10

WALLINGFORD

SN3   SN6

WANTAGE

OX12

OX11

RG9

SWINDON

HENLEY-ON-
THAMES

SN4

GORING

RG4

RG10

SN8

RG17

RG20

READING

RG5

RG8

READING

NEWBURY

RG18

RG7

RG
31

RG
30

RG1

RG
6

WOKINGHAM

HAMPSHIRE

Major administrative and post code boundaries

–·–·–·–·–	County and Unitary Boundaries
••••••••••	District Boundaries
————	Post Code Boundaries
▨	Area covered by this atlas

0   5   10
Kilometres

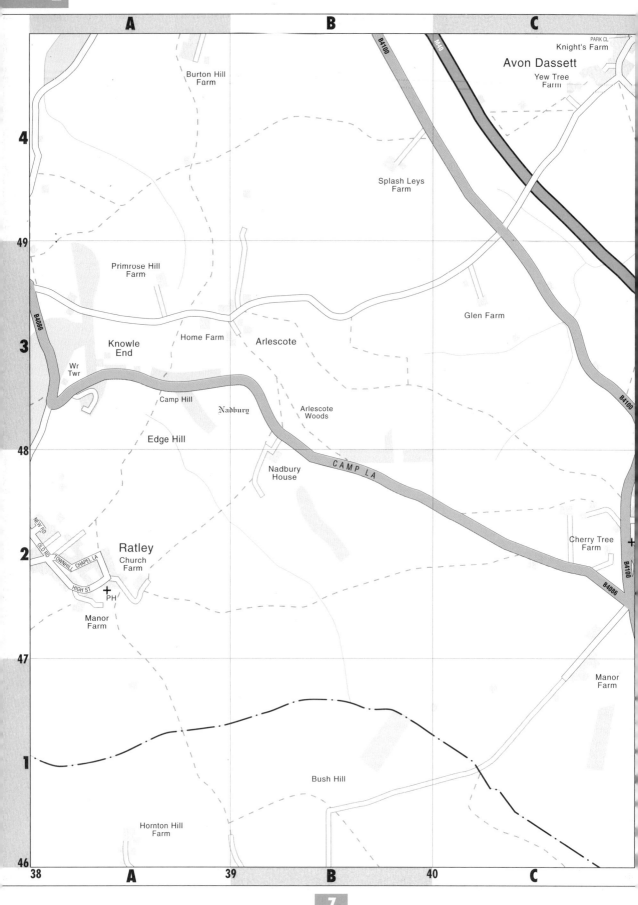

A   **B**   **C**

Knight's Farm

PARK CL

Avon Dassett

Yew Tree
Farm

Burton Hill
Farm

4

Splash Leys
Farm

49

Primrose Hill
Farm

Glen Farm

3

Knowle
End

Home Farm

Arlescote

Wr
Twr

Camp Hill

Nadbury

Arlescote
Woods

Edge Hill

48

Nadbury
House

CAMP LA

NEW RD

OLD RD

TOWNHILL

CHAPEL LA

Ratley

Church
Farm

Cherry Tree
Farm

2

HIGH ST

PH

B4086

Manor
Farm

47

Manor
Farm

1

Bush Hill

Hornton Hill
Farm

46

38   **A**   39   **B**   40   **C**

A **B** **C**

Farnborough Hill Farm

Claydon Crossing

Manor Farm

MANOR PARK

BIGNOLDS CL

Filter Bed

Claydon Locks

Farnborough Hill

4

Lawn Hill

Firs Farm

Priory (remains of)

49

Clattercote

Oxford Canal

Towing Path

3

A423

Clattercote Reservoir

Oathill Farm

Cropredy Lawn

Lambert's Barn

48

Beecham's Cottages

ROUNDHILL RD

SOUTHAM RD

Mollington

2

ROUNDHILL RD

BLACKSMITHS LA

CHURCH
CHURCH LA

THE HOLLOWAY

IVY LA

MAIN ST

CHESTNUT RD

ORCHARD PIECE

Manor Farm

Mill Farm

OXHEY HILL

CLAYDON RD

Cropredy Hill

Oxhay Farm

Cemy

47

CREAMPOT CRES

KYETTS CNR

CREAMPOT LA

ORCHARD VIEW

HIGH ST

RED LION ST

ORCHARD LA

CUP AND SAUCER PH

Cropredy

VICARAGE GDNS

THE PLANTATION

1

STATION RD

Oxford Canal

River Cherwell

Thickthorn Farm

A423

Sch

46

44   **A**   45   **B**   46   **C**

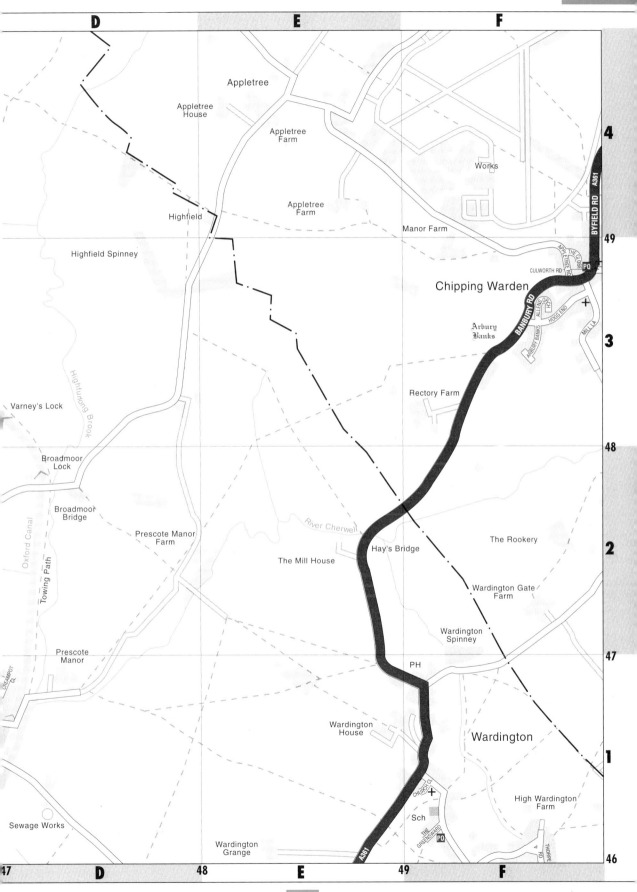

Appletree

Appletree
House

Appletree
Farm

Appletree
Farm

Highfield

Highfield Spinney

Manor Farm

Works

BYFIELD RD
A361

49

CULWORTH RD

Chipping Warden

Arbury
Banks

BANBURY RD

THE CLOSE
APPLETREE RD
PO

ALLENS
SCH
HOGG END

ARBURY BANKS

MILL LA

+

3

Rectory Farm

48

Varney's Lock

Broadmoor
Lock

Broadmoor
Bridge

Prescote Manor
Farm

Highfurlong Brook

River Cherwell

The Mill House

Hay's Bridge

The Rookery

2

Oxford Canal

Towing Path

Wardington Gate
Farm

Wardington
Spinney

47

Prescote
Manor

CREAMPOT LA

PH

Wardington
House

Wardington

1

Sewage Works

Wardington
Grange

A361

CHURCH CL

Sch

+

THE GREENSWARD
PO

High Wardington
Farm

THORPE RD

46

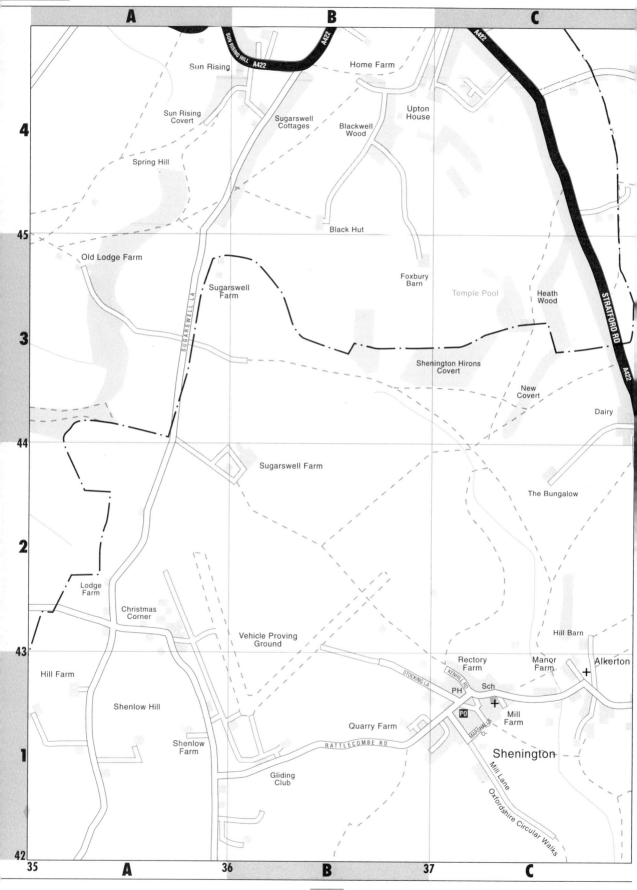

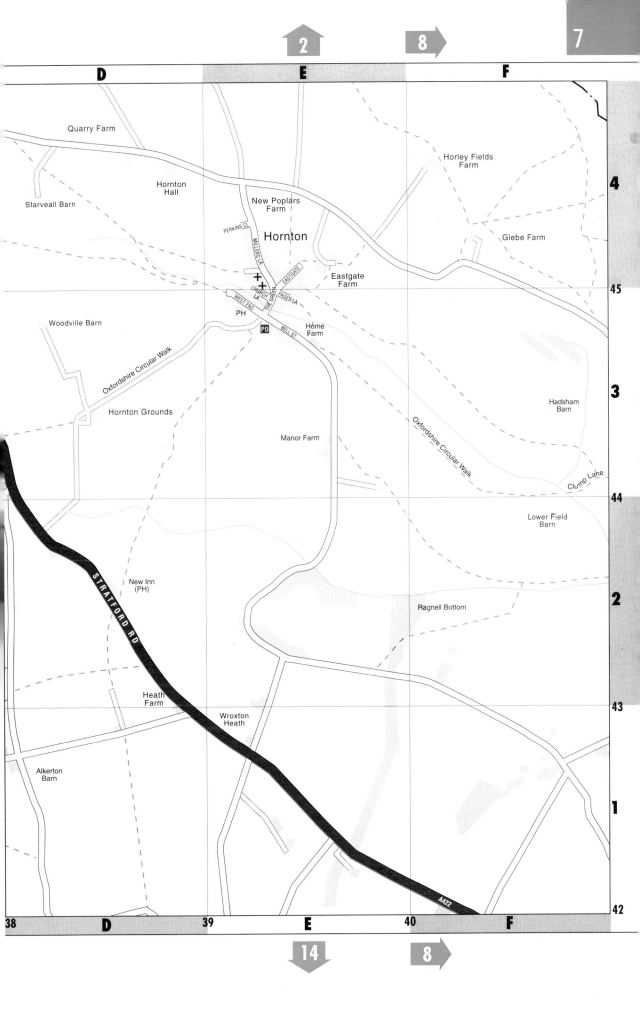

A **B** **C**

B4100

4

Slated Barn

Slade Barn

Laurel Farm

MOLLINGTON RD

SNUFF LA

NEW RD

MIDDLE LA

BAGHOUSE LA

Bury Court Farm

✝

Shotteswell

M40

45

Sor Brook

3

Hadsham House Manor Farm

Horley House

Clump Lane

Water Tower

44

MANOR ORCH

✝

PH

LANE CL

PO

GULLIVER'S CL

Bramhill Park Farm

Horley

Hanwell

SPRINGFIELD

HANWELL CT

MAIN ST

PARK CL

CHURCH LA

✝

Hanwell Castle

SACKVILLE CL

GULLICOTE LA

Park Farm

2

WARWICK RD

43

Oxfordshire Circular Walk

Cemy

Drayton Lodge

1

Lord's Spinney

HORLEY PATH RD

Golf Course

B4100

HARDWICK PARK

PYE CL

CHELSEA CL

BARCOMBE CL

HIGHLANDS

CHEVIOT WAY

HORSHAM CL

SUSSEX PL

ROMNEY RD

42

QUEEN S CRES.

A422

41 **A** 42 **B** 43 **C**

D E F

A423

Great
Bourton

Bourton
House

STANWELL
RD
CHURCH CL
SWAN LA
VALLEY VIEW
MANOR RD
THE GREEN
Hillside
House

PH

SCHOOL LA
CROW LA

THE
CLOSE

SOUTH VIEW

Little Mill
Crossing
LC

Bourtonfields
Farm

Mill Lane

Cemy

Slack Barn

Littlegood
Farm

4

45

M40

Little
Bourton

3

Old Manor
Farm

SPRING LA
BUZZARDS CL
PH
Park
Farm

CHAPEL LA

UPLAND
RISE

Little Bourton
House

44

Lock

2

SOUTHAM RD

Hardwick Hill
House

River Cherwell

Towing Path

Oxford Canal

Cemy

Hardwick
Hill

Hardwick
Gorse

Hardwick
Farm

43

1 GUERNSEY WAY
2 JERSEY DR
3 KERRY CL
4 AYRSHIRE CL
5 TROIKA CL
6 DURHAM MEWS
7 MONIQUE CT
8 BETTINA CRES
9 CHICHESTER WLK
10 AMBERLEY CT

Hardwick
Lock

Works

1 ACACIA WLK
2 AZALEA WLK
3 FORSYTHIA WLK
4 FUCHSIA WLK
5 THE WISTERIA
6 JAPONICA WLK
7 HYDRANGEA WLK

Hanwell
Fields

SYRINGA WLK

Hardwick

HEREFORD
FRENSHAM CL
DALE AVE
PASCALI
STARINA
CROFT
REGINA
CONIFER
THE CAMEL
THE MAGNOLIAS
HIGHLANDS

SALVIA
ERICA CL
HARLEQUIN
JUNIPER
THE RISE

HIGHLANDS
WAY
ALFRISTON PL
GLYNDEBOURNE GDNS
BANESBERIE CL
SUSSEX DR
FERRITON
FORGEWAY
LAVENDER CL
HEARTHWAY

BEAUMONT CL
BEAUMONT RD
PENLWAY

Beaumont
Ind Est

Reservoir

WILDMERE RD
ACORN WAY
DAVENTRY RD

Ind
Est

M40

1

42

A423

A B C

Lower Lodge

Williamscot
House

Williamscot
Village Spinney

A361

Mount Pleasant

Bennetts Farm

Trent Farm

CHELMSCOT ROW

Barn Farm

Upper Wardington

THORPE RD

4

Weir

Oxford Canal

Peewit Farm

Dawkins's Barn

45

Bell Land

WARDINGTON RD

River Cherwell

Williamscot Hill Farm

3

Coton Farm

Bridge Lake Fisheries

WILLIAMSCOT HILL

Redlunch Barn

Marsh Barn Farm

Works

Chacombe

SILVER ST NORTH

SILVER ST

BEAUFF BLDG

POPLARS RD

BENNETTS CL

Sch

44

The Priory

CHURCH LA

PH

WESLEY

THORPE RD

BANBURY RD

THE SWAN

PO

THORNHILL

MIDDLETON RD

BANBURY RD

2

Chacombe House

Golf Course

CH

43

Castle Farm

Huscote Farm

1

Seale's Farm

Yew Tree Cottage

BANBURY LA

CHENEY GDNS

STILE

STILE GDNS

CHACOMBE RD

HIGH ST

GLOVERS LA

CHURCH LA

RECTORY LA

M40

A361

Stanwell Lea 1
Stanwell Dr 2

Windmill Farm

42

B4525

47 A 48 B 49 C

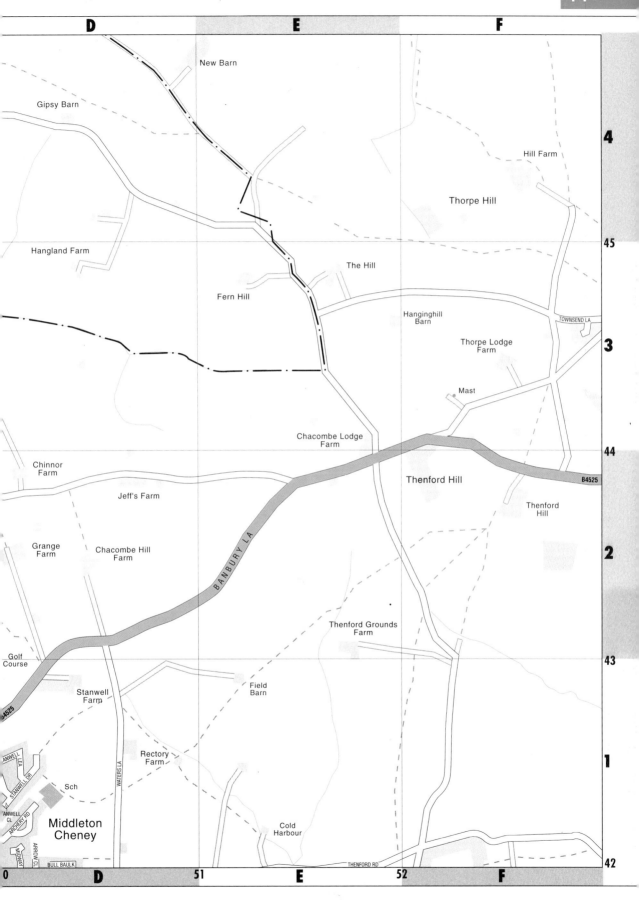

D

E

F

New Barn

Gipsy Barn

Hill Farm

4

Thorpe Hill

45

Hangland Farm

The Hill

Fern Hill

Hanginghill
Barn

TOWNSEND LA

Thorpe Lodge
Farm

3

Mast

Chacombe Lodge
Farm

44

Chinnor
Farm

Thenford Hill

B4525

Jeff's Farm

Thenford
Hill

Grange
Farm

Chacombe Hill
Farm

2

BANBURY LA

Thenford Grounds
Farm

Golf
Course

43

Stanwell
Farm

Field
Barn

B4525

STANWELL LEA

STANWELL DR

WATERS LA

Rectory
Farm

ARCHERY RD

1

STANWELL
CL

Sch

STANWELL RD

**Middleton
Cheney**

MIDWAY

ARROW CL

BULL BAULK

Cold
Harbour

THENFORD RD

42

0

D

51

E

52

F

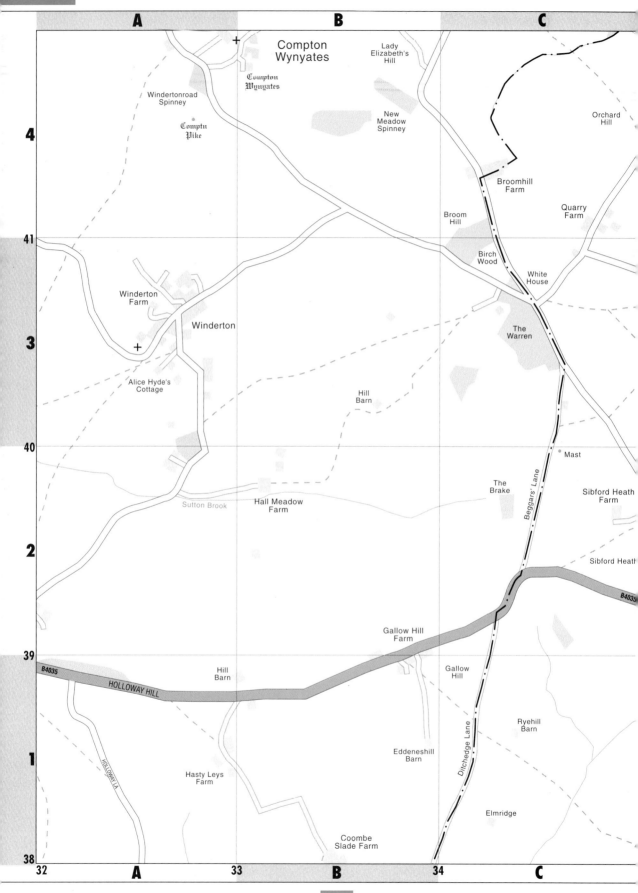

Compton Wynyates

Windertonroad Spinney

Comptn Pike

Compton Wynyates

Lady Elizabeth's Hill

New Meadow Spinney

Orchard Hill

Broomhill Farm

Broom Hill

Quarry Farm

Birch Wood

White House

Winderton Farm

Winderton

The Warren

Alice Hyde's Cottage

Hill Barn

Mast

The Brake

Sibford Heath Farm

Beggars' Lane

Sutton Brook

Hall Meadow Farm

Sibford Heath

B4035

Gallow Hill Farm

B4035

Holloway Hill

Hill Barn

Gallow Hill

Ryehill Barn

Ditchedge Lane

Holloway La

Hasty Leys Farm

Eddeneshill Barn

Elmridge

Coombe Slade Farm

A   B   C

Rough Hill

Rough Hill Farm

OC Walks

Epwell Hill

Yarn Hill Farm

Field Barn

4

Lower Barn

Epwell Grounds Farm

Rectory Farm

Yarn Hill

41

Shutford Grounds Farm

Epwell

BIRDS LA

Long Hill

EPWELL RD

3

THE CLOSE

+ PO

THATCHERS CL

Epwell Mill

Cranes Farm

PH

Gage Farm

Slatters Barn

Cemy

Bottle Barn

Woodington Spinney

40

Heath Plantation

Woodington Barn

Chillaway Barn

Barton Hill

Farmington Farm

Heathnell Spinney

2

Lake Spinney

SIBFORD RD

Blenheim Farm

39

Handywater Farm

Redland Barn

POUND LA

Brakelands Farm

1

Tyne Hill

HIGH MEADOW

BACKSIDE LA

Tyne Hill Farm

B4035

38

A   B   C

Oxfordshire Circular Walk

Ash Farm
PH

Balscote

MIDDLE LA

Priory Farm

Manor House

A422
STRATFORD RD
A42

Guide Post

4

Alkerton Hill Farm

41

Sewage Works

Maidenhill Cottage

Padsdon Bottom

Castle Bank Enclosure

Shutford

Balscote Mill

PLOT RD

PO

THE PLAIN RD

LOWER END

Beggars' Barn

Wroxton Mill

Tythe Farm

Claydonhill Covert

Claydo Hill

3

COOK'S HILL

THE DAIRYGROUND

MALTHOUSE LA

WEST ST

WEAVERS ROW

BANBURY RD

Five Ways

Cemy

EPWELL RD

SIBFORD RD

HIGH ST

PH

Manor House

Claydon Hill Bungalow

SHUTFORD RD

40

Barton Hill Farm

Shutford Bridge

Welshcroft Hill

Round Hill

Jester's Barn

Broughton Grounds Farm

2

Jester's Hill

Langley Hill

Madmarston Hill

39

Castle Brow

Upper Lea Farm

Sandfine Wood

SANDFINE RD

SHUTFORD RD

1

Swalcliffe Mill

Fulling Mill Farm

Swalcliffe Lea

GREEN LA

Preedys Farm

38

38   A   39   B   40   C

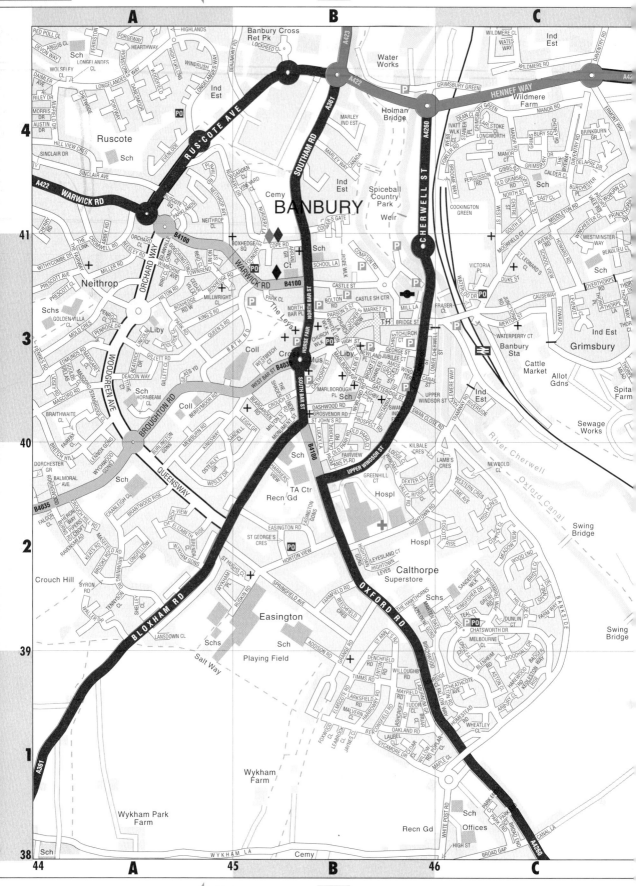

D E F

M40

A361

11

A422

Overthorpe Hall (Sch)

BANBURY LA

B4525

BULL BAULK

CHURCH LA

TENLANDS

QUEEN ST

HIGH ST

SWAN CL

Sch
Liby

PO

MANSION HILL

MAIN RD

BARNETT RD

THE MOORS DR

A422

BLACKLOCKS HILL

Brinsall

Nethercote

WARKWORTH RD

Allot Gdns

4

MIDDLETON RD

The Willows

Home Farm

41

Industrial Estate

ERMONT WAY

CATTERBURY CL

LOMBARD WAY

WALTHAM GDNS

Overthorpe

Longacre

THORPE DR

OVERTHORPE RD

The Bowling Green (PH)

Warkworth Farm

ASTROP RD

THORPE CL

Warkworth House

3

Warkworth

THORPE MEAD

Home Farm

Sewage Works

Grove Lodge

40

Warkworth Hall Farm

Blackpits Farm

2

Farthinghoe Stream

39

Towing Path

River Cherwell

Swing Bridge

1

Oxford Canal

Grant's Lock

Sutton Lodge Farm

38

47 D 48 E 49 F

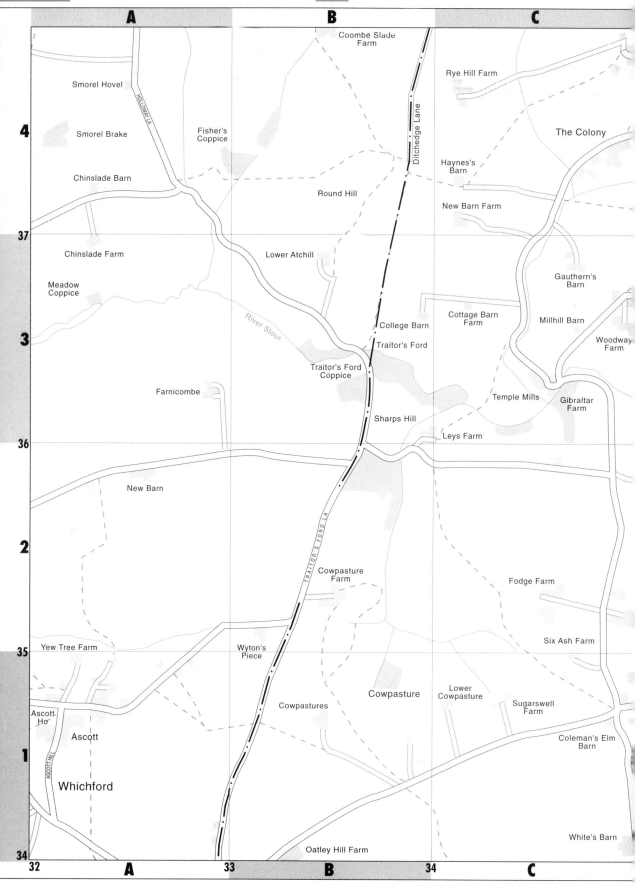

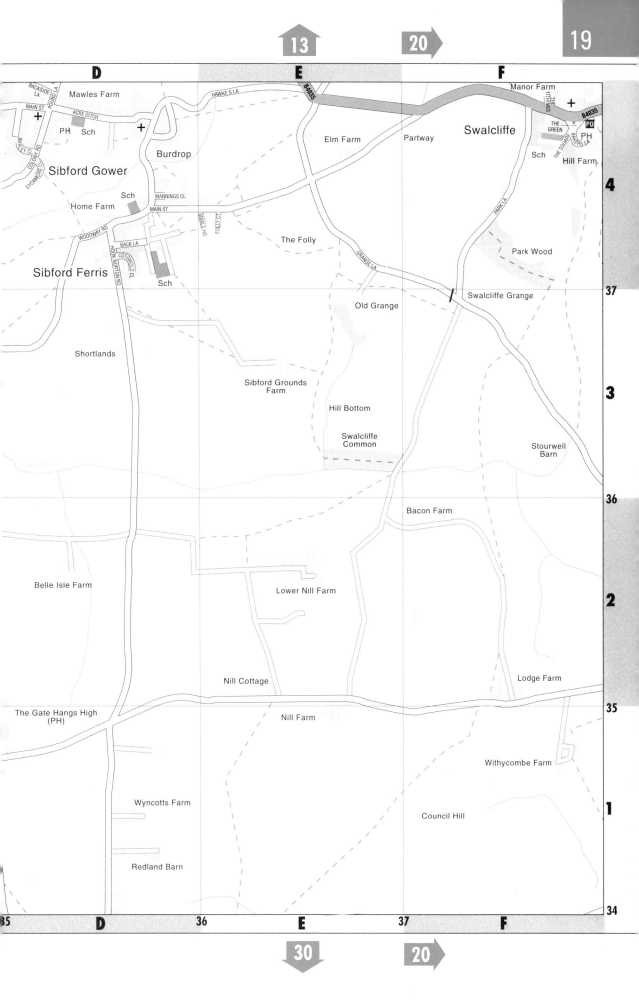

D

E

F

Mawles Farm

BACKSIDE LA

POUND LA

MAIN ST

ACRE DITCH

HAWKE S LA

B4035

PH

Sch

BAILEY CL

COTLOW RD

SYCAMORE CL

Sibford Gower

Burdrop

Elm Farm

Partway

Swalcliffe

Manor Farm

THE TITHINGS

THE GREEN

THE SQUARE

B4035

PO

BAKERS LA

PH

Sch

Hill Farm

4

Sch

MANNINGS CL

Home Farm

MAIN ST

SWALLI HO

FOLLY CT

The Folly

Park Wood

PARK LA

Woodway RD

BACK LA

HOOK NORTON RD

COTSWOLD CL

Sibford Ferris

Sch

GRANGE LA

Swalcliffe Grange

37

Old Grange

Shortlands

Sibford Grounds
Farm

Hill Bottom

3

Swalcliffe
Common

Stourwell
Barn

36

Bacon Farm

Belle Isle Farm

Lower Nill Farm

2

Lodge Farm

Nill Cottage

The Gate Hangs High
(PH)

35

Nill Farm

Withycombe Farm

Wyncotts Farm

Council Hill

1

Redland Barn

34

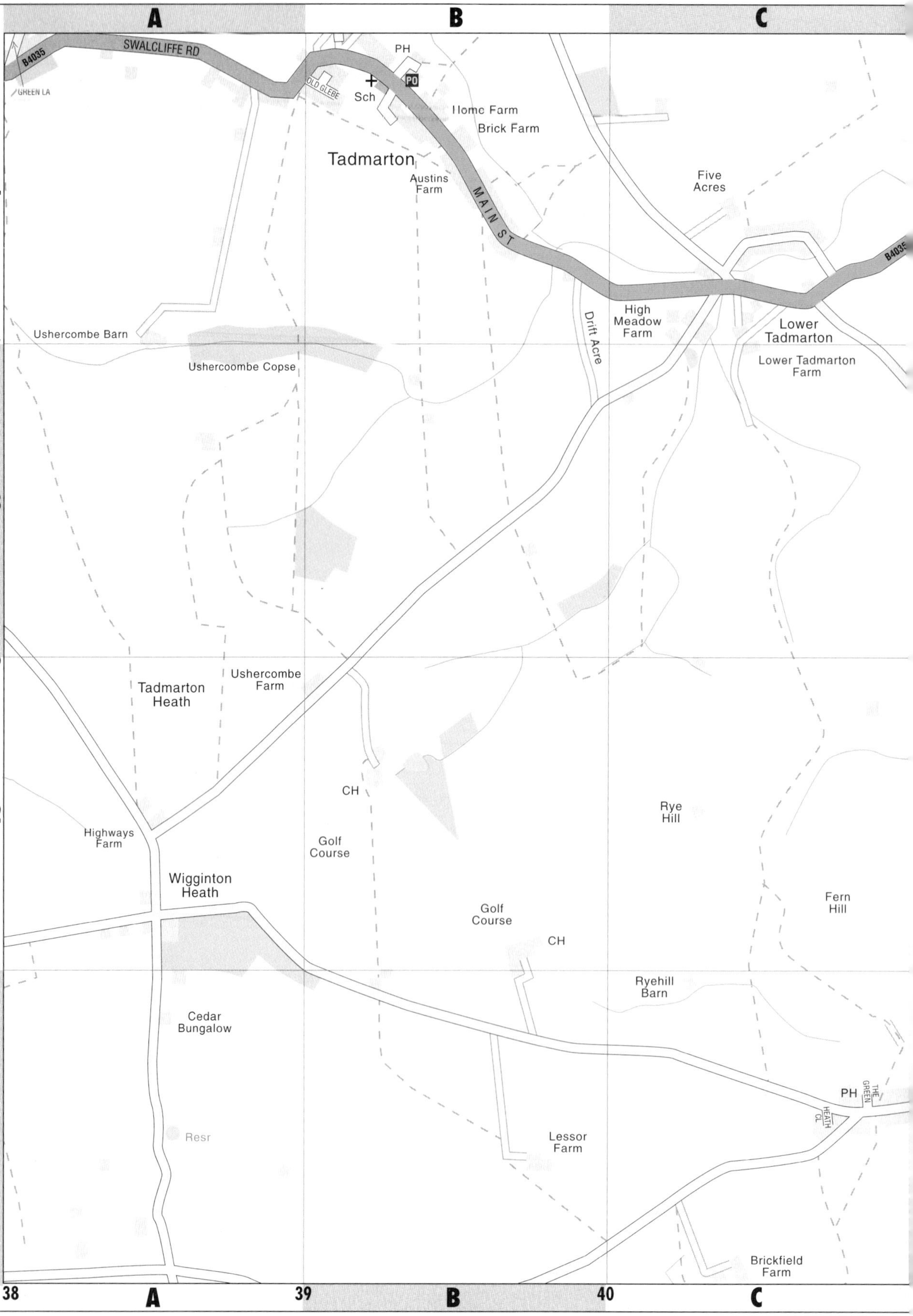

A

B

C

B4035
SWALCLIFFE RD
GREEN LA

PH

PO

OLD GLEBE

Sch

Home Farm

Brick Farm

Tadmarton

Austins
Farm

Five
Acres

M A I N S T

B4035

Ushercombe Barn

Drift Acre

High
Meadow
Farm

**Lower
Tadmarton**

37

Ushercoombe Copse

Lower Tadmarton
Farm

3

36

Ushercombe
Farm

Tadmarton
Heath

CH

Rye
Hill

2

Highways
Farm

Golf
Course

Wigginton
Heath

Golf
Course

CH

Fern
Hill

35

CH

Ryehill
Barn

Cedar
Bungalow

PH

THE
GREEN

HEATH
CL

1

Resr

Lessor
Farm

34

38

A

39

B

40

C

Brickfield
Farm

4

D   E   F

B4035

Broughton
Grange

Wykham Mill
Farm

BLOXHAM RD A361

Sch

Castle
Farm

Wykham
Mill

4

Sor Brook

Chaddle Barn
Farm

Tadmarton
Lodge

Nayland
Farm

Ell's
Farm

ELL'S LA

37

BANBURY RD

BLOXHAM GROVE RD

Tadmarton House Farm
(Industrial Estate)

Hobb
Hill

Sch

Playing
Field

Firs Hill
Farm

Woollen
Hale

CHIPPERFIE

PALMINN CL

LAWRENCE LEYS

BUTLER

OAK HO

SCHOFIELD WAY

GREENS
GARTH

3

TADMARTON RD

Firs Hill

Playing
Fields

GAUNTLETS
CL

STRAW
BERRY
HILL

STRAWBERRY
TERR

Park Farm

Bloxham

THE POUND

BRICKLE LA

WATER LA

Sch

BARLEY CL

Sch

COURTINGTON LA

The
Gogs

LITTLE BRIDGE RD

STONE
HILL

ROSE BANK

HIGH ST

HUMBER

A HOGG END

CHAPEL ST

THE RIDGE

36

THE AVENUE

HORNTON
HOLLOW

PAINT

FROG LA

LITTLE

UNICORN

BRIDGE RD

STEEPLE
CL

Yew Tree
Piggeries

WINTERS WAY

QUARRY CL

CUMBERFORD CL

GREEN HAWK

KINGS RD

GREEN

CHURCH ST

PH

MERRIVALE'S
LA

Sewage
Works

2

BROOKSIDE WAY

CHERRY'S
CL

GREENHILLS PARK

MALTINGS

QUEENS ST

GOOSE
WLK

Coates's Spinney

HYDE GR

COLESBOURNE
GR

WESTBOURNE
CL

ORCHARD
GR

LUDFORD
GDNS

MILTON RD

35

Milcombe
Hall

BLOXHAM RD

Factory

FERNHILL
CL

PO

PARADISE LA

HOR LA

CHURCH LA

MANNING
CL

GASCOIGNE WAY

MAULE
CL

BARFORD RD

Milcombe

PORT
LAND RD

Brompton
Farm

Happy Valley
Farm

Mast

BARU LOW

LONG

Wireless
Station

1

Hollie's
Barn

SOUTH NEWINGTON RD

Mast

Mast

A361

34

A

B

C

Sch

Cemy

PADDOCK FARM LA
PH
MALTHOUSE LA

RYDES CL

THE RYDES

Cottage Farm

OXFORD RD

A4260

GOSSE LA

HIGH ST

CHAPEL LA

WEEPING CROSS

EAST ST

WALTON CL

PH

ROOKERY CL

WISE CL

Bodicote

DEERS CL

RED HOUSE

BLACKWO

SIDELEIGH RD

LOWER CL

CHURCH ST

PO

4

FREEMANS RD

AUSTIN RD

MOLYNEUX DR

KEYSER RD

WARDS CRES

TOWN FURLONG

SEFTON PL

Cotefield
House

DEER'S FARM

Bodicote Mill
House

Water Works

Lower Grove
Mill

Upper Grove
Mill

37

Old Barn Farm

BLOXHAM GROVE RD

Bloxham
Grove

Sor Brook

Windmill

3

Wayhouse Farm

36

Brickhouse
Farm

2

MANOR RD

CROSS HILL RD

NEW RD

PO

Adderbury
Park

DOG CL

ROUND CLOSE RD

HORN HILL RD

PH

Recn G

West Adderbury

TANNERS LA

THE LEYS

Manor Farm

Works

Milton

Church Farm

CHAPEL LA

PH

BERRY HILL RD

NORRIS CL

ST MARY'S CL

35

MILTON RD

1

Mast

Wyatt's Barn

OXFORD RD

Airfield
(disused)

Wireless Station

A4260

Mast

34

44

A

45

B

46

C

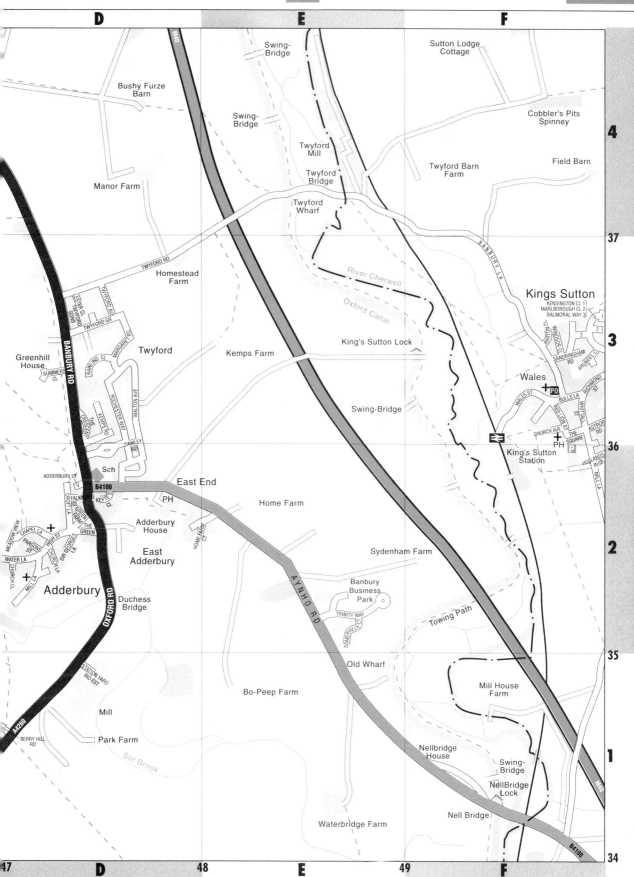

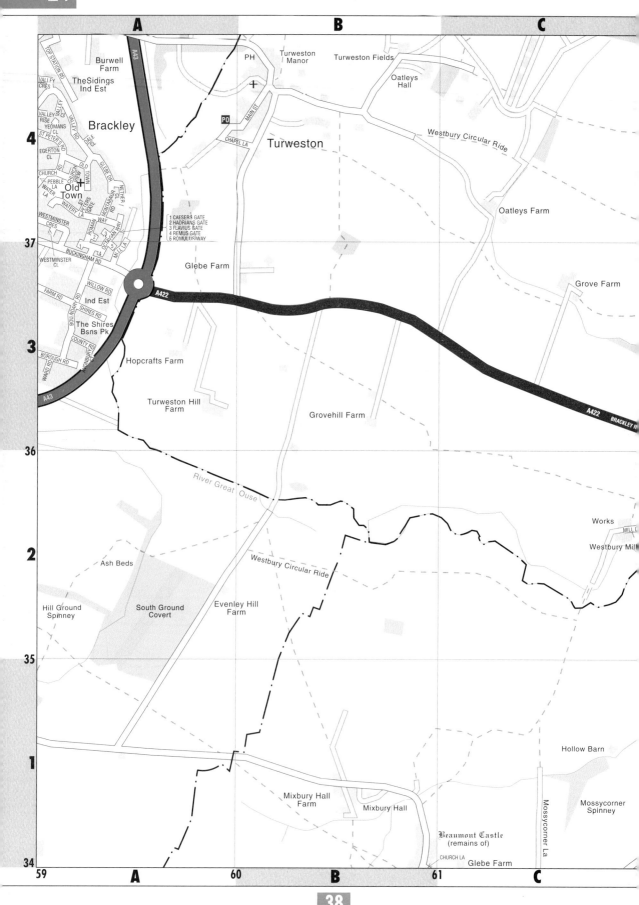

Burwell Farm
TheSidings Ind Est

VALLEY CRES
VALLEY RISE
YEOMANS CL
ST PETERS RD
EGERTON CL
LITTLE
VALLEY RD

Brackley

TOP STATION RD

CHURCH
PEBBLE
WATER LA

Old Town

WESTMINSTER CRES
WESTMINSTER CL
FARM RD
BOUNDARY RD
BOROUGH RD
WARD RD
COUNTY RD

Ind Est
WILLOW RD
SHIRES RD
The Shires Bsns Pk

OLD TOWN
GLEBE DR
NETHER
MONTAGU
OCTAVIAN WAY
ROMAN WAY
M W LA

1 CAESERS GATE
2 HADRIANS GATE
3 FLAVIUS GATE
4 REMUS GATE
5 ROMULUS WAY

PO
CHAPEL LA
MAIN ST
PH
Turweston Manor
Turweston Fields
Oatleys Hall

Turweston

Westbury Circular Ride

Oatleys Farm

Glebe Farm

Grove Farm

A43
A422
A422 BRACKLEY R

Hopcrafts Farm

Turweston Hill Farm

Grovehill Farm

River Great Ouse

Ash Beds

Hill Ground Spinney

South Ground Covert

Evenley Hill Farm

Westbury Circular Ride

Works
Westbury Mill
MILL L

Hollow Barn

Mixbury Hall Farm

Mixbury Hall

Beaumont Castle
(remains of)

CHURCH LA

Glebe Farm

Mossycorner La

Mossycorner Spinney

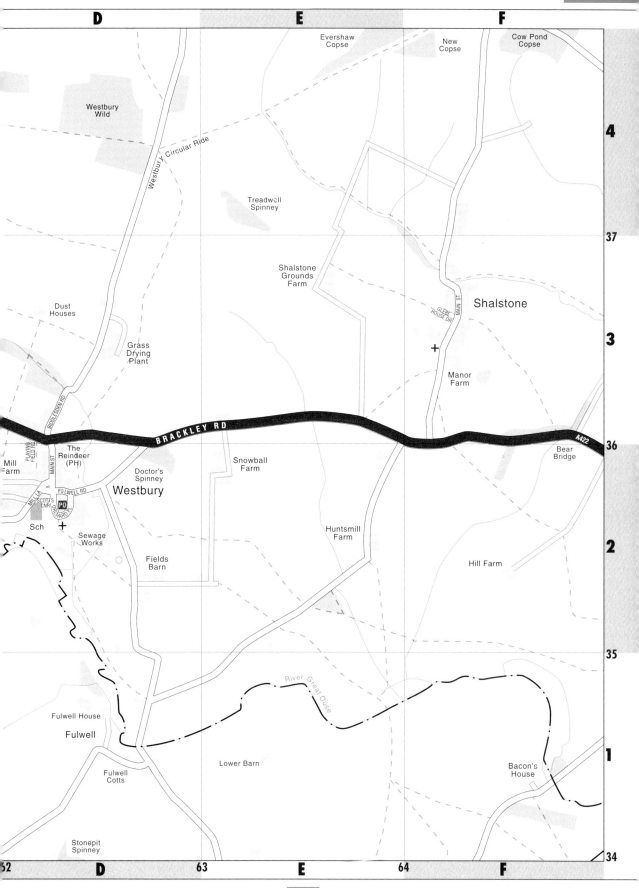

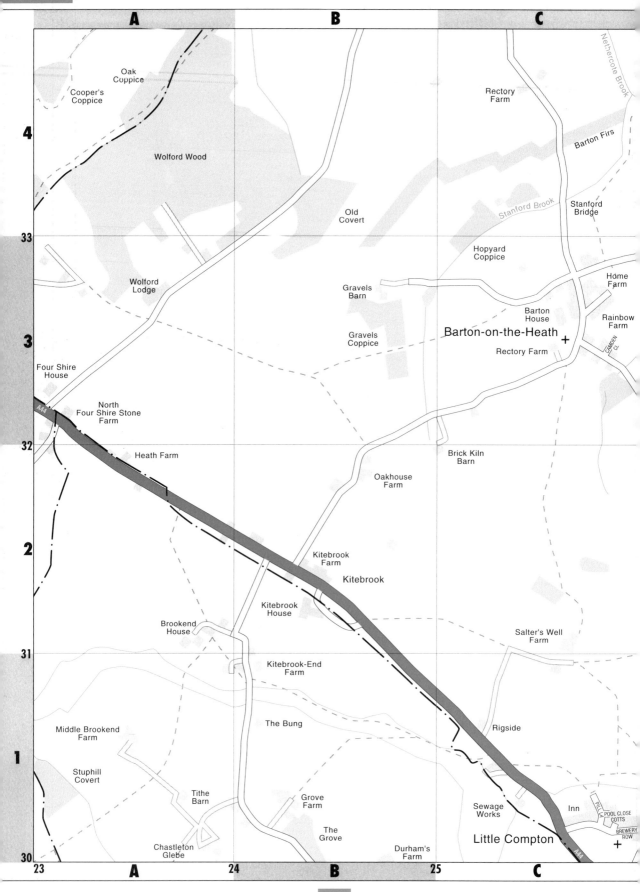

Oak
Coppice

Cooper's
Coppice

Wolford Wood

Rectory
Farm

Barton Firs

Nethercole Brook

Old
Covert

Stanford Brook

Stanford
Bridge

Hopyard
Coppice

Home
Farm

Gravels
Barn

Barton
House

Barton-on-the-Heath

Rainbow
Farm

Wolford
Lodge

Gravels
Coppice

Rectory Farm

CAMDEN CL.

Four Shire
House

A44

North
Four Shire Stone
Farm

Heath Farm

Brick Kiln
Barn

Oakhouse
Farm

Kitebrook
Farm

Kitebrook

Salter's Well
Farm

Kitebrook
House

Brookend
House

Kitebrook-End
Farm

Middle Brookend
Farm

The Bung

Rigside

Stuphill
Covert

Tithe
Barn

Grove
Farm

Sewage
Works

Inn

PILL CL.
POOL CLOSE
COTTS

BREWERY
ROW

Chastleton
Glebe

The
Grove

Durham's
Farm

Little Compton

A44

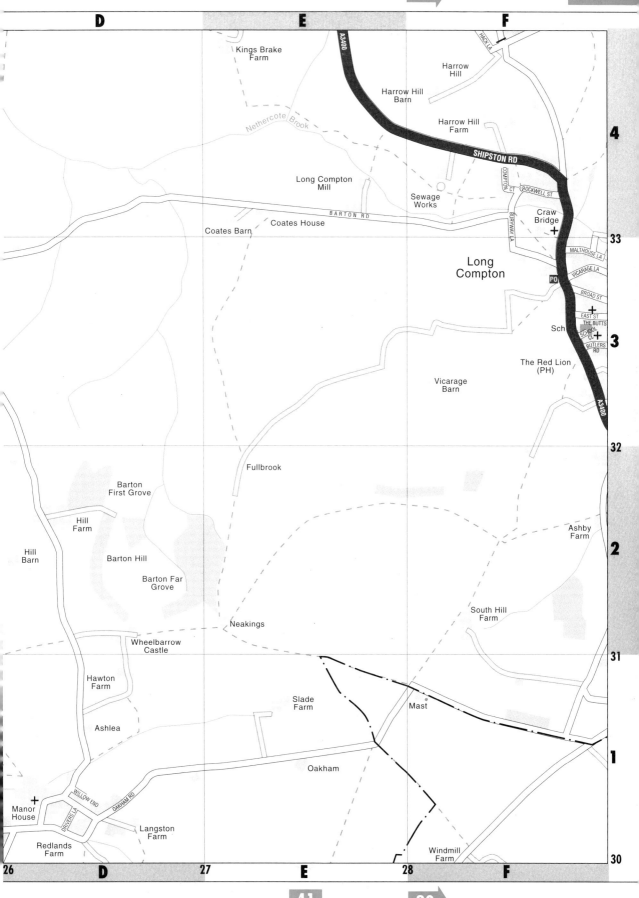

D   E   F

Kings Brake Farm

Harrow Hill

Harrow Hill Barn

Nethercote Brook

Harrow Hill Farm

SHIPSTON RD

A3400

HACK LA

4

Long Compton Mill

Sewage Works

COMPTON CT

CROCKWELL ST

Craw Bridge

BARTON RD

Coates House

Coates Barn

BURYWAY LA

33

Long Compton

MALTHOUSE LA

VICARAGE LA

PO

BROAD ST

EAST ST

THE BUTTS

SCHOOL CL

BUTLERS RD

Sch

3

Vicarage Barn

The Red Lion (PH)

A3400

32

Fullbrook

Barton First Grove

Hill Farm

Ashby Farm

2

Hill Barn

Barton Hill

Barton Far Grove

Neakings

South Hill Farm

Wheelbarrow Castle

31

Hawton Farm

Slade Farm

Mast

Ashlea

Oakham

1

Manor House

WILLOW END

DRIVERS LA

OAKHAM RD

Langston Farm

Redlands Farm

Windmill Farm

30

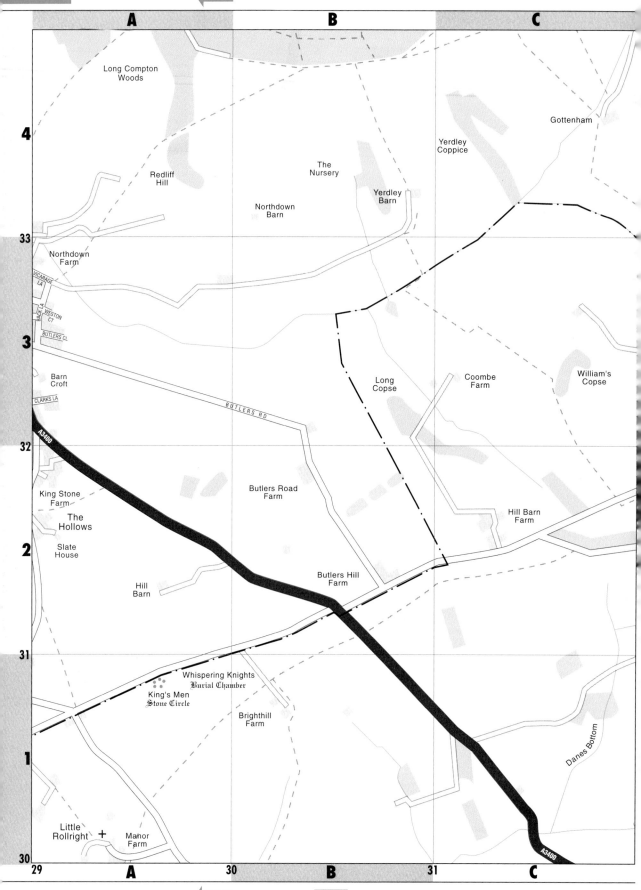

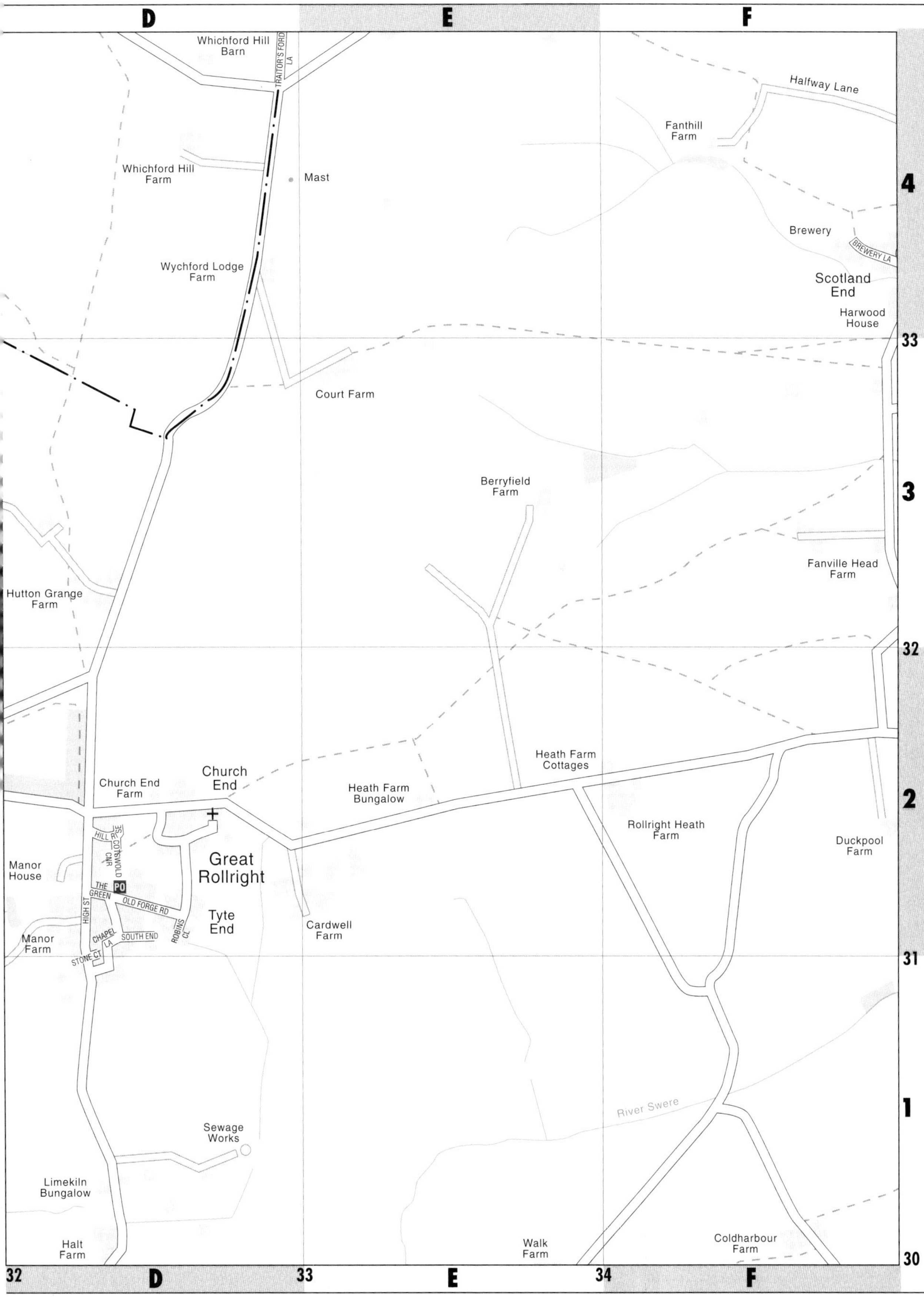

D
E
F

Whichford Hill Barn

TRAITOR'S FORD LA

Halfway Lane

Fanthill Farm

Whichford Hill Farm

Mast

4

Brewery

BREWERY LA

Wychford Lodge Farm

Scotland End

Harwood House

33

Court Farm

Berryfield Farm

3

Fanville Head Farm

Hutton Grange Farm

32

Heath Farm Cottages

Church End Farm

Church End

Heath Farm Bungalow

2

Manor House

HILL RD
COTSWOLD CNR

Great Rollright

Rollright Heath Farm

Duckpool Farm

THE GREEN
PO
OLD FORGE RD

Tyte End

Manor Farm

HIGH ST
CHAPEL LA
SOUTH END
ROBBINS CT

Cardwell Farm

STONE CT

31

Sewage Works

River Swere

1

Limekiln Bungalow

Halt Farm

Walk Farm

Coldharbour Farm

30

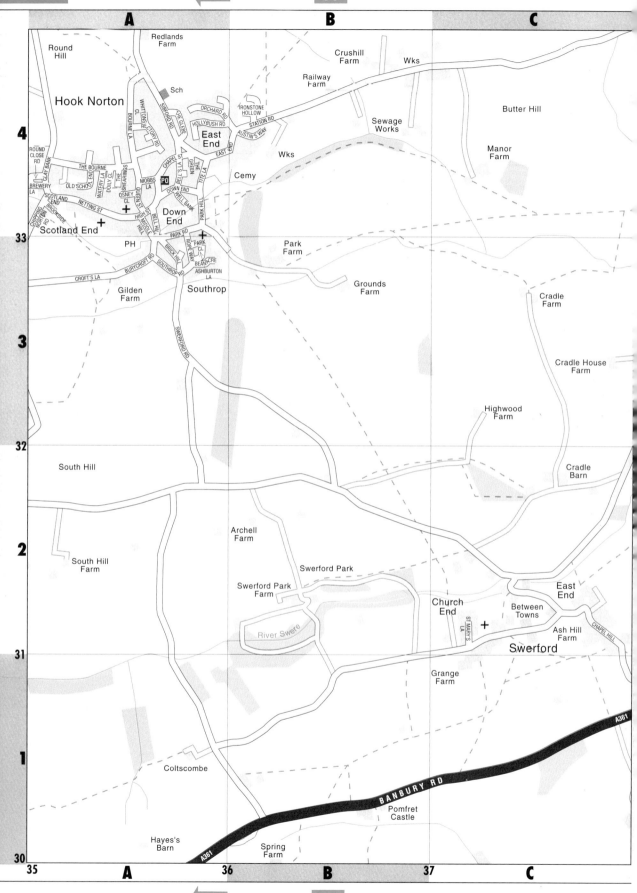

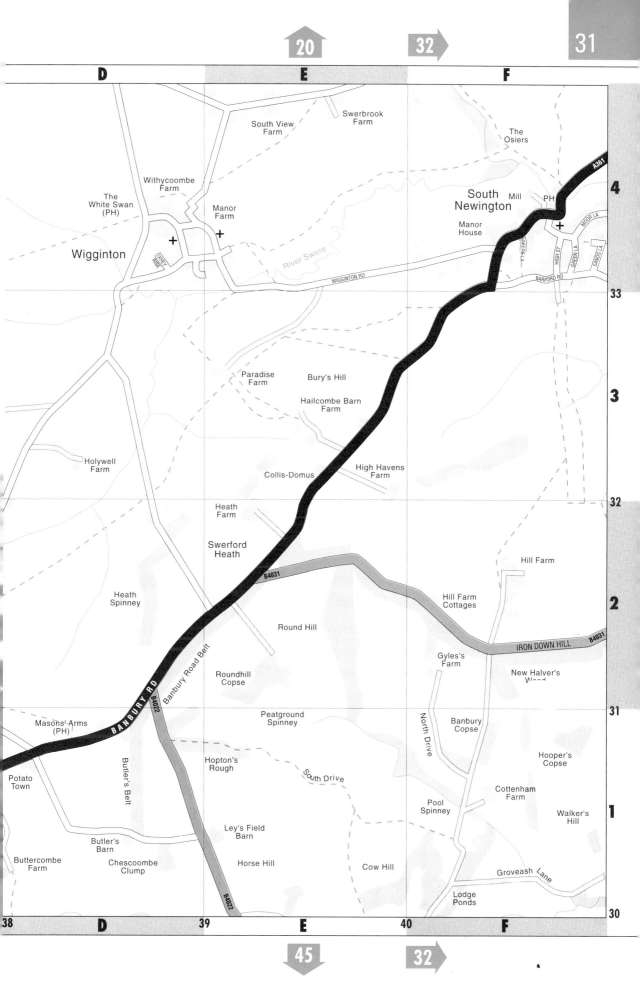

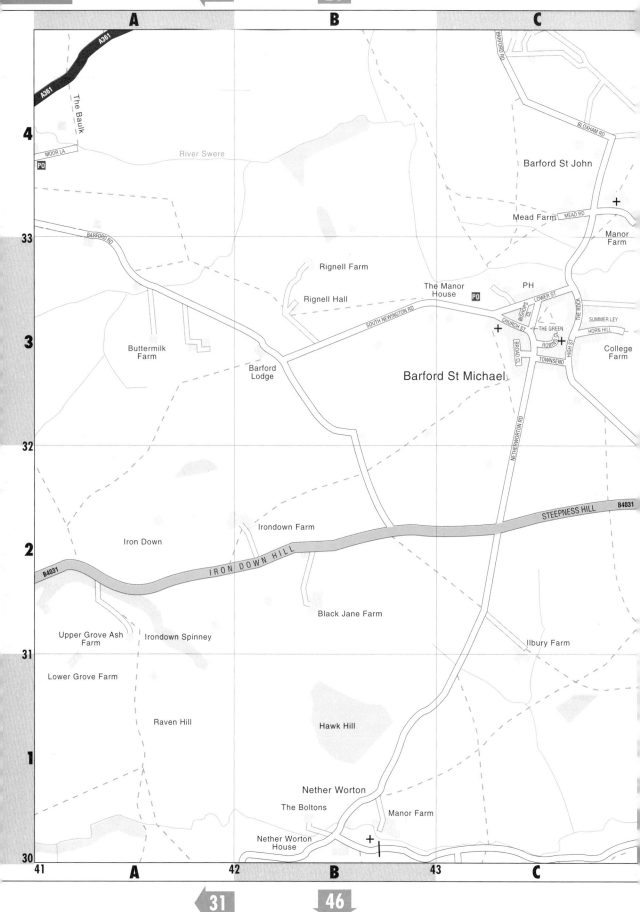

A B C

4

The Baulk

A361

A361

MOOR LA

PO

River Swere

Barford St John

BARFORD RD

BLOXHAM RD

Mead Farm   MEAD RD

Manor Farm

33

BARFORD RD

Rignell Farm

Rignell Hall

The Manor House   PO

PH

LOWER ST

SOUTH NEWINGTON RD

CHURCH ST

BISHOPS CL

THE GREEN

SUMMER LEY

HORN HILL

THE ROCK

3

Buttermilk Farm

Barford Lodge

Barford St Michael

BROAD CL

ROBINS CL

HIGH ST

TOWNSEND

College Farm

32

NETHERWORTON RD

STEEPNESS HILL   B4031

2

Iron Down

Irondown Farm

Black Jane Farm

Ilbury Farm

IRON DOWN HILL

B4031

B4031

Upper Grove Ash Farm

Irondown Spinney

31

Lower Grove Farm

Raven Hill

Hawk Hill

1

Nether Worton

The Boltons

Manor Farm

Nether Worton House

30

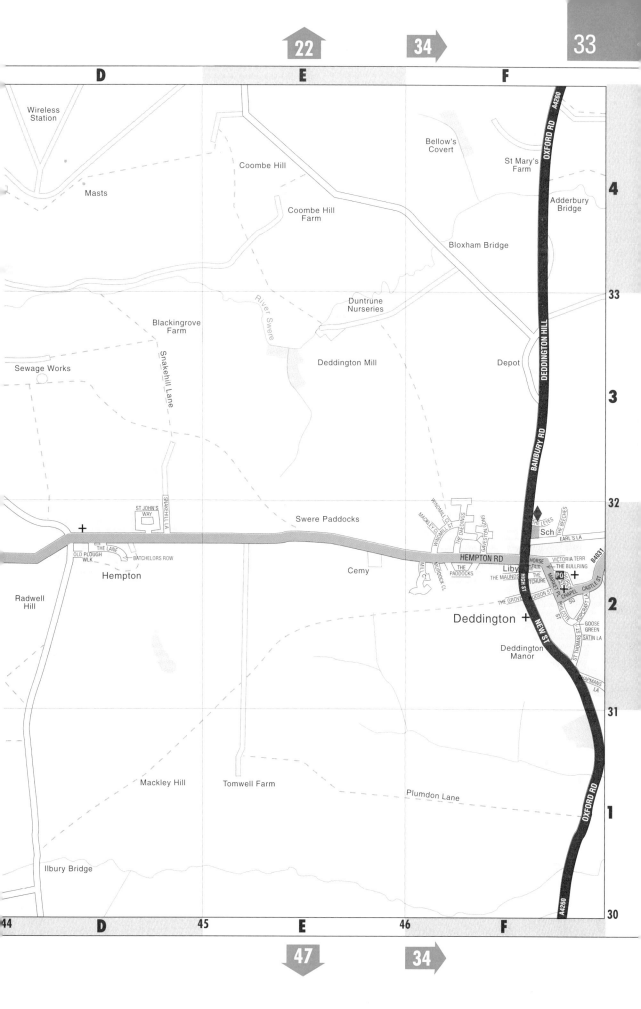

D
E
F

Wireless
Station

Coombe Hill

Bellow's
Covert

St Mary's
Farm

OXFORD RD A4260

Masts

Coombe Hill
Farm

Adderbury
Bridge

4

Bloxham Bridge

DEDDINGTON HILL

33

Blackingrove
Farm

River Swere

Duntrune
Nurseries

Sewage Works

Snakehill Lane

Deddington Mill

Depot

BANBURY RD

3

ST JOHN'S
WAY

THE LEYES
THE BEECHES

32

SNAKEHILL LA

Sch

WINDMILL CL ST

THE DADDINGS

MACKLEY CL

GAVESTON GDNS

EARL'S LA

Swere Paddocks

B4031

THE LANE

OLD PLOUGH
WLK

BATCHELORS ROW

THE
PADDOCKS

HEMPTON RD

Liby

HORSE
FAIR

THE BULLRING

VICTORIA TERR

HIGH ST

Hempton

MILL CL

MURDOCK CL

Cemy

THE MAUNDS

THE
THATCHURE

MARKET PL

CHAPEL
SQ

PO

CASTLE ST

2

Radwell
Hill

THE GROVE

HUDSON ST

BULLCOTE

Deddington

NEW ST

ST THOMAS ST

HORCROFT LA

GOOSE
GREEN

SATIN LA

Deddington
Manor

CHAPMANS
LA

31

Mackley Hill

Tomwell Farm

Plumdon Lane

OXFORD RD

1

Ilbury Bridge

A4260

30

44
D
45
E
46
F

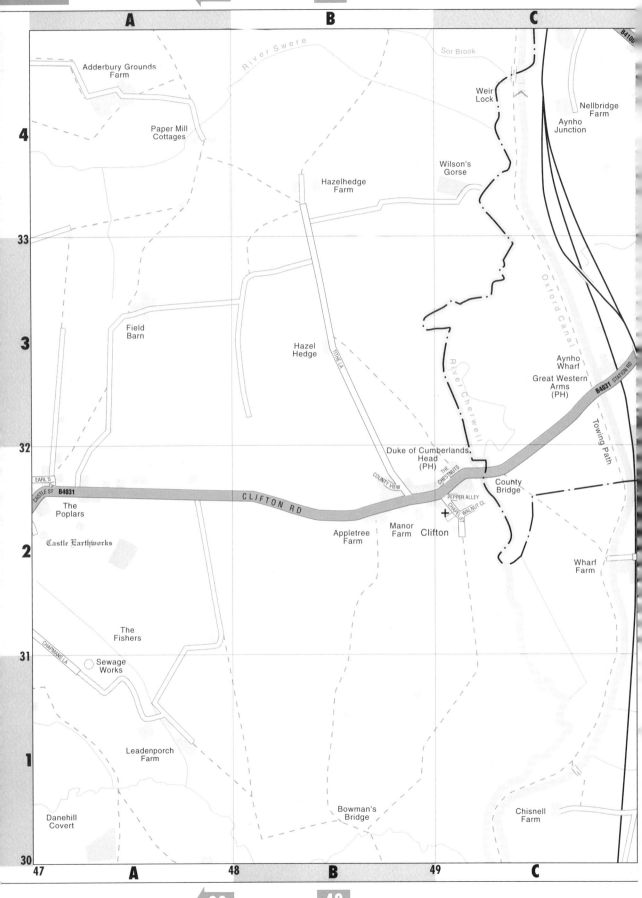

Adderbury Grounds Farm

River Swere

Sor Brook

Weir Lock

Nellbridge Farm

Aynho Junction

4

Paper Mill Cottages

Wilson's Gorse

Hazelhedge Farm

B4100

33

Oxford Canal

3

Field Barn

Hazel Hedge

TITHE LA

River Cherwell

Aynho Wharf

Great Western Arms (PH)

B4031 STATION RD

32

Duke of Cumberlands Head (PH)

Towing Path

EARL'S

CASTLE ST

B4031

COUNTY VIEW

THE CHESTNUTS

County Bridge

CLIFTON RD

The Poplars

PEPPER ALLEY

CHAPEL ST

WALNUT CL.

2

Castle Earthworks

Appletree Farm

Manor Farm

Clifton

Wharf Farm

The Fishers

31

CHAPMANS LA

Sewage Works

1

Leadenporch Farm

Danehill Covert

Bowman's Bridge

Chisnell Farm

30

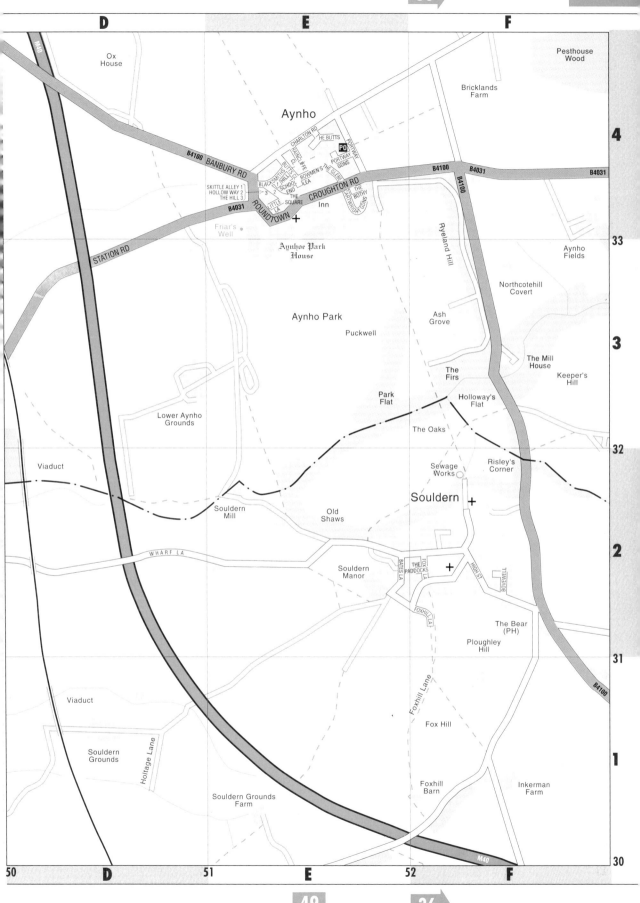

Pesthouse
Wood

Bricklands
Farm

Ox
House

Aynho

4

CHARLTON RD
HE BUTTS
PO
PORTWAY
GDNS
PRINCE FE
BUTTS CL
BLACKSMITHS
HILL CL
SCHOOL
BOWMEN'S
THE GLEBE
LEA
THE
CARTWISCK
CARTWISCK
THE
BOTHY

B4100 BANBURY RD
B4100
B4031
B4031

SKITTLE ALLEY 1
HOLLOW WAY 2
THE HILL 3
3
END
THE
SQUARE
LITTLE
LA
CROUGHTON RD
Inn

ROUNDTOWN
B4031
B4100

+

Friar's
Well

33

Aynhoe Park
House

Ryeland Hill

Aynho
Fields

Northcotehill
Covert

Aynho Park

Ash
Grove

The Mill
House

Keeper's
Hill

3

Puckwell

The Firs

Park
Flat

Holloway's
Flat

Lower Aynho
Grounds

The Oaks

32

Viaduct

Sewage
Works

Risley's
Corner

Souldern

+

Souldern
Mill

Old
Shaws

2

WHARF LA

Souldern
Manor

BATES LA
THE
PADDOCKS
FOX LA
+

HIGH ST
BOVEWELL

Viaduct

FOXHILL LA

The Bear
(PH)

Ploughley
Hill

31

B4100

Souldern
Grounds

Holtage Lane

Foxhill Lane

Fox Hill

1

Souldern Grounds
Farm

Foxhill
Barn

Inkerman
Farm

M40

30

Croughton

Warren Farm

Home Farm

Cemy

BRACKLEY RD

The Moors

WHEELER'S RISE

Blackbird (PH)

Sch

HIGH ST

PO

CHAPEL END

CHURCH END

CHURCH LA

YEW TREE RISE

PARK END

B403

BLENHEIM

B4031

The Green

MILL LA

Ford

PORTWAY CRES

PORTWAY

PORTWAY DR

Old Down Covert

Old Down Pond

Sewage Works

Park Farm

SIXTH ST

FIFTH AVE

Schs

FIFTH ST

BLANKSDALE AVE

FIFTH ST E

FOURTH AVE

FOURTH ST

THIRD ST

SECOND ST

ST ANDREWS AVE

FIRST ST

Padbury's Bottom

Smanhill Covert

New Buildings

Masts

Middle Covert

Upper Aynho Grounds

Crook's Firs

Ockley Brook

Pimlico Farm

Thriftwood House

Tower Farm

B4100

Horwell Corner

Round Hill

Roundhill Farm

Lower Rookery

A43

Horwell Farm

Wr Twr

Oxford Lodge

Park Farm

Hermitage Belt

Sharmans Pit

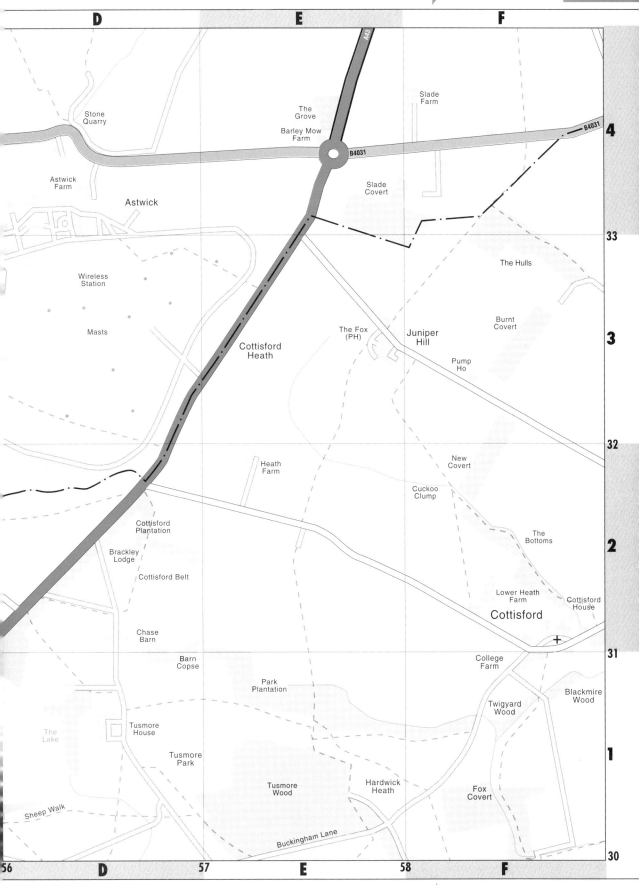

D   E   F

Stone
Quarry

A43

The
Grove

Slade
Farm

Barley Mow
Farm

B4031

B4031   4

Astwick
Farm

Astwick

Slade
Covert

33

Wireless
Station

The Hulls

Masts

Cottisford
Heath

The Fox
(PH)

Juniper
Hill

Burnt
Covert

Pump
Ho

3

32

Heath
Farm

New
Covert

Cuckoo
Clump

Cottisford
Plantation

Brackley
Lodge

Cottisford Belt

The
Bottoms

2

Lower Heath
Farm

Cottisford
House

Chase
Barn

Cottisford

Barn
Copse

College
Farm

31

Park
Plantation

Twigyard
Wood

Blackmire
Wood

The
Lake

Tusmore
House

Tusmore
Park

1

Sheep Walk

Tusmore
Wood

Hardwick
Heath

Fox
Covert

Buckingham Lane

30

A   **B**   **C**

Barrow Hill

Mixbury

CHURCH LA

The Bowling Green

Mixbury Lodge Farm

B4031

4

Monk's House

Monk's House Barn

B4031

Mixbury Plantation

Middle Farm

The Pits

3

FEATHERBED LA

Park Thorns

Diggings Wood

32

Coldharbour Farm

2

Shelswell Plantation

Cottisford Pond

Pondhead

Wr Twr

LAKE VIEW →

HETHE RD

The View

31

The Belt

Shelswell Park

Home Farm

Spilsmere Wood

Windmill Hook

The Cut

Shelswell

Hethe Spinney

1

30

59   **A**   **60**   **B**   **61**   **C**

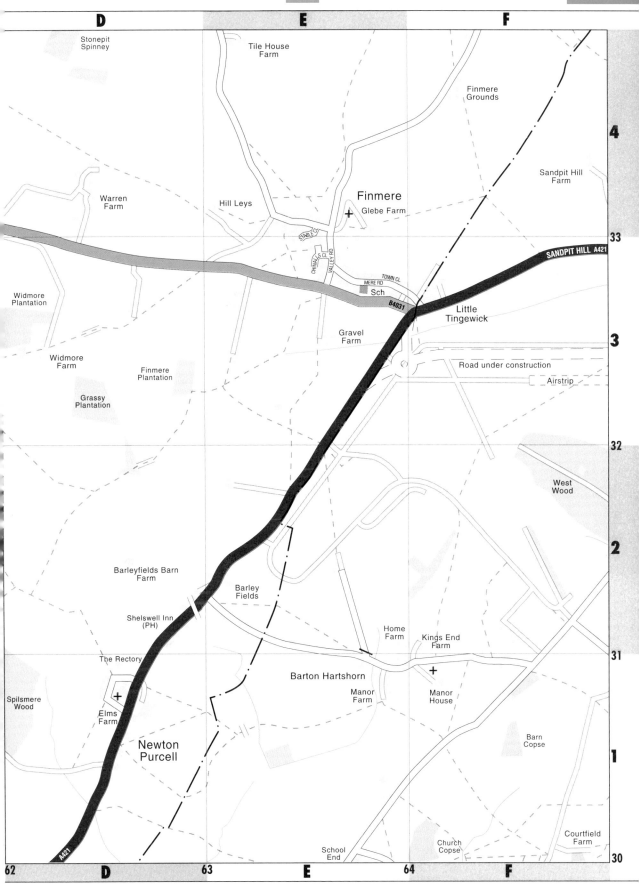

D

E

F

4

Stonepit
Spinney

Tile House
Farm

Finmere
Grounds

Sandpit Hill
Farm

Warren
Farm

Hill Leys

Finmere

Glebe Farm

STABLE CL

CHINALLS CL

VALLEY RD

TOWN CL

MERE RD

Sch

B4031

SANDPIT HILL   A421

Little
Tingewick

33

3

Widmore
Plantation

Gravel
Farm

Road under construction

Airstrip

Widmore
Farm

Finmere
Plantation

Grassy
Plantation

West
Wood

32

2

Barleyfields Barn
Farm

Barley
Fields

Home
Farm

Kings End
Farm

Shelswell Inn
(PH)

31

The Rectory

Barton Hartshorn

Manor
Farm

Manor
House

Spilsmere
Wood

Elms
Farm

Newton
Purcell

Barn
Copse

1

A421

School
End

Church
Copse

Courtfield
Farm

30

62

D

63

E

64

F

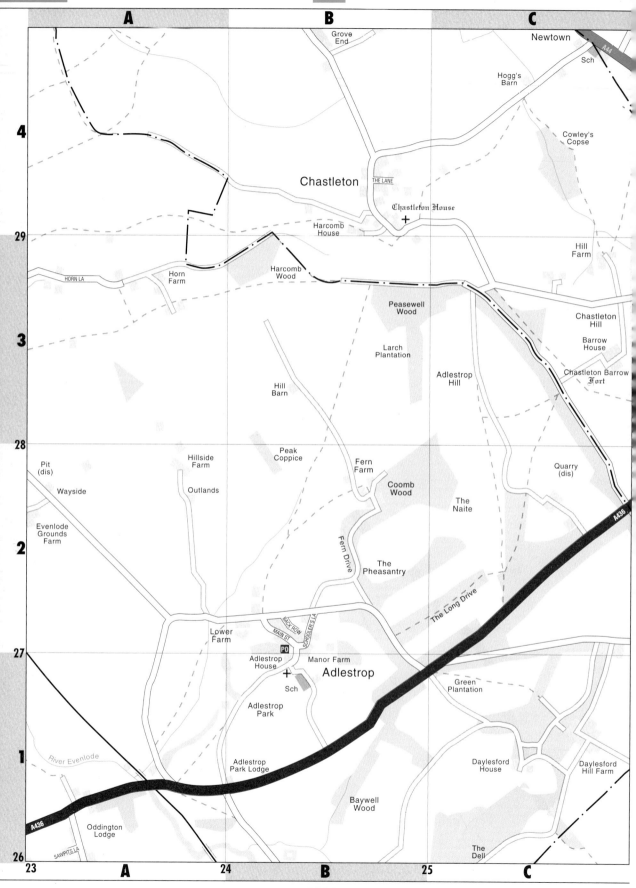

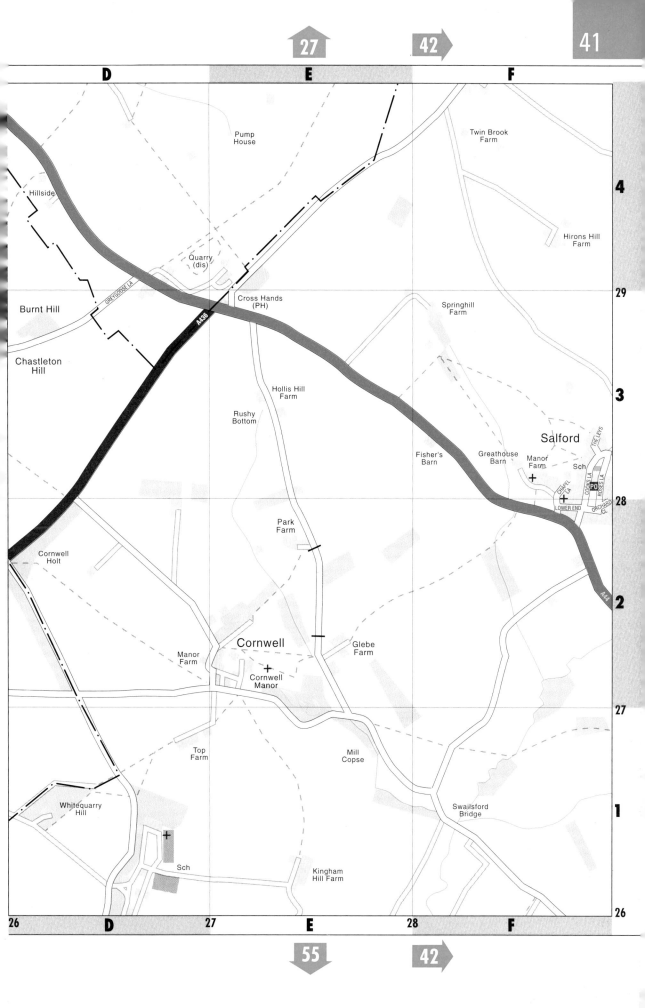

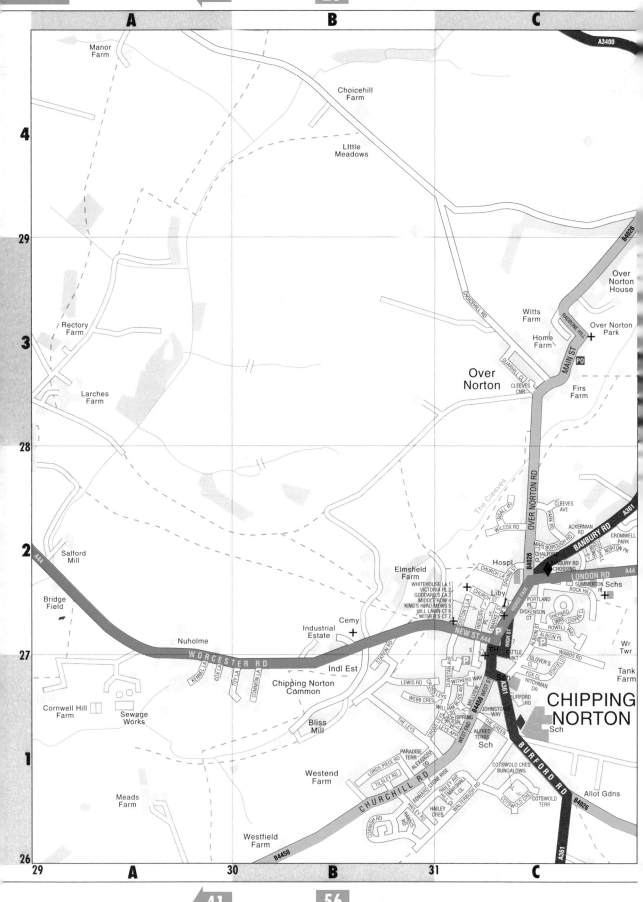

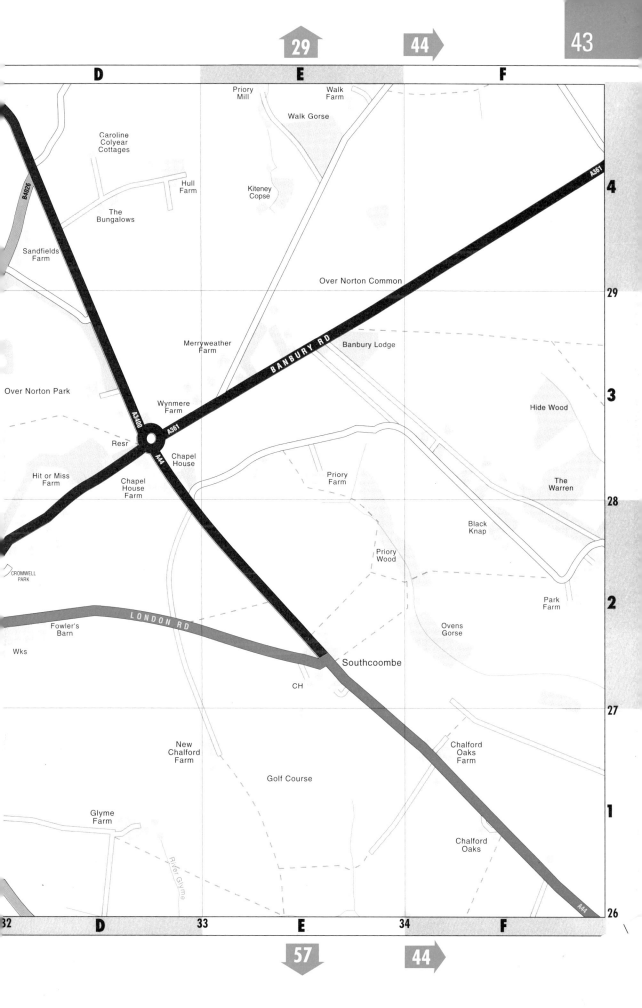

D
E
F

Priory
Mill

Walk
Farm

Walk Gorse

Caroline
Colyear
Cottages

Hull
Farm

A361

4

Kiteney
Copse

The
Bungalows

Sandfields
Farm

Over Norton Common

29

Merryweather
Farm

BANBURY RD

Banbury Lodge

Over Norton Park

Hide Wood

3

Wynmere
Farm

A3400

A361

Resr

Chapel
House

Priory
Farm

The
Warren

Hit or Miss
Farm

A44

Chapel
House
Farm

28

Black
Knap

Priory
Wood

CROMWELL
PARK

Park
Farm

2

LONDON RD

Fowler's
Barn

Ovens
Gorse

Wks

Southcoombe

CH

27

New
Chalford
Farm

Chalford
Oaks
Farm

Golf Course

Glyme
Farm

1

Chalford
Oaks

River Glyme

A44

26

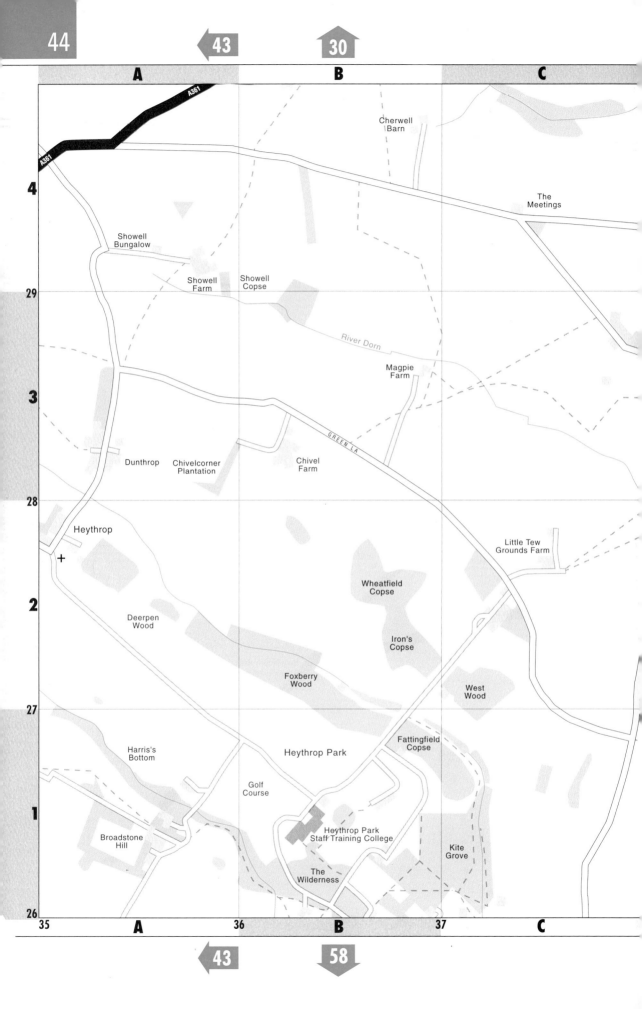

A   **B**   **C**

Newhouse
Farm

4

Flighthill
Farm

Over Worton

Worton
House

Rest Hill Farm

Flighthill
Cottage

Grange
Farm

Hobbshole
Farm

29

Lark
Rise

The Bungalow

3

Hangman's Hill

Cockley Brook

Brae

Ledwell

Heath Farm

Close
Farm

28

Worton Wood

Conygree
Wood

Parkend
Cottages

2

Heath Cottage
Farm

Cricket
Ground

High
Ley

27

Down Hill
Farm

Park Farm

Sandford Park

Sandford
St Martin

River Dorn

Brandon
Farm

Mill

1

Manor
House

Manor
Farm

ORCHARD WAY

HILLSIDE RD

WORTON RD

Middle
Barton

MANOR RD

HOLLIERS CRES

26

Manor
House

BALLARD CL

41   **A**   **42**   **B**   **43**   **C**

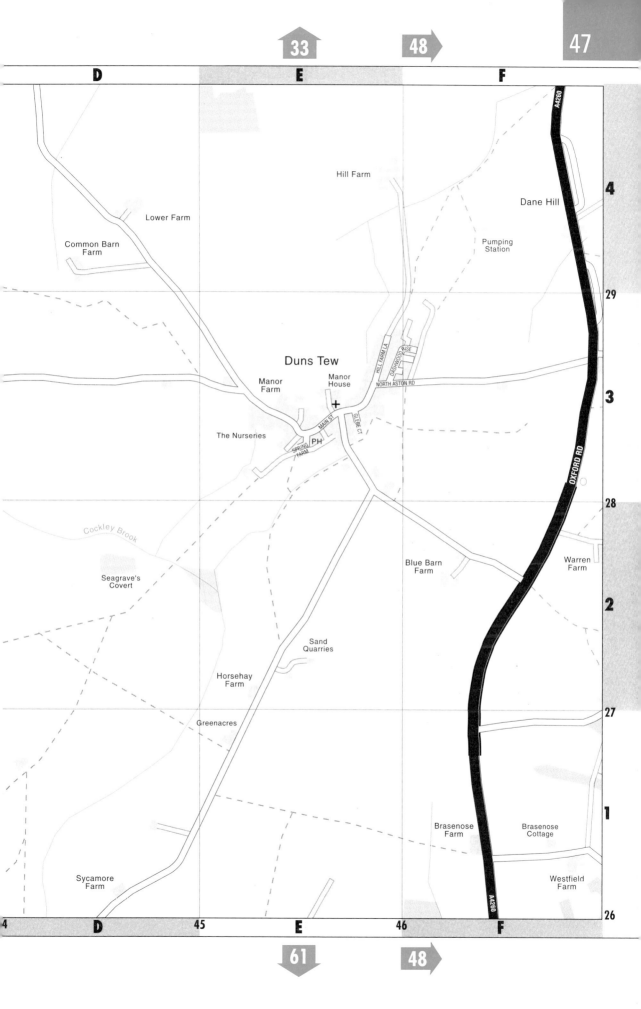

Hill Farm

Dane Hill

Lower Farm

Common Barn Farm

Pumping Station

4

29

Duns Tew

Manor Farm

Manor House

HILL FARM LA
DASHWOOD RISE
NORTH ASTON RD

3

The Nurseries

SPRING FARM
PH
MAIN ST
GLEBE CT

28

Cockley Brook

Seagrave's Covert

Blue Barn Farm

Warren Farm

2

Sand Quarries

Horsehay Farm

OXFORD RD

A4260

Greenacres

27

Brasenose Farm

Brasenose Cottage

1

Sycamore Farm

Westfield Farm

A4260

26

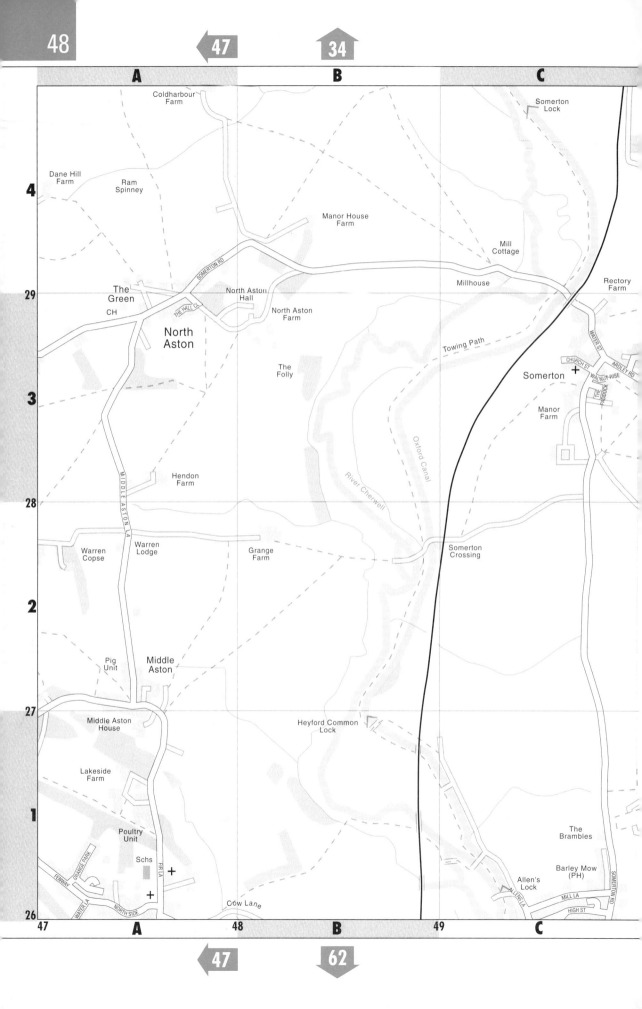

A B C

Coldharbour Farm

Somerton Lock

Dane Hill Farm

Ram Spinney

4

Manor House Farm

Mill Cottage

SOMERTON RD

Millhouse

Rectory Farm

29

The Green

North Aston Hall

North Aston Farm

CH

THE HALL CL

WATER ST

North Aston

Towing Path

CHURCH ST

ARDLEY RD

Somerton

WALNUT RISE

THE PADDOCK

The Folly

3

Manor Farm

Oxford Canal

River Cherwell

Hendon Farm

28

MIDDLE ASTON LA

Warren Copse

Warren Lodge

Grange Farm

Somerton Crossing

2

Pig Unit

Middle Aston

27

Middle Aston House

Heyford Common Lock

Lakeside Farm

1

The Brambles

Poultry Unit

Barley Mow (PH)

Schs

FIR LA

Allen's Lock

SOMERTON RD

ALLEN'S LA

MILL LA

TENWAY

GRANGE PARK

WATER LA

NORTH SIDE

Cow Lane

HIGH ST

26

47 A 48 B 49 C

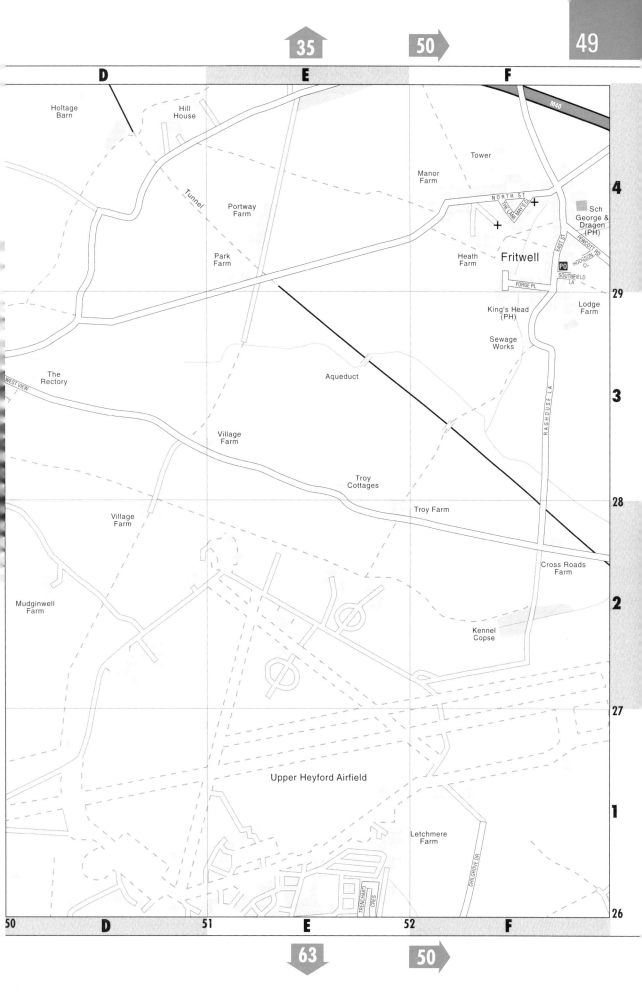

D E F

Holtage Barn
Hill House
M40
Tunnel
Tower
Manor Farm
Portway Farm
NORTH ST
THE LANE
MAY'S CL
Sch
George & Dragon (PH)
Park Farm
Heath Farm
Fritwell
EAST ST
FEWCOTT RD
HODGSON CL
PO
SOUTHFIELD LA
FORGE PL
29
King's Head (PH)
Lodge Farm
Sewage Works
WEST VIEW
The Rectory
Aqueduct
RAGHOUSE LA
3
Village Farm
Troy Cottages
Village Farm
Troy Farm
28
Cross Roads Farm
Mudginwell Farm
2
Kennel Copse
27
Upper Heyford Airfield
1
Letchmere Farm
CHILGROVE DR
TRENCHARD CRES
26

A B C

4

Horwell

Green Farm

M40

B4100

Baynards Green Farm

A43

Park Farm Belt

29

Medkre

Baynard House

Baynard's Green

Lone Barn

3

Fewcott

Manor Farm

Fewcott Farm

Sewage Works

Sycamore Grove

A43

Stoke Wood

B4100

28

FRITWELL RD

PLOUGHLEY CL

WATER LA

PADDOCK RD

ORCHARD RD

RUSSET RD

KEEY'S CL

ARDLEY RD

B430

10

Cherwell Services

Woodbine Cottage

SOMERTON RD

CASTLE FIELDS

Ardley

PH

2

Ardley Wood

Manor Farm

STATION RD

CHURCH RD

Kilby's Barn

27

Kilby's Copse

Nevilles Farm

1

Ashgrove Farm

M40

Digging Copse

Woodlands Farm

B430

Ardley Fields Farm

26

53 A 54 B 55 C

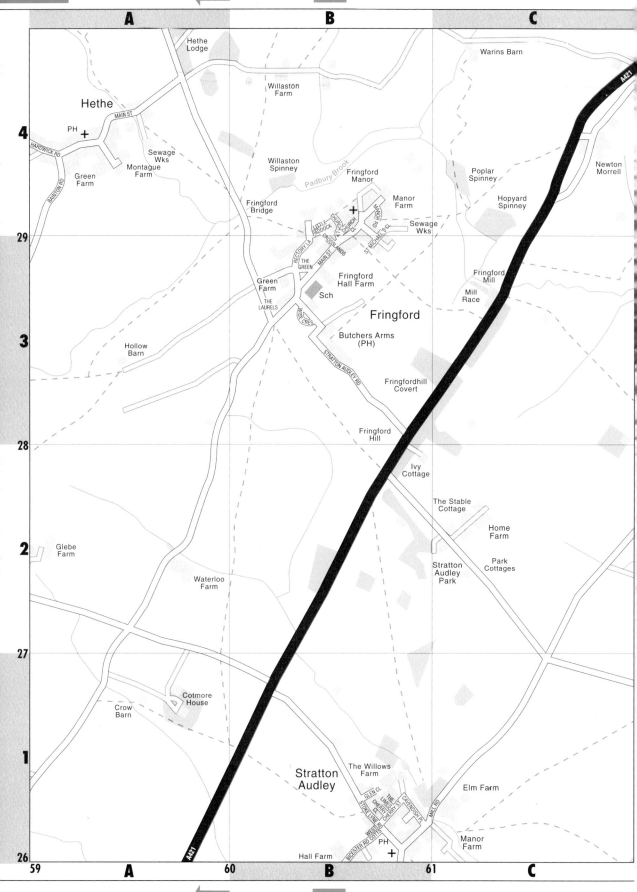

A | B | C

Hethe Lodge

Willaston Farm

Hethe

PH +

MAIN ST

HARDWICK RD

BAINTON RD

Green Farm

Sewage Wks

Montague Farm

Willaston Spinney

Padbury Brook

Fringford Bridge

Warins Barn

A421

Newton Morrell

Poplar Spinney

Hopyard Spinney

Fringford Manor

Manor Farm

Sewage Wks

Fringford Mill

Mill Race

LITTLE PADDOCK

CHURCH LA

CHURCH CL

CROSS LANDS

RECTORY LA

THE GREEN

MAIN ST

ST MICHAEL'S CL

MANOR RD

Green Farm

THE LAURELS

Fringford Hall Farm

Sch

WISE CRES

Fringford

Butchers Arms (PH)

STRATTON AUDLEY RD

Fringfordhill Covert

Hollow Barn

Fringford Hill

Ivy Cottage

The Stable Cottage

Home Farm

Park Cottages

Glebe Farm

Waterloo Farm

Stratton Audley Park

Crow Barn

Cotmore House

Stratton Audley

The Willows Farm

GLEN CL

THE LIMES

CHERRY ST

CHERRY ST

CAVENDISH PL

Elm Farm

STOKE LYNE RD

WEST CL

BICESTER RD COTTS

MILL RD

PH +

Manor Farm

Hall Farm

A421

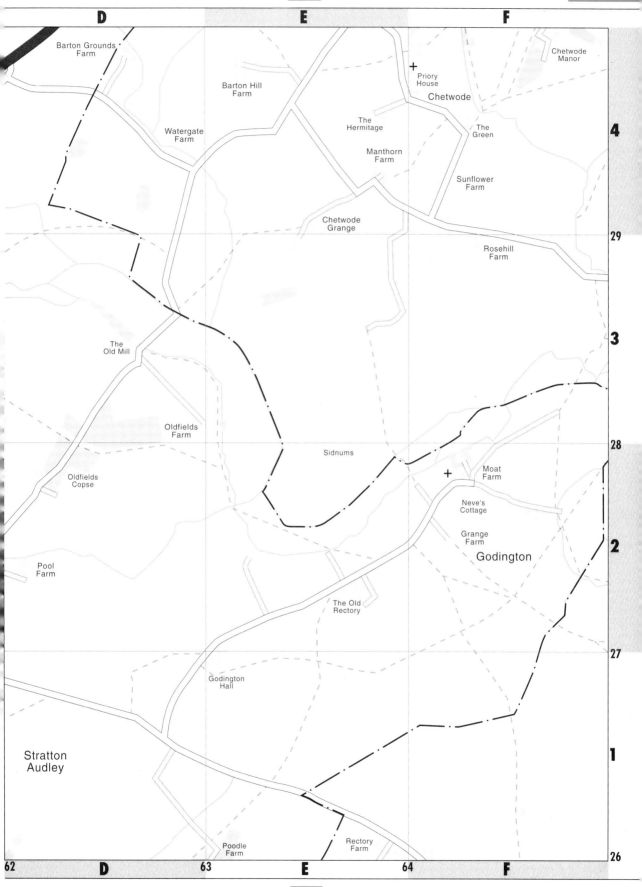

D

E

F

Barton Grounds
Farm

Barton Hill
Farm

+ Priory
House

Chetwode
Manor

Chetwode

Watergate
Farm

The
Hermitage

The
Green

4

Manthorn
Farm

Sunflower
Farm

Chetwode
Grange

29

Rosehill
Farm

The
Old Mill

3

Oldfields
Farm

Sidnums

28

+

Moat
Farm

Oldfields
Copse

Neve's
Cottage

Grange
Farm

Godington

2

Pool
Farm

The Old
Rectory

27

Godington
Hall

Stratton
Audley

1

Poodle
Farm

Rectory
Farm

26

62

D

63

E

64

F

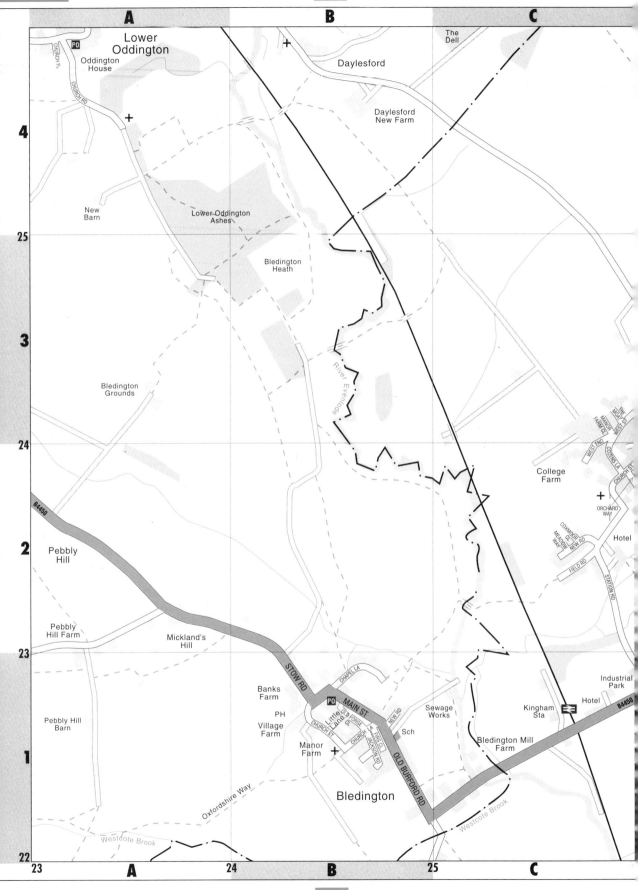

A   B   C

4

25

3

24

2

23

1

22

23   A   24   B   25   C

Lower
Oddington

PO

Oddington House

CHURCH PL

CHURCH RD

New
Barn

Lower Oddington
Ashes

Bledington
Heath

Bledington
Grounds

River Evenlode

Daylesford

The
Dell

Daylesford
New Farm

College
Farm

THE MALT HSE
MANOR FARM CL
WEST END ST
WEST END
COZENS LA
CHURCH ST

ORCHARD
WAY

Hotel

COXMOOR CL
MEADOW WAY
NEW RD
FIELD RD
STATION RD

Pebbly
Hill

B4450

Pebbly
Hill Farm

Mickland's
Hill

STOW RD

Banks
Farm

PH
Village
Farm

Pebbly Hill
Barn

PO
MAIN ST
Little
Lane CL
OLD FORGE CL
CHURCH ST
FIRS CL
CHURCH LA
JACKSON RD
NEW RD

Chapel La

CHAPEL LA

Sewage
Works

Sch

Manor
Farm

Bledington

Oxfordshire Way

Westcote Brook

OLD BURFORD RD

Bledington Mill
Farm

Westcote Brook

Industrial
Park

Hotel

Kingham
Sta

B4450

D
E
F

Slade Farm

Warden's House

Lower Kingham Hill Cottages

Churchill Grounds Farm

Churchill Grounds Cottages

B4450

4

25

Churchill Mill

Sarsden Halt

Grange Farm

3

Mount Farm

Sch

CHURCHILL RD

The Caravan

Churchill Crossing

SIDINGS RD

HASTINGS HILL

KINGHAM RD

Meadow Place

Hill View

Churchill

WEST ST

PO

CHAPEL LA

CHURCH ST

Kingham

ORCHARD WAY

FOWLER'S RD

PH

Churchill Farm

LANGSTON CL

HARKERS LA

WILLIAM SMITH CL

JUNCTION RD

24

Mount Farm

The Mount

The Lodge

2

York Cottage

Home Farm

Sarsden

STATION RD

23

Sarsden House

Rynehill Farm

Sars Brook

1

Churchill Heath Farm

Churchill Heath Bungalow

Lower Buildings

22

6
D
27
E
28
F

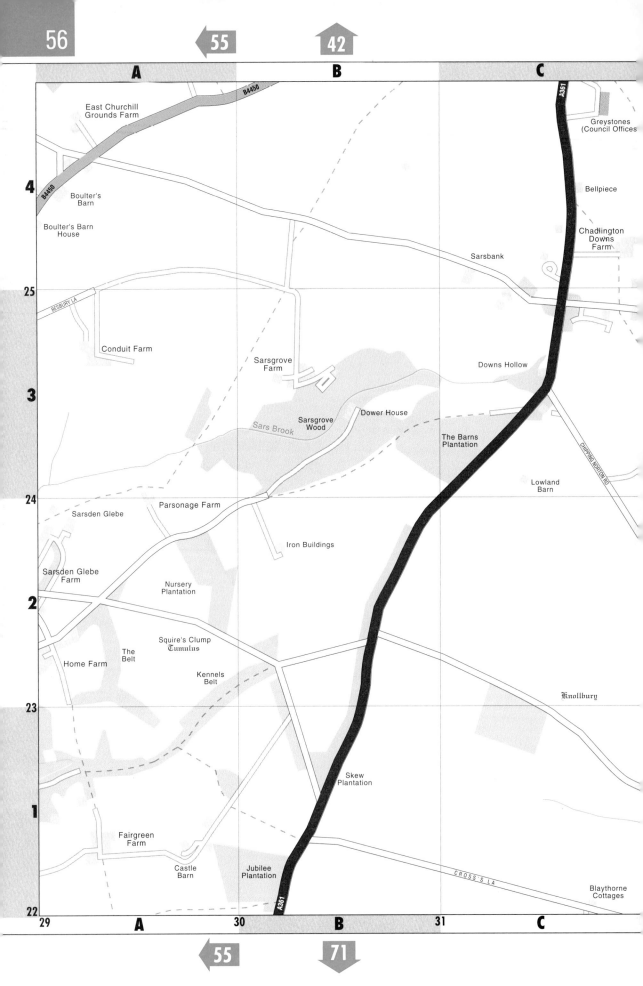

A
B
C

B4450

East Churchill
Grounds Farm

Greystones
(Council Offices

A361

Bellpiece

4

B4450

Boulter's
Barn

Chadlington
Downs
Farm

Boulter's Barn
House

Sarsbank

25

BESBURY LA

Conduit Farm

Downs Hollow

Sarsgrove
Farm

3

Sars Brook

Sarsgrove
Wood

Dower House

The Barns
Plantation

CHIPPING NORTON RD

Lowland
Barn

24

Parsonage Farm

Sarsden Glebe

Iron Buildings

Sarsden Glebe
Farm

Nursery
Plantation

2

Squire's Clump
Tumulus

Home Farm

The
Belt

Kennels
Belt

Knollbury

23

Skew
Plantation

1

Fairgreen
Farm

Castle
Barn

Jubilee
Plantation

CROSS'S LA

Blaythorne
Cottages

22

A361

29
A
30
B
31
C

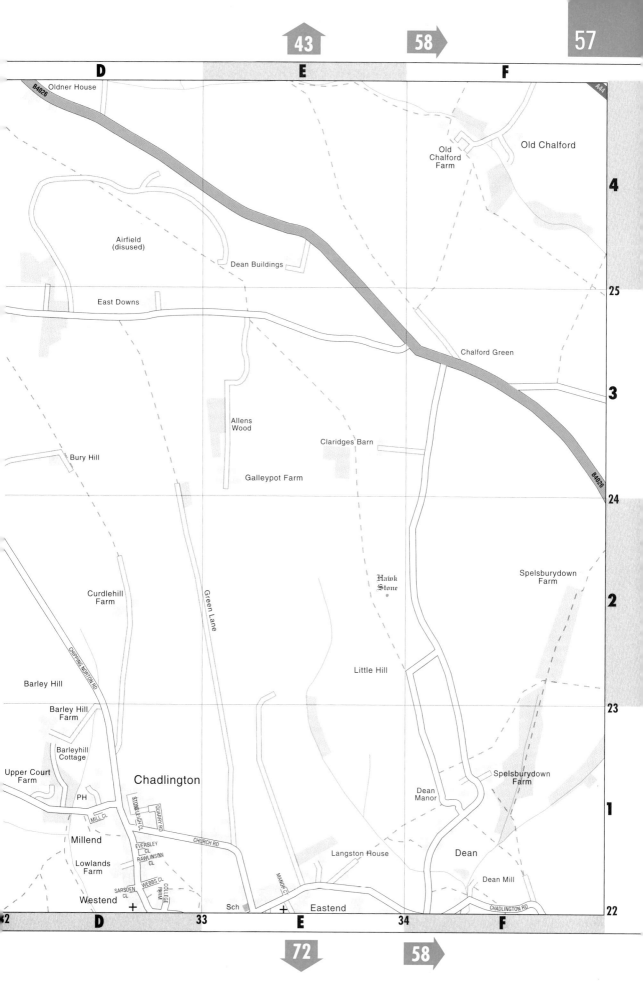

4

Oldner House

Old Chalford Farm

Old Chalford

Airfield (disused)

Dean Buildings

25

East Downs

Chalford Green

3

Allens Wood

Claridges Barn

Bury Hill

Galleypot Farm

24

Hawk Stone

Spelsburydown Farm

2

Curdlehill Farm

Green Lane

Little Hill

Barley Hill

23

Barley Hill Farm

Barleyhill Cottage

Upper Court Farm

Spelsburydown Farm

Chadlington

Dean Manor

1

CHIPPING NORTON RD

PH

STONELEIGH CL

QUARRY RD

MILL CL

CHURCH RD

Millend

EVERSLEY CL

RAWLINSON CL

Lowlands Farm

Langston House

Dean

Dean Mill

SARSDEN CL

WEBBS CL

COLLEGE PRIM

MANOR CL

Westend

Sch

Eastend

CHADLINGTON RD

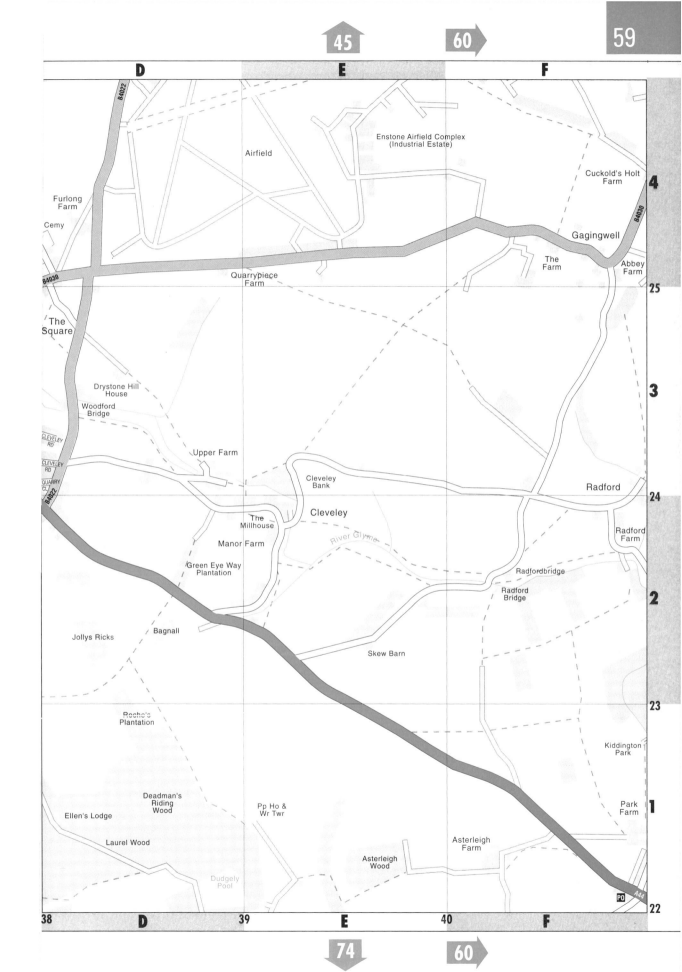

D
E
F

B4022

Furlong
Farm

Cemy

Airfield

Enstone Airfield Complex
(Industrial Estate)

Cuckold's Holt
Farm

4

B4030

Gagingwell

The
Farm

Abbey
Farm

B4030

Quarrypiece
Farm

25

The
Square

Drystone Hill
House

3

Woodford
Bridge

CLEVELEY
RD

CLEVELEY
RD

Upper Farm

Cleveley
Bank

Radford

QUARRY
CL

B4022

Cleveley

24

The
Millhouse

River Glyme

Radford
Farm

Manor Farm

Green Eye Way
Plantation

Radfordbridge

Radford
Bridge

2

Jollys Ricks

Bagnall

Skew Barn

23

Roche's
Plantation

Kiddington
Park

Deadman's
Riding
Wood

Pp Ho &
Wr Twr

Park
Farm

1

Ellen's Lodge

Asterleigh
Farm

Laurel Wood

Asterleigh
Wood

Dudgely
Pool

PO

A44

22

38
D
39
E
40
F

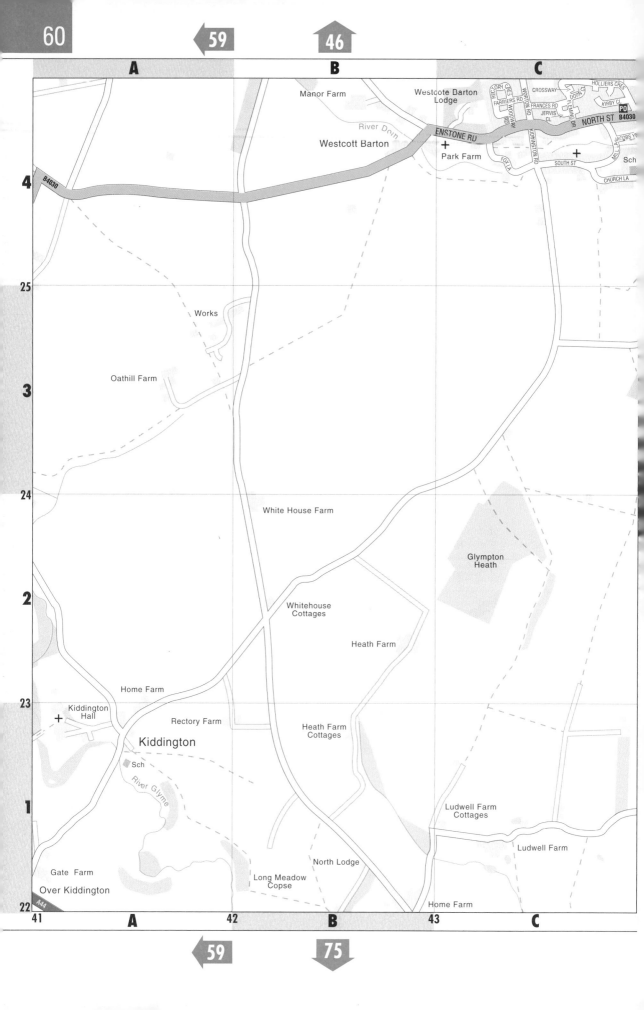

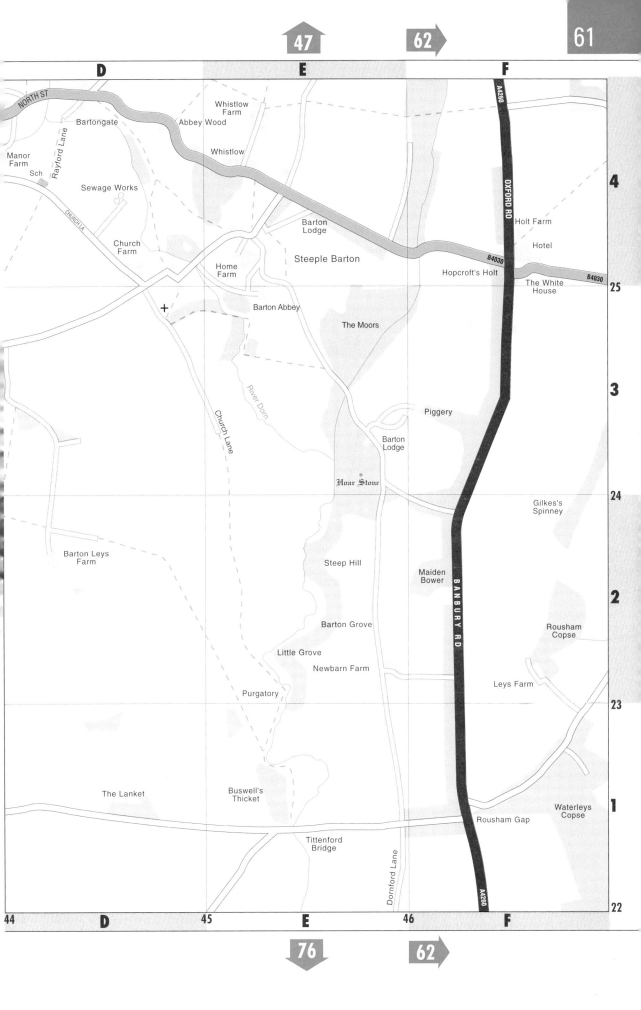

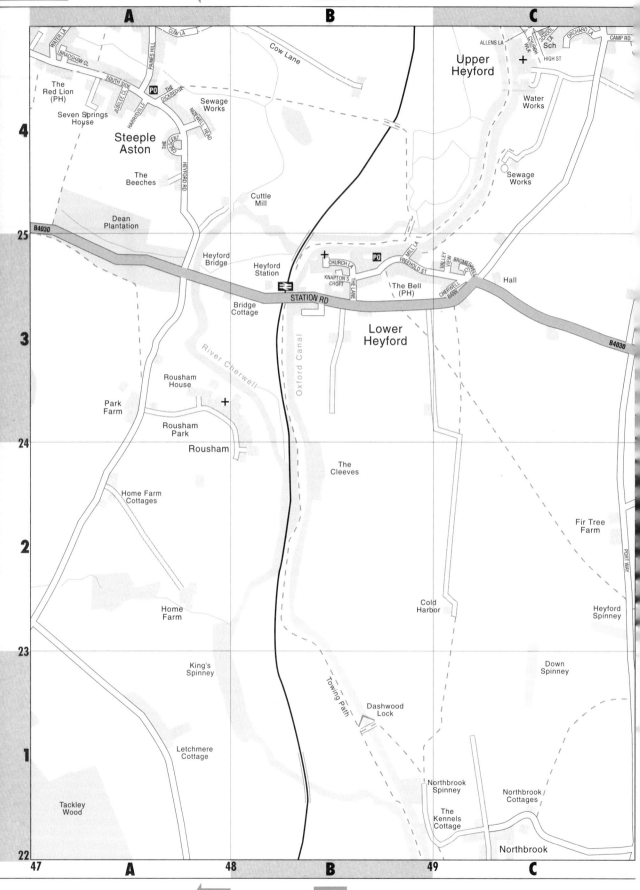

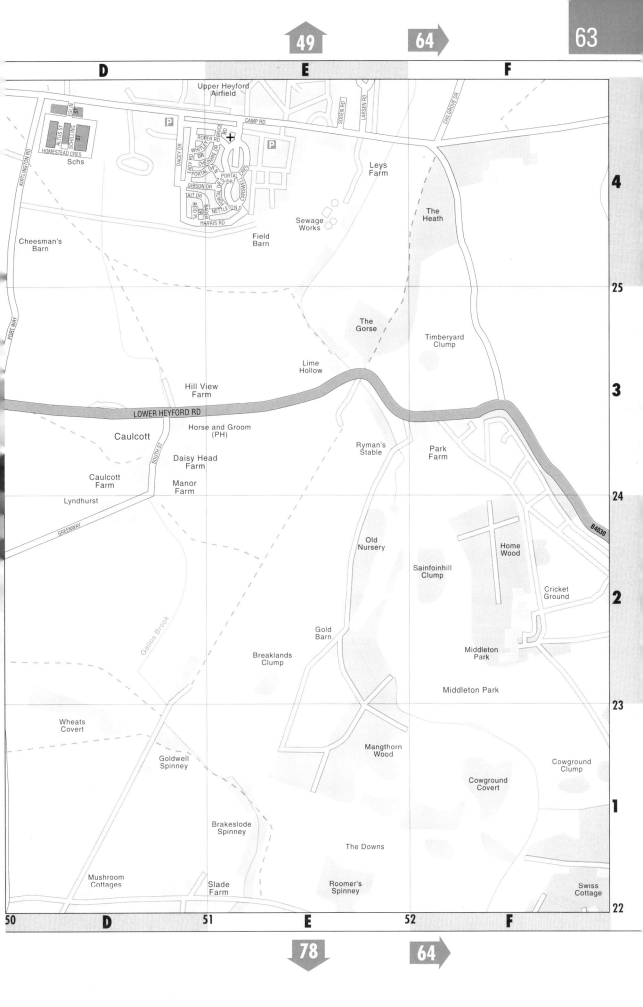

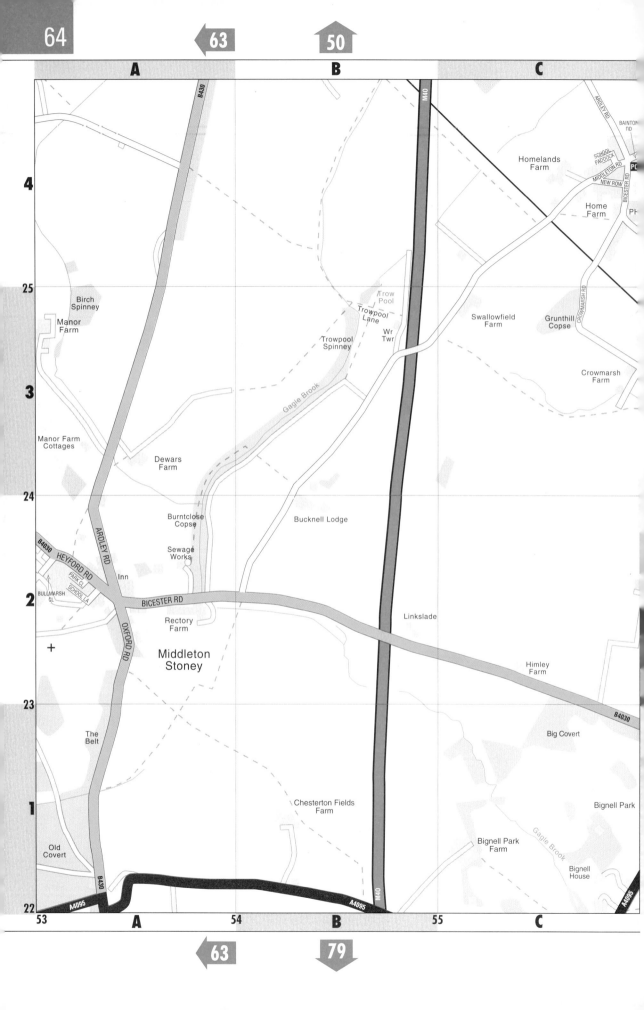

A   B   C

4

25

Homelands
Farm

ARDLEY RD

BAINTON
nD

SCHOOL
PADDOCK

MIDDLETON RD

BICESTER RD

Home
Farm

PC

Ph

NEW ROW

Birch
Spinney

Manor
Farm

Trow
Pool

Trowpool
Lane

Wr
Twr

Swallowfield
Farm

Grunthill
Copse

CROWMARSH RD

3

Trowpool
Spinney

Crowmarsh
Farm

Manor Farm
Cottages

Gagle Brook

Dewars
Farm

24

Burntclose
Copse

Bucknell Lodge

B4030

HEYFORD RD

ARDLEY RD

Inn

Sewage
Works

BULLMARSH
CL

PARK CL

SCHOOL LA

2

BICESTER RD

Linkslade

Rectory
Farm

OXFORD RD

+

Middleton
Stoney

Himley
Farm

23

The
Belt

Big Covert

B4030

1

Chesterton Fields
Farm

Bignell Park

Old
Covert

Bignell Park
Farm

Gagle Brook

Bignell
House

22

B430

A4095

A   B   C

53   54   55

A4095

A4095

M40

A   B   C

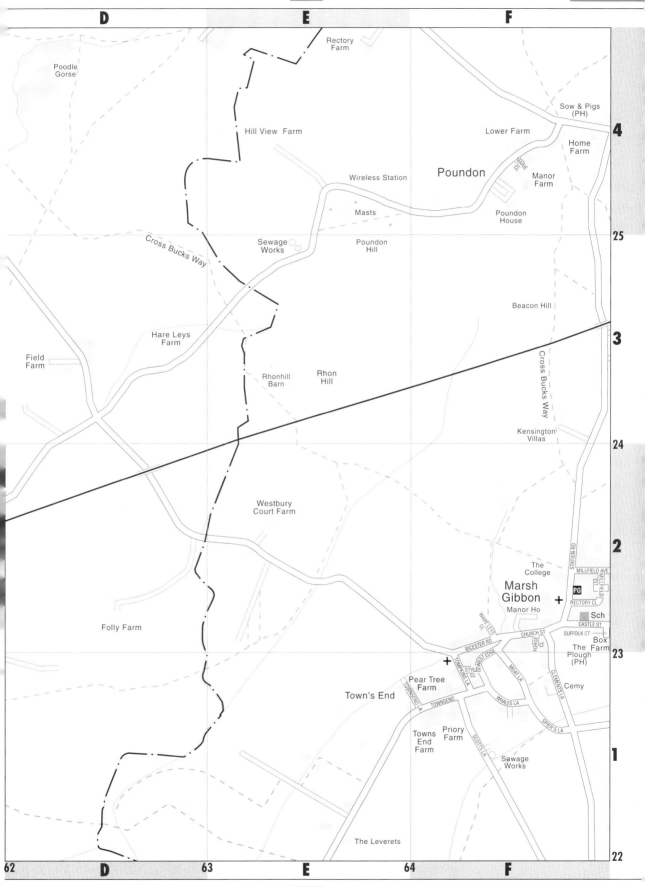

Poodle
Gorse

Rectory
Farm

Sow & Pigs
(PH)

Hill View Farm

Lower Farm

Home
Farm

4

Wireless Station

Poundon

Manor
Farm

MARIE CL

Masts

Poundon
House

25

Cross Bucks Way

Sewage
Works

Poundon
Hill

Beacon Hill

Hare Leys
Farm

Cross Bucks Way

3

Field
Farm

Rhonhill
Barn

Rhon
Hill

Kensington
Villas

24

Westbury
Court Farm

2

The
College

Millfield Ave

Marsh
Gibbon

PO

MILLFIELD CL

STATION RD

Folly Farm

Manor Ho

RECTORY CL

Sch

WARE LEYS CL

CHURCH ST

FORGE CT

CASTLE ST

SUFFOLK CT

Box
The
Farm

BICESTER RD

The
Plough
(PH)

23

Pear Tree
Farm

WEST EDGE

TOMPKINS LA

STYLES CL

MOAT LA

CLEMENTS LA

Cemy

Town's End

TOWNSEND LA

TOWNSEND

WHALES LA

SPIER'S LA

Towns
End
Farm

Priory
Farm

SCOTTS LA

Sewage
Works

1

The Leverets

22

A   B   C

A24

Booth's Barn

Westcote Brook

Oxfordshire Way

Gawcombe

4

Gawcombe
Woods

Wyck Beacon
Farm

21

Hawkwell

Wyck Beacon

Court
Hayes
Farm

Church
Westcote

New Inn (PH)

3

Far Hill
Coppice

Far Hill
Barn

Nether
Westcote

DE HAVILLAND RD

SISKIN RD

Bunting's Hill
Copse

VICKERS RD

WRIGHT CL

Little Glebe
Farm

BRISTOL RD

AVRO RD

WRIGHT RD

FOLLAND DR

SOPWITH RD

FARMAN

CRES

20

Brookfield

BLERIOT RD

HAWKER ST

DOUGLAS DR

SNIPE RD

GREENE SQ

Peak's
Coppice

SANDY LA

SMITH BARRY RD

SMITH BARRY CRES

Westcote Hill

Idbury

Ansell's Hill
Copse

SANDY LANE
CT

GERRARD RD

LONGMORE AVE

FULTON RD

Imjin
Barracks
(dis)

KIRBY RD

2

Collier's Hill
Barn

SOUTH GATE
CT

A P ELLIS RD

LIDDERDALE RD

LITHGOW RD

RANDALL RD

A24

Workham
Farm

19

Workham
Bottom

1

Little Rissington Airfield
(disused)

Limekiln
Plantation

Ram
Plantation

Warren
Farm

18

20   A   21   B   22   C

A
B
C

Sarsden Lodge
Cottages

The Norrells.

Churchill Heath
Wood

Merriscourt
Farm

4

Sarsden
Lodge

Lyneham Heath
Farm

Sarsden
Gorse

21

Cocksmoor
Copse

LC

Lyneham
Farm

Lyneham

3

HIGH ST

Bruern Abbey

PRIORY LA

Priory
Farm

PRIORY RD

Mill

20

Conduit
Copse

Meadow
Copse

Bruern
Wood

The
Crossings

Round
Pound

A361

Pool
Copse

Outside
Copse

2

BRUERN RD

Mast

River Evenlode

Pyrton
Farm

Littlecott

Heath
Farm

Glebe
Farm

LYNEHAM RD

Oxfordshire Way

19

Cemy

Shipton
Station

The Heath

Mill

1

Cottage
Farm

Heath
Farm

GREEN LA

STATION RD

PEAR TREE CL

Sewage
Works

CHURCH MEADOW

CHURCH RD

BRADFORD CL

PH

PO

Littlebrook Meadow

Reynolds CL

Meadow LA

SHIPTON RD

READE

WOODLANDS CL

FROG LA

FETTIPLACE CL

MILTON RD

A361

Willis Gorton Playne

1ST MICHAELS CL

2 COOMBES CL

HIGH ST

Liby

JUBILEE LA

WYCHWOOD CL

THE SANDS

FOREST

ASSEL WAY

Sch

PO

2 TOTHILL

CHURCH WLK

18

26
A
27
B
28
C

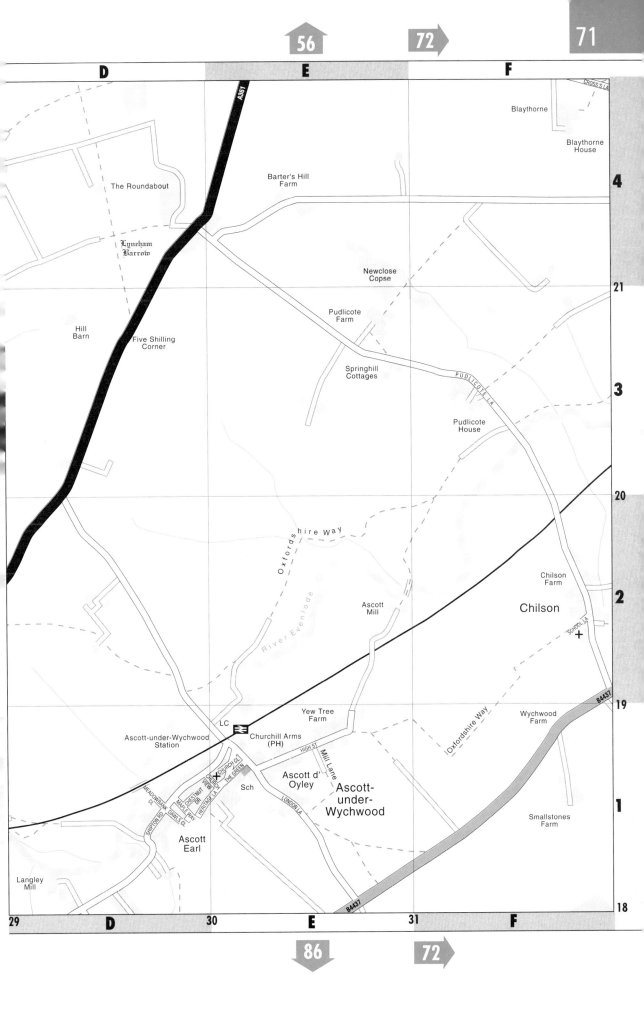

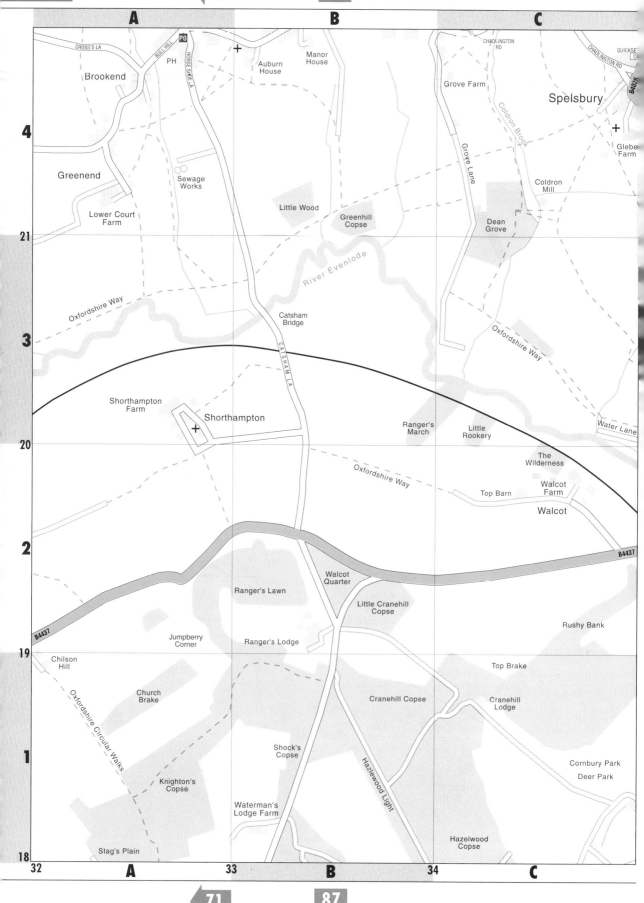

A   **B**   **C**

CROSS'S LA

Brookend

BULL HILL

PH

PO

HORSE SHOE LA

Auburn House

Manor House

CHADLINGTON RD

Grove Farm

QUICKSE CI

B4026

Spelsbury

CHADLINGTON RD

Glebe Farm

4

Greenend

Sewage Works

Little Wood

Greenhill Copse

Grove Lane

Coldron Brook

Dean Grove

Coldron Mill

Lower Court Farm

21

Oxfordshire Way

River Evenlode

Oxfordshire Way

Catsham Bridge

CATSHAM LA

Water Lane

3

Shorthampton Farm

Shorthampton

Ranger's March

Little Rookery

The Wilderness

Oxfordshire Way

Walcot Farm

20

Oxfordshire Way

Top Barn

Walcot

2

B4437

Ranger's Lawn

Walcot Quarter

Little Cranehill Copse

Rushy Bank

B4437

Jumpberry Corner

Ranger's Lodge

Top Brake

19

Chilson Hill

Church Brake

Cranehill Copse

Cranehill Lodge

Oxfordshire Circular Walks

Hazelwood Light

Shock's Copse

Cornbury Park

Deer Park

1

Knighton's Copse

Waterman's Lodge Farm

Hazelwood Copse

Stag's Plain

18

32   **A**   33   **B**   34   **C**

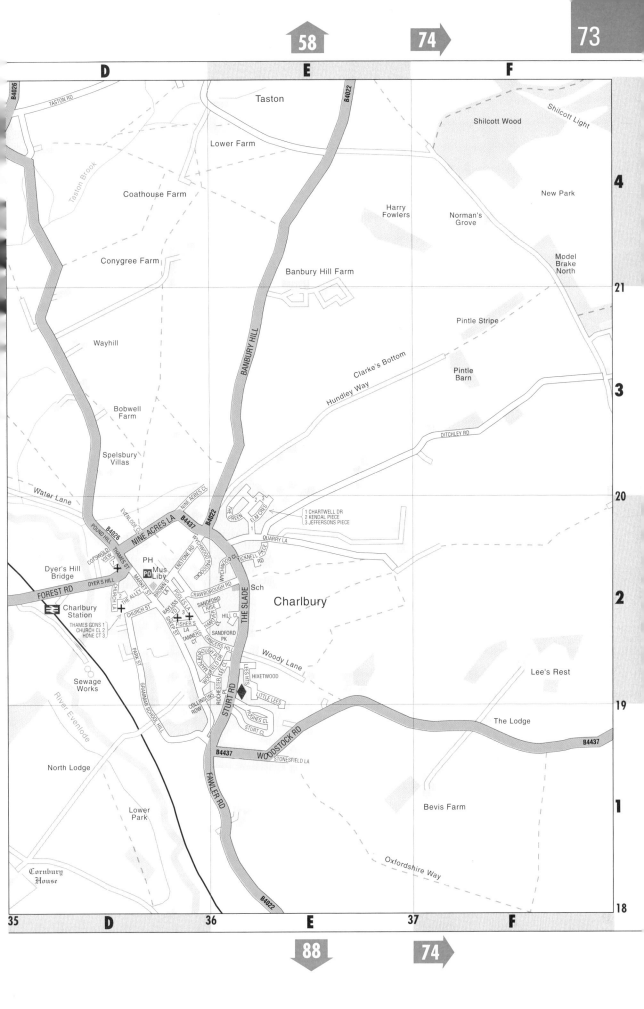

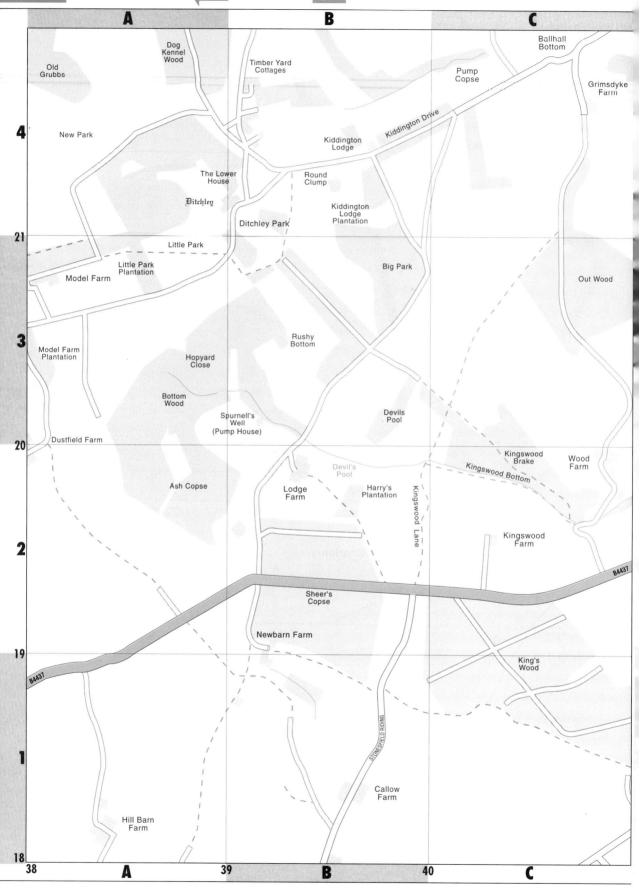

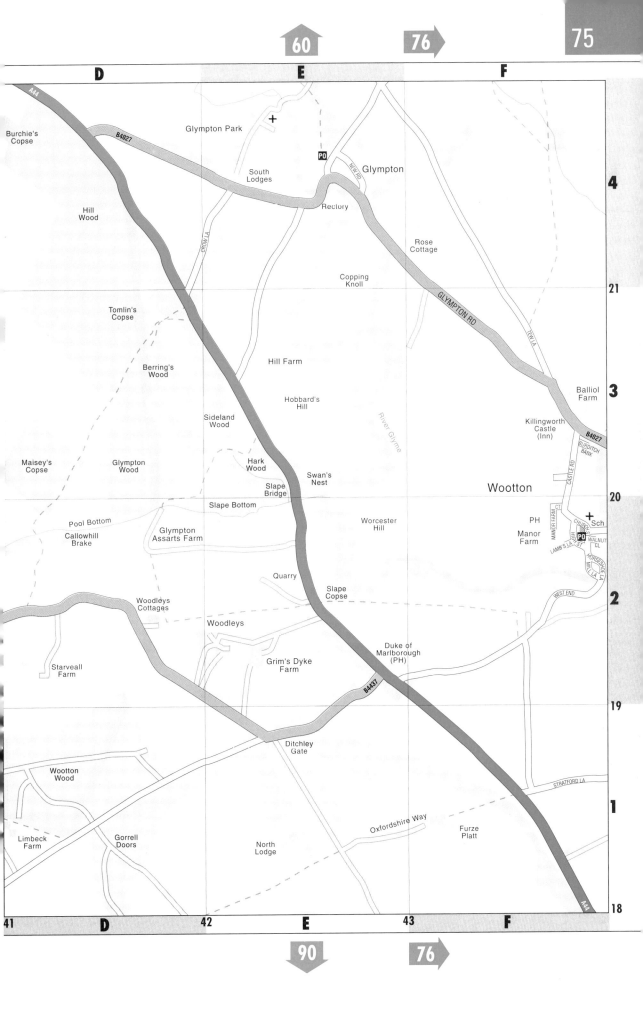

A   B   C

4

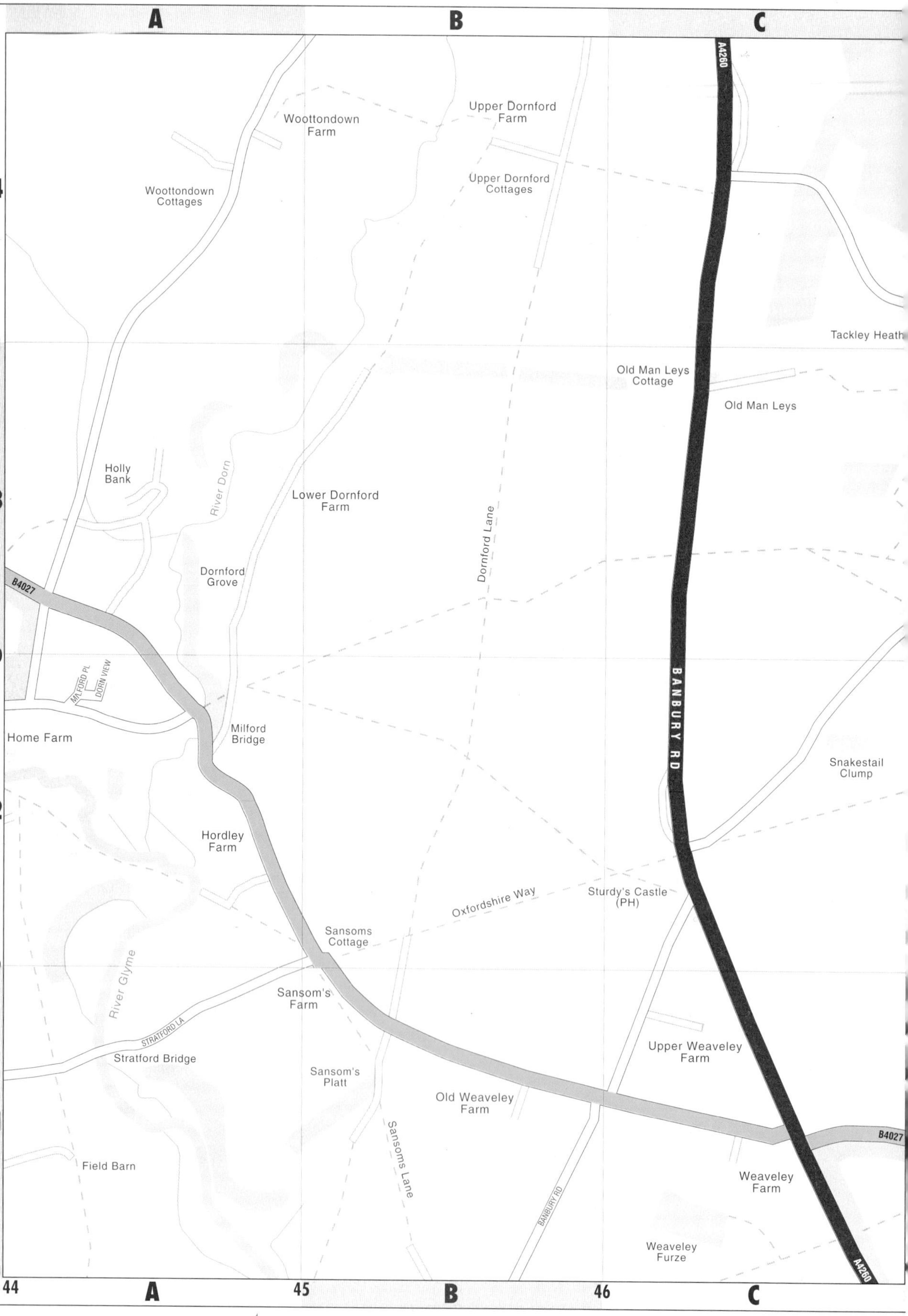

Woottondown
Farm

Upper Dornford
Farm

Woottondown
Cottages

Upper Dornford
Cottages

21

Tackley Heath

Old Man Leys
Cottage

Old Man Leys

Holly
Bank

River Dorn

Lower Dornford
Farm

3

Dornford Lane

A260

Dornford
Grove

B4027

20

MILFORD PL
DORN VIEW

BANBURY RD

Milford
Bridge

Home Farm

Snakestail
Clump

2

Hordley
Farm

Sturdy's Castle
(PH)

Oxfordshire Way

Sansoms
Cottage

19

Sansom's
Farm

River Glyme

STRATFORD LA

Upper Weaveley
Farm

Stratford Bridge

Sansom's
Platt

Old Weaveley
Farm

1

B4027

Sansoms Lane

Field Barn

Weaveley
Farm

BANBURY RD

Weaveley
Furze

A260

18

44   A   45   B   46   C

D E F

Tackley Wood

Northbrook
Bridge

North Brook
Lock

Morar

Wood House

4

Wood Farm

ROUSHAM RD

21

Malt House
Farm

Fox Hill

Nethercott

NETHERCOTE RD

BALLIOL CL.

Crowcastle Lane

BAKER JAMES RD

MEDCROFT RD

ST NICHOLAS RD

TWYNHAMS RD

Sch

PO

THE
GREEN

BALL LANE

ST JOHN'S RD

CHALUMY RD

Tackley
Station

LC

River Cherwell

Oxford Canal

3

Peter's
Cross

Court
Farm

Tackley

HARBORNE RD

LIME KILN RD

CHURCH HILL

+

Tackley Park

Park Farm

Quarry
(disused)

PINK CLOSE

A4095

HEYFORD RD

20

Washford
Pits

Oxfordshire Way

POUND CL.

HATCH END

Telephone
Exchange

Old Whitehill
Farm

Sewage
Works

Weir

MILL LA.

DASHWOOD MEWS

HATCH WAY

HATCH
CL.

Kirtlington

OXFORD RD

HEYFORD RD

A4095

2

Fords

Flight's
Mill

OXFORD CL.

PO

Pound Hill

Weir

Field Barn

Pigeon Lock

South
Farm

BICESTER RD

KIRTLINGTON RD

CRUTCHMORE CRES

Pinsey
Bridge

Vicarage
Farm

19

Lower Whitehill
Farm

Towing Path

LINCE LA.

Sewage Works

Quarry
(disused)

1

B4027

Enslow
Bridge

Enslow

Woodstock
Gap

BUNKERS HILL A4095

Weir

Quarry
Bank

PH

Gibraltar

B4027

18

A B C

4

21

3

20

2

19

1

18

50 A 51 B 52 C

PORT WAY

Hoarstone
Spinney

Greatfield
Spinney

Gallos Brook

Middleton
Park

A409

Stud
Farm

Cranmoor
Plantation

The
Grove

The
Bushes

Werghill
Copse

HEYFORD RD A4095

AKEMAN CL

Polo Ground

Home
Farm

Kirtlington Park

Park
Farm

Gallosbrook
Plantation

Gallos Brook

Kemsley
Barn

Mill
Mound

THE CHESTNUTS

Inn

A4095

CHURCH LA

Kirtlington
Park

Cockshot
Copse

Long
Plantation

Ford

Stonepit
Hills

BLETCHINGDON RD

+

Manor House
Farm

Oxfordshire Way

CRUTCHMORE CRES

Walkers Farm
Buildings

Stonehouse
Farm

Kirtlington Park

Cordle
Bushes

Winterlake

Cordle
Door

Newbridge
Farm

Brookside
Farm

Sch

SPRINGWELL HILL

Bletchingdon
Park

+

Ash
Wood

Tollbrook
Corner

Staplehurst
Farm

4

Home Farm

Gagle Brook

ALCHESTER RD

+ 1 CHESTNUT CL
2 FORTESCUE DR

GREEN LA

2

TUBBS LA

The Red Cow (PH)

Chesterton Lodge

21

Lodge Farm

Foxey Leys Copse

OXFORD RD

A41

A421

A41

PINGLE DR

Recn Grd

MCKAY TRADING ESTATE

B4100

Bicester Town Station

Bicester Village Retail Park

TALISMAN RD

LONDON RD

The Talisman Business Centre

MARTIN CL

Langford Park Farm

Rodney House

Works

Wendlebury Farm

Promised Land Farm

3

Bowler's Copse

LC

LANGFORD LA

Alchester ROMAN TOWN (site of)

LCs

Depot

CIRCULAR RD

Graven Hill

Gravenhill Wood

20

A41

RECTORY CL

OLD RECTORY CT

CHURCH LA

Red Lion (PH)

Elm Tree Farm

ST GILES CL

FARRIER'S MEAD

Wendlebury

2

College Farm

Langford Lane

Merton Grounds

19

1

M40

Astley Bridge Cottage

18

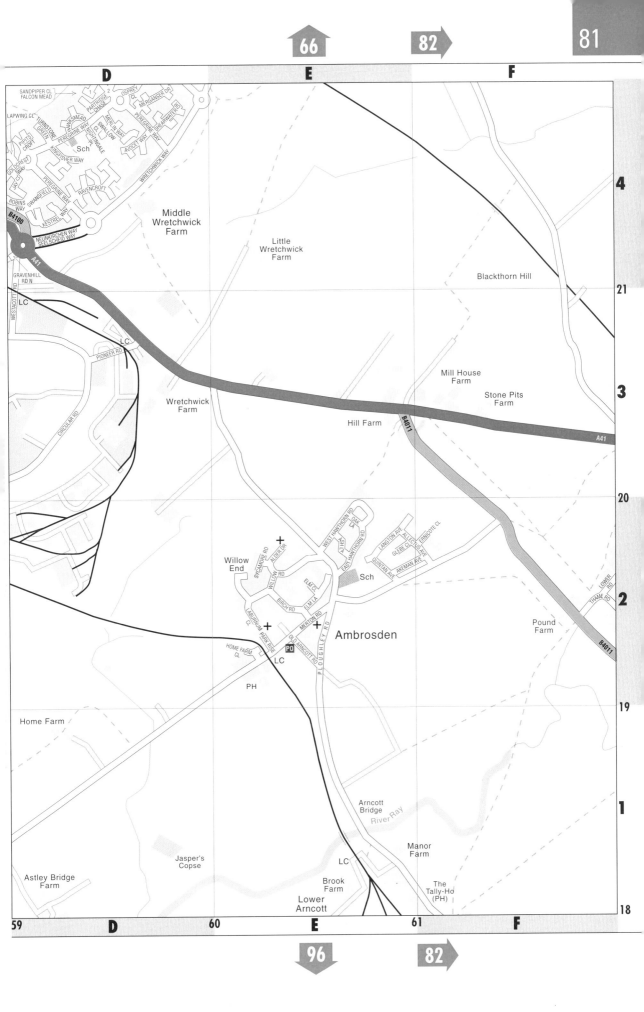

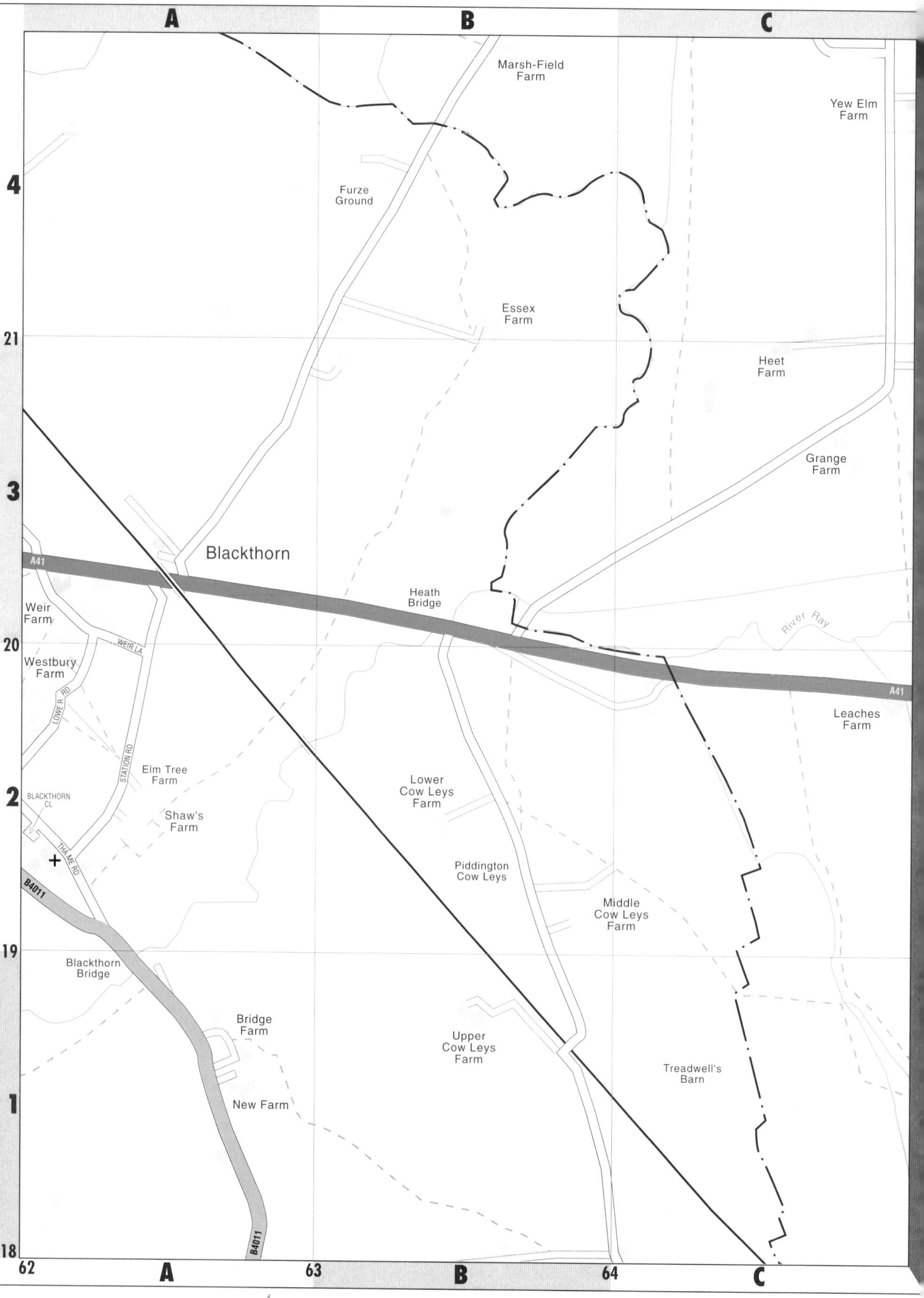

A B C

4

21

Marsh-Field Farm

Yew Elm Farm

Furze Ground

Essex Farm

Heet Farm

3

Grange Farm

A41

Blackthorn

Weir Farm

Heath Bridge

River Ray

20

WEIR LA

Westbury Farm

LOWER RD

A41

Leaches Farm

STATION RD

Elm Tree Farm

Lower Cow Leys Farm

2

BLACKTHORN CL

Shaw's Farm

THAME RD

Piddington Cow Leys

Middle Cow Leys Farm

+

B4011

19

Blackthorn Bridge

Bridge Farm

Upper Cow Leys Farm

Treadwell's Barn

1

New Farm

B4011

18

62 A 63 B 64 C

D
E
F

Great Rissington Farm

Airfield (disused)

Littlehill Bank

Choake's Brake

North Lodge

Great Rissington Hill

4

Choake's Barn

Resr

The Follies

Ell Brake

Sch

17

Washpool Copse

Barrington Bushes

Downs Cottages

Hazelford Brook

3

Taynton Bushes

Mill Hill

Hill Barn

16

Bromham Plantation

Miletree Clump

2

15

1

Comb Hill Plantation

Grosvenor Plantation

Barrington Park

Mortar Pits

14

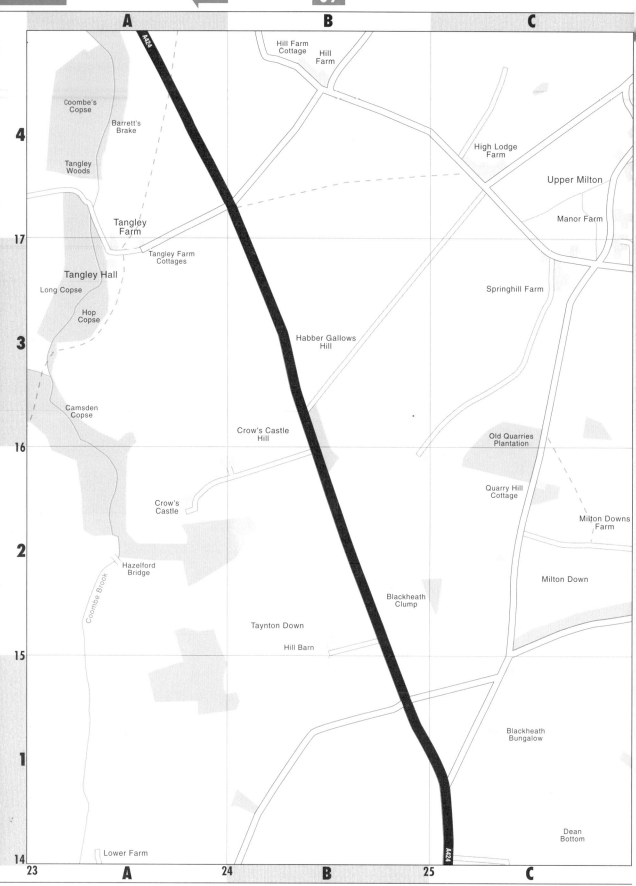

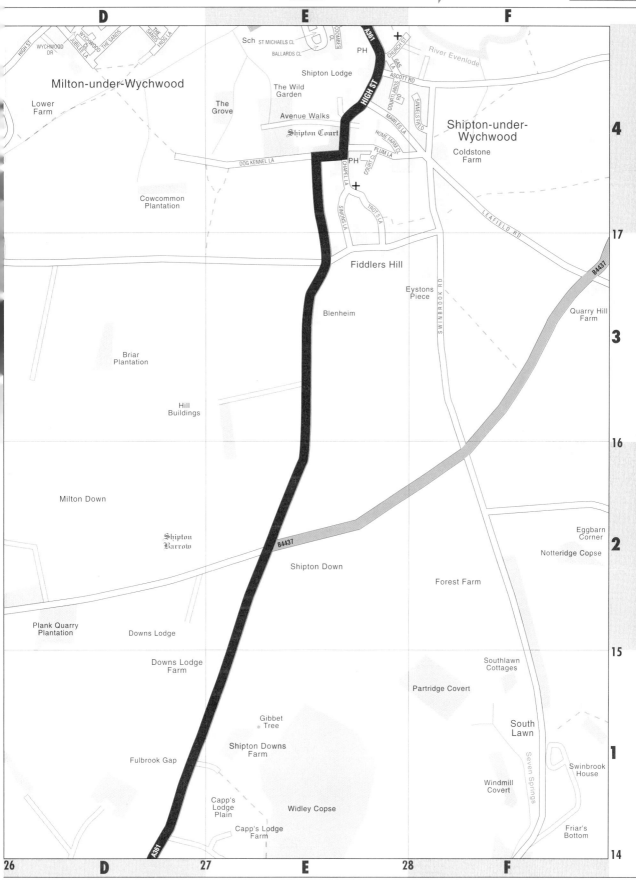

D   E   F

4

17

3

16

2

15

1

14

Milton-under-Wychwood

Lower Farm

Sch   ST MICHAELS CL
BALLARDS CL

Shipton Lodge

The Wild Garden

The Grove

Avenue Walks

Shipton Court

DOG KENNEL LA

Cowcommon Plantation

HIGH ST

A361

PH

CHURCH ST
GAS
COURTLANDS RD
ASCOTT RD
SINNELS FIELD

MAWLES LA

HOME FARM CL

PLUM LA

PH

COURT CL

CHAPEL LA

SIMONS LA

TROT LA

River Evenlode

Shipton-under-Wychwood

Coldstone Farm

LEAFIELD RD

Fiddlers Hill

Eystons Piece

Blenheim

SWINBROOK RD

B4437

Quarry Hill Farm

Briar Plantation

Hill Buildings

Milton Down

Shipton Barrow

B4437

Shipton Down

Eggbarn Corner

Notteridge Copse

Forest Farm

Plank Quarry Plantation

Downs Lodge

Downs Lodge Farm

Southlawn Cottages

Partridge Covert

Gibbet Tree

Shipton Downs Farm

South Lawn

Fulbrook Gap

Seven Springs

Swinbrook House

Windmill Covert

Capp's Lodge Plain

Widley Copse

Capp's Lodge Farm

A361

Friar's Bottom

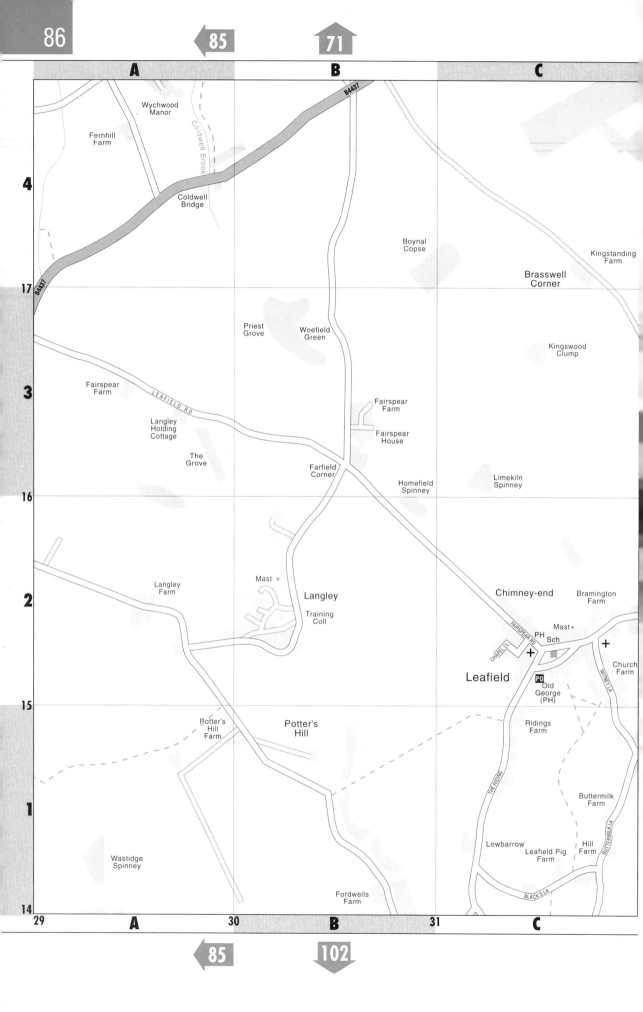

A   B   C

Wychwood
Manor

Fernhill
Farm

Coldwell Brook

B4437

4

Coldwell
Bridge

Boynal
Copse

Kingstanding
Farm

Brasswell
Corner

17

B4437

Priest
Grove

Woefield
Green

Kingswood
Clump

Fairspear
Farm

3

LEAFIELD RD

Langley
Holding
Cottage

Fairspear
Farm

The
Grove

Fairspear
House

Farfield
Corner

Homefield
Spinney

Limekiln
Spinney

16

Langley
Farm

Mast

Langley

Chimney-end

Bramington
Farm

2

Training
Coll

FAIRSPEAR RD

Mast

CHAPEL CL

PH
Sch

✝

Church
Farm

Leafield

PO

WITNEY LA

Old
George
(PH)

15

Potter's
Hill
Farm

Potter's
Hill

Ridings
Farm

THE RIDING

Buttermilk
Farm

1

BUTTERMILK LA

Wastidge
Spinney

Lowbarrow

Leafield Pig
Farm

Hill
Farm

BLACK'S LA

Fordwells
Farm

14

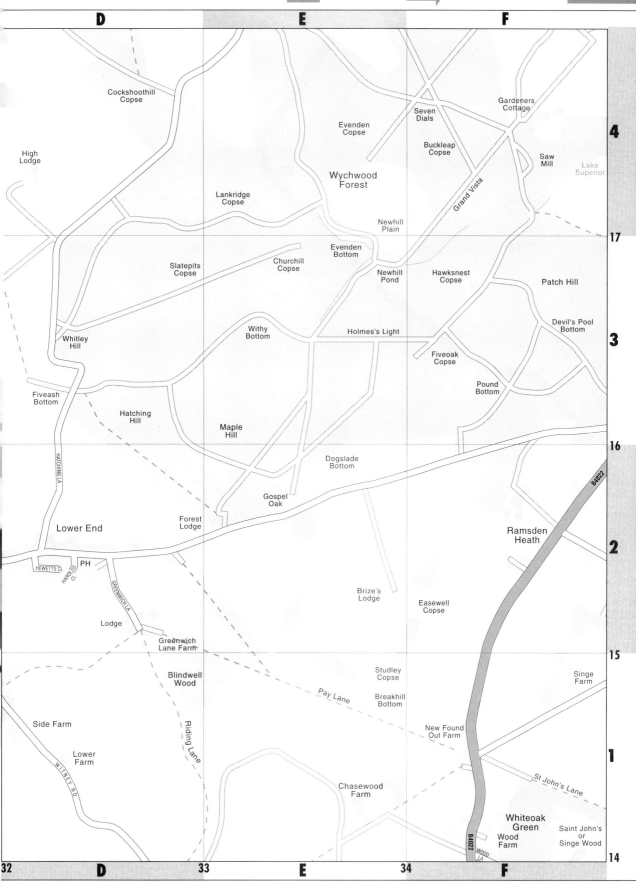

Cockshoothill
Copse

Seven
Dials

Gardeners
Cottage

Evenden
Copse

Buckleap
Copse

High
Lodge

Saw
Mill

Lake
Superior

4

Wychwood
Forest

Lankridge
Copse

Newhill
Plain

Grand Vista

17

Slatepits
Copse

Churchill Copse

Evenden
Bottom

Hawksnest
Copse

Patch Hill

Newhill
Pond

Devil's Pool
Bottom

Withy
Bottom

Holmes's Light

3

Fiveoak
Copse

Whitley
Hill

Fiveash
Bottom

Pound
Bottom

Hatching
Hill

Maple
Hill

16

HATCHING LA

Dogslade
Bottom

B4022

Lower End

Gospel
Oak

Forest
Lodge

Ramsden
Heath

2

HEWETTS CL

PH

HARDLUS CL

GREENWICH LA

Brize's
Lodge

Easewell
Copse

Lodge

Greenwich
Lane Farm

15

Blindwell
Wood

Studley
Copse

Singe
Farm

Pay Lane

Breakhill
Bottom

Side Farm

Riding Lane

New Found
Out Farm

Lower
Farm

St John's Lane

1

WITNEY RD

Chasewood
Farm

Whiteoak
Green

Saint John's
or
Singe Wood

B4022

Wood
Farm

WOOD LA

14

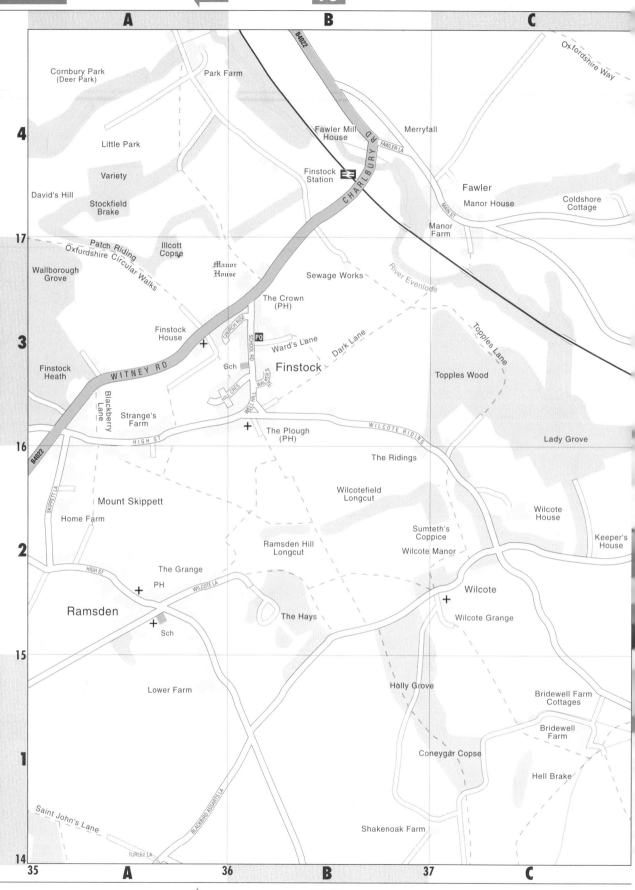

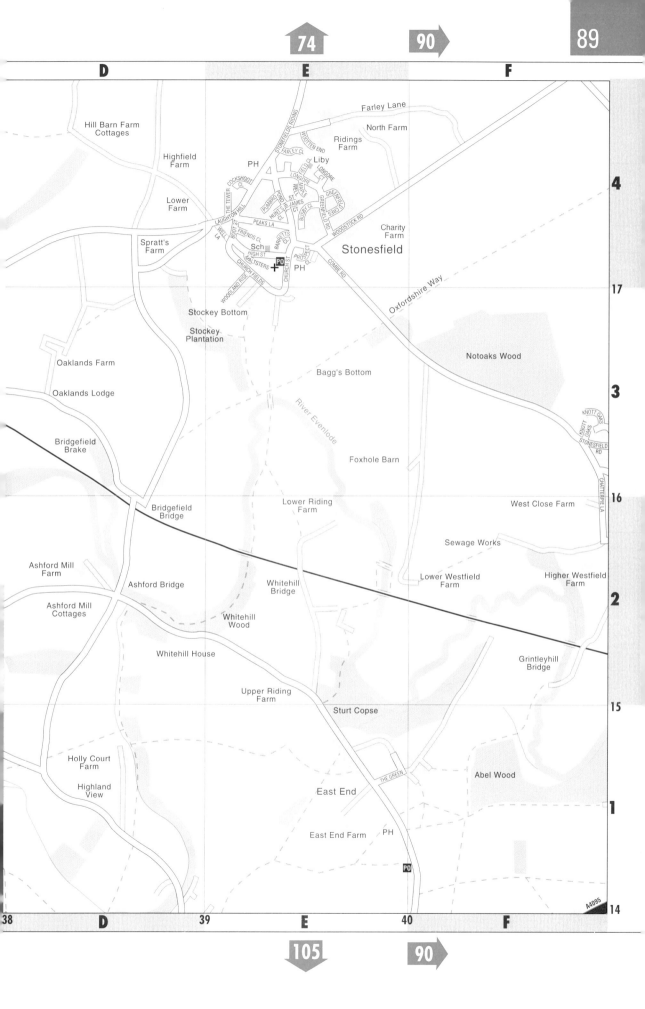

D
E
F

Hill Barn Farm
Cottages

Highfield
Farm

Lower
Farm

Spratt's
Farm

PH

Farley Lane

North Farm

Ridings
Farm

Liby

Sch

Stonesfield

Charity
Farm

Oxfordshire Way

Notoaks Wood

Stockey Bottom

Stockey
Plantation

Oaklands Farm

Oaklands Lodge

Bagg's Bottom

River Evenlode

Foxhole Barn

West Close Farm

KNOTT OAKS

STONESFIELD RD

CHATTERPIE LA

Bridgefield
Brake

Bridgefield
Bridge

Lower Riding
Farm

Sewage Works

Ashford Mill
Farm

Ashford Bridge

Whitehill
Bridge

Lower Westfield
Farm

Higher Westfield
Farm

Ashford Mill
Cottages

Whitehill
Wood

Whitehill House

Upper Riding
Farm

Sturt Copse

Grintleyhill
Bridge

Holly Court
Farm

Highland
View

The Green

East End

Abel Wood

East End Farm

PH

PO

A4095

4

17

3

16

2

15

1

14

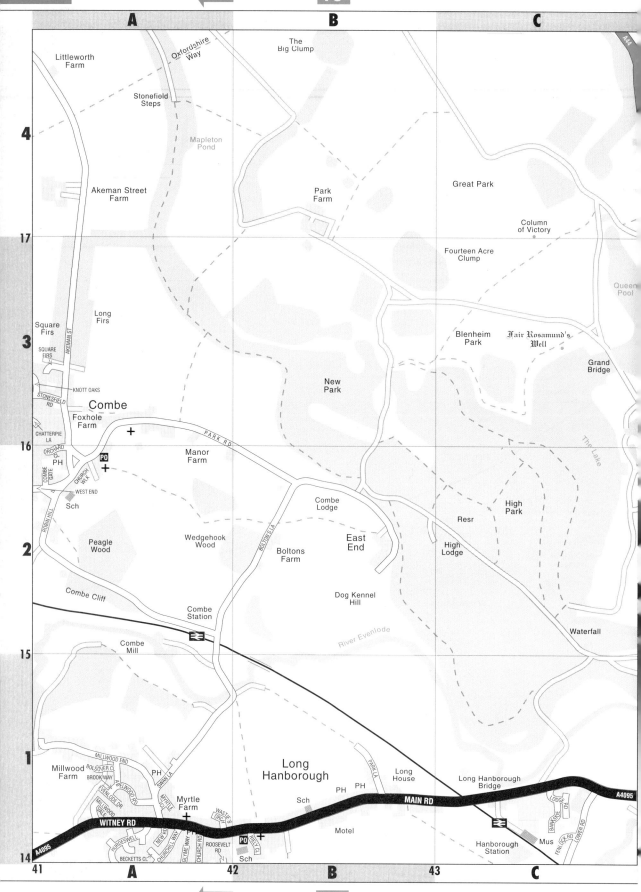

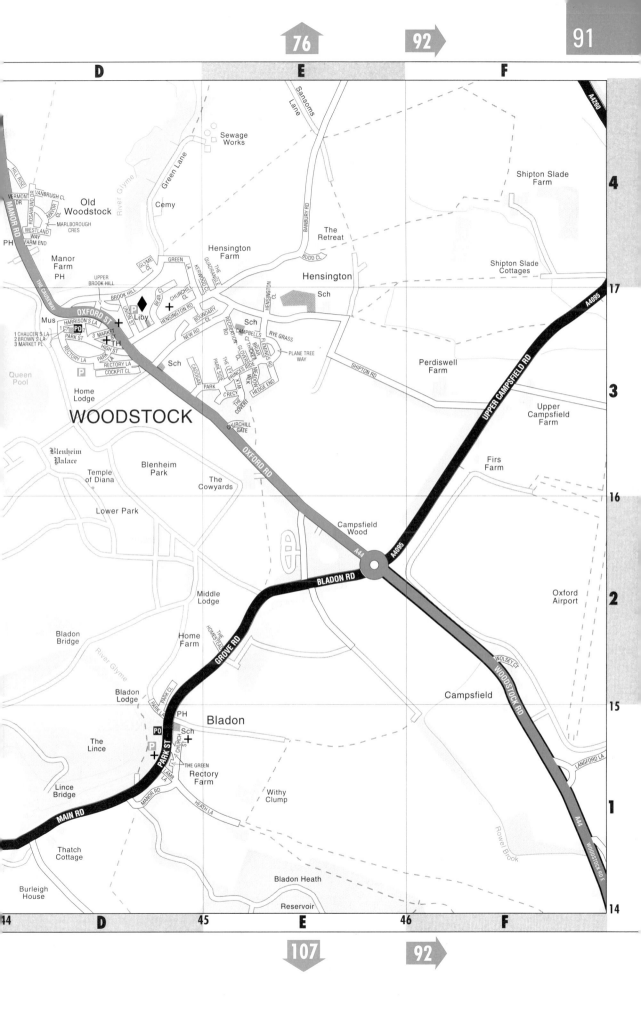

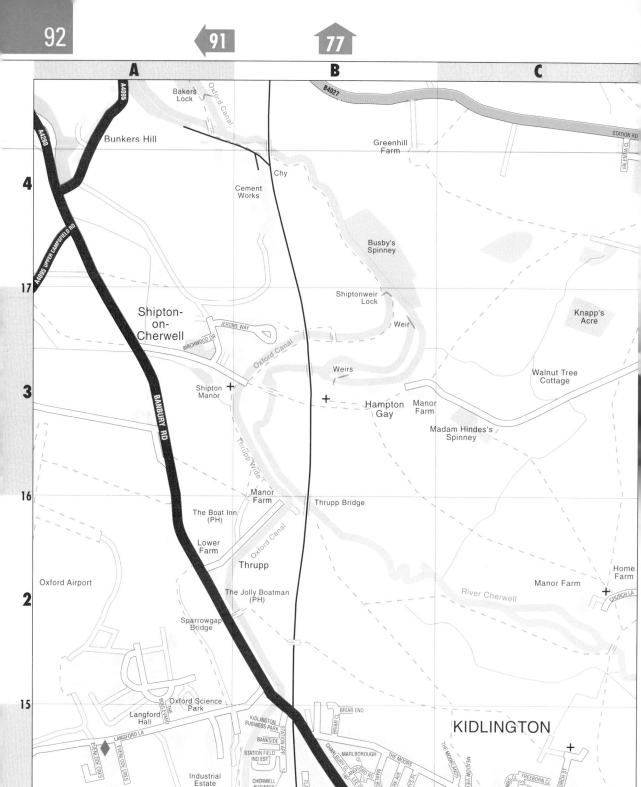

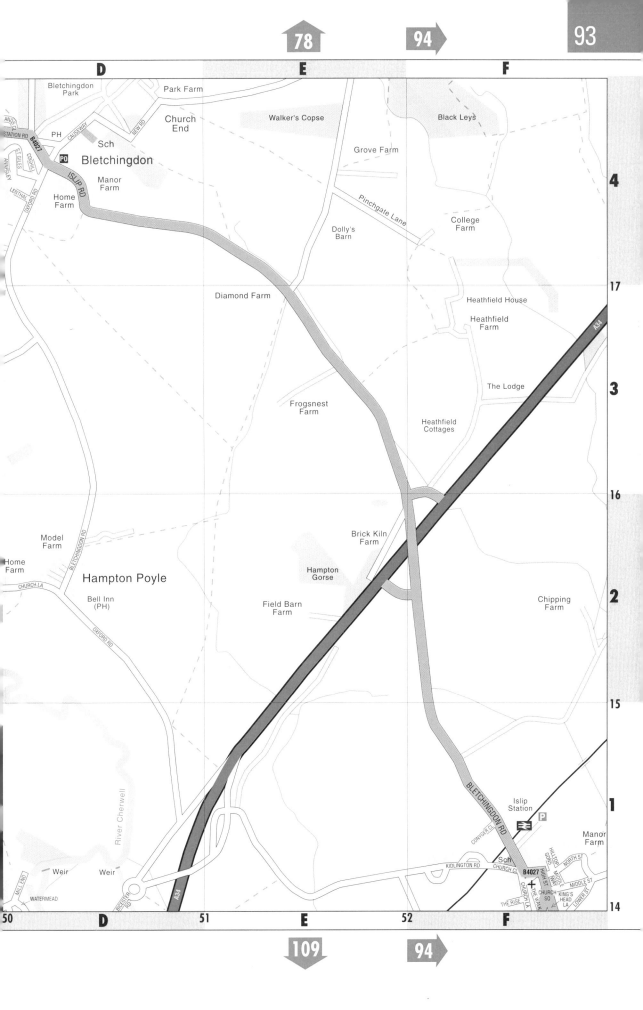

Bletchingdon
Park
Park Farm
Walker's Copse
Black Leys
Church
End
Grove Farm
PH
Sch
Bletchingdon
PO
Manor
Farm
Home
Farm
Pinchgate Lane
College
Farm
Dolly's
Barn
Diamond Farm
Heathfield House
Heathfield
Farm
Frogsnest
Farm
The Lodge
Heathfield
Cottages
Brick Kiln
Farm
Model
Farm
Home
Farm
Hampton Poyle
Hampton
Gorse
Chipping
Farm
Bell Inn
(PH)
Field Barn
Farm
River Cherwell
Islip
Station
Manor
Farm
Weir
Weir
Islip
Station
P
WATERMEAD
Kidlington Rd
Sch
Bicester Rd
A34
B4027
BLETCHINGDON RD
CONYGER CL

ST GILES
COGHILL
ANNESLEY
LENTHAL
OXFORD RD
STATION RD
B4027
ISLIP RD
CAUSEWAY
NEW RD
BLETCHINGDON RD
OXFORD RD
CHURCH LA
MILL END

4
17
3
16
2
15
1
14

50
D
51
E
52
F

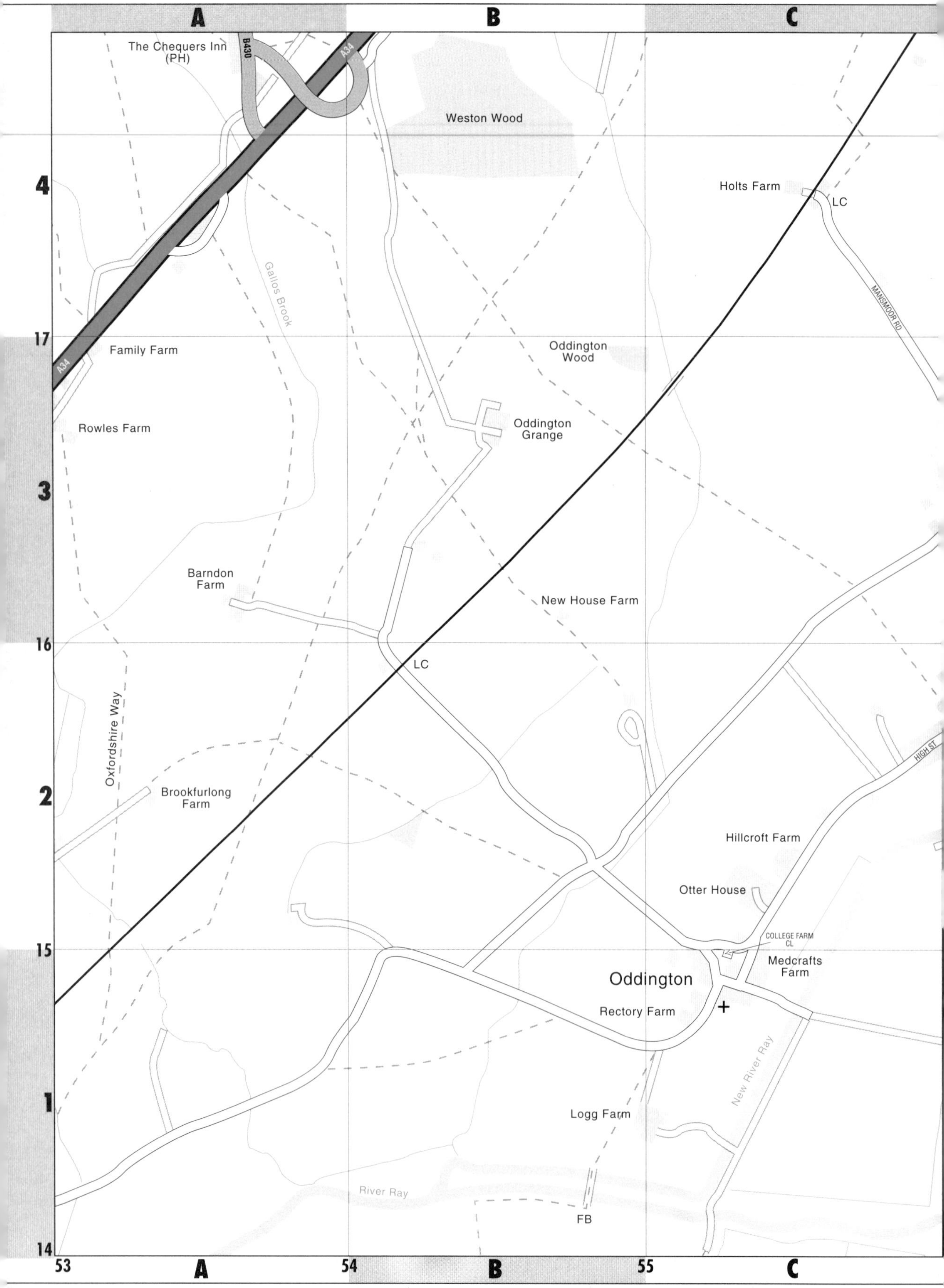

A
B
C

The Chequers Inn
(PH)

B430

A34

Weston Wood

Holts Farm
LC

MANSMOOR RD

4

Gallos Brook

17

A34

Family Farm

Oddington
Wood

Rowles Farm

Oddington
Grange

3

Barndon
Farm

New House Farm

16

LC

Oxfordshire Way

HIGH ST

2

Brookfurlong
Farm

Hillcroft Farm

Otter House

COLLEGE FARM
CL

15

Medcrafts
Farm

Oddington

Rectory Farm

+

New River Ray

1

Logg Farm

River Ray

FB

14

53
A
54
B
55
C

M40

Sewage Works

West End Farm

West End La

The Butts

Church Cl

Manor Farm

Forge Cl

PO PH

The Orchard

Merton

4

River Ray

17

Street Hill

Mansmoor Rd

3

M40

The Homestead

Newgate Rd

Fencott Bridge

Bridge House Farm

Bull's Lane

Pound Lane

Mill Lane

Mill Cl

Wks

Fencott

Murcott

Field La

Sch

Fencott Rd

Manor Farm

16

The Broadway

Church View

Church La

Moor Lands

Blacksmith La

High St

Fiveacres

PH

Charlton-on-Otmoor

The Chine

Pigeonhouse Farm

PH

2

Otmoor La

New River Ray

Pigeonhouse La

15

1

Danger Area

Ot Moor

14

A   **B**   **C**

Astley Bridge Farm

LC

The Plough (PH)

Bridge Farm

PALMER AVE

PLOUGHLEY CL

LC

LC

River Ray

4

LC

PATRICK HAUGH RD

MORRIS RD

Upper Arncott

GREEN LA

CL

Depot

HOPCRAFT CL

EAGLE CL

MILL HILL

LSIDE CL

BUCHANAN RD

Arncott Hill

CH

CONSTABLE'S CROFT

HARPER CL

GREENFIELDS

WOODPIECE RD

Arncott Wood

17

LCs

MURCOTT RD

Arncott Hill Farm

Depot

LC

LC

LC

ARNCOTT WOOD RD

3

M40

FIELD RD

LC

LC

Boarstall Lane

16

New Park Farm

Red House Farm

Murcott

Oldhouse Spinney

2

Marlake House

Latchmeads

Four Winds Farm

Panshill Farms

Pans Hill

Whitecross Green

15

Manor Farm

Upper Panshill Farm

Whitecross Green Wood

Nature Reserve

1

M40

Upper Wood

Oriel Wood

14

59   **A**   60   **B**   61   **C**

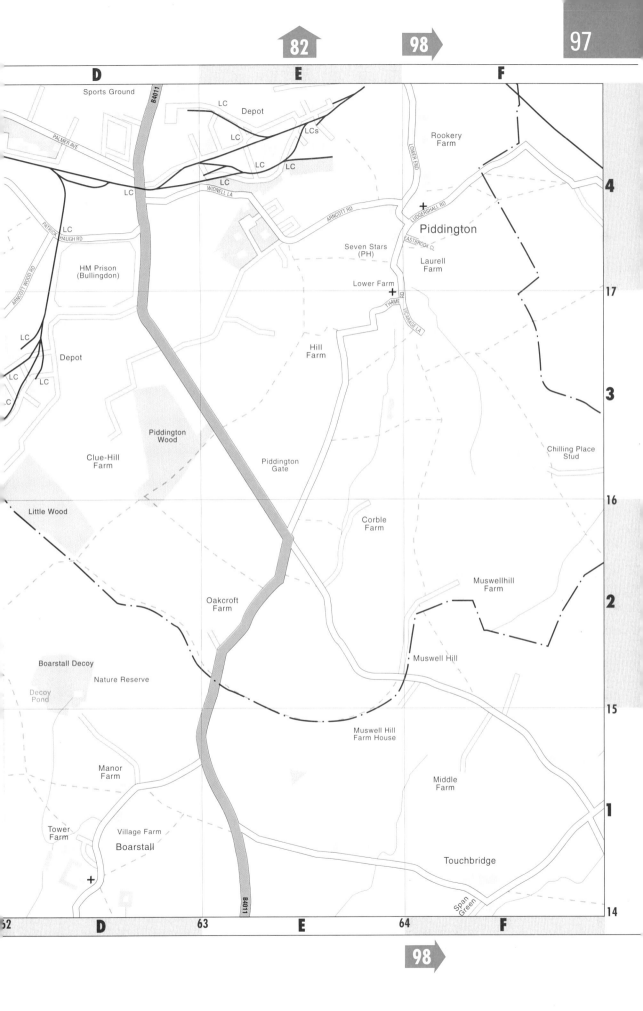

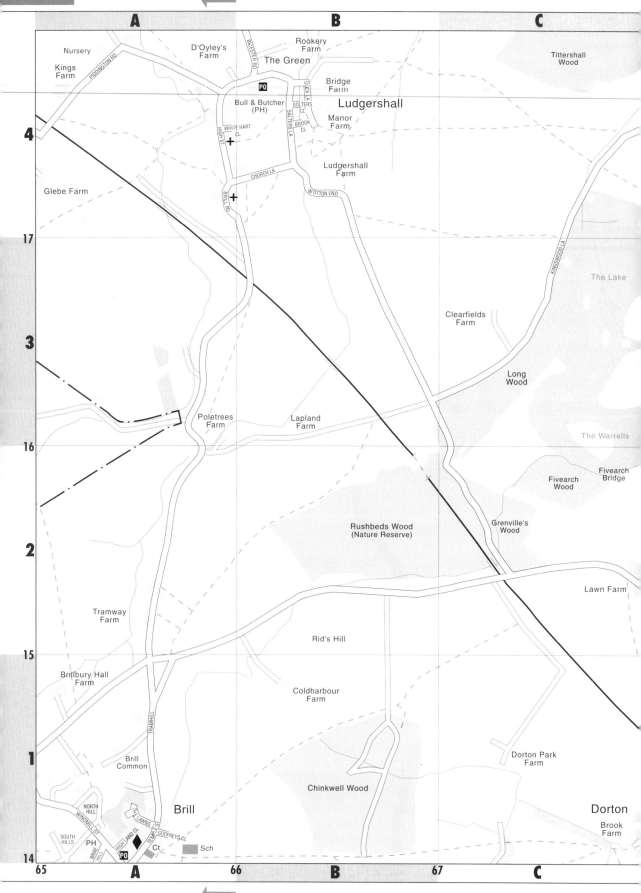

A | B | C

Nursery

Kings
Farm

PIDDINGTON RD

D'Oyley's
Farm

Rookery
Farm

The Green

BICESTER RD

PO

Bull & Butcher
(PH)

Bridge
Farm

DUCK LA

Ludgershall

SOLTERS
CL

Manor
Farm

WHITE HART
CL

4

HIGH ST

SALTERS LA

BROOK
CL

Tittershall
Wood

Glebe Farm

BRILL RD

CHURCH LA

WOTTON END

Ludgershall
Farm

17

KINGSWOOD LA

The Lake

Clearfields
Farm

3

Long
Wood

The Warrells

Poletrees
Farm

Lapland
Farm

16

Fivearch
Wood

Fivearch
Bridge

Rushbeds Wood
(Nature Reserve)

Grenville's
Wood

2

Tramway
Farm

Lawn Farm

Rid's Hill

15

Brillbury Hall
Farm

Coldharbour
Farm

TRAMHILL

1

Brill
Common

Dorton Park
Farm

NORTH
HILL

Chinkwell Wood

Dorton

Brill

WINDMILL ST

THE LAWNS

GODFREYS CL

TEMPLE ST

Brook
Farm

SOUTH
HILLS

PH

BRAE HILL

HIGHLAND CL

PO

Ct

Sch

14

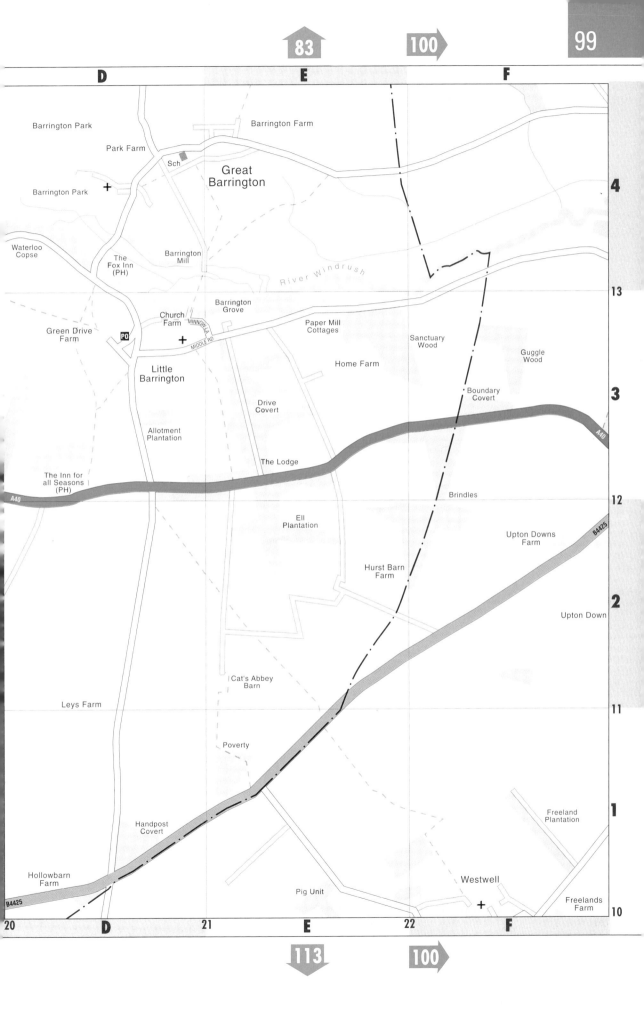

D
E
F

Barrington Park

Park Farm

Sch

Great
Barrington

Barrington Farm

4

Barrington Park

Waterloo
Copse

The
Fox Inn
(PH)

Barrington
Mill

Barrington
Mill

River Windrush

13

Green Drive
Farm

PO

Church
Farm

MINNOW LA

MIDDLE RD

Barrington
Grove

Paper Mill
Cottages

Sanctuary
Wood

Guggle
Wood

Little
Barrington

Home Farm

Drive
Covert

Boundary
Covert

3

A40

Allotment
Plantation

The Inn for
all Seasons
(PH)

A40

The Lodge

Brindles

12

Upton Downs
Farm

B4425

Ell
Plantation

Upton Down

2

Hurst Barn
Farm

Cat's Abbey
Barn

Leys Farm

11

Poverty

Freeland
Plantation

1

Handpost
Covert

Hollowbarn
Farm

B4425

Pig Unit

Westwell

Freelands
Farm

10

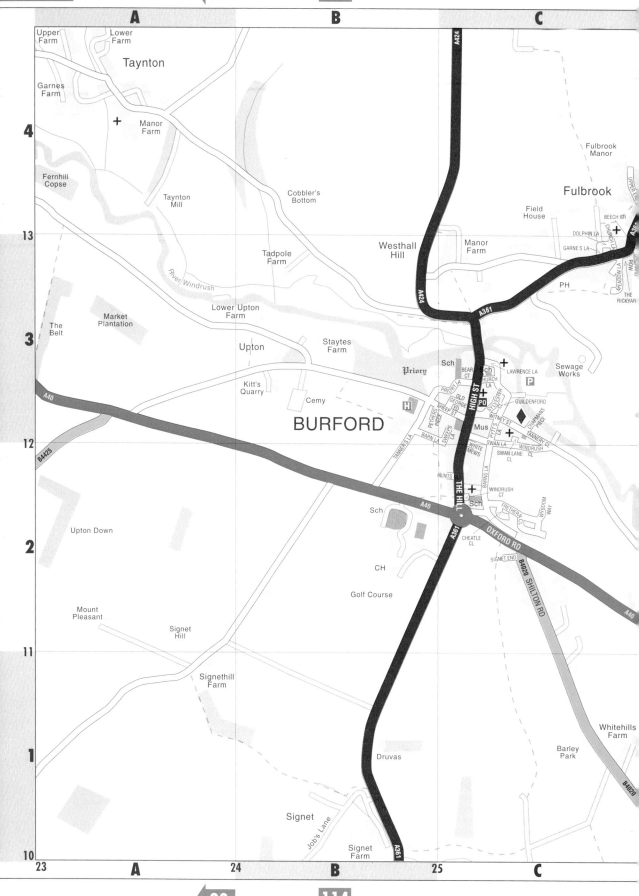

Upper Farm
Lower Farm
Taynton
Garnes Farm
Manor Farm
Fernhill Copse
Taynton Mill
Cobbler's Bottom
Tadpole Farm
River Windrush
Lower Upton Farm
Market Plantation
The Belt
Upton
Staytes Farm
Kitt's Quarry
Cemy
Priory
Sch
BURFORD
Westhall Hill

Fulbrook Manor
Fulbrook
Field House
BEECH BR
DOLPHIN LA
GARNE'S LA
Manor Farm
PH
THE RICKYAR
Sewage Works
Lawrence La
BEAR CT
CHURCH
OLD GEORGE YD
PRIORY LA
PETERS PIECE
SHEEP ST
SWEEPS LA
BARN LA
TANNER S LA
HIGH ST
PO
SILKESTER
WITNEY ST
PYTT'S LA
Mus
WHITE MEWS
SWAN LA
HUNTS
BARNS LA
THE HILL
Sch
Guildenford
CHAPMANS PIECE
TANNERY CL
WINDRUSH CL
SWAN LANE CL
WINDRUSH CT
FRETHERN CL
WYSDOM WAY
CHEATLE CL
Sch
CH
Golf Course
OXFORD RD
SHILTON RD
Signet End
Upton Down
Mount Pleasant
Signet Hill
Signethill Farm
Whitehills Farm
Barley Park
Druvas
Signet
Jobs Lane
Signet Farm
A40
A361
A24
A361
B4425
B4020

101
86

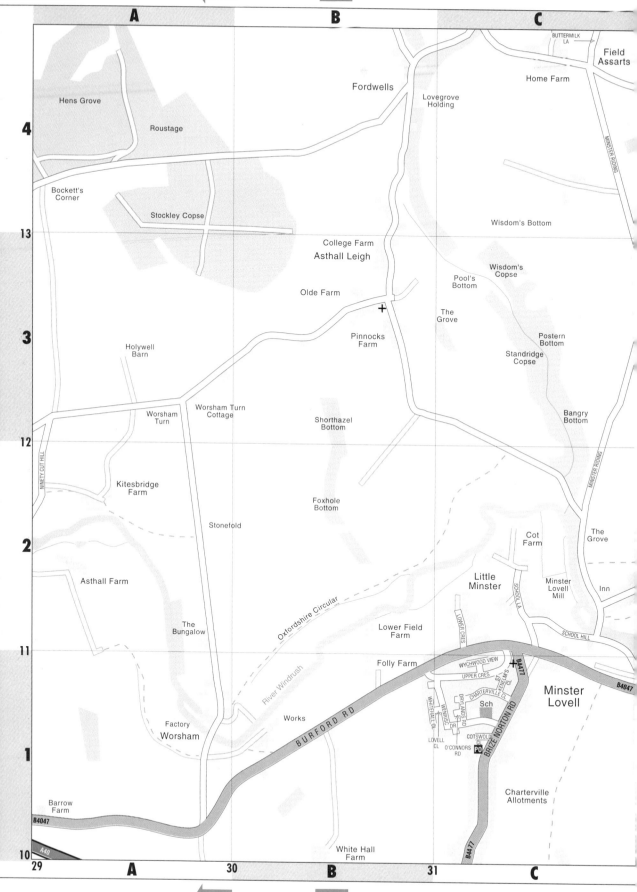

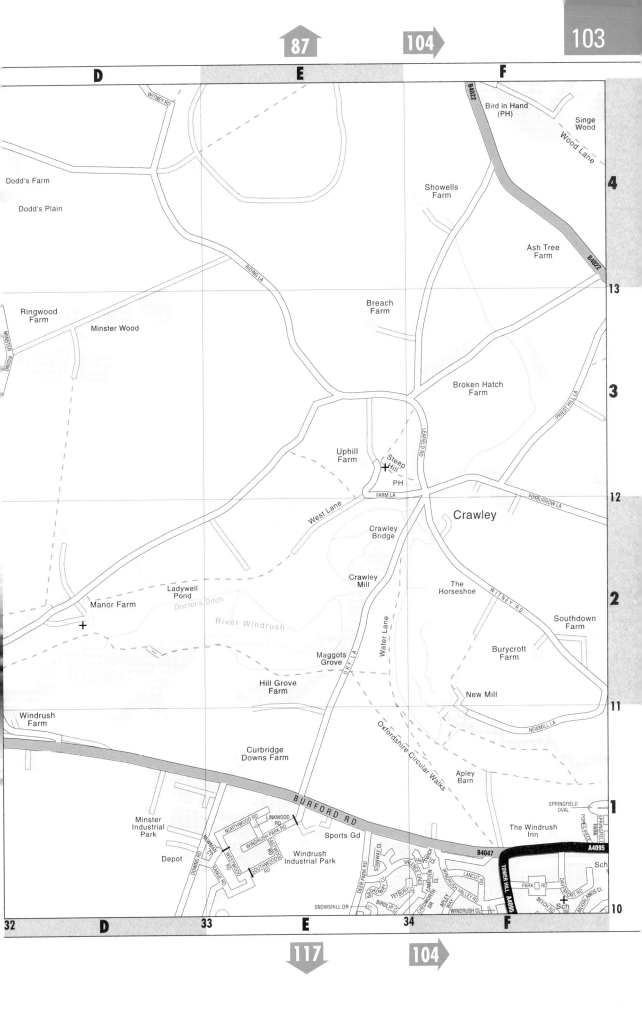

A   B   C

Turley Farm

Gigley Farm

The Bungalow

North Leigh

4

Delly End

Common Leys Farm

Taylor's Copse

TURLEY LA

WHITINGS LA

WOOD LA

DELLY CL

Hickrall

New Yatt Farm

New Yatt

HATFIELD PITS LA

NEW YATT LA

Manor House

The Hydes

BREACH LANE

Keepers Cottage

Business Centre

KITE Lane

GREEN LA

13

Breach Farm

Job's Copse

PH

Moorland Farm

DELLY HILL

B4022

Middletown

Home Farm

Heath Holm Farm

GREENHILLS LA

HICKS CL

FISHERS CL

Sch PH

FLOREY'S CL

NEW RD

Hailey

Poffley End

Spicers Lane

CHURCH LA

+

3

SWANHALL LA

Swanhall Farm

CHAPEL LA

POFFLEY END LA

Witheridge Farm

Witheridge Cross

Water Lane

WATER LANE

12

FOXBURROW LA

FOX CL

University Farm

Downhill Farm

Osney Hill Farm

A4095

DOWNHILL LA

MILKING LA

Highcroft Farm

Merryfield Farm

The Bungalow

2

Sch

SCHOFIELD GDNS

Middlefield Farm

Sch

Cogges Wood

HOYLE CL

SCHOFIELD AVE

EASTFIELD RD

NEW YATT RD

HAILEY RD

QUARRY

WESTFIELD RD

TAPHOUSE AVE

VINER RD

TARRANT AVE

WOODSTOCK RD

11

CHESTNUT CL

FARMERS CL

VINER CL

EARLY RD

CRAWLEY RD

B4022

FARMERS CL

FARMERS CL

SYCAMORE CL

MADLEY CL

River Windrush

BAKERS PIECE

THE CRESCENT

Northfield Farm

Springfield Oval

Wks

WEST END

WOODGREEN HILL

+

WOODLANDS RD

Sch

1

Springfield Park

Mills

WEST END RD

PO

Woodgreen

WITNEY

BURFORD RD

A4095

MILL ST

RIVERSIDE GDNS

BRIDGE ST

MADLEY BROOK

MOOR AVE

DARK LA

PUCK LA

JACOBS

GLOUCESTER PL

THE OLD COACHYARD

NEWLAND

Newland

PENSCLOSE

Sch

MOORLAND RD

H

GLOUCESTER COURT MEWS

WITAN WAY

THE WILLOWS

NEWLANDS MILL

COURTS GDNS

KINGSFIELD CRES

KINGSFIELD GDNS

+

B4022

10

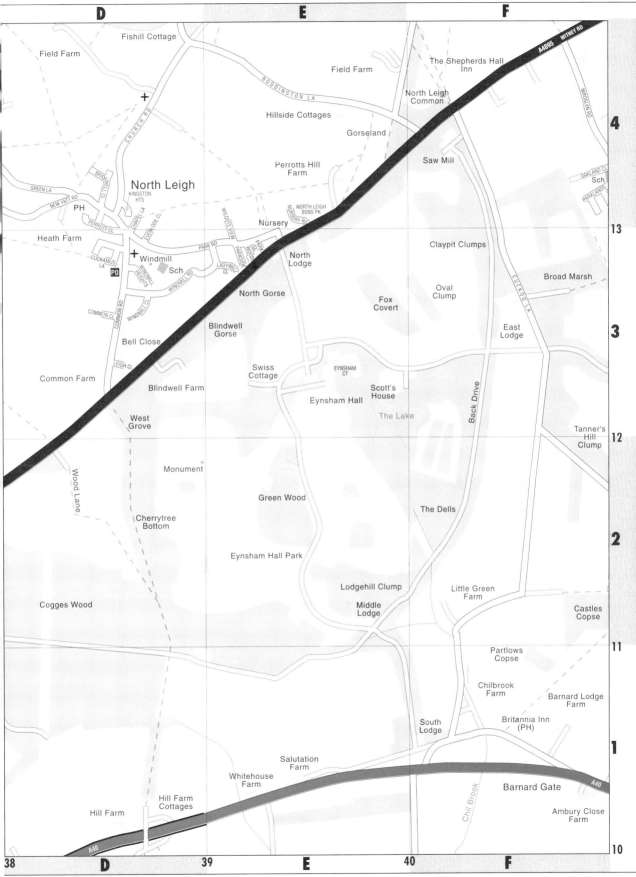

Field Farm

Fishill Cottage

Field Farm

The Shepherds Hall Inn

A4095 WITNEY RD

WROSLYN RD

North Leigh Common

4

BODDINGTON LA

Hillside Cottages

Gorseland

Saw Mill

OAKLAND CL
Sch

PARKLANDS

CHURCH RD

Perrotts Hill Farm

Green La

New Yatt Rd

BRIDEWELL CL

North Leigh

KINGSTON HTS

CHAPEL LA

ELVENDEN CL

PH

PERROTT CL

WILCOTE VIEW

PARK RD

NORTH LEIGH BSNS PK

NURSERY RD

Nursery

13

Claypit Clumps

CUCKOO LA

Broad Marsh

Heath Farm

CUCKAMUS LA

PO

Windmill
Sch

WINDMILL HEIGHTS

WINDMILL RD

PARKSIDE

WILCOTE WOOD

LADYWELL CL

North Lodge

North Gorse

Fox Covert

Oval Clump

East Lodge

3

COMMON CL

COMMON RD

WINDMILL CL

Bell Close

Blindwell Gorse

Swiss Cottage

EYNSHAM CT

Scott's House

LEIGH CL

Common Farm

Blindwell Farm

Eynsham Hall

The Lake

Back Drive

Tanner's Hill Clump

12

West Grove

Monument

Green Wood

The Dells

2

Wood Lane

Cherrytree Bottom

Eynsham Hall Park

Lodgehill Clump

Little Green Farm

Castles Copse

Cogges Wood

Middle Lodge

11

Partlows Copse

Chilbrook Farm

Barnard Lodge Farm

South Lodge

Britannia Inn (PH)

1

Salutation Farm

Whitehouse Farm

Barnard Gate

A40

Chil Brook

Hill Farm Cottages

Hill Farm

A40

Ambury Close Farm

10

A   B   C

LOWER RD

HURDSWELL

GLYME WAY
CHURCHILL WAY
ROOSEVELT RD
PINSLEY RD

Allot
Gdns

Pinsley
Wood

Mill
Farm

4

Cook's Corner
Farm

Cemy

CHURCH RD

OAKLAND CL

Sch
PO   PARKLANDS

Freeland

WROSLYN RD
HURST RD
NASH LA
WOODLANDS
THE
THE ASH
CHURCH RD
WALKERS
BLENHEIM LA
JACOB
MARSH LA
WEBSTER'S CL
PH

Little
Blenheim

Sewage
Works

MANSELL CL

Church
Hanborough

PH

College
Farm

13

+

+
PH

Whitehouse
Farm

PIGEON HOUSE LA

+

Dreydon
House

3

Freeland
House

Elm
Farm

The
Thrift

Goose Eye
Farm

The
Green

Oxfordshire Circular Walks

12

Lady
Grove

New Barn
Farm

River Evenlode

Vincents
Wood

CUCKOO LA

2

Oxfordshire Circular Walks

CUCKOO LA

Bowles
Farm

City
Farm

11

Eynsham
Mill

Acre Hill
Farm

New Wintles
Farm

Mill Lane

1

A40

Evenlode
Farm

Acre Hill
House

A40

Chil Brook

10

41   A   42   B   43   C

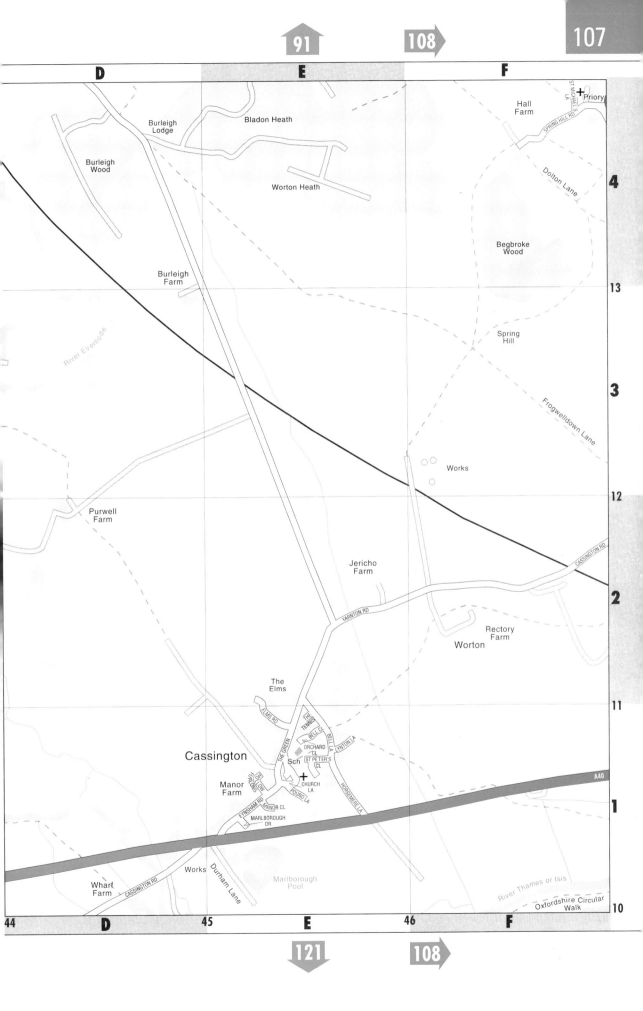

D
E
F

4
13
3
12
2
11
1
10

Hall Farm
Priory
ST MICHAEL'S LA
SPRING HILL RD
Dolton Lane

Burleigh Lodge
Bladon Heath

Burleigh Wood

Worton Heath

Begbroke Wood

Burleigh Farm

River Evenlode

Spring Hill

Frogwelldown Lane

Works

Purwell Farm

CASSINGTON RD

Jericho Farm

YARNTON RD

Rectory Farm

Worton

The Elms

ELMS RD
THE TENNIS
BELL CL
BELL LA
LYNTON LA
ORCHARD CL
ST PETER'S CL

Cassington

THE GREEN
Sch

Manor Farm

CHURCH LA

LOW FURLONG
MANOR CL
POUND LA
HORSEMERE LA

EYNSHAM RD
MARLBOROUGH DR

A40

Wharf Farm

CASSINGTON RD
Works
Durham Lane
Marlborough Pool

River Thames or Isis

Oxfordshire Circular Walk

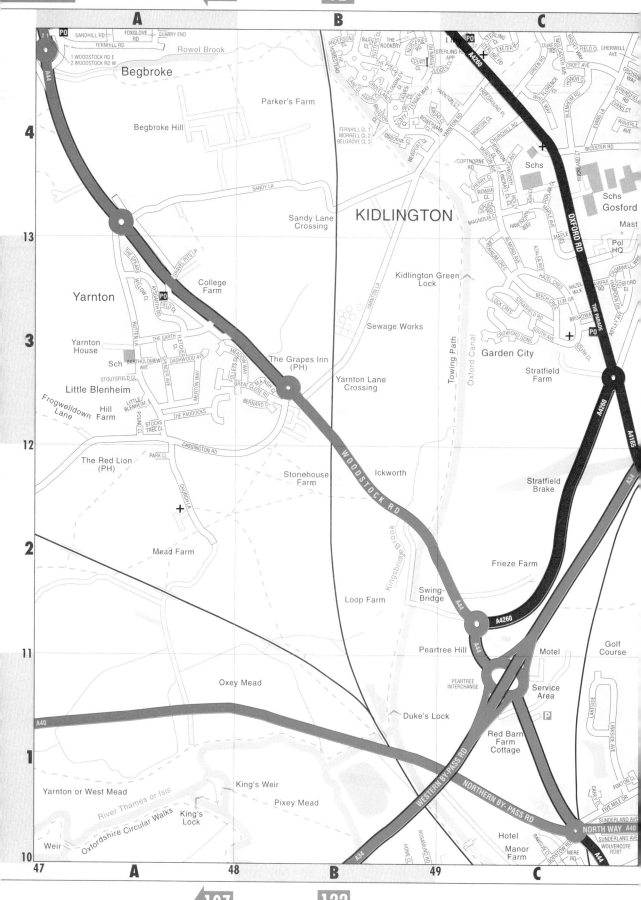

D
E
F

A34

WATERMEAD
WOODLANDS
CHERWELL AVE
QUEEN'S AVE
WAVERLEY AVE
SPRINGFIELD RD
EDINBURGH DR
KINGS WAY
LOVELACE DR
BICESTER RD
CLEVELAND DR
BEAGLES CL
CROMWELL WAY
WATER EATON LA
CH
KIRK CL
ROTHA FIELD RD
FIVE MILE DR
SUNDERLAND AVE
BLANDFORD AVE
CUTTESLOWE RDBT
OAVENANT RD
SUNDERLAND AVE

Gosford Bridge

Gosford Farm

Mill Farm
LC
LC

River Ray
Weir

COLLICE ST
BRIDGE ST
LOWER ST
B4027

Islip

WHEATLEY RD

B4027

4

Northfield Farm

Hillside Farm

13

Water Eaton Crossing

River Cherwell

Middle Farm

3

Water Eaton
+

12

Sparsey Bridge

2

St Frideswide Farm

11

OXFORD RD

Oxford Business Park

Cutteslowe

Cemy
+

HASLEMERE GDNS
HAYWARD RD
TALBOT RD
HARBORD RD
MARRIOTT CL
BOURNE CL
HAREFIELDS
DAVID WALTER CL
JORDAN HILL
PARK CL
PENNYWELL DR
TEMPLAR RD
MILLER'S ACRE
KENDAL
SPARSEY PL
CRES
PRIOR'S FORGE
HOLT WEER CL

P
P
PO
P

Sports Ground

Cutteslow Park

Sescut Farm

1

BANBURY RD

NORTH WAY
ELSFIELD WAY
NORTHERN BY-PASS RD
A40

Bayswater Brook

Sch
HAWKSMOOR RD
WYATT RD
SOUTHDALE RD
CARLTON RD
JACKSON RD
CAVENDISH RD
WOLSEY RD
BUCKLER RD
SCOTT RD
WREN RD
WHITE RD

10

50
D
51
E
52
F

A4165

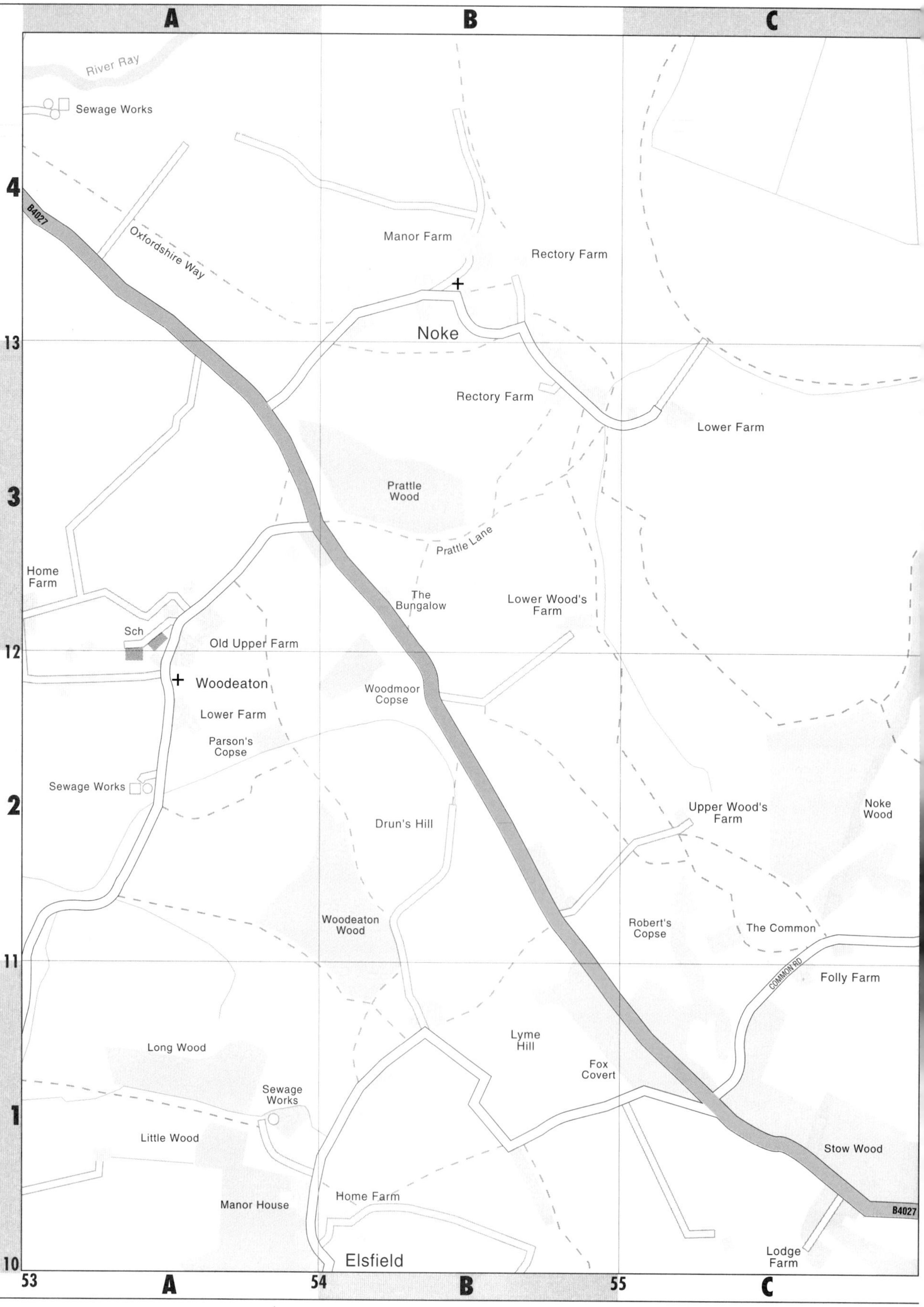

A   B   C

River Ray

Sewage Works

4

B4027

Oxfordshire Way

Manor Farm

Rectory Farm

✝

Noke

13

Rectory Farm

Lower Farm

Prattle Wood

3

Prattle Lane

Home Farm

The Bungalow

Lower Wood's Farm

Sch

Old Upper Farm

12

Woodmoor Copse

✝ Woodeaton

Lower Farm

Parson's Copse

Drun's Hill

Sewage Works

Upper Wood's Farm

Noke Wood

2

Woodeaton Wood

Robert's Copse

The Common

11

COMMON RD

Folly Farm

Long Wood

Lyme Hill

Fox Covert

Sewage Works

Stow Wood

1

Little Wood

B4027

Manor House

Home Farm

Lodge Farm

10

Elsfield

53   A   54   B   55   C

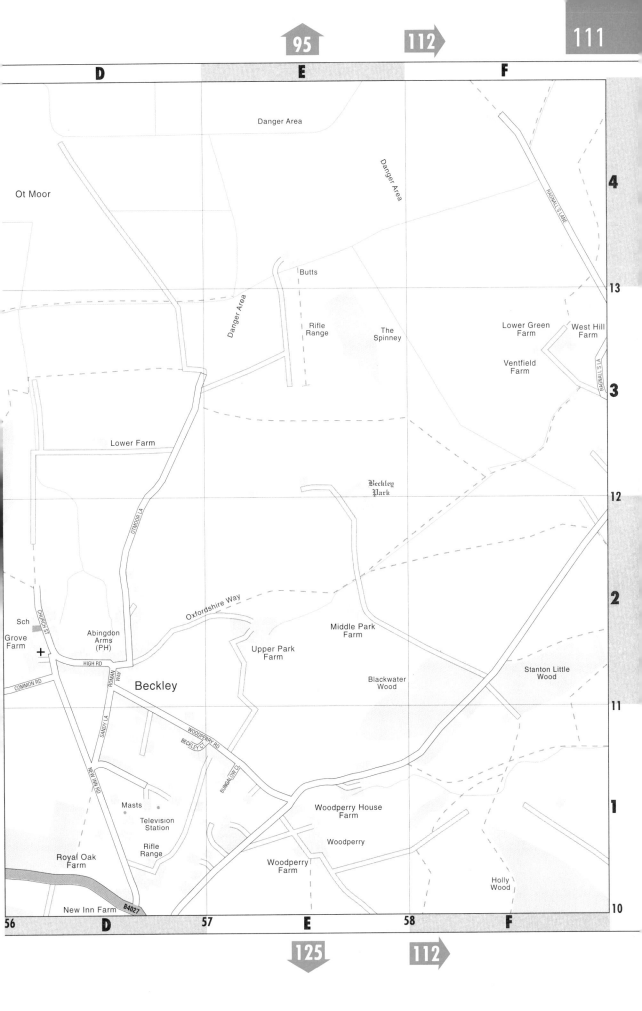

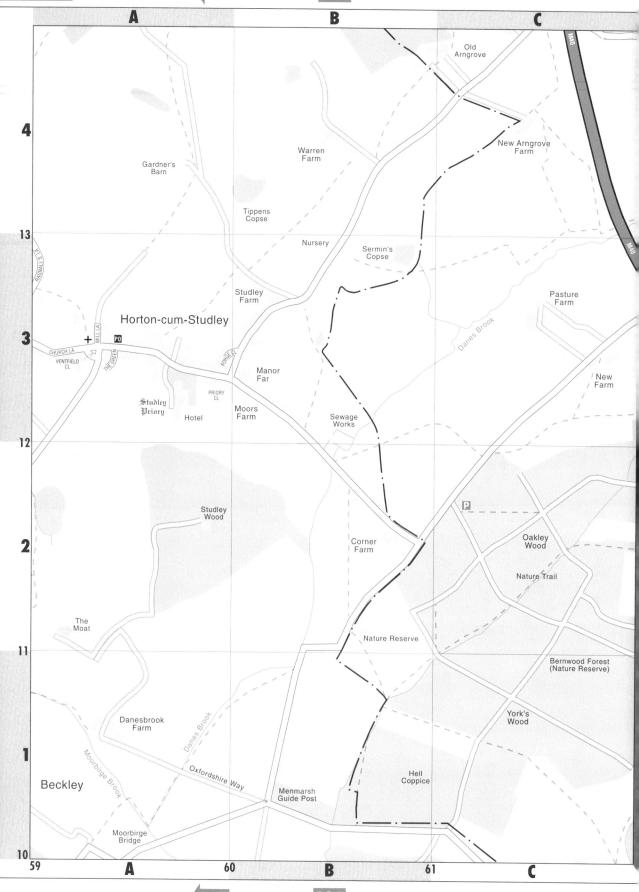

A   B   C

4

Old Arngrove

New Arngrove
Farm

M40

Gardner's
Barn

Warren
Farm

Tippens
Copse

13

Nursery

Sermin's
Copse

Pasture
Farm

Studley
Farm

Danes Brook

Horton-cum-Studley

MILL LA
PO

New
Farm

3

CHURCH LA

VENTFIELD
CL

THE GREEN

FORGE CL

Manor
Far

RAGNALL'S LA

Studley
Priory

PRIORY
CL

Hotel

Moors
Farm

Sewage
Works

12

Studley
Wood

P

Oakley
Wood

2

Corner
Farm

Nature Trail

The
Moat

Nature Reserve

Bernwood Forest
(Nature Reserve)

11

York's
Wood

Danesbrook
Farm

Danes Brook

1

Moorbirge Brook

Oxfordshire Way

Hell
Coppice

Beckley

Menmarsh
Guide Post

Moorbirge
Bridge

10

59   A   60   B   61   C

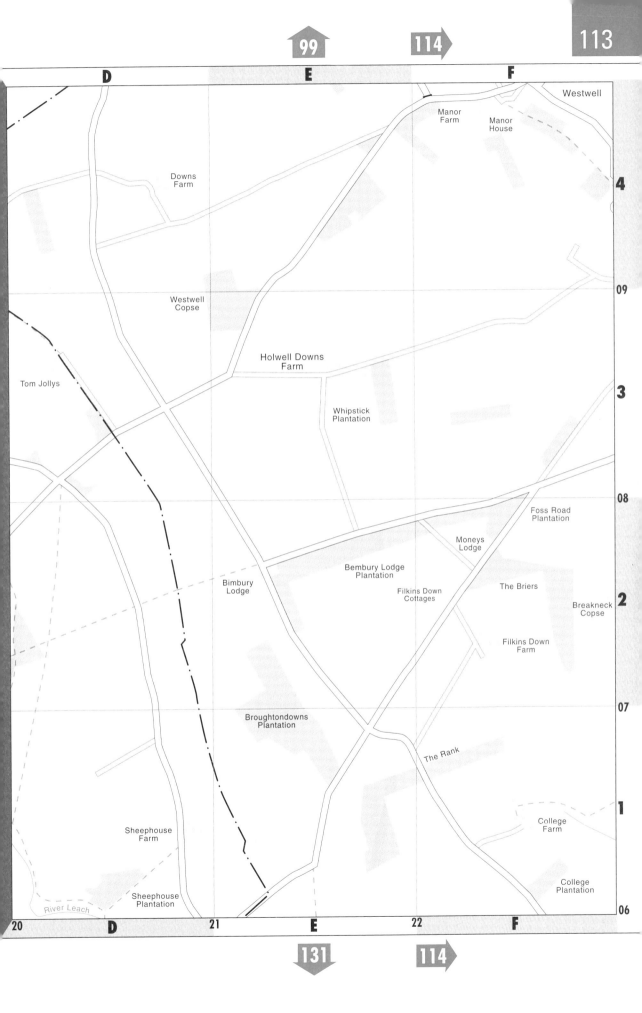

D
E
F

Westwell

Manor
Farm

Manor
House

Downs
Farm

4

09

Westwell
Copse

Holwell Downs
Farm

Tom Jollys

3

Whipstick
Plantation

08

Foss Road
Plantation

Moneys
Lodge

Bembury Lodge
Plantation

Bimbury
Lodge

The Briers

Breakneck
Copse

2

Filkins Down
Cottages

Filkins Down
Farm

07

Broughtondowns
Plantation

The Rank

1

College
Farm

Sheephouse
Farm

College
Plantation

River Leach

Sheephouse
Plantation

06

20
D
21
E
22
F

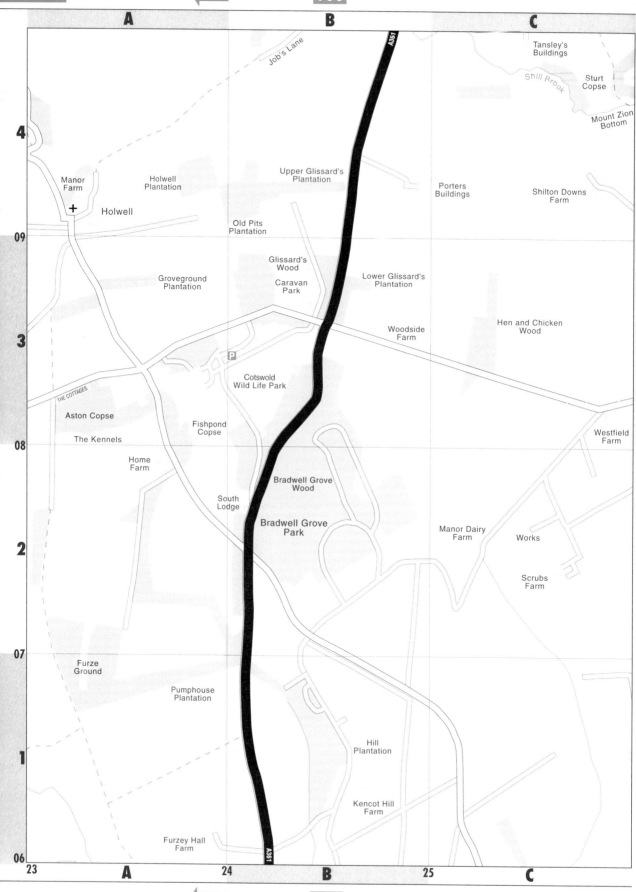

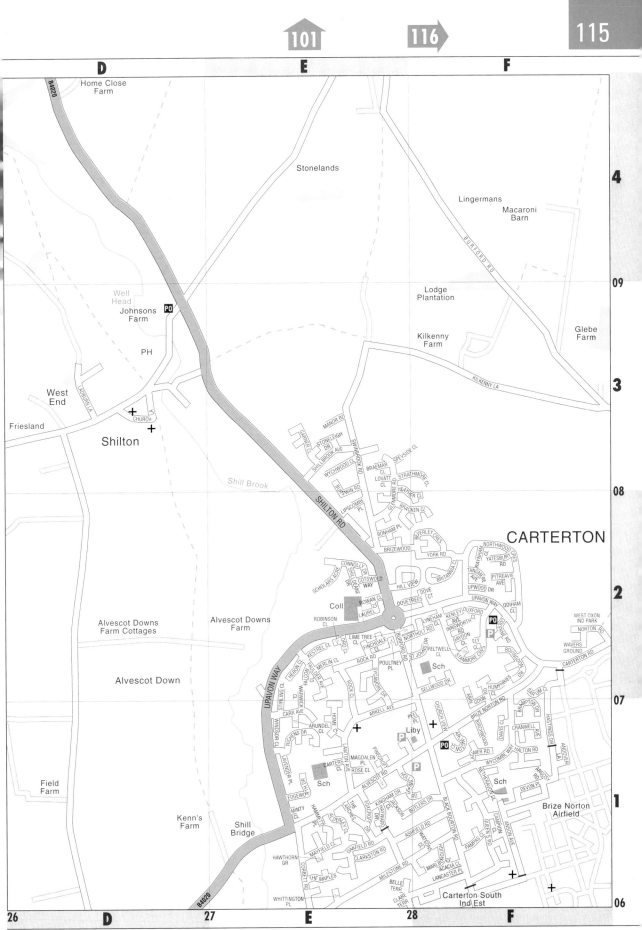

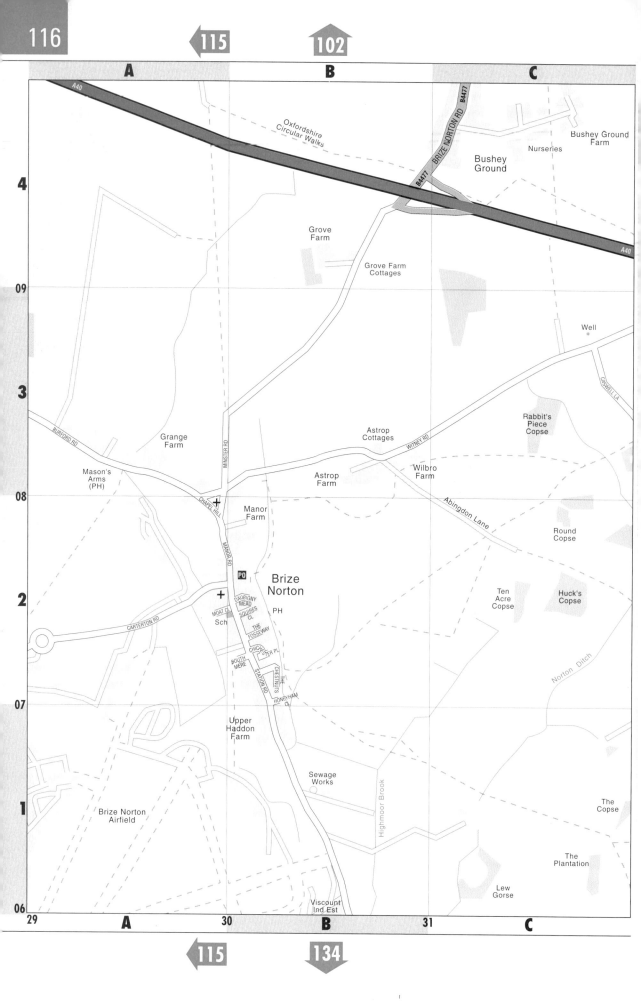

A   B   C

A40

Oxfordshire
Circular Walks

BRIZE NORTON RD   B4477

B4477

Bushey Ground
Farm

Nurseries

Bushey
Ground

4

A40

Grove
Farm

Grove Farm
Cottages

Well

09

CASWELL LA

3

Rabbit's
Piece
Copse

BURFORD RD

Grange
Farm

MINSTER RD

Astrop
Cottages

WITNEY RD

Wilbro
Farm

Mason's
Arms
(PH)

Astrop
Farm

Abingdon Lane

Round
Copse

08

CHAPEL HILL

Manor
Farm

MANOR RD

PO

Brize
Norton

Ten
Acre
Copse

Huck's
Copse

2

DAUBIGNY
MEAD

SQUIRES
CL

MOAT CL

PH

Sch

CARTERTON RD

THE
FOSSEWAY

CHICHESTER PL

Norton Ditch

SOUTH
MERE

STATION RD

THE
CHESTNUTS

07

HONEYHAM
CL

Upper
Haddon
Farm

Sewage
Works

Highmoor Brook

The
Copse

1

Brize Norton
Airfield

The
Plantation

Lew
Gorse

06

Viscount
Ind Est

29   A   30   B   31   C

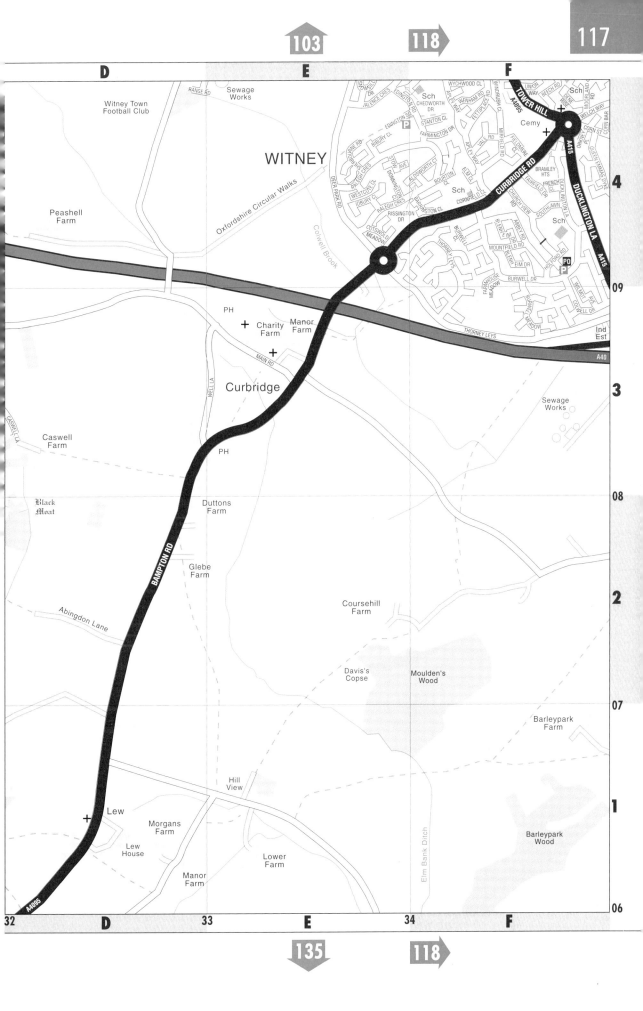

D
E
F

RANGE RD
Sewage Works

Witney Town Football Club

WITNEY

Peashell Farm

Oxfordshire Circular Walks

DEER PARK RD

Colwell Brook

SNOWSHILL DR
JALENCE CRES
EDINGTON SQ
STANTON CL
Sch
CHEDWORTH DR
WYCHWOOD CL
WENMAN RD
WINDRUSH RD
EDINGTON RD
FARMINGTON DR
BECK CL
PINE RISE
DENE RISE
MOOR LAND
WELCH WAY
UNION WAY

TOWER HILL

Cemy

BRAMLEY HTS

CORN BAR
CORN ST
QUEEN EMMAS DYKE
A415

CRANE RD
BIBURY CL
WESTCOTE CL
IDBURY CL
RALEGH CRES
RALEGH CRES
FLOW AVE
ALDSWORTH CT
BOURTON
ELM CL
VALE RD
ARLEY WAY
MIRFIELD RD
FETTIPLACE RD
FELLINGRE
Sch
CORNFIELD CL
BARRINGTON CL
FAIRFIELD
FRENCH
CHURCH VIEW
SOUTHLAWN
A415
DUCKLINGTON LA

CURBRIDGE RD

Sch
BURWELL
BLENH ELM
BLENH ELM DR
MOUNTFIELD RD
ABBEY RD
Sch
HOLFORD RD
WILMOT
COLWELL DR
BURWELL AVE
BURWELL MEADOW

4

RISSINGTON DR
COTSWOLD MEADOW

THORNEY LEYS

FARMHOUSE MEADOW
BURWELL DR

PO
P

09

PH
Charity Farm
Manor Farm

THORNEY LEYS
Ind Est

A40

MAIN RD
WELL LA

Curbridge

3

Sewage Works

CASWELL LA
Caswell Farm

PH

Black Moat

Duttons Farm

08

BAMPTON RD

Glebe Farm

Coursehill Farm

2

Abingdon Lane

Davis's Copse
Moulden's Wood

07

Barleypark Farm

Hill View

Elm Bank Ditch

Lew

1

Morgans Farm

Lower Farm

Barleypark Wood

Lew House

Manor Farm

A4095

06

32
D
33
E
34
F

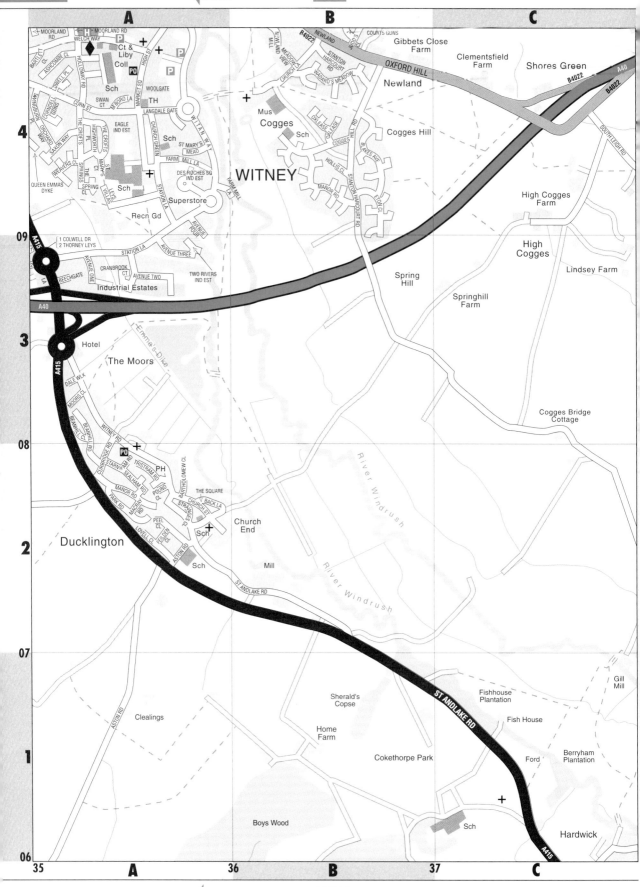

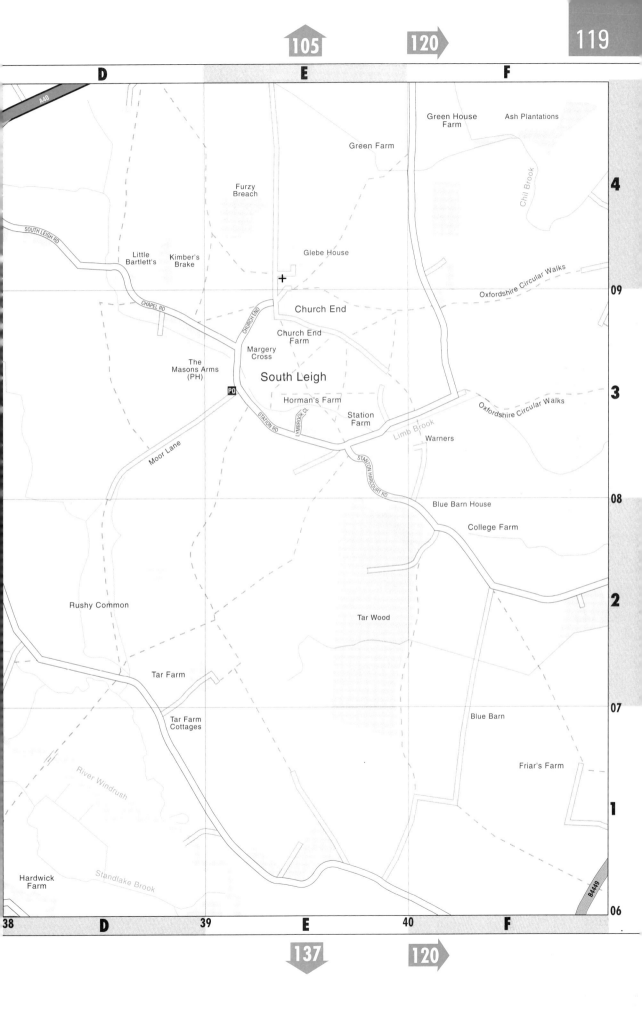

105
120

D
E
F

A40

4

SOUTH LEIGH RD

CHAPEL RD

Little
Bartlett's

Kimber's
Brake

Furzy
Breach

Green Farm

Green House
Farm

Ash Plantations

Chil Brook

Glebe House

Oxfordshire Circular Walks

09

CHURCH END

Church End

Church End
Farm

Margery
Cross

The
Masons Arms
(PH)

South Leigh

PO

Horman's Farm

STATION RD

LYMBROOK CL

Station
Farm

Limb Brook

Oxfordshire Circular Walks

3

Warners

Moor Lane

STANTON HARCOURT RD

Blue Barn House

College Farm

08

Rushy Common

Tar Wood

2

Tar Farm

Tar Farm
Cottages

Blue Barn

07

Friar's Farm

1

River Windrush

Hardwick
Farm

Standlake Brook

B4449

06

38
D
39
E
40
F

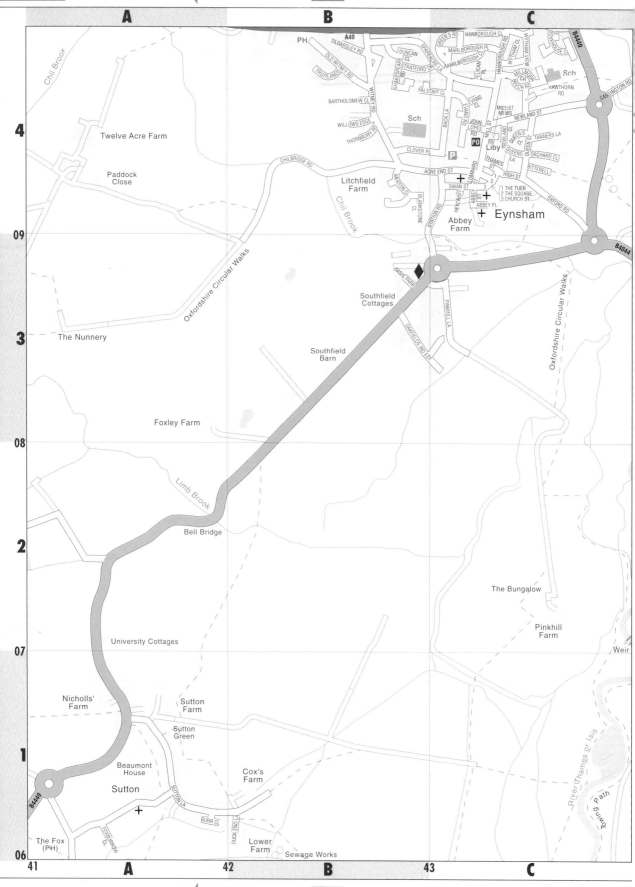

D E F

4

CASSINGTON RD

Cassington Mill

River Evenlode

Old Canal

Towing Path

Ten Acre Copse

Oxfordshire Circular Walks

Hither Clay Hill

Thorney Croft

River Thames or Isis

Great Ash Hill

09

PH

Wharf Stream

Further Clay Hill

Wytham Great Wood

Common Piece

Weir

Great Plain

Keepers Cottage

Swinford Bridge (Toll)

Lock

Water Works

Little Ash Hill

3

Swinford

Hill Copse

OXFORD RD

Swinford Farm

The Five Sisters

Wytham Hill

08

Beacon Hill

My Lady's Seat

Towing Path

Woodcroft Copse

Radbrook Common

Stroud Copse

Rough Copse

2

Nealing's Copse

The Plantation

Pinkhill Lock

Farmoor

PO

Cowleaze Copse

07

CHURCH CL

MEADOW CL

B4017

Woodend Farm

Oaken Holt

MAYFIELD RD

Bean Wood

Hill End Camp

CUMNOR RD

Valley Farm

EYNSHAM RD

Hill End Camp Farm House

1

Farmoor Reservoir

P

B4044

B4017

Red House Farm

06

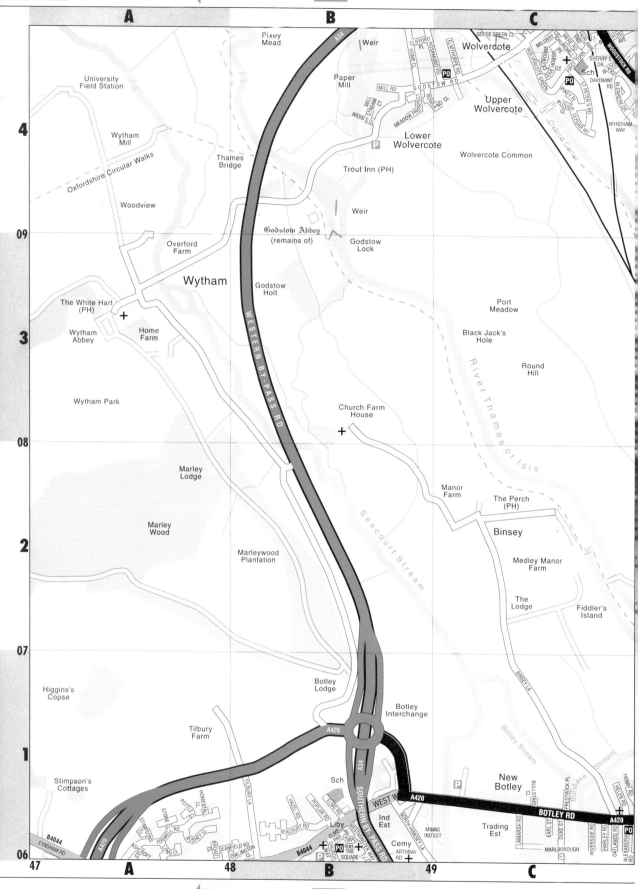

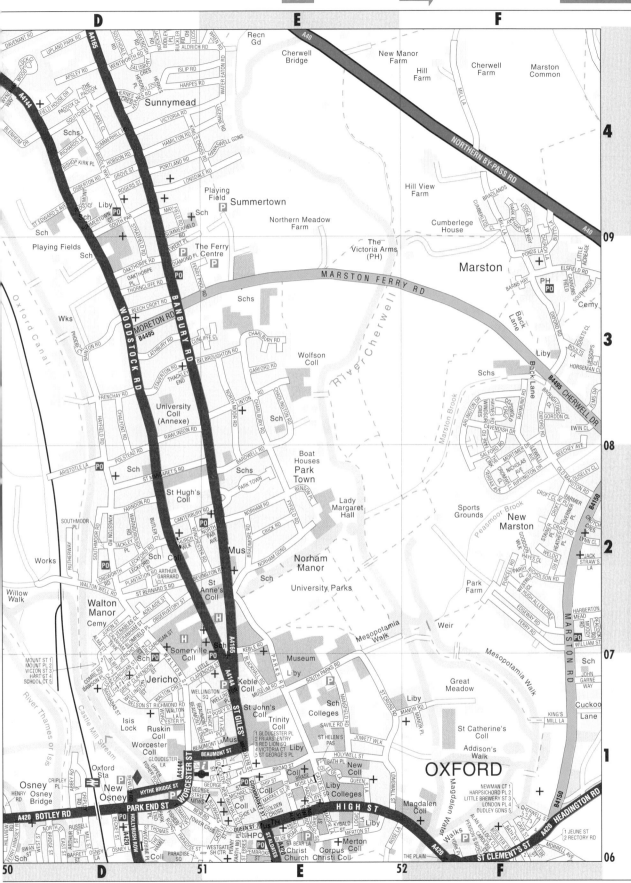

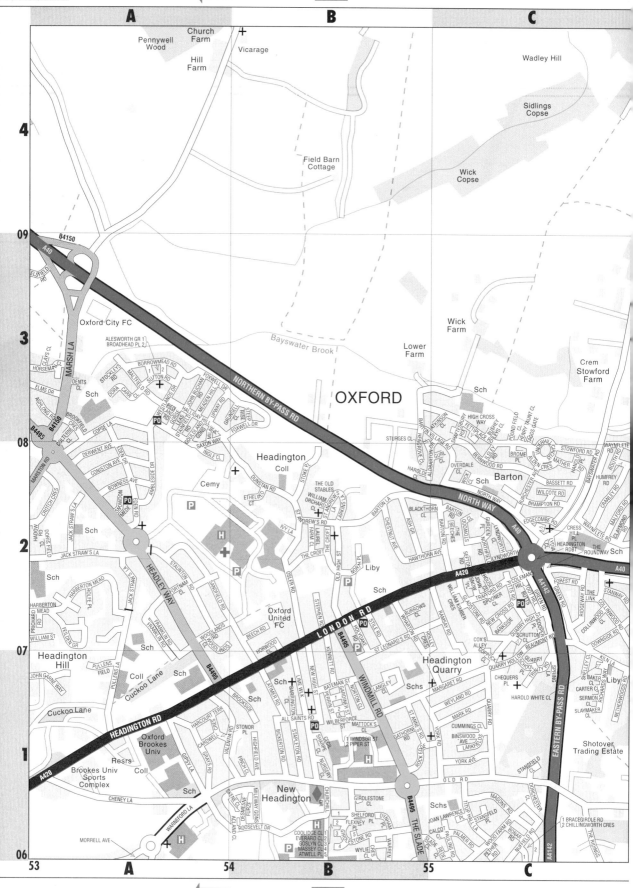

D   E   F

4

Stanton
St John

Stanton
Great Wood

New Inn
Farm

B4027

BAYSWATER RD

Stanton
House

Mill
Farm

Sewage
Works

Kennels

POUND LA
SNOWS LA

MILL ST
SILVER
BIRCHES

Rectory
Farm

COCKS LA

PO

PH

HILLCRAFT RD

COURTFIELD RD

09

PH

Shepherd's
Pit

Sch

Recn
Gd

Ashen
Copse

Breach
Farm

3

Bayswater
Mill

Minchin
Court Farm

08

Bayswater
Farm

1 HUMFREY RD
2 MALFORD RD
3 CLAYMOND RD

Sewage
Works

MICKLE WAY

STANTON RD

POLECAT END LA

Vent
Farm

WATERMILL WAY
BAYSWATER RD
WATERMILL FARM RD

Sandhills

Manor
Farm

BADGER CL

PO

MILTON CRES

POWELL CL

Forest
Hill

WHEATLEY RD

GREEN CL
SSPDN
COLWELL DR
MEREWOOD AVE
ROBERTS CL
BURDELL AVE
HILL VIEW
DELBUSH AVE

Sch

The
Vicarage

Cemy

ROWER C BURSILL CL

Sch

BURLINGTON CRES

LONDON RD

P

Red Hill
Farm

Red
Hill

2

THE LARCHES

DOWNSIDE END

Nielsen
House

Swilly

Thornhill
Farm

Lodge

A40

DOWNSIDE RD
RINGWOOD RD
STANWAY RD

PO

Risinghurst

GROVELANDS RD
FOLLYWOOD RD

07

Pointed
Covert

Shotover
House

LEWIS CL
KILN LA
WYCHWOOD LA

Monk's
Wood

Thorn
Hill

Obelisk

1

Monk's
Farm

Shotover
Hill

Forest
Farm

The
Spinney

Home
Farm

OLD RD

P

Shotover Plain

Ochre
Pits

06

56   D   57   E   58   F

A B C

4

Wood Farm

Clearsale
Hursthill

Waterperry Common

Bernwood Forest

Commonleys Farm

Waterperry Wood

09

Park Farm

Polecat End

Park Farm House

Drunkard's Corner

3

Polecat End Hollows

Marsh Copse

Parson's Farm

Ledall Cottage

08

Holton Wood

Buryhook Barn

Holton Brook

2

Warren Farm

Keeper's Cottage

Pond Farm

Warren Wood

Old Park Farm

07

Lyehill Quarries (disused)

BURYHOOK CNR

Cottage Copse

Warwick Close Farm

Recn Gd

Sch

The Rectory

Holton Place

1

Liby

Holton

Sch

Church Farm

Garden Copse

Coll

06

59

A

60

B

61

C

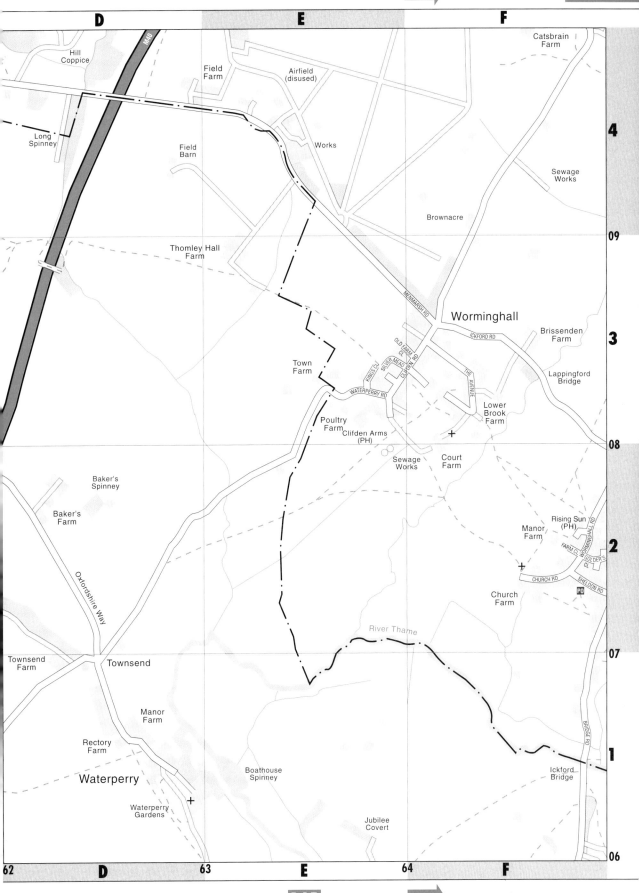

Catsbrain Farm

Hill Coppice

M40

Field Farm

Airfield (disused)

4

Long Spinney

Field Barn

Works

Sewage Works

Brownacre

09

Thomley Hall Farm

MEN MARSH RD

Worminghall

Brissenden Farm

ICKFORD RD

3

OLD FARM CL

CLIFDEN RD

Town Farm

SILVER-MEAD

Lappingford Bridge

KINGS CL

WATERPERRY RD

THE AVENUE

Lower Brook Farm

Poultry Farm

Clifden Arms (PH)

Sewage Works

Court Farm

+

08

Baker's Spinney

Rising Sun (PH)

WORMINGHALL RD

Baker's Farm

Manor Farm

FARM CL

GOLDER'S CL

2

Oxfordshire Way

CHURCH RD

SHELDON RD

PO

Church Farm

River Thame

Townsend Farm

Townsend

07

Manor Farm

BRIDGE RD

Rectory Farm

Waterperry

Boathouse Spinney

Ickford Bridge

1

Waterperry Gardens

+

Jubilee Covert

06

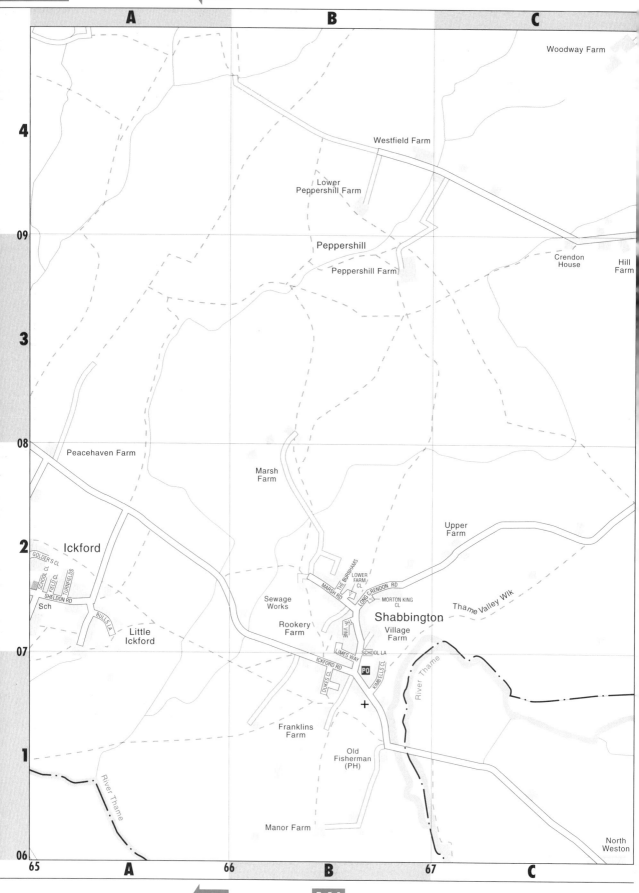

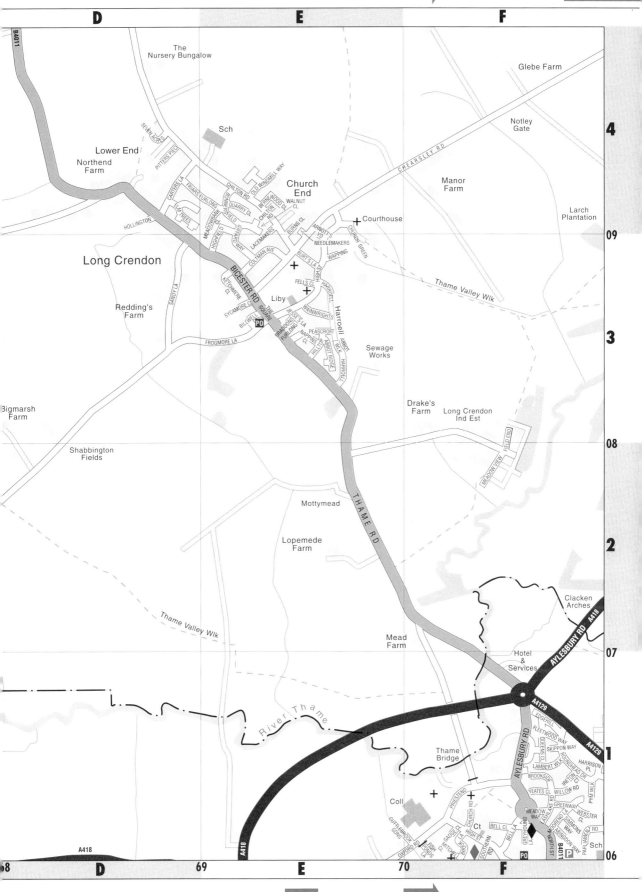

D

E

F

4

09

3

08

2

07

1

06

B4011

The Nursery Bungalow

Glebe Farm

Notley Gate

Sch

CHEARSLEY RD

Manor Farm

Larch Plantation

Lower End

Northend Farm

SEVEN ACRES

PITTERS PIECE

Church End

WALNUT CL

Courthouse

CARTERS LA

FRIARS FURLONG

BONNERSFIELD

QUARRY LA

CHILTON RD

OLD WINDMILL WAY

BERNEWOOD CL

CHILTON RD

BURNS CL

ARNOTT'S YD

NEEDLEMAKERS

CHURCH GREEN

ELM TREES

HOLLINGTON

MEADOWBANK

HIGHFIELD

STANDROW WAY

COLTMAN AVE

LACEMAKERS

BURT'S LA

ST JOHN

WAPPING

Thame Valley Wlk

Long Crendon

KETCHMERE CL

BICESTER RD

FELLS CL

HARROELL

Redding's Farm

SANDY LA

SYCAMORE CL

BILLWELL

THE SQUARE

WAINWRIGHTS

Liby

PO

BRADMOORS LA

DORSET LA

FURLONG

PEASCROFT

NAPPING CL

HILLTOP

ABBOT RIDGE

HARROELL

MILL

ABBOT

Sewage Works

FROGMORE LA

Harroell

Bigmarsh Farm

Drake's Farm

Long Crendon Ind Est

FIELD END

MEADOW VIEW

Shabbington Fields

THAME RD

Mottymead

Lopemede Farm

Thame Valley Wlk

Clacken Arches

AYLESBURY RD

A418

Mead Farm

Hotel & Services

07

A4129

River Thame

LEDGEHILL

AYLESBURY RD

FLEETWOOD WAY

SKIPPON WAY

ROUNDHEAD DR

HARRISON PL

Thame Bridge

LAMBERT WY

BROOKSIDE

YEATES CL

WILLOW RD

IRETON CT

PYM WLK

GREENWAY

WEBSTER CL

SUMMONS WAY

PARLIAMENT RD

Coll

PRIESTEND

LASHLAKE RD

CHURCH RD

HIGH ST

BELL CL

MEADOW WAY

ABINGDON RD

NORTH ST

Sch

CUTTLEBROOK GDNS

OXFORD RD

GADGE CL

MITCHEL

SOUTHERN RD

Ct

BELL LA

GREYHOUND LA

PO

B4011

P

A4129

Ct

A418

A418

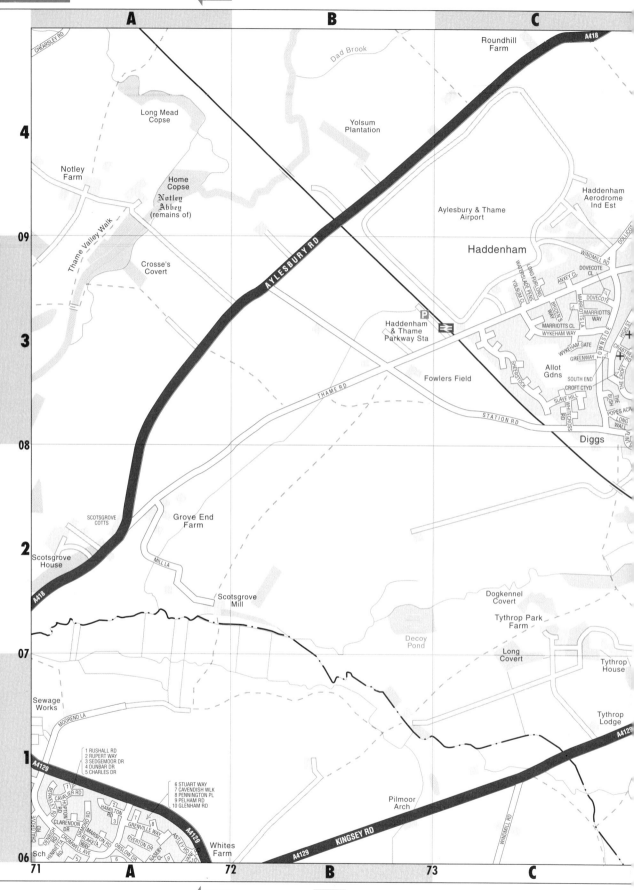

D
E
F

4

Eastleach
Turville

+

Sch   Eastleach Martin

+

THE
BOURNE

Coate
Farm

Oxleaze
Farm

The
Cottages

Field Barn

05

Kings Hay

Oxleaze
Common

The Pills

3

Coate Mill

Shire
Gate

Broadwell Brook

The Bungalow

Greenhill
Barn

Coate
Farm

04

Baxter's
Farm

Fyfield

PH

Langford
Downs Farm

Sch

2

Manor House

Manor Farm

River Leach

Southrop

A361

Langford
Downs
House

03

Rottonborough
Copse

Common Barn
Farm

1

Furzy Knoll
Plantation

A361

02

0
D
21
E
22
F

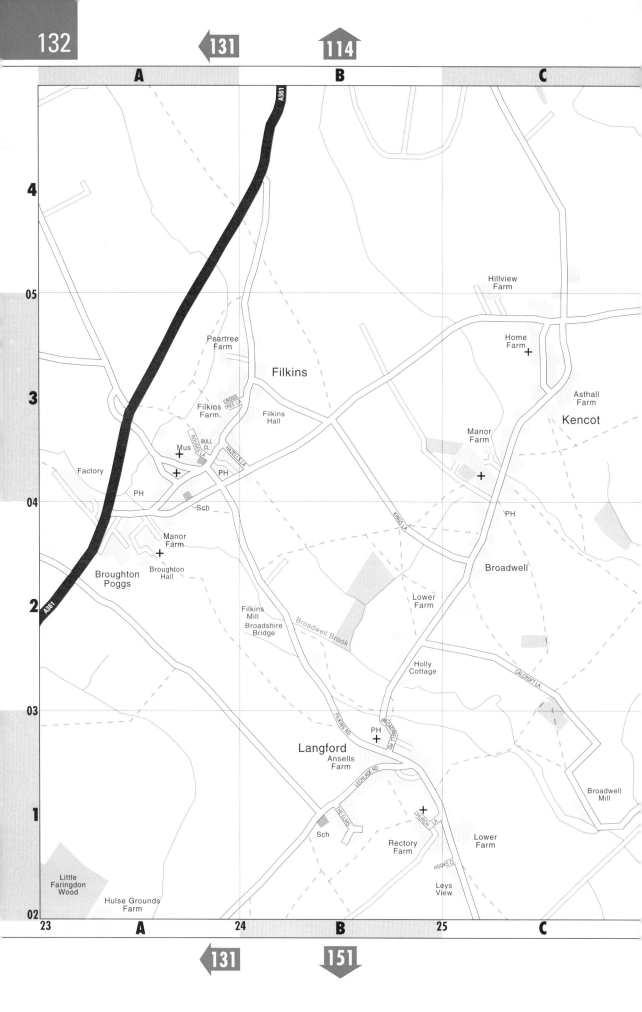

A   B   C

4

05

Hillview
Farm

Peartree
Farm

Home
Farm

Filkins

Asthall
Farm

3

Kencot

CROSS TREE LA

Filkins
Farm

Filkins
Hall

Manor
Farm

BULL CL

ROUSE'S LA

Mus

HAZELL'S LA

Factory

PH

PH

04

Sch

KINGS LA

PH

Broadwell

Manor
Farm

Broughton
Poggs

Broughton
Hall

Lower
Farm

Filkins
Mill

Broadshire
Bridge

Broadwell Brook

Holly
Cottage

CALCROFT LA

03

FILKINS RD

PH

BROADWELL RD

Langford

Ansells
Farm

Broadwell
Mill

LECHLADE RD

CHURCH LA

1

Sch

THE ELMS

Rectory
Farm

Lower
Farm

HOOKS CL

Little
Faringdon
Wood

Hulse Grounds
Farm

Leys
View

02

23   A   24   B   25   C

D
E
F

B4020

CORBETT RD
THE CRESCENT
AIRSFIELD CL
MILESTONE RD
CLARE TERR

Shill Brook

Brize Norton
Airfield

4

Elmwood
House

The
Poplars

05

Springfield
House

Sewage
Works

Home
Farm

MILL LA

BURFORD RD

Mill
House

Black
Bourton

PH

MILL LA

Butlers
Court
Farm

Alvescot

Glebe
Farm

Piggery

3

Sch

PH

THE GREEN
PRESCOTT CL
THORPES FIELD

CHURCH CL

Bedwell
Pond

Park
Farm

College

SCHOOL LA

OAKEY CL

STATION RD

04

Lower End

SHILBROOK
MANOR

Glebe
Farm

Manor
Farm

Long
Copse

2

Langhat Ditch

Clanfield Brook

Black Bourton Brook

03

Bazeland

CALCROFT LA

1

Edgerly
Farm

B4020

BLACK BOURTON RD

Chestlion
Farm

MORTON CL
PH

BAMPTON RD

MARSH LA

POUND LA
A4095

02

6
D
27
E
28
F

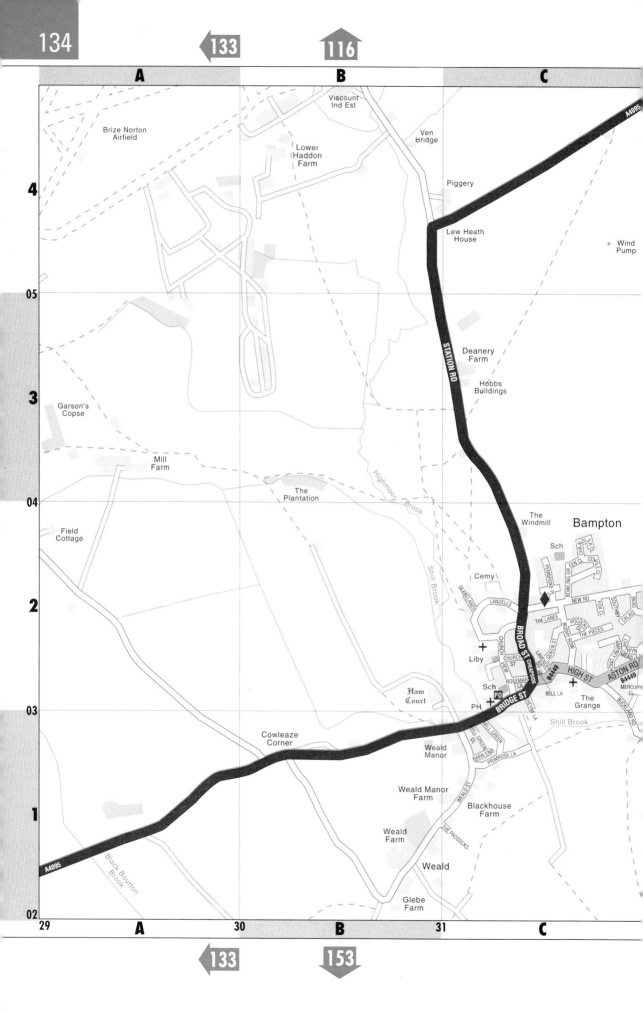

A **B** **C**

4

Brize Norton
Airfield

Viscount
Ind Est

Lower
Haddon
Farm

Ven
Bridge

Piggery

A4095

Lew Heath
House

Wind
Pump

05

3

Garson's
Copse

Mill
Farm

STATION RD

Deanery
Farm

Hobbs
Buildings

Highmoor Brook

Shill Brook

04

The
Plantation

The
Windmill

Bampton

Field
Cottage

Sch

KFLD
KFLD

COLE CL

NORMAN GN

NEW RD

SOUTHBY

CALAIS DENE

GLEBELANDS

Cemy

PEMBROKE PL

LANDELL'S

THE LANES

NEW RD

FOX CL

POCOCKS

THE PIECES

BUSHY ROW

AMPNEY MEAD

NYMM CL

2

Church

GREEN ST

LANCHE

MERCURY CL

BROAD ST

Liby

CHEAPSIDE

CHURCH VIEW

ROSEMARY LA

HIGH ST

ASTON RD

B4449

BELL LA

MILL GREEN

The
Grange

BUCKLAND RD

Sch

Ham
Court

PH

PO

BRIDGE ST

CHENE LA

B4449

Shill Brook

03

Cowleaze
Corner

Weald
Manor

BARN END

PRIMROSE LA

WEALD ST

Weald Manor
Farm

Blackhouse
Farm

1

A4095

Black Bourton Brook

Weald
Farm

THE PADDOCKS

Weald

Glebe
Farm

02

D
E
F

University
Farm

Rushy
Butts

Claywell
Hill

Ditcham
Wood

4

Newhouse
Farm

Elm Bank Ditch

ASTON RD

Lew
Lodge

05

Newhouse
Farm Cottages

Mount Owen
Farm

Far
Horizons

3

Coalpit
Farm

04

White
Owl
Farm

NEW RD

Cote Ditch

2

CALAIS DENE

MOUNT OWEN RD

North Street
Farm

TALBOT
FIELDS

Aston Ditch

MERCURY CL

KILN CL
BACK LA

Aston

ASTON RD

GREENACRES

LA

BOVINGTON'S
YD

NORTH ST

FOXWOOD CL
FOXWOOD CL

B4449

COTE RD

Kingsway
Farm

Home
Farm

Sch

Calais Oak
Farm

LAUNDRY LA

HIGH ST

THE
SQUARE

03

PO

SMITH'S CL

WOODBRIDGE CL

MANOR CL
SAXE CL

VICARAGE CL

WALTERS

BULL ST

BULL LA

Lower
Farm

Sewage
Works

SOUTHLANDS

FARM CL

Nursery

Bull Inn
(PH)

Paradise
Farm

BUCKLAND RD

Shill Brook

Westmoor Lane

HAM LA

1

Nursery

Kennels

Rainbow
Farm

Hedgefields
Farm

02

32
D
33
E
34
F

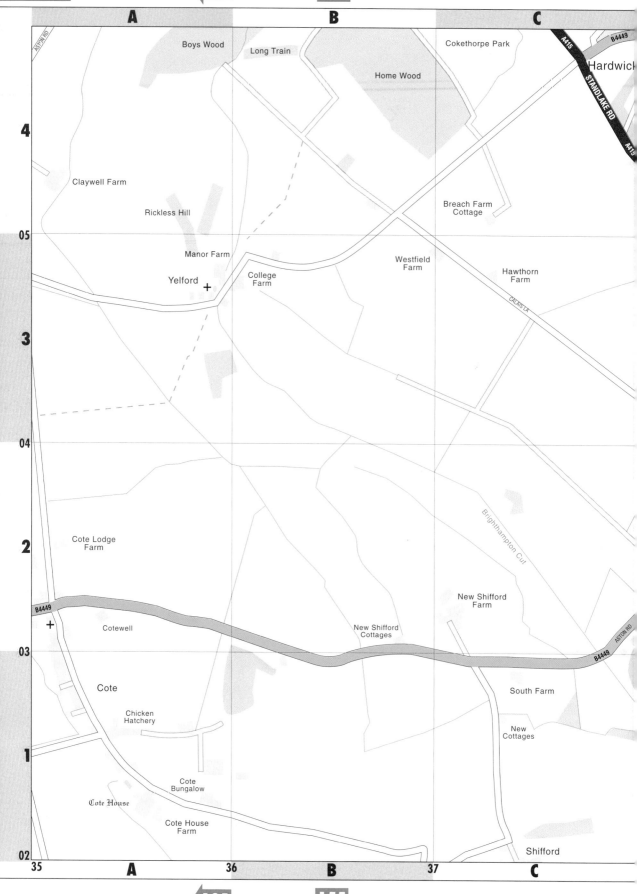

A   B   C

4

Boys Wood

Long Train

Cokethorpe Park

Home Wood

Hardwick

A415

B4449

STANDLAKE RD

A415

Claywell Farm

Rickless Hill

05

Manor Farm

Breach Farm
Cottage

Yelford +

College
Farm

Westfield
Farm

Hawthorn
Farm

CALAIS LA

3

04

Brighthampton Cut

Cote Lodge
Farm

2

New Shifford
Farm

B4449 +

Cotewell

New Shifford
Cottages

ASTON RD

03

B4449

Cote

South Farm

Chicken
Hatchery

New
Cottages

1

Cote
Bungalow

Cote House

Cote House
Farm

Shifford

02

35   A   36   B   37   C

ASTON RD

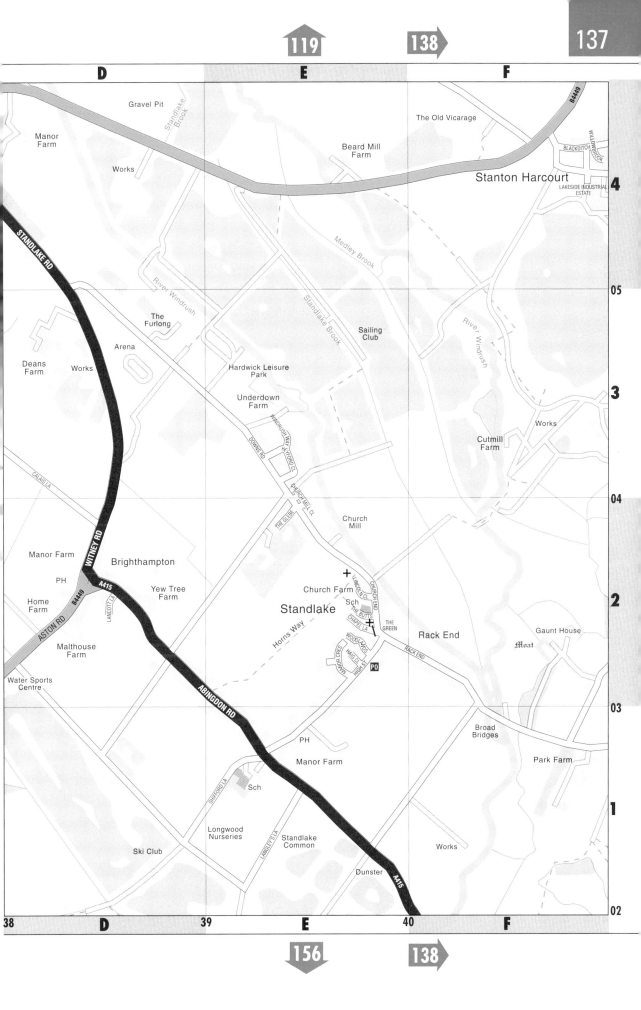

Gravel Pit

The Old Vicarage

Standlake Brook

Manor Farm

Beard Mill Farm

BLACKDITCH

WILLOWBROOK

B4449

Works

Stanton Harcourt

LAKESIDE INDUSTRIAL ESTATE

4

STANDLAKE RD

Medley Brook

05

River Windrush

The Furlong

Standlake Brook

Sailing Club

River Windrush

Arena

Hardwick Leisure Park

Deans Farm

Works

3

Underdown Farm

Works

Cutmill Farm

WINDRUSH WAY

DOWNS RD

YEFORD CL

CALAIS LA

CHURCH MILL CL

04

Church Mill

THE GLEBE

CHURCH END

Manor Farm

Brighthampton

+

Church Farm

LINCOLN CL

PH

WITNEY RD

A415

Yew Tree Farm

Sch

Standlake

THE BUTTS

2

Gaunt House

Home Farm

B4449

LANGOTT LA

Horns Way

CHAPEL LA

THE GREEN

Rack End

Moat

ASTON RD

Malthouse Farm

WOODLANDS

RACK END

MANOR CRES

MAG CL

HIGH ST

PO

Water Sports Centre

ABINGDON RD

03

Broad Bridges

PH

Park Farm

Manor Farm

Sch

SHIFFORD LA

1

LANGLEYS LA

Longwood Nurseries

Works

Ski Club

Standlake Common

Dunster

A415

02

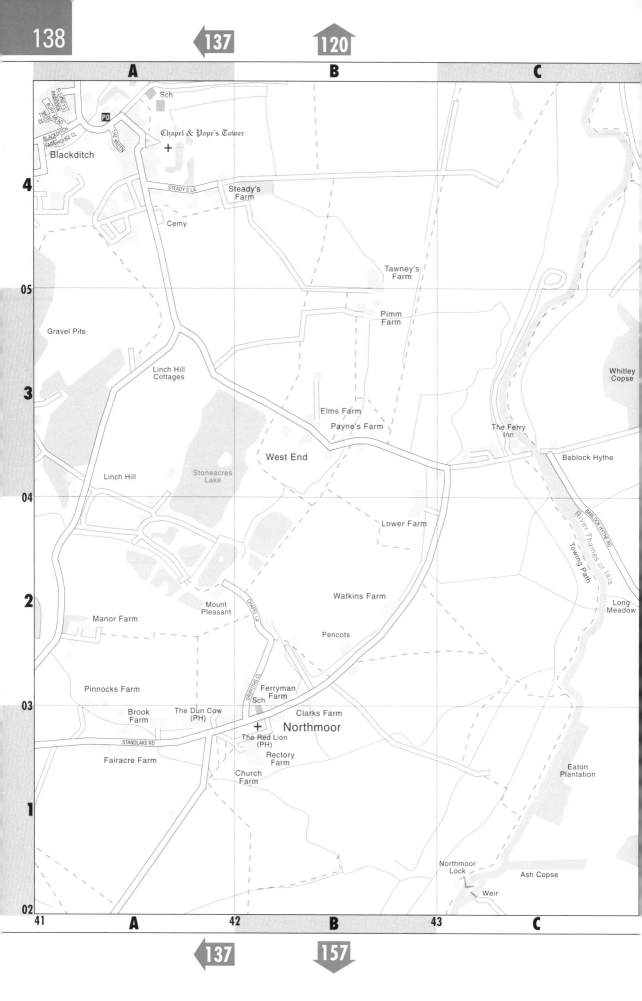

137
120

A   **B**   **C**

Sch

PO

FLEMER'S
PADDOCK
THE
BURH
MEAD
CLOSE
BLACKDITCH
FARMHOUSE CL

THE GREEN

Chapel & Pope's Tower

Blackditch

4

STEADY'S LA

Steady's
Farm

Cemy

Tawney's
Farm

05

Pimm
Farm

Gravel Pits

Linch Hill
Cottages

3

Elms Farm

Payne's Farm

The Ferry
Inn

West End

Bablock Hythe

Linch Hill

Stoneacres
Lake

04

BABLOCK HYTHE RD

Lower Farm

River Thames or Isis

Towing Path

Watkins Farm

Long
Meadow

2

Mount
Pleasant

CHAPEL LA

Manor Farm

Pencots

Pinnocks Farm

Ferryman
Farm

GRIFFITHS CL

Sch

Clarks Farm

03

Brook
Farm

The Dun Cow
(PH)

Northmoor

The Red Lion
(PH)

STANDLAKE RD

Rectory
Farm

Fairacre Farm

Church
Farm

Eaton
Plantation

1

Northmoor
Lock

Ash Copse

Weir

02

137
157

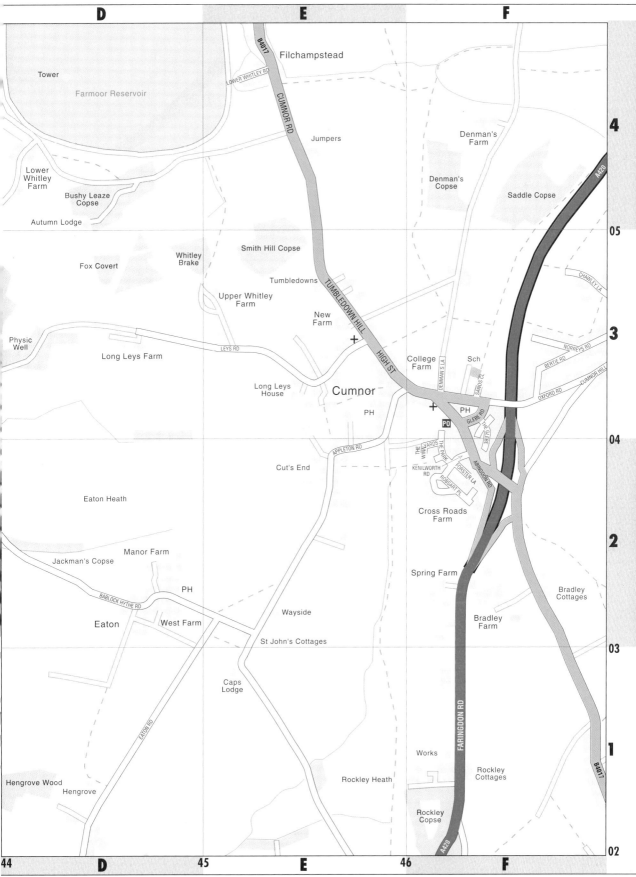

D E F

Filchampstead

Tower

Farmoor Reservoir

Lower
Whitley
Farm

Bushy Leaze
Copse

Autumn Lodge

LOWER WHITLEY RD

B4017

CUMNOR RD

Jumpers

Denman's
Farm

Denman's
Copse

Saddle Copse

A420

CHAWLEY LA

Fox Covert

Whitley
Brake

Smith Hill Copse

Tumbledowns

Upper Whitley
Farm

New
Farm

TUMBLEDOWN HILL

NORREYS RD

Physic
Well

Long Leys Farm

LEYS RD

Long Leys
House

Cumnor

HIGH ST

College
Farm

Sch

DENMAN'S LA

SANDS CL

BERTIE RD

OXFORD RD

CUMNOR HILL

PH

PH

PO

GLEBE RD

THE GLEBE

Cut's End

APPLETON RD

THE WHARF

THE PARK

KENILWORTH
RD

ROBSART PL

FORSTER LA

ABINGDON RD

Cross Roads
Farm

Eaton Heath

Manor Farm

Jackman's Copse

BABLOCK HYTHE RD

PH

Eaton

West Farm

EATON RD

Wayside

St John's Cottages

Caps
Lodge

Spring Farm

Bradley
Cottages

Bradley
Farm

Rockley Heath

FARINGDON RD

Works

Rockley
Cottages

Hengrove Wood

Hengrove

Rockley
Copse

A420

B4017

4

05

3

04

2

03

1

02

44 45 46

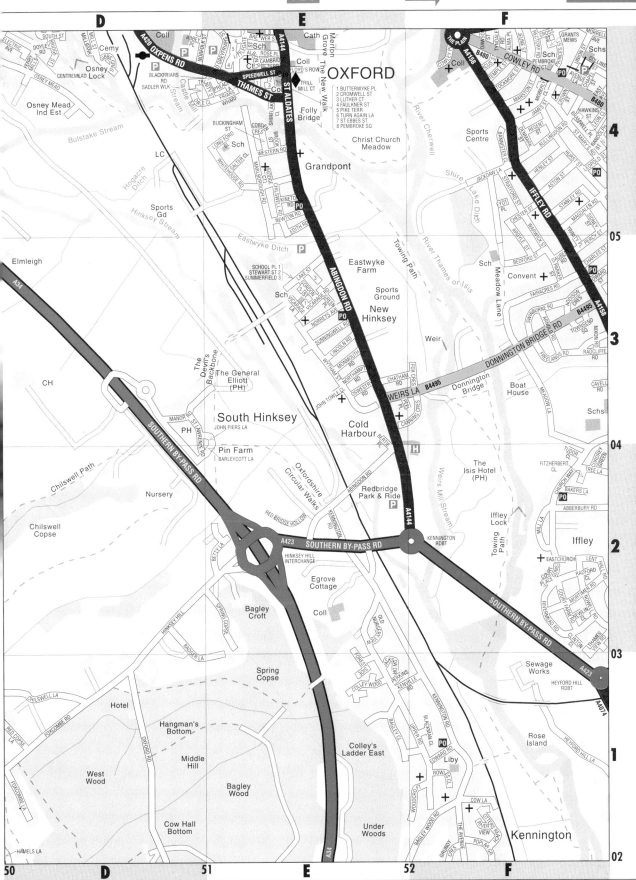

OXFORD

1 BUTTERWYKE PL
2 CROMWELL ST
3 LUTHER CT
4 FAULKNER ST
5 PIKE TERR
6 TURN AGAIN LA
7 ST EBBES ST
8 PEMBROKE SQ

Osney Mead
Ind Est

Elmleigh

South Hinksey

Christ Church
Meadow

Grandpont

Eastwyke
Farm

Sports
Ground

New
Hinksey

Weir

Sports Centre

Convent

Donnington
Bridge

Boat
House

Cold
Harbour

The Isis Hotel
(PH)

Iffley
Lock

Iffley

Chilswell Path

Chilswell Copse

Nursery

The Devil's
Backbone

The General
Elliott
(PH)

Pin Farm

Oxfordshire
Circular Walks

Redbridge
Park & Ride

Kennington
RDBT

Sewage
Works

CH

Bagley
Croft

Egrove
Cottage

Coll

Spring
Copse

Heyford Hill
RDBT

Rose
Island

Hotel

Hangman's
Bottom

Middle
Hill

Bagley
Wood

Colley's
Ladder East

West
Wood

Cow Hall
Bottom

Under
Woods

Kennington

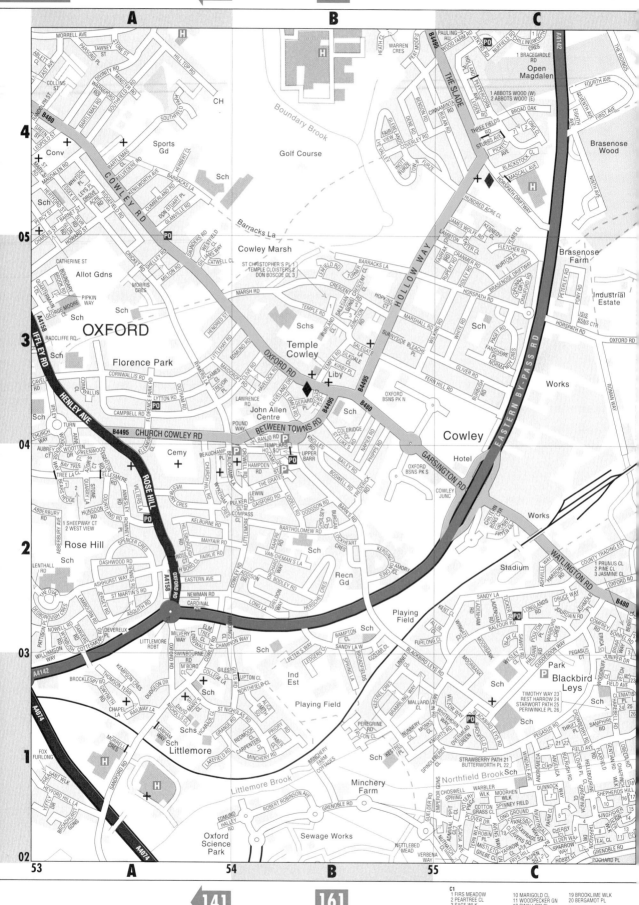

C1
1 FIRS MEADOW
2 PEARTREE CL
3 SAGE WLK
4 CORIANDER WAY
5 COLTSFOOT SQ
6 CELANDINE PL
7 BLUEBELL CT
8 BUTTERCUP SQ
9 BLACKSMITHS MEADOW
10 MARIGOLD CL
11 WOODPECKER GN
12 SWALLOW CL
13 NORMAN SMITH RD
14 JACK ARGENT CL
15 MOLE PL
16 CAMPION CL
17 SWIFT CL
18 PRIMROSE PL
19 BROOKLIME WLK
20 BERGAMOT PL

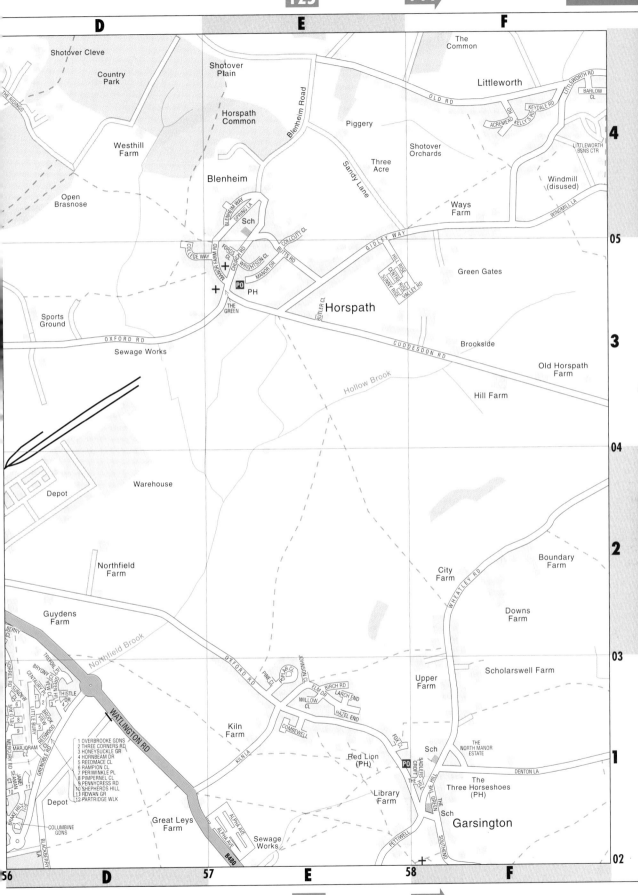

Shotover Cleve

Country Park

THE RIDINGS

Shotover Plain

Blenheim Road

The Common

Littleworth

LITTLEWORTH RD

BARLOW CL

KEYDALE RD

KELLY'S RD

ACREMEAD

Horspath Common

Piggery

Shotover Orchards

4

Westhill Farm

Blenheim

Three Acre

Sandy Lane

LITTLEWORTH BSNS CTR

Windmill (disused)

Open Brasnose

BLENHEIM WAY

SPRING LA

Sch

COLLEGE WAY

MARSH FARM RD

FORDS CL

CHURCH RD

WRIGHTSON CL

BUTTS RD

COLLCUTT CL

MANOR DR

Ways Farm

WINDMILL LA

05

THE GREEN

PO

PH

BUTLER CL

GIDLEY WAY

HILL RISE

CENTRE RISE

SUNNY RISE

VALLEY RD

Green Gates

Horspath

Sports Ground

OXFORD RD

Sewage Works

CUDDESDON RD

Brookside

Old Horspath Farm

3

Hollow Brook

Hill Farm

04

Depot

Warehouse

Northfield Farm

City Farm

WHEATLEY RD

Boundary Farm

Downs Farm

2

Guydens Farm

Northfield Brook

BERRY CL

OXFORD RD

PINE CL

POPLAR CL

TO OXFORD

ELM DR

BIRCH RD

LARCH END

WILLOW CL

HAZEL END

Upper Farm

Scholarswell Farm

03

TREFOIL

BRYONY CL

GREEN PL

CENTAURY PL

THISTLE DR

BROOK VIEW

REDWOOD

SORREL RD

FIELD CL

LITTLE BURY

WATLINGTON RD

KILN LA

Kiln Farm

COMBEWELL

Red Lion (PH)

PO

FOX CL

SADLERS CROFT

Sch

THE NORTH MANOR ESTATE

DENTON LA

1

MARJORAM

MERCURY RD

SAMIAN CT

GRENOBLE RD

1 OVERBROOKE GDNS
2 THREE CORNERS RD
3 HONEYSUCKLE GR
4 HORNBEAM DR
5 REEDMACE CL
6 RAMPION CL
7 PERIWINKLE PL
8 PIMPERNEL CL
9 PENNYCRESS RD
10 SHEPHERDS HILL
11 ROWAN GR
12 PARTRIDGE WLK

Depot

COLUMBINE GDNS

BRAKE HILL

BLACKBERRY LA

Great Leys Farm

ALPHA AVE

ALPHA AVE

B480

Sewage Works

Library Farm

PETTIWELL

THE GREEN

SOUTHEND

Sch

The Three Horseshoes (PH)

Garsington

02

143
126

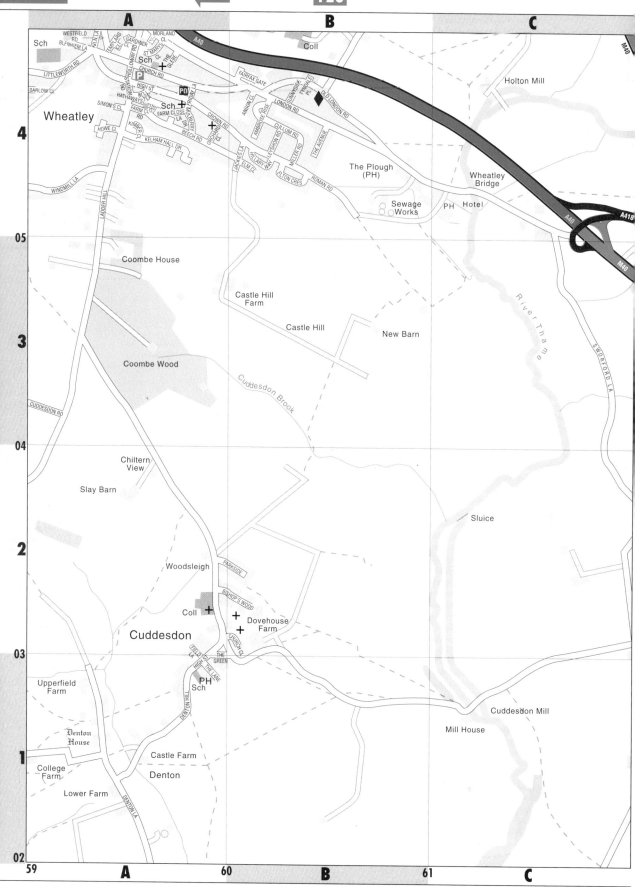

143
163

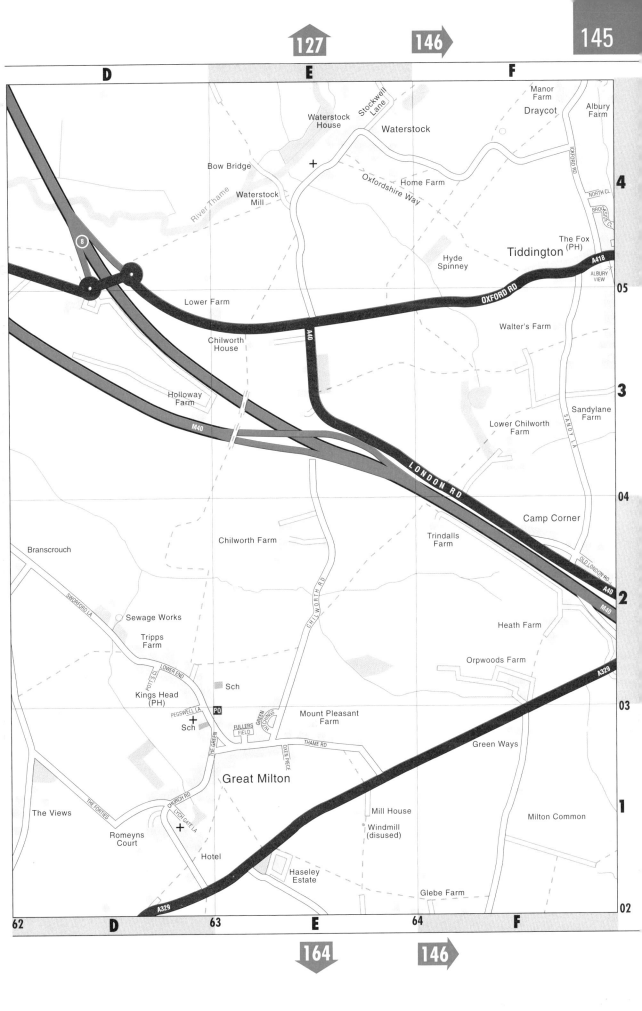

D
E
F

Manor Farm
Draycot
Albury Farm

Waterstock House
Stockwell Lane
Waterstock

4

Bow Bridge
Home Farm
Oxfordshire Way

Ickford Rd
North Cl
Brookside Cl

River Thame
Waterstock Mill

The Fox (PH)
Tiddington
A418
Albury View

Hyde Spinney

8

Lower Farm
Oxford Rd
05

A40
Chilworth House

Walter's Farm

Holloway Farm
M40

Sandy La
Sandylane Farm

3

Lower Chilworth Farm

London Rd
04

Camp Corner

Chilworth Farm

Trindalls Farm

Old London Rd
A40
M40
2

Branscrouch
Swhorford La

Heath Farm

Sewage Works
Chilworth Rd

Orpwoods Farm
A329

Tripps Farm

Lower End
Potts Cl

Kings Head (PH)
Pegswell La
PO
Sch
Green Hatchings
Mount Pleasant Farm

03

Green Ways

Sch
Fullers Field
The Green
Thame Rd
Oxen Piece

Great Milton

The Views
The Forties
Church Rd
Lych Gate La

Mill House
Milton Common

1

Romeyns Court

Windmill (disused)

Hotel

Haseley Estate

Glebe Farm

A329
02

62
D
63
E
64
F

145
128

A **B** **C**

A418

North Weston

WESTON LA

4

River Thame

Tiddington

Colesheath Copse

BROOKSIDE CL

A418

Albury Ct

Albury

Thame Valley Walk

The Red House

The Old Kennels

05

FERNHILL CL

Oxfordshire Way

ALBURY VIEW

SCHOOL LA

Home Farm

Tower

Rycote

Ryecote Lake

Causeway

Field Farm

Fernhill Wood

+ Chapel

Rycote Park

3

A329

Old Paddock

Lever's Brake

Lobbersdown Farm

RYCOTE LA

04

Long Copse

Rycotelane Farm

Lobbersdown Hill

Hotel

Poultry Farm

2

A40

Wr Twr

M40

PH

Milton Common

Heath House

London Rd

A329

7

LONDON RD

Lower Farm

Hill Farm

03

Milton Pools

Harrington Field Farm

Gate House

The Old Cottage

1

Lobb Farm

Godwin's Copse

A40

02

Great Haseley

Tetsworth

M40

65 **A** **66** **B** **67** **C**

145
165

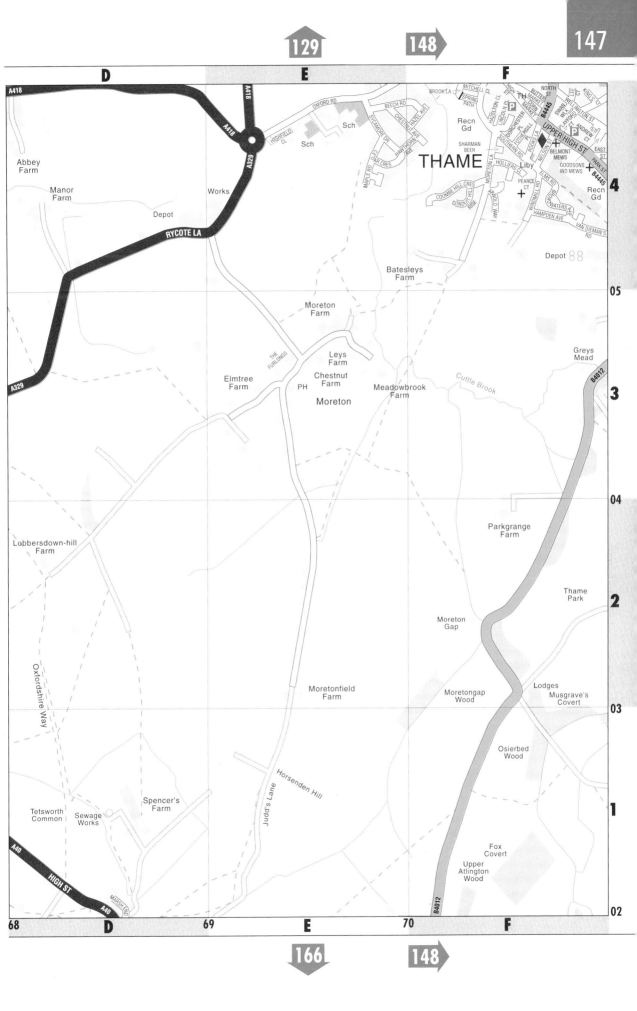

D
E
F

A418

Abbey
Farm

Manor
Farm

Depot

RYCOTE LA

A329

A418

A329

Works

HIGHFIELD
CL

OXFORD RD

BEECH RD

Sch

Sch

Sch

SYCAMORE DR

MAPLE RD

HAWTHORN
AVE

CHESTNUT AVE

HAZEL AVE

COAR CRES

MORETON LA

THE FURLONGS

Elmtree
Farm

PH

Leys
Farm

Moreton
Farm

Chestnut
Farm

Moreton

Meadowbrook
Farm

Batesleys
Farm

Cuttle Brook

THAME

Recn
Gd

SHARMAN
BEER

Liby

BROOK LA

SPRING
PATH

MITCHELL CL

BUTTER
MARKET

NORTH ST

CORN
MARKET

HIGH ST

SWAN

WELLINGTON ST

LEE ST

KING'S
CL

PARK ST

B4445

UPPER HIGH ST

BELMONT
MEWS

GOODSONS
IND MEWS

Recn
Gd

B4445

Depot

Greys
Mead

B4012

SOUTHERN RD
HOLLIERS

COOMBE HILL CRES

CONDUIT
HILL

COMBE HILL RISE

ARNOLD WAY

PEARCE
CT

ELMS RD

WINDMILL RD

BUCKNELL AVE

HAMPDEN AVE

WATERS AVE

VAN DIEMAN'S
RD

Lobbersdown-hill
Farm

Oxfordshire Way

Parkgrange
Farm

Thame
Park

Moreton
Gap

Moretonfield
Farm

Moretongap
Wood

Lodges

Musgrave's
Covert

Judd's Lane

Horsenden Hill

Spencer's
Farm

Tetsworth
Common

Sewage
Works

A40

HIGH ST

A40

MARSH END

Osierbed
Wood

Fox
Covert

Upper
Atlington
Wood

B4012

05

04

3

04

2

03

1

02

68
D
69
E
70
F

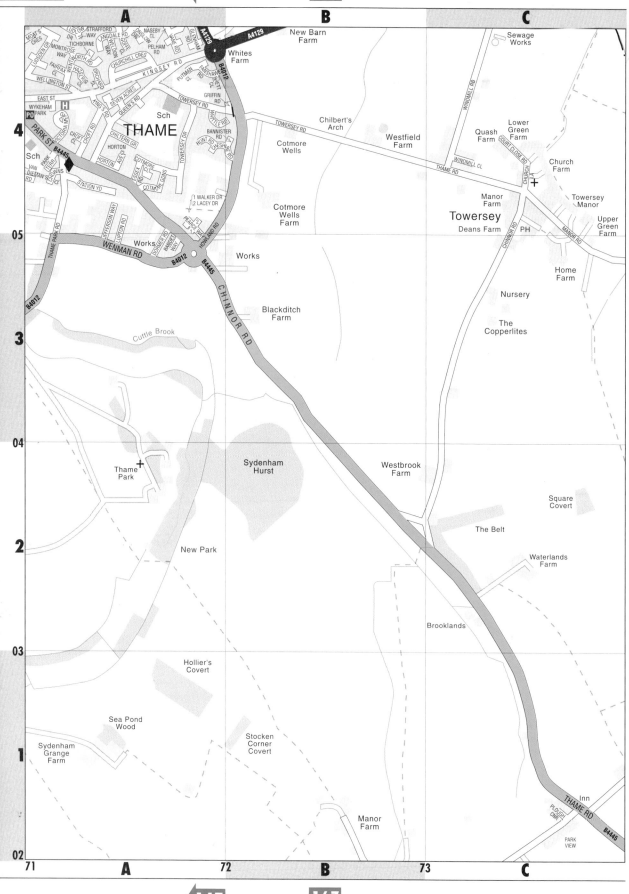

A
B
C

New Barn
Farm

Sewage
Works

MOAT'S
CRES
LUDTON
DR
STRAFFORD
WAY
GLENHAM
RD
NELSON
OXLOW
NASEBY RD
TICHBORNE
NORTH RD
WENTWORTH
CHURCHILL CRES
PELHAM
RD
JANE RD
A4129
Whites
Farm

MONTROSE
WAY
ORCHARD
HAZELRIG
KINGSEY RD
FANSHAWE
PUTMAN RD
B4012
Windmill Rd

FAIRFAX
CL
WELLINGTON ST
QUEEN'S RD
SEVEN ACRES
KING'S RD
TOWERSEY RD
GRIFFIN
RD
Towersey Rd

Chilbert's
Arch

Quash
Farm
Lower
Green
Farm

EAST ST
WYKEHAM
PARK
H
PO
PARK
Sch
THAME
CHILTERN GR
BANNISTER
RD
WHITTLE RD
TOWERSEY DR
HUNT RD
OKESHARP RD
Cotmore
Wells

Westfield
Farm

Church
Farm

4

Sch
VAN
DIEMAN'S
RD
PARK ST
VICTORIA WAY
CROFT
HORTON
HORTON AVE
ESSEX CL
COTMORE CL
COTMORE RD
Cotmore
Wells
Farm
Thame Rd
Windmill Cl
Towersey
Church La
Towersey
Manor

STATION YD
1 WALKER DR
2 LACEY DR
Manor
Farm
Upper
Green
Farm

05
THAME PARK RD
JEFFERSON WAY
LUPTON RD
PEARCE WAY
B4012
Works
B4445
Works
Deans Farm
Chinnor Rd
Manor Rd
PH
Home
Farm

B4012
WENMAN RD
CHINNER RD
BANDET WAY
HOWLAND RD
CHINNOR RD
Nursery

Blackditch
Farm
The
Copperlites

3

Cuttle Brook

04
Thame
Park
Sydenham
Hurst
Westbrook
Farm

Square
Covert

2
New Park
The Belt

Waterlands
Farm

Brooklands

03
Hollier's
Covert

Sea Pond
Wood
Stocken
Corner
Covert

Inn
THAME RD
PLOUGH
CNR
1
Sydenham
Grange
Farm
Manor
Farm
B4445
PARK
VIEW

02
71
A
72
B
73
C

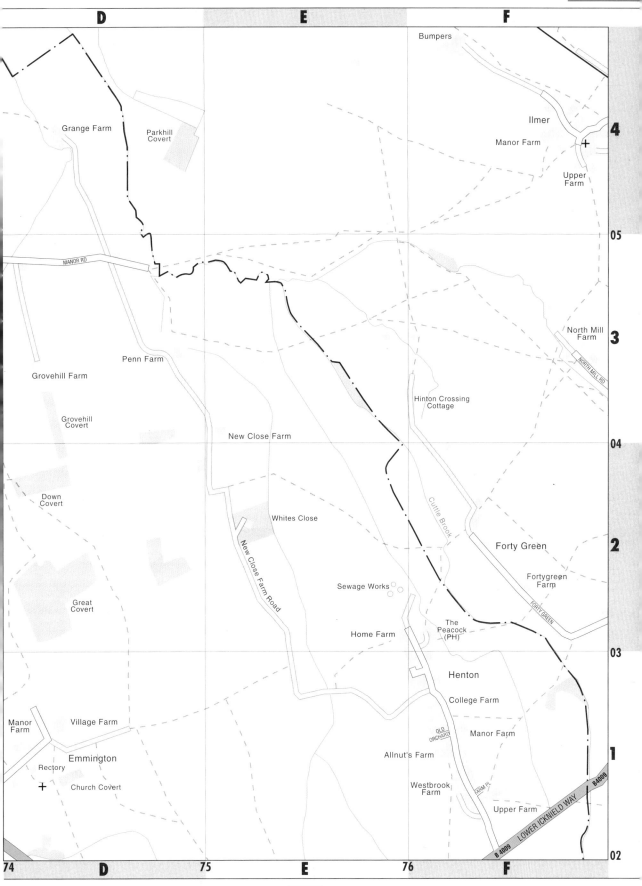

D   E   F

Bumpers

Grange Farm

Parkhill Covert

Ilmer

Manor Farm

Upper Farm

4

MANOR RD

05

North Mill Farm

3

Penn Farm

NORTH MILL RD

Grovehill Farm

Hinton Crossing Cottage

Grovehill Covert

New Close Farm

04

Down Covert

Whites Close

Cuttle Brook

Forty Green

2

Fortygreen Farm

Great Covert

New Close Farm Road

Sewage Works

FORTY GREEN

Home Farm

The Peacock (PH)

03

Henton

Manor Farm

Village Farm

College Farm

OLD ORCHARD

Manor Farm

Allnut's Farm

1

Emmington

Rectory

Westbrook Farm

FARM PL

Church Covert

Upper Farm

B 4009

LOWER ICKNIELD WAY

B4009

02

74   D   75   E   76   F

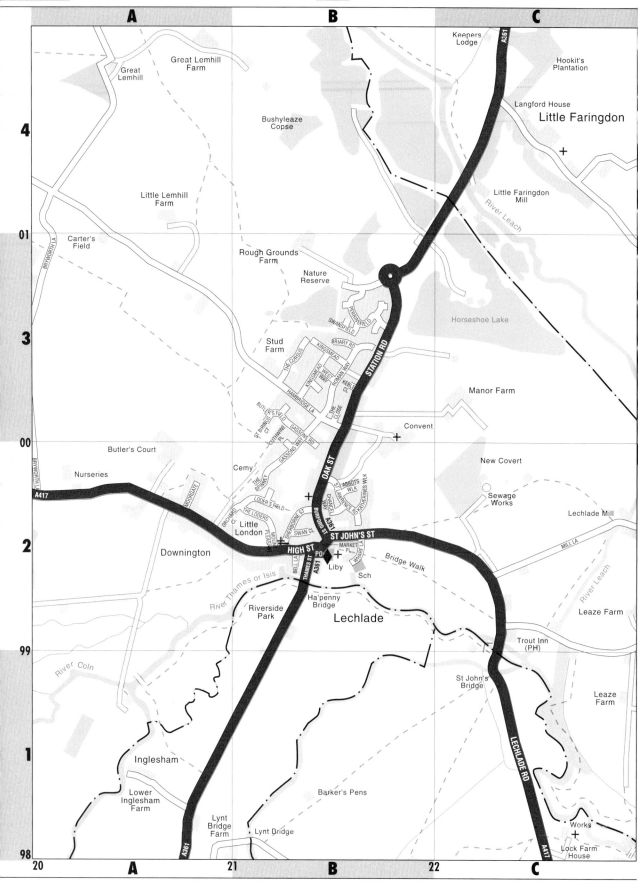

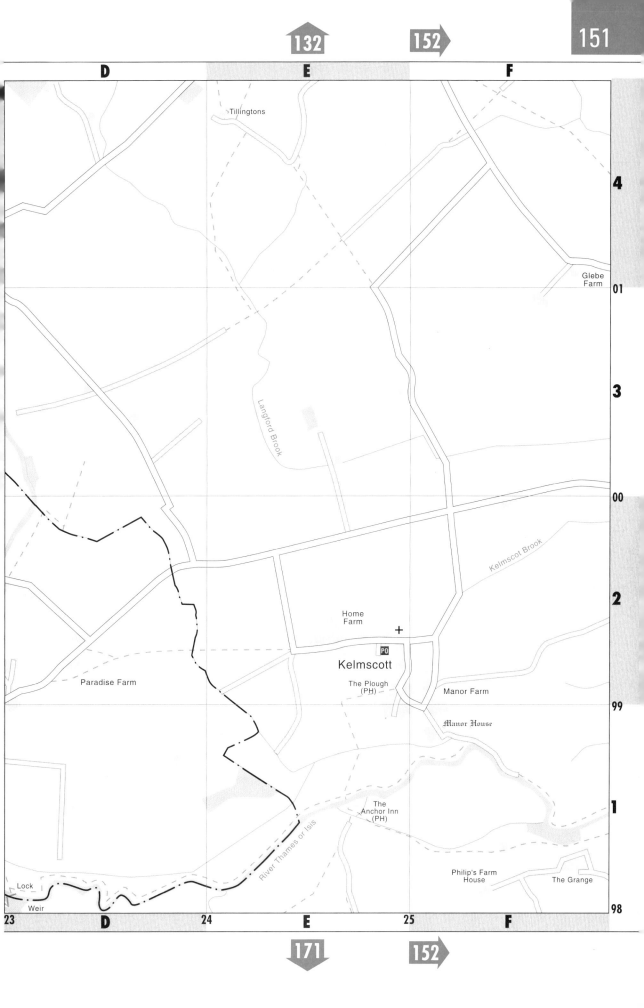

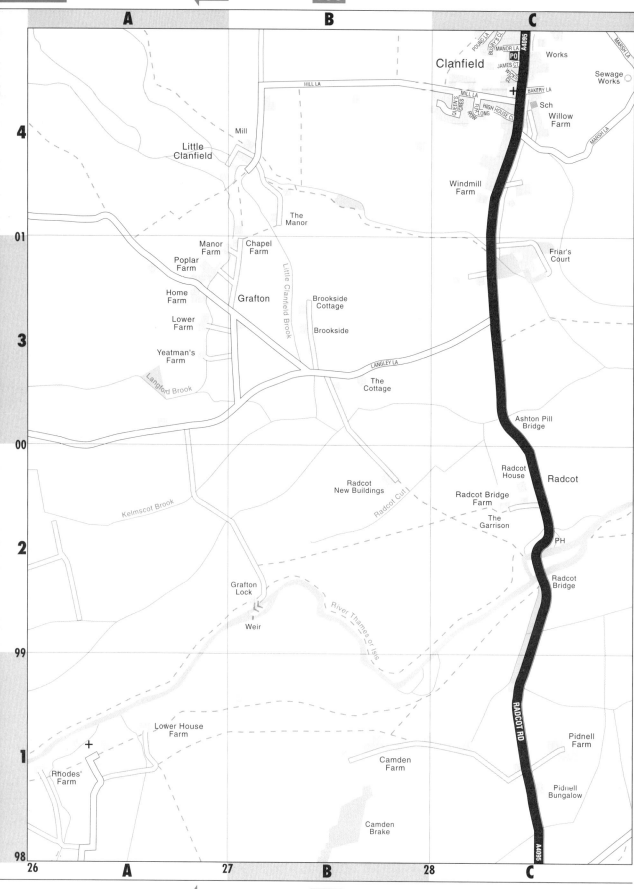
POUND LA
BUSBY'S CL
MANOR LA
JAMES CT
WICKS
PO

Clanfield

Works

HILL LA

Sewage
Works

MILL LA
QUEEN'S CRES
HIGH HOUSE CL
BAKERY LA
FURLONG
ROW

Sch

Willow
Farm

4

Mill

MARSH LA

Little
Clanfield

Windmill
Farm

The Manor

01

Manor
Farm

Chapel
Farm

Friar's
Court

Poplar
Farm

Little Clanfield Brook

Home
Farm

Grafton

Brookside
Cottage

3

Lower
Farm

Brookside

Yeatman's
Farm

LANGLEY LA

Langford Brook

The
Cottage

Ashton Pill
Bridge

00

Radcot
House

Radcot

Radcot
New Buildings

Radcot Bridge
Farm

Kelmscot Brook

Radcot Cut

The
Garrison

2

PH

Radcot
Bridge

Grafton
Lock

River Thames or Isis

Weir

99

Lower House
Farm

RADCOT RD

Pidnell
Farm

1

Camden
Farm

Rhodes'
Farm

Pidnell
Bungalow

Camden
Brake

98

A4095

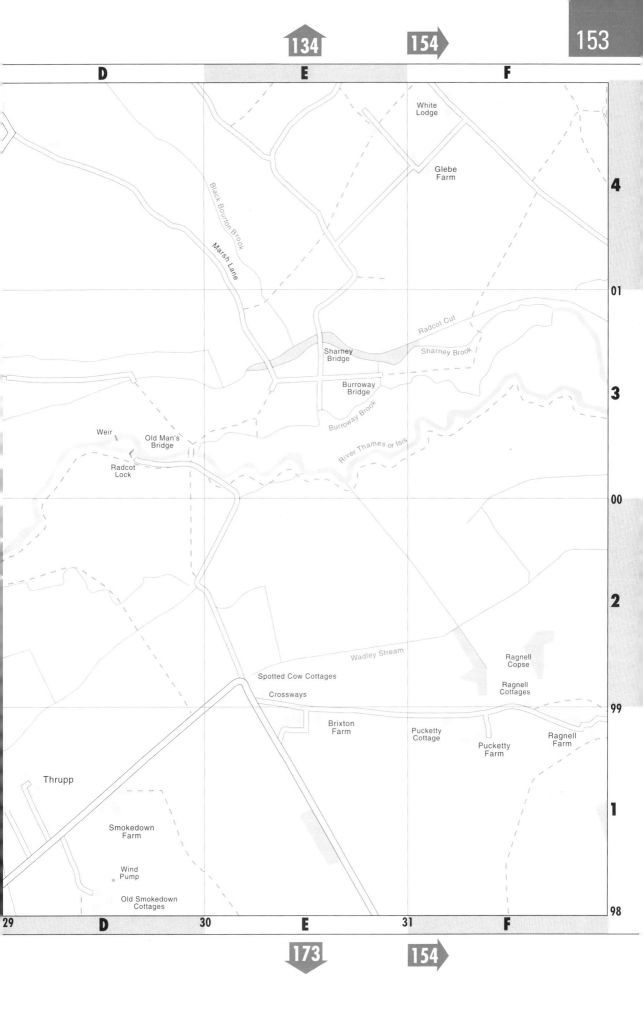

White
Lodge

Glebe
Farm

4

Black Bourton Brook

Marsh Lane

01

Radcot Cut

Sharney
Bridge

Sharney Brook

3

Burroway
Bridge

Burroway Brook

Weir

Old Man's
Bridge

River Thames or Isis

Radcot
Lock

00

2

Wadley Stream

Ragnell
Copse

Spotted Cow Cottages

Ragnell
Cottages

Crossways

99

Brixton
Farm

Pucketty
Cottage

Ragnell
Farm

Pucketty
Farm

Thrupp

1

Smokedown
Farm

Wind
Pump

Old Smokedown
Cottages

98

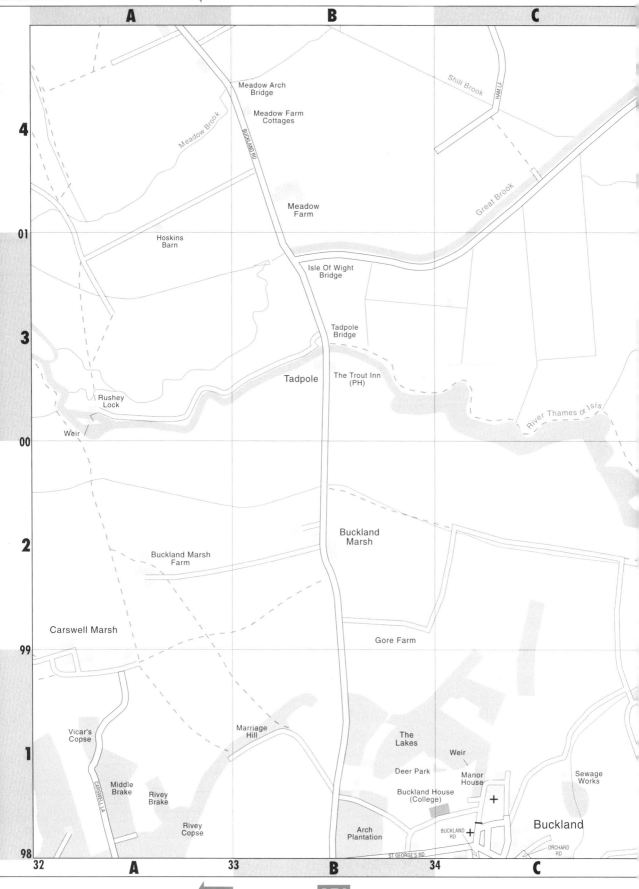

A   B   C

Meadow Arch
Bridge

Meadow Farm
Cottages

Shill Brook

HAM LA

BUCKLAND RD

Meadow Brook

4

Meadow
Farm

Great Brook

01

Hoskins
Barn

Isle Of Wight
Bridge

3

Tadpole
Bridge

Tadpole

The Trout Inn
(PH)

River Thames or Isis

Rushey
Lock

Weir

00

Buckland
Marsh

2

Buckland Marsh
Farm

Carswell Marsh

Gore Farm

99

Vicar's
Copse

Marriage
Hill

The
Lakes

Weir

1

CARSWELL LA

Middle
Brake

Rivey
Brake

Deer Park

Manor
House

Sewage
Works

Buckland House
(College)

Rivey
Copse

BUCKLAND RD

Buckland

Arch
Plantation

ORCHARD
RD

98

ST GEORGE'S RD

32   A   33   B   34   C

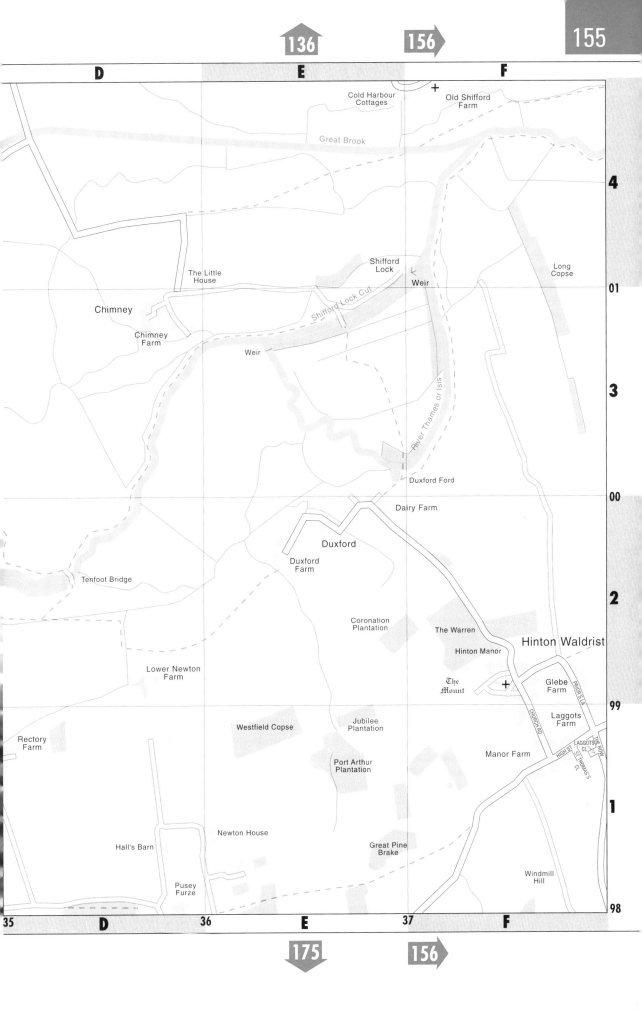

D
E
F

Cold Harbour
Cottages

Old Shifford
Farm

Great Brook

4

Shifford
Lock

The Little
House

Long
Copse

Weir

01

Chimney

Shifford Lock Cut

Chimney
Farm

Weir

River Thames or Isis

3

Duxford Ford

00

Dairy Farm

Duxford

Duxford
Farm

Tenfoot Bridge

Coronation
Plantation

2

The Warren

Hinton Waldrist

Hinton Manor

Lower Newton
Farm

The
Mount

Glebe
Farm

PRIOR'S LA

99

Laggots
Farm

Rectory
Farm

Westfield Copse

Jubilee
Plantation

CHURCH RD

LAGGOTS
CL

THE ROW

Port Arthur
Plantation

Manor Farm

HIGH ST

ST. THOMAS'S
CL

1

Newton House

Great Pine
Brake

Hall's Barn

Windmill
Hill

Pusey
Furze

98

35
D
36
E
37
F

155
137

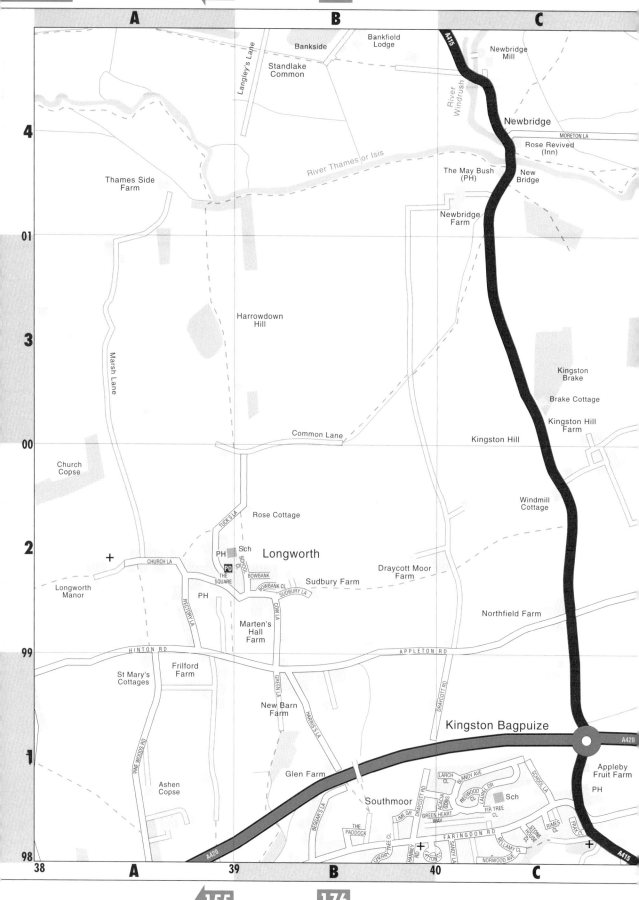

155
176

4

Stonehenge Farm

Moreton

Water Furze

Towing Path

River Thames or Isis

Cowslip Close

The Fold

Cheer's Farm

Woodlands

01

MILLWAY LA

Appleton Lower Common

The Lanket

Nurseries

3

North Audley Copse

NETHERTON RD

North Audley Farm House

Field Farm

Tubney Wood

Rose Hill

Marsh Farm

Sandhill Cottage

00

Sewage Works

MARSH LA

Appleton Upper Common

Church Copse

2

A420

Stone's Farm

Tubworth Barn

Tubney Lodge

Netherton

Bullock's Farm

Painton's Farm

NETHERTON LA

99

Manor House

Manor Farm

Piling Hill

Tubney

Sch

ST JOHN'S CL

PO

Tubney House

PH

MAIN RD

DIGGING LA

Fyfield

Diginglane Cottages

Sandy Wood

Tubney Farm

1

The Spinney

Golf Course

Woodhouse Fruit Farm

DIGGING LA

98

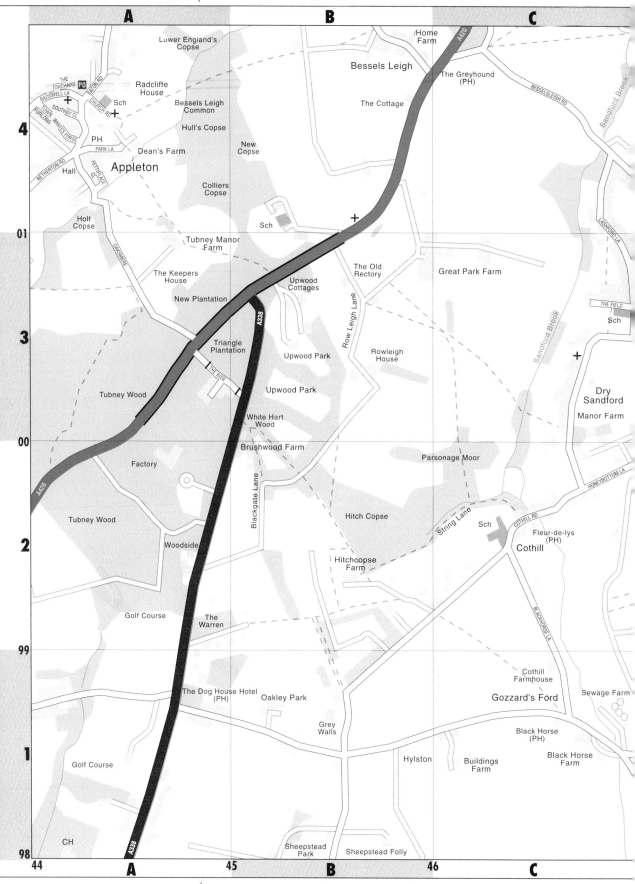

Lower England's Copse

Home Farm

Bessels Leigh

The Greyhound (PH)

THE ORCHARD
PO
BADSWELL LA
SOUTHBY CL
TOWN WHITES FORGE FURLONG
EATON RD
CHURCH RD
Sch

Radcliffe House

Bessels Leigh Common

The Cottage

BESSELSLEIGH RD

Hull's Copse

PH
PARK LA

Dean's Farm

New Copse

METHERTON RD
Hall
FETTIPLACE CL

Appleton

Colliers Copse

4

Holt Copse

OAKMERE

Sch

The Old Rectory

Great Park Farm

LASHFORD LA

THE FIELD
Sch

01

Tubney Manor Farm

The Keepers House

Upwood Cottages

Row Leigh Lane

Sandford Brook

New Plantation

A338

Triangle Plantation

Upwood Park

Rowleigh House

3

THE RIDE

Dry Sandford

Manor Farm

Tubney Wood

Upwood Park

White Hart Wood

Brushwood Farm

00

Factory

Parsonage Moor

HONEYBOTTOM LA

Blackgate Lane

Tubney Wood

Hitch Copse

String Lane
Sch

COTHILL RD

Fleur-de-lys (PH)

Woodside

Hitchcopse Farm

Cothill

BLACKHORSE LA

2

Golf Course

The Warren

99

Cothill Farmhouse

The Dog House Hotel (PH)

Oakley Park

Gozzard's Ford

Sewage Farm

Grey Walls

Black Horse (PH)

Black Horse Farm

1

Golf Course

Hylston

Buildings Farm

CH

A338

Sheepstead Park

Sheepstead Folly

98

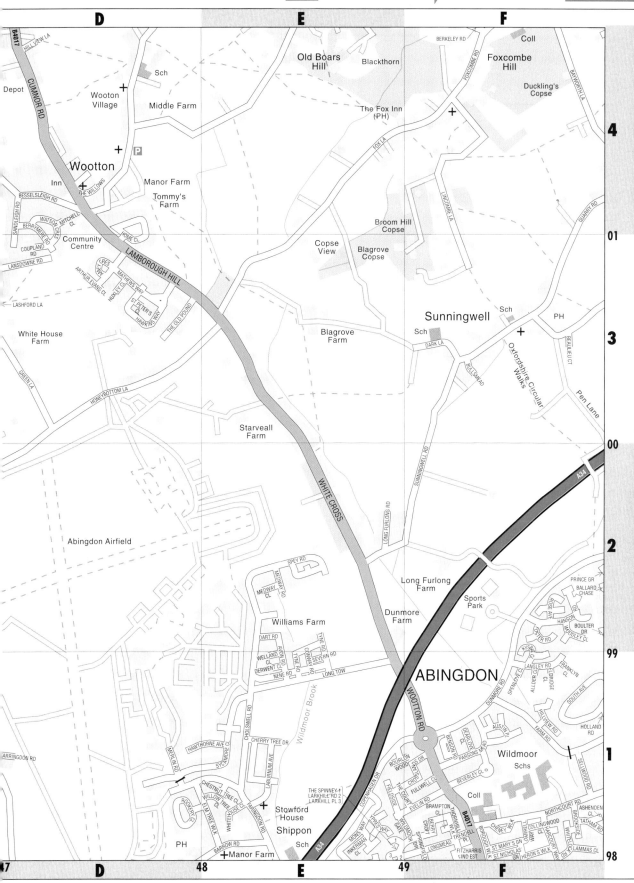

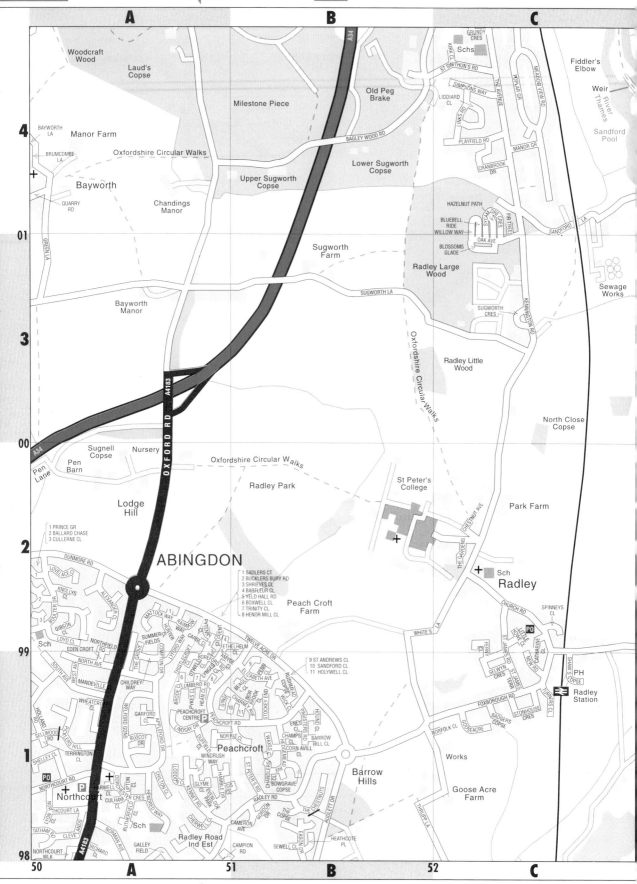

D E F

Orchard House

SANDFORD RD

ROCK KEENE CL
FARM LA

A4074

GRENOBLE RD

KILN CL

THE CRESCENT
MAIN AVE

Sewage Works

FIELDFARE RD 1
WAYFARING CL 2
ANEMONE CL 3
OXEYE CT 4
HYACINTH WLK 5
SPRUCE GDNS 6
FIRS MEADOW 7
APPLETREE CL 8

VIOLET WAY
FRYS HILL
GRENOBLE RD

El Sub Sta

CHURCH RD
PO

HENLEY RD

Caravan Park

Catherine Wheel (PH)

RIVER VIEW
BURRA CL
PH

Lock

Sandford-on-Thames

Bushy Copse

4

SANDFORD LA

01

Lower Farm

3

Towing Path

River Thames or Isis

Nineveh Farm

00

Upper Farm

Nuneham Courtenay

Hop Garden Copse

2

Harcourt Arms (PH)

Sandpits Covert

Pumping Station

Lower Radley

PO

BALDON LA

Fish Pond

99

Lower Farm

Boat House

The Rectory

Old Common

New Close Copse

Nuneham Park

1

Rectory Cottage

The Lake

Sewage Works

Home Farm

Windmill Hill

Bluebell Wood

Nuneham House

Rose Nursery

A4074

98

53 D 54 E 55 F

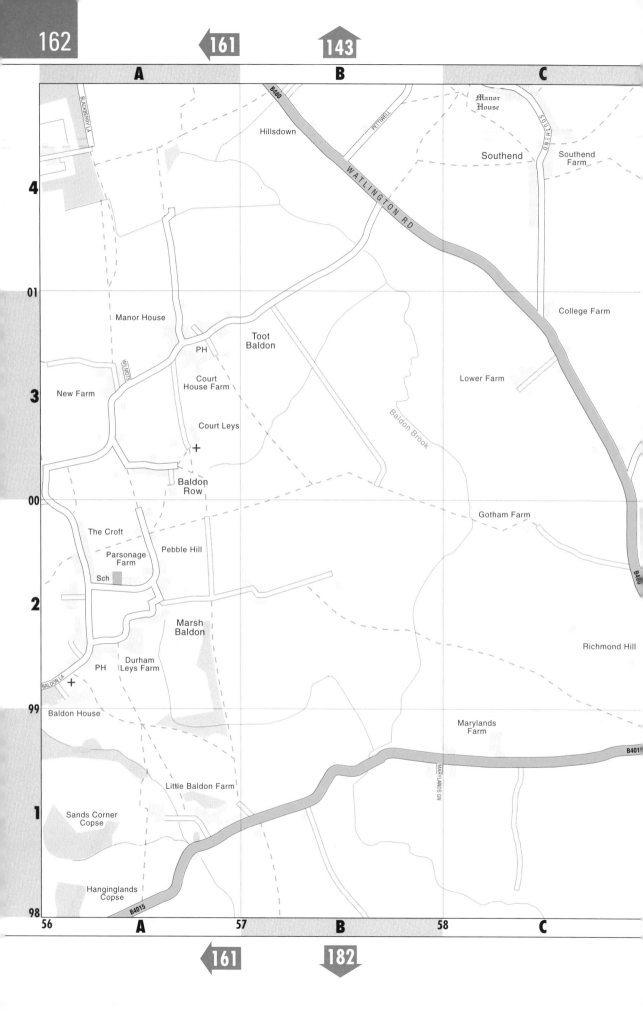

A
B
C

BLACKBERRY LA

B480

Hillsdown

PETTIWELL

Manor House

Southend

SOUTHEND

Southend Farm

WATLINGTON RD

4

01

Manor House

College Farm

PH

Toot Baldon

WILMOTS

Court House Farm

Lower Farm

New Farm

3

Court Leys

Baldon Brook

+

Baldon Row

00

Gotham Farm

The Croft

Pebble Hill

B480

Parsonage Farm

Sch

2

Marsh Baldon

Richmond Hill

BALDON LA

PH

Durham Leys Farm

+

99

Baldon House

Marylands Farm

B401

Little Baldon Farm

MARYLANDS GN

1

Sands Corner Copse

Hanginglands Copse

B4015

98

56
A
57
B
58
C

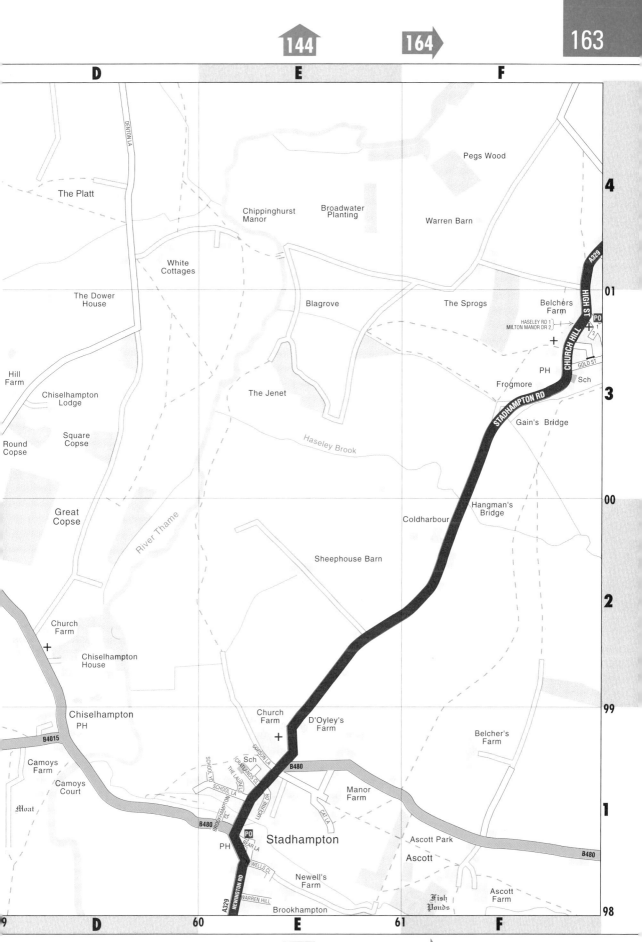

D   E   F

The Platt

DENTON LA

Chippinghurst Manor

Broadwater Planting

Pegs Wood

Warren Barn

White Cottages

4

A329

01

The Dower House

Blagrove

The Sprogs

Belchers Farm

HIGH ST

PO

HASELEY RD 1
MILTON MANOR DR 2

CHURCH HILL

Hill Farm

PH

GOLD ST

Chiselhampton Lodge

The Jenet

Frogmore

Sch

3

STADHAMPTON RD

Round Copse

Square Copse

Haseley Brook

Gain's Bridge

Great Copse

River Thame

Coldharbour

Hangman's Bridge

00

Sheephouse Barn

Church Farm

2

Chiselhampton House

Church Farm

D'Oyley's Farm

99

Belcher's Farm

Chiselhampton
PH

B4015

Camoys Farm

Sch

B480

Manor Farm

GARSON LA

CRATLANDS CL

THE LAURELS

SCHOOL RD

SCHOOL LA

LUCERNE DR

CAT LA

Camoys Court

Moat

1

B480

BROOKHAMPTON CL

Stadhampton

Ascott Park

B480

PH

PO

BEAR LA

Ascott

Ascott Farm

NEWINGTON RD

A329

EWELLS CL

WARREN HILL

Newell's Farm

Fish Ponds

98

Brookhampton

9   D   60   E   61   F   98

163
145

A   **B**   **C**

The Sands

A329

THAME RD

Back Way

MILL LA

LEWINGTON CL

RECTORY RD

The Farm
Sch

HORSE CLOSE

COTES

PH

THAME RD

Church
Farm

CHURCH HILL

Sands
Farm

Great
Haseley

4

OLD FIELD

CHILTERN VIEW

LATCHFORD LA

Haseley Wood

Sainfoin
Close

01

Wells Farm

Little Milton

Stone's
Farm

Haseley
Court

BLENHEIM

Sewage
Works

3

Canker
Leaze

Little
Haseley

Court
Farm

Ditchend
Farm

Carter's
Copse

Stoney Lane

00

Warren
Copse

Standhill
Farm

2

Whitford
Copse

Haseley Brook

Rof
Ford

ROFFORD LA

Cowleaze
Copse

Chalgrove Common

99

Sewage
Works

New
Barn

Rofford
Farm

Rofford

Rofford
Hall

1

Lane
Farm

Manor
Farm
House

Warpsgrove

B480

Chalgrove Airfield

98

62   **A**   63   **B**   64   **C**

D
E
F

M40

Manor
Farm

Jointer's
Farm

Goldpits
Farm

Latchford House

Oxhouse
Farm

4

LATCHFORD LA

Latchford
Farm

Latchford

Latchford
Copse

Haseley Brook

01

Sheepbridge
Copse

Peggs
Farm

3

Cornwell
Copse

Stoke Grange

The
Island

00

Poppets
Hill

Oxfordshire Way

2

Poppets
Hill Farm

Stoke
Talmage

Stoney Lane

Manor
Farm

99

Clare

1

Clare
Copse

Manor
Farm

98

5
D
66
E
67
F

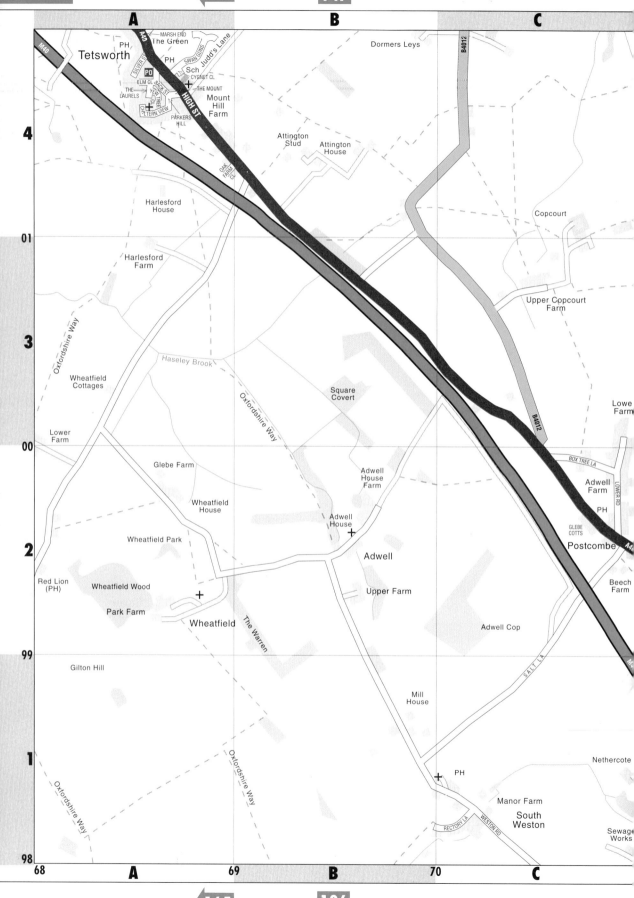

M40
Tetsworth
MARSH END
The Green
PH
Judd's Lane
SWAN GDNS
PH
PO
Sch
CYGNET CL
ELM CL
SILVER ST
BACK ST
THE LAURELS
YEW TREE
CHILTERN VIEW
PARKERS HILL
THE MOUNT
Mount Hill Farm
HIGH ST
Dormers Leys
B4012

Attington Stud
Attington House

OAK FARM CL

Copcourt

Harlesford House

Upper Copcourt Farm

01

Harlesford Farm

Oxfordshire Way

Wheatfield Cottages

Haseley Brook

3

Oxfordshire Way

Square Covert

B4012

Lowe Farm

Lower Farm

00

Glebe Farm

Adwell House Farm

BOX TREE LA

Adwell Farm

LOWER RD

Wheatfield House

Adwell House

PH

GLEBE COTTS

Wheatfield Park

Adwell

Postcombe

A40

2

Red Lion (PH)

Wheatfield Wood

Upper Farm

Beech Farm

Park Farm

Wheatfield

The Warren

Adwell Cop

99

Gilton Hill

SALT LA

Mill House

1

Oxfordshire Way

Oxfordshire Way

PH

Nethercote

Manor Farm
South Weston

Sewage Works

RECTORY LA
WESTON RD

98

4

2

A B C

4

01

3

00

99

2

1

98

B4445
B4009
THAME RD
LOWER ICKNIELD WAY
B4009
LOWER RD
B4009

Lane Farm
HOTLAND CL
ELDERDENE
New Farm
SPRINGFIELD GDNS
LEYBOURNE GDNS
MALYNS CL
DOVELEAF
P
PH
Sch
Liby
DUCK SQ
BENTON DR
DITCH DR
HIGH ST
Sch
Sch
MUSGRAVE RD
RECTORY MEADOW
CHURCH RD
Chinnor
Icknield Line
LC
Lower Wainhill
Hempton Wainhill
Bledlow Cross
LC

Middle Farm
MILL LA
CLEAVERS
MILLERS TURN
FORESTERS WAY
HEDGERLEY
HAILEY CFT
CONIGRE
CONIGRE
COMP ACRE
BEECH RD
CHERRY TREE RD
WILLOW
LACEMAKERS
HILLWRENC
BENWELLS
STATION RD
LIME GR
PH
ROBINS PLATT
ASHRIDGE LA
HUNTERS POINT
RIDERS WAY
FOX COVER
PENLEY CL
FLINT HOLLOW
OAKLEY LA
ST ANDREW'S RD
ELM DR
ELM CL
PLUMBERS GR
GREENWOOD AVE
DRUDGE WLK
GLYNSWOOD
GREENWOOD CL
RAVENSMEAD
TIMBER WAY
ORCHARD WAY
OMO RD
WHEELER RD
WOODVILLE
Saw Mill
MEADOW RD
WYKEHAM RISE
GOLDEN HILLS
HILL RD
THE AVENUE
KEENS LA
PO
HILL FARM CFT
Oakley
Oakley RD
Oakley

Crowell End Farm
Quarry
Chinnor Hill
Works
Crowell Farm
CHINNOR RD
Crowell
ICKNIELD CL
HIGH ST
B4009
PH

Ridgeway
CHINNOR HILL
Woodlands Farm
RED LA

Aston Rowant
Chalk Quarries
Oakley Hill
Manor Farm

99
Sunley Wood

Swan's Way
Race Course
Venus Wood
Venus Wood

1
Crowellhill Wood
Crowell Hill
Sprig's Alley
Crowellhill Farm
Grove Farm
KINGSTON HILL
SPRIGS HOLLY LA

98
Kingston Wood

74 A 75 B 76 C

Icknield Line

Midshires Way

The Warren

The Cop

Thickthorne Wood

Dean Plantation

Bledlow Great Wood

Home Wood

Frenche's Wood

Beechgrove Farm

Hedgerley Wood

SPRIGS HOLLY LA

Keeper's House

Ridgeway

Shimmell's Farm

Callow Down Farm

Wigan's Farm

Harper's Farm

Bledlow Ridge

Radnage Bottom Farm

Daws Hill Farm

CHINNOR RD

RADNAGE LA

CHURCH LA

Frogmore Farm

ODDLEY LA

BLEDLOW RIDGE RD

WIGAN'S LA

Bedlow Circular Ride

BLEDLOW RD

Church Farm

Home Farm

Golf Course

CH

Parsonage Farm

Lodge Hill

LEE RD

Lodge Hill Farm

Rout's Green

RETREAT LA

CHAPEL LA

The Boot (PH)

Studmore Farm

4

01

3

00

2

99

1

98

D 77

D 78

E 79

F

A   B   C

Buscot Wick

Weston
Cottages

Buscot Wick
Farm

A417

LECHLADE RD

The
Rectory

A417

River Thames or Isis

Weir

4

Weston
Farm

97

Upper
Inglesham

Manor
Farm

3

Lynt
Farm

LYNT RD

River Cole

Snowswick
Cottages

SNOWSWICK LA

Broadleaze
Farm

96

Snowswick
Farm

Snowswick
Copse

College
Farm

2

Pennyswick
Farm

95

1

Worsall
Farm

LECHLADE RD

A361

Roundhill
Farm

94

20   21   22

A   B   C

D

E

F

Buscot Wharf

Buscot

P

PO

PH

Kilmester Farm

Eaton Hastings

4

West Lodge

Taylor's Hill

Stud Farm

Little Lake

LECHLADE RD

97

A417

Buscot House

The Lake

Roadside Cottages

Resr

Buscot Park

Canada Wood

Bury Hill

3

Cannon Hill

Old Wood

Cannonhill Wood

Black Plantation

Eaton Wood

Bushy Heath

Heath Barn

Resr

Longmead Plantation

Woodacre Wood

96

Oldfield Farm

Rowleaze Wood

Gorse Hill

2

Brimstone Farm

95

Coxwell Wood

Middle Leaze Farm

Fern Copse

1

B4019

Cuckoopen Plantation

B4019

Colleymore Farm

94

23

D

24

E

25

F

A   B   C

4

Thrupp Turn

Hatton Farm

Crabbe-Tree Farm

Tudor Farm

Northfield Farm

A4095

Northfield New Covert

Northfield Old Covert

Northfield Farm Cottages

97

A417

Manor Farm

RADCOT RD

Eaton Wood

Sewage Works

Step Farm Cottages

LECHLADE RD

3

Badbury Forest

Nursery Cottage

Step Farm

Edmonds's Pen

Faringdon Park

Collins's Ground

Faringdon House

96

Oak Wood

CORNMARKET 1
GLOUCESTER MEWS 2
SOUTHAMPTON ST 3
GOODLAKE AVE 4
WHITE HART WLK 5

WOODVIEW

REGENT MEWS

Sch
Liby

FARINGDON

Sch

GLOUCESTER ST 1

A4095 CHURCH ST

SWAN LA

LONDON

2

Wood House

CANADA LA

THE PINES

CEDAR RD

CHESTNUT AVE

ASH CL

MEADOW

GRAVEL WLK

PULLINGS

MARLBOROUGH ST

STATION RD

PORTLAND ST

HART AVE

FERNDALE

WESTBROOK

BENNETT

SOUTHAMPTON ST

REGAL WAY

Smallgains Copse

OLD

MAPLE

BEECH CL

COXWELL

WALNUT CL

WILLES CL

Sch

Sch

EAGLES CL

SAWMILLS RD

B4019

COXWELL GDNS

MARLBOROUGH RD

PARK RD

PIONEER RD

REGAL WAY

BUTTS

Badbury Hill House

95

Badbury Hill

Highden Farm

HIGHWORTH RD

COXWELL RD

A417

ORCHARD HILL

HAWTHORN RD

ELM RD

MARLBOROUGH GDNS

MARLBOROUGH PL

MARINES DR

SAND VIEW

TOWN END RD

Badbury

WESTLAND RD

CLOCK TWR CL

FOLLY VIEW CRES

FOLLY VIEW RD

TOWER VIEW

1

B4019

Badburyhill Copse

LEAMINGTON DR

Sch

Leisure Centre

THE HOLLOW RD

CARTER CRES

TOLLINGTON CT

FERNHAM RD

COXWELL HALL MEWS

Coxwell Lodge

MEADOW WAY

Steeds Farm

Gipsy Lane

Coxwell Lodge Works

FERNHAM RD

94

Great Barn

A420

26   A   27   B   28   C

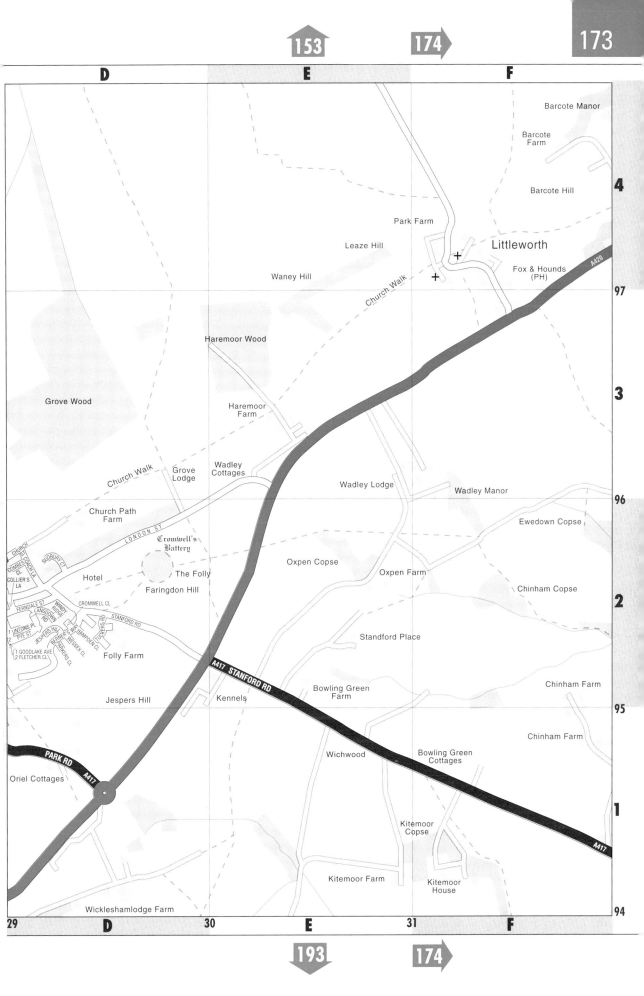

D
E
F

Barcote Manor

Barcote
Farm

Barcote Hill

4

Park Farm

Leaze Hill

Littleworth

Church Walk

Waney Hill

Fox & Hounds
(PH)

A420

97

Haremoor Wood

3

Grove Wood

Haremoor
Farm

Church Walk

Grove
Lodge

Wadley
Cottages

Wadley Lodge

Wadley Manor

96

Church Path
Farm

Ewedown Copse

LONDON ST

Cromwell's
Battery

CHURCH ST
COMBES
CL
COACH LA
SUDBURY CT
COLLIER'S
LA

Hotel

The Folly

Oxpen Copse

Oxpen Farm

Chinham Copse

2

FERNDALE ST
LANSDOWN
MINDY
RIDGE
CROMWELL CL
BENNER'S RD
STANFORD RD

Faringdon Hill

UNTONS PL
PYE ST
JESPERS HILL
BEGNER'S WAY
WESSEX CL
HAMPDEN CL
BARKERS CL

1 GOODLAKE AVE
2 FLETCHER CL

Folly Farm

Standford Place

Chinham Farm

Jespers Hill

A417 STANFORD RD

Kennels

Bowling Green
Farm

95

PARK RD

Wichwood

Bowling Green
Cottages

Chinham Farm

A417

Oriel Cottages

1

Kitemoor
Copse

A417

Kitemoor Farm

Kitemoor
House

Wickleshamlodge Farm

94

29
D
30
E
31
F

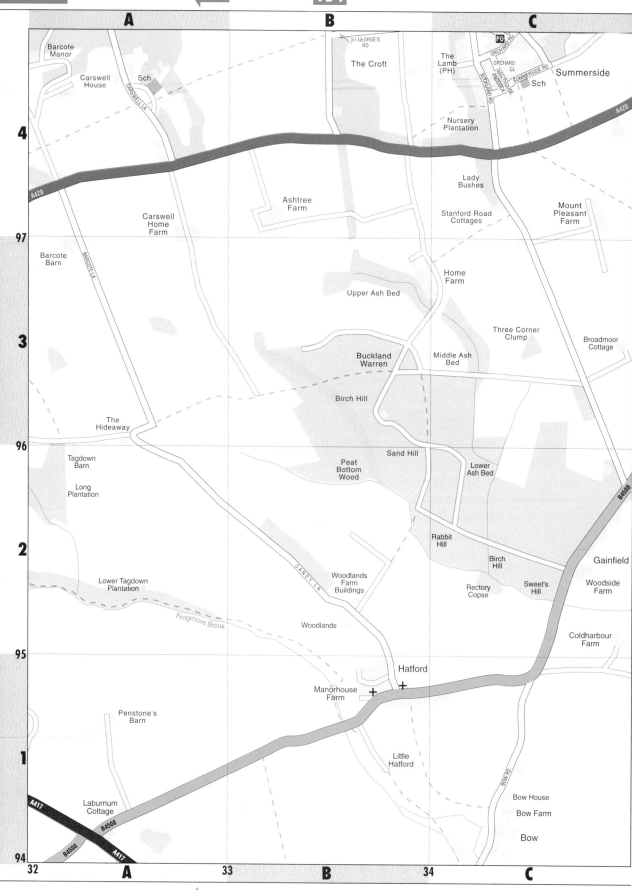

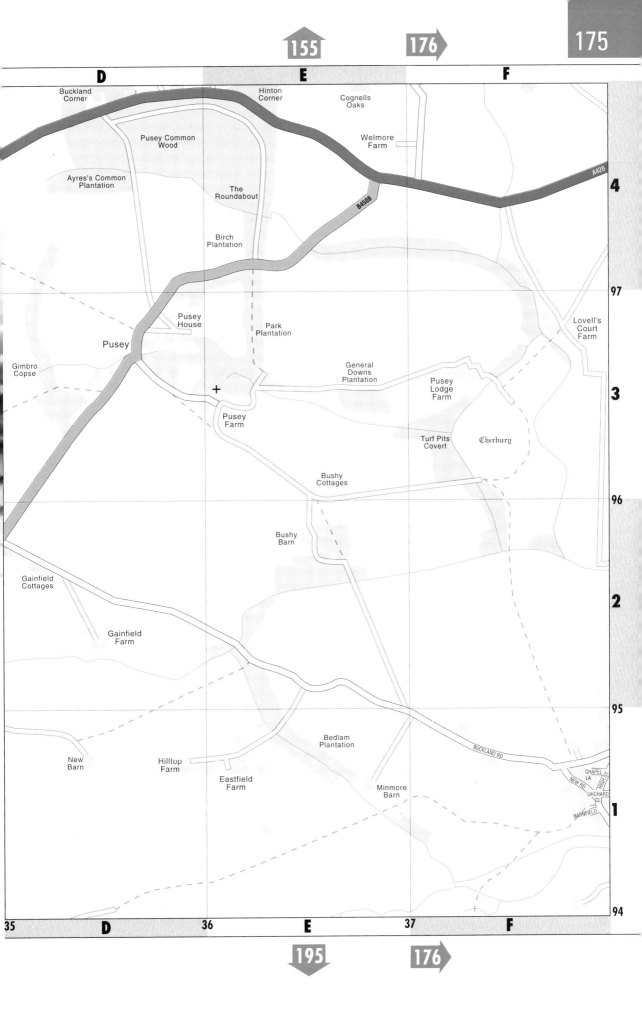

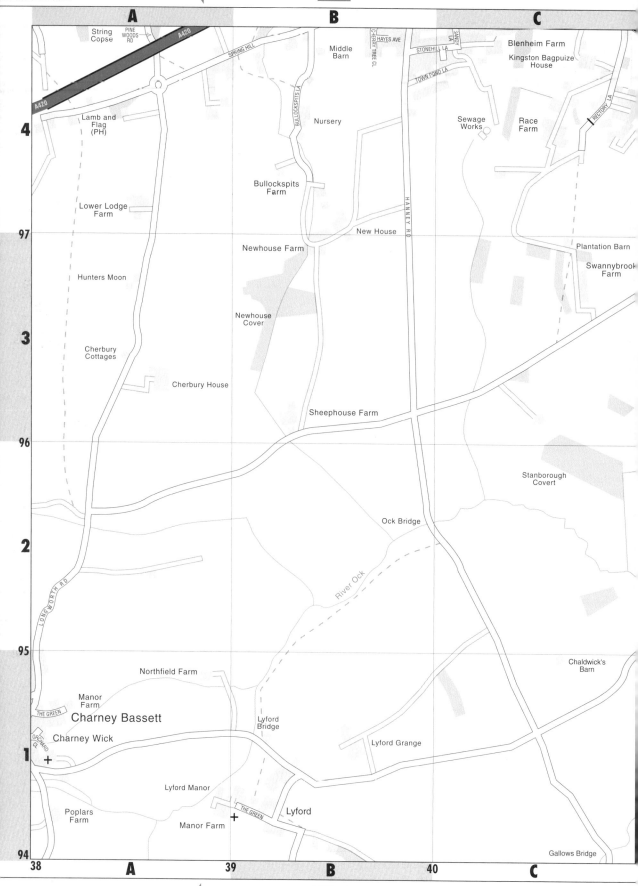

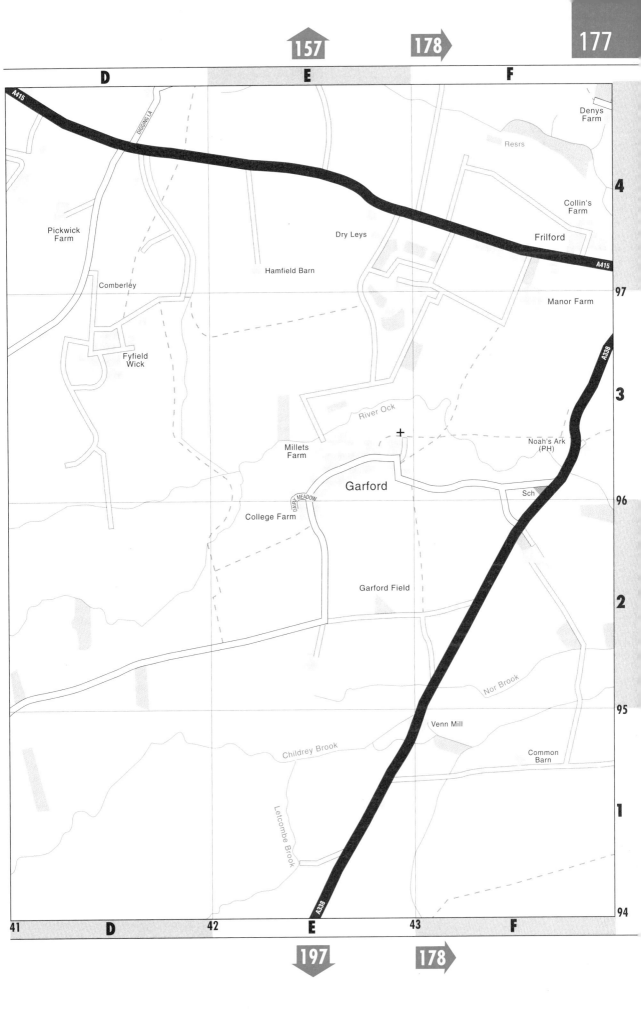

D
E
F

A415

DIGGING LA

Denys Farm

Resrs

4

Collin's Farm

Pickwick Farm

Dry Leys

Frilford

Comberley

Hamfield Barn

A415

97

Manor Farm

A338

Fyfield Wick

3

River Ock

Noah's Ark (PH)

+

Millets Farm

Garford

Sch

DAIRY MEADOW

96

College Farm

Garford Field

2

Nor Brook

95

Venn Mill

Childrey Brook

Common Barn

1

Letcombe Brook

A338

94

41
D
42
E
43
F

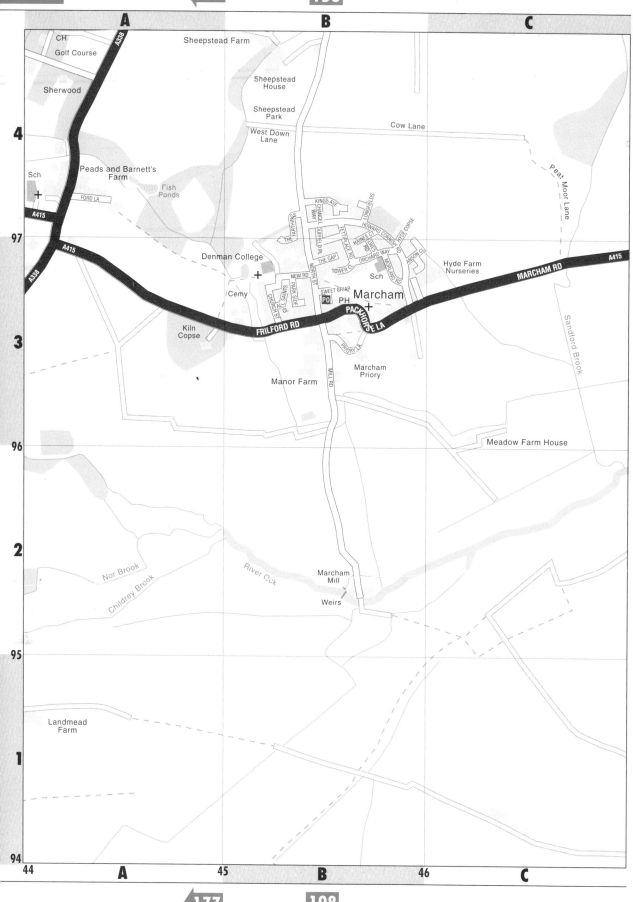

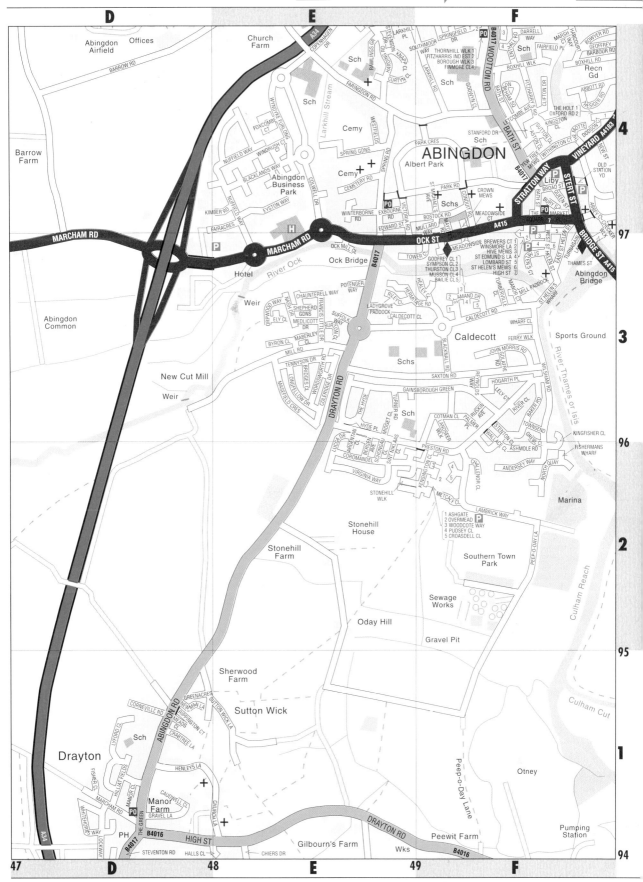

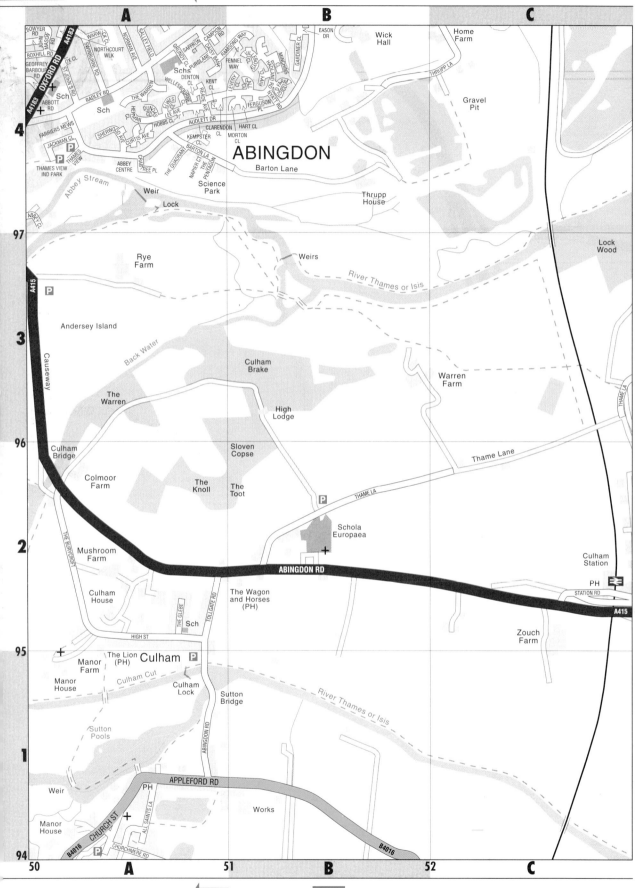

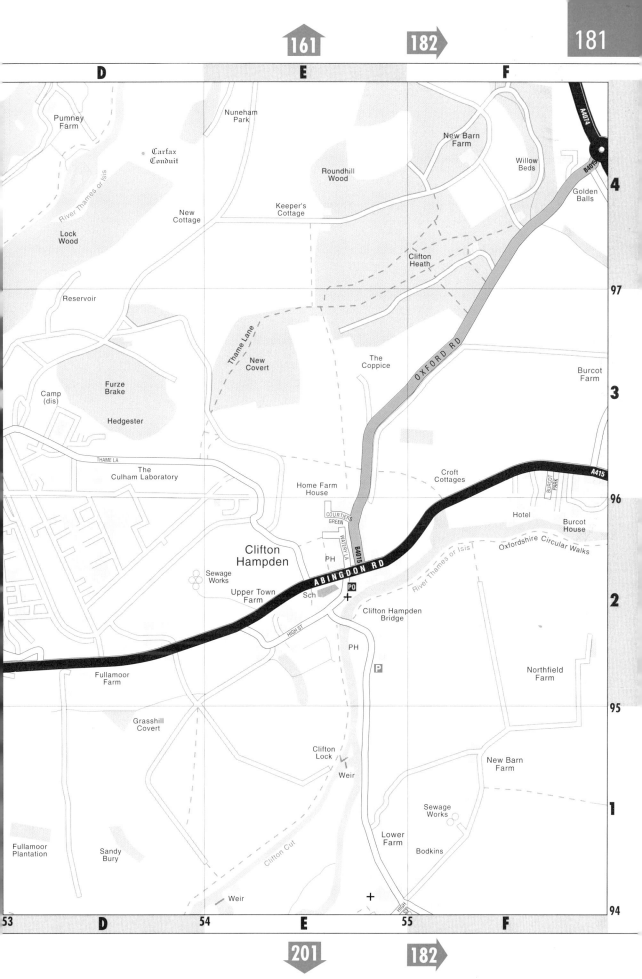

D
E
F

Pumney Farm

Nuneham Park

New Barn Farm

Carfax Conduit

Roundhill Wood

Willow Beds

Golden Balls

4

A4074

B4015

New Cottage

Keeper's Cottage

Lock Wood

Clifton Heath

97

Reservoir

Thame Lane

New Covert

The Coppice

OXFORD RD

Burcot Farm

3

Camp (dis)

Furze Brake

Hedgester

THAME LA

The Culham Laboratory

Home Farm House

Croft Cottages

A415

BURCOT PARK

96

Hotel

Burcot House

COURTIERS GREEN

Clifton Hampden

Oxfordshire Circular Walks

WATERY LA

B4015

PH

Sewage Works

ABINGDON RD

River Thames or Isis

Upper Town Farm

Sch

PO

2

Clifton Hampden Bridge

HIGH ST

PH

Fullamoor Farm

Northfield Farm

P

95

Grasshill Covert

Clifton Lock

Weir

New Barn Farm

1

Sewage Works

Fullamoor Plantation

Sandy Bury

Clifton Cut

Lower Farm

Bodkins

Weir

HIGH ST

94

53
D
54
E
55
F

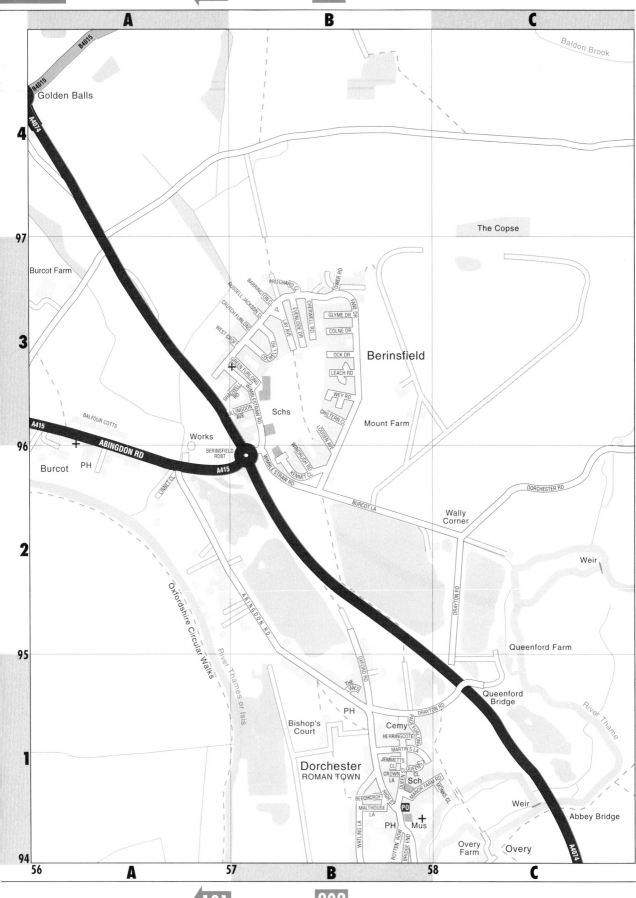

Baldon Brook

4

Golden Balls

97

The Copse

Burcot Farm

RUSSELL JACKSON CL
BARRINGTON CL
PRITCHARD CL
TOWER RD
CRUTCH FURLONG
CHERWELL RD
EVERLODE DR
LAY AVE
FANE RD
WEST CROFT
GLYME DR
COLNE DR
3
COURT RD
GREEN FURLONG
OCK DR
Berinsfield
SHADWELL RD
TIMBLESTRAW RD
LEACH RD
LULLINGDON AVE
WEY RD
Schs
CHILTERN CL
BALFOUR COTTS
LODDEN AVE
Mount Farm
96
Works
WINDRUSH RD
A415 ABINGDON RD
Berinsfield
RDBT
Burcot
PH
KENNET CL
WIMBLE STRAW RD
A415
Burcot La
Dorchester Rd
LINNET CL
Wally
Corner

2
Weir

DRAYTON RD

ABINGDON RD

95
Queenford Farm

Oxfordshire Circular Walks

OXFORD RD
Queenford
Bridge

River Thames or Isis
THE LIMES
PH
DRAYTON RD
River Thame
Bishop's
Court
Cemy
PAGE FURLONG
HERRINGCOTE
MARTIN'S LA
1
JEMMETTS
CL
QUEENS
CL
Dorchester
ROMAN TOWN
CROWN
LA
Sch
QUEEN ST
MANOR FARM RD
BYONGS CL
BEECHCROFT
HIGH ST
Weir
MALTHOUSE
LA
PO
ROTTEN ROW
WATLING LA
PH Mus
Abbey Bridge
BRIDGE END
Overy
Farm
Overy
A4074
94

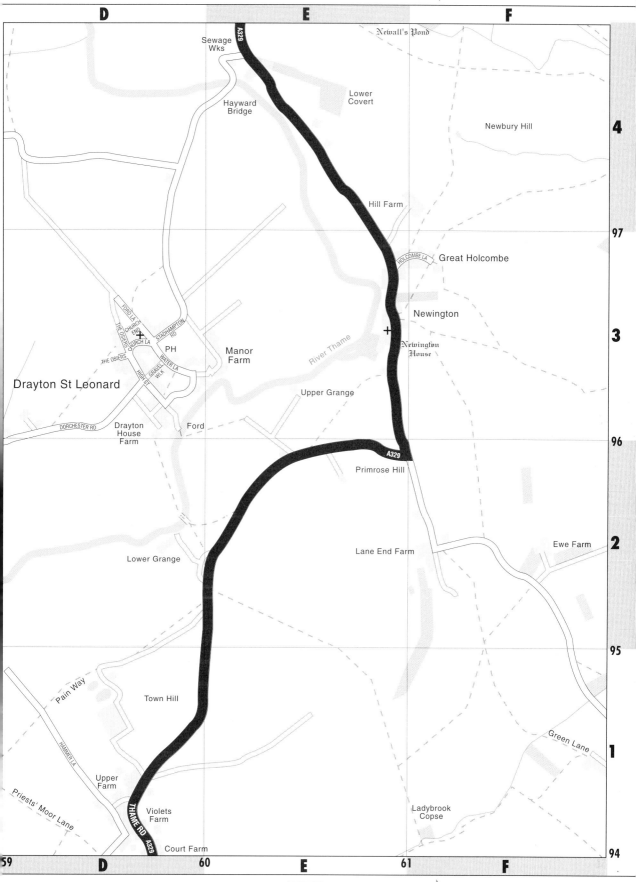

D
E
F

A329

Sewage
Wks

Newall's Pond

Hayward
Bridge

Lower
Covert

Newbury Hill

4

Hill Farm

97

HOLCOMBE LA

Great Holcombe

Newington

3

River Thame

Newington
House

FORD LA

THE OSIERS

CHURCH END

STADHAMPTON RD

CHURCH LA

PH

Manor
Farm

Upper Grange

Drayton St Leonard

THE OSIERS

HIGH ST

WATER LA

GRAVEL WLK

DORCHESTER RD

Drayton
House
Farm

Ford

A329

96

Primrose Hill

Lower Grange

Lane End Farm

Ewe Farm

2

95

Pain Way

Town Hill

HAMMER LA

Green Lane

1

Upper
Farm

Priests' Moor Lane

THAME RD

A329

Violets
Farm

Ladybrook
Copse

Court Farm

94

59
D
60
E
61
F

A B C

B480

Chalgrove
Airfield

Newberry
Hill

4

Chalgrove
Field

Hitchcox
Poultry
Farm

Hampden's
Monument

MONUMENT IND

MONUMENT PARK

POPLAR FARM RD

BOWER END
BROOKSIDE ESTATE
MARLEY LA
CINNAMON CL
HIGH ST
The Lamb
(PH)

Fox
Covert

Little Holcombe
Covert

ORCHARD
BRIMKINFIELD RD
SAGE CL
VICAR CL
LADBE
LODDON RD
FRENCH LAURENCE WAY
OXPENNY LA

97

Manor

Mill
House

Langley
Hall

Langley Field
Farm

FLEMMING AVE
ADEANE RD
QUARTERMAIN RD
TILLERS
LANT CL
ECCLES LA
PADDOCK CL
LANGLEY RD
HARDINGS
THE GREEN
SWINSTEAD CT
Sch
CHIRNALL DR
ST MARTS
CHURCHMEAD
WILLOW MEAD
CHURCH LA
FRANKLIN CL
HAMPDEN
CHAPEL LA
MAYFIELD
IRETON CL
RUPERT RD
FAIRFAX RD
BEVERLEY
ARGOSY CL
MONUMENT RD
FARM CL
CHILTERN CL

Chalgrove

CROMWELL CL

BERRICK RD

B480

3

Church
Farm

Chalgrove
Farm

96

Hares
Leap

Southfield
Barn

Cadwell La

Hollandstide
House

Cadwell
Covert

Cadwell
Farm

2

Whitehouse
Farm

95

Lonesome
Farm

Manor
Farm

Rumbolds Lane

1

Berrick
Prior

Green
Lane

Hollandtide Bottom

PH
Ivyhouse
Farm

Berrick
Salome

94

A   B   C

185
166

WESTON RD

Moor Court

Stokefield
Farm

Brookside
Covert

4

Knightsbridge
Farm

Model Farm

B4009

97

Field Farm
House

Oxfordshire Way

3

Shirburn
Farm

WATLINGTON RD

New
Farm

Home Farm

The Plough
(PH)

KNIGHTSBRIDGE LA

HALL CL

Shirburn
Castle

96

Cemy

CHURCH LA

Pyrton

+

CASTLE RD

BLENHEIM RD

MAFEKING
ROW

Pyrton
Manor

Shirburn

Lower
Farm

2

Ridgeway

Pyrton Field
Farm

Middle Way
Plantation

Swan's Way

95

Oxfordshire Way

B480

SYCAMORE
CL

Sch

Eastfield Farm

BEECH
CL

WILLOW CL

ASH CL

PYRTON LA

ST LEONARDS CL

LOVE LA

ORCHARD WLK

SHIRBURN RD

SHIRBURN ST

CUXHAM RD

THE MEADOWS

PROSPECT PL

NEW
RD

CHURCH
ST

CHAPEL
ST

PAULS WAY

SAUNDERS

LETTS
ALLEY

WATLINGTON
IND EST

BROOKSIDE

GORWELL

HIGH ST

BARNHOUSE
MEWS

CHESTNUT

Watlington

1

HURDLERS
GREEN

Liby

PO

Sch

+

Carriers Arms
(PH)

BRITWELL RD

THE
GOGGS

ALLNUT CL

BARNACRE

BROOK ST

B4009

COUCHING ST

WATCOMBE RD

P

SPRING LA

SPRINGFIELD
CL

HILL RD

White
House
Farm

INGHAM
LA

Watcombe
Manor

HOWE RD

B480

CHILTERN GDNS

STONOR GH

+

Chiltern
Farm

H

Pyrton Hill
House

94

B4009

68   A   69   B   70   C

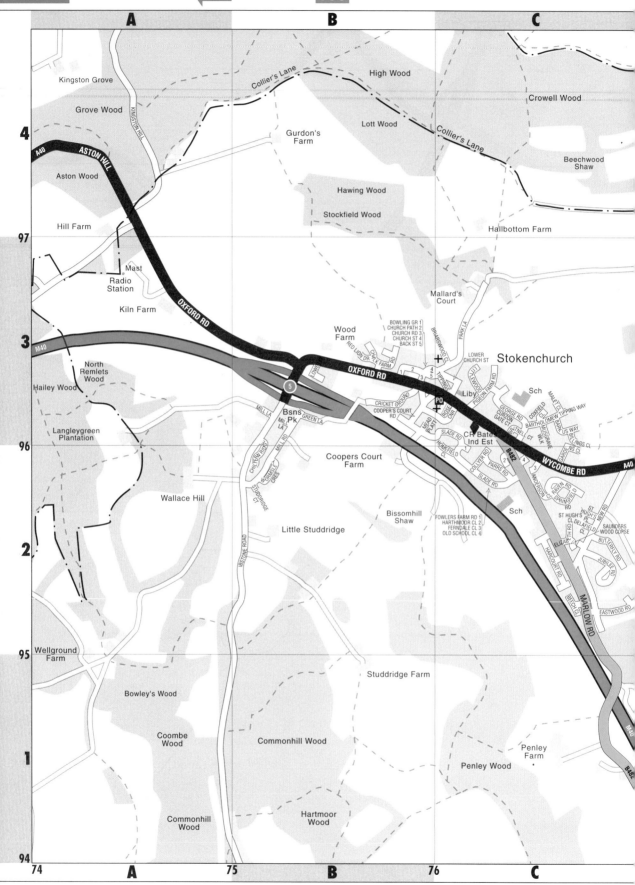

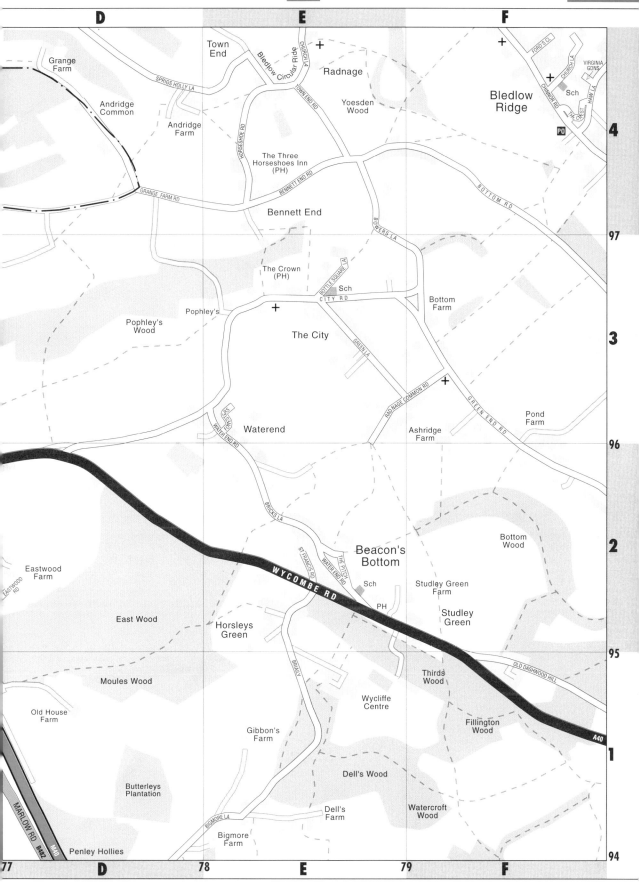

D E F

Grange
Farm

Town
End

Radnage

Bledlow
Ridge

Ford's Cl.

VIRGINIA
GDNS

Sch

PO

4

Andridge
Common

SPRIGS HOLLY LA

Andridge
Farm

Yoesden
Wood

HORSESHOE RD

The Three
Horseshoes Inn
(PH)

BENNETT END RD

BLEDLOW CIRCULAR RIDE

TOWN END RD

CHURCH LA

CHINNOR RD

CHURCH LA

HAW LA

THE CREST

BOTTOM RD

GRANGE FARM RD

Bennett End

BOWERS LA

97

The Crown
(PH)

BOTTLE SQUARE LA

Sch

CITY RD

Bottom
Farm

Pophley's

Pophley's
Wood

The City

GREEN LA

3

RADNAGE COMMON RD

GREEN END RD

Pond
Farm

Waterend

WATER END RD

SPRIGS...

Ashridge
Farm

96

WYCOMBE RD

BRICKS LA

Bottom
Wood

2

Eastwood
Farm

EASTWOOD RD

ST FRANCIS RD

WATER END RD

THE PITCH

Beacon's
Bottom

Sch

Studley Green
Farm

Studley
Green

East Wood

Horsleys
Green

PH

95

Moules Wood

BRIARY

Thirds
Wood

OLD DASHWOOD HILL

Old House
Farm

Wycliffe
Centre

Fillington
Wood

A40

1

MARLOW RD

B482

M40

Butterleys
Plantation

Gibbon's
Farm

Dell's Wood

Dell's
Farm

Watercroft
Wood

Penley Hollies

BIGMORE LA

Bigmore
Farm

94

77 D 78 E 79 F

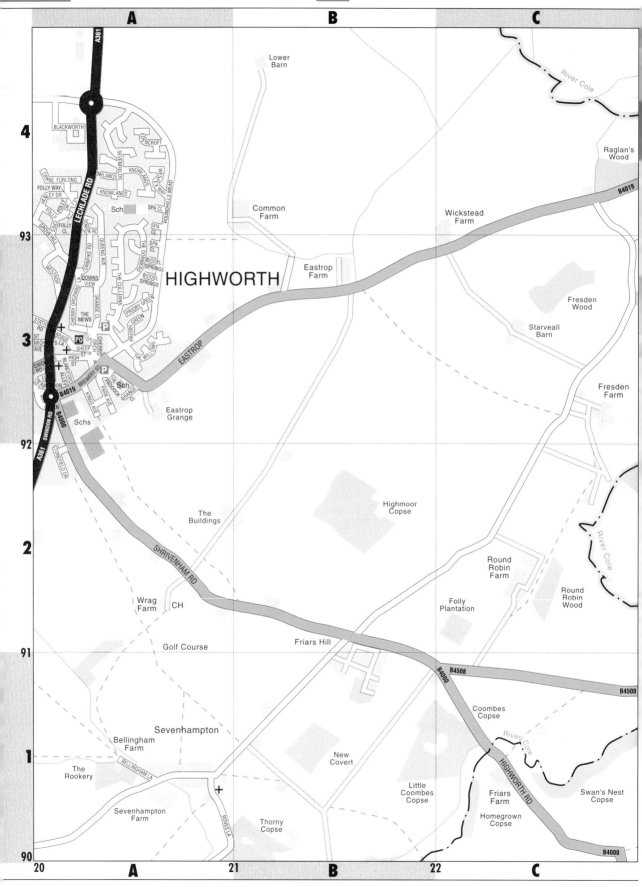

HIGHWORTH

D
E
F

Coleshill

SCHOOL LA
CHURCH LA
+ PH
PO

Coleshill Bridge

Home Farm

4

B4019

Colleymore Farm

Long Shrubbery

Coleshill Park

Ashen Copse Farm

Flamborough Wood

Ashen Copse

93

Fresden Barn

River Cole

Waterloo Copse

Ashencopse Cottage

Tellhard's Copse

Vinthill Withy Bed

3

Waterloo Lodge

Grove Copse

Strattenborough Castle Farm

Watchfield Common Wood (Nature Reserve)

92

Pea Pits Copse

Tithe Farm

2

A420

Southdown Farm

Westmill Bridge

91

MAJORS RD
B4508

Westmill Farm

B4508
B4508

BOWER GREEN
BOWER GRN

Pennyhooks Brook

SHRIVENHAM HUNDRED

MAJORS RD

MEADOW RD

FARRINGTON RD

BOWER

1

Pennyhooks Farm

STAR LA
EAGLE LA
PH
PO

OAK RD
CHAPEL HILL

BARRINGTON AVE

Watchfield

FOLLY AXIS RD
SHORT ST

Pennyhooks Lane

OXFORD SQ

+
HIGH ST

Sch
NORTH ST
SOUTH ST
HILL RD
WELLINGTON SQ

Royal Military College of Science

Ratcoombe Copse

SQUIRES RD
MAIDEN'S CL
THE MEWS
BARRINGTON RD

Golf Course

HOME LEAZE RD

+

Bower Brook

90

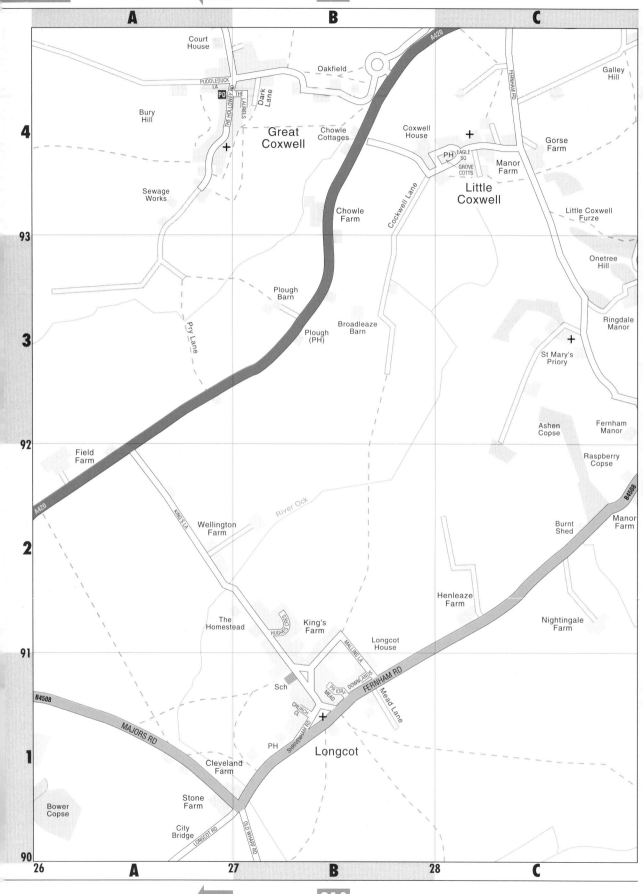

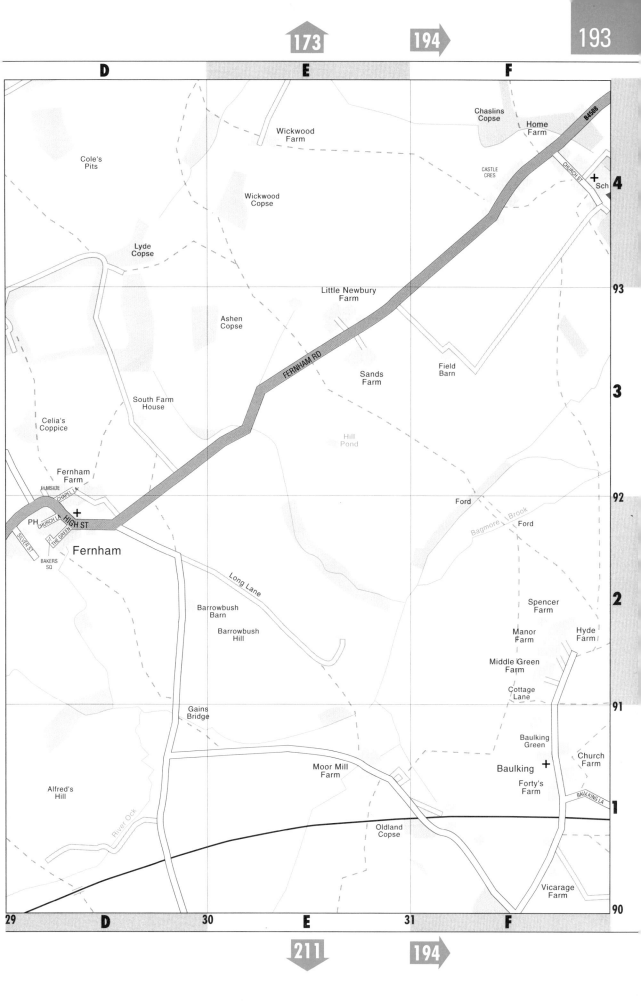

D
E
F

Chaslins
Copse

Home
Farm

B4508

Wickwood
Farm

Cole's
Pits

CASTLE
CRES

CHURCH ST

+ Sch

4

Wickwood
Copse

Lyde
Copse

Little Newbury
Farm

93

Ashen
Copse

FERNHAM RD

Field
Barn

3

Sands
Farm

South Farm
House

Hill
Pond

Celia's
Coppice

Fernham
Farm

Ford

ELMSIDE

CHAPEL LA

Ford

92

PH

CHURCH LA

HIGH ST

Bagmore Brook

Ford

SILVER ST

THE GREEN

Fernham

BAKERS
SQ

Spencer
Farm

2

Long Lane

Manor
Farm

Hyde
Farm

Barrowbush
Barn

Middle Green
Farm

Barrowbush
Hill

Cottage
Lane

Gains
Bridge

91

Baulking
Green

Church
Farm

Alfred's
Hill

Moor Mill
Farm

Baulking

+

Forty's
Farm

BAULKING LA

1

River Ook

Oldland
Copse

Vicarage
Farm

90

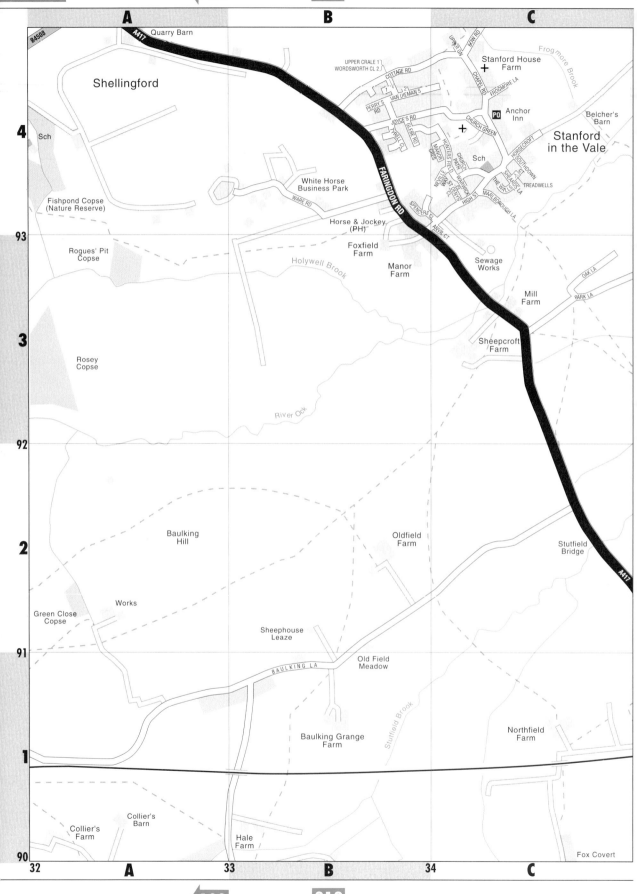

B4508
A417
Quarry Barn

Shellingford

Sch

Fishpond Copse
(Nature Reserve)

Rogues' Pit
Copse

Rosey
Copse

River Ock

Holywell Brook

White Horse
Business Park

WARE RD

Horse & Jockey
(PH)

Foxfield
Farm

Manor
Farm

FARINGDON RD

UPPER CRALE 1
WORDSWORTH CL 2

COTTAGE RD

PERRY'S RD

VAN DIEMAN'S

JOYCE'S RD

GLEBE RD

TYRELL CL

UPPER GN

ROW RD

CHAPEL RD

Stanford House
Farm

FROGMORE LA

Frogmore Brook

Anchor
Inn

PO

CHURCH GREEN

Belcher's
Barn

Stanford
in the Vale

Sch

HUNTERS FIELD

MANOR
GDNS

CHURCH
PATH

WARWICK
MTLINO

ST DENYS

HIGH ST

HORSECROFT

SOUTHDOWN

THE WALLS

SHEARES LA

MARLBOROUGH LA

Treadwells

SPENCERS CL

ANVIL CT

Sewage
Works

Mill
Farm

OAK LA

PARK LA

Sheepcroft
Farm

Baulking
Hill

Oldfield
Farm

Stutfield
Bridge

A417

Green Close
Copse

Works

Sheephouse
Leaze

Old Field
Meadow

BAULKING LA

Stutfield Brook

Northfield
Farm

Baulking Grange
Farm

Collier's
Farm

Collier's
Barn

Hale
Farm

Fox Covert

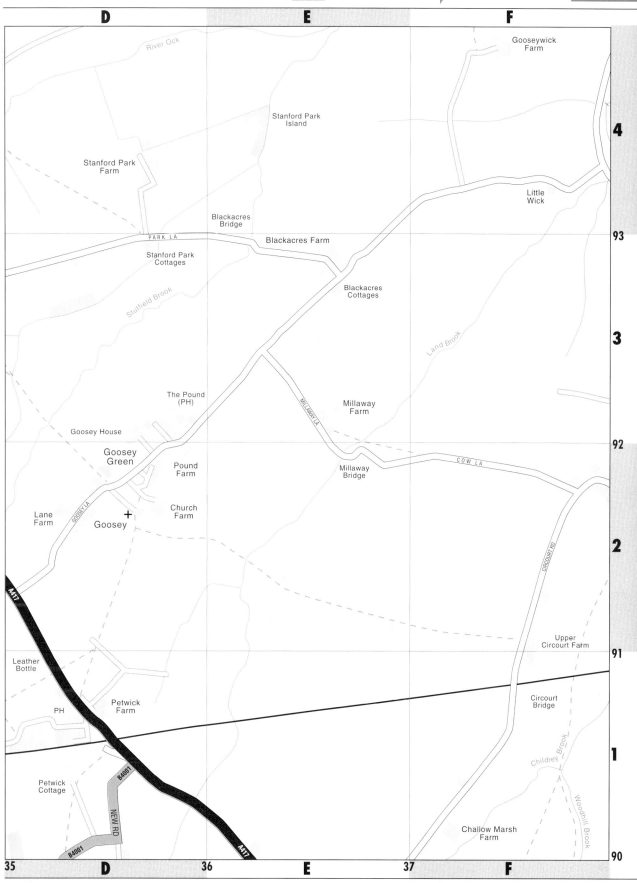

Gooseywick
Farm

4

Stanford Park
Island

Stanford Park
Farm

Little
Wick

Blackacres
Bridge

PARK LA

Blackacres Farm

93

Stanford Park
Cottages

Blackacres
Cottages

Stutfield Brook

Land Brook

3

The Pound
(PH)

Millaway
Farm

Goosey House

MILLAWAY LA

Goosey
Green

92

Pound
Farm

Millaway
Bridge

COW LA

GOOSEY LA

Lane
Farm

Church
Farm

+
Goosey

CIRCOURT RD

2

Upper
Circourt Farm

91

Leather
Bottle

Circourt
Bridge

PH

Petwick
Farm

Childrey Brook

1

Petwick
Cottage

B4001

NEW RD

Woodhill Brook

B4001

Challow Marsh
Farm

A417

A417

90

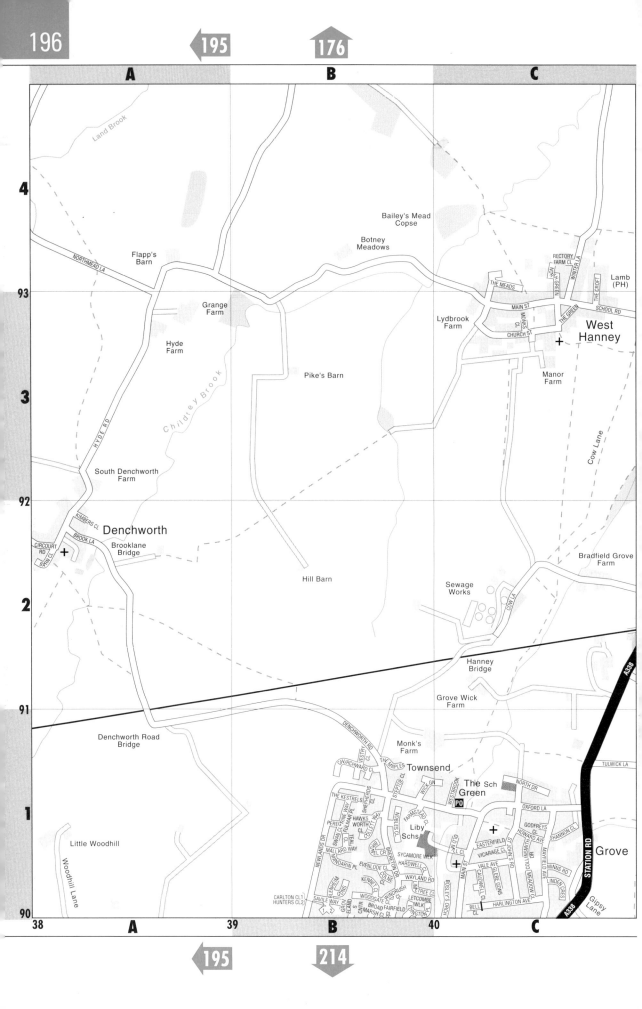

A **B** **C**

4

Land Brook

Northmead La

Flapp's Barn

Bailey's Mead Copse

Botney Meadows

RECTORY FARM LA
NORTH GREEN
WINTER LA
THE CROFT
Lamb (PH)

93

Grange Farm

THE MEADS

MAIN ST

Lydbrook Farm

MONKS CL

CHURCH ST

West Hanney

THE GREEN
SCHOOL RD

Hyde Farm

HYDE RD

Childrey Brook

Pike's Barn

Manor Farm

3

Cow Lane

South Denchworth Farm

92

Bradfield Grove Farm

KIMBERS CL

Denchworth

BROOK LA

CIRCOURT RD
BAY CL

Brooklane Bridge

Hill Barn

Sewage Works

COW LA

2

Hanney Bridge

A338

Grove Wick Farm

91

Denchworth Road Bridge

DENCHWORTH RD

Monk's Farm

Townsend

TULWICK LA

VESTRY CL
CHURCHWARD CL

THE MAPLES

STEEPDOE CL

WICK GN

NORTH DR

The Sch Green
PO

OXFORD LA

1

Little Woodhill

Woodhill Lane

THE KESTRELS
SHEPHERDS CL

NEW ARDS DR

PEREGRINE WAY
SWAN CL
FULMAR CL
HAWKS WORTH CL
TEAL
KNIVEL
MALLARD WAY
MANDARIN PL

NOBLES CL

COLLETT WAY

BRENTON DR
EVENLODE
COLNE

KENNET CL

WOODGATE CL

SYCAMORE WLK

HARDWELL CL

WAYLAND RD

Liby Schs

FARMSTEAD CL

BOSLEY'S ORCH

OLD CL CL
MAIN ST

EASTERFIELD

VICARAGE CL

ST JOHN'S RD

VALE AVE

CAUDWELL CL

GLEBE GDNS

Godfreys CL
HOWARD AVE
HUNTINGDON MEADOW CL

SHANNON CL

MAYFIELD CL

MINNS RD

LINDEN CRES

Grove

STATION RD

A338

Gipsy Lane

CARLTON CL
HUNTERS CL

SAVILE WAY

BLENHEIM GDNS

GROV ELAND
S
C MARSH CL

BROAD FAIRFIELD

WINDRUSH CL

LETCOMBE
WLK

LIME TREE CL

LIVINGTON

BELL CL

HARLINGTON AVE

90

38 **A** 39 **B** 40 **C**

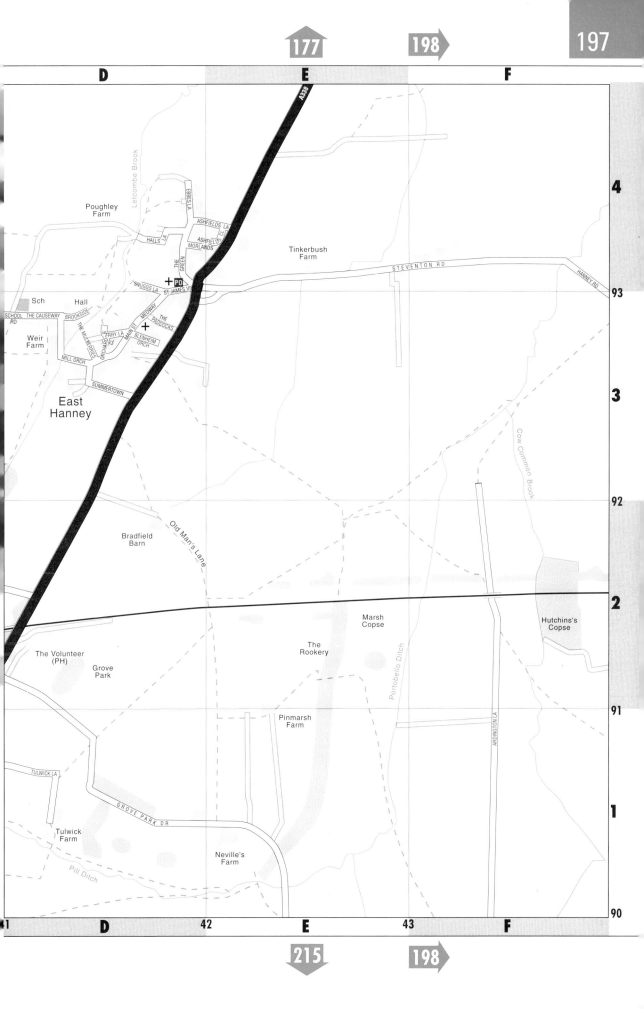

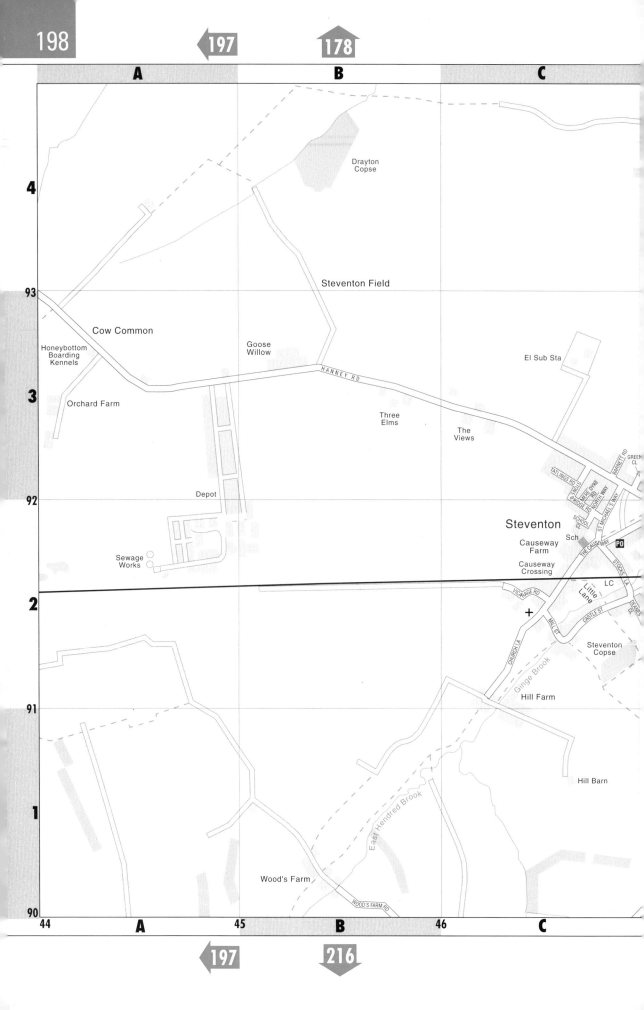

Drayton
Copse

Steventon Field

Cow Common

Honeybottom
Boarding
Kennels

Goose
Willow

El Sub Sta

HANNEY RD

Orchard Farm

Three
Elms

The
Views

TATLINGS RD
MERE DYKE RD
HIDE & RIDGE RD
NORTH WAY
ST MICHAEL'S WAY
BARNETT RD
GREEN
CL

Depot

SCHOOL
CL

Steventon

Sch

THE CAUSEWAY

PO

Causeway
Farm

Sewage
Works

Causeway
Crossing

STOCKS LA

BEARES CL

LC

Little
Lane

VICARAGE RD

CASTLE ST

Steventon
Copse

CHURCH LA

MILL ST

Ginge Brook

Hill Farm

Hill Barn

East Hendred Brook

Wood's Farm

WOOD'S FARM RD

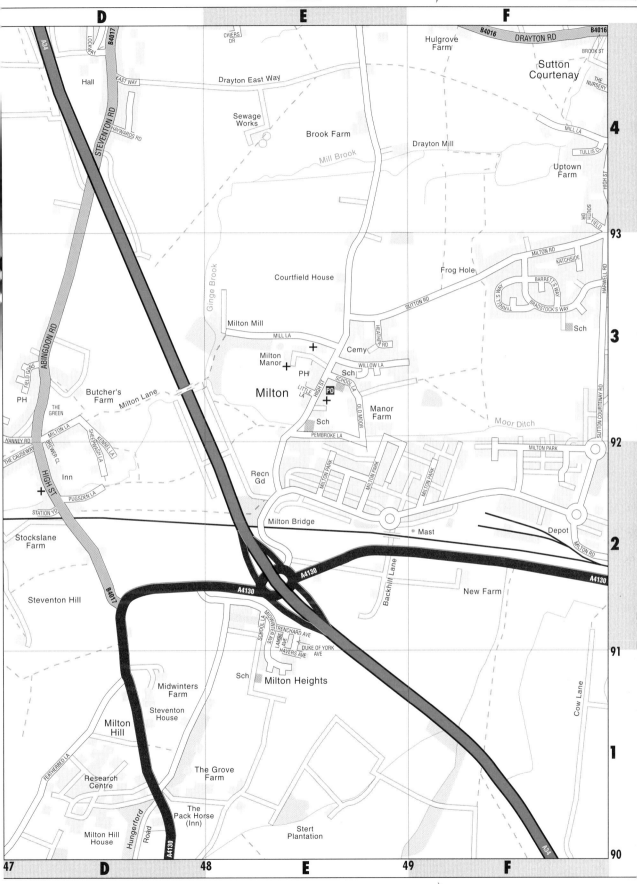

B4016 DRAYTON RD B4016

Hulgrove Farm

BROOK ST

Sutton Courtenay

THE NURSERY

CHIERS DR

Drayton East Way

Drayton Mill

MILL LA

TULLIS CL

4

LOONY
EAST WAY
B4017

Hall

Sewage Works

Brook Farm

Mill Brook

Uptown Farm

HIGH ST

HAYWARDS RD

STEVENTON RD

A34

SOUTH DR

93

Ginge Brook

Courtfield House

Frog Hole

Sutton Rd

MILTON RD

KATCHSIDE

BARRETT'S WAY

BRADSTOCK'S WAY

Sch

HARWELL RD

ABINGDON RD

Milton Mill

MILL LA

Cemy

HEATHER RD

WILLOW LA

TYRRELL'S WAY

3

FIELD GDNS

Butcher's Farm

Milton Manor

PH

Sch

Milton Lane

Milton

LITTLE LA
HIGH ST
PO
SCHOOL LA

Sch

Manor Farm

OLD MOOR

Moor Ditch

SUTTON COURTENAY RD

THE GREEN

MILTON LA

SHEEPWASH LA

KENNELL LA

BREWER CL

PH

Sch

Pembroke La

MILTON PARK

MILTON PARK

MILTON PARK

MILTON PARK

MILTON PARK

92

HANNEY RD

THE CAUSEWAY

Inn

PUGSDEN LA

Recn Gd

HIGH ST

STATION YD

Stockslane Farm

Milton Bridge

Mast

Depot

MILTON RD

Backhill Lane

A4130

A4130

New Farm

A4130

2

B4017

Steventon Hill

A4130

SCHOOL LA

MIDWINTERS LA

TRENCHARD AVE

LAMBE AVE

DUKE OF YORK AVE

HAVERS AVE

91

Midwinters Farm

Steventon House

Sch

Milton Heights

Cow Lane

Milton Hill

FEATHERBED LA

Research Centre

The Grove Farm

1

Hungerford Road

A4130

The Pack Horse (Inn)

Stert Plantation

A34

Milton Hill House

90

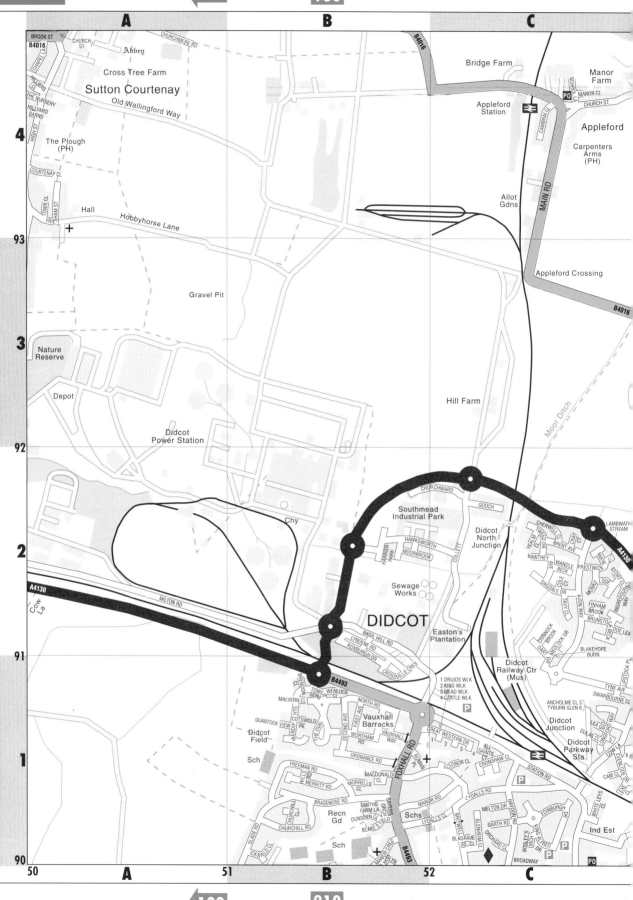

199
180

A   B   C

BROOK ST
B4016
CHAPEL LA
CHURCH ST
Abbey
CHURCHMERE RD
B4016
Bridge Farm
Manor Farm
SCHOOL LA
PO
MANOR CL
Cross Tree Farm
THE NURSERY
HILLIERS CL
Sutton Courtenay
Old Wallingford Way
Appleford Station
CAMBRAI CL
CHURCH ST
Appleford
HIGH ST
HILLYARD BARNS
4
The Plough (PH)
Carpenters Arms (PH)
COURTENAY CL
MAIN RD
TOWN CL
FRILSHAM ST
Hall
Hobbyhorse Lane
Allot Gdns
93
Appleford Crossing
B4016
Gravel Pit
3
Nature Reserve
Hill Farm
Moor Ditch
Depot
92
Didcot Power Station
Chy
Southmead Industrial Park
CHURCHWARD
GOOCH
Didcot North Junction
LAMBWATH STREAM
CHERWELL CL
CRAY
TWEED DR
BRENT AVE
A4130
2
HARRIER PARK
HAWKSWORTH
MOORBROOK
COLLETT
RAWTHEY
YELM
WANDLE BECK
PRESTWICK
MOONS
LODE
NENE
STORT CL
INGREBOURNE WAY
A4130
COLE CT
COLE CL
DAGDALE DR
AVON WAY
TAVY CL
FINHAM BROOK
BRUNSTON BECK
DOE LEA
Sewage Works
Easton's Plantation
CRIMNOCK BROOK
MEDLOCK GR
TAVY CL
BLAKEHOPE BURN
A4130
Cow La
MILTON RD
91
B4493
Didcot Railway Ctr (Mus)
DIDCOT
BASIL HILL RD
LYNDENE RD
ROXBURGH DR
CROSSVILLE CRES
Didcot Junction
TYNE AVE
SWARBOURNE CL
ANCHOLME CL 5
TYBURN GLEN 6
LEA GR
DULAS CT
COW LA
CAM CL
1 DRUIDS WLK
2 KING WLK
3 MEAD WLK
4 CASTLE WLK
P
BRENDON CL
TOWE GDNS
WENLOCK CL
MALVERN CL
NORTH RD
COTSWOLD PK
QUANTOCK VIEW
THE OVAL
SECOND AVE
FIRST AVE
WORTHAM RD
Vauxhall Barracks
VAUXHALL WAY
GREAT WESTERN DR
ALL SAINTS
Didcot Parkway Sta
1
Didcot Field
Sch
ORDNANCE RD
FOXHALL RD
ROMAN PL
CONDR CL
CRONSHAW CL
STATION RD
P
WHITE LEYS CL
EXE CL
KING ALFRED DR
EDINBURGH DR
Ind Est
FREEMAN RD
WILLS RD
MERRITT RD
BRASENOSE RD
SAYERS
MACDONALD CL
MANOR RD
LYDALLS RD
HAYDON
MELTON DR
GARTH RD
BOSLEY'S ORCH
PO
Recn Gd
CHURCHILL RD
SLADE RD
ICKN CL
SMITHS FARM LA
DUNSDEN CL
BLAKE'S FIELD
Schs
LYDALLS CL
BRITWELL RD
BLAGRAVE CL
ORCHARD CL
BROADWAY
P
P
90
Sch
MANOR CRES
B4493

50   A   51   B   52   C

199
218

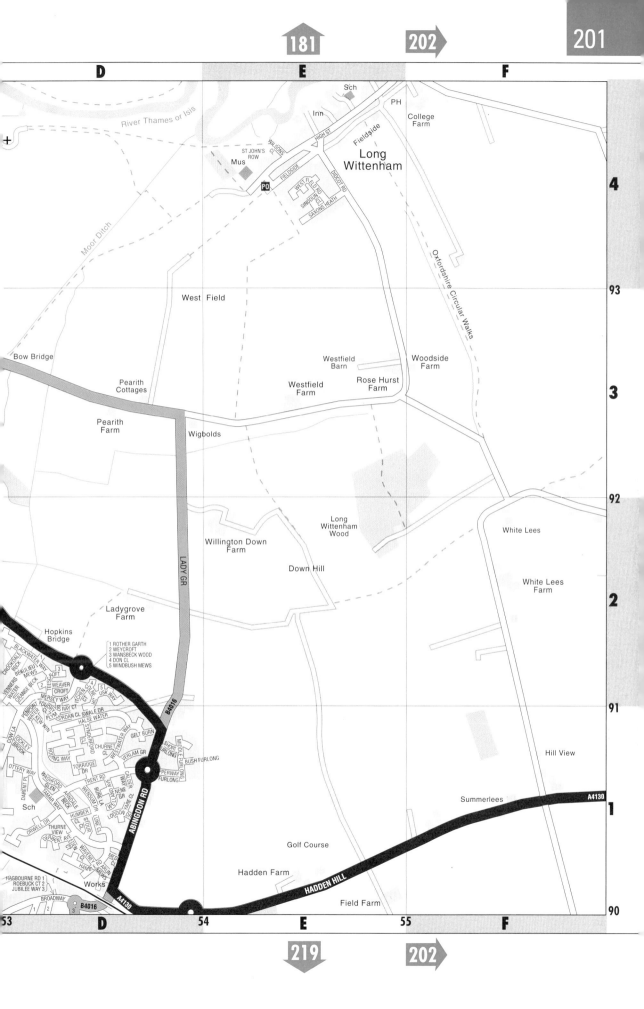

A B C

SAMIAN WAY

WATLING LA

TENPENNY

HAVEN CL

ORCHARD HAVEN

P

Dorchester
Bridge

Overy

Bridge End

Duke Hills

Sewage
Works

River Thame

Weir

Day's Lock

MEADSIDE

HENLEY RD

4

+

Little Wittenham
Bridge

Little Wittenham

Oxfordshire Circular Walks

River Thames

A4074

Little Wittenham Wood

93

Oxfordshire Circular Walks

Lowerhill
Farm

Star Walk

Wittenham
Clumps

Hill Farm

Felmore
Copse

North Farm

3

Castle Hill

P

Picnic
Site

Sinodun
Hills

92

Brightwell
Barrow

Redgate
Farm

2

Highlands
Farm

Sinodun
Hill

Style
Acre

Watermans Lane

HIGH RD

GREENMERE

KINGS CL

91

DIDCOT RD

THORNE LA

WEST END

CHURCH LA

Sch

WELLSPRINGS

BELL LA

MONKS MEAD

HATCHET LA

AKERS LA

GM

A4130

Frogs' Island
Farm

North
Farm

Kibble Ditch

Brightwell-cum-Sotwell

Frogs' Island

PO

BRIGHTWELL ST

Brightwell Manor

PH

+

+

SOTWELL ST

+

PENNYGREEN
LA

Croft Path

1

A4130

LONG WITTENHAM RD

MACKNEY LA

Slade End

Park Farm

Mackney Court
Farm

90

56 A 57 B 58 C

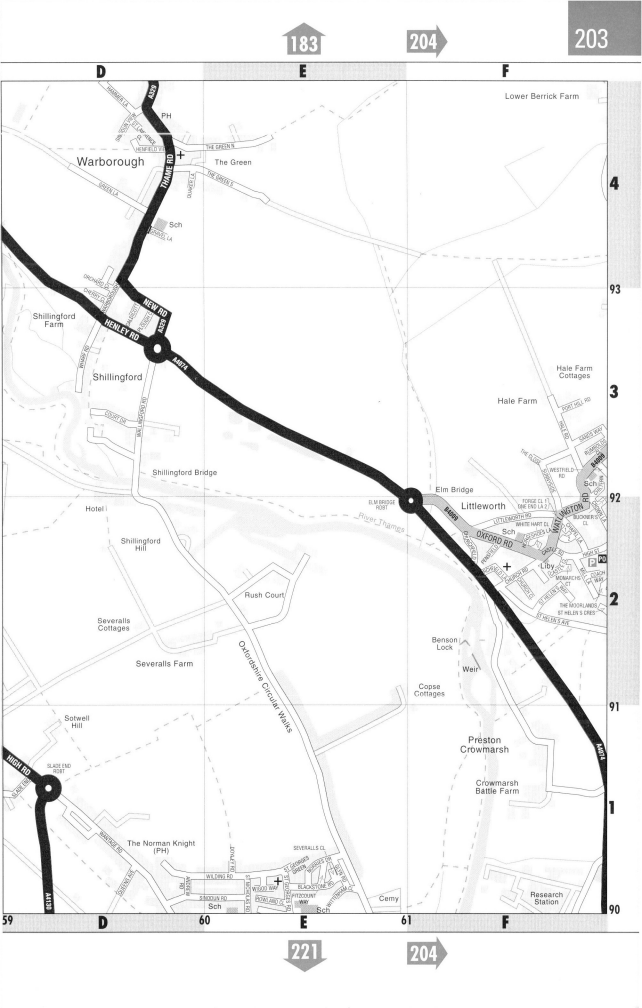

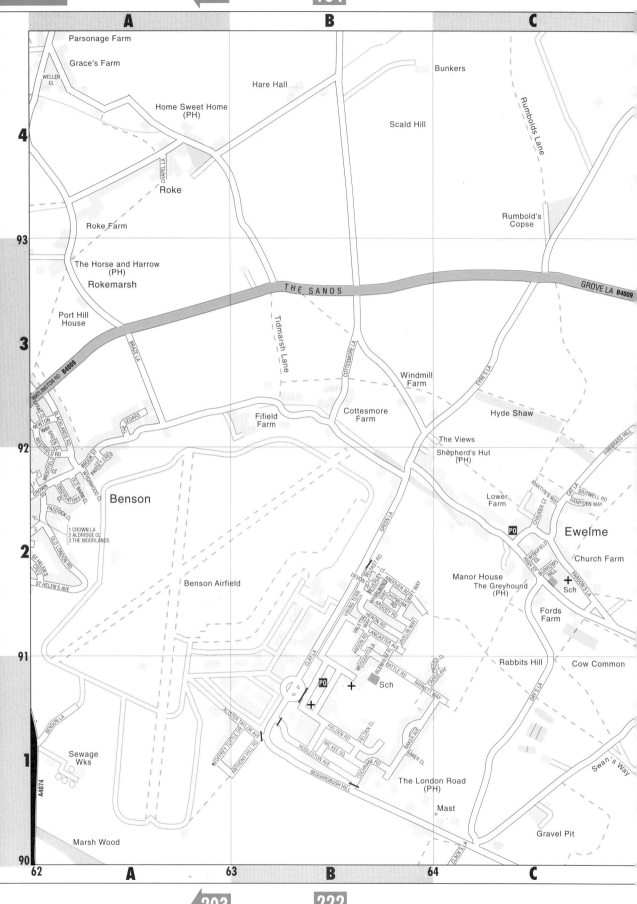

Parsonage Farm

Grace's Farm

Hare Hall

Bunkers

WELLER CL

Scald Hill

Home Sweet Home (PH)

4

CHAPEL LA

Roke

Rumbolds Lane

Roke Farm

Rumbold's Copse

93

The Horse and Harrow (PH)

Rokemarsh

THE SANDS

GROVE LA B4009

Port Hill House

BRAZIL LA

Tidmarsh Lane

3

WATLINGTON RD B4009

Windmill Farm

EYRES LA

CYPRAS CL
NEWTON
BLACKLANDS RD
GREEN CL
WAY

THE CEDARS

Fifield Farm

Cottesmore Farm

Hyde Shaw

FIREBRASS HILL

WESTFIELD RD
BROOK ST
HITCHWOOD CL
PASSEY CRES

The Views

92

WESTFIELD CL
CROWN SQ
OLD BARN CL
OBSERVATORY

Shepherd's Hut (PH)

MARTYN'S WAY
CAT LA
BRITWELL RD
HAMPDEN WAY

Benson

PADDOCK CL

1 CROWN LA
2 ALDRIDGE CL
3 THE MOORLANDS

Lower Farm

CHAUCER CT

Ewelme

OLD LONDON RD

PO

Church Farm

2

ST HELEN'S CRES
ST HELEN'S AVE

Benson Airfield

GREEN LA

Manor House
The Greyhound (PH)

WINGFIELD CL
HIGH ST
BURROWS HILL
PARSON'S LA

Sch

DEVON CL
BELFAST RD
BEVERLEY CL
ANDOVER RD
LOWESTOFT WAY

Fords Farm

WHIRLWIND RD
VIA CHIPMUNK
ARGOSY RD

91

VIKING TERR
HERON WAY
VALETTA RD
JAVELIN WAY

Rabbits Hill

Cow Common

ANSON RD
MOSQUITO LA
LANCASTER AVE
BLENHEIM TERR
BATTLE RD
BARNETT WAY

DAY'S LA

CLAY LA

PO

CROSS CL
CROSS AVE

Sch

Swan's Way

A4074

ALISTER TAYLOR AVE
GEOFFREY TUTTLE DR
ANTHONY HILL RD

FIELDEN RD
MCKEE SQ
FIELDEN CL

BAKER AVE
BAKER CL

1

BENSON LA

Sewage Wks

HUDLESTON AVE
COOKHAM RD

BEGGARSBUSH HILL

The London Road (PH)

Mast

Gravel Pit

Marsh Wood

CLACK'S LA

90

D
E
F

B4009

Turner's Green Lane

Lower Farm

The Old Rectory

✚

The Priory

Cooper's Farm

4

Heath Plantation

Ashley's Wood

Turner's Green

Britwell Salome

Grove Farm

Brightwell Grove

PH

93

Home Farm

GROVE LA

Mon •

3

Britwell Salome House

Brockholes Lane

Mon •

Brockholes Covert

Icknield Way

92

North Farm

Ridgeway

Huntingland

Swan's Way

Icknieldbank Plantation

2

Lower Warren

Swyncombe Downs

Warren Bottom

Sliding Hill

91

The Nuttery

Lower Farm

Down Farm

Littleworth Hill

Lowerfarm Cottages

1

Grindon Lane

Ladies Walk

Potters Lane

Colliers Hill

Ewelme Downs

Colliers Bottom

90

5
D
66
E
67
F

205
186

A **B** **C**

4

Cobditch
Hill

White Mark
Farm

White
Mark

Watlington Hill

P

H O W E R D

Springfield
Farm

Icknield House

HILL RD

93

Piggery

Swan's Way

Ridgeway

Lys Farm
House

Lower
Dean

Lower Deans
Wood

3

Dame Alice
Farm

Dumble
Dore

Watlington
Park

Greenfield
Copse

The
Howe

Howe
Combe

92

Britwell Hill

Howe
Farm

Britwell Hill
Farm

Howe Wood

Ridgeway

Woods
Farm

Dean
Wood

2

Mast

Greenfield
Manor

Westernend
Shaw

The Jolly Ploughman
(PH)

Lower Greenfield
Farm

91

B481

Coates
Farm

COATES LA

Coates Copse

PATEMORE LA

RED LA

Grove
Farm

1

White
Hill

The Rectory

CHURCH LA

Water
Tower

Cookley
Green

RECTORY HILL

Church
Wood

Colliers
Hill

+

Reading Lane

Sch

Van
Diemans

Ladies
Walk

Swyncombe
House

Cookley
Farm

B481

90

68
A
69
B
70
C

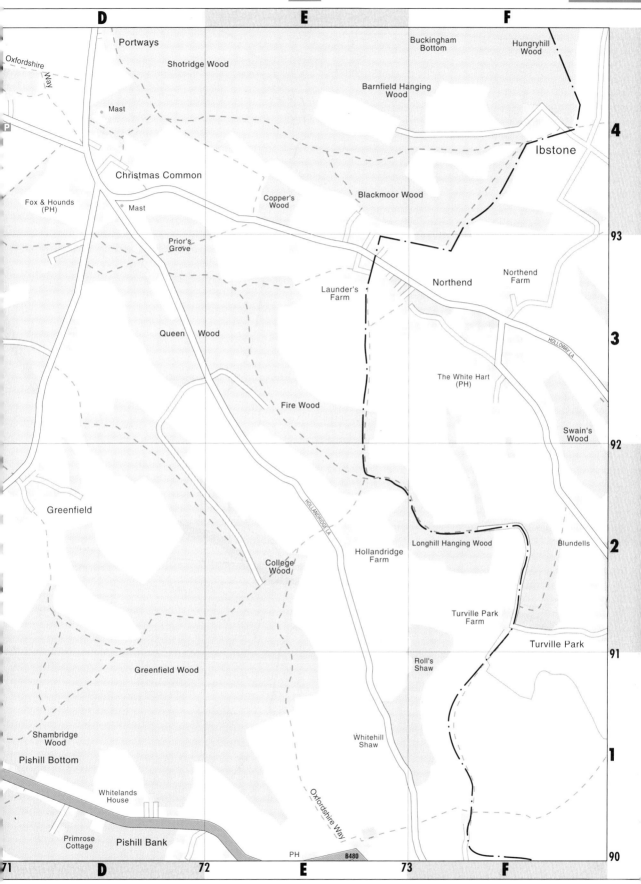

D
E
F

Portways
Oxfordshire Way
Shotridge Wood
Buckingham Bottom
Hungryhill Wood
Mast
Barnfield Hanging Wood
4
Ibstone
P
Christmas Common
Copper's Wood
Blackmoor Wood
93
Fox & Hounds (PH)
Mast
Prior's Grove
Launder's Farm
Northend
Northend Farm
HOLLOWAY LA
3
Queen Wood
The White Hart (PH)
Fire Wood
Swain's Wood
92
Greenfield
HOLLANDRIDGE LA
Hollandridge Farm
Longhill Hanging Wood
Blundells
2
College Wood
Turville Park Farm
Turville Park
91
Greenfield Wood
Roll's Shaw
Shambridge Wood
Whitehill Shaw
1
Pishill Bottom
Whitelands House
Oxfordshire Way
Primrose Cottage
Pishill Bank
PH
B480
90

71
D
72
E
73
F

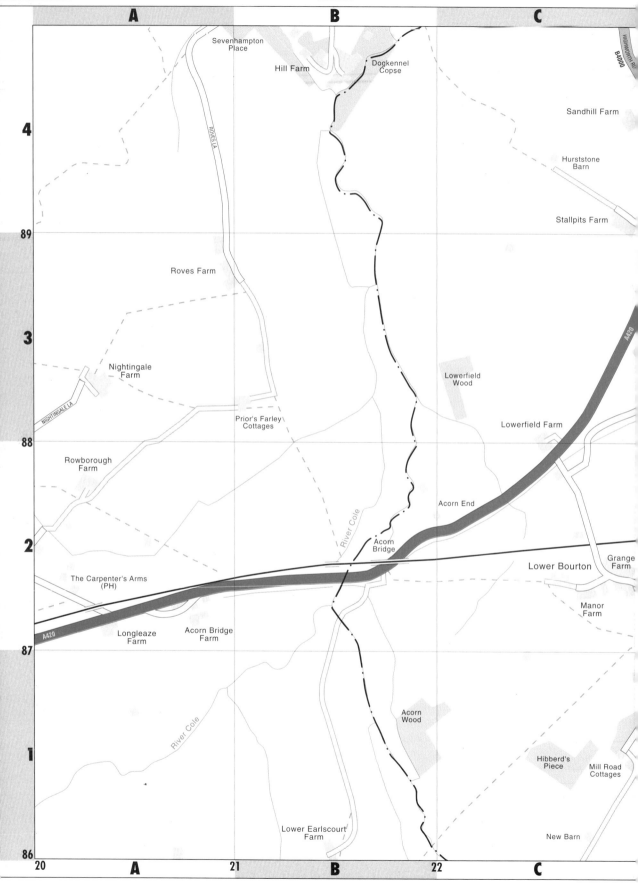

A   B   C

4

Sevenhampton
Place

Hill Farm

Dogkennel
Copse

Sandhill Farm

Hurststone
Barn

89

ROVES LA

Stallpits Farm

Roves Farm

3

A420

Nightingale
Farm

Lowerfield
Wood

NIGHTINGALE LA

Lowerfield Farm

Prior's Farley
Cottages

88

Rowborough
Farm

Acorn End

River Cole

2

Acorn
Bridge

Lower Bourton

Grange
Farm

The Carpenter's Arms
(PH)

A420

Manor
Farm

Longleaze
Farm

Acorn Bridge
Farm

87

River Cole

Acorn
Wood

1

Hibberd's
Piece

Mill Road
Cottages

Lower Earlscourt
Farm

New Barn

86

20   A   21   B   22   C

HIGHWORTH RD

B4000

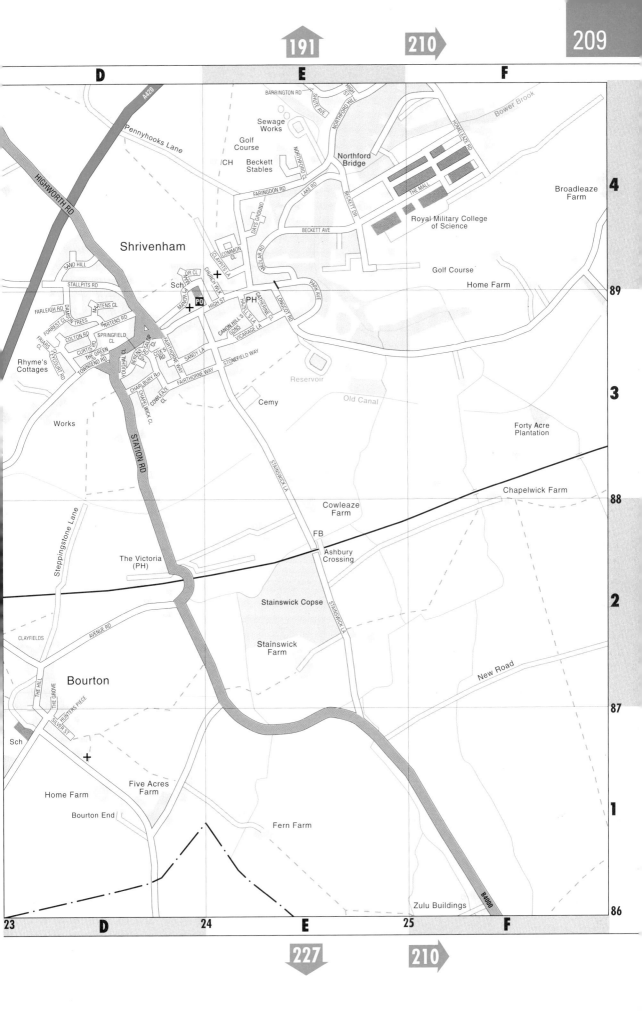

209
192

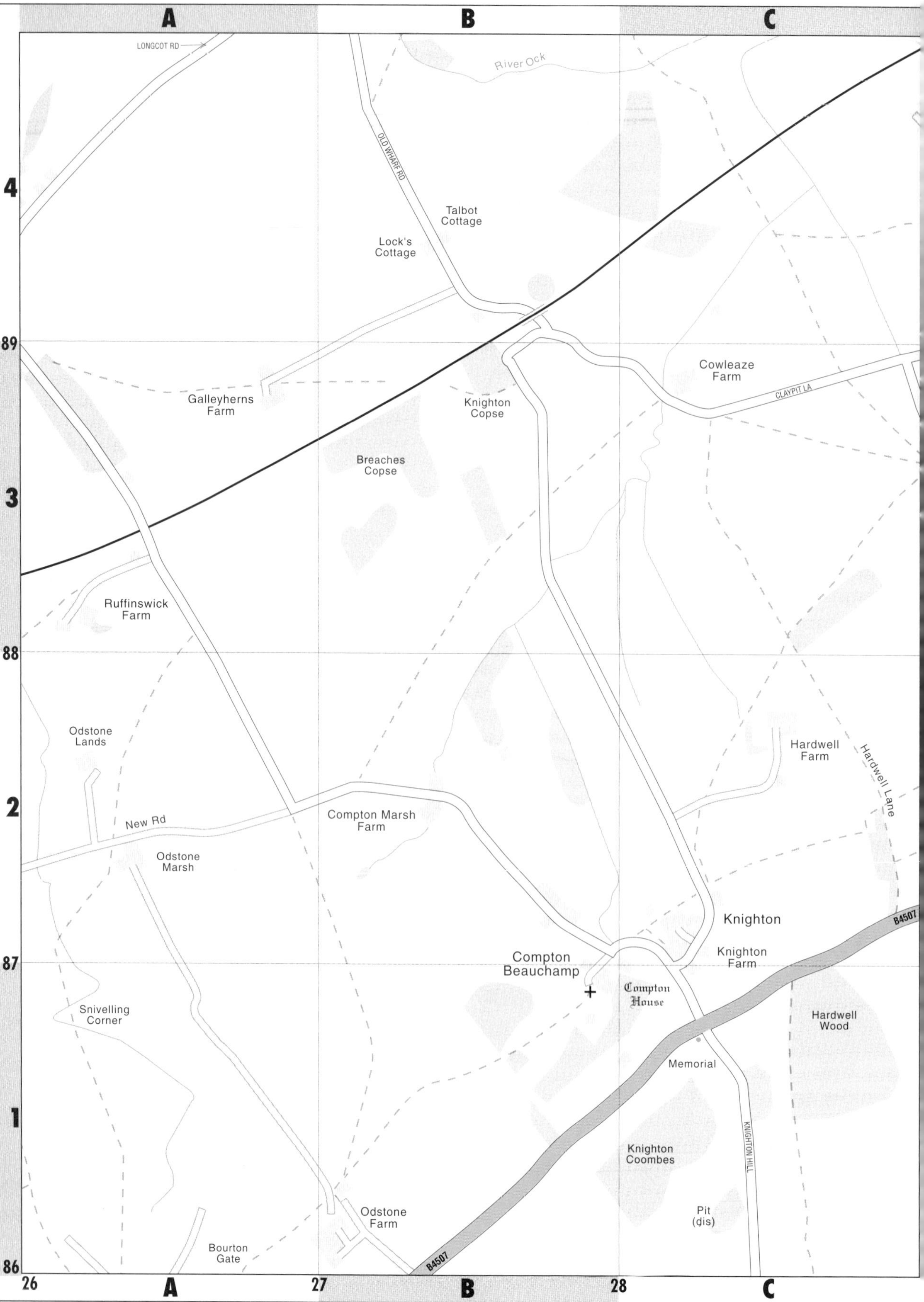

A **B** **C**

LONGCOT RD

River Ock

OLD WHARF RD

Talbot
Cottage

Lock's
Cottage

4

Cowleaze
Farm

CLAYPIT LA

89

Galleyherns
Farm

Knighton
Copse

Breaches
Copse

3

Ruffinswick
Farm

88

Odstone
Lands

Hardwell
Farm

Hardwell Lane

2

New Rd

Compton Marsh
Farm

Odstone
Marsh

Knighton

B4507

87

Compton
Beauchamp

Knighton
Farm

Compton
House

Snivelling
Corner

Hardwell
Wood

Memorial

KNIGHTON HILL

1

Knighton
Coombes

Odstone
Farm

Pit
(dis)

86

Bourton
Gate

B4507

26 27 28

A **B** **C**

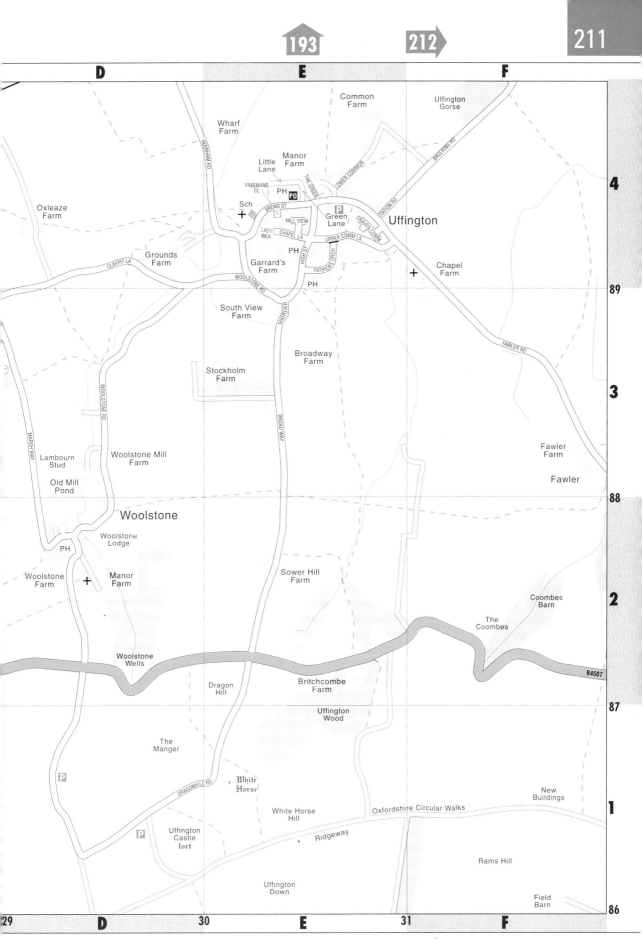

D
E
F

4

Common
Farm

Uffington
Gorse

Wharf
Farm

BADDING RD

Little
Lane

Manor
Farm

FERNHAM RD

Oxleaze
Farm

Freemans
CL

PH
PO

Sch

Broad St

The Green

Lower Common

Station Rd

Uffington

Green
Lane

P

Grounds
Farm

CLAYPIT LA

Hill View

Lady
Wlk

Chapel La

PH

Draven Comm

Garrard's
Farm

High St

Patricks Orch

Upper Comm La

Chapel
Farm

89

Woolstone Rd

PH

South View
Farm

SNOTOVER

Fawler Rd

Broadway
Farm

Stockholm
Farm

3

Woolstone Rd

Broad Way

Marsh Way

Lambourn
Stud

Woolstone Mill
Farm

Fawler
Farm

Old Mill
Pond

Fawler

88

Woolstone

Woolstone
Lodge

PH

Sower Hill
Farm

Coombes
Barn

2

Woolstone
Farm

Manor
Farm

The
Coombes

Woolstone
Wells

B4507

Dragon
Hill

Britchcombe
Farm

87

Uffington
Wood

The
Manger

P

Dragonhill Rd

White
Horse

New
Buildings

Oxfordshire Circular Walks

1

P

Uffington
Castle
fort

White Horse
Hill

Ridgeway

Rams Hill

Uffington
Down

Field
Barn

86

211
194

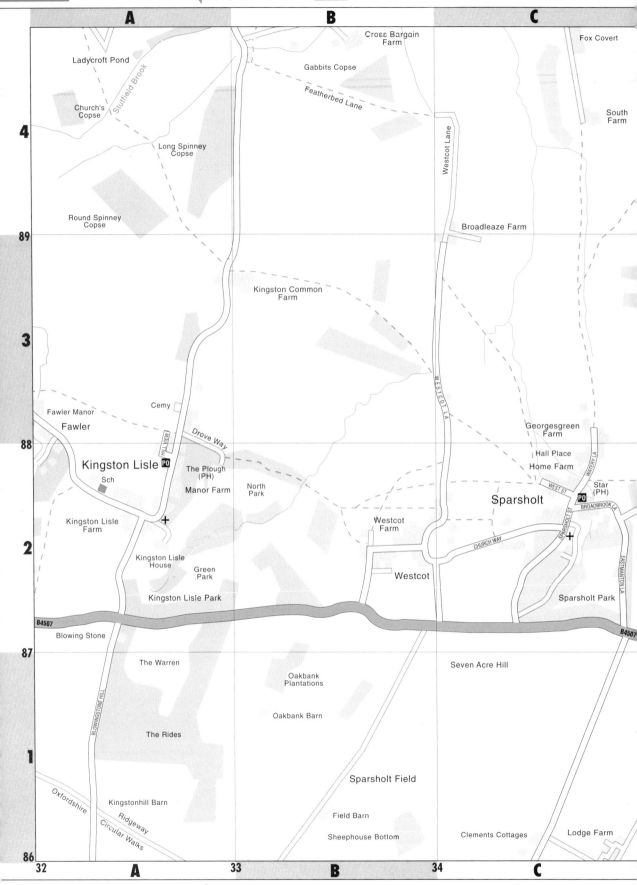

211
230

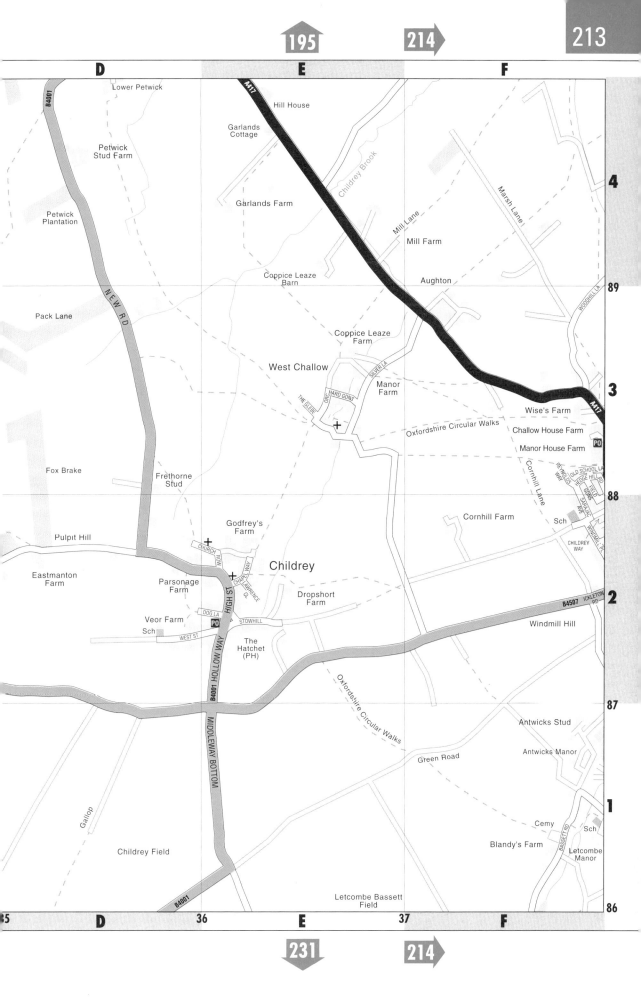

213 **196**

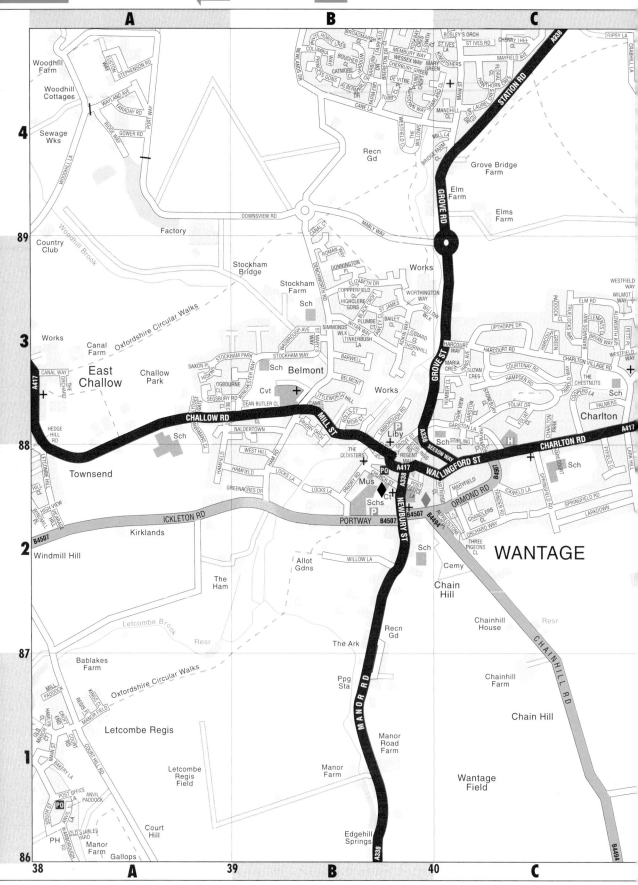

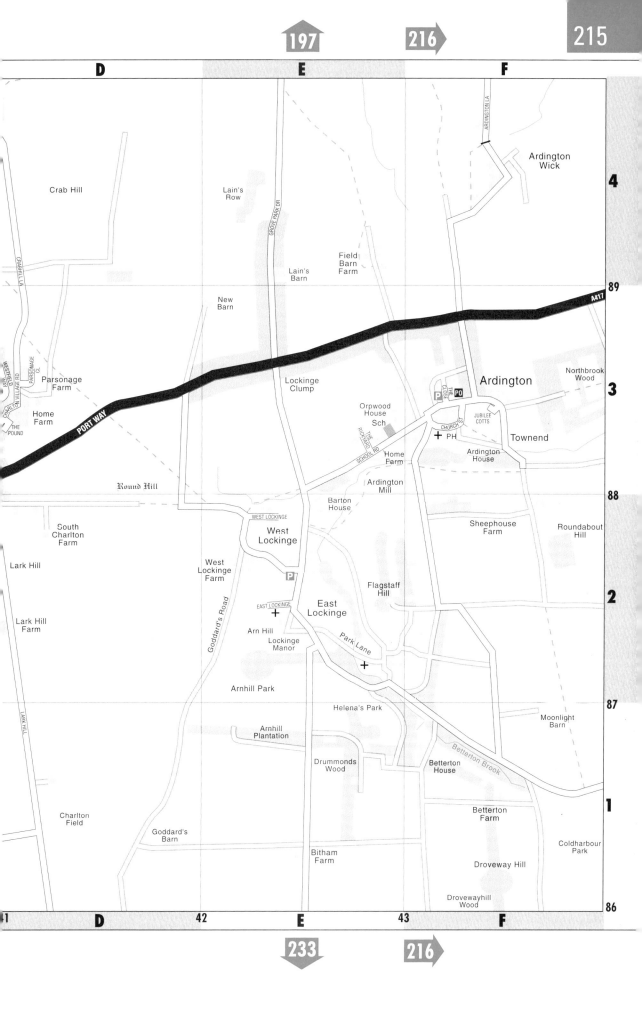

D E F

4

89

Crab Hill

Lain's Row

Field Barn Farm

Ardington Wick

Northbrook Wood

New Barn

Lain's Barn

GROVE PARK DR

A417

Ardington

3

WESTFIELD WAY

PARSONAGE CL

CRABHILL LA

CHARLTON/ LYDE RD

Parsonage Farm

Lockinge Clump

THE CLOSE

PO

JUBILEE COTTS

Townend

Home Farm

THE POUND

PORT WAY

Orpwood House Sch

THE RICKYARD

SCHOOL RD

PH

CHURCH ST

Ardington House

Round Hill

Home Farm

Ardington Mill

88

South Charlton Farm

Barton House

WEST LOCKINGE

West Lockinge

Sheephouse Farm

Roundabout Hill

Lark Hill

West Lockinge Farm

GODDARD'S ROAD

P

EAST LOCKINGE

East Lockinge

Flagstaff Hill

2

Lark Hill Farm

Arn Hill

Lockinge Manor

Park Lane

87

LARK HILL

Arnhill Park

Helena's Park

Moonlight Barn

Charlton Field

Arnhill Plantation

Drummonds Wood

Betterton Brook

Betterton House

Betterton Farm

1

Goddard's Barn

Bitham Farm

Coldharbour Park

Droveway Hill

Drovewayhill Wood

86

215
198

A **B** **C**

4

Quab Hill

Quab Hill
Farm

FEATHERBELA

WOOD'S FARM RD

East Hendred Brook

Ludbridge Mill
(disused)

Greensands

New Barn

Lud Bridge

A417

The Hare
Inn

READING RD

Sheephouse
Barn

SMITHS
RICKYARD

ALLIN'S LA

HOME FARM CL

COULINGS CL

ORCHARD LA

WHITE RD

East
Hendred

89

A417

THE GREENWAY

BANKSIDE

PO

MILL LA

MILL LA

Recreation
Ground

ORCHARD LA

CHAPEL SQ

OLD RD

Chapel

Eyston Arms
(PH)

PO

Sewage
Works

FORD LA

CAT ST

HIGH ST

West Hendred

The Mill

Sch

Hendred
House

Lydebank
Plantation

3

Hall

MANOR LA

THE MILLHAM

Lockinge Brook

The Moors

THE LYNCH

CHURCH ST

HORN LA

ST MARY'S RD

Sch

NEWBURY RD

Hill Farm

Cow Road

Red Barn

Goldbury
Hill

Park Hill

88

Ginge Brook

Park Hill
Row

Icknield

Aldfield Common

Pump
House

Shadwell's Row

2

Black Mills
Row

Parsonage
Barn

Stileway Road

87

Lower Farm

Ellaway's
Barn

TWENTIETH ST

West
Ginge

Ginge
House

East
Ginge

1

Upper Farm

Ginge
Manor

Deer Park

Stileway Road

Meashill
Plantation

White Way

Downs
Cottage

86

44 **A** 45 **B** 46 **C**

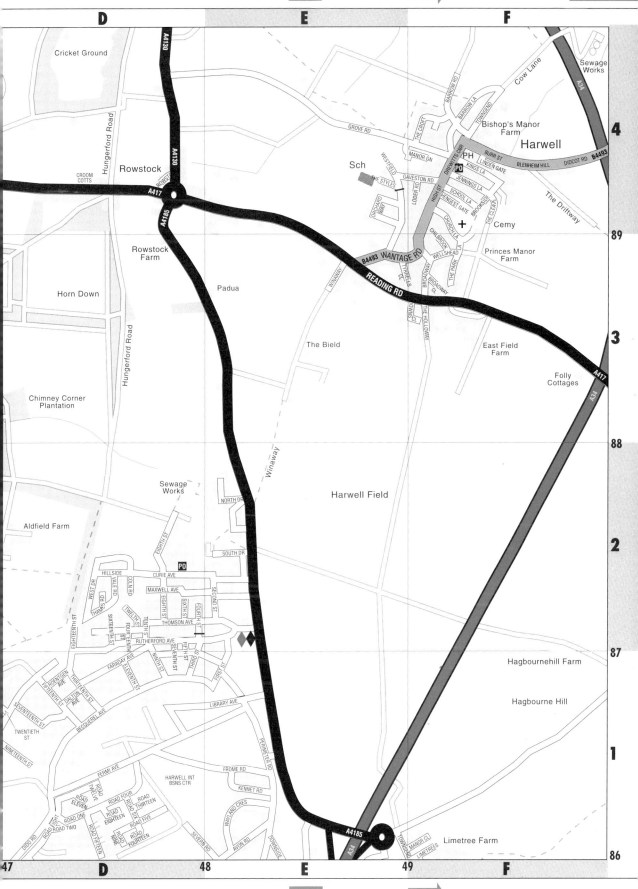

A   **B**   **C**

WANTAGE RD   B4493

OXFORD CRES

PIXTON CL   SHERWOOD   MANOR CRES   ELTN AVE

St ADE RD   COLLINGWOOD RD   DRAKE AVE   COLBORNE RD

Broadway

St PETER'S RD   VICARAGE   CHURCH ST   CHURCH ST

St ANDREW'S RD   WESSEX RD   BOURNE ST   HIGH ST

Ct Liby

Zulu Farm

DIDCOT RD

B4493

Alma Barn

Down Farm

H

ELBOURNE   BARLEYFIELDS

WHEATFIELDS   MEADOW WAY   BRUNEL RD

NORREYS RD   PARK CL   GARDEN CL

PORTWAY

PARK RD

Edmunds Park

Swimming Pool

BONNESS AVE   SOUTH PARK   TAVISTOCK AVE   DOWNS AVE

WARNER CRES   EDWIN RD   MORSE RD   LOYD RD

COCKCROFT RD   QUEENSWAY   BARNES RD   BARNES RD

MOWBRAY RD   GREEN RD   GREEN CL

EDMONDS CT   SAMOR WAY

OATLAND RD

FAIRACRES RD   FRIES RD

NEWLANDS AVE   CLARENCE PL   GLEBE RD

HILLARY   DRT   CHURCH WAY   ABBOTT RD   ABBOTT CL   ABBOTT RD

LYMMOUTH RD

HARDINGS STRINGS

PO

Cemy

LABURNUM GR

KYNASTON RD

MERELAND RD   RICHMERE RD   RIDGEWAY RD   SINODUN RD   THE CROFT

Schs

ROYAL BERKSHIRE CT

BISHOPS CL

DIDCOT

Sch

Playing Field

East Hagbourne

The Driftway

West Hagbourne Field

A34

A417

Coscote

Yew Tree Farm

WINDSOR CRES

LAKE RD   HARWOOD RD   WILCHER CL

UPPER CROSS LA 1   SHOE LA 2

Hall

MAIN RD

Sch

NORTH CROFT   THE CROFT

PO

BAKERS LA

KINGSHOLME

Hakka's Brook

Manor Farm

MANOR CL

YORK RD   BROOK LA

PO

FOXGLOVE LA

Grove Farm

MAIN ST

Manor Farm

Pumping Station

PH

Pumping Station

West Hagbourne

NEWMANS CL

Common Barn

Common Lane

CHILTON RD

BEECHING CL   STATION RD   PROSPECT RD   ALEXANDER CL

FIELDSIDE   POND LA   ORCHARD CL

PO

CHURCH ST   STREAM RD

Owlscote Manor Farm

Frogalley Farm

Sewage Works

PH

HIGH ST

Upton

Lynch Way

Hollow Way

Upton Lodge

LONDON RD

A417

WESTBROOK ST

Sch

A   **B**   **C**

D　　**E**　　**F**

A4130

CHURCH ST

ROEBUCK

KIBBLE CL

FLEET WAY

EAST ST

HADDON HILL

Fulscot Copse

B4016

HAGBOURNE RD

BRIDGE

NUFFIELD CL

DIRAC PL

JUBILEE WAY

EXETER CT

REGENT GDNS

BEAUFORT CT

SOMERSET

MERTON CT

MAGDALEN CT

ORIEL CT

North Moreton

Alders Farm

LONG WITTENHAM RD

QUEENS WAY

4

RUSKIN CL

WINDSOR

BALMORAL CL

BUCKINGHAM

SANDRINGHAM DR

MANSFIELD DR

CAMPION HALL DR

Fulscot Bridge

PEBBLE

HOMEFIELD

SAXONS WAY

VIKING DR

CROMWELL DR

ST ANNES CT

ST HILDAS

ST HUGHS RISE

89

NEW RD

Shortlands Farm

RYMANS CRES

Fulscot Farm

SANDS RD

KIRBY CL

3

HIGGS CL

Hakka's Brook

CLEMENTS GREEN

Sch

PH

FIELDSIDE

Tadley

South Moreton

CHURCH LA

88

Mill Brook

Brookside

Hagbourne Mill Farm

2

West Hagbourne Moor

BLEWBURY RD

Blewbury Mill

Sheencroft Farm

87

HAGBOURNE RD

Aston Upthorpe

MORETON RD

Ham Cottages

1

The Old Mill

Bridus Way

B4016

BESSELS WAY

Upthorpe Farm

THE CROFT

BERRY LA

MILLBROOK

BRIDUS WAY

BRIDUS MEAD

SOUTH

Winterbrook Farm

Blewburton Hill

Thorpe Farm

THORPE ST

FULLERS RD

PH

ASTON ST

RECTORY LA

CHURCH END

BESSELS LEA

LONGFIELD

BAKER ST

86

53　　**D**　　54　　**E**　　55　　**F**

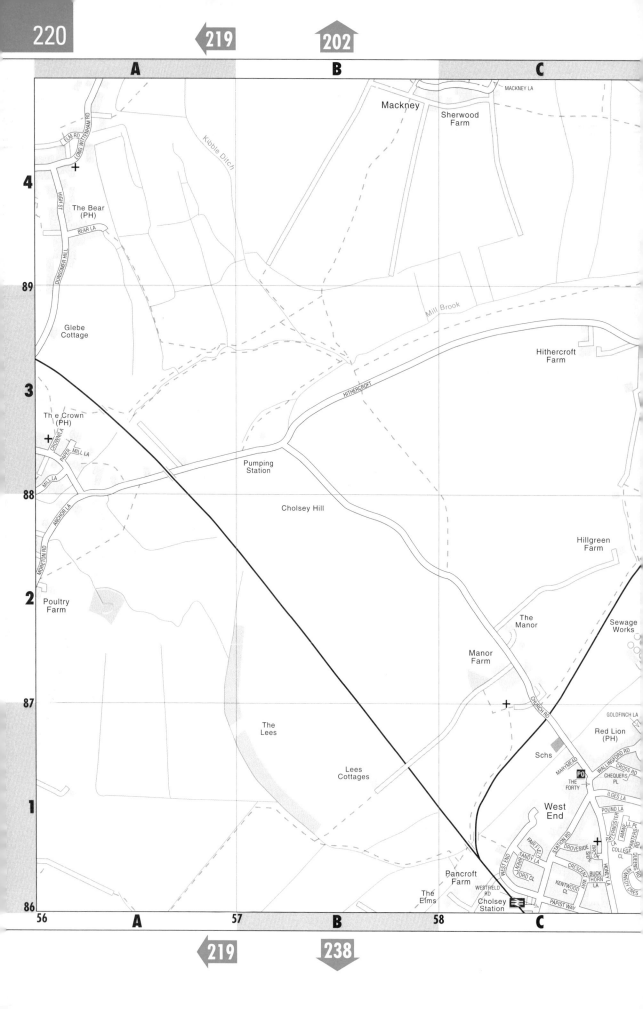

A   B   C

Mackney

Sherwood
Farm

MACKNEY LA

Kibble Ditch

4

+

The Bear
(PH)

BEAR LA

89

ELM RD

LONG WITTENHAM RD

HIGH ST

DUNSOMER HILL

Mill Brook

Hithercroft
Farm

Glebe
Cottage

3

HITHERCROFT

Th e Crown
(PH)

+

CROWN LA

PAPER MILL LA

Pumping
Station

88

MILL LA

Cholsey Hill

Hillgreen
Farm

ANCHOR LA

MORETON RD

The
Manor

Sewage
Works

2

Poultry
Farm

Manor
Farm

87

+

CHURCH RD

GOLDFINCH LA

The
Lees

Red Lion
(PH)

WALLINGFORD RD

CROSS RD

Schs

MARYMEAD

PO

THE
FORTY

CHEQUERS
PL

Lees
Cottages

ILGES LA

1

West
End

POUND LA

STATION RD

DROVESIDE

PYTHWINSTER

AMWELL

L PL

COLLEGE
CL

QUEENS RD

TWENTY CRES

WEST END

SANDY LA

OXFORD CL

CRESCENT WAY

HONEY LA

BUCK
THORN
LA

BROOK

FAIR F CL

Pancroft
Farm

WESTFIELD
RD

KENTWOOD
CL

PAPIST WAY

The
Elms

Cholsey
Station

86

56   57   58

A   B   C

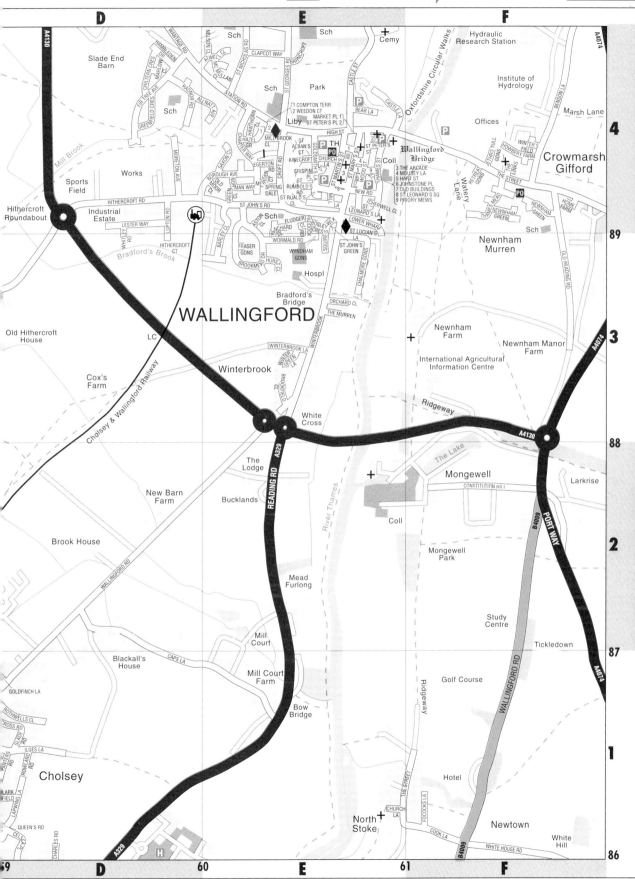

221
204

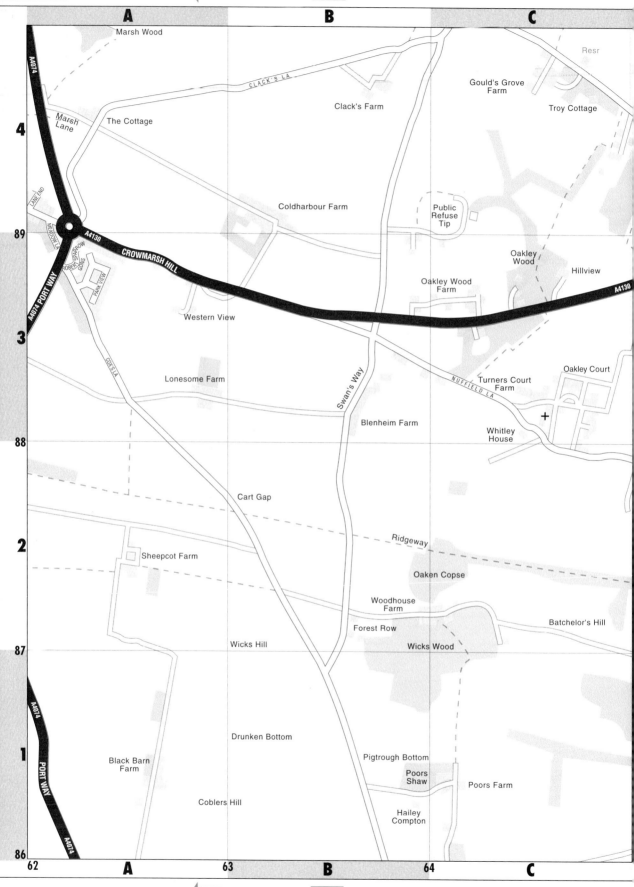

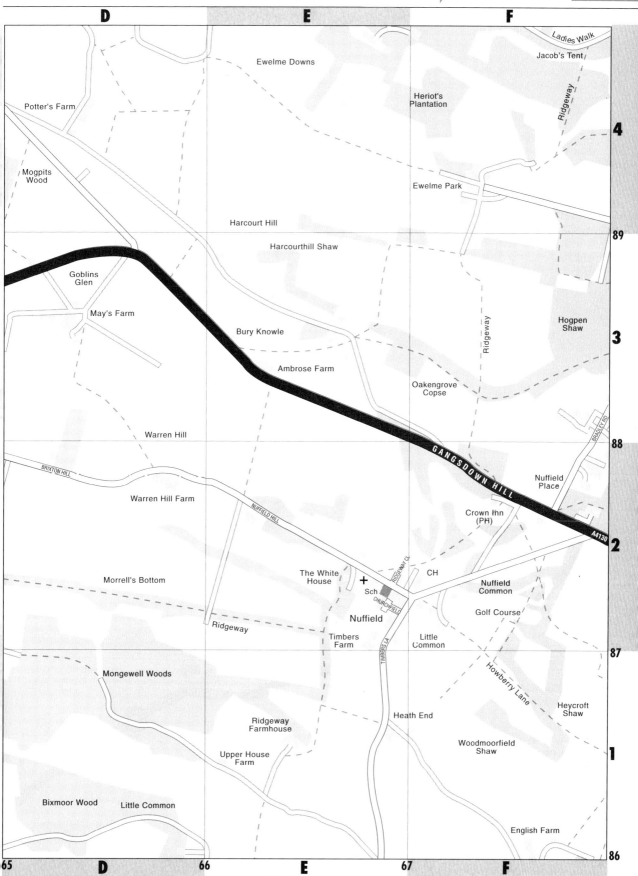

D E F

Ladies Walk
Jacob's Tent
Heriot's Plantation
Ridgeway
Ewelme Downs
Potter's Farm
Ewelme Park
Mogpits Wood
Harcourt Hill
Harcourthill Shaw
Goblins Glen
Hogpen Shaw
May's Farm
Bury Knowle
Ridgeway
Ambrose Farm
Oakengrove Copse
BRADLEY RD
Warren Hill
BRIXTON HILL
GANGSDOWN HILL
Nuffield Place
Warren Hill Farm
NUFFIELD HILL
Crown Inn (PH)
A4130
Morrell's Bottom
The White House
CH
Nuffield Common
RIDGEWAY CL
Sch
Golf Course
CHURCHFIELD
Ridgeway
Nuffield
Little Common
Timbers Farm
Mongewell Woods
TIMBERS LA
Howberry Lane
Heath End
Heycroft Shaw
Ridgeway Farmhouse
Woodmoorfield Shaw
Upper House Farm
Bixmoor Wood
Little Common
English Farm

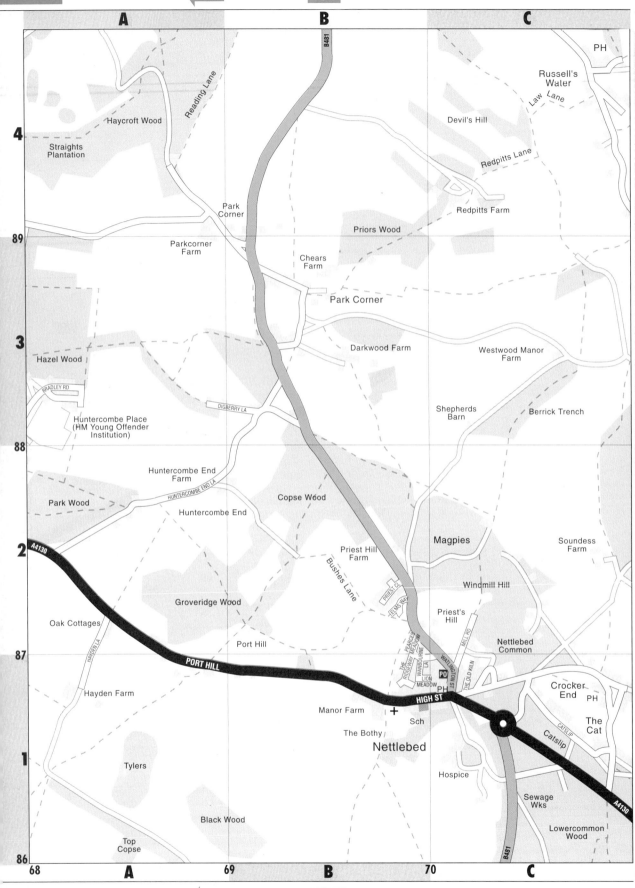

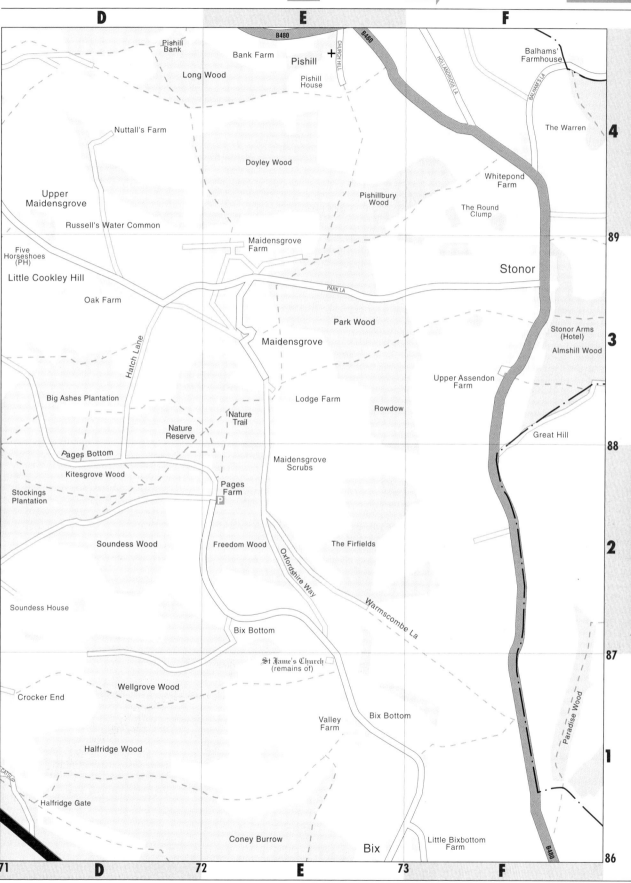

D E F

B480

Pishill
Bank

Bank Farm

Long Wood

Pishill +

CHURCH HILL

B480

HOLLANDRIDGE LA

BALHAM'S LA

Balhams'
Farmhouse

Pishill
House

4

Nuttall's Farm

Doyley Wood

The Warren

Pishillbury
Wood

Whitepond
Farm

Upper
Maidensgrove

The Round
Clump

89

Russell's Water Common

Five
Horseshoes
(PH)

Maidensgrove
Farm

Stonor

Little Cookley Hill

PARK LA

Oak Farm

Park Wood

Stonor Arms
(Hotel)

3

Hatch Lane

Maidensgrove

Almshill Wood

Upper Assendon
Farm

Big Ashes Plantation

Lodge Farm

Rowdow

Nature
Trail

Nature
Reserve

Great Hill

88

Pages Bottom

Maidensgrove
Scrubs

Kitesgrove Wood

Pages
Farm

Stockings
Plantation

P

Soundess Wood

Freedom Wood

The Firfields

2

Oxfordshire Way

Soundess House

Warmscombe La

Bix Bottom

87

St Jame's Church
(remains of)

Wellgrove Wood

Crocker End

Bix Bottom

Paradise Wood

Valley
Farm

1

Halfridge Wood

CATSLIP

Halfridge Gate

Coney Burrow

Bix

Little Bixbottom
Farm

B480

86

71 D 72 E 73 F

225

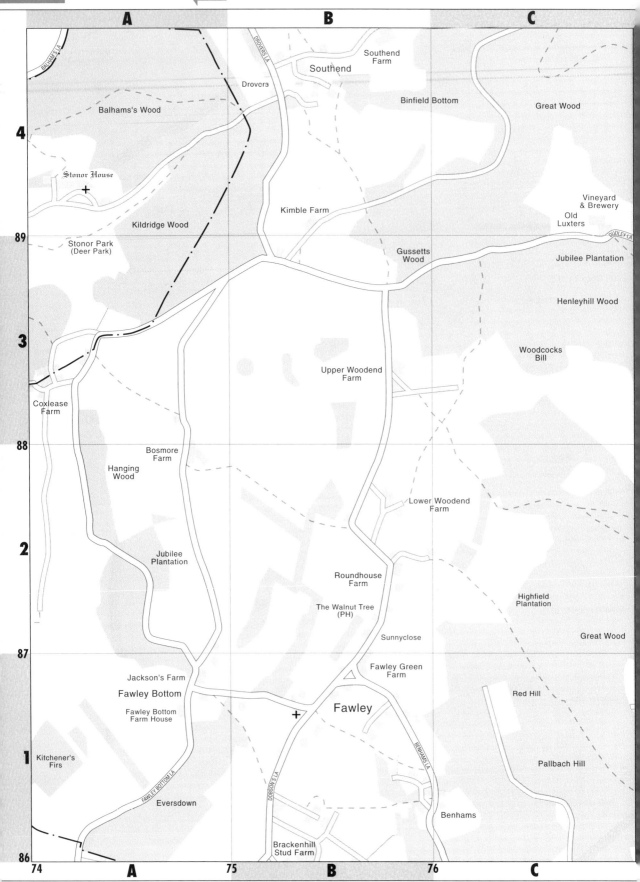

225
244

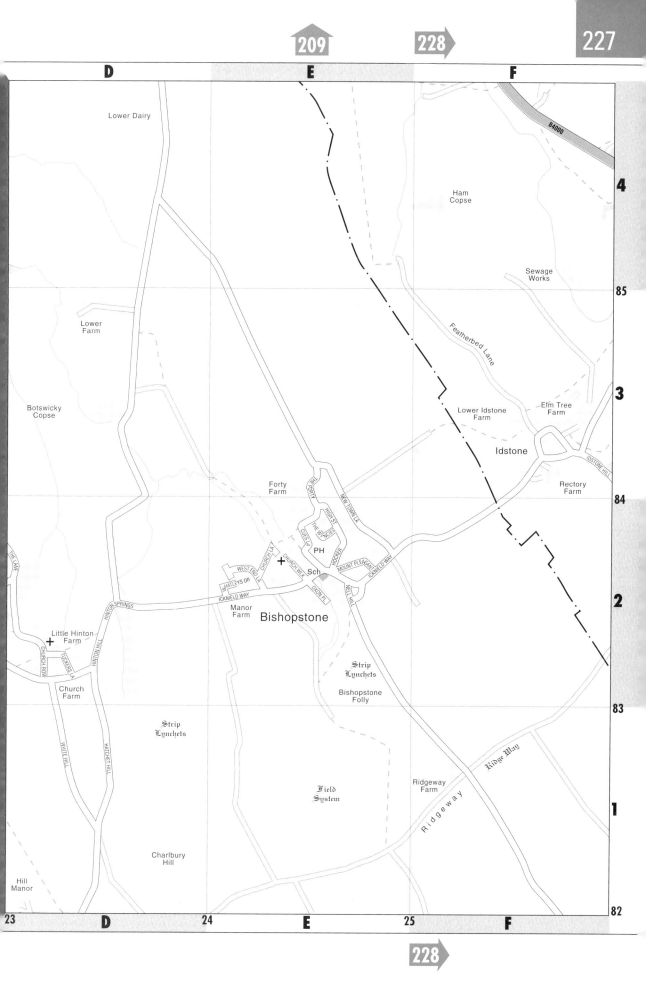

Lower Dairy

Ham
Copse

B4000

4

Sewage
Works

85

Lower
Farm

Featherbed Lane

Botswicky
Copse

Lower Idstone
Farm

Elm Tree
Farm

3

Idstone

Forty
Farm

THE FORTY

HIGH ST

NEW TOWN LA

Rectory
Farm

84

THE WINCHES

CUES LA

CHURCH LA

CHURCH WLK

PH

HOOKER

MOUNT PLEASANT

ICKNIELD WAY

THE LAKE

WEST END LA

Sch

DIXON PL

HATLEYS OR

NELL HILL

HINTON SPRINGS

ICKNIELD WAY

Manor
Farm

Bishopstone

2

Little Hinton
Farm

TUCKERS LA

HINTON HILL

CHURCH ROW

Strip
Lynchets

Church
Farm

Bishopstone
Folly

83

WHITE HILL

HATCHET HILL

Strip
Lynchets

Ridge Way

Field
System

Ridgeway
Farm

Ridgeway

1

Charlbury
Hill

Hill
Manor

82

227
210

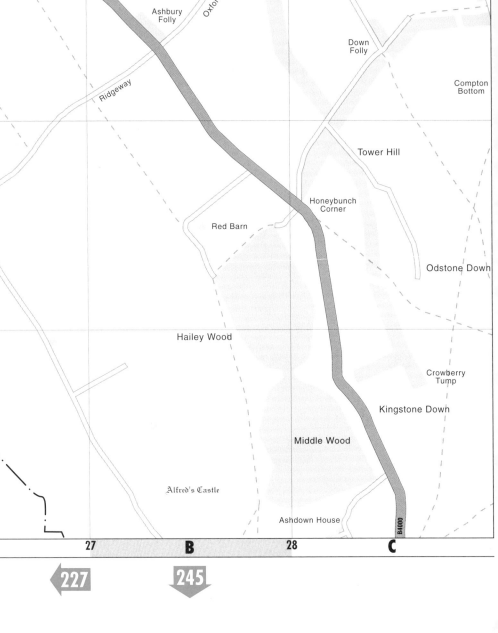

A B C

B4507

Odstone Hill

Kingstone Winslow

Winslow
Bank

Odstone
Coombes

Wayland's Smithy
Long Barrow

Kingstone
Farm

B4000

4

STATION RD

POUND PIECE

MALTHOUSE CL

WALNUT TREES HILL

Knighton
Barn

Ashbury

Berrycroft

KINGS
CL

Sch

MALTHOUSE

HIGH ST

PO

Kingstone Coombes

Odstone Barn

CHAPEL RD

85

PH

ASHBURY HILL

Resr

Kingstone
Barn

Oxfordshire Circular Walks

IDSTONE RD

Ashbury
Folly

Down
Folly

3

Compton
Bottom

Idstone
Plantation

Ridgeway

IDSTONE HILL

84

Tower Hill

Honeybunch
Corner

2

Red Barn

Odstone Down

83

Hailey Wood

Crowberry
Tump

Kingstone Down

1

Middle Wood

Alfred's Castle

Ashdown House

B4000

82
26 A 27 B 28 C

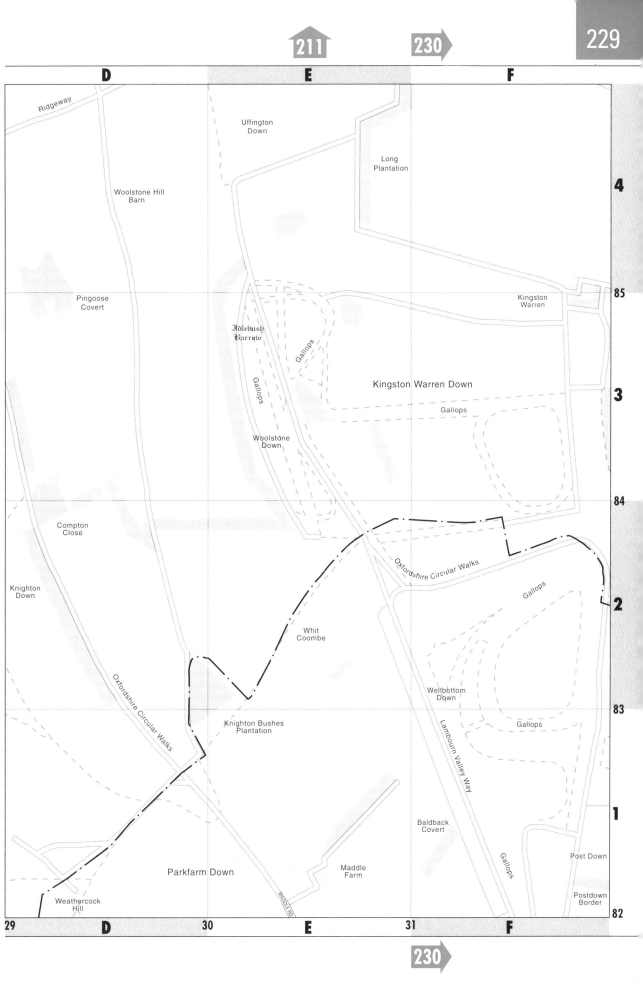

D E F

4

85

Ridgeway

Uffington
Down

Long
Plantation

Woolstone Hill
Barn

Kingston
Warren

Pingoose
Covert

Idlebush
Barrow

Gallops

Gallops

Kingston Warren Down

Gallops

3

Woolstone
Down

84

Compton
Close

Oxfordshire Circular Walks

Knighton
Down

Gallops

2

Whit
Coombe

Wellbottom
Down

Gallops

83

Oxfordshire Circular Walks

Knighton Bushes
Plantation

Lambourn Valley Way

Gallops

1

Baldback
Covert

Post Down

Parkfarm Down

Maddle
Farm

Gallops

Postdown
Border

Weathercock
Hill

MADDLE RD

82

229
212

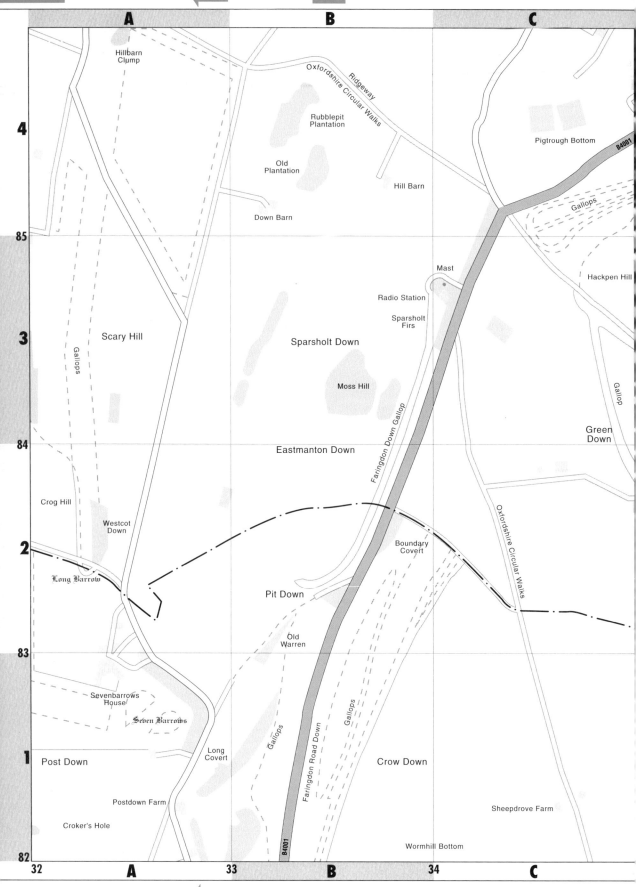

229

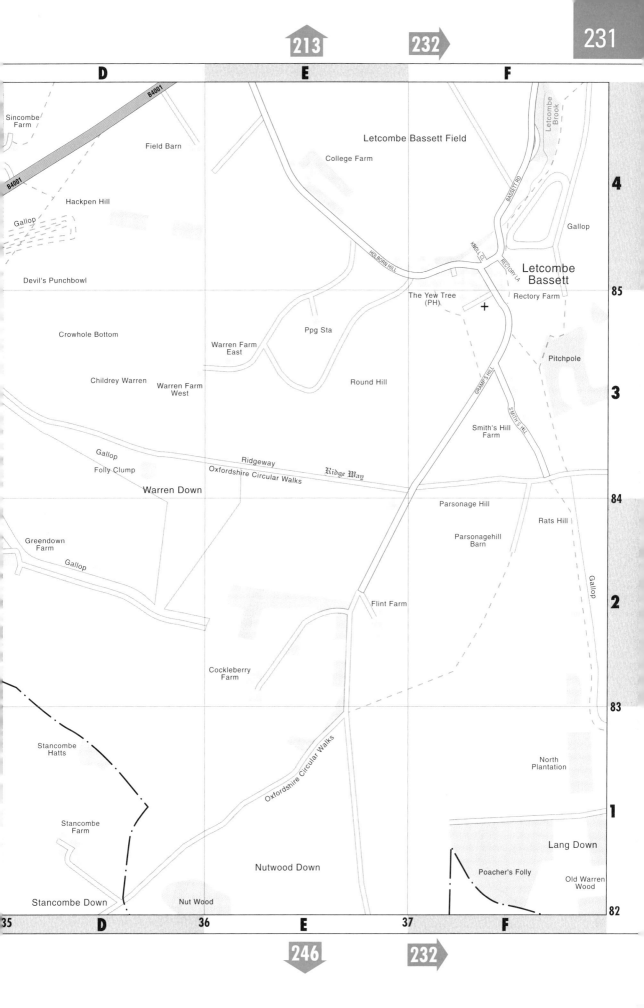

D | **E** | **F**

4

B4001

Sincombe Farm

Field Barn

Hackpen Hill

Gallop

Devil's Punchbowl

Letcombe Bassett Field

College Farm

Letcombe Brook

BASSETT RD

KNOLL CL

RECTORY LA

HOLBORN HILL

Gallop

Letcombe Bassett

85

The Yew Tree (PH)

Rectory Farm

Crowhole Bottom

Warren Farm East

Ppg Sta

Round Hill

Pitchpole

Childrey Warren

Warren Farm West

GRAMP'S HILL

SMITH'S HILL

Smith's Hill Farm

3

Gallop

Folly Clump

Ridgeway

Oxfordshire Circular Walks

Ridge Way

Warren Down

84

Parsonage Hill

Rats Hill

Greendown Farm

Gallop

Parsonagehill Barn

2

Gallop

Flint Farm

Cockleberry Farm

83

Stancombe Hatts

North Plantation

Oxfordshire Circular Walks

1

Stancombe Farm

Lang Down

Stancombe Down

Nut Wood

Nutwood Down

Poacher's Folly

Old Warren Wood

82

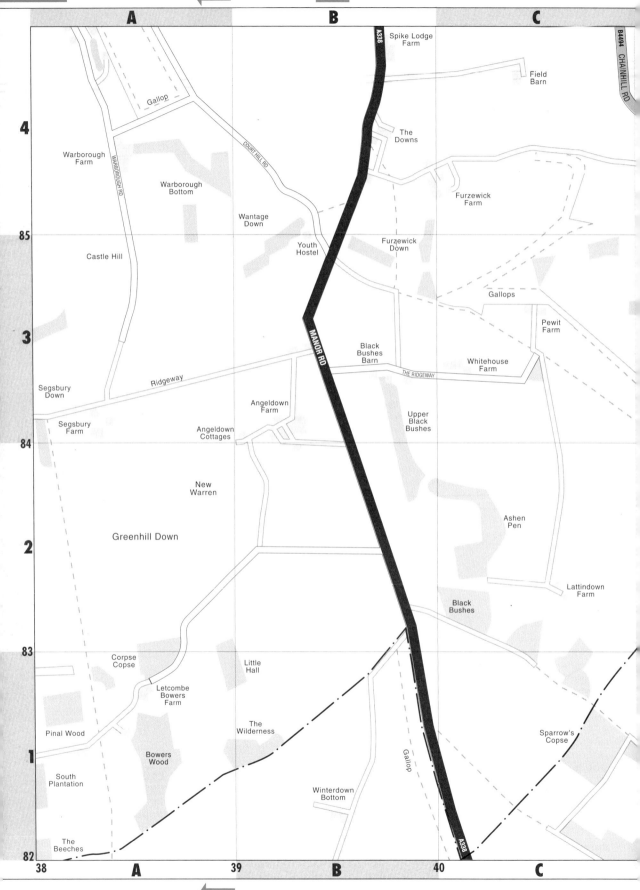

A   B   C

A338

Spike Lodge Farm

B4494 CHAINHILL RD

Field Barn

The Downs

4

Warborough Farm

COURT HILL RD

WARBOROUGH RD

Gallop

Warborough Bottom

Furzewick Farm

Wantage Down

85

Youth Hostel

Furzewick Down

Castle Hill

Gallops

3

MANOR RD

Pewit Farm

Black Bushes Barn

THE RIDGEWAY

Whitehouse Farm

Segsbury Down

Ridgeway

Angeldown Farm

Segsbury Farm

Angeldown Cottages

Upper Black Bushes

84

New Warren

Ashen Pen

Greenhill Down

2

Lattindown Farm

Black Bushes

83

Corpse Copse

Little Hall

Letcombe Bowers Farm

Sparrow's Copse

Pinal Wood

The Wilderness

Gallop

1

Bowers Wood

South Plantation

Winterdown Bottom

A338

The Beeches

82

38   A   39   B   40   C

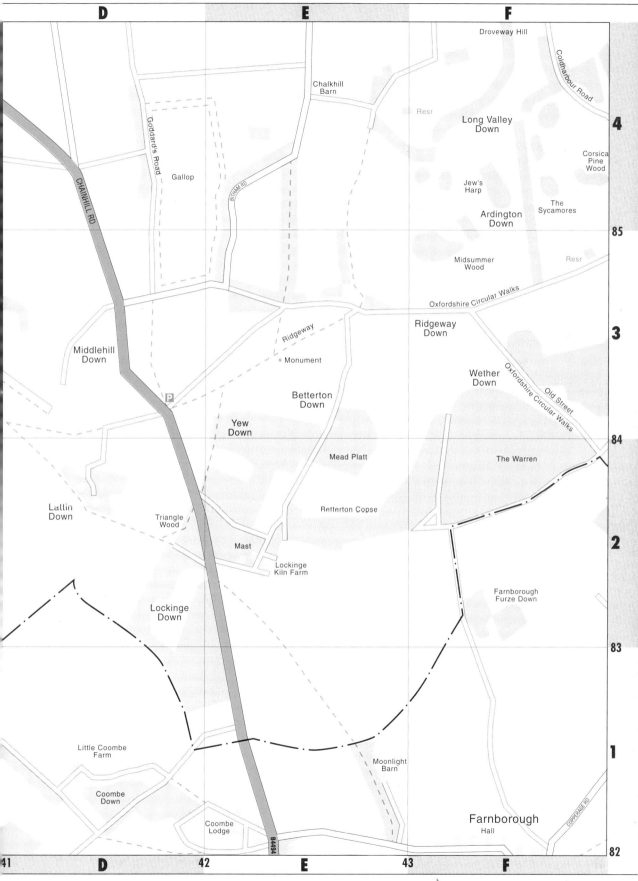

D E F

Droveway Hill

Coldharbour Road

Chalkhill
Barn

Resr

Long Valley
Down

4

Goddard's Road

Gallop

Corsica
Pine
Wood

BITHAM RD

Jew's
Harp

The
Sycamores

Ardington
Down

85

CHAINHILL RD

Midsummer
Wood

Resr

Oxfordshire Circular Walks

Ridgeway

Ridgeway
Down

3

Middlehill
Down

Monument

Wether
Down

Old Street

Oxfordshire Circular Walks

Betterton
Down

Yew
Down

84

Mead Platt

The Warren

Lattin
Down

Betterton Copse

2

Triangle
Wood

Mast

Lockinge
Kiln Farm

Farnborough
Furze Down

Lockinge
Down

83

Little Coombe
Farm

Moonlight
Barn

1

Coombe
Down

COPPERAGE RD

Coombe
Lodge

Farnborough
Hall

B4494

82

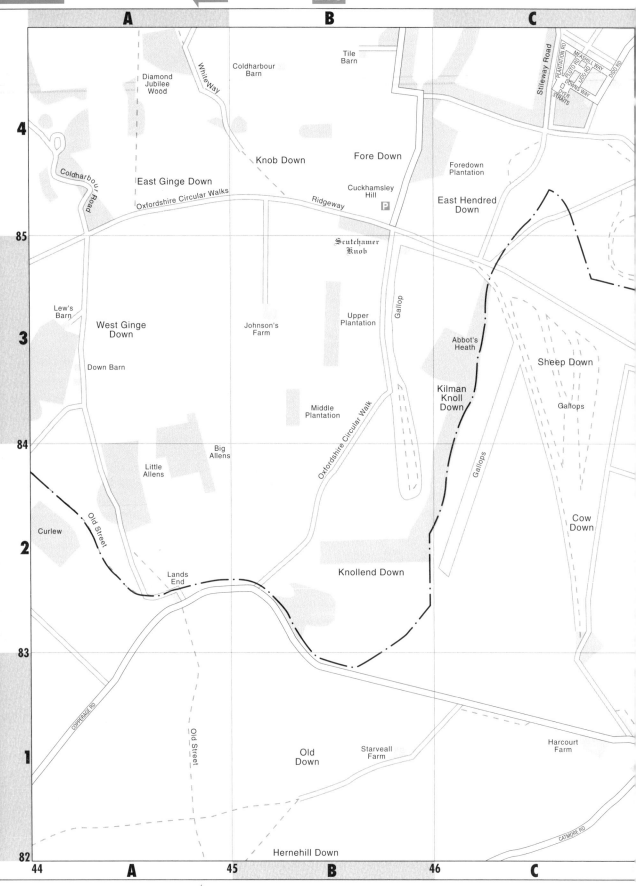

A   B   C

4

Silleway Road

Plantation Rd

Meashill Way

Pluto Rd

Lido Rd

Dido Rd

Downs Way

Dyer

Straits

Tile Barn

Diamond Jubilee Wood

White Way

Coldharbour Barn

Knob Down

Fore Down

Foredown Plantation

Coldharbour Road

East Ginge Down

Oxfordshire Circular Walks

Ridgeway

Cuckhamsley Hill

P

East Hendred Down

85

Scutchamer Knob

Lew's Barn

West Ginge Down

Johnson's Farm

Upper Plantation

Gallop

Abbot's Heath

Sheep Down

3

Down Barn

Middle Plantation

Oxfordshire Circular Walk

Kilman Knoll Down

Gallops

84

Big Allens

Little Allens

Cow Down

Curlew

Old Street

Gallops

2

Lands End

Knollend Down

83

Copperage Rd

Old Street

Harcourt Farm

1

Old Down

Starveall Farm

Catmore Rd

82

44   A   45   B   46   C

Hernehill Down

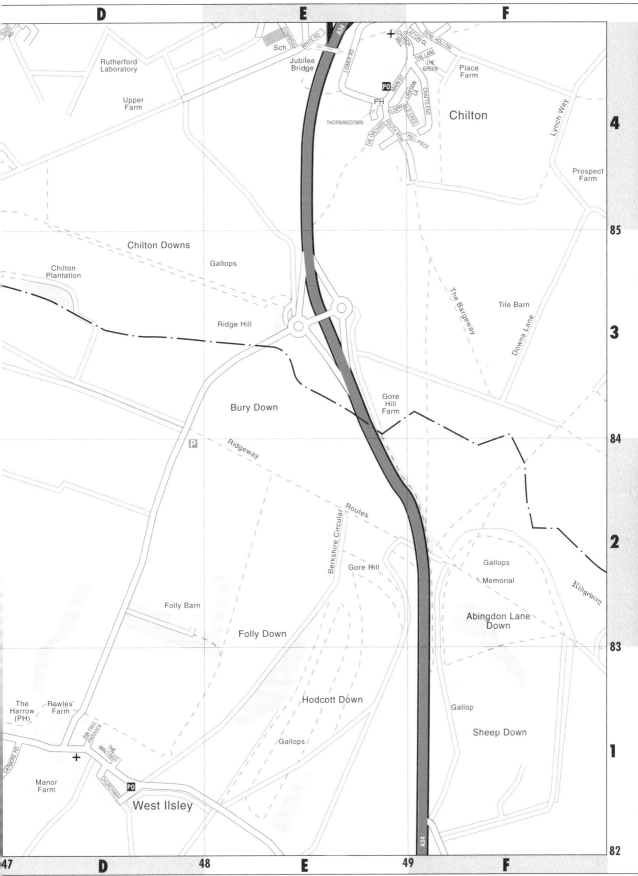

D   E   F

Rutherford
Laboratory

Upper
Farm

Sch

Jubilee
Bridge

White Rd

Lower Rd

A34

Dene Hollow
Latton Cl
Church Hill
The Lane
The Green
Place
Farm

PO

Main St

PH

Lawson La
Old Cres
Crafts End

Lynch Way

Chilton

Thorningdown

The Orchids
Eldene
South Row
Hill Piece

Prospect
Farm

Chilton Downs

Gallops

Chilton
Plantation

Ridge Hill

Bury Down

The Bargeway

Tile Barn

Downs Lane

Gore
Hill
Farm

P

Ridgeway

Berkshire Circular
Routes

Gore Hill

Gallops

Memorial

Ridgeway

Folly Barn

Folly Down

Abingdon Lane
Down

The
Harrow
(PH)

Rowles'
Farm

Cathmore Rd

Fir Tree
Paddock

The
Maltings

Churchway

Manor
Farm

PO

West Ilsley

Hodcott Down

Gallops

Gallop

Sheep Down

A34

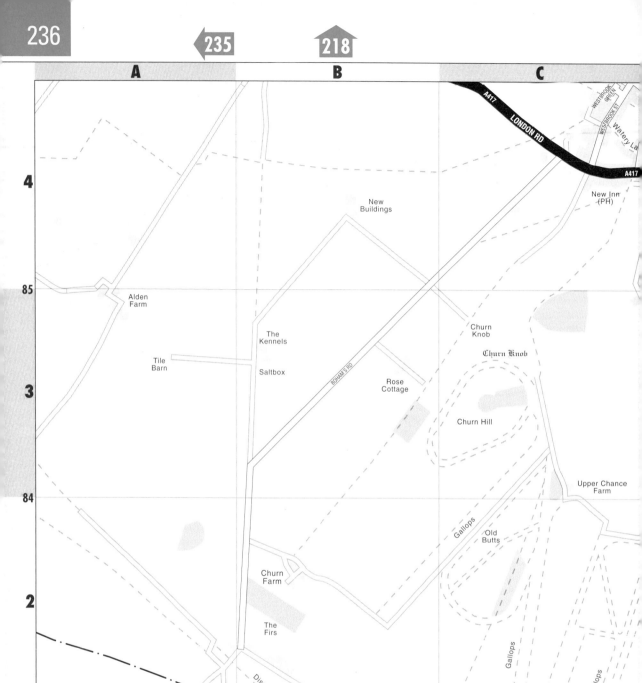

A417 LONDON RD

WESTBROOK GREEN
WESTBROOK ST
Watery La
A417

New Inn
(PH)

4

New
Buildings

85

Alden
Farm

Churn
Knob

The
Kennels

Churn Knob

Tile
Barn

BOHAM'S RD

Saltbox

Rose
Cottage

Churn Hill

3

84

Upper Chance
Farm

Gallops

Old
Butts

Churn
Farm

2

The
Firs

Gallops

Dismantled Railway

Gallops

83

Several
Down

Gallops

Lower Chance
Farm

Ridgeway

Compton
Downs

Gallop

Blewbury
Down

Gallop

1

Gallops

Berkshire Circular Routes

Ridgeway

Ridgeway

Berkshire
Circular
Routes

82

D
E
F

Blewbury

CHURCH END
WATT'S LA
BRAHAM...
CHURCH ST
DIBLEYS
SOUTH ST
EASTFIELD
BESSEL'S WAY
CHAPEL LA
PO
B4016
LONDON RD
RUMSEY'S LA

Copsestile Farm
Sch
RECTORY LA
BAKER ST
PO
SPRING LA
Aston Tirrold
ASTON LA
CHALK HILL

BLEWBURY HILL

Blewbury Barn

Hunt's Grave
Golf Driving Range

WOODWAY RD

Downside Farm

Baldon Hill

Lid's Down

Gallop

4

A417

85

Carrimers Farm

WHITE SHOOT

Riddle Hill

Chalk Hill Bottom

3

Woodway Hostel

Sheepcot Farm

Woodway

Lower Hill Barn

Hogtrough Bottom

84

Gallop

Upper Hill Barn

Oven Bottom

Langdon Hill

Big Bull Hill

The Plantation

2

Gallop

Gallops

Aston Upthorpe Downs

83

The Fair Mile

Gallops

Fuller's Firs

Berkshire Circular Route

1

Lowbury Hill

Dean's Bottom

Berkshire Circular Route

Ridgeway

82

A **B** **C**

PAPIST WAY

Westfield
Farm

4

Lollingdon
Farm

The
Lynch

Lollingdon
Hill

85

A417

Bowslade

WESTFIELD RD

Offlands
Court

Sheephouse
Farm

3

Breach
House

Breach
Farm

HALFPENNY LA

WILLOW COURT LA

Sch

THE STREET

Stormerbank
Kennels

Westfield
Stables

GLEBE CL.

84

Moulsford

Kingstanding
Hill

SHORTLANDS HILL

MEADOW CL.

Cholsey
Downs

NORTH RD

UNHILL RD

2

North Unhill
Bank

Starveall
Farm

Moulsford
Bottom

Unhill
Bottom

Greenlands
Farm

COW LA.

83

South Unhill
Bank

Lingley
Knoll

Moulsford
Downs

Well
Barn

1

WANTAGE RD

A417

Unhill
Wood

Ridge
Roads

82

56 **A** 57 **B** 58 **C**

D   **E**   **F**

WHITE HOUSE RD

CHARLES RD
PAPIST WAY
CELSEA PL   PH
ABBOTTS MEAD
A329
H
H

Cholsey

Cholsey Marsh
(Nature Reserve)

B4009

Barracks
Farm

4

Inn

The
Gables

Littlestoke
Manor
Farm

Ash
Cottage

85

READING RD

HALFPENNY LA

Middle
Barn

Swan's Way

Offlands
Farm

The
Oak

Watch
Folly

3

THE STREET

Sch

River Thames

Ridgeway

WALLINGFORD RD

White Hill

84

Sch

Lower
Farm

Freedom
Cottages

WOODCOTE RD

Ivol
Barn

NORTH RD

Hotel

FERRY LA

FERRY   RD

**South
Stoke**

2

UNDERHILL

FERRY LA

PO

THE BIER PATH
THE STREET

CHAPEL CL

CROSS KEYS RD

PH

THE GARDENS

Lower
Cadley's

COW LA

Sowberry
Court

The
Old
Vicarage

Glebe
Cottages

DEACONFIELD

South
Bank

83

Runsford
Hole

Sewage
Works

Grove Farm
House

Grove
House

WALLINGFORD RD

Grove
Farm

Icknield Way

1

PH

Spring
Farm

A329

Streatley
Farm

B4009

Spring Farm
Cottages

ICKNIELD RD

BEECH LA

82

9   **D**   **60**   **E**   **61**   **F**

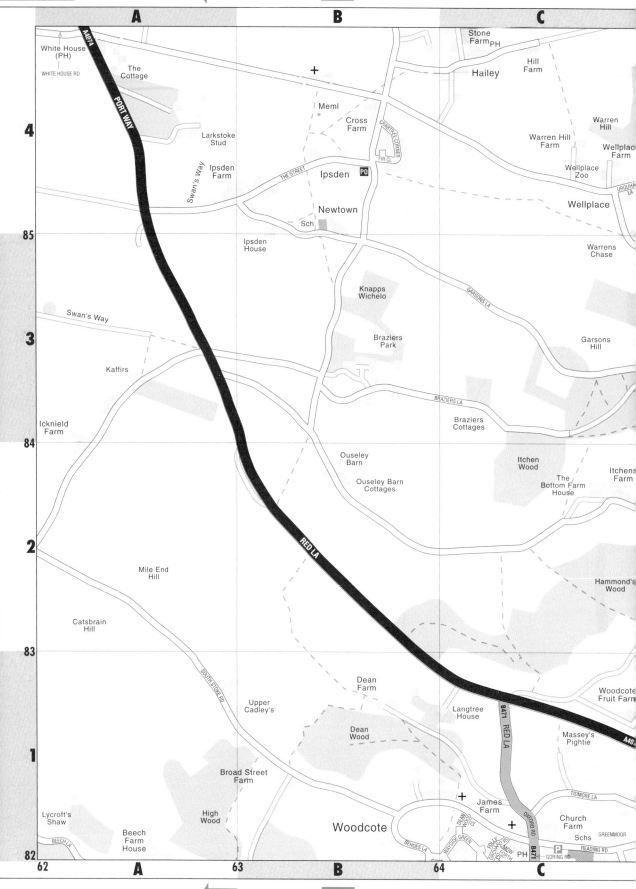

241
224

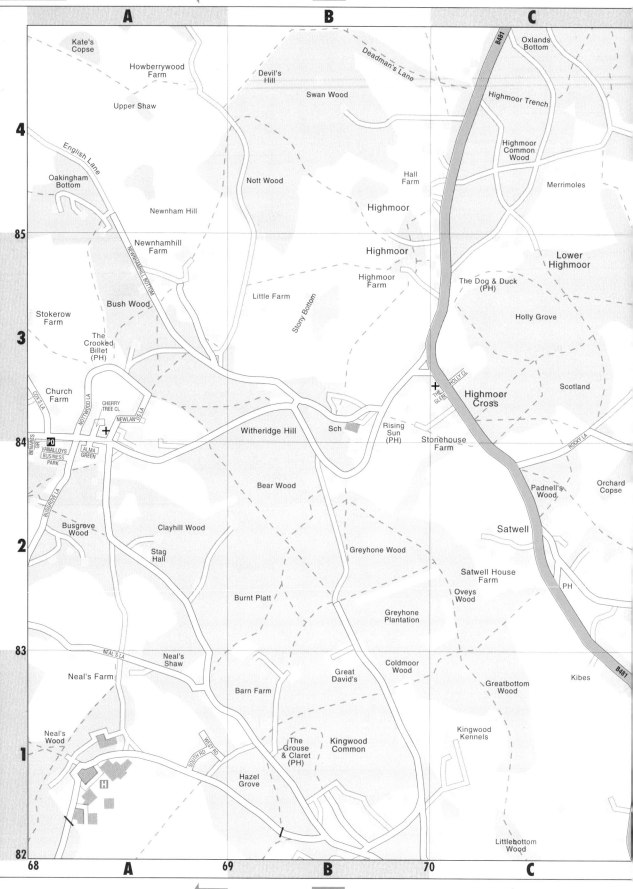

241
252

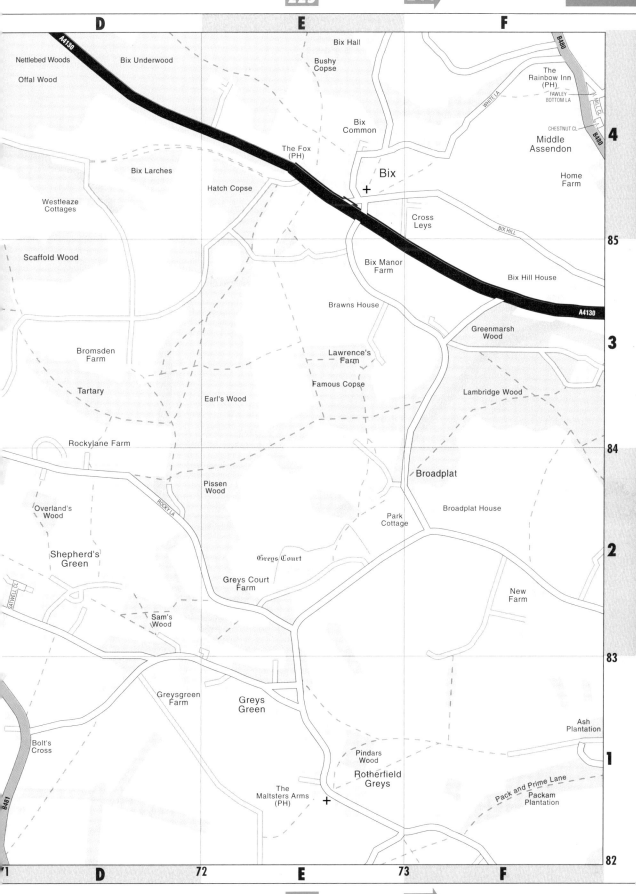

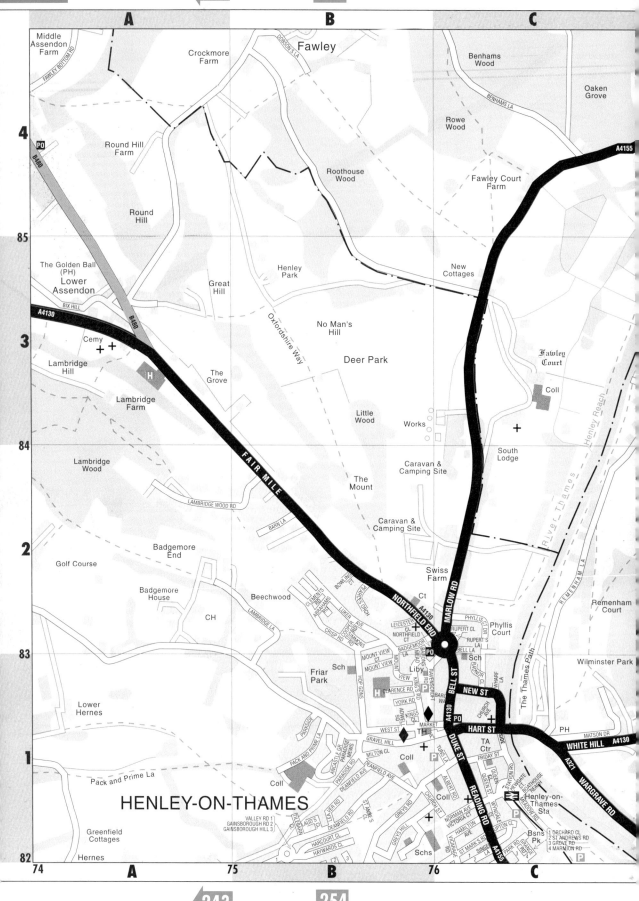

A | B | C

Middle
Assendon
Farm

Crockmore
Farm

Fawley

DOBSON'S LA

Benhams
Wood

Oaken
Grove

4 PO

FAWLEY BOTTOM RD

Round Hill
Farm

Round
Hill

Roothouse
Wood

Rowe
Wood

A4155

Fawley Court
Farm

BENHAMS LA

85

The Golden Ball
(PH)
Lower
Assendon

BIX HILL

Henley
Park

New
Cottages

Great
Hill

BIX HILL

A4130

B480

Oxfordshire Way

No Man's
Hill

Fawley
Court

3 Cemy

Lambridge
Hill

H

The
Grove

Deer Park

Coll

Lambridge
Farm

Little
Wood

Works

South
Lodge

Henley Reach

River Thames

84

Lambridge
Wood

FAIR MILE

The
Mount

Caravan &
Camping Site

LAMBRIDGE WOOD RD

BARN LA

Caravan &
Camping Site

REMENHAM LA

2 Golf Course

Badgemore
End

Beechwood

BOWLING CT
CLEMENTS END
ABRAHAMS

Swiss
Farm

MARLOW RD

Remenham
Court

Badgemore
House

CH

LAMBRIDGE LA

LUKER AVE
TOPS
SIMMONS
CRISP RD
PARKES ORCH

NORTHFIELD END

Ct

A4130

PHYLLIS CT
RUPERT CL
RUPERT S

Phyllis
Court

Wilminster Park

83 Friar
Park

Sch

MOUNT VIEW
CT
MOUNT VIEW

Liby

Leicester
CL
NORTHFIELD
CT

BADGEMOOR
LA
MEAD
BELL LA

PO

Sch

WHARF
LA

The Thames Path

H

CLARENCE RD

RAZNOR CL

BELL ST

Lower
Hernes

PARKSIDE

PARADISE
MEWS
PACK AND PRIME LA

HOP GDNS

YORK RD
KINGS

RAVENSCROFT
RD

P

NEW ST

A4130

CHURCH AVE

PO

PH

MATSON DR

1

Pack and Prime La

ANGCASTLE CT
PARADISE RD
MILTON CL

DEANFIELD AVE
DEANFIELD RD

WEST ST

Coll

GRAVEL HILL

TH

HART ST

TUNS CT

DUKE ST

TA
Ctr
FRIDAY ST

WHITE HILL

A4130

A321

A4130

WARGRAVE RD

Coll

HENLEY-ON-THAMES

Greenfield
Cottages

ST ANNE'S
CL

RIVER RD

LAUD S

VALLEY RD 1
GAINSBOROUGH RD 2
GAINSBOROUGH HILL 3

DEANFIELD RD

GREYS RD

GREYS HILL

CHURCH ST

READING RD

ALBERT RD

NORMAN AVE
VICTORIA CT

HAMILTON
AVE

STATION RD

QUEEN ST

NEWGATE

BOATHOUSE
REACH

Henley-on-
Thames
Sta

P

Bsns
Pk

1 ORCHARD CL
2 ST ANDREWS RD
3 GROVE RD
4 MARMION RD

Hernes

82

HARCOURT CL

HAYWARDS CL

VICARAGE
RD

ST MARK'S RD

SINGE

PARK RD

UPTON CL

A4155

GRANGE RD

P

74 | A | 75 | B | 76 | C

D   **E**   **F**

Starveall Farm

Swinley Down

Swinley Copse

B4000

Ashdown Farm

4

Oxfordshire Circular Walks

Harley Bushes

Upper Wood

Pumping Station

B4000

81

Whiteshere

Bishopstone Downs

Idstone Down

Botley Bottom

3

Dean Bottom

Botley Copse

Russley Park

Bailey Hill

80

Goor Lane Farm

GOOR LA

Bailey Hill Copse

2

Peaks Down

Hazelbury Farm

M4

Peaks Wood

Bailey Hill Farm

79

Gallop

1

Baydon

Westfield Farm

Finche's Farm

M4

BAYDON RD

East Leaze Farm

DOWNSMEAD

PO

Sch

FINCHES LA

78

6   **D**   **27**   **E**   **28**   **F**

231

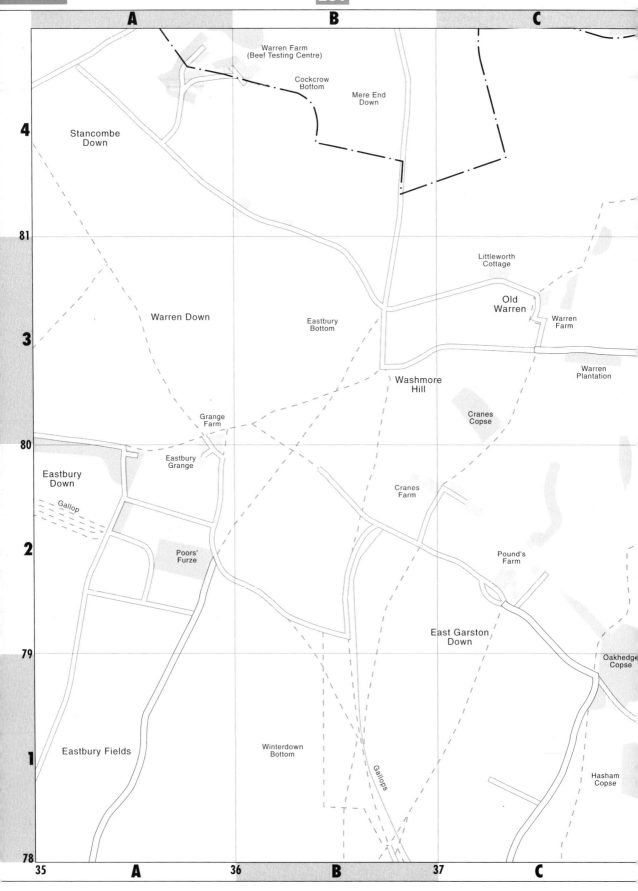

A

B

C

Warren Farm
(Beef Testing Centre)

Cockcrow
Bottom

Mere End
Down

4

Stancombe
Down

81

Littleworth
Cottage

Old
Warren

Warren Down

Eastbury
Bottom

Warren
Farm

3

Warren
Plantation

Washmore
Hill

Cranes
Copse

Grange
Farm

80

Eastbury
Grange

Eastbury
Down

Cranes
Farm

Gallop

Pound's
Farm

2

Poors'
Furze

East Garston
Down

79

Oakhedge
Copse

Eastbury Fields

Winterdown
Bottom

1

Gallops

Hasham
Copse

78

35   **A**   **36**   **B**   **37**   **C**

Roden
Downs

Warren
Farm

Town
Copse

4

Ridgeway

Berkshire Circular Routes

81

Starveall

Streatley
Warren

Crows
Foot

3

Bower
Farm

Grey
Ladies

80

Lower
Farm

The
Bell Inn
(PH)

Hungerford
Green

DOWNS RD

AMBURY RD

The
Red Lion
(PH)

Applepie
Hill

Parsonage
Green

BELL LA

THE GLEBE

2

TOWNSEND RD

Pibworth
Farm

Dumworth
Farm

Aldworth

READING RD

Woodrows
Farm

79

Fayleys
Border

Aces
High

Four
Points

The
Four Points
(PH)

Foxborough
Copse

Southfield
Shaw

Lower Point
Cottage

1

HAW LA

De La
Beche

Thorn
Hill

B4009

78

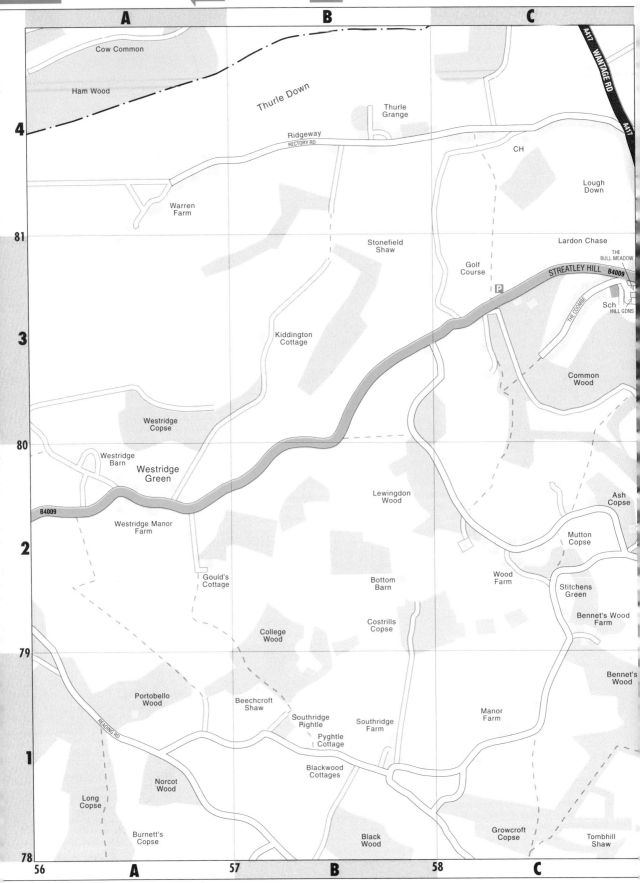

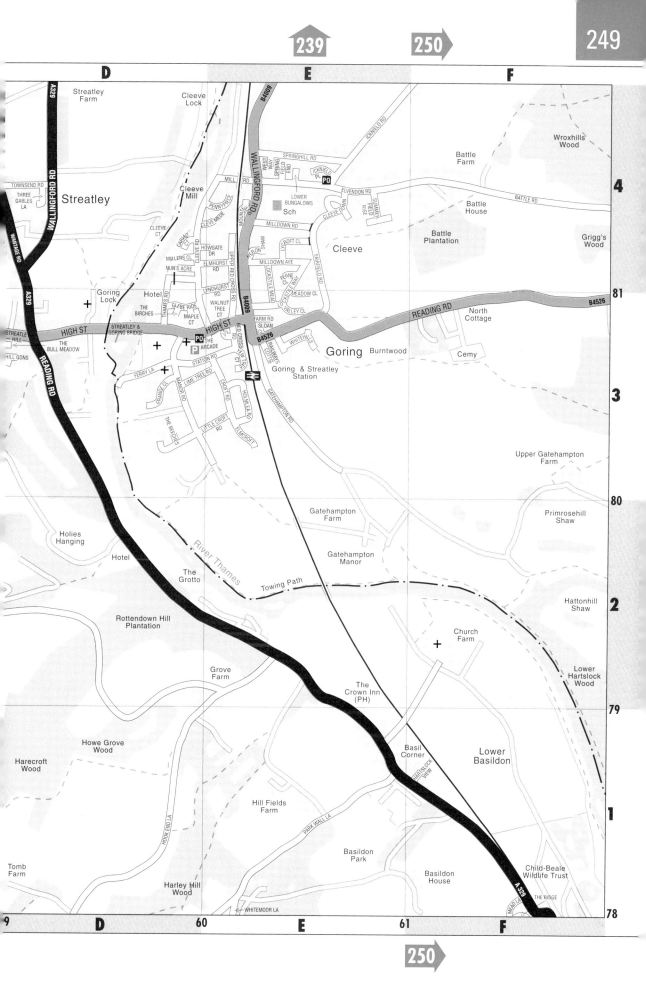

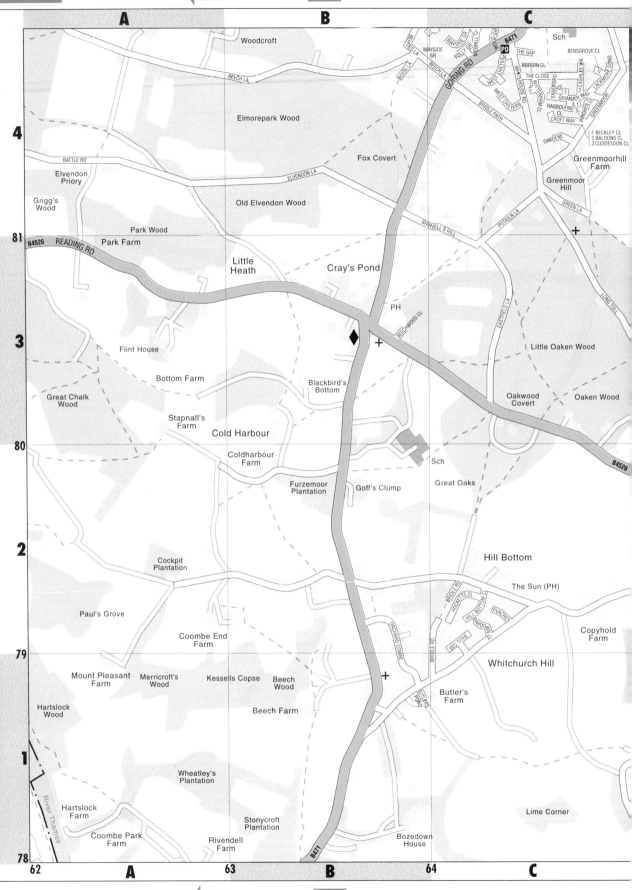

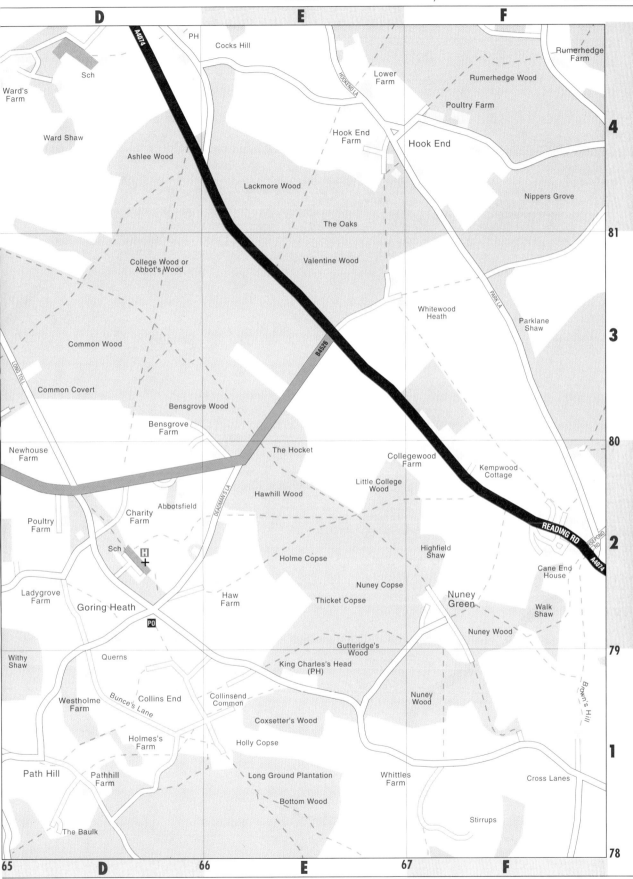

D
E
F

4

81

3

80

2

79

1

78

65
D
66
E
67
F

Ward's Farm
Sch
Ward Shaw
Ashlee Wood
Common Wood
Common Covert
Newhouse Farm
Poultry Farm
Ladygrove Farm
Sch
H
Goring Heath
PO
Charity Farm
Abbotsfield
Withy Shaw
Westholme Farm
Querns
Bunce's Lane
Collins End
Holmes's Farm
Path Hill
Pathhill Farm
The Baulk
LONG TOLL
DEADMAN'S LA
Bensgrove Wood
Bensgrove Farm
The Hocket
Hawhill Wood
Haw Farm
Holme Copse
PH
Cocks Hill
HOOKEND LA
Lackmore Wood
The Oaks
Valentine Wood
Lower Farm
Hook End Farm
Hook End
B4526
College Wood or Abbot's Wood
Collinsend Common
Coxsetter's Wood
Holly Copse
Long Ground Plantation
Bottom Wood
King Charles's Head (PH)
Gutteridge's Wood
Thicket Copse
Nuney Copse
Little College Wood
Collegewood Farm
Whitewood Heath
Highfield Shaw
Nuney Green
Nuney Wood
Nuney Wood
Whittles Farm
Stirrups
Cross Lanes
Walk Shaw
Cane End House
Kempwood Cottage
PARK LA
Parklane Shaw
Nippers Grove
Poultry Farm
Rumerhedge Wood
Rumerhedge Farm
Brown's Hill
READING RD
ROSEPOND RD
A4074
A4074

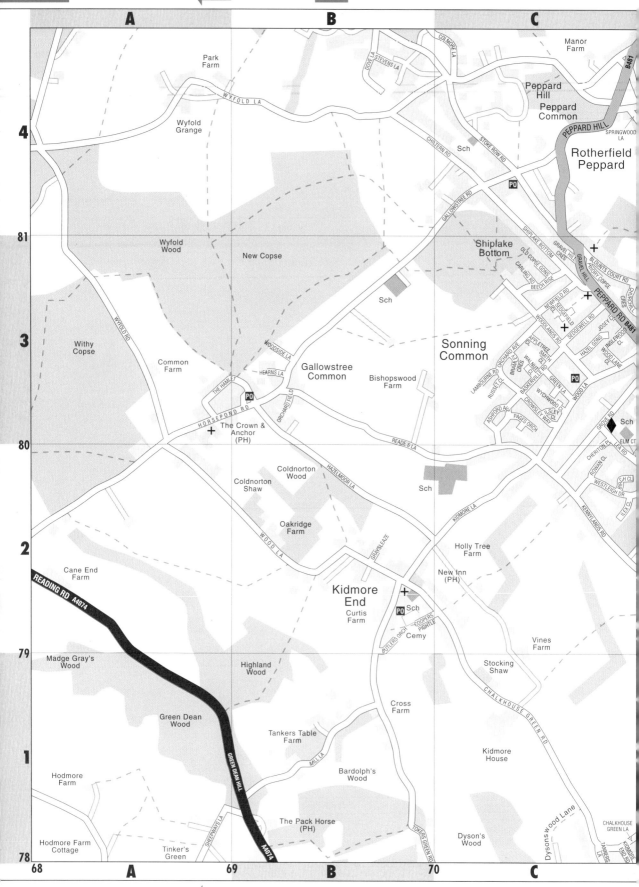

A   **B**   **C**

Manor Farm

Park Farm

WYFOLD LA

Wyfold Grange

COLMORE LA

DOLE LA   STEVENS LA

CHILTERN RD

STOKE ROW RD

Sch

Peppard Hill

Peppard Common

PEPPARD HILL

SPRINGWOOD LA

B481

Rotherfield Peppard

PO

4

Wyfold Wood

New Copse

GALLOWSTREE RD

Shiplake Bottom

GRAVEL HILL

PRIORY COPSE

BLOUNTS COURT RD

PEPPARD RD B481

CHURCHILL CRES

SHIPLAKE BOTTOM

OLD COPSE GDNS

CARLING RD

BEECH RISE

GRAVEL HILL CRES

81

Withy Copse

WYFOLD RD

Common Farm

WOODSIDE LA

HEARNS LA

THE HAMLET

Gallowstree Common

Bishopswood Farm

Sch

Sonning Common

NEWFIELD RD

SEDGEWELL RD

WOODLANDS RD

LAMBOURNE RD

ORCHARD AVE

APPLETREE CL

WALNUT

SMITH

BRAMAS CRES

RUSSET CT

BASKERVILLE RD

HAZEL GDNS

INGLEWOOD CL

WOOD LANE

GREEN LA

WYCHWOOD

JOSEY CL

WOOD RD

PO

3

PO

The Crown & Anchor (PH)

HORSEPOND RD

ORCHARD FIELD

READE'S LA

CROWSLEY WAY

ILSLEY CL

PAGES ORCH

ASHFORD AV

Sch

GROVE RD

ELM CT

LEA RD

80

Coldnorton Wood

Coldnorton Shaw

HAZELMOOR LA

WOOD LA

Sch

KIDMORE LA

CHERITON PL

ROWAN CL

WESTLEIGH DR

KENNYLANDS RD

2

Oakridge Farm

GRAYSLEAZE

Holly Tree Farm

New Inn (PH)

Cane End Farm

READING RD A4074

Kidmore End

Curtis Farm

PO Sch

BUTLERS ORCH

Cemy

COOPERS PIGHTLE

Vines Farm

79

Madge Gray's Wood

Highland Wood

Cross Farm

CHALKHOUSE GREEN RD

Stocking Shaw

GREEN DEAN HILL

Green Dean Wood

Tankers Table Farm

MILL LA

Bardolph's Wood

TOKERS GREEN RD

Kidmore House

1

Hodmore Farm

Hodmore Farm Cottage

SHEEPWAYS LA

Tinker's Green

A4074

The Pack Horse (PH)

Dyson's Wood

DYSONS WOOD LANE

TANNERS LA

KIDMORE END RD

CHALKHOUSE GREEN LA

78

68   **A**   69   **B**   70   **C**

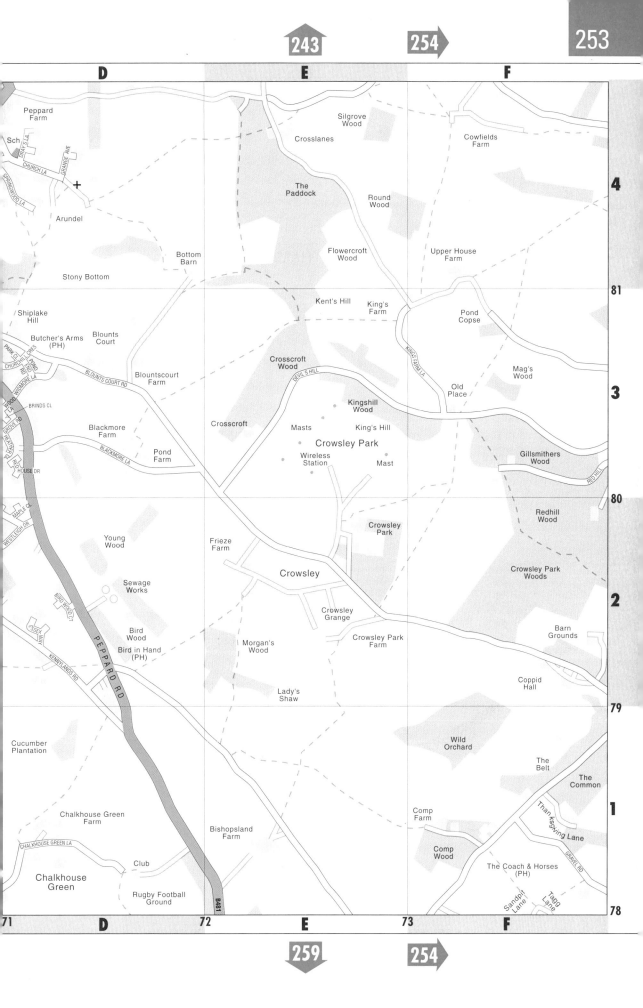

D E F

4

Peppard
Farm

Sch

DRAY'S LA

CHURCH LA

GRANGE AVE

SPRINGWOOD LA

+

Arundel

Silgrove
Wood

Crosslanes

Cowfields
Farm

The
Paddock

Round
Wood

Bottom
Barn

Flowercroft
Wood

Upper House
Farm

81

Stony Bottom

Shiplake
Hill

Kent's Hill

King's
Farm

Pond
Copse

Butcher's Arms
(PH)

Blounts
Court

PARK CL

CHURCHILL CRES

POND

WIDMORE LA

BLOUNTS COURT RD

Blountscourt
Farm

Crosscroft
Wood

DEVIL'S HILL

KINGS FARM LA

Mag's
Wood

3

WOOD LA

BRINDS CL

GROVE RD

HEATHER RD

Blackmore
Farm

BLACKMORE LA

Crosscroft

Kingshill
Wood

Old
Place

Masts

King's Hill

HOUSE DR

Pond
Farm

Crowsley Park

Wireless
Station

Mast

Gillsmithers
Wood

REDHILL

80

MAPLE CL

WESTLEIGH DR

Young
Wood

Frieze
Farm

Crowsley
Park

Redhill
Wood

Sewage
Works

Crowsley

Crowsley Park
Woods

2

BIRD WOOD CT

ESSEX WAY

Bird
Wood

Morgan's
Wood

Crowsley
Grange

Barn
Grounds

PEPPARD RD

KENNYLANDS RD

Bird in Hand
(PH)

Crowsley Park
Farm

Coppid
Hall

Lady's
Shaw

79

Cucumber
Plantation

Wild
Orchard

The
Belt

The
Common

Chalkhouse Green
Farm

Comp
Farm

Thanksgiving Lane

1

CHALKHOUSE GREEN LA

Bishopsland
Farm

Comp
Wood

GRAVEL RD

Chalkhouse
Green

Club

The Coach & Horses
(PH)

Sandpit
Lane

Tagg
Lane

Rugby Football
Ground

B481

78

71 D 72 E 73 F

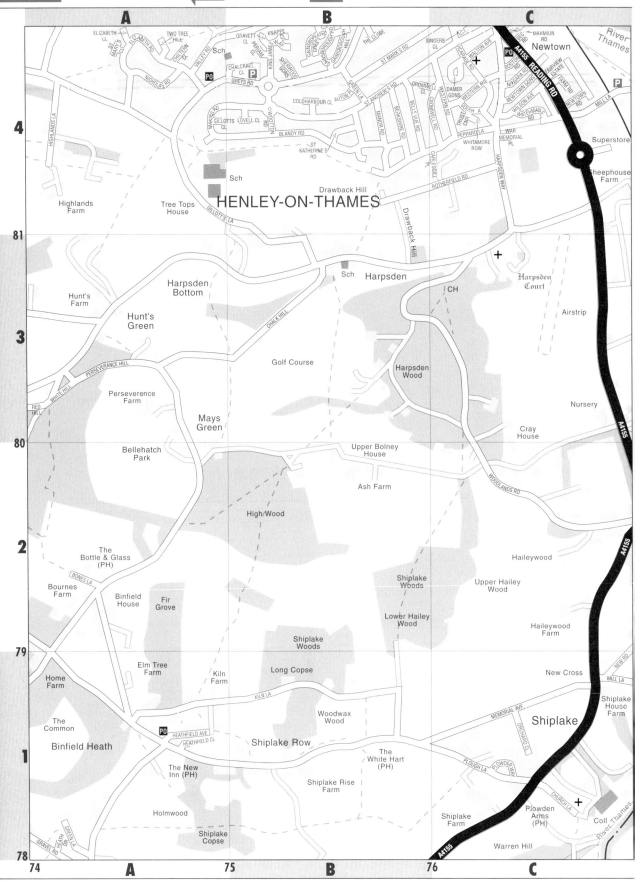

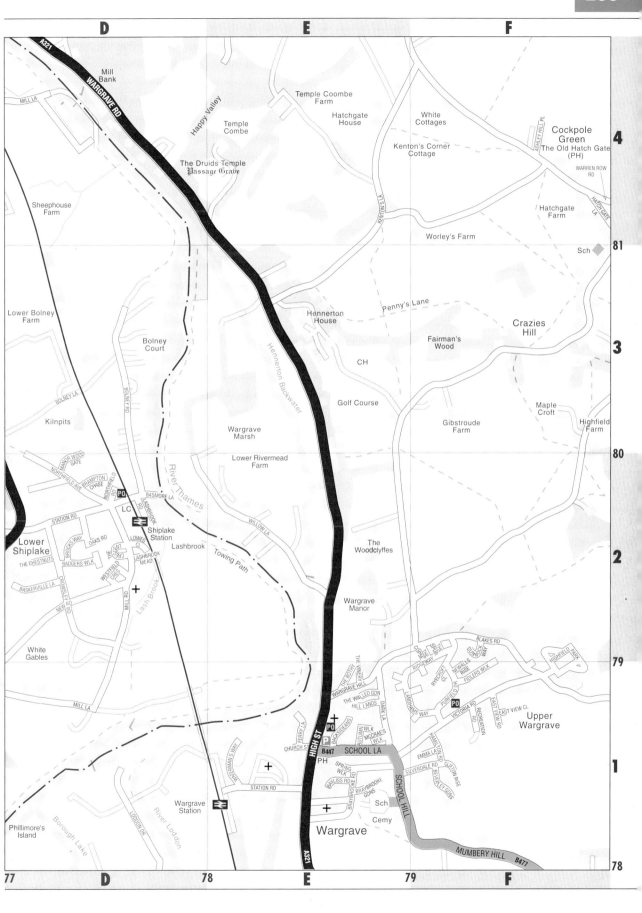

D E F

4

Mill Bank

MILL LA

WARGRAVE RD

A321

Happy Valley

Temple Combe Farm

Temple Combe

Hatchgate House

White Cottages

Kenton's Corner Cottage

Cockpole Green
The Old Hatch Gate (PH)

ASHLEY HILL PL

WARREN ROW RD

The Druids Temple
Passage Grave

KENTON'S LA

Hatchgate Farm

HATCHGATE LA

Sheephouse Farm

Worley's Farm

Sch

81

Lower Bolney Farm

Hennerton House

Penny's Lane

Crazies Hill

3

Bolney Court

Hennerton Backwater

Fairman's Wood

BOLNEY LA

BOLNEY RD

CH

Maple Croft

Kilnpits

Golf Course

Gibstroude Farm

Highfield Farm

Wargrave Marsh

Lower Rivermead Farm

80

MANOR WOOD GATE

NORTHFIELD AVE

BRAMPTON CHASE

NORTHFIELD RD

PO

BASMORE LA

River Thames

STATION RD

LC

LASHBROOK RD

Shiplake Station

Willow LA

Lower Shiplake

BRICKS WAY

OAKS RD

THE SALT

LOWES CL

LASHBROOK MEAD

Lashbrook

Towing Path

The Woodclyffes

2

THE CHESTNUTS

BADGERS WLK

WESTFIELD CRES

Lash Brook

BASKERVILLE LA

CROWSLEY RD

NEW RD

MILL RD

White Gables

Wargrave Manor

BLAKES RD

HIGHFIELD PARK

79

MILL LA

THE BOTTY

WARGRAVE HILL

THE VINERY

THE WALLED GDN

HILL LANDS

DARK LA

RIDGEWAY

THE CORSE

PRIEST HILL

LANDHAMS WAY

RYECROFT CL

NEWALLS RISE

GUINS WLK

FIDLERS WLK

PURFIELD DR

VICTORIA RD

RECREATION RD

EAST VIEW CL

Upper Wargrave

WATERMAN'S WAY

FERRY LA

CHURCH ST

HIGH ST

PO
P

BACKSIDEANS

AUTUMN WLK

McCRAE'S WLK

B447

SCHOOL LA

PH

SPRING WLK

BAYLISS RD

BRAYBROOKE RD

BRAYBROOKE GDNS

Sch

SCHOOL HILL

SILVERDALE RD

EMMA LA

HAMILTON RD

BEVERLEY GDNS

CLIFTON RISE

EAST VIEW RD

1

STATION RD

Wargrave Station

River Loddon

LONDON DR

Wargrave

Cemy

MUMBERY HILL

B477

Phillimore's Island

Borough Lake

78

77 D 78 E 79 F 78

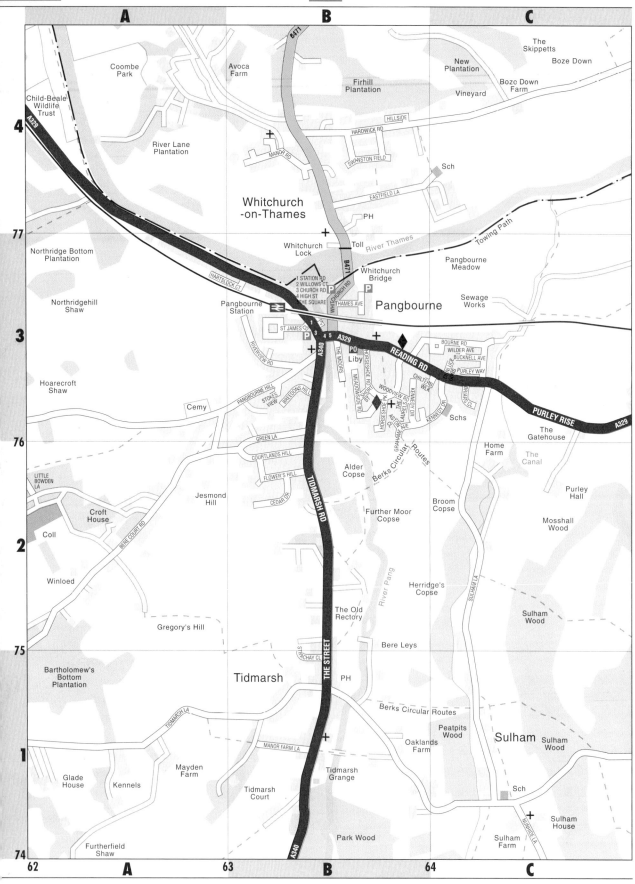

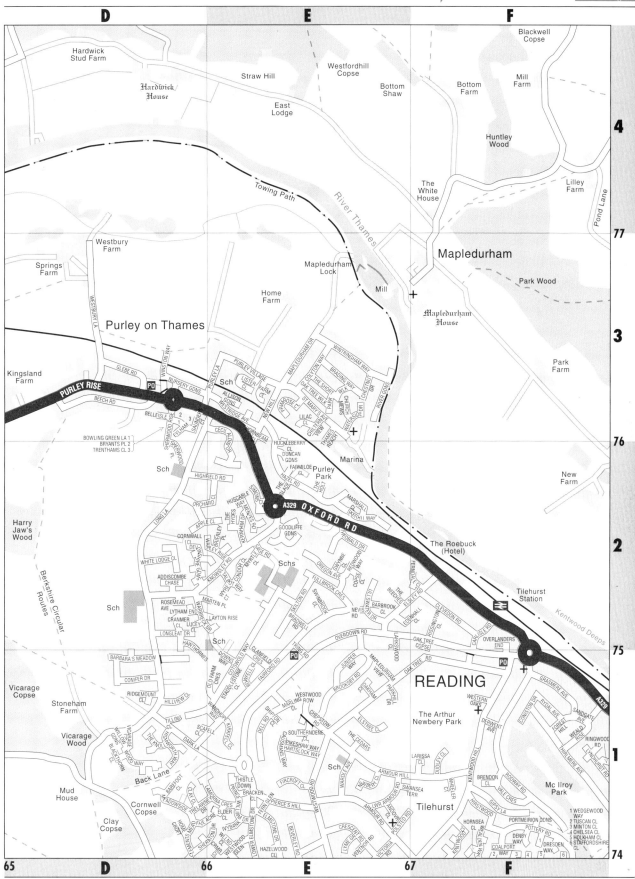

D
E
F

4

77

3

76

2

75

1

74

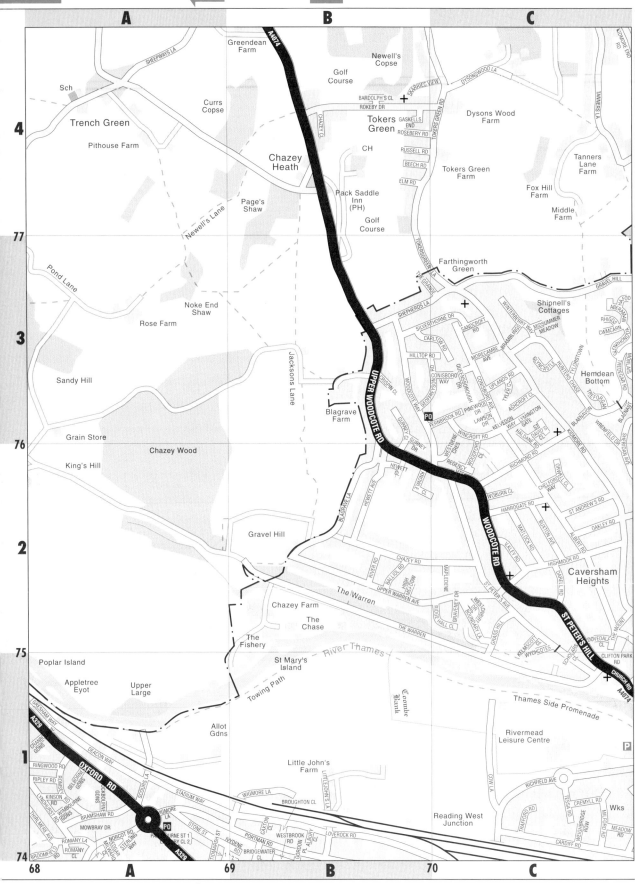

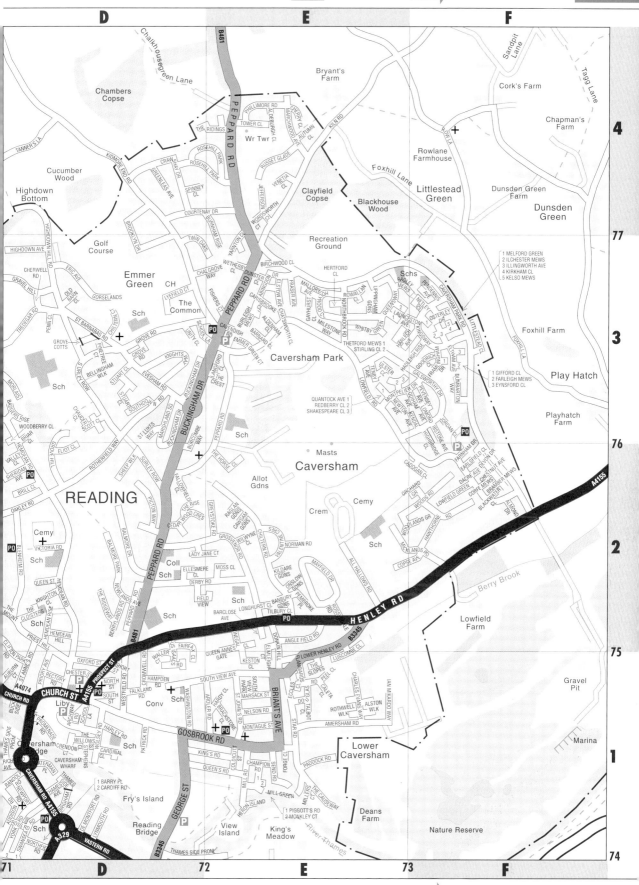

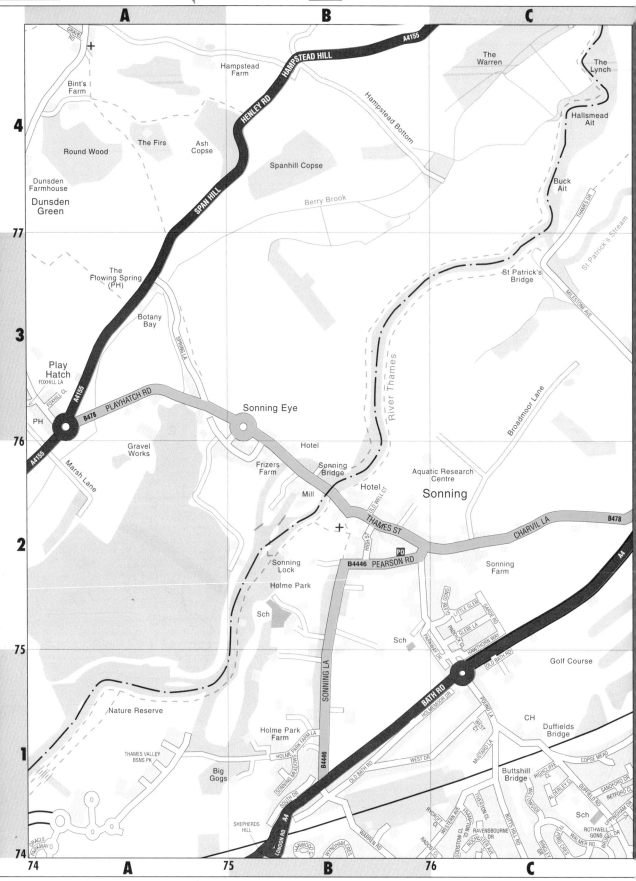

Street names are listed alphabetically and show the locality, the Postcode District, the page number and
a reference to the square in which the name falls on the map page

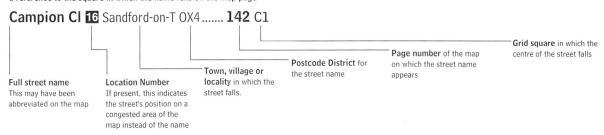

Campion Cl 16 Sandford-on-T OX4 .... 142 C1

Full street name
This may have been
abbreviated on the map

Location Number
If present, this indicates
the street's position on a
congested area of the
map instead of the name

Town, village or locality in which the
street falls.

Postcode District for
the street name

Page number of the map
on which the street name
appears

Grid square in which the
centre of the street falls

Abbreviations used in the index

App	Approach	Cl	Close	Ent	Enterprise	La	Lane	Rdbt	Roundabout
Arc	Arcade	Comm	Common	Espl	Esplanade	N	North	S	South
Ave	Avenue	Cnr	Corner	Est	Estate	Orch	Orchard	Sq	Square
Bvd	Boulevard	Cotts	Cottages	Gdns	Gardens	Par	Parade	Strs	Stairs
Bldgs	Buildings	Ct	Court	Gn	Green	Pk	Park	Stps	Steps
Bsns Pk	Business Park	Ctyd	Courtyard	Gr	Grove	Pas	Passage	St	Street, Saint
Bsns Ctr	Business Centre	Cres	Crescent	Hts	Heights	Pl	Place	Terr	Terrace
Bglws	Bungalows	Dr	Drive	Ho	House	Prec	Precinct	Trad Est	Trading Estate
Cswy	Causeway	Dro	Drove	Ind Est	Industrial Estate	Prom	Promenade	Wlk	Walk
Ctr	Centre	E	East	Intc	Interchange	Ret Pk	Retail Park	W	West
Cir	Circus	Emb	Embankment	Junc	Junction	Rd	Road	Yd	Yard

Town and village index

Abingdon 180 B4
Adderbury 23 D2
Adlestrop 40 B1
Aldworth 247 F2
Alvescot 133 E3
Ambrosden 81 E2
Appleton 158 A4
Ardington 215 F2
Ardley 50 B2
Ascott-under-Wychwood . 71 E1
Ashbury 228 A4
Aston 135 F2
Aston Rowant 167 E1
Aston Tirrold 237 F4
Avon Dassett 2 C4
Aynho 35 E4
Bampton 134 C2
Banbury 16 B4
Barford St Michael 32 C3
Barton-on-the-Heath 26 C3
Baydon 245 F1
Beacon's Bottom 189 E2
Beckley 111 D2
Begbroke 108 A4
Benson 204 A2
Berinsfield 182 B3
Berrick Salome 184 A1
Bicester 65 F2
Bishopstone 227 E2
Bix 243 E4
Black Bourton 133 F3
Blackthorn 82 A3
Bladon 91 B1
Bledington 54 B1
Bledlow Ridge 189 F4
Bletchingdon 93 D4
Blewbury 237 D4
Bloxham 21 E3
Bodicote 22 B4
Bourton 209 D2
Brackley 24 A4
Brightwell-cum-Sotwell 202 B1
Brill 98 A1
Brize Norton 116 B2
Broughton 15 E1
Buckland 154 C1
Bucknell 65 D4
Burford 100 B3
Buscot 171 D4
Carterton 115 F2
Cassington 107 E1
Caversham 259 D2
Chacombe 10 C2
Chadlington 57 D1
Chalgrove 184 C3
Charlbury 73 D2
Charlton-on-Otmoor 95 D2
Charney Bassett 176 A1
Chastleton 40 B4
Checkendon 241 E2
Chesterton 79 F4
Childrey 213 E2

Chilson 71 F2
Chilton 235 F4
Chinnor 168 B4
Chipping Norton 42 C1
Chipping Warden 5 F3
Cholsey 221 D1
Church Westcote 68 B3
Churchill 55 F3
Clanfield 152 C4
Claydon 1 B1
Clifton Hampden 181 E2
Cockpole Green 255 F4
Coleshill 191 D4
Combe 90 A3
Compton Wynyates 12 B4
Cottisford 37 F2
Crawley 103 F2
Cropredy 4 C1
Croughton 36 B4
Crowmarsh Gifford 221 F4
Cuddesdon 144 A2
Culham 180 A1
Cumnor 139 E3
Curbridge 117 E3
Cutteslowe 109 D1
Cuxham 185 E2
Deddington 33 F2
Denchworth 196 A2
Didcot 218 C4
Dorchester 182 B1
Drayton 179 D1
Drayton (Banbury) 15 E4
Drayton St Leonard 183 D3
Ducklington 118 A2
Duns Tew 47 E3
East Challow 214 A3
East Hagbourne 218 C3
East Hanney 197 D3
East Hendred 216 C4
Eastleach Martin 131 D4
Enstone 58 C3
Epwell 13 D3
Ewelme 204 C2
Eynsham 120 C4
Faringdon 172 C2
Farnborough (Berks) 233 F1
Farnborough (Warks) 3 F4
Fawley 226 B1
Fernham 193 D2
Fifield 69 E1
Filkins 132 B3
Finmere 39 E4
Finstock 88 B3
Forest Hill 125 F2
Freeland 106 A4
Fringford 52 B3
Fritwell 49 F4
Fulbrook 100 C4
Fyfield 157 E1
Garford 177 E3
Garsington 143 F1
Glympton 75 E4

Goring 249 E3
Great Barrington 99 E4
Great Bourton 9 E4
Great Coxwell 192 B4
Great Haseley 164 C4
Great Milton 145 E1
Great Rollright 29 D2
Great Tew 45 E4
Grove 196 C1
Haddenham 130 C3
Hailey 104 A3
Hampton Poyle 93 D2
Hanwell 8 C2
Hardwick 51 E4
Harwell 217 F4
Henley-on-Thames 244 B1
Hethe 52 A4
Highworth 190 A3
Hinton Waldrist 155 F2
Holton 126 B1
Hook Norton 30 A4
Horley 8 A2
Hornton 7 E4
Horspath 143 E3
Horton-cum-Studley 112 A3
Ibstone 207 F4
Ickford 128 A2
Idbury 69 D2
Islip 109 F4
Kencot 132 C3
Kennington 141 F1
Kidlington 92 C1
Kidmore End 252 B2
Kingham 55 D2
Kings Sutton 23 F3
Kingston Bagpuize 156 C1
Kingston Lisle 212 A2
Kirtlington 77 F2
Langford 132 B1
Launton 66 B1
Leafield 86 C2
Lechlade 150 B2
Letcombe Bassett 231 F4
Lewknor 187 D4
Little Compton 26 C1
Little Coxwell 192 C4
Little Milton 164 A3
Little Tew 45 D3
Long Compton 27 F3
Long Crendon 129 D3
Long Hanborough 90 B1
Long Wittenham 201 E4
Longcot 192 B1
Longworth 156 B2
Lower Basildon 249 F1
Lower Heyford 62 B3
Lower Odington 54 A4
Ludgershall 98 B4
Lyneham 70 C3
Mapledurham 257 F3
Marcham 178 B3
Marsh Gibbon 67 F2

Marston 123 F3
Merton 95 E4
Middle Barton 46 C1
Middleton Cheney 11 D1
Middleton Stoney 64 A2
Milcombe 21 D1
Milton (Abingdon) 199 E3
Milton (Banbury) 22 B2
Milton-under-Wychwood 85 D4
Minster Lovell 102 C1
Mixbury 38 B4
Mollington 4 A2
Moulsford 238 C2
Murcott 95 F2
Nettlebed 224 B1
North Aston 48 A3
North Hinksey Village 140 C4
North Leigh 105 D4
North Moreton 219 F4
North Newington 15 D2
Northmoor 138 B1
Nuneham Courtenay 161 F2
Oddington 94 C1
Over Norton 42 C3
Oxford 123 F1
Pangbourne 256 B3
Piddington 97 F4
Poundon 67 F4
Purley on Thames 257 D3
Radley 160 C2
Ramsden 88 A2
Ratley 2 A2
Reading 259 D2
Rotherfield Peppard 252 C4
Salford 41 F3
Sandford-on-Thames 161 D4
Shabbington 128 B2
Shalstone 25 F3
Shellingford 194 A4
Shenington 6 C1
Shilton 115 D3
Shiplake 254 C1
Shipton-on-Cherwell 92 A3
Shipton-under-Wychwood 85 F4
Shotteswell 8 B4
Shrivenham 209 D4
Shutford 14 A3
Sibford Ferris 19 D4
Sibford Gower 19 D4
Sonning 260 C2
Sonning Common 252 C3
Souldern 35 F2
South Hinksey 141 E3
South Leigh 119 E3
South Moreton 219 F3
South Newington 31 F4
South Stoke 239 E2
Southend 226 B4
Sparsholt 212 C2
Spelsbury 72 C4
Stadhampton 163 E1
Standlake 137 E2

Stanford in the Vale 194 C4
Stanton Harcourt 137 F4
Stanton St John 125 F4
Steeple Aston 62 A4
Steventon 198 C2
Stoke Lyne 51 D3
Stoke Row 241 F2
Stoke Talmage 165 F2
Stokenchurch 188 C3
Stonesfield 89 E4
Stonor 225 F3
Stratton Audley 52 B1
Streatley 249 D4
Sunningwell 159 F3
Sutton Courtenay 200 A4
Swalcliffe 19 F4
Swerford 30 C2
Swinbrook 101 F3
Sydenham 167 E4
Tackley 77 E3
Tadmarton 20 B4
Tetsworth 166 A4
Thame 147 F4
Tiddington 145 F4
Tidmarsh 256 B1
Towersey 148 C4
Turweston 24 B4
Uffington 211 E4
Upper Arncott 96 C4
Upper Heyford 62 C4
Upton 218 B1
Wallingford 221 E3
Wantage 214 C2
Warborough 203 D4
Wardington 5 F1
Wargrave 255 E1
Warmington 3 D2
Watchfield 191 F1
Watlington 186 B1
Wendlebury 80 A2
West Hagbourne 218 B2
West Hanney 196 C3
West Ilsley 235 D1
Westbury 25 D2
Weston-on-the-Green 79 D1
Wheatley 144 A4
Whichford 18 A1
Whitchurch-on-Thames . 256 B4
Wigginton 31 D4
Witney 104 B1
Woodcote 240 B1
Woodstock 91 D3
Woolstone 211 D2
Wootton 75 F3
Wootton (Oxford) 159 D4
Worminghall 127 F3
Wroxton 15 D4
Wytham 122 A3
Yarnton 108 A3

A P Ellis Rd GL54 ..... 68 A2
Abberbury Ave OX4 ..... 142 A2
Abberbury Rd OX4 ..... 141 F2
Abbey Centre OX14 ..... 180 A4
Abbey Cl OX14 ..... 179 F4
Abbey Pl Eynsham OX8 ..... 120 C4
  Oxford OX3 ..... 141 D4
Abbey Rd Banbury OX16 ..... 16 A4
  Oxford OX2 ..... 123 D1
  Witney OX8 ..... 117 F4
Abbey St OX8 ..... 120 C4
Abbot Ridge HP18 ..... 129 E3
Abbot Wlk HP18 ..... 129 E3
Abbots Wlk GL7 ..... 150 B2
Abbots Wood (E) OX3 ..... 142 C4
Abbots Wood (W) OX3 ..... 142 C4
Abbott Cl OX11 ..... 218 C4
Abbott Rd Abingdon OX14 ..... 179 F4
  Didcot OX11 ..... 218 C4
Abelwood Rd OX8 ..... 90 A1
Aberaman OX8 ..... 258 C3
Abingdon Dr RG4 ..... 259 E3
Abingdon Rd
  Carterton OX18 ..... 115 F2
  Clifton Hampden OX14 ..... 181 E2
  Culham OX14 ..... 180 B2
  Cumnor OX2 ..... 139 F2
  Didcot OX11 ..... 201 D1
  Dorchester OX10 ..... 182 B2
  Drayton OX14 ..... 179 D1
  Kennington Ox1 ..... 141 E2
  Oxford OX1, OX2 ..... 141 E3
  Standlake OX8 ..... 137 E2
  Steventon OX13 ..... 199 D3
  Sutton Courtenay OX14 ..... 180 A1
Abingdon Way OX9 ..... 129 F1
Ablett Cl OX4 ..... 142 A4
Abotts Mead OX10 ..... 239 D4
Abrahams Rd RG9 ..... 244 B2
Acacia RG9 ..... 244 B1
Acacia Ave OX4 ..... 142 C1
Acacia Cl OX18 ..... 115 F1
Acacia Gdns OX13 ..... 156 C1
Acacia Wlk Banbury OX16 ..... 9 D1
  Bicester OX6 ..... 65 F3
Ackerman Rd OX7 ..... 42 C2
Acland Cl OX3 ..... 124 B1
Acorn Cl OX6 ..... 65 F3
Acorn Way OX16 ..... 9 F1
Acre Ditch OX15 ..... 19 D4
Acre End St OX8 ..... 120 C4
Acremead Rd OX33 ..... 143 F4
Adderbury Ct OX17 ..... 23 D2
Adderbury Park OX17 ..... 22 C2
Addiscombe Chase RG31 ..... 257 D2
Addison Cres OX4 ..... 141 F3
Addison Dr OX4 ..... 142 B2
Addison Rd Banbury OX16 ..... 16 B2
  Reading RG1 ..... 259 D1
Adeane Rd OX44 ..... 184 B4
Adelaide St OX2 ..... 123 D2
Adkin Way OX12 ..... 214 B3
Admiral Cl OX4 ..... 142 C1
Adwell Sq RG9 ..... 244 B1
Akeman Ave OX6 ..... 81 E2
Akeman Cl OX5 ..... 78 A3
Akeman St OX8 ..... 90 A3
Akers La OX10 ..... 202 C1
Alan Bullock Cl OX4 ..... 123 F1
Albermarle St OX12 ..... 214 B4
Albert Rd Caversham RG4 ..... 258 C2
  Henley-on-T RG9 ..... 244 C1
Albert St Banbury OX16 ..... 16 B3
  Oxford OX2 ..... 123 D1
Albion Pl Chipping Norton OX7 42 C2
  Oxford OX1 ..... 141 E4
Albion St OX7 ..... 42 C2
Albury Cl RG30 ..... 258 B1
Albury View OX9 ..... 146 A3
Alchester Rd OX6 ..... 80 A4
Alchester Terr OX6 ..... 65 F1
Aldbarton Dr OX3 ..... 124 C2
Aldbourne Cl OX6 ..... 65 E1
Aldeburgh Cl RG4 ..... 259 E4
Alden Cres OX3 ..... 124 C2
Aldenham Cl RG4 ..... 259 E3
Alder Dr OX6 ..... 81 E2
Aldergate Rd OX6 ..... 65 E1
Alderley Cl Carterton OX18 .. 115 E1
  Woodstock RG5 ..... 260 C1
Aldrich Rd OX2 ..... 123 D4
Aldridge Cl OX10 ..... 204 A2
Aldsworth Ct OX8 ..... 117 F4
Aldworth Ave OX12 ..... 214 C3
Alesworth Gr OX3 ..... 124 A3
Alexander Cl
  Abingdon OX14 ..... 160 A2
  Upton OX11 ..... 218 B1
Alexandra Rd OX2 ..... 122 C1
Alexandra Sq OX7 ..... 42 B1
Alfred St Oxford OX1 ..... 123 E1
  Wantage OX12 ..... 214 B2
Alfred Terraces OX7 ..... 42 C1
Alfredstone Pl OX12 ..... 214 C2
Alfriston Pl OX16 ..... 9 D1
Alice Smith Sq OX4 ..... 142 B1
Alister Taylor Ave OX10 ..... 204 B1
All Hallows Rd RG4 ..... 259 E2
All Saints Cl OX13 ..... 178 B3
All Saints Ct OX11 ..... 200 C1
All Saints La OX14 ..... 180 A1
All Saints Rd OX3 ..... 124 B1
Allam St OX2 ..... 123 D2
Allder Cl OX14 ..... 159 F1
Allectus Ave OX6 ..... 81 E2

Allens La OX6 ..... 48 C1
Allens Orch OX17 ..... 5 F3
Alley The OX7 ..... 73 D2
Allin Cl OX4 ..... 142 C2
Allin's La OX12 ..... 216 B4
Allison Gdns RG8 ..... 257 E3
Allnatt Ave OX10 ..... 221 E4
Allnut Cl OX9 ..... 186 A1
Alma Green RG9 ..... 242 A2
Alma Pl OX4 ..... 141 F4
Almond Ave OX5 ..... 108 C3
Almond Dr RG4 ..... 259 F2
Almond Rd OX6 ..... 65 F2
Alpha Ave OX44 ..... 143 E1
Alston Wlk RG4 ..... 259 E1
Altus St OX6 ..... 63 D4
Alvescot Rd OX18 ..... 115 E1
Alvis Gate OX16 ..... 15 F4
Amberley Ct OX6 ..... 9 D1
Ambleside Dr OX3 ..... 124 A2
Ambrose Rise OX33 ..... 144 B4
Ambury Rd RG8 ..... 247 F2
Amersham Rd RG4 ..... 259 E1
Amey Cres OX13 ..... 159 D3
Amory Cl OX4 ..... 142 B2
Amos Ct OX16 ..... 16 B3
Ampney Orch OX18 ..... 134 C2
Amwell Pl OX10 ..... 220 C1
Amyoe Ct OX14 ..... 160 A1
Ancastle Gr RG9 ..... 244 B1
Ancholme Cl OX11 ..... 200 C1
Anchor La OX11 ..... 220 A2
Ancil Ave OX6 ..... 66 B1
Andersey Way OX14 ..... 179 F2
Anderson Cl HP14 ..... 188 C2
Andersons Cl OX5 ..... 108 B4
Andover Cl Bicester OX6 ..... 66 A2
  Reading RG31 ..... 257 E1
Andover La OX18 ..... 115 F1
Andover Rd OX10 ..... 204 B2
Andrew Rd OX10 ..... 203 D1
Andrews Ave NN13 ..... 36 C3
Andromeda Cl OX4 ..... 142 C1
Anemone Cl OX4 ..... 161 F4
Angelica Cl OX4 ..... 142 C1
Angle Field Rd RG4 ..... 259 E2
Anglesey Ct HP14 ..... 188 C3
Angus Cl OX16 ..... 16 A4
Anne Greenwood Cl OX4 .. 142 A2
Annesley Cl OX5 ..... 93 D4
Annesley Rd OX4 ..... 142 A2
Ansell Way OX7 ..... 70 A1
Anson Ave OX18 ..... 115 F1
Anson Cl Marcham OX13 ... 178 B3
  Wheatley OX33 ..... 144 B4
Anson Rd OX10 ..... 204 B2
Anson Way OX6 ..... 66 A2
Anthony Hill Rd OX10 ..... 204 B1
Anvil Ct SN7 ..... 194 C4
Anvil La OX12 ..... 214 A1
Anvil Paddock OX12 ..... 214 A1
Anxey Cl HP17 ..... 130 C3
Apley Way OX8 ..... 117 F4
Apple Cl RG31 ..... 257 D2
Appleby Cl OX16 ..... 15 F4
Appleford Dr OX14 ..... 160 A1
Appleford Rd OX14 ..... 180 A1
Appleton Rd Cumnor OX2 ... 139 E2
  Kingston Bagpuize OX13 .. 156 B2
  Longworth OX13 ..... 156 B2
Appletree Cl
  Sandford-on-T OX4 ..... 161 F4
  Sonning Common RG4 ..... 252 C3
Appletree Rd OX17 ..... 5 F3
Approach The OX6 ..... 65 E2
Apsley Rd OX2 ..... 123 D4
Arbury Banks OX17 ..... 5 F3
Arbury Cl OX16 ..... 16 C1
Arcade The Goring RG8 ..... 249 E3
  Wallingford OX10 ..... 221 E4
Archery Rd OX17 ..... 11 D1
Archway Rd RG4 ..... 259 D1
Ardington La OX12 ..... 197 D1
Ardler Rd RG4 ..... 259 E1
Ardley Rd Ardley OX6 ..... 50 B2
  Bucknell OX6 ..... 64 A2
  Upper Heyford OX6 ..... 48 C3
Argentan Cl OX14 ..... 179 E2
Argosy Cl OX44 ..... 184 C3
Argosy Rd Benson OX10 ..... 204 B2
  Carterton OX18 ..... 115 F1
Argyle St OX4 ..... 141 F3
Aristotle La OX2 ..... 123 D2
Arkell Ave OX18 ..... 115 E1
Arkwright Rd OX6 ..... 66 A2
Arlington Cl OX18 ..... 115 F1
Arlington Dr OX3 ..... 123 F3
Armour Hill RG31 ..... 257 E1
Armour Rd RG31 ..... 257 E1
Armour Wlk RG31 ..... 257 E1
Arncott Rd OX6 ..... 97 E4
Arncott Wood Rd OX6 ..... 96 C3
Arndale Beck OX11 ..... 201 D1
Arnold Rd OX4 ..... 141 F3
Arnold Way OX9 ..... 147 F4
Arnold's Way OX2 ..... 140 B4
Arnott's Yd HP18 ..... 129 E3
Arran Gr OX16 ..... 16 B3
Arrow Ct OX17 ..... 11 D1
Arthray Rd OX2 ..... 140 B4
Arthur Evans Cl OX13 ..... 159 D3
Arthur Garrard Cl OX2 ..... 123 D2
Arthur St OX2 ..... 123 D1
Arun Mews OX11 ..... 201 D1
Arundel Cl Carterton OX18 .. 115 E1
  Kings Sutton OX17 ..... 23 F3
Arundel Pl OX16 ..... 15 F3
Ascott Hill OX15 ..... 18 A1

Ascott Rd OX7 ..... 85 E4
Ash Cl Faringdon SN7 ..... 172 C2
  Kidlington OX5 ..... 108 C4
  Watlington OX9 ..... 186 A1
Ash Gr Chesterton OX6 ..... 79 F4
  Oxford OX3 ..... 124 B2
Ash La OX12 ..... 81 E2
Ashburton La OX15 ..... 30 A3
Ashbury Hill SN6 ..... 228 A3
Ashby Ct OX16 ..... 16 B3
Ashby Rd OX6 ..... 65 E1
Ashcombe Cl OX8 ..... 118 A4
Ashcroft Cl
  Caversham RG4 ..... 258 C3
  N Hinksey Vill UX2 ..... 122 A1
Ashcroft Rd OX16 ..... 16 B1
Ashdene Rd OX6 ..... 65 E1
Ashdown Way OX12 ..... 214 B4
Ashenden Cl OX11 ..... 159 F1
Ashfield Rd OX18 ..... 115 F1
Ashfields Cl OX12 ..... 197 E4
Ashfields La OX12 ..... 197 E4
Ashford Ave RG4 ..... 252 C3
Ashgate OX17 ..... 179 F2
Ashhurst Way OX4 ..... 142 A2
Ashlee Wk RG8 ..... 250 C4
Ashley Hill Pl RG10 ..... 255 F4
Ashlong Rd OX3 ..... 124 A3
Ashmole Pl OX4 ..... 142 C2
Ashmole Rd OX14 ..... 179 F2
Ashridge OX9 ..... 168 A3
Ashridge Cl OX16 ..... 16 B1
Ashville Way OX4 ..... 142 C2
Aspen Cl OX4 ..... 65 F3
Aspen Sq OX4 ..... 142 C1
Asquith Rd OX4 ..... 142 A2
Astley Ave OX5 ..... 108 C3
Astley Rd OX3 ..... 130 A1
Aston Ave RG31 ..... 257 D3
Aston Cl Abingdon OX14 ..... 179 F4
  Banbury OX16 ..... 16 C1
  Pangbourne RG8 ..... 256 B3
Aston Gdns OX9 ..... 167 E2
Aston Hill OX9 ..... 187 F4
Aston Park OX9 ..... 167 E1
Aston Rd Ducklington OX8 ... 118 A1
  Standlake OX8 ..... 137 D2
Aston St Aston Tirrold OX11 . 237 F4
  Oxford OX4 ..... 141 F4
Astrop Rd Kings Sutton OX17 . 23 F3
  Middleton Cheney OX17 .... 17 F3
Atkinson Cl OX3 ..... 124 C3
Atkyns Rd OX3 ..... 142 C4
Atnho Rd OX17 ..... 23 E2
Atwell Cl OX10 ..... 221 E4
Atwell Pl OX3 ..... 124 B1
Aubrey Ct OX4 ..... 142 A2
Audlett Dr OX14 ..... 180 A4
Austen Wlk OX6 ..... 65 E1
Austin Dr OX16 ..... 15 F4
Austin Pl OX14 ..... 159 F1
Austin Rd OX15 ..... 22 C4
Austin's Way OX15 ..... 30 B4
Auton Pl RG9 ..... 254 B4
Autumn Cl RG4 ..... 259 E4
Autumn Wlk RG10 ..... 255 E1
Avens Way OX4 ..... 142 C1
Avenue Four OX8 ..... 118 A4
Avenue La OX4 ..... 141 F4
Avenue One OX8 ..... 118 A3
Avenue Rd Banbury OX16 ... 16 C3
  Bourton SN6 ..... 209 D2
Avenue The Bloxham OX15 .. 21 E2
  Chinnor OX9 ..... 168 B3
  Great Tew OX7 ..... 45 E4
  Kennington OX1 ..... 160 C4
  Wheatley OX33 ..... 144 B4
  Wormingball HP18 ..... 127 F4
Avenue Three OX8 ..... 118 A3
Avenue Two OX8 ..... 118 A3
Avington Cl RG31 ..... 257 D3
Avocet Way Banbury OX16 ... 16 C2
  Bicester OX6 ..... 81 D4
Avon Carrow OX17 ..... 3 D4
Avon Cres OX6 ..... 65 D2
Avon Rd Abingdon OX13 .... 159 E1
  Harwell OX11 ..... 217 E1
Avon Way OX11 ..... 200 C2
Avonbury Ct NN13 ..... 24 A3
Avro Rd GL54 ..... 68 A3
Axis Rd SN6 ..... 191 F1
Axtell Cl OX5 ..... 92 B1
Aylesbury Rd
  Haddenham HP17,HP18 .. 130 B3
  Thame OX9 ..... 130 B3
Ayrshire Cl OX16 ..... 9 D1
Aysgarth Rd OX5 ..... 108 A3
Azalea Ave OX5 ..... 108 C3
Azalea Wlk OX16 ..... 9 D1
Azor's Ct OX4 ..... 142 A2

Bablock Hythe Rd OX13 ... 139 D2
Back La Aston OX18 ..... 135 E2
  Ducklington OX8 ..... 118 A2
  Eynsham OX8 ..... 120 C4
  Long Compton CV36 ..... 28 A3
  Sibford Ferris OX15 ..... 19 D4
Back Row OX12 ..... 40 B2
Back St Stokenchurch HP14 .. 188 B3
  Tetsworth OX9 ..... 166 A4
Backside La OX15 ..... 19 D4
Backsideans RG10 ..... 255 E1
Bader Dr OX6 ..... 63 E4
Badgemoor La RG9 ..... 244 B2
Badger Cl OX33 ..... 125 F2
Badger La OX1 ..... 141 D1
Badger Way OX16 ..... 16 C1

Badgers Copse OX14 ..... 160 C1
Badgers Rise RG4 ..... 259 D3
Badgers Wlk RG9 ..... 255 D2
Badswell La OX13 ..... 158 A4
Bagley Cl OX1 ..... 141 E1
Bagley Wood Rd OX1 ..... 160 B4
Bailey Cl OX12 ..... 214 B3
Bainton Rd Bucknell OX6 .... 65 D4
  Hethe OX6 ..... 52 A4
  Oxford OX2 ..... 123 D3
Bakehouse La OX17 ..... 8 B4
Baker Ave OX10 ..... 204 B1
Baker Cl Benson OX10 ..... 204 B1
  Bicester OX6 ..... 65 F4
  Oxford OX3 ..... 124 C1
Baker Rd OX14 ..... 179 F4
Baker St OX11 ..... 237 F4
Baker's Piece OX9 ..... 167 F2
Bakers La
  East Hagbourne OX11 ..... 218 C3
  Oxford OX1 ..... 141 F2
  South Newington OX15 .... 31 F4
  Swalcliffe OX15 ..... 19 F4
  Tadmarton OX15 ..... 20 B4
Bakers Piece OX8 ..... 104 A1
Bakers Sq SN7 ..... 193 D2
Bakery La Clanfield OX18 ... 152 C4
  Letcombe Bassett OX12 ... 214 A1
Baldon La OX44 ..... 161 F2
Baldons Cl RG8 ..... 250 C4
Balfour Cotts OX14 ..... 182 A3
Balfour Rd OX4 ..... 142 C2
Balfour's Field RG8 ..... 241 E3
Balham's La Ibstone RG9 .... 225 F4
  Stonor RG9 ..... 225 F2
Ball La OX5 ..... 77 D3
Ballard Chase OX14 ..... 160 A2
Ballard Cl OX7 ..... 46 C1
Ballards Cl OX7 ..... 85 E4
Balliol Cl OX5 ..... 77 E3
Balliol Dr OX11 ..... 219 D4
Balliol Rd Bicester OX6 ..... 65 F4
  Caversham RG4 ..... 258 B2
Balmoral Ave Banbury OX16 . 15 F3
  Banbury, Crouch Hill OX16 . 15 F2
Balmoral Cl OX11 ..... 219 D4
Balmoral Way OX17 ..... 23 F3
Balmore Dr RG4 ..... 259 D2
Bampton Cl OX4 ..... 142 B2
Bampton Rd Aston OX18 .... 135 E1
  Clanfield OX18 ..... 133 F1
  Curbridge OX8 ..... 117 D2
Banbury Gdns RG4 ..... 259 E4
Banbury Hill OX7 ..... 73 E3
Banbury La
  Kings Sutton OX17 ..... 23 F3
  Middleton Cheney OX17 .... 10 C1
Banbury Rd Adderbury OX17 . 23 D3
  Aynho OX17 ..... 35 E4
  Bicester OX6 ..... 65 F2
  Bloxham OX15 ..... 21 F3
  Chacombe OX17 ..... 10 B2
  Chipping Norton OX7 ..... 42 C2
  Chipping Warden OX17 .... 5 F3
  Cutteslowe OX2 ..... 109 D1
  Deddington OX15 ..... 33 F3
  Kidlington OX5 ..... 92 B1
  North Newington OX15 .... 15 E2
  Over Norton OX7 ..... 43 E3
  Oxford OX2 ..... 123 D2
  Shipton-on-C OX5 ..... 92 A3
  Shutford OX15 ..... 14 A3
  Swerford OX7 ..... 30 B1
  Tackley OX5 ..... 76 C2
  Warmington OX17 ..... 3 D1
  Woodstock OX20 ..... 91 E4
Bandet Way OX9 ..... 148 A3
Banjo Rd OX4 ..... 142 B3
Banks Furlong OX6 ..... 79 F4
Bankside Banbury OX16 ..... 16 C2
  East Hendred OX12 ..... 216 A3
  Kidlington OX5 ..... 92 B1
  Long Hanborough OX8 ..... 90 C1
  Oxford OX3 ..... 124 C2
Bannister Cl OX4 ..... 141 F4
Bannister Rd OX9 ..... 148 B4
Barbaras Meadow RG31 ... 257 D1
Barbrook Cl RG31 ..... 257 E2
Barbury Dr OX12 ..... 214 B4
Barclose Ave RG4 ..... 259 E2
Barcombe Cl OX8 ..... 8 C1
Barcote La SN7 ..... 174 A3
Bardolphs Rd RG4 ..... 258 B4
Bardwell Rd OX2 ..... 123 E2
Bardwell Terr OX6 ..... 65 F1
Barefoot Cl RG31 ..... 257 D1
Barfleur Ct OX14 ..... 160 A2
Barford Rd Bloxham OX15 ... 21 F1
  South Newington OX15 ... 32 A3
Barkdale Ave NN13 ..... 36 C3
Barkus Way HP14 ..... 188 C3
Barley Cl Lewknor OX9 ..... 187 D4
  Sibford Gower OX15 ..... 19 D4
  Wallingford OX10 ..... 221 E3
Barleycott La OX1 ..... 141 E2
Barleyfields OX11 ..... 218 B4
Barleyfields OX11 ..... 218 B4
Barlow Cl Milcombe OX15 ... 21 D1
  Wheatley OX33 ..... 143 F4
Barn Cl Denchworth OX12 ... 196 A2
  Kidlington OX5 ..... 108 B2
Barn End OX18 ..... 134 C1
Barn La Burford OX18 ..... 100 B3
  Henley-on-T RG9 ..... 244 B2
Barn's Rd OX4 ..... 142 B2

Barnacre OX9 ..... 186 A1
Barnard Cl RG4 ..... 259 E3
Barnards Way OX12 ..... 214 C3
Barncroft OX10 ..... 221 E4
Barnes Cl OX11 ..... 218 C4
Barnes Rd OX11 ..... 218 C3
Barnett Rd
  Middleton Cheney OX17 ..... 17 F4
  Steventon OX13 ..... 198 C3
Barnett Way OX10 ..... 204 B1
Barnfield OX12 ..... 175 F1
Barnfield Cl OX6 ..... 65 F3
Barns Cl OX2 ..... 140 A3
Barns Hay OX3 ..... 123 F3
Barns La OX18 ..... 100 C2
Baroma Way RG9 ..... 244 C1
Baronhurst Dr OX44 ..... 184 B3
Barons Mead RG9 ..... 244 B1
Barracks La Oxford OX4 ..... 142 A4
  Oxford OX4 ..... 142 B3
Barrett St OX2 ..... 123 C1
Barrett's Way OX14 ..... 199 F3
Barretts Cl OX8 ..... 89 E4
Barrington Ave SN6 ..... 191 F1
Barrington Cl
  Berinsfield OX10 ..... 182 B3
  Oxford OX3 ..... 124 B1
  Witney OX8 ..... 117 F4
Barrington Rd SN6 ..... 209 E4
Barrow Hill Cl OX14 ..... 160 B1
Barrow Cl OX11 ..... 217 F4
Barrow Rd Abingdon OX13 .. 179 D4
  Harwell OX11 ..... 217 F4
Barry Ave OX6 ..... 65 E2
Barry Pl RG4 ..... 259 D1
Bartholomew Ave OX5 ..... 108 A3
Bartholomew Cl
  Ducklington OX8 ..... 118 A2
  Eynsham OX8 ..... 120 B4
Bartholomew Rd OX4 ..... 142 B2
Bartholomew Tipping Way
  HP14 ..... 188 C3
Bartlemas Cl OX4 ..... 142 A4
Bartlemas Rd OX4 ..... 142 A4
Bartlett Cl OX8 ..... 118 A4
Barton Cl OX17 ..... 23 F3
Barton La Abingdon OX14 .... 180 A4
  Oxford OX3 ..... 124 B2
Barton Rd
  Long Compton CV36 ..... 27 D1
  Oxford OX3 ..... 124 C2
Barton Village Rd OX3 ..... 124 B3
Barwell OX12 ..... 214 B3
Basil Hill Rd OX11 ..... 200 B2
Baskerville La RG9 ..... 255 D2
Baskerville Rd RG4 ..... 252 C3
Basmore La RG9 ..... 255 D2
Basset Way OX5 ..... 108 C4
Bassett Ave OX6 ..... 65 F2
Bassett Rd
  Letcombe Bassett OX12 ... 231 F4
  Oxford OX3 ..... 124 C2
Batchelors Row OX15 ..... 33 D2
Bateman St OX3 ..... 124 B1
Bates La OX6 ..... 35 E2
Bath Pl OX1 ..... 123 E1
Bath Rd Banbury OX16 ..... 16 B3
  Sonning RG4 ..... 260 C1
Bath St Abingdon OX14 ..... 179 F4
  Oxford OX4 ..... 123 F1
Battle Cl OX6 ..... 66 A2
Battle Rd Benson OX10 ..... 204 B1
  Goring RG8 ..... 249 F4
Baulking La OX12 ..... 194 B1
Baulking Rd SN7 ..... 211 F4
Bay Rd OX6 ..... 65 E1
Bay Tree Cl OX4 ..... 142 A2
Baydon Rd RG17 ..... 245 D3
Bayliss Rd RG10 ..... 255 E1
Bayswater Farm Rd OX3 ... 125 D2
Bayswater Rd Oxford OX3 .. 124 C2
  Stanton St John OX3 ..... 125 D4
Bayworth La OX1 ..... 159 F4
Beaconsfield Rd OX16 ..... 16 B1
Beagle Cl OX14 ..... 160 B1
Beagles Cl OX5 ..... 109 D4
Beanacre Rd OX15 ..... 30 A3
Beanfurlong OX17 ..... 10 C2
Beanhill Cl OX8 ..... 118 A4
Beanhill Rd OX8 ..... 118 A3
Bear Cl OX20 ..... 91 D3
Bear Ct OX18 ..... 100 C3
Bear La
  North Moreton OX11 ..... 220 A4
  Oxford OX1, OX44 ..... 123 E1
  Stadhampton OX44 ..... 163 E1
  Wallingford OX10 ..... 221 E4
Beargarden Rd OX16 ..... 16 B3
Bears Hedge OX4 ..... 142 A2
Beatrice Dr OX16 ..... 16 A3
Beauchamp La OX4 ..... 142 B2
Beauchamp Pl OX4 ..... 142 A2
Beaufort Cl Bicester OX6 .... 66 A2
  Didcot OX11 ..... 219 D4
Beaulieu Cl OX16 ..... 16 C3
Beaulieu Ct OX13 ..... 159 F3
Beaulieu Mews OX11 ..... 201 D2
Beaumaris Cl OX16 ..... 15 F1
Beaumont Bldgs OX1 ..... 123 D1
Beaumont Cl OX16 ..... 9 E1
Beaumont La OX1 ..... 123 E1
Beaumont Pl OX1 ..... 123 E1
Beaumont Rd Banbury OX16 ... 9 E1
  Oxford OX3 ..... 124 C2
Beaumont St OX1 ..... 123 E1
Bec Cl OX12 ..... 214 A3

Bec Tithe RG8 .... 250 C2
Beckdale Cl OX6 .... 65 D2
Becket St OX1 .... 123 D1
Beckett Ave SN6 .... 209 E4
Beckett Dr SN6 .... 209 E4
Becketts Cl OX8 .... 90 A1
Beckley Cl RG8 .... 250 C4
Beckley Ct OX3 .... 111 D1
Bedford Cl OX16 .... 15 F4
Bedford St OX4 .... 141 F3
Bedwells Heath OX1 .... 140 B1
Beech RG9 .... 244 B1
Beech Cl Faringdon SN7 .... 172 C2
Stokenchurch HP14 .... 188 C2
Watlington OX9 .... 186 A1
Beech Cres OX5 .... 108 C3
Beech Croft Rd OX2 .... 123 D3
Beech Gr OX18 .... 100 C3
Beech La RG8 .... 250 B4
Beech Rd Chinnor OX9 .... 168 B3
Eynsham OX8 .... 120 C4
Mapledurham RG4 .... 258 B4
N Hinksey Vill OX2 .... 140 B4
Oxford OX3 .... 124 B2
Purley on T RG8 .... 257 D3
Thame OX9 .... 147 E4
Wheatley OX33 .... 144 A4
Witney OX8 .... 117 F4
Beech Rise RG4 .... 252 C3
Beechcroft OX10 .... 182 B1
Beeches The
Deddington OX15 .... 33 F2
Goring RG8 .... 249 D3
Oxford OX3 .... 124 C2
Reading RG8 .... 257 E2
Beechey Ave OX3 .... 123 F2
Beechfield Cres OX16 .... 16 B2
Beechgate OX8 .... 118 A3
Beeching Cl OX11 .... 218 B1
Beechwood Cl RG8 .... 250 B3
Beesley Rd OX16 .... 16 A3
Beeson Cl RG8 .... 250 C4
Begbroke Cres OX5 .... 92 A1
Begbroke La OX5 .... 92 A1
Beggar's La OX13 .... 156 B1
Beggarsbush Hill OX10 .... 204 B1
Behoes La OX9 .... 240 B1
Beir Path The RG8 .... 239 D2
Belbroughton Rd OX2 .... 123 E3
Belfast Rd OX10 .... 204 B2
Belgrove Cl OX5 .... 108 B4
Bell Cl Cassington OX8 .... 107 D1
Grove OX12 .... 196 C1
Thame OX9 .... 129 F1
Bell Hill OX15 .... 30 A4
Bell La Aldworth RG8 .... 247 F2
Bampton OX18 .... 134 C2
Bicester OX6 .... 65 F1
Brightwell-cum-S OX10 .... 202 C1
Cassington OX8 .... 107 E1
Henley-on-T RG9 .... 244 C2
Lechlade GL7 .... 150 B2
Thame OX9 .... 129 F1
Wheatley OX33 .... 144 A4
Bell Lane Henley-on-T RG9 .... 244 C1
Hornton OX15 .... 7 E3
Bell's La OX15 .... 30 A4
Bellamy Cl OX13 .... 156 C1
Belle Terr OX18 .... 115 E1
Belle Vue Rd RG9 .... 254 B4
Bellenger Way OX5 .... 108 B4
Bellingham La SN6 .... 190 A1
Bellingham Wlk RG4 .... 259 D3
Belmont OX18 .... 214 B3
Belmont Mews OX9 .... 147 F4
Belvedere Rd OX4 .... 142 A4
Ben Cl OX5 .... 92 C1
Benares Gr RG4 .... 242 A2
Benhams La RG9 .... 226 B1
Bennett Cl OX17 .... 10 C2
Bennett End Rd HP14 .... 189 E4
Bennett Rd SN7 .... 172 C2
Bensgrove Cl RG8 .... 250 C4
Benson Cl OX6 .... 66 A2
Benson La Benson OX10 .... 204 A1
Crowmarsh G OX10 .... 221 F4
Benson Pl OX2 .... 123 E2
Benson Rd Abingdon OX14 .... 159 F1
Oxford OX3 .... 142 B4
Bentley Cl OX16 .... 15 F4
Benton Dr OX9 .... 168 B4
Benwells OX9 .... 168 B3
Bere Court Rd RG8 .... 256 B2
Berens Rd SN6 .... 209 D3
Bergamot Pl [20] OX4 .... 142 C1
Bergamot Pl OX4 .... 142 C1
Bergen Ave OX4 .... 179 E2
Berins Hill OX10 .... 241 D3
Berinsfield Rdbt OX10 .... 182 A2
Berkeley Cl OX16 .... 15 F4
Berkeley Rd
Sunningwell OX1 .... 140 C1
Thame OX9 .... 130 A1
Berkshire Rd RG9 .... 254 B4
Bernard Cl OX5 .... 108 B3
Berner's Way SN7 .... 173 D2
Bernewood Cl HP18 .... 129 E4
Bernwood Rd Bicester OX6 .... 65 F1
Oxford OX3 .... 124 C2
Berrick Rd OX44 .... 184 B3
Berry Cl OX4 .... 142 C2
Berry Croft OX14 .... 159 F1
Berry Hill Rd OX17 .... 22 C1
Berry La Blewbury OX11 .... 219 D1
East Hanney OX12 .... 197 D3
Berrylands Rd RG4 .... 259 D2

Berrymere Rd OX13 .... 159 D4
Berrymoor Rd OX16 .... 16 A3
Bertie Pl OX1 .... 141 E3
Bertie Rd OX1 .... 139 F3
Besbury La OX7 .... 55 F3
Bessels Lea OX11 .... 219 D1
Bessels Way OX11 .... 237 D4
Besselsleigh Rd
Appleton OX13 .... 158 C4
Wootton (Oxford) OX13 .... 159 D4
Bessemer Rd OX6 .... 66 A1
Bettina Cres OX16 .... 9 D1
Betty La OX1 .... 141 E2
Between Towns Rd OX4 .... 142 B3
Beverley Cl
Abingdon OX14 .... 159 F1
Benson OX10 .... 204 B2
Chalgrove OX44 .... 184 C3
Beverley Cres OX18 .... 115 F2
Beverley Gdns
Bicester OX6 .... 66 A2
Wargrave RG10 .... 255 F1
Beverley Rd RG31 .... 257 E1
Bevington Rd OX2 .... 123 E2
Bibury Cl OX8 .... 117 E4
Bicester Rd Bucknell OX6 .... 64 C4
Enstone OX7 .... 58 C3
Kidlington OX5 .... 109 D4
Launton OX6 .... 66 B1
Long Crendon HP18 .... 129 E3
Ludgershall HP18 .... 98 B4
Marsh Gibbon OX6 .... 67 F2
Middleton Stoney OX6 .... 64 A2
Stratton Audley OX6 .... 66 B4
Bickerton Rd OX3 .... 124 B1
Biddel Springs SN6 .... 190 A3
Biddlesden Rd NN13 .... 25 D3
Bigmore La HP14 .... 189 E1
Bignell View OX6 .... 79 F4
Bignolds Cl OX17 .... 4 B4
Billings Cl HP14 .... 188 C3
Billwell HP18 .... 129 E3
Bingley Gr RG5 .... 260 C1
Binsey La OX2 .... 122 C1
Binswood Ave OX3 .... 124 C1
Birch Cl RG4 .... 252 C2
Birch Rd Ambrosden OX6 .... 81 E2
Garsington OX44 .... 143 E1
Birchen Cl RG8 .... 250 C4
Birches The RG8 .... 249 D3
Birchfield Cl OX4 .... 142 C1
Birchwood Banbury OX16 .... 16 B2
Carterton OX18 .... 115 F1
Birchwood Cl RG4 .... 259 E3
Birchwood Dr OX5 .... 92 B3
Birchwood The RG31 .... 257 D3
Bird Cl OX16 .... 16 A3
Bird Wood Ct RG4 .... 253 D2
Birdlip Cl OX8 .... 103 E1
Birds La OX15 .... 13 D3
Bishop Kirk Pl OX2 .... 123 D4
Bishop's Wood OX44 .... 144 B2
Bishops Cl OX15 .... 32 C3
Bishops Orch OX11 .... 218 C4
Bisley Cl OX6 .... 66 A2
Bitham Rd Ox12 .... 233 E4
Bitterell OX8 .... 120 C4
Bix Hill Bix RG9 .... 243 F4
Henley-on-T RG9 .... 244 A3
Black Bourton Rd
Carterton OX18 .... 115 F1
Clanfield OX18 .... 133 F1
Black Croft OX12 .... 214 B3
Black's La OX8 .... 86 C1
Blackberry La OX4 .... 162 A4
Blackbird Assarts La OX7 .... 88 A1
Blackbird Leys Rd OX4 .... 142 B1
Blackburn Wlk OX4 .... 66 A2
Blackditch OX8 .... 138 A4
Blackfriars Rd OX1 .... 141 D4
Blackhorse La OX13 .... 158 C2
Blackhall Rd OX1 .... 123 E1
Blacklands Rd OX10 .... 204 A3
Blacklands Way OX14 .... 179 E4
Blacklocks Hill OX17 .... 17 D4
Blackman Cl OX1 .... 141 F1
Blackmore La RG4 .... 253 D3
Blacknall Rd OX14 .... 179 F3
Blacksmith La OX5 .... 95 D2
Blacksmiths Hill OX17 .... 35 E4
Blacksmiths Meadow [9]
OX4 .... 142 C1
Blackstock Cl OX3 .... 142 C4
Blackstone Rd OX10 .... 203 E1
Blackthorn Cl
Blackthorn OX6 .... 82 A2
Oxford OX3 .... 124 C2
Reading RG31 .... 257 D1
Blackthorn Rd OX6 .... 66 C1
Blackwater Cl RG4 .... 259 F2
Blackwater Way OX11 .... 201 D2
Blackwood Pl OX15 .... 22 C4
Blackworth SN6 .... 190 A4
Bladon Cl OX2 .... 122 C4
Bladon Rd OX20 .... 91 E2
Blaenant RG4 .... 258 C3
Blaenavon RG4 .... 258 C3
Blagrave Cl OX11 .... 200 C1
Blagrave La RG4 .... 258 B2
Blake Rd OX6 .... 65 F2
Blake Way OX9 .... 130 A1
Blake's Field OX11 .... 200 B1
Blakehope Burn OX11 .... 200 C2
Blakes Ave OX18 .... 118 B4
Blakes Rd RG10 .... 255 F2
Blandford Allcy SN6 .... 190 A3
Blandford Ave OX2 .... 109 D1

Blandford Rd OX5 .... 92 B1
Blandy Ave OX13 .... 156 C1
Blandy Rd RG9 .... 254 B4
Blankstone Cl OX8 .... 120 B4
Blay Cl OX4 .... 142 C2
Bleache Pl OX4 .... 142 B3
Bledlow Rd HP27 .... 169 F4
Bledlow Ridge Rd HP27 .... 169 E4
Blencowe Cl OX6 .... 65 F3
Blenheim NN13 .... 36 A4
Blenheim Cl OX11 .... 200 C1
Blenheim Dr Bicester OX6 .... 65 E2
Cutteslowe OX2 .... 123 D4
Launton OX6 .... 66 C1
Witney OX8 .... 117 F4
Blenheim Gdns OX12 .... 196 B1
Blenheim Hill OX11 .... 217 F4
Blenheim La OX8 .... 106 A3
Blenheim Orch OX12 .... 197 D3
Blenheim Pl OX10 .... 204 B1
Blenheim Rd
Banbury OX16 .... 16 C1
Caversham RG4 .... 259 D2
Kidlington OX5 .... 108 C4
Lewknor OX9 .... 186 B2
LIttle Milton OX44 .... 164 A3
Blenheim Rise OX17 .... 23 F3
Blenheim Way OX33 .... 143 E4
Blenhiem La OX33 .... 144 A4
Bleriot Rd GL54 .... 68 A2
Bletchingdon Rd
Bletchingdon OX5 .... 78 A2
Hampton Poyle OX5 .... 93 D2
Islip OX5 .... 93 F1
Blewbury Hill OX11 .... 237 E4
Blewbury Rd OX11 .... 219 D2
Blomfield Pl OX2 .... 123 D2
Blossoms Glade OX4 .... 160 C3
Blounts Court Rd RG4 .... 253 D3
Blowings The OX6 .... 106 A4
Blowingstone Hill OX12 .... 212 A1
Bloxham Grove Rd OX15 .... 22 A3
Bloxham Rd
Banbury OX15, OX16 .... 16 A2
Barford St M OX15 .... 32 C4
Bloxham OX15 .... 21 D1
Milcombe OX15 .... 21 D1
Blue Boar St OX1 .... 123 E1
Bluebell Ct [7] OX4 .... 142 C1
Bluebell Ride OX4 .... 160 C4
Blythe Pl OX6 .... 65 D2
Boathouse Reach RG9 .... 244 C1
Bobby Fryer Cl OX4 .... 142 C2
Boddington La OX8 .... 105 E4
Bodley Pl OX2 .... 123 D4
Bodley Rd OX4 .... 142 B2
Bohams Rd OX11 .... 236 B3
Bolney La RG9 .... 255 D3
Bolney Rd RG9 .... 255 D3
Bolsover Cl OX8 .... 90 A1
Bolton Rd OX16 .... 16 B3
Bolton's La OX8 .... 90 B2
Bonar Rd OX3 .... 124 C1
Bones La RG9 .... 254 A2
Bonham Pl OX18 .... 115 E2
Bonnersfield HP18 .... 129 E4
Boot St OX6 .... 89 E4
Boreford Rd OX14 .... 160 A1
Borough Ave OX10 .... 221 E4
Borough Rd NN13 .... 24 A3
Borough Wlk OX14 .... 159 F1
Borrowmead Rd OX3 .... 124 A3
Bosley Cres OX10 .... 221 E4
Bosley's Orch
Didcot OX11 .... 200 C1
Grove OX12 .... 196 C1
Bostock Rd OX14 .... 179 F4
Boston Rd Bicester OX6 .... 66 A1
Henley-on-T RG9 .... 254 C2
Boswell Rd OX4 .... 142 B2
Bothy The Aynho RG10 .... 35 E4
Wargrave RG10 .... 255 E1
Botley Rd OX2 .... 122 C1
Bottle Square La HP14 .... 189 E3
Bottom La RG8 .... 241 D2
Bottom Rd HP14 .... 189 E4
Boucher Cl OX12 .... 214 B4
Boulevard The OX5 .... 92 A1
Boulter Dr OX14 .... 160 A2
Boulter St OX4 .... 123 F1
Boults Cl OX3 .... 123 F3
Boults La OX3 .... 123 F3
Boundary Brook Rd OX4 .... 142 A3
Boundary Cl OX20 .... 91 E3
Boundary La RG4 .... 258 C2
Boundary Rd NN13 .... 24 A3
Bourlon Wood OX14 .... 159 E1
Bourne Cl Bicester OX6 .... 65 E1
Cutteslowe OX2 .... 109 D1
Bourne Rd OX15 .... 30 A4
Bourne Rd RG8 .... 256 C3
Bourne St OX11 .... 218 C4
Bourne The
Eastleach Martin GL7 .... 131 D4
Hook Norton OX15 .... 30 A4
Bourton Cl Clanfield OX18 .... 133 F1
Witney OX8 .... 117 F4
Bovewell OX6 .... 35 F2
Bovingdon Rd OX18 .... 115 F2
Bovington's Yd OX18 .... 135 E2
Bow Rd SN7 .... 174 C1
Bowbank OX13 .... 156 B2
Bowbank OX13 .... 156 B2
Bower Green SN6 .... 191 F1
Bowerman Cl OX5 .... 108 B4
Bowers La HP14 .... 189 E4
Bowfell Cl RG31 .... 257 E1
Bowgrave Copse OX14 .... 160 B1

Bowling Ct RG9 .... 244 B2
Bowling Gr HP14 .... 188 B3
Bowling Green Cl OX18 .... 134 C2
Bowling Green La RG8 .... 257 D3
Bowmen's Lea OX4 .... 35 E4
Bowmont Sq OX5 .... 65 D1
Bowness Ave Didcot OX11 .... 218 B4
Oxford OX3 .... 124 A2
Bowyer Rd OX14 .... 179 F4
Box Tree La OX9 .... 166 C2
Boxhedge Rd OX16 .... 16 A3
Boxhedge Rd W OX16 .... 16 A3
Boxhedge Sq OX16 .... 16 A3
Boxhill Rd OX14 .... 179 F4
Boxhill Wlk OX14 .... 179 F4
Boxwell Cl OX14 .... 160 A1
Bracegirdle Rd OX3 .... 124 C1
Bracken Cl
Carterton OX18 .... 115 E2
Reading RG31 .... 257 E1
Brackley Rd
Croughton NN13 .... 36 B4
Westbury NN13 .... 25 D3
Bradburys The OX6 .... 66 B4
Braddons Furlong HP18 .... 129 E3
Brading Way RG8 .... 257 E3
Bradlands OX3 .... 123 E4
Bradley Rd RG9 .... 224 A3
Bradley's St RG8 .... 241 D2
Bradmore Rd OX2 .... 123 E2
Bradshaw Cl OX5 .... 62 A4
Bradstock's Way OX14 .... 199 F3
Bradwell Rd RG31 .... 257 E2
Brae Hill HP18 .... 98 A1
Braemar Ct OX18 .... 115 E3
Braithwaite Cl OX16 .... 16 A3
Brake Hill OX4 .... 143 D1
Bramber Cl OX16 .... 15 F4
Bramber Mews RG4 .... 259 F2
Brambling Way OX4 .... 142 B1
Bramblings RG4 .... 258 C3
Bramblings The OX6 .... 66 A1
Bramley Cres RG4 .... 252 C3
Bramley Hts OX8 .... 117 F4
Brampton Chase RG9 .... 255 D2
Brampton Cl OX14 .... 159 F1
Brampton Dr OX18 .... 115 F1
Brampton Rd OX3 .... 124 C2
Bramshaw Rd RG30 .... 258 A1
Bramwell Pl OX4 .... 141 F4
Brandon Cl OX5 .... 108 B4
Brantwood Rise OX16 .... 16 A2
Brasenose Dr OX5 .... 92 C1
Brasenose Driftway
OX4 .... 142 C3
Brasenose La OX1 .... 123 E1
Brasenose Rd OX11 .... 200 B1
Brashfield Rd OX6 .... 65 F2
Braybrooke Cl OX7 .... 58 C3
Braybrooke Gdns RG10 .... 255 E1
Braybrooke Rd RG10 .... 255 E1
Braze La OX10 .... 204 A3
Braziers La OX10 .... 240 C3
Breedons Hill RG8 .... 256 B3
Brenda Cl OX16 .... 16 A2
Brendon Cl Didcot OX11 .... 200 B1
Reading RG30 .... 257 F1
Brentford Cl OX10 .... 220 C1
Brereton Dr OX12 .... 196 B1
Bretch Hill OX16 .... 15 F3
Brett Cl OX9 .... 148 A4
Brewer Rd OX13 .... 199 D2
Brewer St OX1 .... 141 E4
Brewers Ct OX4 .... 179 F3
Brewery La OX15 .... 29 F4
Brewery Row GL56 .... 26 C1
Brewery St SN6 .... 190 A3
Briaily HP14 .... 189 E1
Briants Ave RG4 .... 259 E1
Briar Cl Banbury OX16 .... 16 B1
Caversham RG4 .... 259 D3
Kidlington OX5 .... 92 B1
Briar Cl OX5 .... 92 B1
Briar Thicket OX20 .... 91 E3
Briar Way OX4 .... 142 C2
Briars Cl RG8 .... 256 C3
Briarswood HP14 .... 188 C3
Briarswood Cl HP14 .... 188 C3
Brice Rd OX6 .... 63 E4
Brick Hill OX15 .... 30 A3
Brickle La OX15 .... 21 F3
Bricks La HP14 .... 189 E2
Briden's Way HP17 .... 130 C3
Bridewell Cl OX8 .... 105 D4
Bridge Cl OX11 .... 219 D4
Bridge End OX10 .... 202 B4
Bridge Farm Cl OX12 .... 214 C4
Bridge Rd HP18 .... 127 F1
Bridge St Abingdon OX14 .... 179 F4
Bampton OX18 .... 134 C2
Banbury OX16 .... 16 B3
Caversham RG4 .... 259 D1
Islip OX5 .... 109 F4
Oxford OX1 .... 123 E1
Witney OX8 .... 104 A1
Bridges Cl OX14 .... 179 E3
Bridgewater Cl RG30 .... 258 B1
Bridle Cl OX16 .... 16 C2
Bridle Path RG8 .... 250 C4
Bridle Rd RG8 .... 250 C4
Bridus Mead OX11 .... 219 D1
Bridus Way OX11 .... 219 D1
Brierley Pl RG31 .... 257 E2
Briggs Cl OX16 .... 15 F2
Brigham Rd RG1 .... 259 D1
Brightwell St OX10 .... 202 C1
Brill Cl RG4 .... 259 D2
Brill Rd HP18 .... 98 A4

Brinds Cl RG4 .... 253 D3
Brinkburn Gr RG4 .... 16 C4
Brinkinfield Rd OX44 .... 184 B4
Bristol Rd Bicester OX6 .... 66 A2
Church Westcote GL54 .... 68 A3
Britannia Cl OX18 .... 115 F2
Britannia Rd OX16 .... 16 B3
Britnell Ct HP14 .... 188 C3
Britwell Rd Didcot OX11 .... 200 C1
Ewelme OX10 .... 204 C2
Watlington OX9 .... 186 A1
Brixton Hill OX10 .... 223 D2
Brize Norton Rd
Carterton OX18 .... 115 F1
Minster Lovell OX8 .... 102 C1
Brizewood OX18 .... 115 E1
Broad Cl Barford St M OX15 .... 32 C3
Kidlington OX5 .... 108 B4
N Hinksey Vill OX2 .... 122 A1
Broad End OX15 .... 16 C1
Broad Gap OX15 .... 16 C1
Broad Marsh La OX8 .... 106 A3
Broad Oak OX3 .... 142 C4
Broad St Abingdon OX14 .... 179 F4
Bampton OX18 .... 134 C2
Banbury OX16 .... 16 B3
Long Compton CV36 .... 27 F3
Oxford OX1 .... 123 E1
Uffington SN7 .... 211 E4
Broad Way SN7 .... 211 E3
Broadbrook La OX12 .... 212 C2
Broadfields OX4 .... 142 B1
Broadhead Pl OX3 .... 124 A3
Broadhurst Gdns OX4 .... 142 A1
Broadmarsh Cl OX12 .... 214 B4
Broadwaters Ave OX9 .... 147 F4
Broadway Didcot OX11 .... 218 C4
Harwell OX11 .... 217 F3
Kidlington OX5 .... 108 C3
Broadway Cl Harwell OX11 .... 217 F3
Witney OX8 .... 103 E1
Broadway The OX5 .... 95 D2
Broadwell Cl OX6 .... 65 E1
Broadwell Rd GL7 .... 132 B1
Brocklesby Rd OX4 .... 142 A1
Brocks Way RG9 .... 255 D2
Brode Cl OX14 .... 160 A1
Brogden Cl OX2 .... 140 C4
Brome Pl OX3 .... 124 C2
Bromeswell Cl OX6 .... 62 C3
Bromsgrove SN7 .... 172 C2
Brook Cl HP18 .... 98 B4
Brook Hill OX20 .... 91 D3
Brook La
Denchworth OX12 .... 196 A2
Thame OX9 .... 129 F1
West Hagbourne OX11 .... 218 B3
Brook Rd Bicester OX6 .... 65 E2
Great Tew OX7 .... 45 E4
Brook St
Aston Rowant OX9 .... 167 F2
Benson OX10 .... 204 A2
Oxford OX1 .... 141 E4
Sutton Courtenay OX14 .... 200 A4
Watlington OX9 .... 186 A1
Brook View OX4 .... 143 D1
Brook Way OX8 .... 90 A1
Brooke Rd OX16 .... 16 A2
Brookfield Cl
Cholsey OX10 .... 221 E3
Milton-u-W OX7 .... 70 A1
Brookfield Cres OX3 .... 124 A3
Brookhampton Cl OX44 .... 163 D1
Brooklime Wlk [16] OX4 .... 142 C1
Brooklyn Dr RG4 .... 259 D3
Brookmead Dr OX10 .... 221 E3
Brooksby Rd RG31 .... 257 E1
Brookside
Abingdon OX14 .... 159 F1
Cholsey OX10 .... 220 C1
East Hanney OX12 .... 197 D3
Great Tew OX7 .... 45 E4
Hook Norton OX15 .... 30 A4
Oxford OX3, OX44 .... 124 B1
Thame OX9 .... 129 F1
Watlington OX9 .... 186 A1
Brookside Cl OX9 .... 145 F4
Brookside Estate OX44 .... 184 B4
Brookside Way OX15 .... 21 E2
Broome Way OX16 .... 16 C4
Broomfield Rd RG30 .... 258 A1
Broughton Cl OX18 .... 258 B1
Broughton Rd OX16 .... 15 F2
Broughtons Cl OX3 .... 123 F3
Brown's La Charlbury OX7 .... 73 D2
Woodstock OX20 .... 91 D3
Browning Dr OX6 .... 65 E2
Browning Rd OX16 .... 16 A2
Browns Cl OX2 .... 140 A4
Brrokside OX11 .... 217 F4
Bruern Rd OX7 .... 70 A2
Brunel Cres OX12 .... 196 B1
Brunel Dr RG5 .... 260 C1
Brunel Rd OX11 .... 218 B4
Brunstock Beck OX11 .... 200 C2
Bryan Way OX12 .... 214 C3
Bryants Pl RG8 .... 257 D3
Bryony Cl OX4 .... 143 C1
Brywarth La GL7 .... 150 A3
Buchan Rd OX6 .... 65 E2
Buchanan Rd OX6 .... 96 C4
Buck Side RG4 .... 259 D1
Buckingham Cl OX11 .... 219 D4
Buckingham Cres OX6 .... 65 F2
Buckingham Dr RG4 .... 259 D3

Buckingham Rd
Bicester OX6 .... 65 F2
Brackley NN13 .... 24 A3
Buckingham St OX1 .... 141 E4
Buckland Ct OX5 .... 108 C4
Buckland Rd
Bampton OX18 .... 154 B4
Buckland SN7 .... 174 C4
Charney Bassett OX12 ... 175 F1
Buckler Rd OX2 .... 123 D4
Bucklers Bury Rd OX14 .. 160 A2
Bucknell Ave RG8 .... 256 C3
Bucknell Rd OX6 .... 65 E2
Buckner's Cl OX13 .... 203 F2
Buckthorn La OX10 ...... 220 C1
Budd Cl OX20 .... 91 E4
Bulan Rd OX3 .... 142 C4
Bull Baulk
Middleton Cheney OX17 .... 11 D1
Middleton Cheney OX17 .... 17 F4
Bull Cl GL7 .... 132 A3
Bull Hill OX7 .... 72 A4
Bull La OX18 .... 135 F1
Bull Meadow The RG8 ... 248 C3
Bull St OX18 .... 135 F1
Bullingdon Ave OX10 .... 182 B3
Bullingdon Rd OX4 ...... 141 F4
Bullmarsh Cl OX6 .... 64 A2
Bullockspits La OX13 .... 176 B4
Bullring The OX15 .... 33 F2
Bulls La Ickford HP18 .... 128 A2
Kings Sutton OX17 .... 23 F3
Bullsmead OX13 .... 159 F3
Bulrush Rd OX4 .... 142 C1
Bulwarks La OX1 .... 123 E1
Bungalow Cl OX3 .... 111 E1
Bunkers Hill OX5 .... 77 D1
Bunyan Rd OX6 .... 65 E2
Burbush Rd OX4 .... 142 C3
Burchester Ave OX3 ..... 124 C2
Burchester Pl OX16 ...... 16 C4
Burcombe Way RG4 ...... 259 D2
Burcot la OX10 .... 182 B2
Burcot Park OX14 .... 181 F3
Burdell Ave OX3 .... 125 D2
Burditch Bank OX20 ..... 75 F3
Bure La OX11 .... 201 D1
Bure Pl OX6 .... 65 F1
Burford Rd
Black Bourton OX18 ...... 133 F3
Brize Norton OX18 .... 115 F4
Carterton OX18 .... 115 E2
Chipping Norton OX7 ..... 42 C1
Curbridge OX8 .... 103 E1
Minster Lovell OX8 ...... 102 B1
Swinbrook OX18 .... 102 B1
Witney OX8 .... 103 E1
Burford St GL7 .... 150 B2
Burgan Cl OX4 .... 142 B2
Burleigh Mews RG4 ...... 259 E2
Burlington Cres OX3 ..... 125 D2
Burlington Gdns OX16 ... 16 A2
Burnhams The HP18 ..... 128 B2
Burns Cl HP18 .... 129 E4
Burns Cres OX6 .... 65 E2
Burns Rd OX16 .... 16 A2
Burr Cl OX8 .... 120 A1
Burr St OX11 .... 217 F4
Burra Cl OX4 .... 161 D4
Burrows Cl OX3 .... 124 B2
Burrows Hill OX10 .... 204 C2
Bursill Cl OX3 .... 125 D2
Burswin Rd OX18 .... 115 E3
Burt's La HP18 .... 129 E3
Burton Cl OX14 .... 179 E3
Burton Pl OX4 .... 142 C1
Burwell Cl OX8 .... 117 F4
Burwell Dr OX8 .... 117 F4
Burwell Meadow OX8 .... 117 F3
Bury Mead OX8 .... 138 A4
Bury St OX14 .... 179 F4
Burycroft Rd OX15 ...... 30 A3
Burycroft The OX14 ..... 180 A2
Buryhook Cnr OX33 ...... 126 B1
Buryway La CV36 .... 27 F4
Busby Cl OX8 .... 89 E4
Busby's Cl OX18 .... 152 C4
Buscot Dr OX14 .... 160 A1
Busgrove La RG9 .... 242 A2
Bush Furlong OX11 ...... 201 D1
Bush The HP17 .... 130 C3
Bushey Cl OX2 .... 122 A1
Bushey Leys Cl OX3 ..... 124 C3
Bushy Row OX8 .... 134 C2
Butcher's Hill OX7 ...... 45 E4
Butcher's Row OX16 ..... 16 B3
Butler Cl Bloxham OX15 .. 21 F3
Horspath OX33 .... 143 E3
Oxford OX2, OX33 ...... 123 D2
Butler's Field GL7 ...... 150 B3
Butlers Cl CV36 .... 28 A3
Butlers Dr OX18 .... 115 F1
Butlers Orch RG8 .... 252 B2
Butlers Pond RG8 ...... 250 B1
Butlers Rd CV36 .... 28 B3
Buttercup Sq 8 OX4 ... 142 C1
Butterfly HP14 .... 188 C2
Buttermarket OX9 ...... 147 F4
Buttermilk La OX8 ...... 86 C1
Butterworth Pl OX4 ..... 142 C1
Butterwyke Pl OX1 ...... 141 E4
Butts Cl OX17 .... 35 E4
Butts Hill Rd RG5 .... 260 C1

Butts La OX3 .... 123 F4
Butts Rd Faringdon SN7 .. 172 C1
Horspath OX33 .... 143 E3
Butts The Aynho OX17 ... 35 E4
Long Compton CV36 ..... 27 F3
Merton OX6 .... 95 E4
Standlake OX8 .... 137 E2
Butts Way OX9 .... 167 E1
Buxton Ave RG4 .... 258 C2
Buzzards Cl OX17 .... 9 E3
Byeway The OX16 .... 16 C4
Byfield Rd OX17 .... 5 F4
Byres The HP17 .... 130 C3
Byron Cl OX14 .... 179 E3
Byron Rd OX16 .... 16 A2
Byron Way OX6 .... 65 E2

Cadogan Cl RG4 .... 259 F2
Cadogan Park OX20 ..... 91 D3
Caernarvon Way OX16 ... 15 F3
Caesers Gate NN13 ..... 24 A3
Calais Dene OX18 .... 134 C2
Calais La OX8 .... 136 C3
Calcot Cl OX3 .... 124 C1
Calcroft La
Clanfield OX18 .... 133 E1
Kencot OX18 .... 132 C2
Caldecott Cl OX14 ...... 179 E3
Caldecott Rd OX14 ..... 179 F3
Calder Cl OX16 .... 16 C4
Calder Way OX11 ...... 201 D1
Caldicott Cl OX10 ...... 203 D3
Caleta Cl RG4 .... 259 E1
Calthorpe Rd OX16 ..... 16 B3
Calthorpe St OX16 ..... 16 B3
Calves Cl OX5 .... 108 B4
Cam Cl OX11 .... 200 C1
Cambrai Cl OX14 ...... 200 C4
Cambridge Terr OX1 .... 141 E4
Camden Cl GL56 .... 26 C3
Camel Cross OX12 ...... 214 B3
Camellias The OX16 .... 9 D1
Cameron Ave OX14 ..... 160 B1
Camp La Ratley OX15 ... 2 B2
Warmington OX17 ...... 2 B2
Camp Rd OX6 .... 63 E4
Campbell Cl OX6 .... 65 F1
Campbell Rd OX4 ...... 142 A3
Campbells Cl OX20 .... 91 E3
Campden Cl OX8 .... 103 F1
Campion Cl
Carterton OX18 .... 115 F1
16 Sandford-on-T OX4 .. 142 C1
Campion Hall Dr OX11 .. 219 D4
Campion Rd OX14 ...... 180 A4
Canada Cl OX16 .... 16 B4
Canada La SN7 .... 172 C2
Canal Ct OX12 .... 214 B4
Canal La OX15 .... 16 C1
Canal St Banbury OX16 .. 16 B3
Oxford OX2 .... 123 D1
Canal Way OX12 .... 214 A3
Cane La OX12 .... 214 B4
Canning Cres OX1 ...... 141 F3
Cannons Field OX3 ..... 123 F3
Canon Hill's Gdns SN6 .. 209 E3
Canterbury Cl OX16 .... 17 D4
Canterbury Rd OX2 .... 123 D2
Capel Cl OX2 .... 123 D4
Caps La OX10 .... 221 D1
Cardiff Rd RG1 .... 258 C1
Cardigan St
Oxford OX2 .... 123 D1
Oxford OX2 .... 123 D2
Cardinal Cl
Caversham RG4 .... 259 D1
Oxford OX4 .... 142 A2
Cardwell Cres OX3 ..... 124 A1
Carey Cl OX2 .... 108 C1
Cariad Ct RG4 .... 249 D4
Carisbrooke Cl RG4 .... 259 E3
Carlesgill Pl RG9 ...... 254 C4
Carling Rd RG4 .... 252 C3
Carlisle Rd RG31 ...... 257 F2
Carlton Cl OX12 ...... 196 B1
Carlton Rd
Caversham RG4 .... 258 C3
Cutteslowe OX2 .... 109 D1
Caroline St OX4 .... 123 F1
Carpenter Cl OX4 ..... 142 B1
Carr Ave OX18 .... 115 E1
Carse Cl OX14 .... 160 A2
Carswell Cres OX6 ..... 63 E4
Carswell La SN7 ...... 154 A1
Carter Cl OX3 .... 124 C1
Carter Cres SN7 ...... 172 C2
Carters Cl OX18 ...... 115 E1
Carters La HP18 ...... 129 D4
Carterton Rd OX18 .... 116 A2
Cartwright Gdns OX17 .. 35 E4
Cassington Rd
Cassington OX8 .... 121 D4
Eynsham OX8 .... 121 D4
Yarnton OX5 .... 108 A3
Castle Cl Benson OX10 .. 203 F2
Bicester OX6 .... 65 E4
Castle Cres SN7 ...... 193 F4
Castle Fields OX6 ..... 50 A2
Castle La OX10 .... 221 E4
Castle Rd Lewknor OX9 .. 186 B2
Wootton OX20 .... 75 F3
Castle Sh Ctr OX16 .... 16 B3
Castle Sq OX10 ...... 203 F2
Castle St
Banbury OX15, OX16 ... 16 B3
Deddington OX15 ...... 33 F2
Marsh Gibbon OX6 ..... 67 F2
Oxford OX1 .... 123 E1

Castle St continued
Steventon OX13 .... 198 C2
Wallingford OX10 ...... 221 E4
Castle Wlk OX11 ...... 200 C1
Caswell La OX8 .... 116 C3
Cat La Ewelme OX10 ... 204 C2
Stadhampton OX44 ..... 163 E1
Cat St OX12 .... 216 B3
Catharine Cl OX14 .... 160 C2
Catherine Cl SN6 ..... 209 E3
Catherine St OX4 ..... 142 A3
Catmore Cl OX12 ..... 214 B4
Catmore Rd RG20 ..... 234 C1
Catsham La
Chadlington OX20 ...... 72 B3
Chilson OX7 .... 72 B3
Catslip RG9 .... 224 C1
Catte St OX1 .... 123 E1
Cattle Mkt OX7 ...... 42 C2
Catwell Cl OX4 ...... 142 A3
Caudwell Cl Drayton OX14 .. 179 D1
Grove OX12 .... 196 C1
Causeway Banbury OX16 .. 16 C3
Bicester OX6 .... 65 F1
Bletchingdon OX5 ..... 93 D4
Causeway The
East Hanney OX12 ..... 197 D3
Steventon OX13 .... 198 C2
Woodstock OX20 ...... 91 D3
Causmans Way RG31 ... 257 E3
Cavalier Rd OX9 ...... 130 A1
Cave St OX1 .... 123 F1
Cavell Rd OX4 .... 142 A3
Cavendish Dr OX3 .... 123 F3
Cavendish Pl OX6 .... 52 B1
Cavendish Rd
Caversham RG4 .... 259 D3
Cutteslowe OX2 .... 123 D4
Cavendish Wlk OX9 ... 130 A1
Caversham Park Rd RG4 .. 259 F3
Caversham Rd RG1 ..... 259 D1
Cawley Rd OX17 ...... 23 D3
Cawsham Gdns RG4 ... 259 E2
Caxton Cl RG30 ...... 258 B1
Caxton Ct RG9 .... 244 C1
Cecil Aldin Dr RG31 ... 257 E2
Cecil Sharpe Cl OX3 .. 124 B1
Cedar RG9 .... 244 B1
Cedar Cl OX16 .... 16 B1
Cedar Cres OX9 ...... 147 E4
Cedar Ct OX4 .... 142 B3
Cedar Dr Bicester OX6 .. 65 F2
Pangbourne RG8 .... 256 B2
Cedar Rd Faringdon SN7 .. 172 C2
N Hinksey Vill OX2 ..... 140 B4
Cedar Villa OX16 ..... 16 A3
Cedar Wood Cres RG4 .. 259 D2
Cedars The Benson OX10 .. 204 A3
Reading RG31 .... 257 E1
Celandine Pl 6 OX4 .. 142 C1
Celsea Pl OX10 ...... 221 D1
Cemetery Rd
Abingdon OX14 .... 179 E4
Bicester OX6 .... 65 F1
Centaury Pl OX4 ..... 143 D1
Centenary Bsns Pk RG9 .. 244 C1
Centre Rise OX33 .... 143 E3
Centre St OX16 ...... 16 C4
Centremead OX2 .... 141 D4
Chacombe Rd OX17 .. 10 C1
Chadlington Rd
Oxford OX2 .... 123 E3
Spelsbury OX7 .... 72 C4
Chaffinch Wlk OX4 ... 142 C1
Chainhill Rd OX12 ... 214 C1
Chalcraft Cl RG9 ..... 254 B4
Chalfont Cl OX2 ..... 123 D3
Chalford Cl OX7 ..... 42 C2
Chalford Rd OX7 .... 167 D2
Chalgrove Rd OX9 ... 130 A1
Chalgrove Way RG4 .. 259 E3
Chalk Farm Rd HP14 .. 188 B3
Chalk Hill
Aston Tirrold OX11 ..... 237 F4
Shiplake RG9 .... 254 B3
Chalkhouse Green La
RG4 .... 253 D1
Chalkhouse Green Rd
RG4 .... 252 C1
Chalkhousegreen La RG4 .. 259 D4
Challenor Cl OX14 ... 179 F2
Challow Rd OX12 .... 214 A3
Chalmore Gdns OX10 .. 221 E3
Chalvey Cl OX6 ...... 65 E1
Chalvey Rd OX6 ..... 65 E1
Chamberlain Pl OX5 .. 92 B1
Champion Rd RG4 .... 259 E1
Champion Way OX4 .. 142 B2
Champs Cl OX14 ..... 160 B1
Chancel Way
Lechlade GL7 .... 150 B2
Marcham OX13 .... 178 B4
Chandler Cl OX18 .... 134 C2
Chandlers Cl
Abingdon OX14 .... 160 B1
Wantage OX12 .... 214 C2
Chapel Cl Leafield OX8 .. 86 C2
South Stoke RG8 ...... 239 E2
Chapel End NN13 .... 36 B4
Chapel Hill
Brize Norton OX18 ..... 116 A2
Swerford OX7 .... 30 C2
Watchfield SN6 .... 191 E1
Chapel La Adderbury OX17 .. 23 D2
Benson OX10 .... 203 F2
Berrick Salome OX10 .. 204 A4
Bledington OX7 .... 54 B1
Bledlow Ridge HP14 .... 169 F1

Chapel La continued
Blewbury OX11 .... 237 D4
Bodicote OX15 .... 22 C4
Chalgrove OX44 .... 184 B3
Charney Bassett OX12 .. 175 F1
Cropredy OX7 .... 4 C1
Enstone OX7 .... 58 C3
Fernham SN7 .... 193 D3
Great Bourton OX17 ... 9 E3
Great Rollright OX7 .... 29 D2
Hailey OX8 .... 104 A3
Kingham OX7 .... 55 D4
Little Tew OX7 .... 45 D3
Milton (Banbury) OX15 .. 22 B2
North Leigh OX8 ...... 105 D4
Northmoor OX8 .... 138 B2
Oxford OX4, OX44 .... 142 A1
Ratley OX15 .... 2 A1
Salford OX7 .... 41 F3
Shipton-u-W OX7 ..... 85 E4
Standlake OX8 .... 137 E2
Sutton Courtenay OX14 .. 200 A4
Turweston NN13 ...... 24 A4
Uffington SN7 .... 211 E4
Warmington OX17 .... 3 D2
Watlington OX9 ...... 186 A1
Chapel Rd Ashbury SN6 .. 228 A4
South Leigh OX8 ...... 119 D3
Stanford in the V SN7 .. 194 C4
Chapel Sq Deddington OX15 .. 33 F2
East Hendred OX12 .... 216 C3
Chapel St Bicester OX6 .. 65 F1
Bloxham OX15 .... 21 F2
Deddington OX15 ...... 34 C2
Hook Norton OX15 .... 30 A4
Oxford OX4 .... 141 F4
Warmington OX17 .... 3 D2
Watlington OX9 ...... 186 A1
Chapel Way Childrey OX12 .. 213 E2
N Hinksey Vill OX2 ..... 122 B1
Chapelwick Cl SN6 .... 209 D3
Chapmans La OX15 ... 34 A2
Chapmans Piece OX18 .. 100 C3
Charbridge La OX6 .... 66 A1
Charbridge Way OX6 .. 66 B1
Charlbury Cl OX5 ..... 92 B1
Charlbury Rd Finstock OX7 .. 88 B4
Oxford OX2 .... 123 E3
Shrivenham SN6 ...... 209 D3
Charles Ct OX16 ..... 16 B3
Charles Dr OX9 ...... 130 A1
Charles Evans Way RG4 .. 259 E1
Charles Rd OX10 .... 239 D4
Charles St OX4 ..... 142 A3
Charlton Park OX12 .. 214 C3
Charlton Rd Aynho OX17 .. 35 E4
Wantage OX12 .... 214 C3
Charlton Village Rd
OX12 .... 214 C3
Charney Ave OX14 ... 160 B1
Charter Way OX10 ... 221 E4
Charterville Cl OX8 ... 102 C1
Chartwell Dr OX7 .... 73 E2
Charvil La RG4 .... 260 C2
Chatham Rd OX1 ..... 141 E3
Chatsworth Cl RG4 ... 259 E3
Chatsworth Dr OX16 .. 16 C2
Chatterpie La OX8 ... 89 F3
Chaucer Cl Bicester OX6 .. 65 E2
Caversham RG4 .... 259 D3
Chaucer Ct OX10 .... 204 C2
Chaucer's La OX20 ... 91 D3
Chaundy Rd OX5 ..... 77 E3
Chaunterell Way OX14 .. 179 E3
Chawley La OX2 ..... 140 A3
Chazey Cl RG4 .... 258 B4
Chazey Rd RG4 ...... 258 B2
Chearsley Rd HP18 .. 129 F4
Cheatle Cl OX18 .... 100 C2
Checker Wlk OX14 ... 179 F4
Chedworth Dr OX8 .. 117 F4
Chelford Way RG4 ... 258 C2
Chelmscot Row OX17 .. 10 C4
Chelsea Cl RG30 .... 257 F1
Cheney Gdns OX10 ... 10 C1
Cheney La OX3 ...... 124 A1
Cheney Rd OX16 .... 16 C4
Cheney Wlk OX14 ... 159 F1
Chepstow Gdns OX16 .. 15 F3
Chepstow Rd RG31 .. 257 F1
Chequers Pl
Cholsey OX10 .... 220 C1
Oxford OX3 .... 124 C2
Cherbury Gr OX12 ... 214 B4
Cheriton Pl RG4 ..... 252 C2
Cherry Cl Caversham RG4 .. 259 E4
Kidlington OX5 .... 108 C4
Sandford-on-T OX4 .... 142 C1
Stratton Audley OX6 .. 52 B1
Warborough OX10 .... 203 D3
Cherry Orch SN6 .... 190 A3
Cherry Orchard La SN6 .. 190 A3
Cherry Rd OX16 .... 16 A4
Cherry St OX6 ...... 52 B1
Cherry Tree Cl Grove OX12 .. 214 C4
Kingston Bagpuize OX13 .. 176 B3
Stoke Row RG9 .... 242 A3
Cherry Tree Dr OX13 .. 159 E1
Cherry Tree Rd OX9 .. 168 B3
Cherrys Cl OX15 .... 21 E2
Cherwell Ave OX5 ... 109 D4
Cherwell Bank OX6 .. 62 C3
Cherwell Business Centre
OX5 .... 92 B1
Cherwell Cl
Abingdon OX14 .... 160 A1
Bicester OX6 .... 65 E1
Didcot OX11 .... 200 C2
Wallingford OX10 ..... 221 E4
Cherwell Dr OX3 .... 123 F3

Cherwell Rd
Berinsfield OX10 ...... 182 B3
Caversham RG4 .... 259 D3
Cherwell st Banbury OX16 .. 16 B4
Oxford OX4 .... 123 F1
Cheshire Dr OX6 .... 63 E4
Cheshire Rd OX9 .... 148 B4
Chester St Caversham RG4 .. 259 E4
Oxford OX4 .... 141 F4
Chester Way OX16 ... 15 F3
Chestnut Ave
Caversham RG4 .... 259 F2
Faringdon SN7 .... 172 C2
Oxford OX3 .... 124 B2
Radley OX14 .... 160 C2
Thame OX9 .... 147 E4
Chestnut Cl Bix RG9 .. 243 F4
Chesterton OX6 ...... 80 A4
Launton OX6 .... 66 B1
Witney OX8 .... 104 A1
Chestnut Dr OX7 .... 71 D1
Chestnut End OX6 ... 65 F3
Chestnut Gr RG8 .... 257 E3
Chestnut Rd
Mollington OX17 ...... 4 A2
N Hinksey Vill OX2 ..... 140 B4
Chestnut Tree Cl OX13 .. 159 E1
Chestnuts The
Abingdon OX14 .... 160 B1
Brize Norton OX18 .... 116 B2
Deddington OX15 ..... 34 C2
Kirtlington OX5 .... 78 A2
Shiplake RG9 .... 255 D2
Wantage OX12 .... 214 C3
Chetwode OX16, OX17 .. 16 A4
Chetwyn Mead OX18 .. 134 C2
Cheviot Way OX16 ... 8 C1
Cheyne La OX18 ..... 134 C2
Chibnall Cl OX44 .... 184 B3
Chichester Cl OX16 .. 65 F1
Chichester Pl OX18 .. 116 B2
Chichester Wlk OX16 .. 9 D1
Chiers Dr OX16 ..... 179 E1
Chilbridge Rd OX8 ... 120 B4
Chilbrook OX11 ..... 217 F3
Childrey Way
Abingdon OX14 .... 160 A1
East Challow OX12 .... 213 F2
Chilgrove Dr OX6 .... 49 F1
Chillingworth Cres OX3 .. 142 C4
Chilswell La
Sunningwell OX1 ...... 141 D1
Wootton (Oxford) OX1 .. 140 C2
Chilswell Rd OX1 .... 141 E4
Chiltern Bsns Ctr OX4 .. 142 C2
Chiltern Cl Benson OX10 .. 203 F3
Berinsfield OX10 ...... 182 B3
Chalgrove OX44 .... 184 C3
Henley-on-T RG9 ...... 254 A4
Chiltern Cres OX10 ... 221 D4
Chiltern Ct RG4 ..... 259 D3
Chiltern Gdns OX9 ... 186 B1
Chiltern Gr OX9 ..... 148 A4
Chiltern Rd
Caversham RG4 .... 259 E2
Rotherfield Peppard RG9 .. 252 C4
Chiltern Ridge HP14 .. 188 B2
Chiltern View
Little Milton OX44 ..... 164 A4
Purley on T RG8 ...... 257 E2
Tetsworth OX9 .... 166 A4
Chiltern Wlk RG8 .... 256 C3
Chilton Cl OX14 ..... 160 A1
Chilton Rd
Long Crendon HP18 ... 129 E4
Upton OX11 .... 218 A1
Chilworth Rd OX44 ... 145 E2
Chinalls Cl MK18 .... 39 E3
Chinnock Brook OX11 .. 200 C2
Chinnor Hill OX9 .... 168 C2
Chinnor Rd
Aston Rowant OX9 ..... 167 E1
Bledlow Ridge HP14 .... 169 E2
Chinnor OX9 .... 168 A2
Thame OX9 .... 148 B3
Towersey OX9 .... 148 C4
Chipmunk Rd OX10 .. 204 B2
Chipperfield Park Rd
OX15 .... 21 F3
Chipping Norton Rd
Chadlington OX7 ...... 57 D2
Hook Norton OX15 .... 30 A4
Choicehill Rd OX7 ... 42 C3
Cholsey Cl OX4 ..... 142 B2
Cholswell Rd OX13 ... 159 E1
Chorefields OX5 ..... 92 B1
Choswell Spring OX4 .. 142 C1
Chowns Cl OX9 ..... 148 A4
Christchurch Ct OX16 .. 16 B3
Church Ave
Henley-on-T RG9 ...... 244 C1
Kings Sutton OX17 .... 23 F3
Church Cl Adderbury OX17 .. 23 D2
Ascott-u-W OX7 ...... 71 E1
Benson OX10 .... 203 F2
Black Bourton OX18 ... 133 F3
Charlbury OX7 .... 73 D2
Cuddesdon OX44 ...... 144 B2
Cumnor OX2 .... 121 E1
East Hagbourne OX11 .. 218 C3
Fringford OX6 .... 52 B4
Great Bourton OX17 ... 9 E3
Islip OX5 .... 93 F1
Longcot SN7 .... 192 B1
Merton OX6 .... 95 E4
Wardington OX17 ..... 5 F1
Weston-on-the-G OX6 .. 79 D1

Church Cowley Rd OX4 ..... 142 A3
Church End
Blewbury OX11 .... 219 D1
Croughton NN13 .... 36 B4
Drayton St L OX10 .... 183 D3
South Leigh OX8 .... 119 E3
Standlake OX8 .... 137 E2
Church Fields OX18 .... 89 E4
Church Furlong OX15 .... 20 B4
Church Green
Long Crendon HP18 .... 129 E4
Stanford in the V SN7 ...... 194 C4
Witney OX8 .... 118 A4
Church Hill Chilton OX11 ... 235 E4
Great Haseley OX44 .... 164 C4
Little Milton OX44 .... 163 F3
Stonor RG9 .... 225 E4
Tackley OX5 .... 77 D3
Warmington OX17 .... 3 D2
Church Hill Rd OX4 .... 142 A2
Church La Adderbury OX17 .. 23 D2
Aston Rowant OX9 .... 167 E2
Banbury OX15, OX16, OX17 .. 16 B3
Bicester OX6 .... 65 F1
Bishopstone SN6 .... 227 E2
Bledington OX7 .... 54 B1
Bledlow Ridge HP14 .... 189 F4
Bledlow Ridge HP14 .... 189 E4
Brackley NN13 .... 24 B1
Brightwell-cum-S OX10 .... 202 C2
Burford OX18 .... 100 C3
Cassington OX8 .... 107 E1
Chacombe OX17 .... 10 C2
Chalgrove OX44 .... 184 B3
Charlbury OX7 .... 73 D2
Charlton-on-O OX5 .... 95 D2
Chinnor OX9 .... 168 B3
Chipping Norton OX7 .... 42 C2
Coleshill SN6 .... 191 D4
Croughton NN13 .... 36 B4
Crowmarsh G OX10 .... 221 E1
Drayton OX14 .... 179 E1
Drayton St L OX10 .... 183 D3
Ewelme RG9 .... 206 A1
Fernham SN7 .... 193 D2
Fringford OX6 .... 52 B4
Fulbrook OX18 .... 100 C3
Hailey OX8 .... 104 A3
Hampton Poyle OX5 .... 93 D2
Hanwell OX17 .... 8 C2
Harwell OX11 .... 217 F4
Hornton OX15 .... 7 E3
Horton-cum-S OX33 .... 112 A3
Islip OX5 .... 93 F1
Kirtlington OX5 .... 78 A2
Langford GL7 .... 132 B1
Longworth OX13 .... 156 A2
Lower Heyford OX6 .... 62 B3
Ludgershall HP18 .... 98 B4
Marston OX3 .... 123 F3
Middle Barton OX7 .... 61 D4
Middleton Cheney OX17 ..... 10 C1
Milcombe OX15 .... 21 D1
Mixbury OX6 .... 38 C4
Mollington OX17 .... 4 A2
Rotherfield Peppard RG9 .. 253 D4
Shilton OX18 .... 115 D3
Shiplake OX9 .... 254 C1
South Moreton OX11 .... 219 F3
Steventon OX13 .... 198 C2
Towersey OX9 .... 148 C4
Wallingford OX10 .... 221 D1
Watlington OX9 .... 186 A2
Wendlebury OX6 .... 80 A2
Weston-on-the-G OX6 ...... 79 D1
Witney OX8 .... 118 B4
Yarnton OX5 .... 108 A2
Church Meadow OX7 .... 70 A1
Church Mews RG8 .... 257 E3
Church Mill OX8 .... 137 E2
Church Path
Stanford in the V SN7 ...... 194 C4
Stokenchurch HP14 .... 188 B3
Church Pl GL56 .... 54 A4
Church Rd Appleton OX13 .. 158 A4
Ardley OX6 .... 50 B2
Benson OX10 .... 203 F2
Brackley NN13 .... 24 A4
Caversham RG4 .... 259 D1
Chadlington OX7 .... 57 E1
Chinnor OX9 .... 168 B3
Cholsey OX10 .... 220 C2
Great Milton OX44 .... 145 D1
Hinton Waldrist SN7 .... 155 F1
Horspath OX33 .... 143 E3
Ickford OX9 .... 127 F2
Lewknor OX9 .... 187 D4
Long Hanborough OX8 ..... 106 B4
Lower Odington GL56 .... 54 A4
Milton-u-W OX7 .... 70 A1
North Leigh OX8 .... 105 D4
Pangbourne RG8 .... 256 B3
Radley OX14 .... 160 C2
Sandford-on-T OX4 .... 161 D4
Stokenchurch HP14 .... 188 B3
Thame OX9 .... 129 F1
Weston-on-the-G OX6 ...... 79 D1
Wheatley OX33 .... 144 A4
Church Rise OX7 .... 88 B3
Church Row
Bishopstone SN6 .... 227 D2
Childrey OX12 .... 213 E2
Church Sq OX5 .... 93 F1
Church St Ardington OX12 .. 215 F3
Bampton OX18 .... 134 C2
Barford St M OX15 .... 32 C3
Beckley OX3 .... 111 D2
Bicester OX6 .... 65 F1

Church St continued
Bladon OX20 .... 91 D1
Bledington OX7 .... 54 B1
Blewbury OX11 .... 237 D4
Bloxham OX15 .... 21 E2
Bodicote OX15 .... 22 C4
Caversham RG4 .... 259 D1
Charlbury OX7 .... 73 D2
Chipping Norton OX7 .... 42 C2
Deddington OX15 .... 33 F2
Didcot OX11 .... 218 C4
Ducklington OX8 .... 118 A2
East Hendred OX12 .... 216 B3
Eynsham OX8 .... 120 C4
Faringdon SN7 .... 172 C2
Fifield OX7 .... 69 D1
Henley-on-T RG9 .... 244 B1
Idbury OX7 .... 69 D2
Kidlington OX5 .... 92 C1
Kingham OX7 .... 55 D2
Marcham OX13 .... 178 B3
Marsh Gibbon OX6 .... 67 F2
Shellingford SN7 .... 193 F4
Shipton-u-W OX7 .... 85 E4
Stokenchurch HP14 .... 188 B3
Stonesfield OX8 .... 89 E4
Sutton Courtenay OX14 .... 180 A1
Upper Heyford OX6 .... 48 C3
Upton OX11 .... 218 B1
Wantage OX12 .... 214 B2
Wargrave RG10 .... 255 E1
Watlington OX9 .... 186 A1
West Hanney OX12 .... 196 A3
Wootton OX20 .... 75 F2
Wroxton OX15 .... 15 D4
Church View
Ascott-u-W OX7 .... 71 E1
Bampton OX18 .... 134 C2
Banbury OX16 .... 16 A2
Brackley NN13 .... 24 A4
Carterton OX18 .... 115 F1
Charlton-on-O OX5 .... 95 D3
Freeland OX8 .... 106 A3
Stoke Row RG9 .... 241 F3
Church View Rd OX8 .... 117 F4
Church Way
N Hinksey Vill OX2 .... 122 B1
Oxford OX4 .... 141 F2
Sparsholt OX12 .... 212 C2
Church Wlk Banbury OX16 .. 16 B3
Bishopstone SN6 .... 227 E2
Combe OX8 .... 90 A2
Oxford OX2 .... 123 D2
Shipton-u-W OX7 .... 70 B1
Shrivenham SN6 .... 209 E4
Upper Heyford OX6 .... 62 C4
Churchfield RG9 .... 223 E2
Churchfield La OX10 .... 203 F2
Churchill Cl Didcot OX11 .. 200 B1
Woodstock OX20 .... 91 D3
Churchill Cres OX9 .... 148 A4
Churchill Dr OX3 .... 124 B1
Churchill Gate OX20 .... 91 E3
Churchill Rd Bicester OX6 .. 65 F2
Chipping Norton OX7 .... 42 B1
Didcot OX11 .... 200 B1
Kidlington OX5 .... 108 C4
Kingham OX7 .... 55 D4
Churchill Way OX8 .... 106 A4
Churchlea OX17 .... 4 A2
Churchmere Rd OX14 ...... 180 A1
Churchward OX11 .... 200 C2
Churchward Cl OX12 .... 196 B1
Churchway RG20 .... 235 D1
Chure The OX5 .... 95 D2
Churnet Cl OX11 .... 201 D1
Cinnaminta Rd OX3 .... 142 C4
Cinnamon Cl OX44 .... 184 B4
Circourt Rd OX12 .... 195 F2
Circular Rd OX6 .... 81 D3
Circus St OX4 .... 141 F4
City Rd HP14 .... 189 E3
Clack's La Benson OX10 ... 222 B4
Crowmarsh G OX10 .... 222 B4
Clanfield Cres RG31 .... 257 E1
Clapcot Way OX10 .... 221 E4
Clare Terr OX18 .... 115 E1
Clarence Pl OX11 .... 218 C4
Clarence Rd RG9 .... 244 B1
Clarendon Cl OX14 .... 180 A4
Clarendon Dr OX9 .... 130 A1
Clarks La CV36 .... 28 A3
Clarkston Rd OX18 .... 115 E1
Clay Bank OX15 .... 30 A4
Clay Cl RG31 .... 257 D1
Clay La OX10 .... 204 B1
Claydon Rd OX17 .... 4 C2
Clayfields SN6 .... 209 D2
Claymond Rd OX3 .... 124 C2
Claypit La SN7 .... 211 D4
Claypits La SN6 .... 209 E4
Clays Cl OX3 .... 124 A3
Cleave The OX11 .... 217 F4
Cleavers OX9 .... 168 A3
Cleavers Sq OX4 .... 142 C1
Cleeve Down RG8 .... 249 E4
Cleeve Rd RG8 .... 249 D4
Cleeves Ave OX7 .... 42 C3
Cleeves Cnr OX7 .... 42 C3
Clematis Pl OX4 .... 142 C1
Clements Cl OX12 .... 214 C3
Clements Green OX11 ...... 219 F3
Clements La OX6 .... 67 F1
Clements Mead RG31 ...... 257 D1
Clements Rd RG9 .... 244 B2
Clerkenwell Cotts HP17 ... 130 C3
Cleve Ct RG8 .... 249 D4

Clevedon Rd RG31 .... 257 F2
Cleveland Cl OX5 .... 109 D4
Cleveland Dr OX4 .... 142 B3
Clevelands OX14 .... 160 A1
Cleveley Rd OX7 .... 58 C3
Clevemede RG8 .... 249 E4
Cleycourt Rd SN6 .... 209 D3
Clifden Rd HP18 .... 127 E3
Clifton Dr OX14 .... 179 F4
Clifton Rd OX15 .... 34 B2
Clifton Rise RG10 .... 255 F1
Clinton Cl OX4 .... 141 F2
Clive Rd OX4 .... 142 B3
Clock Tower SN7 .... 172 C1
Cloisters The
Caversham RG4 .... 259 D2
Wantage OX12 .... 214 B2
Close The Ardington OX12 .. 215 F3
Benson OX10 .... 203 F3
Chipping Warden OX17 ...... 5 F3
Epwell OX15 .... 13 D3
Great Bourton OX17 .... 9 E4
Henley-on-T RG9 .... 254 B4
Lechlade GL7 .... 150 B3
Stanton Harcourt OX8 ..... 138 A4
Woodcote RG8 .... 250 C4
Closes The OX5 .... 92 C1
Clover Cl OX2 .... 140 A3
Clover Pl Eynsham OX8 ... 120 B4
Oxford OX4 .... 142 C1
Coach La SN7 .... 173 D2
Coach Way OX10 .... 203 F2
Coalport Way RG30 .... 257 F1
Coates La RG9 .... 206 B3
Cobden Cres OX1 .... 141 E4
Cochrane Cl OX14 .... 204 B1
Cockcroft Rd OX11 .... 218 C4
Cockington Green OX16 ... 16 C4
Cockpit Cl OX20 .... 91 D3
Cocks La OX33 .... 125 E4
Cockshoot Cl OX8 .... 89 E4
Coggs Hill Rd OX8 .... 118 B4
Coghill OX5 .... 93 D4
Coker Cl OX5 .... 65 F1
Colborne Rd OX11 .... 218 B4
Coldharbour Cl RG9 .... 254 B4
Coldicutt St RG4 .... 259 E1
Cole Ct OX11 .... 200 C2
Colegrave Rd OX15 .... 21 F3
Colegrove Down OX2 ...... 140 A3
Colemans Hill OX3 .... 124 C2
Coleridge Cl Bicester OX6 .. 65 D2
Oxford OX4 .... 142 B3
Coleridge Dr OX14 .... 179 E3
Colerne Rd OX18 .... 115 F2
Coles La OX44 .... 184 B4
Colesbourne Rd OX15 ..... 21 E2
Collcutt Cl OX33 .... 143 E4
College Cl Cholsey OX10 .. 220 C1
Holton OX33 .... 126 B1
College Farm OX7 .... 57 D1
College Farm Cl OX5 .... 94 C2
College La Oxford OX4 ..... 123 E1
Oxford, Littlemore OX4 ... 142 A1
College The OX18 .... 101 F2
College Way OX33 .... 143 D3
Collett OX11 .... 200 C2
Collett Way OX12 .... 196 B1
Colley Wood OX1 .... 141 F1
Collice St OX5 .... 109 F4
Collier's La SN7 .... 173 D2
Collingwood Cl OX14 ...... 159 F1
Collingwood Rd OX11 ..... 218 B4
Collins St OX4 .... 141 F4
Collinsmith Dr OX12 ...... 196 C1
Collinsons Row OX7 .... 73 D2
Collinwood Cl OX3 .... 124 C2
Collinwood Rd OX3 .... 124 C2
Collyer Rd HP14 .... 188 C2
Colmore La RG9 .... 252 C4
Coln Rd OX11 .... 217 D2
Colne Cl Bicester OX6 ...... 65 E1
Grove OX12 .... 196 B1
Colne Dr Berinsfield OX10 .. 182 B3
Didcot OX11 .... 201 D2
Colony Rd OX15 .... 19 C4
Colterne Cl OX3 .... 124 A3
Coltman Ave HP18 .... 129 E3
Colton Rd SN6 .... 209 D3
Coltsfoot Sq 5 OX4 .... 142 C1
Columbia Way OX12 ...... 214 B4
Columbine Gdns OX4 ..... 143 D1
Colvile Cl OX18 .... 134 C2
Colwell Dr Abingdon OX14 . 179 E4
Oxford OX4 .... 125 D2
Witney OX8 .... 117 F3
Colwell Rd OX10 .... 182 B3
Colyton Way RG8 .... 257 E3
Combe Gate OX8 .... 90 A2
Combe Rd Oxford OX2 .... 123 D1
Stonesfield OX8 .... 89 E4
Combes SN7 .... 173 D2
Combewell OX44 .... 143 E1
Comfrey Rd OX4 .... 142 C1
Common Cl
North Leigh OX8 .... 105 D3
Shrivenham SN6 .... 209 E4
Common La OX7 .... 42 B1
Common Rd Beckley OX3 .. 110 C2
North Leigh OX8 .... 105 D3
Compass Cl OX4 .... 142 B3
Compton Ave RG31 .... 257 D3
Compton Ct CV36 .... 27 F4
Compton Dr OX14 .... 160 A1
Compton Rd OX16 .... 16 B3
Compton Terr OX10 .... 221 F4
Condor Cl RG31 .... 257 E2

Conduit Hill Rise OX9 .... 147 F2
Conduit Rd OX14 .... 179 F4
Conifer Cl OX2 .... 140 B4
Conifer Dr Bicester OX6 ... 65 F3
Reading RG31 .... 257 D1
Conifer Rise OX16 .... 9 D1
Conigre OX9 .... 168 A3
Conisboro Ave RG4 .... 258 C3
Conisboro Way RG4 ...... 258 C3
Coniston Ave OX11 .... 124 A2
Coniston Dr RG30 .... 257 F1
Connolly Dr OX18 .... 115 E2
Constable's Croft OX6 .... 96 C4
Constitution Hill OX10 ... 221 F2
Conway Dr OX6 .... 15 F3
Conway Rd OX13 .... 159 E1
Conyger Cl OX5 .... 93 F1
Cook La OX10 .... 221 F1
Cook's Hill OX15 .... 14 A3
Cooks La OX7 .... 41 F3
Coolidge Cl OX3 .... 124 B1
Coombe Hill Cres OX9 ... 147 F4
Coombe The RG8 .... 248 C3
Coombes Cl OX7 .... 85 E4
Cooper Cl OX7 .... 42 C2
Cooper Pl OX3 .... 124 C2
Cooper Rd RG9 .... 244 B2
Cooper's Court Rd HP14 .. 188 B3
Coopers Gate OX16 .... 16 B4
Coopers Gn OX6 .... 65 F3
Coopers La OX12 .... 214 C3
Coopers Pightle RG4 ..... 252 B2
Cope Cl OX2 .... 140 B4
Cope Rd OX16 .... 16 B3
Copenhagen Dr OX13 .... 159 E1
Copperage Rd OX11 ..... 234 A1
Coppice Cl OX16 .... 16 C2
Coppock Cl OX3 .... 124 C1
Copperfield Cl OX12 ..... 214 B3
Copse Ave RG4 .... 259 F2
Copse Cl RG31 .... 257 E2
Copse La OX3 .... 124 A3
Copse Mead RG5 .... 260 C1
Copse The Abingdon OX14 .. 160 B1
Wargrave RG10 .... 255 F2
Copson La OX44 .... 163 E1
Copthorne Rd OX5 .... 108 C4
Corbett Rd OX18 .... 115 E1
Cordrey Green OX4 ...... 141 F2
Corfe Mews RG4 .... 259 F2
Coriander Way 4 OX4 ... 142 C1
Corn Avill Cl OX14 .... 160 B1
Corn Bar OX8 .... 117 F4
Corn St OX8 .... 118 A4
Cordell Gdns OX8 .... 118 A4
Corneville Rd OX14 ...... 179 D1
Cornfield Cl OX8 .... 117 F4
Cornish Rd OX7 .... 42 B1
Cornmarket
Faringdon SN7 .... 172 C2
Thame OX9 .... 147 F4
Cornmarket St OX1 ...... 123 E1
Cornwall Cl RG31 .... 257 D2
Cornwallis Cl OX4 .... 142 A3
Cornwallis Rd OX4 .... 142 A3
Coromandel OX14 .... 179 E2
Corunna Cres OX4 .... 142 C3
Cosford Gdns OX6 .... 66 A2
Costar Cl OX4 .... 142 B1
Cot's Gn OX5 .... 92 B1
Cote Rd OX18 .... 135 F2
Cothill Rd OX13 .... 158 C2
Cotman Cl OX14 .... 179 F3
Cotmore Cl OX9 .... 148 A4
Cotmore Gdns OX9 ...... 148 A4
Cotshill Gdns OX7 .... 42 C2
Cotswold Cl
Minster Lovell OX8 .... 102 C1
Sibford Ferris OX15 .... 19 D4
Cotswold Cnr OX7 .... 29 C2
Cotswold Cres
Chipping Norton OX7 ...... 42 C1
Marston OX3 .... 123 F3
Cotswold Cres Bglws OX7 . 42 C1
Cotswold Meadow OX8 ... 117 E4
Cotswold Pk OX11 .... 200 B1
Cotswold Rd OX2 .... 140 A3
Cotswold Terr OX7 .... 42 C1
Cotswold View OX7 .... 73 D2
Cotswold Way
Carterton OX18 .... 115 E2
Reading RG31 .... 257 E1
Cottage Rd SN7 .... 194 B4
Cottages The GL7 .... 114 A3
Cottesmore La OX10 .... 204 B3
Cottesmore Rd OX4 ..... 142 A2
Cotton Grass Cl OX4 .... 142 C1
Couching St OX9 .... 186 A1
Coulings Cl OX12 .... 216 B4
Council Houses OX7 ...... 45 E4
County Rd NN13 .... 24 A3
County Trading Est OX4 .. 142 C2
County View OX15 .... 34 B2
Coupland Rd OX13 .... 159 D3
Court Cl Kidlington OX5 .. 108 B4
Shipton-u-W OX7 .... 85 E4
Warmington OX17 .... 3 D2
Court Close Rd OX9 ..... 148 C4
Court Dr OX10 .... 203 D3
Court Farm Rd OX4 ...... 141 F2
Court Hill Rd OX12 .... 214 A1
Court Pl Gdns OX4 .... 141 F2
Court Place Gdns OX4 ... 141 F2
Court The OX14 .... 159 F2
Courtenay Cl OX14 ...... 200 A4
Courtenay Dr RG4 .... 259 D4
Courtenay Rd OX12 ..... 214 C3
Courtfield Rd OX33 ...... 125 E4

Courthouse HP18 .... 129 E4
Courtiers Green OX14 ... 181 E2
Courtington La OX15 ...... 21 E3
Courtland Rd OX4 .... 142 A2
Courtlands Hill RG8 ..... 256 B2
Courtlands Rd OX7 .... 85 E4
Courts Gdns OX8 .... 118 B4
Covent Cl OX14 .... 160 A2
Coverley Rd OX3 .... 142 B4
Covert The OX20 .... 91 E3
Cow La Denchworth OX12 . 195 F2
Didcot OX11 .... 201 D1
Grove OX12 .... 196 C2
Kennington OX1 .... 141 F1
Longworth OX13 .... 156 B2
Moulsford OX10 .... 238 C2
Reading RG1 .... 258 C1
Steeple Aston OX6 .... 62 A4
Cowell Pl OX8 .... 118 A4
Cowleaze OX9 .... 168 A3
Cowleaze Cl SN6 .... 209 D3
Cowley Junc OX4 .... 142 C2
Cowley Pl OX4 .... 141 F4
Cowley Rd Oxford OX4 .. 142 A2
Oxford, Littlemore OX4 .. 142 A4
Cowper Cl OX6 .... 65 D2
Cox La OX7 .... 42 A1
Cox's Alley OX3 .... 124 C2
Cox's La
Crowmarsh G OX10 ..... 222 A3
Stoke Row RG9 .... 241 F3
Cox's Rd SN6 .... 209 D3
Coxfield Cl HP14 .... 188 C3
Coxmoor Cl OX7 .... 54 C2
Coxwell Gdns OX7 .... 172 C2
Coxwell Hall Mews SN7 .. 172 C1
Coxwell Rd SN7 .... 172 C1
Coxwell St SN7 .... 172 C2
Cozens La OX7 .... 54 C2
CR Bates Ind Est HP14 .. 188 C3
Crabhill La OX12 .... 215 D4
Crabtree Cnr OX10 ...... 240 B4
Crabtree La OX14 .... 179 D1
Crabtree Pl OX14 .... 180 A4
Crabtree Rd
Haddenham HP17 .... 130 C3
N Hinksey Vill OX2 ...... 140 B4
Crafts End OX11 .... 235 F4
Cranbourne Gdns RG30 .. 258 A1
Cranbrook Ct OX8 .... 118 A3
Cranbrook Dr OX1 .... 160 C4
Crane Furlong SN6 ...... 190 A4
Cranesbill Way OX4 ..... 142 C1
Cranham St OX2 .... 123 D2
Cranham Terr OX2 .... 123 D2
Cranleigh Cl OX16 .... 16 A2
Cranley Rd OX3 .... 124 C2
Cranmer Cl RG31 .... 257 D2
Cranmer Rd OX4 .... 142 C3
Cranwell Ave OX18 ..... 115 F1
Cratlands Cl OX44 ...... 163 E1
Craufurd Rd OX4 .... 142 C3
Craven Comm SN7 ...... 211 E4
Craven Way OX11 .... 218 C4
Crawborough Rd OX7 .... 73 E2
Crawley Rd OX8 .... 104 A1
Crawshay Dr RG4 .... 259 D4
Cray Ct OX11 .... 200 C2
Creampot Cl OX17 .... 4 C1
Creampot Cres OX17 ...... 4 C1
Creampot La OX17 .... 4 C1
Crecy Wlk OX20 .... 91 E3
Cremyll Rd RG1 .... 258 C1
Crescent Cl OX4 .... 142 B3
Crescent Rd Oxford OX4 .. 142 B3
Reading RG31 .... 257 E1
Crescent The
Adderbury OX17 .... 23 D3
Bicester OX6 .... 65 E2
Carterton OX18 .... 133 E4
Sandford-on-T OX4 ..... 161 E4
Shiplake RG9 .... 255 D2
Steeple Aston OX6 .... 62 A4
Witney OX8 .... 104 B1
Crescent Way OX10 .... 220 C1
Cress Hill Pl OX3 .... 124 C2
Crest The
Bledlow Ridge HP14 .... 189 F4
Caversham RG4 .... 259 E3
Crick Rd OX2 .... 123 E2
Cricket Ground HP14 ... 188 B3
Cricket Rd OX4 .... 142 A3
Cricklade Rd SN6 .... 190 A3
Cripley Dr OX2 .... 123 D1
Cripley Rd OX2 .... 123 D1
Crisp Rd RG9 .... 244 B2
Crispin Cl RG4 .... 258 B3
Crispin Pl OX10 .... 221 E4
Croasdell Cl OX14 ..... 179 F2
Crockwell Cl OX6 ...... 65 F1
Crockwell St CV36 ...... 27 F4
Croft Ave OX5 .... 108 C4
Croft Cl Merton OX6 .... 95 E4
Oxford OX3 .... 123 F2
Thame OX9 .... 148 A4
Croft Ctyd HP17 .... 130 C3
Croft End OX12 .... 214 A1
Croft La OX17 .... 23 D2
Croft Rd Goring RG8 ... 249 E3
Oxford OX3 .... 123 F2
Thame OX9 .... 148 A4
Wallingford OX10 ..... 221 D4
Croft The
Aston Tirrold OX11 .... 219 F1
Didcot OX11 .... 218 C4

Croft The continued
East Hagbourne OX11 .... **218** C3
Haddenham HP17 .... **130** C3
Harwell OX11 .... **217** F4
Oxford OX3, OX44 .... **124** B2
West Hanney OX12 .... **196** C4
Croft Way RG8 .... **250** C4
Croft's La OX15 .... **30** A3
Crofts The OX8 .... **118** A4
Cromer Cl RG31 .... **257** E1
Cromwell Cl
Chalgrove OX44 .... **184** C3
Faringdon SN7 .... **173** D2
Henley-on-T RG9 .... **254** C4
Marston OX3 .... **123** F2
Cromwell Dr OX11 .... **219** D4
Cromwell Park OX7 .... **42** C2
Cromwell Rd
Banbury OX16 .... **16** A3
Caversham RG4 .... **259** D1
Henley-on-T RG9 .... **254** C4
Cromwell St OX4 .... **141** E4
Cromwell Way OX5 .... **109** D4
Cronshaw Cl OX11 .... **200** C1
Crookdale Beck OX11 .... **201** D2
Croom Cotts OX11 .... **217** D4
Cross Ave OX10 .... **204** B1
Cross Cl OX10 .... **204** C1
Cross Hill Rd OX17 .... **22** C2
Cross Keys Rd RG8 .... **239** E2
Cross Leys OX7 .... **42** C1
Cross Rd OX10 .... **220** C1
Cross St OX4 .... **141** E4
Cross Tree La GL7 .... **132** A3
Cross's La OX7 .... **56** C1
Crosslands OX6 .... **52** B3
Crosslands Dr OX14 .... **159** F1
Crossville Cres OX11 .... **200** B1
Crossway OX7 .... **60** C4
Crotch Cres OX3 .... **124** A2
Crouch Hill Rd OX16 .... **16** A2
Crouch St OX16 .... **16** B3
Croughton Rd OX17 .... **35** E4
Crow La OX17 .... **9** E4
Crowberry Rd OX4 .... **142** C1
Crowell Rd OX4 .... **142** B2
Crowmarsh Hill OX10 .... **222** A3
Crowmarsh Rd OX6 .... **64** C3
Crown La Benson OX10 .... **203** F2
Dorchester OX10 .... **182** B1
South Moreton OX11 .... **220** A3
Crown Mews OX14 .... **179** F4
Crown Rd Kidlington OX5 ..... **108** B4
Wheatley OX33 .... **144** A4
Crown Sq OX10 .... **204** A2
Crown St OX4 .... **141** F4
Crown Wlk OX6 .... **65** F1
Crowsley Rd RG9 .... **255** D2
Crowsley Way RG4 .... **252** C3
Croxford Gdns OX5 .... **108** C3
Crozier Cl OX2 .... **140** B4
Crumps Butts OX6 .... **65** F1
Crutch Furlong OX10 .... **182** B3
Crutchmore Cres OX5 .... **78** A2
Cuckamus La OX8 .... **105** D3
Cuckoo Cl OX6 .... **65** F3
Cuckoo La Eynsham OX8 ... **106** A2
Freeland OX8 .... **106** A2
Cuddesdon Cl RG8 .... **250** C4
Cuddesdon OX33 .... **143** F3
Cuddesdon Way OX4 .... **142** C1
Cues La SN6 .... **227** E2
Culham Cl OX14 .... **160** A1
Cullerne Cl OX14 .... **160** A2
Cullerns The SN6 .... **190** A3
Cullum Rd OX33 .... **144** B4
Culworth Rd OX17 .... **5** F3
Cumberford Cl OX15 .... **21** E2
Cumberford Cl OX15 .... **21** E2
Cumberford Hill OX15 .... **21** E2
Cumberland Rd OX4 .... **142** A4
Cumberlege Cl OX3 .... **123** F4
Cummings Cl OX3 .... **124** C1
Cumnor Hill Cumnor OX2 ... **140** A4
N Hinksey Vill OX2 .... **140** A4
Cumnor Rd Cumnor OX2 ..... **139** E4
Wootton (Oxford) OX13 ...... **159** D4
Cumnor Rise Rd OX2 .... **140** B4
Cunliffe Cl OX2 .... **123** E3
Cup & Saucer OX17 .... **4** C1
Curbridge Rd
Ducklington OX8 .... **118** A2
Witney OX8 .... **117** F1
Curie Ave OX11 .... **217** D2
Cursus The GL7 .... **150** B3
Curtis Ave OX14 .... **180** A4
Curtis Rd Kidlington OX5 ...... **92** C1
Shrivenham SN6 .... **209** D3
Curtiss Cl OX6 .... **66** A2
Curtyn Cl OX14 .... **179** E4
Curzon Gate Ct HP14 .... **188** C3
Cuthwine Pl GL7 .... **150** B3
Cutteslowe Rdbt OX2 .... **109** D1
Cuttlebrook Gdns OX9 .... **129** F1
Cuxham Rd OX9 .... **186** A1
Cwmcarn RG4 .... **258** C2
Cygnet Cl OX4 .... **166** A4
Cypress Gdns OX6 .... **65** F3

Dacey Dr OX6 .... **63** D4
Dacre Ave RG4 .... **259** F2
Daedings The OX15 .... **33** F2
Dagdale Dr OX11 .... **200** C2
Daimler Ave OX16 .... **15** F4

Dairy Meadow OX13 .... **177** E3
Dairyground The OX15 .... **14** A3
Daisy Bank OX14 .... **180** A4
Dale Cl Brackley NN13 .... **24** A4
Oxford OX1 .... **141** D4
Dale Pl OX5 .... **92** C1
Dale Wlk OX8 .... **118** A3
Dalton Ave OX11 .... **217** D1
Damer Gdns RG9 .... **254** C2
Damson Trees SN6 .... **209** D3
Dancers Hill OX7 .... **73** E2
Danes Rd OX6 .... **65** E1
Danesmoor OX16 .... **16** A4
Danvers Cl OX15 .... **15** E1
Danvers Rd
Broughton OX15 .... **15** E1
Oxford OX4 .... **142** A2
Darell Rd RG4 .... **258** C2
Darent Pl OX11 .... **201** D1
Dark La Reading RG31 .... **257** D1
Sunningwell OX13 .... **159** F3
Wargrave RG10 .... **255** E1
Witney OX8 .... **104** A1
Wroxton OX15 .... **15** D4
Darrell Way OX14 .... **159** F1
Dart Dr OX11 .... **200** C2
Dart Rd OX11 .... **159** E2
Dashwood Ave OX5 .... **108** A3
Dashwood Mews OX5 .... **77** F2
Dashwood Rd
Banbury OX16 .... **16** B3
Oxford OX4 .... **142** A2
Dashwood Rise OX6 .... **47** E3
Datchet Gn OX10 .... **202** C1
Daubeny Rd OX4 .... **141** F3
Daubigny Mead OX18 .... **116** B2
Davenant Rd OX2 .... **123** D4
Davenport Rd OX8 .... **103** F1
Daventry Rd OX16 .... **16** C4
David Nicholls Cl OX4 .... **142** A1
David Walter Cl OX2 .... **109** D1
Davis Cl OX18 .... **115** F1
Davis Gdns OX6 .... **65** F4
Dawls Cl OX7 .... **71** D1
Dawson Pl OX2 .... **123** D1
Dawson St OX4 .... **141** F4
Day's La OX10 .... **204** C1
Days Ground SN6 .... **209** E4
De Havilland Rd GL54 .... **68** A3
De Montfort Rd RG1 .... **259** D1
De Vitre Pl OX12 .... **214** B4
Deacon Way Banbury OX16 ... **16** A3
Reading RG30 .... **258** A1
Deaconfield RG8 .... **239** E2
Deadman's La RG8 .... **251** E2
Deafort Cl OX5 .... **92** C1
Dean Butler Cl OX12 .... **214** B3
Dean Cl OX16 .... **16** C4
Dean Court Rd OX2 .... **140** A4
Dean Wood Cl RG8 .... **240** C1
Deanes Cl OX13 .... **198** C2
Deanfield Ave RG9 .... **244** B1
Deanfield Rd
Henley-on-T RG9 .... **244** B1
N Hinksey Vill OX2 .... **122** A1
Deans Cl OX6 .... **65** F1
Dearlove Cl OX14 .... **159** F1
Deddington Hill OX15 .... **33** F3
Deene Cl OX17 .... **23** D2
Deer Park Rd OX8 .... **117** E4
Deer Wlk OX4 .... **142** C1
Deer's Farm OX15 .... **22** C4
Deer's La RG8 .... **241** E1
Deers Cl OX15 .... **22** C4
Defiant Cl OX6 .... **66** A2
Delafield Cl HP14 .... **188** C2
Delamare Way OX2 .... **140** A4
Delapre Dr OX16 .... **16** C4
Dell Rd RG31 .... **257** E1
Delly Cl OX8 .... **104** A4
Denbigh Cl OX16 .... **15** F2
Denbigh Rd OX9 .... **130** A1
Denby Way RG30 .... **257** F1
Denchfield Rd OX16 .... **16** B1
Denchworth Rd
Grove OX12 .... **196** B1
Wantage OX12 .... **214** B3
Dene Hollow OX11 .... **235** F4
Dene Rd OX3 .... **142** B4
Dene Rise OX8 .... **117** F4
Denman's La OX2 .... **139** F3
Denmark St OX4 .... **141** F4
Denton Cl Abingdon OX14 ... **180** A4
N Hinksey Vill OX2 .... **140** A4
Denton Hill OX44 .... **144** A4
Denton La Cuddesdon OX44 ... **144** A1
Garsington OX44 .... **143** F1
Dents Cl OX3 .... **124** A3
Derby Rd RG4 .... **259** D2
Derwent Ave Didcot OX11 ... **201** D1
Oxford OX3 .... **124** A2
Reading RG30 .... **257** F1
Derwent Cl OX13 .... **159** E1
Derwent Rd OX6 .... **65** D2
Des Roches Sq Ind Est
OX8 .... **118** A4
Desborough Cres OX4 .... **142** A2
Desmesne Furze OX3 .... **124** B1
Devereux Pl OX4 .... **142** A2
Devil's Hill RG4 .... **253** E3
Devon Cl OX10 .... **204** B2
Devon Rd RG4 .... **259** F2
Devon Pl OX18 .... **115** F1
Devon Way OX16 .... **16** A4
Devonshire Gdns RG31 ...... **257** D2
Dexter Cl OX16 .... **16** B2
Diamond Pl OX2 .... **123** D3
Dickens Cl OX6 .... **65** E2

Dickenson Ct OX7 .... **42** C2
Dickredge The OX6 .... **62** A4
Didcot Rd
Brightwell-cum-S OX10 ..... **202** B2
Harwell OX11 .... **218** A4
Long Wittenham OX14 .... **201** E4
Dido Rd OX11 .... **217** D1
Digberry La RG9 .... **224** B3
Digging La OX13 .... **157** E1
Dirac Pl OX11 .... **219** D4
Diston's La OX7 .... **42** C2
Ditchley Rd OX7 .... **73** F3
Divinity Rd OX4 .... **142** A4
Dobson's La RG9 .... **244** B4
Dobson's La RG9 .... **244** B4
Dodd Dr GL54 .... **68** A2
Dodgson Rd OX4 .... **142** B2
Dodson Ct OX14 .... **179** F4
Doe Lea OX11 .... **200** C2
Dog Cl OX17 .... **22** C2
Dog Kennel La OX7 .... **85** E4
Dog La OX12 .... **213** E2
Doily Cl OX15 .... **30** A4
Dollicot HP17 .... **130** C4
Dolphin La OX18 .... **100** C3
Don Boscoe Cl OX4 .... **142** B3
Don Cl OX11 .... **201** D2
Don Stuart Pl OX4 .... **142** A4
Donegal Cl RG4 .... **259** E2
Donkin Hill RG4 .... **259** E2
Donnington Bridge Rd
OX4 .... **141** F3
Donnington Cl OX8 .... **117** E4
Donnington Pl OX12 .... **214** B3
Dora Carr Cl OX3 .... **124** A3
Dorchester Cl OX3 .... **124** C1
Dorchester Cres OX14 .... **160** A1
Dorchester Gr OX16 .... **15** F2
Dorchester Pl OX7 .... **147** F4
Dorchester Rd
Berinsfield OX10 .... **182** C2
Drayton St L OX10 .... **183** D3
Doris Field Cl OX3 .... **124** A2
Dormer Rd OX9 .... **148** A3
Dormers The SN6 .... **190** A3
Dorn Cl OX7 .... **60** C4
Dorn View OX20 .... **76** A2
Douglas Rd RG4 .... **259** E1
Dove Ct OX18 .... **115** F2
Dove Green OX6 .... **65** D2
Dove House Cl OX2 .... **122** C4
Dove La RG9 .... **252** B4
Dovecote HP17 .... **130** C3
Dovecote Cl HP17 .... **130** C3
Dovedale Cl RG4 .... **258** C2
Dovehouse Cl OX8 .... **120** C4
Doveleat OX9 .... **168** B4
Dover Ave OX16 .... **15** F3
Dovetrees OX18 .... **115** F2
Down End OX15 .... **30** A4
Downhill La OX8 .... **104** A2
Downlands SN7 .... **192** B1
Downs Cl OX11 .... **217** F3
Downs Rd Aldworth RG20 ... **247** D2
Curbridge OX8 .... **103** D1
Didcot OX11 .... **218** B4
Standlake OX8 .... **137** E3
Downs View OX11 .... **190** A3
Downs Way Chilton OX11 .... **234** C4
Reading RG31 .... **257** E1
Downside OX11 .... **217** E1
Downside End OX3 .... **125** D2
Downside Rd OX3 .... **125** D2
Downsmead SN8 .... **245** E1
Downsview Rd OX12 .... **214** B4
Doyley Rd Oxford OX2 .... **141** D4
Wallingford OX10 .... **203** E1
Dragonhill Rd SN7 .... **211** D1
Drake Ave OX11 .... **218** B4
Dray's La RG9 .... **253** D4
Draycott Rd OX13 .... **156** B1
Draymans Croft OX6 .... **65** F1
Drayton Rd
Abingdon OX14 .... **179** E3
Dorchester OX10 .... **182** B1
Milton (Abingdon) OX14 .... **199** F4
Dresden Way RG30 .... **257** F1
Drewitts Cnr OX11 .... **217** F4
Drive The OX7 .... **58** C3
Drivers La GL56 .... **27** D1
Drove Acre Rd OX4 .... **142** A4
Drover's La RG9 .... **226** B4
Droveside OX10 .... **220** C1
Druce Way OX4 .... **142** C2
Druids Wlk Chinnor OX9 ..... **168** B3
Didcot OX11 .... **200** C1
Dry La Crawley OX8 .... **103** E2
Curbridge OX8 .... **103** E2
Dryden Ave OX6 .... **65** D2
Drylands Rd OX3 .... **102** C1
Duck End La OX8 .... **120** B1
Duck La HP18 .... **98** B4
Duck Sq OX9 .... **168** B3
Ducklington La OX8 .... **117** F4
Dudgeon Dr OX4 .... **142** A1
Dudley Cl OX16 .... **257** F1
Dudley Gdns OX4 .... **123** F1
Dudley La RG9 .... **226** C4
Dudley Mews RG31 .... **257** F1
Duffield Cl OX14 .... **160** A1
Duffield Pl OX13 .... **178** B4
Duffield Rd RG5 .... **260** C1
Duke Of York Ave OX14 ..... **199** E2
Duke St Banbury OX16 .... **16** C3
Henley-on-T RG9 .... **244** C1
Oxford OX1 .... **122** C1
Dukes Cl HP18 .... **128** B1
Dukes Cl OX5 .... **108** C4

Dulas Cl OX11 .... **200** C1
Dumas Cl OX6 .... **65** E1
Dumbarton Way RG4 .... **259** F3
Dunbar Dr OX9 .... **130** A1
Duncan Cl OX8 .... **120** B4
Duncan Gdns RG8 .... **257** E2
Dundas Cl OX14 .... **180** A4
Dunlin Ct OX10 .... **16** C2
Dunluce Gdns RG8 .... **256** C3
Dunmore Rd OX14 .... **159** F1
Dunnock Way
Sandford-on-T OX4 .... **142** C1
Wargrave RG10 .... **255** F2
Dunsden Cl OX11 .... **200** B1
Dunsomer Hill OX11 .... **220** A4
Dunstan Ave OX7 .... **42** C1
Dunstan Rd OX3 .... **124** B2
Dunster Cl RG4 .... **259** E3
Durham Mews OX16 .... **9** D1
Duxford Cl Bicester OX6 ...... **66** A2
Carterton OX18 .... **115** F2
Dyer Straits OX11 .... **234** C4
Dyer's Hill OX7 .... **73** D2
Dynham Pl OX3 .... **124** B1
Dysonswood La RG4 .... **258** C3

Eady Rd OX6 .... **63** D4
Eagle Ind Est OX8 .... **118** A4
Eagle La SN6 .... **191** E1
Eagle Sq SN7 .... **192** C4
Eagles SN7 .... **172** C2
Earl St OX2 .... **122** C1
Earl's La OX15 .... **33** F2
Earlsfield Cl RG4 .... **259** F2
Earlstoke Cl OX16 .... **16** C4
Early Rd OX8 .... **104** B1
Easington Gdns OX16 .... **16** B2
Easington Rd OX16 .... **16** B2
Eason Dr OX14 .... **160** B1
East Ave OX4 .... **142** A4
East Cl OX16 .... **16** C4
East End OX15 .... **30** A4
East Hawthorn Rd OX6 .... **81** E2
East Lockinge OX12 .... **215** E2
East St Banbury OX15, OX16 ... **16** C4
Bicester OX6 .... **65** E2
Bodicote OX15 .... **22** C4
Didcot OX11 .... **219** D4
Fritwell OX6 .... **49** F4
Long Compton CV36 .... **27** F3
Oxford OX2 .... **123** D1
Thame OX9 .... **148** A4
East St Helen St OX14 .... **179** F3
East View Cl RG10 .... **255** F1
East View Rd RG10 .... **255** F1
East Way OX14 .... **199** D4
Eastbrook Cl OX6 .... **97** F4
Eastbury Ave RG31 .... **257** D3
Eastchurch OX4 .... **141** F2
Easterfield OX12 .... **196** C1
Eastern Ave OX4 .... **142** A2
Eastern By-pass Rd OX4 ... **142** C3
Eastfield OX11 .... **237** D4
Eastfield La
Whitchurch RG8 .... **256** B4
Woodcote RG8 .... **250** C3
Eastfield Rd OX4 .... **104** A2
Eastgate OX1 .... **7** E4
Eastmanton La OX12 .... **212** C2
Eastrop SN6 .... **190** A3
Eastwood Rd
Curbridge OX8 .... **103** E1
Stokenchurch HP14 .... **188** C2
Eaton Rd OX12 .... **139** D1
Ebbes La OX12 .... **197** D4
Eccles Cl RG4 .... **259** E1
Eden Croft OX14 .... **160** A1
Eden Ct OX11 .... **201** D1
Eden Dr OX3 .... **124** A2
Eden Rd OX3 .... **124** A2
Eden Way OX6 .... **65** D1
Edencroft SN6 .... **190** A4
Edenhall Cl RG31 .... **257** E2
Edgar Milward Cl RG30 ..... **258** A1
Edgecombe Rd OX3 .... **124** C2
Edgehill OX9 .... **129** F1
Edgeway Rd OX3 .... **123** F2
Edgeworth Dr OX18 .... **115** E1
Edinburgh Cl OX16 .... **15** F4
Edinburgh Dr
Didcot OX11 .... **200** C1
Kidlington OX5 .... **109** D4
Edinburgh Way OX16 .... **15** F3
Edington Pl OX12 .... **196** B1
Edington Rd OX8 .... **117** E4
Edington Sq OX8 .... **117** E4
Edith Rd OX1 .... **141** E4
Edmonds Ct OX11 .... **218** B4
Edmund Halley Rd OX4 ...... **142** A1
Edmund Rd OX4 .... **142** B3
Edmunds Rd OX16 .... **15** F3
Edward Rd OX1 .... **141** F1
Edward St Abingdon OX14 ... **179** E4
Banbury OX16 .... **16** C3
Edward Stone Rise OX7 .... **42** B1
Edwin Rd OX11 .... **218** B4
Egerton Cl NN13 .... **24** A4
Egerton Rd Oxford OX4 ...... **142** A2
Wallingford OX10 .... **221** E4
Eglin St OX5 .... **63** D4
Eighteenth St OX11 .... **217** D2
Eighth Ave OX4 .... **142** C4
Eighth St OX11 .... **217** D2
Elbourne OX11 .... **218** B4
Elder Cl RG31 .... **257** E1
Elder Way OX4 .... **142** C1
Elderdene OX9 .... **168** B4
Elderfield Cres OX11 .... **235** E4

Elderfield Rd OX6 .... **65** F4
Eldridge Cl OX14 .... **159** F1
Eleanor Cl OX4 .... **142** A2
Electric Ave OX2 .... **141** D4
Eleventh St OX11 .... **217** D1
Eliot Cl RG4 .... **259** D2
Elizabeth Ave OX14 .... **160** B1
Elizabeth Cl RG4 .... **254** A4
Elizabeth Dr OX12 .... **214** B3
Elizabeth Rd
Henley-on-T RG9 .... **254** A4
Stokenchurch HP14 .... **188** C2
Elizabeth Rise OX16 .... **16** A2
Ell's La OX15 .... **21** E4
Ellesmere Cl RG4 .... **259** D2
Ellesmere Rd OX4 .... **142** A2
Elm Bridge Rdbt OX10 .... **203** F2
Elm Cl Ambrosden OX6 .... **81** E2
Bicester OX6 .... **65** F2
Chinnor OX9 .... **168** B3
Tetsworth OX9 .... **166** A4
Wheatley OX33 .... **144** B4
Witney OX8 .... **117** F4
Elm Cres OX7 .... **73** E2
Elm Ct RG4 .... **252** C2
Elm Dr Chinnor OX9 .... **168** B3
Garsington OX44 .... **143** E1
Elm Gr OX5 .... **108** C3
Elm La OX6 .... **81** E2
Elm Rd Faringdon SN7 .... **172** C2
Mapledurham RG4 .... **258** B4
North Moreton OX11 .... **220** A4
Wantage OX12 .... **214** C3
Elm Tree Cl OX4 .... **142** A2
Elm Tree Wlk OX13 .... **159** E1
Elm Trees HP18 .... **129** D4
Elmcroft RG8 .... **249** E3
Elmhurst Rd RG8 .... **249** E4
Elmleigh Ct RG4 .... **259** E2
Elms Dr OX3 .... **124** A3
Elms Par OX2 .... **122** B1
Elms Rd Cassington OX8 ..... **107** E1
N Hinksey Vill OX2 .... **122** B1
Thame OX9 .... **147** F4
Elms The Highworth SN6 ..... **190** A3
Langford GL7 .... **132** B1
Elms Way RG9 .... **224** B2
Elmscote Rd OX16 .... **16** B1
Elmstone Dr RG31 .... **257** E1
Elmthorpe Rd OX2 .... **122** C4
Elsfield Rd OX3 .... **123** F3
Elsfield Way OX2 .... **109** D1
Elsley Rd RG31 .... **257** F2
Elstow Ave RG4 .... **259** E3
Elstree Cl RG31 .... **257** E1
Elswith Cl OX12 .... **214** B4
Eltham Ave RG4 .... **259** F3
Elton Cres OX33 .... **144** B4
Elton Rd OX16 .... **16** C1
Elvendon La RG8 .... **250** B4
Elvendon Rd RG8 .... **249** E4
Elwes Cl OX14 .... **180** A4
Elwes Rd OX13 .... **178** B3
Ely Cl Abingdon OX14 .... **179** E3
Carterton OX18 .... **115** F2
Emma La RG10 .... **255** F1
Emmens Cl RG8 .... **241** E2
Emmer Green Ct RG4 .... **259** E3
Emperor Gdns OX4 .... **142** C1
Eney Cl OX14 .... **160** B1
Enstone Rd
Charlbury OX7 .... **73** D2
Little Tew OX7 .... **45** D3
Middle Barton OX7 .... **60** C4
Epwell Rd OX15 .... **13** F3
Eric Ave RG4 .... **259** D3
Erica Cl Banbury OX16 .... **9** D1
Oxford OX4 .... **142** C2
Ermont Way OX16 .... **16** C4
Ernest Rd OX11 .... **218** C4
Ernicote Cl OX6 .... **81** F2
Essex Rd OX9 .... **148** A4
Essex St OX4 .... **142** A4
Essex Way RG4 .... **253** D2
Estover Way OX9 .... **168** A3
Ethelhelm Cl OX14 .... **160** B2
Ethelred Ct OX3 .... **124** B2
Eton Cl OX8 .... **118** B4
Euston Way OX12 .... **214** A4
Evans Cl OX8 .... **120** C4
Evans Ct OX5 .... **108** C4
Evans La OX5 .... **108** C4
Evans Rd OX8 .... **120** C4
Evelin Rd OX14 .... **159** F1
Evelyn Ct OX2 .... **140** A4
Evenlode Cl OX6 .... **16** A4
Evenlode Dr
Berinsfield OX10 .... **182** B3
Didcot OX11 .... **200** C1
Long Hanborough OX8 .... **90** A1
Evenlode Park OX14 .... **160** A1
Evenlode Rd Bicester OX6 ... **65** E1
Charlbury OX7 .... **73** D2
Grove OX12 .... **196** B1
North Leigh OX8 .... **105** D3
Evenlode Cres OX5 .... **92** C1
Everard Cl OX3 .... **124** B1
Eversley Cl OX7 .... **57** D1
Evesham Rd RG4 .... **259** D3
Ewart Cl OX6 .... **65** E2
Ewert Pl OX2 .... **123** D3
Ewin Cl OX3 .... **123** F3
Exbourne Rd OX14 .... **179** E4
Exe Cl OX11 .... **200** C1
Exeter Ct OX11 .... **219** D4
Eylham RG8 .... **257** D3
Eynsford Cl RG4 .... **259** F3
Eynsham Cl OX8 .... **105** E3

Eynsham Rd
Cassington OX8 .... 107 E1
Cumnor OX2 .... 121 F1
N Hinksey Vill OX2 .... 140 A4
Eyot Pl OX4 .... 141 F4
Eyre's La OX10 .... 204 C3
Eyston Way OX14 .... 179 E4

Faber Cl OX4 .... 142 B1
Fair Cl OX6 .... 65 F2
Fair Mile RG9 .... 244 B2
Fair View OX3 .... 142 B4
Fairacres OX4 .... 179 E4
Fairacres Rd Didcot OX11 ...... 218 C4
Oxford OX4 .... 141 F3
Fairfax Ave OX3 .... 123 F2
Fairfax Cl Banbury OX16 .... 16 A3
Caversham RG4 .... 259 D2
Thame OX9 .... 148 A4
Fairfax Gate OX33 .... 144 B4
Fairfax Rd Chalgrove OX44 ..... 184 B3
Kidlington OX5 .... 108 C3
Oxford OX4, OX44 .... 142 C3
Fairfield OX12 .... 220 C1
Fairfield Cl OX12 .... 214 B4
Fairfield Dr OX8 .... 117 F4
Fairfield Pl OX14 .... 179 F4
Fairfield Rd RG8 .... 249 E4
Fairford Rd RG31 .... 257 E1
Fairford Way OX6 .... 66 A2
Fairhaven Rd OX6 .... 65 F4
Fairlawn End OX2 .... 122 C4
Fairlie Rd OX4 .... 142 A2
Fairmile Ct RG4 .... 244 B2
Fairspear Rd OX8 .... 86 C2
Fairthorne Way SN6 .... 209 D3
Fairview Rd OX16 .... 16 B2
Fairway The OX16 .... 16 A3
Falcon Cl Banbury OX16 .... 16 A2
Carterton OX18 .... 115 E2
Oxford OX4 .... 142 B1
Falcon Mead OX6 .... 81 D4
Falkland Rd RG4 .... 259 D1
Falkner's Cl OX17 .... 23 D2
Fallow Way OX16 .... 16 C1
Fallowfield Cl RG4 .... 259 D2
Fallowfields OX6 .... 65 F1
Falstaff Cl OX8 .... 120 C4
Fane Cl OX6 .... 65 E2
Fane Dr OX10 .... 182 B3
Fane Rd OX3 .... 123 F3
Fanshawe Pl OX4 .... 142 C3
Fanshawe Rd OX9 .... 148 A4
Faraday Ave OX11 .... 217 D1
Faraday Rd OX12 .... 214 A4
Faringdon Rd
Appleton OX13 .... 139 F1
Kingston Bagpuize OX13 .... 156 C1
Shrivenham SN6 .... 209 E4
Stanford in the V SN7 .... 194 B4
Watchfield SN6 .... 191 F1
Farleigh Mews RG4 .... 259 F3
Farleigh Rd SN6 .... 209 D3
Farley Cl OX8 .... 89 E4
Farm Cl Aston OX18 .... 135 F1
Chalgrove OX44 .... 184 A3
Kidlington OX5 .... 92 C1
Purley on T RG8 .... 257 E3
Sandford-on-T OX4 .... 142 C1
Farm Close La OX14 .... 144 A4
Farm Close Rd OX33 .... 144 A4
Farm End Grove OX12 .... 214 B4
Woodstock OX20 .... 91 D4
Farm La OX8 .... 103 E3
Farm Mill La OX8 .... 118 A4
Farm Pl OX9 .... 149 F1
Farm Rd Abingdon OX14 ..... 159 F1
Brackley NN13 .... 24 A3
Goring RG8 .... 249 E3
Henley-on-T RG9 .... 254 C4
Farm Way OX6 .... 16 C2
Farman Cres GL54 .... 68 A2
Farmer Pl OX3 .... 123 F2
Farmers Cl OX8 .... 104 A1
Farmfield Rd OX16 .... 16 B2
Farmhouse Cl OX8 .... 104 B4
Farmhouse Meadow OX8 .... 117 F4
Farmhouse Mews OX9 .... 186 A1
Farmiloe Cl RG8 .... 257 E2
Farmington Dr OX8 .... 117 F4
Farmstead Cl OX12 .... 196 B1
Farndon Rd OX2 .... 123 D2
Farnham Dr RG4 .... 259 F2
Farrier's Mead OX6 .... 80 A2
Farriers Mews OX14 .... 180 A4
Farriers Rd OX7 .... 60 C4
Farringdon Rd OX14 .... 159 D1
Farthings The OX13 .... 178 B4
Faulder Ave OX18 .... 115 E2
Faulkner St OX1 .... 141 E4
Fawler La OX7 .... 88 B4
Fawler Rd Charlbury OX7 ... 73 E1
Kingston Lisle OX12 .... 211 F3
Uffington SN7 .... 211 F3
Fawley Bottom La RG9 .... 226 A1
Fawley Cl OX12 .... 214 B3
Fawley Court RG9 .... 244 C3
Featherbed La
East Hendred OX12 .... 216 C4
Milton (Abingdon) OX14 .... 199 D1
Mixbury OX6 .... 38 B3
Fecott Rd OX5 .... 95 D2
Fenlock Rd OX8 .... 90 C1

Fennel Way OX14 .... 180 B4
Fenny Compton Rd OX17 .... 1 B1
Fenway OX6 .... 48 A1
Ferguson Pl OX14 .... 180 B4
Fergusson Rd OX16 .... 16 C4
Fermi Ave OX11 .... 217 D1
Fern Glen RG31 .... 257 E1
Fern Hill Rd OX4 .... 142 B3
Fernbrook Rd RG4 .... 258 C3
Ferndale Reading RG31 .... 257 E2
Stokenchurch HP14 .... 188 C2
Ferndale Rd OX16 .... 15 F4
Ferndale St SN7 .... 173 D2
Ferne Cl RG8 .... 249 E4
Fernham Rd
Faringdon SN7 .... 172 B1
Fernham SN7 .... 193 E3
Little Coxwell SN7 .... 192 C4
Longcot SN7 .... 192 B1
Shellingford SN7 .... 193 E3
Fernhill Cl Kidlington OX5 ..... 108 B4
Milcombe OX15 .... 21 D1
Tiddington OX9 .... 146 A3
Fernhill Rd OX5 .... 108 A4
Ferny Cl OX14 .... 160 C2
Ferriston OX16 .... 9 D1
Ferry Hinksey Rd OX2 .... 123 D1
South Stoke RG8 .... 239 D2
Wargrave RG10 .... 255 F1
Ferry Mills OX2 .... 141 D4
Ferry Pool Rd OX2 .... 123 D3
Ferry Rd Oxford OX3 .... 123 F2
South Stoke RG8 .... 239 E2
Ferry Wlk OX14 .... 179 F3
Fetti Pl OX12 .... 214 C3
Fettiplace OX7 .... 70 A1
Fettiplace Cl OX13 .... 158 A4
Fettiplace Rd
Marcham OX13 .... 178 B3
Oxford OX3 .... 124 C3
Witney OX8 .... 117 F4
Fewcott Rd OX6 .... 49 F4
Fidlers Wlk RG10 .... 255 F1
Field Ave OX4 .... 142 C1
Field Cl Ickford HP18 .... 128 A2
Kidlington OX5 .... 108 C4
Stonesfield OX8 .... 89 E4
Yarnton OX5 .... 108 A3
Field End
Long Crendon HP18 .... 129 F3
Wargrave RG10 .... 255 F1
Field Gdns
East Challow OX12 .... 213 F3
Steventon OX13 .... 199 D3
Field House Dr OX2 .... 123 D4
Field La Cuddesdon OX44 ... 144 A2
Murcott OX6 .... 95 F2
Field Rd OX7 .... 54 C2
Field St OX6 .... 65 F1
Field The OX13 .... 158 C3
Field View RG4 .... 259 D2
Fielden Cl OX10 .... 204 B1
Fielden Rd OX10 .... 204 B1
Fieldfare Rd OX4 .... 161 F4
Fieldmere Cl OX8 .... 117 F4
Fieldside Abingdon OX14 .... 159 E1
East Hagbourne OX11 .... 219 D3
Long Wittenham OX11 .... 201 E4
Upton OX11 .... 218 B1
Fiennes Rd Banbury OX16 .... 16 A3
Oxford OX4 .... 142 A2
Fifteenth St OX11 .... 217 D1
Fifth Ave NN13 .... 36 C4
Fifth St Croughton NN13 .... 36 C4
Harwell OX11 .... 217 D2
Fifth St E NN13 .... 36 C4
Filkins Rd GL7 .... 132 B1
Finch Cl OX4 .... 124 B1
Finchdale Cl OX18 .... 115 E2
Finches La OX6 .... 65 E1
Finchley La OX6 .... 65 E1
Finham Brook OX11 .... 200 C2
Finmore Cl OX14 .... 179 F4
Finmore Rd OX2 .... 140 B4
Finsbury Pl OX7 .... 42 C2
Fir Cl OX10 .... 240 B4
Fir La OX6 .... 48 A1
Fir Tree Ave OX10 .... 221 D4
Fir Tree Cl OX13 .... 156 C1
Fir Tree Paddock RG20 .... 235 D1
Fir Trees OX14 .... 160 C4
Fircroft OX6 .... 65 F3
Fircroft Cl RG31 .... 257 E1
Firebrass Hill OX10 .... 204 C3
Firs Cl OX7 .... 54 B1
Firs Meadow **1** OX4 .... 142 C1
Firs The OX15 .... 15 D4
First Ave Didcot OX11 .... 200 B1
Horspath OX33 .... 142 C4
First St Croughton NN13 .... 36 C3
Harwell OX11 .... 217 D1
First Turn OX2 .... 122 C4
Fish Ponds La OX9 .... 129 F1
Fisher Cl OX14 .... 179 D1
Fisher Row OX1 .... 123 D1
Fisher's La OX7 .... 73 D2
Fishermans Wharf OX14 .... 179 F2
Fishers Cl OX8 .... 104 A3
Fishers Ct RG4 .... 259 E3
Fitzcount Way OX10 .... 203 E2
Fitzharris Ind Est OX14 .... 179 F4
Fitzhary's Rd OX14 .... 179 F4
Fitzherbert Cl OX4 .... 141 F2
Five Acre RG31 .... 257 E1
Fiveacres OX6 .... 95 F2
Flambards RG4 .... 259 E1

Flatford Pl OX5 .... 92 B1
Flavius Gate NN13 .... 24 A4
Flaxfield Rd OX4 .... 142 C1
Fleet Way OX11 .... 219 D1
Fleetwood Way OX9 .... 129 F1
Fleming Cl OX6 .... 65 E2
Fleming Dr OX7 .... 60 C4
Flemings Rd OX20 .... 91 E3
Flemming Ave OX44 .... 184 B4
Fletcher Cl Faringdon SN7 .. 173 D2
Yarnton OX5 .... 108 A3
Fletcher Rd OX4 .... 142 C3
Flexney Pl OX3 .... 124 B1
Flexneys Paddock OX8 .... 138 A4
Flint Hollow OX9 .... 168 A3
Flint St HP17 .... 130 C3
Floral Cl OX12 .... 214 C4
Florence Cl OX5 .... 108 C4
Florence Park Rd OX4 .... 142 A3
Florey's St OX14 .... 42 A3
Flowers Hill RG8 .... 256 B2
Floyd's Row OX1 .... 141 E4
Fludger Cl OX10 .... 221 E4
Fococks La OX10 .... 221 F1
Fogwell Rd OX2 .... 122 A1
Foliat Cl OX12 .... 214 C3
Foliat Dr OX12 .... 214 C3
Folland Dr GL54 .... 68 A3
Follets Cl OX5 .... 108 A3
Folly Cl SN6 .... 190 A4
Folly Cres Highworth SN6 ... 190 A4
Watchfield SN6 .... 191 F1
Folly Ct OX15 .... 19 E4
Folly Dr SN6 .... 190 A4
Folly Gr RG8 .... 250 A4
Folly Orchard Rd RG8 .... 240 C1
Folly View Cres SN7 .... 172 C1
Folly View Rd SN7 .... 172 C1
Folly Way SN6 .... 190 A4
Ford La Drayton St L OX10 .... 183 D3
East Hendred OX12 .... 216 B3
Garford OX13 .... 178 A4
Ford's Cl HP14 .... 189 F4
Fords Cl OX33 .... 143 E3
Forest Cl Launton OX6 .... 66 B1
Milton-u-W OX7 .... 70 A1
Forest Rd RG30 .... 257 F1
Forest Rd Charlbury OX7 .... 73 D2
Oxford OX3 .... 124 C2
Forest Side OX1 .... 141 F1
Foresters
Beacon's Bottom HP14 .... 189 E3
Chinnor OX9 .... 168 A3
Forge Cl Benson OX10 .... 203 F2
Caversham RG4 .... 259 E1
Horton-cum-S OX33 .... 112 A3
Marsh Gibbon OX6 .... 67 F2
Merton OX6 .... 95 E4
Forge Pl OX4 .... 49 F4
Forgeway OX16 .... 9 D1
Forrest Cl SN6 .... 209 D3
Forster La OX2 .... 139 F2
Forsythia Cl OX6 .... 65 F3
Forsythia Wlk OX16 .... 9 D1
Fortescue Dr OX6 .... 80 A4
Forties The OX44 .... 145 D1
Fortnam Cl OX3 .... 124 A2
Forty Green OX9 .... 149 F2
Forty The
Bishopstone SN6 .... 227 E3
Cholsey OX10 .... 220 C1
Foscote Rise OX16 .... 16 C2
Fosseway The OX18 .... 116 B2
Foster Rd OX14 .... 159 F2
Fothergill Pl OX9 .... 147 F4
Foudry Cl OX11 .... 201 D1
Foundry St OX16 .... 16 B3
Fourteenth St OX11 .... 217 D2
Fourth Ave
Croughton NN13 .... 36 C3
Horspath OX33 .... 142 C4
Fourth St Croughton NN13 .. 36 C3
Harwell OX11 .... 217 D2
Fowler Rd OX16 .... 16 C4
Fowler's Rd OX7 .... 55 D2
Fowlers Farm Rd HP14 .... 188 C2
Fox Cl Bampton OX18 .... 134 C2
Chipping Norton OX7 .... 42 C1
Garsington OX44 .... 143 E1
Hailey OX8 .... 104 A2
Fox Cover OX9 .... 168 B3
Fox Cres OX1 .... 141 F3
Fox Furlong OX4 .... 142 A1
Fox La Bicester OX6 .... 65 E1
Middle Barton OX7 .... 60 C4
Souldern OX6 .... 35 F2
Wootton (Oxford) OX13 .... 159 E4
Foxborough Rd OX14 .... 160 C1
Foxburrow Cl OX8 .... 120 A1
Foxburrow La
Crawley OX8 .... 103 F2
Hailey OX8 .... 103 F2
Foxcombe Ct OX14 .... 179 E4
Foxcombe La OX1 .... 141 D1
Foxcombe Rd OX1 .... 140 C1
Foxcroft Dr OX18 .... 115 E1
Foxdown Cl OX5 .... 92 C1
Foxfield OX7 .... 42 C1
Foxglove La OX11 .... 218 B2
Foxglove Rd OX5 .... 108 A4
Foxhall Rd OX11 .... 200 B1
Foxhill Cl RG4 .... 260 A3
Foxhill La
Caversham RG4 .... 259 F3
Souldern OX6 .... 35 F2
Foxton Cl OX2 .... 108 C1
Foxwell Dr OX3 .... 124 A3
Foxwood OX18 .... 135 F2

Foxwood Cl Aston OX18 ..... 135 F2
Banbury OX16 .... 16 B1
Framlands Cl OX12 .... 214 B3
Framlingham Dr RG4 .... 259 F3
Frampton Cl RG5 .... 260 C1
Frances Rd OX7 .... 60 C4
Francis Little Dr OX14 .... 179 E3
Franklin Cl
Chalgrove OX44 .... 184 B3
Kidlington OX5 .... 92 C1
Franklin Rd OX3 .... 124 A2
Franklyn Cl OX14 .... 159 F1
Fraser Ave RG4 .... 259 E3
Fraser Cl OX6 .... 16 C3
Fraser Gdns OX10 .... 221 E3
Frax Cl OX13 .... 156 C1
Frederick Rd OX4 .... 142 B2
Freeborn Cl OX5 .... 92 C1
Freehold St OX6 .... 62 B3
Freelands Rd OX4 .... 141 F3
Freeman Rd OX11 .... 200 B3
Freemans Cl SN7 .... 211 E4
Freemans Rd OX6 .... 22 C4
French Cl OX8 .... 117 F4
French Laurence Way
OX44 .... 184 B3
Frenchay Rd OX2 .... 123 D3
Frensham Cl OX16 .... 9 D1
Frethern Cl OX18 .... 100 C2
Friars Cl SN6 .... 209 D3
Friars' Entry OX1 .... 123 E1
Friars Furlong HP18 .... 129 D4
Friars Wharf OX1 .... 141 E4
Friday Ct OX9 .... 129 F1
Friday La OX33 .... 144 A4
Friday St RG9 .... 244 C1
Friends Cl OX8 .... 89 E4
Frilford Rd OX13 .... 178 B3
Frilsham St OX14 .... 200 A4
Fritwell Rd OX6 .... 50 A2
Frog La OX7 .... 70 A1
Frogmore La SN7 .... 194 C4
Frome Rd OX11 .... 217 E1
Fruitlands OX8 .... 120 B4
Frys Hill OX4 .... 142 C1
Fuchsia Wlk OX16 .... 9 D1
Fullbrook Cres RG31 .... 257 E2
Fullers Field OX44 .... 145 E1
Fullers Rd OX11 .... 219 F1
Fullwell Cl OX14 .... 159 F1
Fulmar Ct OX6 .... 66 A2
Fulmar Pl OX12 .... 196 B1
Fulton Rd GL54 .... 68 A2
Fulwell Rd NN13 .... 25 D2
Furlong Cl OX4 .... 142 B2
Furlong Row OX18 .... 152 C4
Furlongs The OX9 .... 147 E3
Fyfield Cl OX12 .... 214 C2
Fyfield Rd OX2 .... 123 E2

Gadge Cl OX9 .... 129 F1
Gainsborough Cres RG9 .... 254 B4
Gainsborough Green
OX14 .... 179 F3
Gainsborough Hill RG9 .... 254 B4
Gainsborough Rd RG9 .... 254 B4
Gaisford Rd OX4 .... 142 B2
Gall Cl OX14 .... 180 B4
Galley Field OX14 .... 180 A4
Gallowstree Rd RG9 .... 252 C4
Galsworthy Dr RG4 .... 259 F3
Gangsdown Hill OX10 .... 223 F2
Gap The Marcham OX13 .... 178 B3
Woodcote RG8 .... 250 C4
Garde Rd RG4 .... 260 C2
Garden Cl Banbury OX16 .... 16 B4
Didcot OX11 .... 218 B4
Gardens Cl HP14 .... 188 C2
Gardens The
Radley OX14 .... 160 C2
South Stoke RG8 .... 239 E2
Gardiner Cl
Abingdon OX14 .... 180 B4
Wheatley OX33 .... 144 A4
Gardiner St OX3 .... 124 B1
Garford Cl OX14 .... 160 A1
Garford Rd OX2 .... 123 E3
Garne's La OX18 .... 100 C3
Garner Cl OX18 .... 115 E3
Garsington Rd OX4 .... 142 C2
Garsons Cl OX10 .... 240 C3
Garston Cl OX12 .... 214 C3
Garston La OX12 .... 214 C3
Garth Rd OX11 .... 200 C1
Garth The
N Hinksey Vill OX2 .... 140 B4
Yarnton OX5 .... 108 A3
Gas La OX7 .... 85 E4
Gascoigne Way OX15 .... 21 F1
Gaskells End RG4 .... 258 B4
Gassons Rd GL7 .... 150 B3
Gassons Way GL7 .... 150 B2
Gatehampton Rd RG8 .... 249 E3
Gathorne Rd OX3 .... 124 B1
Gatteridge St OX16 .... 16 B3
Gauntlets Cl OX15 .... 21 F3
Gaveston Gdns OX15 .... 33 F2
Gaveston Rd OX11 .... 217 F4
Gavray Dr OX6 .... 66 A1
Gaydon Cl OX18 .... 115 F2
Gaydon Wlk OX6 .... 66 A2
Gayhurst Cl RG4 .... 259 E3
Gelt Burn OX11 .... 201 D1
Gentian Rd OX4 .... 142 C1
Geoffrey Barbour Rd
OX14 .... 179 F4
Geoffrey Tuttle Dr OX10 ...... 204 B1
Geoffreyson Rd RG4 .... 258 C3

George Moore Cl OX4 .... 142 A3
George Rd HP14 .... 188 C3
George St Banbury OX16 .... 16 B3
Bicester OX6 .... 65 E2
Caversham RG4 .... 259 E1
Oxford OX1 .... 123 E1
George Street Mews
OX1 .... 123 D1
Gerard Pl OX4 .... 142 B3
Gerrard Rd GL54 .... 68 A2
Gibbs Cres OX2 .... 141 D4
Gibbs Rd OX16 .... 16 C4
Gibson Cl OX14 .... 160 A2
Gibson Dr OX6 .... 63 E4
Gidley Way OX33 .... 143 E4
Giernalls La OX8 .... 104 A3
Giffard Way HP18 .... 129 E4
Gifford Cl RG4 .... 259 F3
Giles Cl OX4 .... 142 A1
Giles Rd OX4 .... 142 B1
Gilkes Yd OX16 .... 16 A3
Gillett Cl OX16 .... 16 A3
Gillett Rd OX16 .... 16 A3
Gillians Way OX4 .... 142 A4
Gillotts Cl RG9 .... 254 A4
Gillotts La RG9 .... 254 B4
Ginge Cl OX14 .... 160 A1
Gipsy La Grove OX12 .... 214 C4
Oxford OX4 .... 124 A1
Reading RG30 .... 257 F1
Girdlestone Cl OX3 .... 124 B1
Girdlestone Rd OX3 .... 124 B1
Glade The RG8 .... 257 E2
Glades The OX6 .... 66 B1
Gladstone Rd OX3 .... 124 C2
Glamis Pl OX16 .... 15 F3
Glanville Gdns OX16 .... 16 A3
Glanville Rd OX4 .... 142 A4
Glebe Cl Ambrosden OX6 ... 81 E2
Moulsford OX10 .... 238 C3
Glebe Cotts OX9 .... 166 C2
Glebe Ct OX6 .... 47 E3
Glebe Dr NN13 .... 24 A4
Glebe Gdns Grove OX12 .... 196 C1
Sonning RG4 .... 260 C2
Glebe House Dr MK18 .... 25 F3
Glebe La RG4 .... 260 C2
Glebe Rd Cumnor OX2 ...... 139 F3
Didcot OX11 .... 218 C4
Purley on T RG8 .... 257 D3
Stanford in the V SN7 .... 194 B4
Glebe Ride RG8 .... 249 D3
Glebe St OX4 .... 123 F1
Glebe The Aldworth RG8 ...... 247 F2
Aynho OX17 .... 35 E4
Culham OX14 .... 180 A2
Cumnor OX2 .... 139 F3
East Challow OX12 .... 213 E3
Hook Norton OX15 .... 30 A4
Lewknor OX9 .... 187 D4
Rotherfield Peppard RG9 ...... 242 C3
Standlake OX8 .... 137 E2
Wheatley OX33 .... 144 A4
Glebelands Bampton OX18 . 134 C2
Oxford OX3 .... 142 B4
Glen Cl OX6 .... 52 B1
Glenham Rd OX9 .... 148 A1
Glenmore Rd OX18 .... 115 E2
Glenrhondda RG4 .... 258 C3
Glimbers Gr OX9 .... 168 B3
Gloucester Court Mews
OX8 .... 104 A1
Gloucester La OX2 .... 123 D1
Gloucester Mews SN7 .... 172 C2
Gloucester Pl Oxford OX8 .... 123 E1
Witney OX8 .... 104 A1
Gloucester St
Faringdon SN7 .... 172 C2
Oxford OX1 .... 123 E1
Glover's Cl OX7 .... 42 C1
Glovers Cl OX20 .... 91 E3
Glovers La OX17 .... 10 C1
Glyme Cl Abingdon OX14 ..... 160 A1
Woodstock OX20 .... 91 D4
Glyme Dr OX10 .... 182 B3
Glyme Way OX8 .... 106 A4
Glympton Rd OX20 .... 75 F3
Glyn Ave OX11 .... 218 B4
Glyn Rd OX10 .... 203 E1
Glyncastle RG4 .... 258 C3
Glyndebourne Gdns OX16 ..... 9 D1
Glynswood OX9 .... 168 B3
Gobles Ct OX6 .... 65 F1
Goddard's La OX7 .... 42 C2
Godfrey Cl OX14 .... 179 F3
Godfreys Cl Brill HP18 ...... 98 A1
Grove OX12 .... 196 C1
Godstow Cl RG5 .... 260 C1
Godstow Rd OX2 .... 122 C4
Godwyn Cl OX14 .... 179 F4
Goffe Cl OX9 .... 148 A4
Goggs The OX9 .... 186 A1
Golafre Rd OX14 .... 179 F3
Gold St OX44 .... 163 F3
Goldcrest Way OX6 .... 81 D4
Golden Cross OX1 .... 123 E1
Golden Hills OX9 .... 168 B3
Golden Rd OX4 .... 142 A4
Golden Villa Cl OX16 .... 16 A3
Golder's Cl HP18 .... 127 F2
Goldfinch La OX10 .... 221 D1
Goldsmith Cl OX6 .... 65 D2
Goldsmith's La OX10 .... 221 E4
Gooch Cl OX11 .... 200 C2
Goodlake Ave SN7 .... 173 D2

Goodliffe Gdns RG31 ...... 257 E2
Goodrich Cl RG4 .... 259 F3
Goodrington Cl OX16 ...... 16 A3
Goodson Wlk OX3 .... 123 F2
Goodsons Ind Mews
  OX9 .... 147 F4
Goor La SN8 .... 245 D2
Goose Green OX15 .... 33 F2
Goose Green Cl OX2 ...... 122 C4
Goose La OX15 .... 22 B4
Goose Wlk OX15 .... 21 E2
Goosacacre OX14 .... 160 C1
Goosey La OX12 .... 195 D2
Gordon Cl OX3 .... 123 F3
Gordon Dr OX14 .... 160 B1
Gordon Pl RG30 .... 258 B1
Gordon St OX1 .... 141 E3
Goring Rd RG8 .... 250 C4
Gorse Leas OX3 .... 124 A3
Gorselands RG4 .... 259 D3
Gorton Playne OX7 ...... 70 B1
Gorwell OX9 .... 186 A1
Gosbrook Rd RG4 .... 259 D1
Gosford Cl OX5 .... 108 C3
Goslyn Cl OX3 .... 124 B1
Gott Cl OX6 .... 66 A3
Gouldland Gdns OX3 .... 124 A3
Goulds Villas OX16 ...... 16 A3
Gower Rd OX12 .... 214 A4
Grafton Ho OX9 .... 168 B4
Grafton Orch OX11 ...... 168 B4
Graham Cl OX11 .... 237 D4
Graham Rd OX6 .... 65 E2
Grahame Ave RG8 .... 256 B3
Grammar School Hill
  OX7 .... 73 D2
Gramps Hill OX12 .... 231 F3
Grange Ave RG9 .... 253 D4
Grange Beck OX11 .... 201 D2
Grange Cl Goring RG8 .... 249 D3
  Highworth SN6 .... 190 A3
Grange Ct OX2 .... 140 A4
Grange Farm Rd HP14 .... 189 D4
Grange La OX15 .... 19 E4
Grange Park OX6 .... 48 A1
Grange Rd Banbury OX16 ...... 16 B2
  Henley-on-T RG9 .... 244 C1
  Oxford OX4 .... 142 A1
Grange The RG4 .... 258 B3
Grants Mews OX4 .... 141 F4
Granville Way OX6 ...... 66 A1
Grasmere Ave RG30 ...... 257 F1
Grass Hill RG4 .... 258 C2
Grates The OX4 .... 142 B2
Gravel Hill
  Caversham RG4 .... 259 D3
  Henley-on-T RG9 .... 244 B1
  Sonning Common RG4 .... 252 C3
Gravel Hill Cres RG4 .... 252 C3
Gravel La Drayton OX14 ...... 179 D1
  Warborough OX10 .... 203 D4
Gravel Pits La OX5 ...... 108 A3
Gravel Rd RG9 .... 253 F1
Gravel Wlk
  Drayton St L OX10 ...... 183 D3
  Faringdon SN7 .... 172 C2
Graveney Dr RG4 .... 258 C2
Gravenhill Rd N OX6 .... 81 D4
Gravett Cl RG4 .... 254 B4
Grays Cl OX44 .... 184 B4
Grays Rd OX3 .... 124 A1
Graysleaze RG4 .... 252 B2
Great Clarendon St OX2 ...... 123 D1
Great Close Rd OX5 ...... 108 B3
Great Western Dr OX11 .... 200 C1
Grebe Cl Abingdon OX14 ...... 179 F3
  Sandford-on-T OX4 ...... 142 C1
Grebe Rd OX16 .... 16 C2
Grebe Sq GL54 .... 68 A2
Green Cl Benson OX10 .... 204 A3
  Bicester OX6 .... 65 F1
  Didcot OX11 .... 218 C3
  Steventon OX13 .... 198 C3
  Wallingford OX10 .... 221 E4
Green Dean Hill RG4 .... 252 B1
Green End Rd HP14 ...... 189 F3
Green Farm OX17 .... 23 D2
Green Furlong OX10 .... 182 B3
Green Heart Way OX13 .. 156 C1
Green Hill OX4 .... 143 D1
Green Hitchings OX44 .. 145 E1
Green La Abingdon OX13 .... 159 D3
  Banbury OX15, OX16, OX17 ... 16 B2
  Bledlow Ridge HP14 .... 189 E3
  Caversham RG9 .... 254 A1
  Chesterton OX6 .... 79 F4
  Ewelme OX10 .... 204 B4
  Henley-on-T RG9 .... 254 B4
  Little Tew OX7 .... 44 B3
  Longworth OX13 .... 156 B1
  Milton-u-W OX7 .... 70 A1
  N Hinksey Vill OX2 ...... 140 A4
  North Leigh OX8 .... 105 D4
  Pangbourne RG8 .... 256 B2
  Sonning Common RG4 .... 252 C3
  South Newington OX15 .. 31 F4
  Stokenchurch HP14 ...... 188 B3
  Sunningwell OX13 .... 160 A3
  Swalcliffe OX15 .... 14 A1
  Upper Arncott OX6 ...... 96 C4
  Warborough OX10 .... 203 D4
  Woodcote RG8 .... 250 C4
  Woodstock OX20 .... 91 D4
Green N The OX10 .... 203 E4
Green Pl OX1 .... 141 E3

Green Rd Didcot OX11 .... 218 C4
  Kidlington OX5 .... 108 C4
  Oxford OX3 .... 124 C2
Green Ridges OX3 .... 125 D2
Green S The OX10 .... 203 E4
Green St OX4 .... 142 A4
Green The Adderbury OX17 ... 23 D2
  Alvescot OX18 .... 133 E3
  Ascott-u-W OX7 .... 71 E1
  Aston Rowant OX9 ...... 167 E2
  Barford St M OX15 ...... 32 C3
  Bladon OX20 .... 91 D1
  Cassington OX8 .... 107 E1
  Chalgrove OX44 .... 184 B3
  Charlbury OX7 .... 73 E2
  Charney Bassett OX12 .. 176 A1
  Chesterton OX6 .... 79 F4
  Chilton OX11 .... 235 F4
  Chipping Norton OX7 .... 42 C1
  Drayton OX14 .... 179 D1
  East Hanney OX12 ...... 197 D4
  Fernham SN7 .... 193 D2
  Fifield OX7 .... 69 E1
  Fringford OX6 .... 52 B3
  Garsington OX44 .... 143 F1
  Great Bourton OX17 .... 9 E4
  Great Milton OX44 ...... 145 D1
  Great Rollright OX7 ...... 29 D2
  Highworth SN6 .... 190 A3
  Hook Norton OX15 ...... 30 A4
  Hornton OX15 .... 7 E3
  Horspath OX33 .... 143 E3
  Horton-cum-S OX33 .... 112 A3
  Launton OX6 .... 66 C1
  Milcombe OX15 .... 20 C1
  North Leigh OX8 .... 89 E1
  Shrivenham SN6 .... 209 D3
  Standlake OX8 .... 137 E2
  Stanton Harcourt OX8 .. 138 A4
  Steventon OX13 .... 199 D3
  Swalcliffe OX15 .... 19 F4
  Tackley OX5 .... 77 D3
  Uffington SN7 .... 211 E4
  West Hanney OX12 ...... 176 B1
  West Hanney OX12 ...... 196 C3
Green's Rd OX8 .... 120 C4
Greenacres OX14 .... 179 D1
Greenacres Dr OX12 .... 214 B2
Greenacres La OX18 .... 135 E2
Greenfield Cres
  Stonesfield OX8 .... 89 E4
  Wallingford OX10 .... 221 D4
Greenfield Rd OX8 ...... 89 E4
Greenfields OX6 .... 96 B4
Greenfinch Cl OX4 ...... 142 C1
Greenhill Ct OX16 .... 16 B2
Greenhills Park OX15 .... 21 E2
Greenleas Ave RG4 ...... 259 D4
Greenmere OX10 .... 202 C2
Greenmoor RG8 .... 250 C4
Greens Garth OX15 ...... 21 F3
Greens Keep HP17 ...... 130 C3
Greensward The OX17 .. 5 F1
Greenway
  Haddenham HP17 .... 130 C3
  Lower Heyford OX6 ...... 63 D2
Greenway The OX8 ...... 216 A3
Greenwich La OX18 ...... 87 C2
Greenwood Ave OX9 .... 168 B3
Greenwood Dr OX6 ...... 65 D2
Greenwood Meadow OX9 .. 168 B3
Gregory Estate OX9 .... 185 E2
Grenoble Rd
  Garsington OX4 .... 143 D1
  Sandford-on-T OX4 ...... 142 B1
Grenville Way OX9 ...... 130 A1
Gresham Way RG30 ...... 258 A1
Greygoose La GL56 ...... 41 D3
Greyhound La OX9 ...... 129 F1
Greys Cl OX16 .... 15 F3
Greys Hill RG9 .... 244 B1
Greys Rd RG9 .... 254 B4
Greystoke Rd RG4 ...... 259 E2
Griffin Rd OX9 .... 148 B4
Griffiths Cl OX8 .... 138 B2
Griffiths Gdns OX6 ...... 66 A4
Grimmer Way RG8 ...... 250 C4
Grimsbury Dr OX16 .... 16 C4
Grimsbury Green OX16 .. 16 C4
Grimsbury Sq OX16 .... 16 C4
Grosvenor Rd
  Banbury OX16 .... 16 B3
  Caversham RG4 .... 259 E2
  N Hinksey Vill OX2 ...... 140 C3
Grove Cotts
  Caversham RG4 .... 259 D3
  Little Coxwell SN7 ...... 192 C4
Grove Hill
  Caversham RG4 .... 259 D2
  Highworth SN6 .... 190 A4
Grove La OX10 .... 205 D3
Grove Park Dr
  Ardington OX12 .... 215 E4
  Grove OX12 .... 197 D4
Grove Rd Bladon OX20 .. 91 E2
  Caversham RG4 .... 259 D3
  Grove OX12 .... 214 C4
  Harwell OX11 .... 217 E4
  Henley-on-T RG9 .... 244 C1
  Sonning Common RG4 .. 252 C3
Grove St Banbury OX16 .. 16 B3
  Cutteslowe OX2 .... 123 D4
  Wantage OX12 .... 214 C4
Grove The Abingdon OX14 .. 160 A1
  Bourton SN6 .... 209 D2
  Deddington OX15 .... 33 F2
Grovelands OX5 .... 108 B4
Grovelands Centre OX12 .. 196 B1

Grovelands Rd OX3 ...... 125 D1
Grundy Cl OX14 .... 180 A4
Grundy Cres OX14 ...... 141 F1
Grunsell Cl OX3 .... 124 B3
Guelder Rd OX4 .... 142 B1
Guildenford OX18 ...... 100 C3
Gullicote La OX17 ...... 8 C2
Gulliver's Cl OX15 ...... 8 A2
Gurden Pl OX3 .... 124 C2
Gurl Cl OX3 .... 124 C2
Gurney Cl RG4 .... 258 B3
Gurney Dr RG4 .... 258 B3
Gwyneth Rd OX4 .... 142 A1
Gwynne Cl RG31 .... 257 E2

Hackers La OX7 .... 55 F2
Hadden Hill OX11 ...... 201 E1
Haddenham Aerodrome
  Ind Est
  HP17 .... 130 C4
Haddenham & Thame
  Parkway Sta HP17 ...... 130 C3
Hadland Rd OX14 .... 180 B4
Hadleigh Rise RG4 ...... 259 F3
Hadow Rd OX3 .... 124 A2
Hadrians Gate NN13 .... 24 A4
Hafod OX2 .... 258 C3
Hagbourne Cl RG8 ...... 250 C4
Hagbourne Rd
  Aston Tirrold OX11 ...... 219 E1
  Didcot OX11 .... 219 D4
  East Hagbourne OX11 .. 219 E1
Hailey Ave OX7 .... 42 C1
Hailey Cft OX9 .... 168 A3
Hailey Cres OX7 .... 42 C1
Hailey Rd
  Chipping Norton OX7 .... 42 B1
  Witney OX8 .... 104 A2
Haines Ct OX13 .... 178 B4
Haldane Rd
  Caversham RG4 .... 258 C3
  Oxford OX4 .... 142 C1
Hale Rd OX10 .... 203 F3
Halfpenny La OX10 ...... 238 C3
Halifax Rd OX6 .... 66 A2
Hall Cl OX9 .... 186 A2
Hall Cl The OX6 .... 48 A3
Halliday Hill OX3 .... 124 A3
Halls Cl Drayton OX14 .. 179 E1
  N Hinksey Vill OX2 ...... 140 A4
Halls La OX12 .... 197 D4
Halse Water OX11 ...... 201 D1
Halton Rd OX18 .... 115 F1
Ham La OX15 .... 135 F1
Ham Rd OX12 .... 214 B2
Hamble Dr OX14 .... 160 A1
Hamble Rd OX11 .... 201 D1
Hambleden Dr OX10 .... 221 D4
Hambleside OX6 .... 65 D1
Hambridge La GL7 ...... 150 B3
Hamel The OX1 .... 123 D1
Hamels La OX1 .... 140 C1
Hamfield OX12 .... 214 A2
Hamilton Ave RG9 ...... 244 C1
Hamilton Rd
  Cutteslowe OX2 .... 123 D4
  Thame OX9 .... 130 A1
  Wargrave RG10 .... 255 F1
Hamlet The RG4 .... 252 A3
Hamlyn Cl OX12 .... 214 A4
Hammer La OX10 .... 183 D1
Hammett Pl OX18 ...... 115 E1
Hampden Ave OX9 ...... 147 F4
Hampden Cl Banbury OX16 .. 15 F3
  Bicester OX6 .... 66 A2
  Chalgrove OX44 .... 184 B3
  Faringdon SN7 .... 173 D2
Hampden Dr OX5 .... 108 C3
Hampden Rd
  Caversham RG4 .... 259 D1
  Oxford OX4 .... 142 B2
  Wantage OX12 .... 214 C3
Hampden Way OX10 .... 204 C2
Hampstead Hill RG4 .... 260 B4
Hampton Dr OX17 ...... 23 F3
Hanborough Cl OX8 .... 120 C4
Hanborough Rd OX8 .... 120 C4
Handlo Pl OX3 .... 124 C2
Hanney Rd
  Kingston Bagpuize OX13 .. 176 B4
  Steventon OX13 .... 198 B3
Hannis Rd OX7 .... 42 B1
Hanover Cl OX7 .... 73 E2
Hanover Gdns OX6 ...... 65 F1
Hans Ave OX12 .... 214 C3
Hanson Rd OX14 .... 159 F2
Hanwell Ct OX17 .... 8 C2
Hanwood Cl RG5 .... 260 B1
Harberton Mead OX3 .. 123 F2
Harbord Rd OX2 .... 109 D1
Harborne Rd OX5 .... 77 E3
Harcourt Cl RG9 .... 244 B1
Harcourt Green OX12 .. 214 C3
Harcourt Hill OX2 ...... 140 C3
Harcourt Rd
  Stokenchurch HP14 .... 188 C2
  Wantage OX12 .... 214 C3
Harcourt Terr OX3 ...... 124 C1
Harcourt Way
  Abingdon OX14 .... 159 F1
  Wantage OX12 .... 214 C3
Hardie Rd OX14 .... 179 E4
Hardings OX44 .... 184 B3
Hardings Cl OX4 .... 142 A3
Hardings Strings OX11 .. 218 C4
Hardwell Cl OX12 ...... 196 B1
Hardwick Ave OX5 ...... 108 C4
Hardwick Park OX16 .... 8 C1

Hardwick Rd Hethe OX6 .. 52 A4
  Whitchurch RG8 .... 256 B4
Hardy Cl RG4 .... 259 E1
Harebell Rd OX4 .... 142 C1
Harecourt OX12 .... 214 C2
Harefields OX12 .... 109 D1
Harewood Rd OX16 .... 16 C1
Harlech Ave RG4 .... 259 E3
Harlech Cl OX16 .... 15 F3
Harlequin Way OX16 .... 9 D1
Harley Rd
  Caversham RG4 .... 259 D1
  Oxford OX2 .... 122 C1
Harlington Ave OX12 .... 196 C1
Harlow Way OX3 .... 123 F4
Harmon Cl OX6 .... 66 A3
Harold White Cl OX3 .... 124 C1
Harolde Cl OX3 .... 124 B2
Harolds Cl OX8 .... 87 D2
Harper Cl OX6 .... 96 B4
Harpes Rd OX2 .... 123 D4
Harpsden Rd RG9 ...... 254 C4
Harpsichord Pl OX4 .... 123 F1
Harrier Park OX11 ...... 200 B2
Harrier Way OX6 .... 66 A2
Harriers View OX16 .... 16 B2
Harris Rd OX6 .... 63 E4
Harris's La OX13 .... 156 B1
Harrison Pl OX9 .... 129 F1
Harrison's La OX20 .... 91 D3
Harrisville OX6 .... 62 A4
Harroell HP18 .... 129 E3
Harrogate Rd RG4 ...... 258 C2
Harrow Rd OX4 .... 142 C2
Harrowby Rd OX16 .... 16 B1
Harsden Way RG9 ...... 254 C4
Hart Ave SN7 .... 172 C2
Hart Cl OX14 .... 180 B4
Hart Pl OX6 .... 66 A2
Hart St Henley-on-T RG9 .. 244 C1
Harthmoor Cl HP14 .... 188 C2
Harts Cl OX5 .... 108 B4
Hartslock Ct RG8 ...... 256 A3
Hartslock View RG8 .... 249 F1
Hartslock Way RG31 .... 257 E1
Harwell Cl OX14 .... 160 A1
Harwell Int Bsns Ctr OX11 217 D1
Harwell Rd OX11 ...... 199 F3
Harwood Rd OX11 ...... 218 C3
Haslemere Gdns OX2 .. 109 D1
Haslemere Way OX16 .. 16 C3
Hastings Cl OX16 ...... 15 F3
Hastings Dr OX16 ...... 115 F1
Hastings Hill OX7 ...... 55 F3
Hastings Rd OX16 ...... 15 F4
Hatch Cl OX5 .... 77 F2
Hatch End OX5 .... 77 F2
Hatch Gate La RG10 .... 255 F4
Hatch Way OX5 .... 77 F2
Hatchet Hill SN6 .... 227 D1
Hatching La OX8 .... 87 D2
Hatfield Pits La OX8 .... 104 B4
Hathaways OX33 .... 144 A4
Havelock Rd OX4 .... 142 B3
Haven Cl OX10 .... 202 B4
Havers Ave OX14 ...... 199 E1
Haw La Aldworth RG8 .. 247 F1
  Bledlow Ridge HP14 .... 189 F4
Hawke La OX15 .... 21 E2
Hawke's La OX15 ...... 19 E4
Hawker Sq GL54 ...... 68 A2
Hawkins St OX4 .... 141 F4
Hawkins Way OX13 .... 159 D3
Hawksmead OX6 ...... 81 D4
Hawksmoor Rd OX2 .. 109 D1
Hawkswell Gdns OX2 .. 123 E4
Hawksworth OX11 .... 200 B2
Hawkworth Cl OX12 .. 196 B1
Hawthorn Ave Oxford OX3 .. 124 B2
  Thame OX9 .... 147 E4
Hawthorn Cl
  N Hinksey Vill OX2 ...... 140 B4
  Wallingford OX10 .... 221 E4
Hawthorn Cres OX12 .. 214 C4
Hawthorn Gr OX18 .... 115 E1
Hawthorn Rd
  Eynsham OX8 .... 120 C4
  Faringdon SN7 .... 172 C2
Hawthorn Way
  Kidlington OX5 .... 108 C4
  Sonning RG4 .... 260 C1
Hawthorne Ave OX13 .. 159 E1
Hawthorne Rd RG4 .... 259 F2
Hawthornes RG31 ...... 257 D2
Hawthorns The OX16 .. 16 B2
Hayden La RG9 .... 224 B2
Haydon Rd OX11 ...... 200 C1
Hayes Ave OX13 .... 176 B4
Hayes Cl OX3 .... 123 F2
Hayfield Rd OX2 .... 123 D3
Haynes Rd OX3 .... 123 F3
Hayward Dr OX18 ...... 115 E1
Hayward Rd OX2 ...... 109 D1
Haywards Cl
  Henley-on-T RG9 .... 244 B1
  Wantage OX12 .... 214 C3
Haywards Rd OX14 .... 199 D4
Hazel Ave OX12 .... 214 B4
Hazel Cres OX5 .... 108 C3
Hazel End OX44 .... 143 E1
Hazel Gr Bicester OX6 .. 65 F3
  Purley on T RG8 .... 257 E2
Hazel N Hinksey Vill OX2 .. 122 B1
Hazel Wlk OX5 .... 108 C3

Hazeldene Gdns OX16 .. 16 B2
Hazell's La SN6 .... 209 E3
Hazells La GL7 .... 132 A3
Hazelmoor La RG4 ...... 252 B2
Hazelnut Path OX14 .... 160 C4
Hazelrig Cl OX9 .... 148 A4
Hazelton Cl OX9 .... 147 F4
Hazelwood Cl RG31 .... 257 E1
Headington Rd OX3 .... 124 A1
Headington Rdbt OX3 .. 124 C2
Headley Way OX3 ...... 124 A2
Healey Cl OX14 .... 179 F3
Hean Cl OX14 .... 160 A1
Hearns La RG4 .... 252 B3
Hearthway OX6 .... 9 D1
Heath Cl Milcombe OX15 .. 20 C1
  Oxford OX3 .... 142 B4
Heath Dr RG9 .... 254 A1
Heath La OX20 .... 91 D1
Heathcote Ave OX16 .... 16 C1
Heathcote Pl OX14 .... 160 B1
Heather Cl
  Carterton OX18 .... 115 E3
  Sonning Common RG4 .. 253 D3
Heather Rd Bicester OX6 .. 65 F3
  Milton (Abingdon) OX14 .. 199 E3
Heathfield Ave RG9 .... 254 A1
Heathfield Cl RG9 ...... 254 A1
Hedge End OX20 ...... 91 E3
Hedge Hill Rd OX12 .... 213 F3
Hedgemead Ave OX14 .. 160 B1
Hedgerley OX9 .... 168 A3
Helen Rd OX2 .... 122 C1
Hellebourine Cl OX4 .. 142 C1
Helwys Pl OX5 .... 92 B1
Hemdean Hill RG4 ...... 259 D2
Hemdean Rd RG4 ...... 259 D2
Hemdean Rise RG4 .... 259 D2
Hemingway Dr OX6 .... 65 E1
Hempton Rd OX15 ...... 33 F2
Hendon Pl OX6 .... 66 A2
Hendred St OX4 .... 142 A3
Hendred Way OX14 .... 160 A1
Henfield View OX10 .... 203 D4
Hengest Gate OX11 .... 217 F4
Hengrove Cl OX3 ...... 124 B2
Henley Ave OX4 .... 142 A3
Henley Dr SN6 .... 190 A4
Henley Gdns OX6 ...... 65 F1
Henley Rd
  Caversham RG4 .... 260 B4
  Dorchester OX10 .... 202 C4
  Sandford-on-T OX4 .... 161 D4
  Shiplake RG4 .... 260 B4
Henley St OX4 .... 141 F4
Henleys La OX14 ...... 179 D1
Hennef Way OX16 ...... 16 C4
Henor Mill Cl OX14 .... 160 A1
Henrietta Rd OX9 ...... 130 A1
Henry Rd OX2 .... 122 C1
Henry Taunt Cl OX3 .... 124 C3
Hensington Cl OX20 .. 91 E3
Hensington Rd OX20 .. 91 D3
Henwood Dr OX1 ...... 140 A1
Herald Way OX6 .... 66 A2
Herbert Cl OX4 .... 142 A4
Hereford Way OX16 .... 9 D1
Heritage Cl OX7 .... 71 D1
Herman Cl OX14 .... 180 A4
Hermitage Rd OX14 .... 179 F3
Hernes Cl OX2 .... 123 D4
Hernes Cres OX2 ...... 123 D4
Hernes Rd OX2 .... 123 D4
Heron Cl OX18 .... 115 E2
Heron Ct OX6 .... 66 A1
Heron Island RG4 ...... 259 E1
Heron Rd OX10 .... 204 B2
Heron Shaw RG8 ...... 249 E4
Heron Way OX6 .... 16 A2
Heron's Wlk OX14 .... 159 F1
Herons Pl OX2 .... 123 D4
Herringcote OX10 ...... 182 B1
Herschel Cres OX4 .... 142 B2
Hertford Cl Bicester OX6 .. 65 F2
  Caversham RG4 .... 259 E3
Hertford St OX4 .... 142 A3
Hethe Rd Cottisford NN13 .. 38 A2
  Hardwick NN13 .... 51 E4
Hewett Ave OX4 .... 258 B2
Hewett Cl RG4 .... 258 B2
Hewetts Cl OX8 .... 87 D2
Hewgate Ct RG9 ...... 244 C1
Heycroft OX8 .... 120 C4
Heydons Terr OX17 .... 3 F4
Heyford Cl OX8 .... 137 E3
Heyford Hill La OX4 .... 141 F1
Heyford Hill Rdbt OX4 .. 141 F1
Heyford Mead OX5 .... 92 B1
Heyford Rd
  Kirtlington OX5 .... 77 F2
  Middleton Stoney OX6 .. 64 A2
  Steeple Aston OX6 ...... 62 A4
Hicks Cl OX5 .... 104 A3
Hid's Copse Rd OX2 .. 140 A4
Higgs Cl OX11 .... 219 D3
High Acres OX16 ...... 16 C2
High Cross Way OX3 .. 124 C3
High Furlong OX6 ...... 16 A4
High House Cl OX13 .. 152 C4
High Land Cl HP18 .... 98 A1
High Meadow
  Caversham RG4 .... 258 B2
  Sibford Gower OX15 .... 13 D1
High Rd Beckley OX3 .. 111 D2
  Brightwell-cum-S OX10 .. 202 C2
  Brightwell-cum-S, Slade End
    OX10 .... 203 D1

High St
Abingdon OX13, OX14 ...... 179 F4
Adderbury OX17 ...... 23 D2
Ascott-u-W OX7 ...... 71 E1
Ashbury SN6 ...... 228 A4
Aston OX18 ...... 135 E2
Aston Rowant OX9 ...... 167 F2
Bampton OX18 ...... 134 C2
Banbury OX15, OX16, OX17 ... 16 B3
Barford St M OX15 ...... 32 C3
Benson OX10 ...... 203 F2
Bishopstone SN6 ...... 227 E2
Bloxham OX15 ...... 21 F3
Bodicote OX15 ...... 22 B4
Burford OX18 ...... 100 C3
Chalgrove OX44 ...... 184 B4
Charlton-on-O OX5 ...... 95 D2
Charney Bassett OX12 ...... 175 F1
Childrey OX9 ...... 213 E2
Chinnor OX9 ...... 168 B4
Chipping Norton OX7 ...... 42 C2
Clifton Hampden OX14 ...... 181 E2
Cropredy OX17 ...... 4 C1
Croughton NN13 ...... 36 B4
Cuddesdon OX44 ...... 144 A1
Culham OX14 ...... 180 A2
Cumnor OX2 ...... 139 E3
Deddington OX15 ...... 33 F2
Didcot OX11 ...... 218 C4
Dorchester OX10 ...... 182 B1
Drayton OX14 ...... 179 D1
Drayton St L OX10 ...... 183 D3
East Hendred OX12 ...... 216 C3
Ewelme OX10 ...... 204 C2
Eynsham OX8 ...... 120 C4
Fernham SN7 ...... 193 D2
Fifield OX7 ...... 69 D1
Finstock OX7 ...... 88 A3
Goring RG8 ...... 249 E3
Great Rollright OX7 ...... 29 D2
Haddenham HP17 ...... 130 C3
Harwell OX11 ...... 217 F4
Highworth SN6 ...... 190 A3
Hinton Waldrist SN7 ...... 155 F1
Hook Norton OX15 ...... 30 A4
Islip OX5 ...... 93 F1
Lechlade GL7 ...... 150 B2
Lewknor OX9 ...... 187 D4
Long Crendon HP18 ...... 129 E3
Long Wittenham OX14 ...... 201 E4
Ludgershall HP18 ...... 98 A4
Middleton Cheney OX17 ...... 17 F4
Milton (Abingdon) OX14 ...... 199 E3
Milton-u-W OX7 ...... 70 A1
Nettlebed RG9 ...... 224 B1
North Moreton OX11 ...... 220 A4
Oxford OX1 ...... 123 E1
Pangbourne RG8 ...... 256 B3
Ramsden OX7 ...... 88 A2
Ratley OX15 ...... 2 A2
Shipton-u-W OX7 ...... 85 E4
Shrivenham SN6 ...... 209 E3
Shutford OX15 ...... 14 A3
Sonning RG4 ...... 260 B2
Souldern OX6 ...... 35 F2
South Newington OX15 ...... 31 F4
Standlake OX8 ...... 137 E2
Stanford in the V SN7 ...... 194 C4
Steventon OX13 ...... 199 D2
Stonesfield OX8 ...... 89 E4
Streatley RG8 ...... 249 D3
Sutton Courtenay OX14 ...... 200 A4
Tetsworth OX9 ...... 166 A4
Thame OX9 ...... 129 F1
Uffington SN7 ...... 211 E4
Upper Heyford OX6 ...... 48 C1
Upton OX11 ...... 218 B1
Wallingford OX10 ...... 221 E4
Wargrave RG10 ...... 255 E1
Watchfield SN6 ...... 191 E1
Watlington OX9 ...... 186 A1
Wheatley OX33 ...... 144 A4
Whitchurch RG8 ...... 256 B4
Witney OX8 ...... 118 A4
Woodstock OX20 ...... 91 D3
Wootton OX20 ...... 75 D2
High View OX12 ...... 214 A2
Highbridge Cl RG4 ...... 259 F2
Highclere Gdns
Banbury OX15 ...... 15 F3
Wantage OX12 ...... 214 B3
Highdown Ave RG4 ...... 259 F4
Highdown Hill Rd
Caversham RG4 ...... 259 D4
Mapledurham RG4 ...... 259 D4
Highfield HP18 ...... 129 E4
Highfield Ave OX3 ...... 124 B1
Highfield Cl OX9 ...... 147 E4
Highfield Park RG10 ...... 255 F1
Highfield Rd RG31 ...... 257 E2
Highlands OX16 ...... 9 D1
Highlands La RG9 ...... 254 A4
Highmoor Rd RG4 ...... 258 C2
Hightown Gdns OX16 ...... 16 B2
Hightown Leyes OX16 ...... 16 B2
Hightown Rd OX16 ...... 16 B2
Highworth Pl OX8 ...... 118 A4
Highworth Rd
Faringdon SN7 ...... 172 C1
Shrivenham SN6 ...... 209 D4
Highworth Way RG31 ...... 257 D1
Hill Bottom Cl RG8 ...... 250 C2
Hill Cl Charlbury OX7 ...... 73 D2
Chipping Norton OX7 ...... 42 C1
East Challow OX12 ...... 214 A2
Hill Cres OX7 ...... 88 B3
Hill Farm Ct OX9 ...... 168 B3
Hill Farm La OX6 ...... 47 E3

Hill Gdns RG8 ...... 249 D3
Hill La OX18 ...... 152 B4
Hill Lands RG10 ...... 255 E1
Hill Piece OX11 ...... 235 F4
Hill Rd Chinnor OX9 ...... 168 B3
Lewknor OX9 ...... 187 D4
Lewknor OX9 ...... 187 E3
Watchfield SN6 ...... 191 E1
Watlington OX9 ...... 206 C4
Hill Rise
Great Rollright OX7 ...... 29 D2
Horspath OX33 ...... 143 E3
Woodstock OX20 ...... 91 D4
Hill The Aynho OX17 ...... 35 E4
Bourton SN6 ...... 209 D2
Burford OX18 ...... 100 C2
Garsington OX44 ...... 143 F1
Hill Top La OX9 ...... 168 C2
Hill Top Rd OX4 ...... 142 A4
Hill View Carterton OX18 ...... 115 E2
Kingston Lisle OX12 ...... 212 A2
Oxford OX3 ...... 125 D2
Uffington SN7 ...... 211 E4
Hill View Cres OX16 ...... 16 A4
Hill View La OX13 ...... 159 D4
Hillary Dr OX11 ...... 218 C4
Hillary Way OX33 ...... 144 B4
Hillcraft Rd OX33 ...... 125 E4
Hilliat Fields OX14 ...... 179 D1
Hilliers Cl OX14 ...... 200 A4
Hillsborough Cl OX4 ...... 142 A2
Hillsborough Rd OX4 ...... 142 A2
Hillside Harwell OX11 ...... 217 D2
Whitchurch RG8 ...... 256 B4
Hillside Cl Banbury OX16 ...... 16 C2
Upper Arncott OX6 ...... 96 C4
Hillside Rd OX4 ...... 46 C1
Hilltop HP18 ...... 129 E3
Hilltop Gdns OX5 ...... 93 F1
Hilltop Rd RG4 ...... 258 B3
Hillview OX7 RG31 ...... 257 D1
Hillview Rd Abingdon OX14 ... 159 F1
Oxford OX4 ...... 123 D1
Hillwerke OX9 ...... 168 B3
Hilly Lawn Ct OX7 ...... 42 C2
Hillyard Barns OX14 ...... 200 A4
Hilton Rd OX16 ...... 16 A3
Hinksey Hill OX1 ...... 141 D2
Hinksey Hill Intc OX1 ...... 141 E2
Hinton Hill SN6 ...... 227 D2
Hinton Rd
Hinton Waldrist OX13 ...... 156 A2
Longworth OX13 ...... 156 A2
Hinton Springs SN6 ...... 227 D2
Hirstwood RG30 ...... 257 F1
Hiskins OX12 ...... 214 A3
Hitchman Dr OX7 ...... 42 C2
Hithercroft Cholsey OX10 ...... 220 B3
South Moreton OX11 ...... 220 B3
Hithercroft Ct OX10 ...... 221 D3
Hithercroft Rd OX10 ...... 221 D4
Hive Mews OX14 ...... 179 F3
Hixet Wood OX7 ...... 73 D2
HM Prison (Bullingdon)
OX6 ...... 97 D3
Hobbs Cl OX14 ...... 180 A4
Hobby Ct OX4 ...... 142 C1
Hobson Rd OX2 ...... 123 D4
Hocker Bench SN6 ...... 227 E2
Hocketts Cl RG8 ...... 250 C2
Hockmore St OX4 ...... 142 B2
Hodge Cl OX1 ...... 141 E4
Hodgson Cl OX4 ...... 49 F4
Hogarth Pl OX14 ...... 179 F3
Hogg End Bloxham OX15 ...... 21 F2
Chipping Warden OX17 ...... 5 F3
Holborn Hill OX12 ...... 231 E4
Holcombe La OX10 ...... 183 E3
Holford Rd OX14 ...... 117 F4
Holis Cl OX3 ...... 118 B4
Holkham Cl RG30 ...... 257 F1
Holland Cl OX9 ...... 168 B4
Holland Pl OX3 ...... 142 C4
Holland Rd OX14 ...... 160 A1
Hollandridge La RG9 ...... 207 E2
Hollands Rise OX17 ...... 23 F2
Holley Cres OX3 ...... 124 C2
Holliers Cl Sydenham OX9 ...... 167 E4
Thame OX9 ...... 147 F4
Holliers Cres OX7 ...... 60 C4
Hollington HP18 ...... 129 E4
Hollow Furlong OX8 ...... 107 E1
Hollow Way Childrey OX12 ...... 213 E2
Oxford OX3, OX4 ...... 142 B3
Holloway Hill OX15 ...... 12 A1
Holloway La
Compton Wynyates OX15 ...... 12 A1
Ibstone RG9 ...... 207 F3
Holloway Rd OX33 ...... 144 A4
Holloway Rd The SN7 ...... 192 A4
Holloway The
Harwell OX11 ...... 217 F3
Mollington OX17 ...... 4 A2
Holly Cl Bicester OX6 ...... 65 F3
Kidlington OX5 ...... 108 C4
Rotherfield Peppard RG9 ...... 242 C3
Hollybush Rd
Carterton OX18 ...... 115 E1
Hook Norton OX15 ...... 30 A4
Hollybush Row OX1 ...... 123 D1
Holm Sq OX6 ...... 65 F3
Holm Way OX6 ...... 65 F3
Holme Park Farm La RG4 ...... 260 B1
Holmemoor Dr RG4 ...... 260 C1
Holmlea Rd RG8 ...... 249 E3
Holoway Rd OX8 ...... 118 A4
Holt The Abingdon OX14 ...... 179 F4

Mollington OX17 ...... 3 F2
Purley on T RG8 ...... 257 E2
Holt Weer Cl OX2 ...... 109 D1
Holyoake Rd OX3 ...... 124 B2
Holyrood Cl RG4 ...... 259 E3
Holywell Cl OX14 ...... 160 B1
Holywell St OX1 ...... 123 E1
Home Cl Carterton OX18 ...... 115 E1
Cutteslowe OX2 ...... 122 B4
Kidlington OX5 ...... 92 C1
Wootton (Oxford) OX13 ...... 159 D3
Home Croft RG31 ...... 257 D1
Home Farm OX10 ...... 221 F4
Home Farm Cl
Ambrosden OX6 ...... 81 E2
East Hendred OX12 ...... 216 B4
Shipton-u-W OX7 ...... 85 E4
Home Farm Ct OX17 ...... 23 D2
Homefield Cl HP14 ...... 188 C2
Homeleaze Rd SN6 ...... 209 F4
Homestall Ct OX4 ...... 122 A1
Homestead Cres OX6 ...... 63 D4
Homestead Rd OX16 ...... 16 C1
Homestead The
Bladon OX20 ...... 91 E2
Kidlington OX5 ...... 108 B4
Thame OX9 ...... 129 F1
Hone Ct OX7 ...... 73 D2
Honey La OX10 ...... 220 C1
Honeybottom La OX13 ...... 159 D3
Honeyham OX18 ...... 116 B2
Honeysuckle Cl OX6 ...... 65 F3
Honeysuckle Gr OX4 ...... 143 D1
Hook End La RG8 ...... 249 D1
Hook Norton Rd OX15 ...... 19 D4
Hookend La RG8 ...... 251 E4
Hooks Cl GL7 ...... 132 C1
Hop Gdns RG9 ...... 244 B1
Hopcraft Cl OX6 ...... 96 C4
Hopcraft La OX15 ...... 33 F2
Hopkins Ct OX4 ...... 142 B3
Hopton Rd OX9 ...... 130 A1
Horley Path Rd OX15 ...... 8 A1
Horn Hill OX15 ...... 32 C3
Horn Hill Rd OX17 ...... 22 C2
Horn La Adlestrop OX12 ...... 40 A3
East Hendred OX12 ...... 216 B3
Hornbeam Cl Banbury OX16 ... 16 A3
Purley on T RG8 ...... 257 E3
Hornbeam Dr OX4 ...... 143 D1
Horne 66 A4
Hornbeam Rd OX6 ...... 65 F3
Hornsea Cl RG30 ...... 257 F1
Hornton Hollow OX15 ...... 21 E2
Horse Cl The RG4 ...... 259 E2
Horse Close Cotts OX44 ... 164 B4
Horse Fair
Banbury OX15, OX16 ...... 16 B3
Chipping Norton OX7 ...... 42 C2
Deddington OX15 ...... 33 F2
Horse Shoe La OX20 ...... 72 A4
Horsecroft SN7 ...... 194 C4
Horseman Cl OX3 ...... 124 A3
Horsemere La OX8 ...... 107 E1
Horsepond Rd RG4 ...... 252 A3
Horseshoe La OX20 ...... 75 F2
Horseshoe Park RG8 ...... 256 B3
Horseshoe Rd
Bledlow Ridge HP14 ...... 189 E4
Pangbourne RG8 ...... 256 B3
Horseshoes La OX10 ...... 203 F2
Horsham Cl OX16 ...... 8 C1
Horspath Driftway OX3 ...... 142 C4
Horspath Rd OX4 ...... 142 C3
Horton Ave OX9 ...... 148 A4
Horton Cl OX9 ...... 148 A4
Horton La OX15 ...... 21 D1
Horton View OX16 ...... 16 B2
Horwood Cl OX3 ...... 124 B2
Hosker Cl OX3 ...... 125 D2
Hound Cl OX14 ...... 160 B1
Howard Cl OX14 ...... 180 A4
Howard Cornish Rd OX13 .. 178 B4
Howard Rd OX16 ...... 16 C3
Howard St OX4 ...... 142 A3
Howbery Farm OX10 ...... 221 F4
Howe Cl OX33 ...... 144 A4
Howe Rd OX9 ...... 206 B4
Howes La OX6 ...... 65 D2
Howgate Dr RG8 ...... 249 D2
Howland Rd OX9 ...... 148 A3
Hoyle Cl OX8 ...... 104 A2
Huckleberry Cl RG8 ...... 257 E2
Hudleston Ave OX10 ...... 204 B1
Hudson St Bicester OX6 ...... 65 E2
Deddington OX15 ...... 33 F2
Hugh Allen Cres OX3 ...... 123 F2
Hughes Cl OX7 ...... 73 E1
Hughes Cres SN7 ...... 192 B2
Humber Cl Didcot OX11 ...... 201 D1
Wantage OX12 ...... 214 C3
Humber St OX15 ...... 21 F2
Humber Wlk OX16 ...... 15 F4
Humfrey Rd OX3 ...... 124 C2
Humphries Cl OX14 ...... 115 F2
Hundred Acre Cl OX14 ...... 142 C4
Hunsdon Rd OX4 ...... 142 A2
Hunt Cl OX6 ...... 65 F1
Hunt Rd OX4 ...... 148 A4
Hunt's Cl OX8 ...... 89 E4
Hunter Cl Abingdon OX14 ...... 160 A2
Oxford OX4 ...... 142 C2
Huntercombe End La
RG9 ...... 224 A2
Hunters Chase RG4 ...... 258 C3
Hunters Cl OX12 ...... 196 B1
Hunters Field SN7 ...... 194 C4

Hunters Piece SN6 ...... 209 D1
Hunters Point OX9 ...... 168 B3
Hunts Cl OX18 ...... 100 C2
Hurdeswell OX8 ...... 90 A1
Hurdlers Green OX9 ...... 186 A1
Hurst OX10 ...... 221 E3
Hurst La Cumnor OX2 ...... 140 A3
Freeland OX8 ...... 106 A4
Hurst Rise Rd OX2 ...... 140 B4
Hurst St OX4 ...... 141 F4
Huscarle Way RG31 ...... 257 E2
Hutchcomb Rd OX2 ...... 140 B4
Hutchcombe Farm Cl
OX2 ...... 140 B4
Huxley Cl Bicester OX6 ...... 65 E2
Wootton (Oxford) OX13 ...... 159 D3
Hyacinth Wlk OX4 ...... 161 F4
Hyde Copse OX13 ...... 178 B4
Hyde Gr OX15 ...... 21 E2
Hyde Pl OX14 ...... 179 E3
Hyde Rd OX12 ...... 196 A3
Hyde The OX14 ...... 179 E3
Hydes The RG31 ...... 257 E2
Hydrangea Wlk OX16 ...... 9 D1
Hythe Bridge St OX1 ...... 123 D1

Ian Mikardo Way RG4 ...... 259 E1
Ibstone Ave RG4 ...... 259 F3
Ibstone Rd HP14 ...... 188 B2
Ickford Rd
Shabbington HP18 ...... 128 B1
Tiddington OX9 ...... 145 F4
Worminghall HP18 ...... 127 F3
Ickleton Rd
East Challow OX12 ...... 214 A2
Wantage OX12 ...... 214 A2
Icknield Cl
Aston Rowant OX9 ...... 168 A2
Didcot OX11 ...... 200 B1
Icknield La OX12 ...... 214 C2
Icknield Pl RG8 ...... 249 E4
Icknield Rd RG8 ...... 249 E4
Icknield Way SN6 ...... 227 E2
Idbury Cl OX8 ...... 117 E4
Idstone Hill SN6 ...... 228 A2
Idstone Rd SN6 ...... 228 A3
Iffley Rd OX4 ...... 141 F4
Iffley Turn OX4 ...... 142 A3
Ilchester Mews RG4 ...... 259 F3
Ilex Cl RG4 ...... 252 C2
Ilges La OX10 ...... 221 D1
Ilkley Rd OX4 ...... 258 C2
Illingworth Ave RG4 ...... 259 F3
Ilsley Cl RG4 ...... 252 C3
Imperial Ct RG9 ...... 244 C1
Independent Bsns Pk
HP14 ...... 188 B3
Ingham La OX9 ...... 186 A1
Ingle Cl OX3 ...... 124 A2
Inglewood Cl RG4 ...... 252 C3
Ingrebourne Way OX11 ...... 200 C2
Inkerman Cl OX14 ...... 159 E1
Innsworth Rd OX18 ...... 115 F2
Inott Furze OX3 ...... 142 B4
Insall Rd OX7 ...... 42 C2
Ireton Cl OX44 ...... 184 B3
Ireton Ct OX9 ...... 129 F1
Iron Down Hill
Barford St M OX15 ...... 32 B2
South Newington OX15 ...... 31 F2
Ironstone Hollow OX15 ...... 30 B4
Ironstones OX16 ...... 16 A4
Isis Ave OX6 ...... 65 D1
Isis Bsns Ctr OX4 ...... 142 C3
Isis Cl Abingdon OX14 ...... 160 B1
Long Hanborough OX8 ...... 106 A4
Islip Rd Bletchingdon OX5 ...... 93 D4
Cutteslowe OX2 ...... 123 D4
Islsley Rd OX3 ...... 124 C2
Itchen Ct OX11 ...... 201 D2
Ivatt Wlk OX16 ...... 16 C4
Ivy La Mollington OX17 ...... 4 A2
Oxford OX3 ...... 124 B2
Ivybank RG31 ...... 257 E1
Ivydene Rd RG30 ...... 258 B1

Jack Argent [14] OX4 ...... 142 C1
Jack Straw's La OX3 ...... 124 A3
Jackdaw La OX4 ...... 141 F4
Jackies La OX33 ...... 144 B4
Jackman Cl OX14 ...... 180 A4
Jackson Cl OX18 ...... 115 E1
Jackson Dr OX1 ...... 141 F1
Jackson Rd Bledington OX7 .. 54 B1
Cutteslowe OX2 ...... 109 D1
Jacobs Cl OX8 ...... 104 A1
Jacobs Yd OX7 ...... 60 C4
James Ct OX18 ...... 152 C4
James St OX4 ...... 141 F4
James Wolfe Rd OX4 ...... 142 C4
Jane Seaman Ct OX4 ...... 143 D1
Japonica Cl OX6 ...... 65 F3
Japonica Wlk OX16 ...... 9 D1
Jarn Way OX1 ...... 140 B1
Jarvis La OX6 ...... 66 A1
Jasmine Cl OX4 ...... 142 C2
Jasmine Pl OX6 ...... 65 F3
Javelin Way OX10 ...... 204 B2
Jay Cl OX6 ...... 81 D4
Jaynes Cl OX16 ...... 16 B1
Jefferson Cl RG4 ...... 259 E1
Jefferson Way OX9 ...... 148 A4
Jeffersons Piece OX7 ...... 73 E2
Jemmetts Cl OX10 ...... 182 B1
Jennings La OX11 ...... 217 F4
Jericho St OX2 ...... 123 D2
Jerome Way OX5 ...... 92 B3
Jersey Dr OX16 ...... 9 D1

Jersey Rd OX4 ...... 142 A2
Jervis Cl OX7 ...... 60 C4
Jespers Hill SN7 ...... 173 D2
Jesse's La HP18 ...... 129 E3
Jessops Cl OX3 ...... 123 F3
Jethro Tull Gdns OX10 ...... 221 E4
Jeune St OX4 ...... 141 F4
Joan Lawrence Pl OX3 ...... 124 C1
John Buchan Rd OX3 ...... 124 A3
John Garne Way OX3 ...... 124 A1
John Lopes Rd OX8 ...... 120 C4
John Mason Rd OX14 ...... 180 A4
John Morris Rd OX14 ...... 179 F3
John Piers La OX1 ...... 141 E3
John Snow Pl OX3 ...... 124 C2
John Towle Cl OX1 ...... 141 E3
Johnson Cl OX44 ...... 143 E1
Johnston's Way OX7 ...... 42 C1
Johnstone Pl OX10 ...... 221 E4
Jordan Cl Caversham RG4 ... 259 F3
Didcot OX11 ...... 201 D1
Jordan Hill OX3 ...... 109 D1
Josey Cl RG4 ...... 252 C3
Jourdain Rd OX4 ...... 142 C2
Jowett Wlk OX1 ...... 123 E1
Joyce's Rd SN7 ...... 194 B4
Jubilee Cl OX6 ...... 62 A4
Jubilee Cotts OX12 ...... 215 F3
Jubilee Ct OX16 ...... 16 B3
Jubilee Rd HP14 ...... 188 C2
Jubilee Way OX11 ...... 219 D4
Jubillee La OX7 ...... 85 D2
Judd's Cl OX8 ...... 118 B4
Judges Cl OX5 ...... 108 C4
Junction Rd Banbury OX16 ... 16 C3
Churchill OX7 ...... 55 F2
Oxford OX4 ...... 142 B3
Juniper Cl OX16 ...... 9 D1
Juniper Dr OX4 ...... 142 C1
Juniper Gdns OX6 ...... 65 F3
Juniper Way RG31 ...... 257 E1
Juxon St OX2 ...... 123 D2

Kames Cl OX4 ...... 142 A3
Katchside OX14 ...... 199 F3
Katherine's Wlk GL7 ...... 150 B2
Keats Cl OX6 ...... 65 D2
Keats Rd OX16 ...... 16 A2
Keble Cl OX7 ...... 150 B3
Keble Rd Bicester OX6 ...... 65 F3
Oxford OX1 ...... 123 E2
Kedleston Rise OX16 ...... 16 C1
Keene Cl OX9 ...... 161 D4
Keens La OX9 ...... 168 B3
Keeys Cl OX6 ...... 50 B2
Kelburne Rd OX4 ...... 142 A2
Kelham Hall Dr OX33 ...... 144 A4
Kelly's Rd OX33 ...... 143 F4
Kelmscott Cl RG4 ...... 258 C2
Kelso Mews RG4 ...... 259 F3
Kelvedon Way RG4 ...... 258 C3
Kemps Rd OX17 ...... 23 D3
Kempson Cres OX44 ...... 142 A1
Kempster Cl OX14 ...... 180 A4
Kendal Ave RG4 ...... 259 F3
Kendal Cl OX2 ...... 109 D1
Kendal Piece OX7 ...... 73 E2
Kenhill Rd OX15 ...... 6 B1
Kenilworth Ave OX4 ...... 142 A2
Kenilworth Rd RG4 ...... 139 F2
Kenilworth Way OX16 ...... 15 F3
Kenley Ave OX18 ...... 115 F2
Kennedy Cl OX4 ...... 142 C4
Kennedy Cres OX10 ...... 220 C1
Kennedy Dr RG8 ...... 256 C3
Kennedy Rd OX6 ...... 65 E1
Kennel La
Chipping Norton OX7 ...... 42 A1
Steventon OX13 ...... 199 D3
Kennet Cl Berinsfield OX10 .. 182 B2
Bicester OX6 ...... 65 E1
Grove OX12 ...... 196 B1
Kennet Rd Abingdon OX14 ... 160 A1
Harwell OX11 ...... 217 E1
Kennett Rd OX3 ...... 124 B1
Kennington Rd
Kennington OX1 ...... 141 F1
Kennington OX1 ...... 160 C3
Radley OX14 ...... 160 C3
Kennington Rdbt OX1 ...... 141 F2
Kennylands Rd RG4 ...... 253 D2
Kensington Cl
Abingdon OX14 ...... 179 F2
Kings Sutton OX17 ...... 23 F3
Kent Cl Abingdon OX14 ...... 180 A4
Oxford OX4 ...... 142 C2
Kentons La RG10 ...... 255 E4
Kentwood Cl
Cholsey OX10 ...... 220 C1
Reading RG30 ...... 257 F1
Kentwood Hill RG31 ...... 257 D1
Kenville Rd OX1 ...... 141 F1
Kernham Dr RG31 ...... 257 E2
Kerry Cl OX16 ...... 9 D1
Kersington Cres OX4 ...... 142 B2
Kerwood Cl OX20 ...... 91 D4
Keston Cl RG4 ...... 259 E1
Kestrel Cl OX18 ...... 115 E2
Kestrel Cres OX4 ...... 142 B1
Kestrel Pl OX4 ...... 142 B1
Kestrel Way OX6 ...... 81 D4
Kestrels The OX12 ...... 196 B1
Ketchmere Cl HP18 ...... 129 E3
Kew Win OX11 ...... 201 D1
Keydale Rd OX33 ...... 143 F4

Keyser Rd OX15 .... 22 C4
Keyte's Cl OX17 .... 23 D2
Kibble Cl OX11 .... 219 D4
Kiddington Rd OX7 .... 60 C4
Kidlington Business Park
  OX5 .... 92 B1
Kidlington Ctr OX5 .... 92 C1
Kidlington Rd OX5 .... 93 F1
Kidmore End Rd
  Caversham RG4 .... 259 D4
  Mapledurham RG4 .... 259 D4
Kidmore La OX44 .... 252 C2
Kidmore Rd RG4 .... 258 C3
Kilbale Cres OX16 .... 16 B2
Kildare Gdns RG4 .... 259 E2
Kilkenny La OX18 .... 115 F3
Kiln Cl OX4 .... 161 E4
Kiln La Garsington OX44 .... 143 E1
  Oxford OX3, OX33, OX44 .... 124 C1
  Shiplake RG9 .... 254 B1
  Wheatley OX33 .... 144 A4
Kiln Rd RG4 .... 259 E4
Kimbells Cl HP18 .... 128 B1
Kimber Cl OX33 .... 144 A4
Kimber Rd OX14 .... 179 E4
Kimbers Cl OX12 .... 196 A2
Kinecroft OX10 .... 221 E4
Kineton Rd OX1 .... 141 E4
King Alfred Dr OX11 .... 200 C1
King Edward St OX1 .... 123 E1
King James Way RG9 .... 254 B4
King St OX2 .... 123 D2
King Wlk OX11 .... 200 C1
King's Ave OX6 .... 65 E1
King's Cl OX9 .... 147 F4
King's Cross OX2 .... 123 D4
King's End OX6 .... 65 E1
King's Head La OX5 .... 93 F1
King's Head Mews OX7 .... 42 C2
King's La SN7 .... 192 A2
King's Mill La OX3 .... 123 F1
King's Rd Banbury OX16 .... 16 A3
  Henley-on-T RG9 .... 244 B1
  Thame OX9 .... 148 A4
Kingfisher Cl OX14 .... 179 F2
Kingfisher Dr OX16 .... 16 C2
Kingfisher Gn OX4 .... 142 C1
Kingfisher Way OX6 .... 81 D4
Kingfishers OX12 .... 214 C4
Kingham Dr OX18 .... 115 E2
Kingham Rd OX7 .... 55 F3
Kings Ave
  Highworth SN6 .... 190 A3
  Marcham OX13 .... 178 B4
Kings Cl Ashbury SN6 .... 228 A4
  Brightwell-cum-S OX10 .... 202 C2
  Henley-on-T RG9 .... 244 B1
  Letcombe Bassett OX12 .... 214 A1
  Worminghall HP18 .... 127 E3
Kings Farm La RG9 .... 253 F3
Kings La Harwell OX11 .... 217 F4
  Kencot OX18 .... 132 B2
Kings Rd Bloxham OX15 .... 21 E2
  Caversham RG4 .... 259 E1
Kings Stile OX17 .... 10 C1
Kings Way Dr OX5 .... 109 D4
Kingsclere Rd OX6 .... 65 E1
Kingsey Rd OX9 .... 130 B1
Kingsholme Cl OX11 .... 218 C3
Kingsley Rd OX6 .... 65 D2
Kingsmead GL7 .... 150 B3
Kingston Cl OX14 .... 179 F4
Kingston Hill OX9 .... 188 A4
Kingston Hts OX8 .... 105 D4
Kingston Rd OX2 .... 123 D2
Kingsway Banbury OX16 .... 16 A3
  Caversham RG4 .... 259 F3
Kingswood La HP18 .... 98 C3
Kinson Rd RG30 .... 258 A1
Kipling Cl OX6 .... 65 E2
Kirby Cl
  Middle Barton OX7 .... 60 C4
  South Moreton OX11 .... 219 F3
Kirby Pl OX4 .... 142 B3
Kirby Rd GL54 .... 68 A2
Kirk Cl Cutteslowe OX2 .... 109 D1
  Kennington OX1 .... 160 C4
Kirkfell Cl RG31 .... 257 E1
Kirkham Cl RG4 .... 259 F3
Kirtlington Rd OX6 .... 63 D4
Kit La RG9 .... 241 E3
Knapp Cl OX14 .... 179 E4
Knappe Cl RG4 .... 254 B4
Knapton's Croft OX6 .... 62 B3
Knighton Cl RG4 .... 259 D2
Knighton Hill SN7 .... 210 C1
Knights Rd OX4 .... 142 B1
Knights Way RG4 .... 259 D3
Knightsbridge La OX9 .... 186 A3
Knoll Cl OX12 .... 231 F4
Knoll The RG31 .... 257 D1
Knolles Rd OX4 .... 142 B2
Knollys Cl OX14 .... 160 A2
Knowlands SN6 .... 190 A4
Knowle Cl RG4 .... 258 B2
Knowle La OX6 .... 79 D1
Knowsley Rd RG31 .... 257 E2
Kybald St OX1 .... 123 E1
Kyetts Cnr OX17 .... 4 C1
Kynaston Rd OX11 .... 218 C4
Kysbie Cl OX14 .... 159 F2

Laburnum Ave OX13 .... 159 E1
Laburnum Cl OX6 .... 81 E2
Laburnum Cres OX5 .... 108 C3

Laburnum Gr
  Banbury OX16 .... 16 B1
  Didcot OX11 .... 218 C4
Laburnum Rd OX2 .... 140 B4
Lacemakers Chinnor OX9 .... 168 B3
  Long Crendon HP18 .... 129 E4
Lacey Dr OX9 .... 148 A4
Lackmore Gdns RG8 .... 250 C4
Ladburn La OX18 .... 115 D3
Ladder Hill OX33 .... 144 A4
Ladenham Rd OX4 .... 142 C2
Lady Gr OX14 .... 201 D2
Lady Jane Ct RG4 .... 259 E2
Lady Wlk SN7 .... 211 E4
Ladygrove Paddock
  OX14 .... 179 E3
Ladywell Cl OX18 .... 105 E3
Laggots Cl SN7 .... 155 F1
Lake Rd
  East Hagbourne OX11 .... 218 C3
  Shrivenham SN6 .... 209 E4
Lake St OX1 .... 141 E3
Lake View NN13 .... 38 A2
Lakefield Rd OX4 .... 142 A1
Lakeside OX2 .... 108 C1
Lakeside Ind Est OX8 .... 137 F4
Lamarsh Rd OX2 .... 122 C1
Lamb La OX20 .... 91 D1
Lamb's Cres OX16 .... 16 C3
Lamb's La OX20 .... 75 F2
Lambe Ave OX14 .... 199 E2
Lambert Wlk OX9 .... 129 F1
Lamborough Hill OX13 .... 159 D3
Lambourn Rd OX4 .... 142 A2
Lambourne Cres OX6 .... 65 F1
Lambourne Rd RG4 .... 252 C3
Lambrick Way OX14 .... 179 F2
Lambridge La RG9 .... 244 B2
Lambridge Wood Rd
  RG9 .... 244 A2
Lambs Cl OX5 .... 92 C1
Lambton Cl OX4 .... 142 C3
Lambwath Stream OX11 .... 200 C2
Lammas St OX14 .... 159 F1
Lamorna Cres RG31 .... 257 E1
Lampitts Green OX15 .... 15 D4
Lancaster Ave OX10 .... 204 B2
Lancaster Cl OX6 .... 66 A2
Lancaster Pl OX18 .... 115 F1
Lanchester Dr OX16 .... 15 F4
Lancott La OX8F 137 D2
Lancut Rd OX8 .... 103 F1
Landells OX18 .... 134 C2
Landseer Wlk OX14 .... 179 F3
Lane Cl Horley OX15 .... 8 A2
  Kidlington OX5 .... 108 B4
Lane End OX10 .... 222 A4
Lane The Bishopstone SN6 .... 227 D2
  Chastleton GL56 .... 40 B4
  Chilton OX11 .... 235 F4
  Cuddesdon OX44 .... 144 A1
  Deddington OX15 .... 33 D2
  Fritwell OX6 .... 49 F4
  Great Tew OX7 .... 45 E4
  Lower Heyford OX6 .... 62 B3
Lanes The OX18 .... 134 C2
Langdale Gate OX18 .... 118 A4
Langdale Rd OX9 .... 148 A4
Langford Cl RG4 .... 259 E1
Langford Gdns OX6 .... 65 E1
Langford La Kidlington OX5 .... 92 A1
  Wendlebury OX5 .... 80 B3
Langhams Way RG10 .... 255 F1
Langley Cl OX18 .... 124 B1
Langley La OX18 .... 152 B3
Langley Rd Abingdon OX14 .... 159 F1
  Chalgrove OX44 .... 184 B3
Langley's La OX18 .... 137 E1
Langston Ct OX17 .... 55 F3
Langton Ave OX16 .... 81 E2
Lanham Way OX4 .... 142 A1
Lansdown Cl OX16 .... 16 A2
Lansdown Rd SN7 .... 173 D2
Lansdowne Rd OX13 .... 159 D3
Lapwing Cl OX6 .... 81 D4
Lapwing La OX10 .... 221 D1
Larch Cl Bicester OX6 .... 65 F3
  Kingston Bagpuize OX13 .... 156 C1
Larch End OX44 .... 143 E1
Larches The
  Carterton OX18 .... 115 E1
  Oxford OX3 .... 125 D2
Larissa Cl RG31 .... 257 D1
Lark Hill OX12 .... 215 D1
Larkdown OX12 .... 214 C2
Larkfield OX10 .... 221 D1
Larkfields OX3 .... 124 C1
Larkhill Pl OX14 .... 179 E4
Larkhill Rd OX14 .... 179 F4
Larkins La OX3 .... 124 B2
Larksfield Cl OX18 .... 133 E4
Larksfield Rd OX16 .... 16 B1
Larkswood Cl RG31 .... 257 E2
Larsen Rd OX6 .... 63 E4
Lashbrook Mead RG9 .... 255 D2
Lashbrook Rd RG9 .... 255 D2
Lashford La OX13 .... 158 C4
Lashford Rd OX13 .... 158 C4
Lashlake Rd OX9 .... 129 F1
Latchford La OX44 .... 164 C4
Lathbury Rd OX2 .... 123 D3
Latimer Rd
  Carterton OX18 .... 115 E1
  Oxford OX3 .... 124 B1
Latton Cl Chilton OX11 .... 235 F4
  Kingston Bagpuize OX13 .... 156 B1
Laud's Cl RG9 .... 244 B1
Laughton Hill OX8 .... 89 E4

Launceston Ave RG4 .... 259 F3
Laundry La OX18 .... 135 E2
Launton Rd Bicester OX6 .... 66 A1
  Stratton Audley OX6 .... 66 B4
Laurel Cl Banbury OX16 .... 16 B1
  Carterton OX18 .... 115 E2
  Chalgrove OX44 .... 184 B4
Laurel Cres OX12 .... 214 C4
Laurel Dr
  Kingston Bagpuize OX13 .... 156 C1
  Reading RG31 .... 257 D3
Laurel Farm Cl OX3 .... 124 B2
Laurels The Fringford OX6 .... 52 B3
  Great Coxwell SN7 .... 192 R4
  Stadhampton OX44 .... 163 E1
  Tetsworth OX9 .... 166 A4
Lavender Cl OX16 .... 9 D1
Lavender Pl OX18 .... 115 E1
Lavender Sq OX18 .... 134 C2
Lawns The HP18 .... 98 A1
Lawrence Cl OX12 .... 213 E2
Lawrence La OX18 .... 100 C3
Lawrence Leys OX15 .... 21 F3
Lawrence Rd OX4 .... 142 B3
Lawrence Way OX6 .... 65 E1
Lawson Dr RG4 .... 258 C3
Lawson La OX11 .... 235 E4
Lawton Ave OX18 .... 115 E1
Lay Ave OX10 .... 182 B3
Laytm Rise RG31 .... 257 E2
Lea Gr OX11 .... 200 C1
Lea Rd RG4 .... 252 C2
Leabrook Cl OX16 .... 16 B1
Leach Rd
  Berinsfield OX10 .... 182 B3
  Bicester OX6 .... 65 E1
Leafield Rd Crawley OX8 .... 103 F3
  Oxford OX4 .... 142 B3
  Shipton-u-W OX7 .... 86 A3
Leamington Dr SN7 .... 172 C1
Leaver Rd RG9 .... 244 B1
Lechlade Rd Buscot SN7 .... 171 E4
  Faringdon SN7 .... 172 B3
  Highworth SN6 .... 190 A4
  Langford GL7 .... 132 B1
Leckford Pl OX1 .... 123 D2
Leckford Rd OX2 .... 123 D2
Ledbury Cl RG30 .... 258 A1
Ledgers Cl OX4 .... 142 B1
Lee Ave OX14 .... 180 A4
Lee Cl Charlbury OX7 .... 73 E2
  Kidlington OX5 .... 92 B1
Lee Ct OX9 .... 147 F4
Lee Rd HP27 .... 169 F3
Lees Hts OX7 .... 73 E2
Lees The SN7 .... 172 C2
Leicester Cl RG9 .... 244 B2
Leiden Rd OX3 .... 142 C4
Leigh Cl OX48 .... 105 D3
Leigh Gr OX16 .... 16 B3
Lely Ct OX14 .... 179 F3
Lennox Gdns OX16 .... 16 A2
Lenthal OX5 .... 93 D4
Lenthall Rd
  Abingdon OX14 .... 179 F4
  Oxford OX4 .... 141 F2
Lenton Rd OX16 .... 16 B1
Leon Cl OX4 .... 141 F4
Leopold St OX4 .... 142 A4
Lerwick Croft OX6 .... 66 A2
Lester Cl OX17 .... 23 D3
Lester Way OX10 .... 221 D4
Letcombe Ave OX14 .... 179 F4
Letcombe Hill OX12 .... 214 A1
Letcombe Wlk OX12 .... 196 B1
Letts Alley OX9 .... 186 A1
Levenot Cl OX16 .... 16 C3
Leverkus Ho OX9 .... 168 B3
Levery Cl OX3 .... 123 F2
Lewell Ave OX3 .... 123 F2
Lewin Cl OX4 .... 142 B2
Lewington Cl OX44 .... 164 B4
Lewis Cl OX3 .... 125 D1
Lewis Rd OX7 .... 42 B1
Lewknor Cl OX9 .... 187 D4
Ley The OX20 .... 91 E3
Leybourne Gdns OX9 .... 168 B4
Leyes The OX15 .... 33 F2
Leyland Ct OX16 .... 16 B2
Leys App OX7 .... 42 C1
Leys Cl OX15 .... 15 D4
Leys Pl OX4 .... 142 A4
Leys Rd OX2 .... 139 E3
Leys The Adderbury OX17 .... 22 C2
  Chipping Norton OX7 .... 42 B1
  Salford OX7 .... 41 F3
Leys Villas OX8 .... 118 A4
Leyshon Rd OX33 .... 144 B4
Library Ave OX11 .... 217 E1
Liddell Rd OX4 .... 142 B2
Lidderdale Rd GL54 .... 68 A2
Liddiard Cl
  Kennington OX1 .... 160 C4
  Wantage OX12 .... 214 C4
Liddon Rd OX44 .... 184 B3
Lido Rd OX11 .... 234 C4
Lidsey Rd OX16 .... 16 A3
Lilac Cl RG8 .... 257 E3
Limborough Rd OX12 .... 214 B3
Lime Ave OX16 .... 16 C2
Lime Cres OX6 .... 65 E1
Lime Gr Chinnor OX9 .... 168 B3
  Kingston Bagpuize OX13 .... 156 B1
Lime Kiln Rd OX5 .... 77 E3
Lime Rd OX2 .... 140 B4
Lime Tree Cl OX18 .... 115 E2
Lime Tree Rd RG8 .... 249 D3
Lime Wlk OX3 .... 124 B1

Limes The
  Dorchester OX10 .... 182 B1
  Stratton Audley OX6 .... 52 B1
Limes Way HP18 .... 128 B1
Limetree Cl OX12 .... 196 B1
Limetrees OX11 .... 217 F1
Linacre Cl OX11 .... 219 D4
Lince La OX5 .... 77 F1
Lincoln Cl Banbury OX16 .... 16 A3
  Bicester OX6 .... 66 A2
  Standlake OX8 .... 137 E2
Lincoln Gdns OX11 .... 219 D4
Lincoln Pl OX9 .... 147 F4
Lincoln Rd OX1 .... 141 E3
Lincombe La OX1 .... 159 F4
Lincraft Cl OX5 .... 108 C4
Linden Cres OX12 .... 196 C1
Linden Gate OX11 .... 217 F4
Linden Rd OX6 .... 65 F1
Lindsay Dr OX14 .... 160 A1
Link The Banbury OX16 .... 16 A3
  Marston OX3 .... 123 F2
  Oxford OX3 .... 124 C2
Links Rd OX1 .... 160 C4
Links The OX10 .... 221 F4
Linkside Ave OX2 .... 108 C1
Linkwood Rd OX8 .... 103 E1
Linnet Cl
  Clifton Hampden OX14 .... 182 A2
  Oxford OX4 .... 142 B1
Linton Rd OX2 .... 123 E3
Lion Meadow RG9 .... 224 B1
Lipscombe Pl OX18 .... 115 E2
Lipstock Pl OX11 .... 200 C1
Lister Cl RG8 .... 257 E3
Litchfield Cl OX7 .... 58 C3
Lithgow Rd GL54 .... 68 A2
Little Acreage OX3 .... 123 F3
Little Blenheim OX5 .... 108 A3
Little Bowden La RG8 .... 256 A2
Little Brewery St OX4 .... 123 F1
Little Bridge Rd OX15 .... 21 E2
Little Bury OX4 .... 143 D1
Little Clarendon St OX1 .... 123 E1
Little Croft Rd RG8 .... 249 E3
Little Glebe RG4 .... 260 C2
Little Green OX15 .... 21 E2
Little Howe Cl OX14 .... 160 C2
Little La Aynho OX17 .... 35 E4
  Milton (Abingdon) OX14 .... 199 E3
Little Lees OX7 .... 73 E2
Little Paddock OX6 .... 52 B4
Littlebrook Meadow
  OX7 .... 70 B1
Littlegate St OX1 .... 141 E4
Littlehay Rd OX4 .... 142 A3
Littlejohns La RG30 .... 258 B1
Littlemore Rd OX4 .... 142 B2
Littlemore Rdbt OX4 .... 142 A2
Littlestead Cl RG4 .... 259 F3
Littlewood Rd HP14 .... 188 C3
Littleworth Bsns Ctr
  OX33 .... 143 F4
Littleworth Hill OX12 .... 214 B3
Littleworth Rd
  Benson OX10 .... 203 F2
  Wheatley OX33 .... 144 A4
Lobelia Rd OX4 .... 142 C1
Lock Cres OX5 .... 108 C3
Lockheart Cres OX4 .... 142 B2
Lockheed Cl OX16 .... 16 B4
Lockinge Ct OX11 .... 218 C4
Locks La OX12 .... 214 B2
Lockstile Mead RG8 .... 249 E3
Lockstile Way RG8 .... 249 E3
Lockway OX14 .... 199 D4
Locombe Hill GL7 .... 131 D3
Lodden Ave OX10 .... 182 B3
Loddon Cl
  Abingdon OX14 .... 160 A1
  Bicester OX6 .... 65 E1
Loddon Dr Didcot OX11 .... 201 D1
  Wargrave RG10 .... 255 D1
Loder Rd OX11 .... 217 F4
Loder's Field GL7 .... 150 B2
Loders The GL7 .... 150 B2
Lodge Cl Banbury OX16 .... 16 B2
  Bicester OX6 .... 65 F3
  Marston OX3 .... 123 F4
Lodge Rd OX8 .... 90 C1
Logic La OX1 .... 123 E1
Lombard St
  Abingdon OX14 .... 179 F4
  Eynsham OX8 .... 120 C4
Lombard Way OX16 .... 17 D3
Lomond Ave RG4 .... 259 F3
London La OX7 .... 71 C4
London Pl OX4 .... 123 F1
London Rd Bicester OX6 .... 80 C4
  Blewbury OX11 .... 236 C4
  Chipping Norton OX7 .... 43 D2
  Great Haseley OX9 .... 146 A2
  Holton OX33 .... 126 A1
  Oxford OX3, OX33 .... 124 B2
  Tiddington OX9 .... 145 F3
  Upton OX11 .... 236 C4
  Wheatley OX33 .... 144 B4
  Woodstock RG5 .... 260 B1
London St SN7 .... 173 D2
Long Cl N Hinksey Vill OX2 .... 122 A1
  Oxford OX3 .... 142 C4
Long Crendon Ind Est
  HP18 .... 129 F3
Long Crendon Rd HP18 .... 128 B2
Long Ford Cl OX1 .... 141 E4
Long Furlong HP17 .... 130 C3
Long Furlong Rd OX13 .... 159 E2
Long Ground OX4 .... 142 C1

Long La Oxford OX4 .... 142 B2
  Purley on T RG31 .... 257 D2
  Reading RG31 .... 257 D2
Long Toll RG8 .... 251 D3
Long Tow OX13 .... 159 E1
Long Wall HP17 .... 130 C3
Long Wittenham Rd
  OX11 .... 220 A4
Longcot Rd Longcot SN7 .... 192 A1
  Shrivenham SN6 .... 209 E3
Longelandes Cl OX16 .... 16 A4
Longelandes Way OX16 .... 16 A4
Longfellow Cl UX6 .... 65 E2
Longfellow Dr OX14 .... 179 E3
Longfellow Rd OX16 .... 16 A2
Longfields Bicester OX6 .... 65 F1
  Marcham OX13 .... 178 B4
Longford Way OX11 .... 200 C1
Longhurst Cl RG4 .... 259 E2
Longlands Rd OX4 .... 142 C2
Longleat Cl OX16 .... 16 C1
Longleat Dr RG31 .... 257 D2
Longmead OX14 .... 159 F1
Longmore Ave GL54 .... 68 A2
Longore OX8 .... 89 E4
Longore Ct OX8 .... 89 E4
Longwall OX4 .... 142 A2
Longwall St OX1 .... 123 E1
Longworth Cl OX16 .... 16 C4
Longworth Rd
  Charney Bassett OX12 .... 176 A2
  Oxford OX2 .... 123 D2
Lonsdale Rd OX2 .... 123 D4
Lord Cl OX18 .... 115 E2
Lords Piece Rd OX7 .... 42 B1
Lovatt Cl OX18 .... 115 E3
Love La OX9 .... 186 A1
Lovegrove's La RG8 .... 241 E2
Lovelace Cl OX14 .... 160 A2
Lovelace Dr OX5 .... 109 D4
Lovelace Rd OX2 .... 109 D2
Lovell Cl Ducklington OX8 .... 118 A2
  Henley-on-T RG9 .... 254 B4
  Swinbrook OX18 .... 102 A2
Loverock Rd RG30 .... 258 B1
Lower Armour Rd RG31 .... 257 E1
Lower Bungalows RG8 .... 249 E4
Lower Cherwell St OX16 .... 16 B1
Lower Church St HP14 .... 188 C3
Lower Cl OX15 .... 22 C4
Lower Common SN7 .... 211 E4
Lower Cres OX6 .... 102 C2
Lower Elmstone Dr RG31 .... 257 E1
Lower End
  Great Milton OX44 .... 145 D2
  Piddington OX6 .... 97 F4
  Salford OX7 .... 41 F2
  Shutford OX15 .... 14 A3
Lower Farm Cl HP18 .... 128 B2
Lower Farm La OX17 .... 3 F2
Lower Hades Rd OX5 .... 77 D3
Lower Henley Rd RG4 .... 259 E1
Lower Heyford Rd OX6 .... 63 D3
Lower Icknield Way OX9 .... 168 B4
Lower Rd
  Aston Rowant OX9 .... 166 C2
  Blackthorn OX6 .... 82 A3
  Chilton OX11 .... 235 E4
  Chinnor OX9 .... 168 B4
  Long Hanborough OX8 .... 90 C1
Lower St
  Barford St M OX15 .... 32 C3
  Islip OX5 .... 93 F1
Lower Wharf OX10 .... 221 E4
Lower Whitley Rd OX2 .... 139 E4
Lowes Cl Shiplake RG9 .... 255 D2
  Stokenchurch HP14 .... 188 B3
Lowfield Green RG4 .... 259 F2
Lowfield Rd RG4 .... 259 F3
Loyd Cl OX14 .... 160 A2
Loyd Rd OX11 .... 218 B3
Lucca Dr OX14 .... 179 E3
Lucern Rd OX2 .... 123 E4
Lucey Cl RG31 .... 257 D2
Lucky La OX16 .... 16 B3
Ludford Gdns OX15 .... 21 E2
Ludgershall Rd OX6 .... 97 F4
Ludlow Dr OX9 .... 148 A4
Ludsden Gr OX9 .... 148 A4
Luker Ave RG9 .... 244 B2
Lumberd Rd OX14 .... 160 A1
Lune Cl OX11 .... 201 D1
Lupton Rd Thame OX9 .... 148 A4
  Wallingford OX10 .... 221 D4
Luscombe Cl RG4 .... 259 E2
Luther Ct OX1 .... 141 E4
Lych Gate La OX44 .... 145 D1
Lycroft Cl RG8 .... 249 E4
Lydalls Cl OX11 .... 200 C1
Lydalls Rd OX11 .... 200 C1
Lydia Cl OX3 .... 124 C2
Lydsee Gate OX12 .... 214 A3
Lye Valley OX3 .... 142 B4
Lyefield Ct RG4 .... 259 D3
Lyford Cl OX14 .... 179 D1
Lyford Way OX14 .... 160 A1
Lymbrook Cl OX8 .... 119 E3
Lyme Gr RG31 .... 257 E1
Lymington Gate RG4 .... 258 C3
Lynch The OX12 .... 216 B3
Lyndene Rd OX11 .... 200 B2
Lyndhurst Rd
  Goring RG8 .... 249 E3
  Reading RG30 .... 258 A1
Lyndworth Cl OX3 .... 124 C2
Lyndworth Mews OX3 .... 124 C2
Lyneham Cl OX18 .... 115 F2

Lyneham Rd Bicester OX6 .... 66 A2
Milton-u-W OX7 .... 70 A2
Lynges Cl OX14 .... 160 A1
Lynmouth Rd Didcot OX11 .. 218 C4
Reading RG1 .... 259 D1
Lynn Cl OX3 .... 123 F2
Lynt Rd SN6 .... 170 A3
Lynton La OX8 .... 107 E1
Lyon Cl OX14 .... 160 A1
Lysander Cl OX6 .... 66 A2
Lytham End RG31 .... 257 D2
Lytton Rd OX4 .... 142 A3

Maberley Cl OX14 .... 179 E3
Mably Way OX12 .... 214 B4
Macaulay Cl OX6 .... 65 E2
Macdonald Cl OX11 .... 200 B1
Mackenzie Cl OX6 .... 65 E2
Mackley Cl OX15 .... 33 F2
Macray Rd OX8 .... 118 A2
Mafeking Row OX9 .... 186 C2
Magdalen Cl OX6 .... 65 F2
Magdalen Ct OX11 .... 219 D4
Magdalen Pl OX18 .... 115 E1
Magdalen Rd OX4 .... 142 A4
Magdalen St OX1 .... 123 E1
Magnolia Cl OX5 .... 108 C4
Magnolias The
  Banbury OX16 .... 9 D1
  Bicester OX6 .... 65 F3
Magpie La OX1 .... 123 E1
Maidcroft Rd OX4 .... 142 B3
Maiden's Cl SN6 .... 191 E1
Maidley Cl OX8 .... 104 B1
Main Ave OX4 .... 161 E4
Main Rd Broughton OX15 ... 15 E1
  Curbridge OX8 .... 117 E3
  East Hagbourne OX11 ...... 218 C3
  Fyfield OX13 .... 157 E1
  Long Hanborough OX8 ...... 90 B1
  Middleton Cheney OX17 ..... 17 F4
  Sutton Courtenay OX14 .... 200 C4
  West Hanney OX12 .... 196 C3
Main St Adlestrop OX12 ..... 40 B2
  Bledington OX7 .... 54 B1
  Chilton OX11 .... 235 E4
  Duns Tew OX6 .... 47 E3
  East Hanney OX12 .... 197 D3
  Finstock OX7 .... 88 C4
  Fringford OX6 .... 52 B3
  Grove OX12 .... 196 C1
  Hanwell OX17 .... 8 C2
  Hethe OX6 .... 52 A4
  Letcombe Bassett OX12 .... 214 A1
  Mollington OX17 .... 4 A2
  North Newington OX15 ..... 15 D2
  Over Norton OX7 .... 42 C3
  Shalstone MK18 .... 25 E3
  Sibford Gower OX15 .... 19 D4
  Sibford Gower OX15 .... 19 D4
  Tadmarton OX15 .... 20 B4
  Turweston NN13 .... 24 B4
  West Hagbourne OX11 ...... 218 B2
  Westbury NN13 .... 25 D2
  Wroxton OX15 .... 15 D4
Majors Rd SN6 .... 191 F1
Makins Rd RG9 .... 254 B4
Malet Cl HP14 .... 188 C3
Malford Rd OX3 .... 124 C2
Mall The SN6 .... 209 F4
Mallard Cl OX4 .... 142 B1
Mallard Way OX12 .... 196 B1
Mallins La SN7 .... 192 B2
Mallory Ave RG4 .... 259 E3
Maltfield Rd OX3 .... 124 A3
Malthouse SN6 .... 228 A4
Malthouse Cl SN6 .... 228 A4
Malthouse La
  Bodicote OX15 .... 22 B4
  Dorchester OX10 .... 182 B1
  Long Compton CV36 .... 27 F3
  Shutford OX15 .... 14 A3
Malthouse Paddock SN7 .. 174 C4
Maltings Cl OX15 .... 21 E2
Maltings The RG20 .... 235 D1
Maltsters OX8 .... 89 E4
Malvern Cl Banbury OX16 ... 16 B1
  Didcot OX11 .... 200 B1
Malyns Cl OX9 .... 168 B4
Mandarin Pl OX12 .... 196 B1
Mandeville Cl OX14 .... 160 A1
Mandhill Cl OX12 .... 214 C4
Manning Cl OX15 .... 21 F1
Mannings Cl OX15 .... 19 D4
Manor Cl Aston OX18 ..... 135 F1
  Cassington OX8 .... 107 E1
  Drayton OX14 .... 179 D1
  Great Bourton OX17 .... 9 E4
  Shrivenham SN6 .... 209 D4
  Sutton Courtenay OX14 .... 200 C4
  West Hagbourne OX11 ..... 218 B2
Manor Cres Didcot OX11 ... 200 B1
  Standlake OX8 .... 137 E2
  Stanford in the V SN7 ..... 194 C4
Manor Ct Abingdon OX14 ... 179 F3
  Banbury OX16 .... 16 C4
  Chadlington OX7 .... 57 E1
Manor Dr OX33 .... 143 E3
Manor Farm Cl
  Kingham OX7 .... 54 C3
  Merton OX6 .... 95 E4
Manor Farm Ct OX20 ..... 75 F2
Manor Farm La RG8 ...... 256 B1
Manor Farm Rd
  Dorchester OX10 .... 182 B1
  Horspath OX33 .... 143 E3
Manor Field OX12 .... 214 A1
Manor Gn OX11 .... 217 E4

Manor Gr OX1 .... 160 C4
Manor La Clanfield OX18 ... 152 C4
  East Hendred OX12 .... 216 A3
  Shrivenham SN6 .... 209 D3
Manor Orch OX15 .... 8 A2
Manor Park OX17 .... 1 B1
Manor Pl OX1 .... 123 F1
Manor Rd Adderbury OX17 ... 22 C2
  Banbury OX16, OX15 ...... 16 C4
  Bladon OX20 .... 91 D1
  Brize Norton OX18 .... 116 A2
  Carterton OX18 .... 115 E3
  Chinnor OX9 .... 149 D3
  Didcot OX11 .... 200 B1
  Ducklington OX8 .... 118 A2
  Fringford OX6 .... 52 B4
  Goring RG8 .... 249 D3
  Great Bourton OX17 .... 9 E4
  Henley-on-T RG9 .... 254 B4
  Middle Barton OX7 .... 46 B1
  Oxford OX1 .... 123 F1
  South Hinksey OX1 .... 141 D3
  Wantage OX12 .... 232 B3
  Whitchurch RG8 .... 256 B4
  Witney OX8 .... 118 B4
  Woodstock OX20 .... 91 D4
Manor Way OX4 .... 92 C1
Manor Wood Gate RG9 ... 255 D2
Manorsfield Rd OX6 .... 65 F1
Mansell Cl OX8 .... 106 B3
Mansfield Gdns OX11 ..... 219 D4
Mansfield Rd OX1 .... 123 E1
Mansion Hill OX17 .... 17 F4
Mansmoor Rd OX5 .... 94 C4
Manston Cl OX6 .... 66 A2
Manzel Rd OX6 .... 66 A3
Maple Ave OX5 .... 108 C4
Maple Cl Banbury OX16 .... 16 C1
  N Hinksey Vill OX2 .... 140 B4
  Sonning Common RG4 ..... 253 D2
Maple Ct Goring RG8 ...... 249 D3
  Kidlington OX5 .... 108 C4
Maple Rd Bicester OX6 .... 65 F1
  Faringdon SN7 .... 172 C2
  Thame OX9 .... 147 E4
Maple Way OX7 .... 71 D1
Maple Well OX8 .... 89 E4
Mapledene RG4 .... 258 C2
Mapledurham Dr RG8 .... 257 E3
Mapledurham View RG31 . 257 E1
Maples The
  Carterton OX18 .... 115 E1
  Grove OX12 .... 196 B1
March Rd OX17 .... 3 E2
Marcham Rd
  Abingdon OX13, OX14 .... 179 D4
  Drayton OX14 .... 179 D1
  Marcham OX13 .... 179 D4
Marchwood Ave OX4 ..... 259 E4
Margaret Cl Banbury OX16 . 16 A3
  Bicester OX6 .... 65 E2
Margaret Rd
  Adderbury OX17 .... 23 D3
  Oxford OX3 .... 124 C1
Maria Cres OX12 .... 214 C3
Marie Cl OX6 .... 67 F4
Marigold Cl 10 OX4 .... 142 C1
Marines Dr SN7 .... 172 C1
Marjoram Cl OX4 .... 143 D1
Mark Rd OX3 .... 124 C1
Market End Way OX6 ..... 65 E2
Market Pl Abingdon OX14 . 179 F4
  Banbury OX15, OX16 ...... 16 B3
  Deddington OX15 .... 33 F2
  Faringdon SN7 .... 172 C2
  Henley-on-T RG9 .... 244 B1
  Lechlade GL7 .... 150 B2
  Wallingford OX10 .... 221 E4
  Wantage OX12 .... 214 B2
  Woodstock OX20 .... 91 D3
Market Sq Bicester OX6 ... 65 F1
  Witney OX8 .... 118 A4
Market St Charlbury OX7 .. 73 D2
  Chipping Norton OX7 ...... 42 C2
  Oxford OX1 .... 123 E1
  Woodstock OX20 .... 91 D3
Marlborough Ave OX5 .... 92 B1
Marlborough Cl
  Carterton OX18 .... 115 F1
  Eynsham OX8 .... 120 C4
  Faringdon SN7 .... 172 C2
  Kidlington OX5 .... 92 B1
  Oxford OX4 .... 142 A1
Marlborough Cr
  Long Hanborough OX8 .... 106 A4
  Woodstock OX20 .... 91 D4
Marlborough Ct OX2 ..... 122 C1
Marlborough Dr OX7 ..... 107 E1
Marlborough Gdns SN7 .. 172 C1
Marlborough La
  Stanford in the V SN7 ... 194 C4
  Witney OX8 .... 118 A4
Marlborough Pl
  Banbury OX16 .... 16 B3
  Charlbury OX7 .... 73 D2
  Eynsham OX8 .... 120 C4
  Faringdon SN7 .... 172 C1
Marlborough Rd
  Banbury OX16 .... 16 B3
  Chipping Norton OX7 ..... 42 C2
  Oxford OX1 .... 141 E4
Marlborough St SN7 ..... 172 C2
Marley Ind Est OX16 ..... 16 B4
Marley La OX44 .... 184 B4
Marley Way OX16 .... 16 B4
Marling Cl RG31 .... 257 E1
Marlow Cl OX10 .... 221 D4

Marlow Rd
  Beacon's Bottom HP14 ... 189 D1
  Henley-on-T RG9 .... 244 C2
Marlowe Cl OX16 .... 15 F3
Marmion Rd RG9 .... 254 C4
Marriott Cl OX2 .... 109 D1
Marriotts Cl HP17 .... 130 C3
Marriotts La HP17 .... 130 C3
Marriotts Way HP17 ..... 130 C3
Marsack St RG4 .... 259 E1
Marsh Cl OX5 .... 108 B3
Marsh Ct OX14 .... 179 F4
Marsh End OX9 .... 147 D1
Marsh La Clanfield OX18 .. 152 C4
  Fyfield OX13 .... 157 D2
  Marston OX3 .... 124 A3
Marsh Rd Oxford OX4 .... 142 B3
  Shabbington HP18 .... 128 B2
Marsh Way SN7 .... 211 D3
Marshall Cl
  Chipping Norton OX7 ..... 42 C1
  Reading RG8 .... 257 E2
Marshall Cres OX7 .... 46 C1
Marshall Rd OX4 .... 142 B3
Marshalls Cl OX15 .... 6 B1
Marshland Sq RG4 ...... 259 D3
Marston Ferry Rd
  Cutteslowe OX2 .... 123 E3
  Marston OX3 .... 123 E3
Marston Rd
  Oxford OX3, OX4 .... 123 F2
  Thame OX9 .... 130 A1
Marston St OX4 .... 141 F4
Marten Gate OX16 .... 16 B2
Marten Pl RG31 .... 257 D2
Martens Cl SN6 .... 209 D3
Martens Rd SN6 .... 209 D3
Martin Cl OX6 .... 80 C4
Martin's La OX10 .... 182 B1
Martyn's Way OX10 .... 204 C2
Maryfield OX12 .... 214 C2
Marygreen OX12 .... 214 B4
Marylands Green OX44 . 162 B1
Marymead OX10 .... 220 C1
Mascall Ave OX3 .... 142 C4
Mascord Cl OX16 .... 16 A3
Mascord Rd OX16 ...... 16 A3
Masefield Cl OX6 .... 65 E2
Masefield Cres OX14 ... 179 E3
Masefield Rd OX16 ..... 16 A2
Masons' Rd OX3 .... 124 C1
Massey Cl OX3 .... 124 B1
Mather Rd OX3 .... 124 C2
Mathews Way OX13 .... 159 D3
Matlock Rd RG4 .... 258 C2
Matson Dr RG9 .... 244 C1
Mattock Way OX14 .... 160 A2
Mattock's Cl OX3 ...... 124 B1
Maud Cl OX5 .... 65 E2
Maule Cl OX15 .... 21 F1
Maunds The OX15 ..... 33 F2
Mavor Cl OX20 .... 91 D4
Mawles La OX7 .... 85 E4
Maxwell Ave OX11 ... 217 D2
May's Cl OX6 .... 49 F4
Mayfair Rd OX4 ...... 142 A2
Mayfield Ave OX16 ... 196 C1
Mayfield Cl
  Carterton OX18 .... 115 E1
  Chalgrove OX44 ...... 184 B3
Mayfield Dr RG4 ...... 259 E2
Mayfield Rd Banbury OX16 . 16 B1
  Cumnor OX2 .... 121 D1
  Cutteslowe OX2 .... 123 D4
Mayott's Rd OX14 .... 179 F4
McCraes Wlk RG10 ... 255 E1
McKee Sq OX10 ...... 204 B1
McMullan Cl OX10 ... 221 E4
Mead La RG8 .... 249 F1
Mead Platt HP14 ..... 188 B3
Mead Rd OX15 .... 32 C4
Mead The OX17 ...... 3 F2
Mead Way OX5 ...... 92 C1
Mead Wlk OX11 ..... 200 C1
Meaden Hill OX3 .... 124 A3
Meadow Bank SN7 .. 172 C2
Meadow Cl Cumnor OX2 .. 121 D2
  Goring RG8 .... 249 E3
  Grove OX12 .... 196 C1
  Moulsford OX10 .... 238 C2
  Shipton-u-W OX7 .... 70 B1
Meadow La
  Crowmarsh G OX10 ... 222 A3
  Fulbrook OX18 .... 100 C3
  Oxford OX4 .... 141 F3
  Shipton-u-W OX7 ... 70 B1
Meadow Prospect OX2 . 122 B4
Meadow Rd Chinnor OX9 . 168 B3
  Henley-on-T RG9 .... 244 B1
  Reading RG1 .... 258 C1
  Watchfield SN6 ..... 191 F1
Meadow View
  Adderbury OX17 .... 23 D2
  Banbury OX16, OX17 .. 16 C2
  Kidlington OX5 ..... 92 C1
  Long Crendon HP18 . 129 F2
  Wendlebury OX6 .... 79 F2
  Witney OX8 .... 118 B4
Meadow View Rd OX1 . 160 C4
Meadow Way Didcot OX11 .. 218 B4
  Faringdon SN7 ...... 172 C2
  Kingham OX7 .... 54 C2
  Thame OX9 .... 129 F1
  Yarnton OX5 .... 108 B3
Meadowbank Cl
  Ascott-u-W OX7 .... 71 D1
  Long Crendon HP18 . 129 E4

Meadows The OX9 ...... 186 A1
Meadowside
  Abingdon OX14 .... 179 F3
  Reading RG31 .... 257 D2
Meadowside Ct OX14 .. 179 F4
Meadowside Rd RG8 .. 256 B4
Meads Cl OX14 .... 179 D1
Meads The OX14 ...... 196 C4
Meadside OX10 .... 202 C4
Meashill Way OX11 ... 234 C4
Medcroft Rd OX5 .... 77 D3
Medhill Cl RG8 .... 250 C4
Medina Cl OX11 ...... 201 D3
Medina Gdns OX6 .... 65 D1
Medlar Rd SN6 .... 209 E4
Medlicott Dr OX14 ... 179 E3
Medlock Gr OX11 .... 200 C2
Medway OX12 .... 197 D3
Medway Cl OX13 .... 159 E2
Medway Rd OX13 ... 159 E2
Melbourne Cl OX16 . 16 C2
Melford Green RG4 . 259 F3
Melton Dr OX11 .... 200 C1
Melville Cl OX6 ..... 65 D1
Membury Way OX12 . 214 B4
Memorial Ave RG9 .. 254 C1
Mendip Hts OX11 ... 200 B1
Menmarsh Rd HP18 . 127 F3
Menpes Rd RG31 ... 257 E2
Mercury Cl OX18 ... 134 C2
Mercury Rd OX4 ... 143 D1
Mere Dyke Rd OX13 . 198 C3
Mere Rd Cutteslowe OX2 . 122 C4
  Finmere MK18 ..... 39 E3
Meredith Cl OX6 ... 65 E2
Mereland Rd OX11 . 218 C4
Merewood Ave OX3 . 125 D2
Merganser Dr OX6 .. 81 D4
Meriden Ct OX10 ... 221 E4
Merlin Cl OX18 .... 115 E2
Merlin Rd Abingdon OX14 . 159 D1
  Oxford OX4 .... 142 C1
Merlin Way OX6 .... 81 D4
Merritt Rd OX11 ... 200 B1
Merrivale's La OX15 . 21 F2
Merrymouth Rd OX7 . 69 D1
Mersey Way OX11 .. 201 D2
Merton Cl Didcot OX11 . 219 D4
  Eynsham OX8 ...... 120 B4
Merton Rd OX6 .... 81 E2
Merton St Banbury OX16 . 16 C3
  Oxford OX1 .... 123 E1
Merton Way OX5 ... 108 A3
Merton Wlk OX6 ... 65 F2
Metcalf Cl OX15 ... 179 E2
Metcalfe Cl OX15 .. 15 E4
Meteor Cl OX6 .... 66 A2
Mewburn Rd OX16 . 16 A3
Mews The Highworth SN6 . 190 A3
  Watchfield SN6 .... 191 E1
Micklands Rd RG4 . 259 F2
Mickle Way OX33 . 125 F2
Middle Aston La
  North Aston OX6 .. 48 A3
  Steeple Aston OX6 . 48 A3
Middle Furlong OX11 . 201 D1
Middle Hill OX15 ... 30 A4
Middle La Shotteswell OX17 . 8 B4
  Wroxton OX15 .... 14 B4
Middle Rd OX18 ... 99 D3
Middle Row OX7 .. 42 C2
Middle St OX5 .... 93 F1
Middle Way Chinnor OX9 . 168 A3
  Cutteslowe OX2 .. 123 D4
  Islip OX5 .... 93 F1
Middleton Rd
  Banbury OX16, OX17 . 16 C4
  Bucknell OX6 ...... 64 C4
  Chacombe OX17 ... 10 C2
Middleton Stoney Rd
  OX6 .... 65 E1
Middleway Bottom OX12 . 213 E1
Middleway Rd OX12 . 213 E1
Midget Cl OX12 .... 179 E2
Midsummer Meadow
  RG4 .... 258 C3
Midway OX17 ...... 11 D1
Miles Dr OX12 .... 214 C4
Milestone Ave RG4 . 260 C3
Milestone Rd OX18 . 115 E1
Milestone Way RG4 . 259 E3
Mileway Gdns OX3 . 124 B1
Milford Rd Reading RG1 . 258 C2
  Wootton OX20 .... 76 A2
Milking La OX8 .... 104 A2
Mill Cl Bix RG9 .... 243 F4
  Chadlington OX7 .. 57 D1
  Charlton-on-O OX5 . 95 D3
  Deddington OX15 . 33 F2
Mill End OX5 ..... 93 D1
Mill Green Bampton OX18 . 134 C1
  Caversham RG4 ... 259 D1
Mill Green Cl OX18 . 134 C1
Mill La Adderbury OX17 . 23 D2
  Alvescot OX18 .... 133 E3
  Banbury OX15, OX16, OX17 . 16 B3
  Benson OX10 ..... 203 F2
  Black Bourton OX18 . 133 F3
  Brackley NN13 ... 24 A3
  Chalgrove OX44 .. 184 B3
  Chinnor OX9 ..... 168 A4
  Chipping Warden OX17 . 5 F3
  Clanfield OX18 ... 152 C4
  Croughton NN13 . 36 B4
  Drayton (Banbury) OX15 . 15 E4
  East Hendred OX12 . 216 A3
  Fast Hendred OX12 . 216 B3
  Great Haseley OX44 . 164 B4

Mill La continued
  Grove OX12 .... 214 C4
  Haddenham HP17 ... 130 A2
  Henley-on-T RG9 .... 254 C4
  Horton-cum-S OX33 . 112 A3
  Kidmore End RG4 ... 252 B1
  Kings Sutton OX17 .. 23 F2
  Kirtlington OX5 ..... 77 F2
  Lechlade GL7 ...... 150 C2
  Lower Heyford OX6 . 62 B3
  Marston OX3 .... 123 F4
  Middle Barton OX7 . 60 C4
  Milton (Abingdon) OX14 . 199 E3
  Oxford
    OX3, OX33, OX4, OX44 . 141 F2
  Shiplake RG9 ...... 255 D1
  South Moreton OX11 . 220 A3
  Stokenchurch HP14 . 188 B3
  Sutton Courtenay OX14 . 199 F4
  Upper Arncott OX6 . 96 C4
  Upper Heyford OX6 . 48 C1
  Wallingford OX10 .. 221 E4
  Westbury NN13 ... 25 D2
  Weston-on-the-G OX6 . 79 D1
  Wootton OX20 ..... 75 F2
Mill Orch OX12 .... 197 D3
Mill Paddock
  Abingdon OX14 ... 179 F3
  Letcombe Bassett OX12 . 214 A1
Mill Rd
  Abingdon OX13, OX14 . 179 E3
  Caversham RG4 ... 259 E1
  Cutteslowe OX2 ... 122 B4
  Goring RG8 .... 249 E4
  Marcham OX13 ... 178 B3
  Nettlebed RG9 ... 224 C2
  Shiplake RG9 .... 255 D2
  Stokenchurch HP14 . 188 B3
  Stratton Auley OX6 . 52 C1
Mill St Eynsham OX8 . 120 C4
  Islip OX5 .... 109 F4
  Kidlington OX5 ... 92 C1
  Oxford OX2, OX33 . 123 D1
  Stanton St John OX33 . 125 F4
  Steventon OX13 .. 198 C2
  Wantage OX12 ... 214 B3
  Witney OX8 ...... 104 A1
Mill St Mews OX8 . 120 C4
Millaway La OX12 . 195 E3
Millbank OX2 ..... 141 D4
Millbrook Cl
  Blewbury OX11 ... 219 D1
  Wallingford OX10 . 221 E4
Milldown Ave RG8 . 249 E4
Milldown Rd RG8 . 249 E4
Miller Rd Banbury OX16 . 16 A3
  Wheatley OX33 ... 144 B4
Miller's Acre OX2 . 109 D1
Millers Cl Chalgrove OX44 . 184 B4
  Goring RG8 ...... 249 D4
Millers La OX15 .... 7 E4
Millers Turn OX9 . 168 A3
Millfield Ave OX6 . 67 F2
Millfield Cl OX6 ... 67 F2
Millham The OX12 . 216 A3
Millmoor Cres OX8 . 120 C4
Mills La OX15 .... 15 D4
Millstream Ct OX2 . 122 B4
Millview OX7 ..... 42 C1
Millway Cl OX2 ... 122 C4
Millway La OX13 . 157 F3
Millwood End OX8 . 90 A1
Millwood Vale OX8 . 90 A1
Millwright Cl OX16 . 16 A3
Milne Pl OX3 ..... 124 A3
Milton Cl Bicester OX6 . 65 E2
  Henley-on-T RG9 . 244 B1
Milton Cres OX33 . 125 F2
Milton La OX13 ... 199 D3
Milton Manor Dr OX44 . 163 F3
Milton Park OX14 . 199 E2
Milton Rd Bloxham OX15 . 21 F2
  Milton (Banbury) OX15 . 22 B1
  Oxford OX4, OX44 . 142 A3
  Shipton-u-W OX7 . 70 B1
  Sutton Courtenay OX14 . 199 F3
  Sutton Courtenay OX14 . 200 A2
Milton St OX16 ... 16 B3
Milvery Way OX4 . 142 A2
Minchery Farm Cotts
  OX4 .... 142 B1
Minchery Rd OX4 . 142 B1
Minchins Cl OX14 . 180 B4
Minnow La OX18 .. 99 E3
Minns Ind Est OX2 . 122 B1
Minns Rd OX12 ... 196 C1
Minster Rd
  Brize Norton OX18 . 116 A3
  Oxford OX4 ...... 142 A4
Minster Riding OX8 . 102 C2
Minton Cl RG30 ... 257 F1
Minty Cl OX18 ... 115 E1
Mirfield Rd OX6 .. 117 F4
Mistletoe Gn OX4 . 142 C1
Mitchell Cl Thame OX9 . 147 F4
  Wootton (Oxford) OX13 . 159 D4
Moat Cl OX18 .... 116 A2
Moat La OX6 ..... 67 F4
Moat The OX7 ... 54 C3
Moat's Cres OX9 . 148 A4
Mobbs La OX15 .. 30 A4
Moberly Cl OX4 .. 141 F4
Moir Ct OX12 .... 214 B3
Mold Cres OX16 . 16 A3
Mole Pl 15 OX4 . 142 C1

Mollington La OX17 .... 3 D2
Molyneux Dr OX15 .... 22 C4
Monarchs Ct OX10 .... 203 F2
Monique Ct OX16 .... 9 D1
Monks Cl
  Dorchester OX10 .... 182 C1
  Oxford OX4 .... 142 B1
  West Hanney OX12 .... 196 C3
Monks Lode OX11 .... 200 C2
Monks Mead OX10 .... 202 C1
Monmouth Rd OX1 .... 141 E3
Mons Way OX14 .... 159 E1
Montabaur Rd NN13 .... 24 A4
Montagu Rd OX2 .... 140 B4
Montague St RG4 .... 259 E1
Montgomery Rd OX6 .... 66 A4
Montpelier Dr RG4 .... 259 E3
Montrose Way OX9 .... 148 A4
Monument Ind Park
  OX44 .... 184 C4
Monument Rd OX44 .... 184 C3
Monument St OX16 .... 16 B3
Moody Rd OX3 .... 123 F2
Moor Ave OX8 .... 104 A1
Moor La OX15 .... 31 F4
Moor Pond Cl OX6 .... 65 F1
Moorbank OX4 .... 142 C2
Moorbrook OX11 .... 200 B2
Moorend La Thame OX9 .... 129 F1
  Thame OX9 .... 130 A1
Moorfield Ct OX16 .... 16 C3
Moorgate GL7 .... 150 A2
Moorhen Wlk OX4 .... 142 C1
Moorland Rd OX8 .... 117 F4
Moorlands Cl OX8 .... 103 F1
Moorlands The
  Benson OX10 .... 204 A2
  Kidlington OX5 .... 92 C1
Moors Cl OX8 .... 118 A3
Moors Drive The OX17 .... 17 F4
Moors The Kidlington OX5 .... 92 B1
  Pangbourne RG8 .... 256 B3
Morecambe Ave RG4 .... 258 C3
Moreton Ave OX10 .... 221 D4
Moreton La Northmoor OX8 .... 156 C4
  Thame OX9 .... 147 F4
Moreton Rd
  Aston Tirrold OX11 .... 219 F1
  Cutteslowe OX2 .... 123 D3
Morgan Cl OX16 .... 15 F4
Morlais RG4 .... 259 D3
Morland Cl OX33 .... 144 A4
Morland Rd OX13 .... 178 B3
Morlands OX12 .... 197 D4
Morrell Ave OX4 .... 142 A1
Morrell Cl OX5 .... 108 B4
Morrell Cres OX4 .... 142 A1
Morrells Cl OX11 .... 200 B1
Morris Cres OX4 .... 142 A3
Morris Dr OX16 .... 15 F4
Morse Rd OX11 .... 218 B3
Mortimer Dr OX3 .... 123 F2
Mortimer Rd OX4 .... 141 F2
Morton Ave OX5 .... 108 C4
Morton Cl Abingdon OX14 .... 180 B4
  Kidlington OX5 .... 108 C4
Morton King Cl HP18 .... 128 B2
Mosquito La OX10 .... 204 B1
Moss Cl RG4 .... 259 E2
Motte The OX14 .... 179 F4
Mount Owen Rd OX18 .... 135 D2
Mount Pl OX2 .... 123 D1
Mount Pleasant
  Bishopstone SN6 .... 227 E2
  Lechlade GL7 .... 150 B2
Mount St OX2 .... 123 D1
Mount The
  Caversham RG4 .... 258 C2
  Tetsworth OX9 .... 166 A4
Mount View RG8 .... 244 B1
Mount View Ct RG9 .... 244 B1
Mountfield RG8 .... 249 E4
Mountfield Rd OX8 .... 117 F4
Mousey La OX10 .... 221 E4
Mowbray Dr
  RG1 & RG30 & RG31 .... 258 A1
Mowbray Rd OX11 .... 218 C3
Mowforth Cl RG8 .... 240 C1
Mulberries The OX12 .... 197 D3
Mulberry Dr Bicester OX6 .... 65 F3
  Wheatley OX33 .... 144 A4
Mulcaster Ave OX5 .... 108 C4
Mullard Way OX14 .... 179 F4
Mumbery Hill RG10 .... 255 F1
Murcott Rd OX6 .... 96 B3
Murdock Cl OX15 .... 33 F2
Murdock Rd OX6 .... 66 A1
Murren The OX10 .... 221 E3
Museum Rd OX1 .... 123 E1
Musgrave Rd OX9 .... 168 B4
Musgrave Wlk HP14 .... 188 C3
Mustard La RG4 .... 260 C1
Myrtle Cl
  Long Hanborough OX8 .... 90 A1
  Reading RG31 .... 257 E2

Naldertown OX12 .... 214 B3
Napier Ct OX14 .... 180 A4
Napier Rd OX4 .... 142 B3
Nappins Cl HP18 .... 129 E3
Naseby OX11 .... 200 B1
Nash Dr OX14 .... 179 E4
Nash La OX8 .... 106 A4
Neal's La RG9 .... 242 A1
Needlemakers HP18 .... 129 E4

Neithrop Ave OX16 .... 16 A4
Neithrop Cl OX16 .... 16 A4
Nell Hill SN6 .... 227 E2
Nelson Rd RG4 .... 259 E1
Nelson St Oxford OX2 .... 123 D1
  Thame OX9 .... 147 F4
Nene Gr OX11 .... 201 D1
Nene Rd OX13 .... 159 E1
Nether Cl NN13 .... 24 A4
Netheravon OX18 .... 115 F1
Nethercote La OX9 .... 167 D1
Nethercote Rd OX5 .... 77 E3
Netherton La OX13 .... 157 E2
Netherton Rd OX13 .... 157 F3
Netherwoods Rd OX3 .... 124 C1
Netherworton Rd OX15 .... 32 C3
Netley Cl RG4 .... 259 F1
Netting St OX15 .... 30 A4
Nettlebed Mead OX4 .... 142 C1
Nettleton Dr OX6 .... 63 E4
Neunkirchen Way OX6 .... 81 D4
Neville Way SN7 .... 194 C4
Nevis RG4 .... 259 D3
New Cotts HP18 .... 129 E3
New Cross Rd OX3 .... 124 C2
New High St OX3 .... 124 B1
New Hill RG8 .... 257 E1
New Inn Hall St OX1 .... 123 E1
New Inn Rd OX3 .... 111 D1
New Pond La OX5 .... 95 D3
New Rd Adderbury OX17 .... 22 C2
  Bampton OX18 .... 134 C2
  Banbury OX15, OX16, OX17 .... 16 B3
  Bledington OX7 .... 54 B1
  Bletchingdon OX5 .... 93 D4
  Charney Bassett OX12 .... 175 F1
  Childrey OX12 .... 213 D3
  East Hagbourne OX11 .... 219 D3
  Great Tew OX7 .... 45 E3
  Hailey OX8 .... 104 A3
  Kingham OX7 .... 54 C2
  Long Hanborough OX8 .... 90 A1
  Marcham OX13 .... 178 B3
  Oxford OX1, OX3 .... 123 D1
  Radley OX14 .... 160 C1
  Ratley OX15 .... 2 A2
  Shiplake RG9 .... 255 D2
  Shotteswell OX17 .... 8 B4
  Stokenchurch HP14 .... 188 C2
  Wallingford OX10 .... 221 E4
  Warborough OX10 .... 203 D3
  Watlington OX9 .... 186 A1
  Woodstock OX20 .... 91 D3
  Wootton OX20 .... 75 E4
New Row OX6 .... 64 C4
New St Abingdon OX14 .... 179 F4
  Bicester OX6 .... 65 F2
  Chipping Norton OX7 .... 42 C2
  Deddington OX15 .... 33 F2
  Henley-on-T RG9 .... 244 C1
New Town La SN6 .... 227 E2
New Yatt La OX8 .... 104 C4
New Yatt Rd Hailey OX8 .... 104 B2
  Witney OX8 .... 104 B2
Newalls Rise RG10 .... 255 F1
Newbery Rd RG31 .... 257 E1
Newbold OX16 .... 16 C2
Newbury Rd OX12 .... 216 C3
Newbury St OX12 .... 214 B2
Newcombe Cl OX15 .... 21 D1
Newells Cl OX44 .... 163 E1
Newfield Rd RG4 .... 252 C3
Newgate Rd OX6 .... 95 F3
Newington Rd OX44 .... 163 E1
Newland OX8 .... 104 B1
Newland Cl OX8 .... 120 C4
Newland Pl OX16 .... 16 B3
Newland Rd OX16 .... 16 B3
Newland St OX8 .... 120 C4
Newlands Ave
  Caversham RG4 .... 259 D2
  Didcot OX11 .... 218 C4
Newlands Dr OX12 .... 196 B1
Newlands La RG9 .... 242 A3
Newlands Mill OX8 .... 104 B1
Newlin Cl OX4 .... 141 F2
Newman Ct Curbridge OX8 .... 103 E1
  Oxford OX4 .... 123 F1
Newman La OX14 .... 179 D1
Newman Rd OX4 .... 142 A2
Newmans Cl OX11 .... 218 B2
Newmill La OX8 .... 103 F1
Newnham Green OX10 .... 221 F4
Newnhamhill Bottom
  RG9 .... 242 A3
Newport Cl OX5 .... 108 B4
Newport Rd RG1 .... 259 D1
Newton Ave RG4 .... 259 E3
Newton Rd OX1 .... 141 E4
Newton Way OX10 .... 204 A3
Newtown Gdns RG9 .... 254 C4
Newtown Rd RG9 .... 254 C4
Niagara Rd RG9 .... 254 C4
Nicholas Ave OX3 .... 123 F2
Nicholas Rd RG9 .... 254 A4
Nicholson Rd OX3 .... 123 F2
Nightingale Ave OX4 .... 142 C1
Nightingale La SN6 .... 208 A3
Nightingale Pl OX4 .... 81 D4
Nine Acres Cl OX7 .... 73 D2
Nine Acres La OX7 .... 73 D2
Nineteenth St OX11 .... 217 D1
Ninety Cut Hill OX18 .... 102 A2
Ninth Ave OX3 .... 142 C4
Ninth St OX11 .... 217 D1
Nixon Rd OX4 .... 141 F3
Nizewell Head OX6 .... 62 A4

Nobles Cl Grove OX12 .... 196 B1
N Hinksey Vill OX2 .... 140 A4
Nobles La OX2 .... 140 A4
Nor Brook Cl OX14 .... 160 B1
Norcot Rd RG30 .... 258 A1
Norfolk Cl OX14 .... 160 C1
Norfolk St OX1 .... 141 F4
Norham Gdns OX2 .... 123 E2
Norham Rd OX2 .... 123 E2
Norman Ave
  Abingdon OX14 .... 160 A1
  Henley-on-T RG9 .... 244 C1
Norman Rd RG4 .... 259 E2
Norman Smith Rd
  13 OX4 .... 142 C1
Norman Way OX10 .... 221 E4
Normandy Cres OX4 .... 142 C3
Norreys Ave OX1 .... 141 E3
Norreys Cl OX11 .... 218 B4
Norreys Rd Cumnor OX2 .... 139 F3
  Didcot OX11 .... 218 B4
Norries Dr OX10 .... 203 E1
Norris Cl Abingdon OX14 .... 160 B1
  Adderbury OX17 .... 22 C1
Norris Rd OX6 .... 96 C4
North Aston Rd OX6 .... 47 E3
North Ave OX14 .... 160 A1
North Bar Pl OX16 .... 16 B3
North Bar St OX16 .... 16 B3
North Cl OX9 .... 145 F4
North Croft OX11 .... 218 C3
North Dr Grove OX12 .... 196 C4
  Harwell OX11 .... 217 E2
North Green OX12 .... 196 C4
North Hill OX18 .... 98 A1
North Hinksey La OX2 .... 140 C4
North Hinksey Village
  OX2 .... 140 C4
North La OX6 .... 79 D1
North Leigh Bsns Pk OX8 .... 105 E4
North Manor Estate The
  OX44 .... 143 F1
North Mill Rd OX9 .... 149 F3
North Parade Ave OX2 .... 123 E2
North Pl OX3 .... 124 B2
North Quay OX14 .... 179 F2
North Rd Didcot OX11 .... 200 B1
  Moulsford OX10 .... 238 C2
North Side OX6 .... 48 A1
North St Aston OX18 .... 135 F2
  Banbury OX15 .... 16 C4
  Bicester OX6 .... 65 F1
  Caversham RG4 .... 259 D1
  Fritwell OX6 .... 49 F4
  Islip OX5 .... 93 F1
  Marcham OX13 .... 178 B3
  Middle Barton OX7 .... 60 C4
  Oxford OX2 .... 123 D1
  Thame OX9 .... 129 F1
  Watchfield SN6 .... 191 E1
North Way Cutteslowe OX2 .... 109 D1
  Oxford OX3 .... 124 C2
  Steventon OX13 .... 198 C2
Northampton Rd OX1 .... 141 E3
Northbrook Rd RG4 .... 259 E3
Northcourt La OX14 .... 160 A1
Northcourt Rd OX14 .... 159 F1
Northcourt Wlk OX14 .... 180 A4
Northern By-pass Rd
  Cutteslowe OX2 .... 108 C1
  Marston OX3 .... 124 B3
  Oxford OX3 .... 124 B3
Northfield Ave RG9 .... 255 D2
Northfield Cl OX4 .... 142 B1
Northfield Ct RG9 .... 244 B2
Northfield End RG9 .... 244 B2
Northfield Rd
  Abingdon OX14 .... 160 A2
  Oxford OX3 .... 124 C2
  Reading RG1 .... 259 D1
  Shiplake RG9 .... 255 D2
Northford Cl SN6 .... 209 E4
Northford Hill SN6 .... 209 E4
Northmead La OX12 .... 196 A4
Northmoor Rd OX2 .... 123 E3
Northolt Rd OX18 .... 115 F2
Northwood Cres OX18 .... 115 F2
Northwood Rd OX8 .... 103 E1
Norton Cl OX3 .... 124 B1
Norton Pk OX7 .... 42 C2
Norton Rd OX18 .... 115 F2
Norwood Ave OX13 .... 156 C1
Nowell Rd OX4 .... 141 F2
Nuffield Cl Bicester OX6 .... 65 F2
  Didcot OX11 .... 219 D4
Nuffield Dr OX16 .... 16 A4
Nuffield Hill RG9 .... 223 E2
Nuffield La OX10 .... 222 C3
Nuffield Rd OX3 .... 124 C1
Nuffield Way OX14 .... 179 E4
Nuneham Sq OX14 .... 179 F4
Nunhide La RG8 .... 256 C1
Nunnery Cl OX4 .... 142 B1
Nuns Acre RG8 .... 249 D4
Nurseries Rd OX5 .... 108 B4
Nursery Cl OX3 .... 124 B1
Nursery Dr OX16 .... 16 B4
Nursery Gdns RG8 .... 257 D3
Nursery La OX16 .... 16 B4
Nursery Rd OX4 .... 105 E4
Nursery The OX14 .... 200 A4
Nuthatch Cl OX4 .... 142 C1
Nyatt Rd OX14 .... 180 B4

Oak Ave OX14 .... 160 C3
Oak Cl OX6 .... 65 F2

Oak Dr OX5 .... 92 C1
Oak End Way OX9 .... 168 B3
Oak Farm Cl OX9 .... 166 A4
Oak La Ambrosden OX6 .... 81 E2
  Stanford in the V SN7 .... 194 C3
Oak Rd SN6 .... 191 E1
Oak St GL7 .... 150 B2
Oak Tree Copse RG31 .... 257 E2
Oak Tree Rd RG31 .... 257 E1
Oak Tree Wlk RG8 .... 257 E3
Oakdene RG8 .... 250 C4
Oakdown Cl RG8 .... 250 C2
Oakey Cl OX18 .... 133 E3
Oakfield Rd OX18 .... 115 E1
Oakfields Ind Est OX8 .... 120 B3
Oakham Cl RG31 .... 257 E1
Oakham Rd GL56 .... 27 D1
Oakland Cl OX8 .... 105 F4
Oakland Rd OX16 .... 16 B1
Oakley La OX9 .... 168 A3
Oakley Rd
  Caversham RG4 .... 258 C2
  Chinnor OX9 .... 168 B3
Oaks Rd RG9 .... 255 D2
Oaksmere OX13 .... 158 A3
Oakthorpe Pl OX2 .... 123 D3
Oakthorpe Rd OX2 .... 123 D3
Oasis Park OX8 .... 120 B3
Oatland Rd OX11 .... 218 C4
Oatlands Rd OX2 .... 122 C1
Observatory Cl OX10 .... 204 A2
Observatory St OX2 .... 123 D2
Ock Dr OX10 .... 182 B3
Ock Mill Cl OX14 .... 179 E3
Ock St OX14 .... 179 F3
Ockley Brook OX11 .... 201 D1
Octavian Way NN13 .... 24 A4
Oddley La HP27 .... 169 E4
Odiham Ave RG4 .... 259 F1
Odiham Cl OX18 .... 115 F2
Offas Cl OX10 .... 204 A3
Ogbourne Cl OX12 .... 214 A3
Old Arncott Rd OX6 .... 81 E2
  Caversham RG4 .... 259 D3
Old Bath Rd RG4 .... 260 B1
Old Bridge Rd OX15 .... 21 F2
Old Buildings OX10 .... 221 E4
Old Burford Rd OX7 .... 54 B1
Old Chapel Cl OX5 .... 92 C1
Old Coachyard The OX8 .... 104 A1
Old Copse Gdns RG4 .... 252 C3
Old Croft OX9 .... 167 F2
Old Dashwood Hill HP14 .... 189 F1
Old Farm Cl
  Abingdon OX14 .... 180 B4
  Worminghall HP18 .... 127 E3
Old Farm Cres RG31 .... 257 E1
Old Field OX44 .... 164 A4
Old Forge Cl OX7 .... 54 B1
Old Forge Rd OX7 .... 29 D2
Old George Yd OX18 .... 100 C3
Old Glebe OX5 .... 20 B4
Old Greyfriars St OX1 .... 141 E4
Old Grimsbury Rd OX16 .... 16 C4
Old High St OX3 .... 124 B2
Old Kiln The RG9 .... 224 C1
Old London Rd
  Benson OX10 .... 204 A2
  Tiddington OX9 .... 145 F2
  Wheatley OX33 .... 144 B4
Old Maltings The OX9 .... 129 F1
Old Manor Ct OX12 .... 214 A1
Old Marston Rd OX3 .... 123 F2
Old Mill Cl OX12 .... 196 C3
Old Moor OX14 .... 199 E3
Old Moor Cl OX10 .... 221 E4
Old Nursery View OX1 .... 141 E2
Old Orchard OX9 .... 149 F1
Old Parr Cl OX16 .... 16 B3
Old Parr Rd OX16 .... 16 B3
Old Place Yd OX6 .... 65 F1
Old Plough Wlk OX15 .... 33 D2
Old Pound The OX13 .... 159 D3
Old Rd East Hendred OX12 .... 216 C3
  Great Tew OX7 .... 45 E4
  Oxford OX3, OX33 .... 124 C1
  Ratley OX15 .... 2 A2
  Wheatley OX33 .... 143 F4
Old Reading Rd OX10 .... 221 F3
Old Rectory Ct OX6 .... 80 A2
Old Sawmills SN7 .... 172 C1
Old Station Yd OX14 .... 179 F4
Old Town NN13 .... 24 A4
Old Wharf Rd SN7 .... 210 B4
Old Windmill Way HP18 .... 129 E4
Old Witney Rd OX8 .... 120 B4
Oliver Rd OX4 .... 142 C1
One End La OX10 .... 203 D2
Onslow Dr OX9 .... 130 A1
Onslow Gdns RG4 .... 259 D2
Oracle Parkway RG4 .... 260 A1
Orange Cl SN6 .... 190 A3
Orchard Ave RG4 .... 252 B3
Orchard Cl Abingdon OX14 . 160 A1
  Banbury OX15, OX16 .... 16 A3
  Bucknell SN7 .... 174 C4
  Cassington OX8 .... 107 D3
  Chalgrove OX44 .... 184 B4
  Charney Bassett OX12 .... 175 F1
  Cholsey OX10 .... 221 D3
  Combe OX8 .... 90 A2

Orchard Cl continued
  Didcot OX11 .... 200 C1
  East Hanney OX12 .... 197 D3
  East Hendred OX12 .... 216 C4
  Eynsham OX8 .... 120 C4
  Henley-on-T RG9 .... 244 C1
  Lechlade GL7 .... 150 B2
  Purley on T RG31 .... 257 E2
  Salford OX7 .... 41 F2
  Shiplake RG9 .... 254 C1
  Thame OX9 .... 148 A4
  Upton OX11 .... 218 B1
  Warborough OX10 .... 203 D4
  Wheatley OX33 .... 144 A4
Orchard Combe RG8 .... 250 B2
Orchard Field RG4 .... 252 B3
Orchard Field La OX20 .... 91 E2
Orchard Gdns OX12 .... 213 E3
Orchard Gr Bloxham OX15 .... 21 E2
  Caversham RG4 .... 259 F2
Orchard Ground OX7 .... 69 E1
Orchard Haven OX10 .... 202 B4
Orchard Hill SN7 .... 172 C2
Orchard La Cropredy OX17 .... 4 C1
  East Hendred OX12 .... 216 B3
  Upper Heyford OX6 .... 62 C4
  Wootton (Oxford) OX1 .... 140 B1
Orchard Piece OX17 .... 4 A2
Orchard Pl NN13 .... 25 D2
Orchard Rd Ardley OX6 .... 50 A2
  Buckland SN7 .... 174 C4
  Hook Norton OX15 .... 30 A4
  N Hinksey Vill OX2 .... 140 A4
Orchard Rise OX6 .... 79 F4
Orchard Row OX18 .... 100 C3
Orchard The
  Appleton OX13 .... 158 A4
  East Challow OX12 .... 214 A3
  Merton OX6 .... 95 E4
Orchard View OX17 .... 4 C1
Orchard Way
  Banbury OX16, OX17 .... 16 A3
  Bicester OX6 .... 65 E2
  Chinnor OX9 .... 168 B3
  Harwell OX11 .... 217 E4
  Kidlington OX5 .... 108 C4
  Kingham OX7 .... 54 C2
  Marcham OX13 .... 178 B3
  Middle Barton OX7 .... 46 C1
  Oxford OX4 .... 142 B2
  Wantage OX12 .... 214 C2
  Witney OX8 .... 118 A4
Orchard Wlk OX6 .... 186 B1
Orchids The OX11 .... 235 E4
Ordnance Rd OX11 .... 200 B1
Oregon Ave RG31 .... 257 E2
Oriel Ct OX11 .... 219 D4
Oriel Sq OX1 .... 123 E1
Oriel St OX1 .... 123 E1
Oriel Way OX6 .... 65 F2
Orkney Pl OX8 .... 117 F4
Ormond Rd Thame OX9 .... 130 A1
  Wantage OX12 .... 214 C2
Orpwood Way OX14 .... 179 E3
Orwell Cl RG4 .... 258 C2
Orwell Dr OX11 .... 201 D1
Osberton Rd OX2 .... 123 D4
Osborne Cl Bicester OX6 .... 65 E1
  Cutteslowe OX2 .... 122 C4
  Kidlington OX5 .... 108 B4
Osiers The OX10 .... 183 D3
Osler Rd OX3 .... 124 B2
Osney Cl OX15 .... 30 A4
Osney La OX1 .... 123 D1
Osney Mead OX2 .... 141 D4
Osprey Cl OX6 .... 81 D4
Osterley Dr RG4 .... 259 F3
Osterley Gr OX16 .... 16 A2
Oswestry Rd OX1 .... 141 E4
Otmoor La Beckley OX3 .... 111 D2
  Charlton-on-O OX5 .... 95 D2
Otters Reach OX1 .... 141 F1
Ottery Way OX11 .... 201 D1
Otwell Cl OX14 .... 160 A1
Ouseley Cl OX3 .... 123 F2
Outram Rd OX4 .... 142 A3
Oval The Bicester OX6 .... 65 E2
  Didcot OX11 .... 200 B1
  Oxford OX4 .... 142 A2
Over Norton Rd OX7 .... 42 C2
Overbrooke Gdns OX4 .... 143 D1
Overdale Cl OX3 .... 124 C2
Overdown Rd RG31 .... 257 E1
Overlanders End RG31 .... 257 F2
Overmead OX14 .... 179 F2
Overmead Green OX4 .... 142 C1
Overstrand Cl OX6 .... 66 A2
Overthorpe Rd OX16 .... 16 C3
Overton Dr OX9 .... 130 A1
Owlington Cl OX2 .... 122 B1
Ox Cl OX14 .... 180 A4
Oxen Piece OX44 .... 145 E1
Oxeye Ct OX4 .... 161 F4
Oxford Bsns Pk N OX4 .... 142 B3
Oxford Bsns Pk S OX4 .... 142 B2
Oxford Cl OX5 .... 77 F2
Oxford Cres OX11 .... 218 B4
Oxford Hill OX8 .... 118 B4
Oxford La OX12 .... 196 C1
Oxford Rd
  Abingdon OX13, OX14 .... 160 A3
  Adderbury OX17 .... 23 D2
  Banbury OX15, OX16, OX17 .... 16 B2
  Benson OX10 .... 203 F2
  Bicester OX6 .... 80 B4
  Bletchingdon OX5 .... 93 D4
  Burford OX18 .... 100 C2
  Clifton Hampden OX14 .... 181 E3

Oxford Rd continued
Cumnor OX2 .... 139 F3
Cumnor, Farmore OX2 ...... 139 F3
Cutteslowe OX2 .... 109 D2
Deddington OX15 .... 33 F1
Dorchester OX10 .... 182 B1
Enstone OX7 .... 58 C3
Eynsham OX8 .... 120 C4
Garsington OX44 .... 143 E1
Hampton Poyle OX5 .... 93 D2
Horspath OX33 .... 143 D3
Kennington OX1 .... 160 A3
Kidlington OX5 .... 108 C4
Kirtlington OX5 .... 77 F2
Marston OX3 .... 123 F3
Middleton Stoney OX6 .... 64 A2
North Aston OX6 .... 47 F3
Oxford, Blackbird Leys OX4 . 142 C2
Oxford, Littlemore OX4 ..... 142 A2
Oxford, Temple Cowley OX4 . 142 B3
Reading RG30 .... 258 A1
Steeple Aston OX6 .... 47 F3
Stokenchurch HP14 .... 188 B3
Thame OX9 .... 147 F4
Tiddington OX9 .... 145 F3
Woodcote RG8 .... 240 C1
Woodstock OX20 .... 91 E3
Oxford Sq SN6 .... 191 E1
Oxford St
Caversham RG4 .... 259 D1
Woodstock OX20 .... 91 D3
Oxhey Hill OX17 .... 4 B2
Oxhey Rise OX15 .... 31 D4
Oxlease OX8 .... 118 B4
Oxon Pl SN6 .... 227 E2
Oxpens Rd OX1 .... 141 D4

Pack & Prime La RG9 .... 244 B1
Packhorse La OX13 .... 178 B3
Paddick Cl RG4 .... 260 C2
Paddock Cl Benson OX10 ... 204 A2
Chalgrove OX44 .... 184 B4
Wantage OX12 .... 214 C3
Paddock Farm La OX15 ..... 22 B4
Paddock Rd Ardley OX6 ..... 50 A2
Caversham RG4 .... 259 E1
Wallingford OX10 .... 221 E4
Paddock The
Highworth SN6 .... 190 A3
Longworth OX13 .... 156 B1
Upper Heyford OX6 .... 48 C3
Paddocks The
Bampton OX18 .... 134 C1
Deddington OX15 .... 33 F2
East Hanney OX12 .... 197 D3
Mollington OX17 .... 3 F2
Souldern OX6 .... 35 F2
Yarnton OX5 .... 108 A3
Paddox Cl OX2 .... 123 D4
Paddox The OX2 .... 123 D4
Page Furlong OX10 .... 182 B3
Pages La OX15 .... 7 E3
Pages Orch RG4 .... 252 C3
Paget Rd OX4 .... 142 C3
Pagisters Rd OX14 .... 160 B1
Paines Hill OX6 .... 62 A4
Painswick Cl OX8 .... 103 F1
Painters Cl OX15 .... 21 E2
Palmer Ave OX6 .... 96 C4
Palmer Pl OX14 .... 179 F3
Palmer Rd OX4 .... 124 C1
Palmers OX12 .... 214 C3
Pampas OX14 .... 115 F1
Panbourne Hill RG8 .... 256 B3
Pangbourne St RG30 .... 258 A1
Panters Rd OX10 .... 221 D1
Paper Mill La OX11 .... 220 A3
Papist Way OX10 .... 238 C4
Parade The OX5 .... 108 C3
Paradise La OX15 .... 21 D1
Paradise Mews RG9 .... 244 B1
Paradise Rd RG9 .... 244 B1
Paradise Sq OX1 .... 123 D1
Paradise St OX1 .... 123 D1
Paradise Terr OX7 .... 42 B1
Park Ave Highworth SN6 ... 190 A3
Kidlington OX5 .... 92 B1
Shrivenham SN6 .... 209 E4
Park Cl
Avon Dassett OX17 .... 2 C4
Banbury OX16, OX17 .... 16 B3
Bladon OX20 .... 91 D2
Cutteslowe OX2 .... 109 D1
Didcot OX11 .... 218 B4
Hanwell OX17 .... 8 C2
Hook Norton OX15 .... 30 A3
Kirtlington OX5 .... 77 F3
Middleton Stoney OX6 .... 64 A2
North Leigh OX8 .... 105 E3
Sonning Common RG4 .... 253 D3
Yarnton OX5 .... 108 A2
Park Cres OX14 .... 179 F4
Park End Bodicote OX15 ..... 16 C1
Croughton NN13 .... 36 B4
Park End Cl OX15 .... 16 C1
Park End Ct OX15 .... 16 C1
Park End Pl OX1 .... 123 D1
Park End St OX1 .... 123 D1
Park Hill Holton OX33 ...... 126 A1
Hook Norton OX15 .... 30 A4
Park La Appleton OX13 ..... 158 A4
Aston Rowant OX9 .... 167 F2
Bladon OX20 .... 91 D1
Checkendon RG8 .... 251 F3
Long Hanborough OX8 .... 90 B1
North Newington OX15 .... 15 E2
Stanford in the V SN7 ...... 195 D3
Stokenchurch HP14 .... 188 C3

Park La continued
Stonor RG9 .... 225 E3
Swalcliffe OX15 .... 19 F4
Woodstock OX20 .... 91 D3
Park Rd Abingdon OX14 .... 179 F4
Banbury OX15, OX16 .... 16 A3
Chipping Norton OX7 .... 42 C2
Combe OX8 .... 90 A3
Didcot OX11 .... 218 B4
Ducklington OX8 .... 118 A2
Faringdon SN7 .... 172 C2
Henley-on-T RG9 .... 244 C1
Hook Norton OX15 .... 30 A4
North Leigh OX8 .... 105 D3
Witney OX8 .... 103 F1
Park Rise OX6 .... 81 E2
Park Side Marcham OX13 ... 178 B3
Woodstock OX20 .... 91 E3
Park St Bladon OX20 .... 91 D1
Charlbury OX7 .... 73 D2
Thame OX9 .... 148 A4
Woodstock OX20 .... 91 D3
Park Terr OX9 .... 148 A4
Park The Cumnor OX2 ...... 139 F2
Harwell OX11 .... 217 F3
Park Town OX2 .... 123 E2
Park View
Crowmarsh G OX10 .... 222 A3
Sydenham OX9 .... 148 C1
Wantage OX12 .... 214 C3
Park Wall La RG8 .... 249 E1
Park Way OX3 .... 123 F4
Park Wlk RG8 .... 257 E3
Parker St OX4 .... 141 F3
Parkers Cl SN7 .... 173 D2
Parkers Hill OX9 .... 166 A4
Parkhill Dr RG31 .... 257 E1
Parklands Banbury OX16 .... 16 A4
Freeland OX8 .... 105 F4
Parks Rd OX1 .... 123 E1
Parkside Cuddesdon OX44 . 144 B2
Henley-on-T RG9 .... 244 B1
North Leigh OX8 .... 105 E3
Parkway Dr RG4 .... 260 C2
Parliament Rd OX9 .... 129 F1
Parrs Rd HP14 .... 188 C2
Parry Cl OX3 .... 123 F2
Parson's La OX10 .... 204 C2
Parson's St OX16 .... 16 B3
Parsonage Rd OX12 .... 215 D3
Parsons Mead OX14 .... 159 F1
Parsons Pl OX4 .... 142 A4
Parsons St OX17 .... 23 D2
Partridge Chase OX6 .... 81 D4
Partridge Cl OX12 .... 214 C2
Partridge Pl OX5 .... 92 B1
Partridge Wlk OX4 .... 143 D1
Pascali Cl OX16 .... 9 D1
Passey Cres OX10 .... 204 A2
Patemore La OX9 .... 206 C1
Paternoster La OX10 .... 220 C1
Patrick Haugh Rd OX6 ...... 96 C4
Patrick Rd RG4 .... 259 D1
Patricks Orch SN7 .... 211 E4
Pattison Pl OX4 .... 142 A2
Pauling Rd OX3 .... 124 C1
Pauls Way OX9 .... 186 A1
Paxmans Pl OX16 .... 16 B2
Paynes End OX6 .... 65 F3
Peachcroft Centre OX14 ... 160 A1
Peachcroft Rd OX14 .... 160 A1
Peacock Rd OX3 .... 123 F2
Peaks La OX18 .... 89 E4
Pear Tree Cl OX7 .... 70 A1
Pearce Ct OX9 .... 147 F4
Pearce Dr OX7 .... 42 C1
Pearce Way OX9 .... 148 A4
Pearces Meadow RG9 ...... 224 B2
Pearces Orch RG9 .... 244 B1
Pearson Rd OX4 .... 260 B2
Peartree Cl 2 OX4 .... 142 C1
Peartree Interchange
OX2 .... 108 C4
Peascroft HP18 .... 129 E3
Peat Moors OX3 .... 142 B4
Pebble Cl OX18 .... 101 E3
Pebble Dr OX11 .... 219 D4
Pebble La NN13 .... 24 A4
Peel Cl Caversham RG4 .... 259 E1
Ducklington OX8 .... 118 A2
Peel Pl Carterton OX18 .... 115 F1
Oxford OX1 .... 141 E3
Peep-o-day La OX14 .... 179 F2
Pegasus Ct OX4 .... 142 C2
Pegasus Rd OX4 .... 142 C1
Pegswell La OX44 .... 145 D1
Pelham Rd OX9 .... 130 A1
Pelican Pl OX8 .... 120 C4
Pembroke Ct OX4 .... 141 F4
Pembroke La OX14 .... 199 E3
Pembroke Pl
Bampton OX18 .... 134 C2
Caversham RG4 .... 259 E2
Pembroke Sq OX1 .... 141 E4
Pembroke St OX1 .... 123 E1
Pembroke Way OX6 .... 65 F2
Pemscott OX18 .... 133 E3
Pen Way OX16 .... 9 E1
Pendennis Ave RG4 .... 259 F1
Penley Cl OX9 .... 168 A3
Penn Cl Abingdon OX14 .... 160 B1
Caversham RG4 .... 259 D3
Pennington Pl OX9 .... 130 A1
Pennycress Rd OX4 .... 143 D1
Pennyfarthing Pl OX1 ...... 123 E1
Pennygreen La OX10 .... 202 C1
Pennypiece RG8 .... 249 E4
Pennywell Dr OX2 .... 109 D1

Penpont Water OX11 .... 201 D1
Penrhyn OX16 .... 15 F4
Penrose Cl OX16 .... 16 A3
Penrose Dr OX16 .... 16 A3
Pensclose OX8 .... 104 B1
Pensfield OX10 .... 203 F2
Pentagon The OX14 .... 180 A4
Penson's Gdns OX4 .... 123 F1
Peppard Hill RG9 .... 252 B3
Peppard La RG9 .... 254 C4
Peppard Rd
Caversham RG4 .... 253 D2
Sonning Common RG4 .... 253 D2
Pepper Alley OX15 .... 34 C2
Peppercorn Ave OX3 .... 142 C4
Percy St OX4 .... 141 F3
Peregrine Rd OX4 .... 142 B1
Peregrine Way
Bicester OX6 .... 81 D4
Grove OX12 .... 196 B1
Periam Cl RG9 .... 254 B4
Perimeter Rd OX11 .... 217 E1
Periwinkle Pl OX4 .... 143 D1
Perkins OX1 .... 141 E1
Perkins Cl OX15 .... 7 E1
Perrin St OX3 .... 124 B1
Perrinsfield GL7 .... 150 B3
Perrott Cl OX8 .... 105 D4
Perry's Rd SN7 .... 194 B4
Perserverance Hill RG9 .... 254 A1
Peter's Way OX4 .... 142 B2
Peterley Rd OX4 .... 142 C3
Pether Rd OX3 .... 124 C1
Pethers Piece OX18 .... 100 B3
Petre Pl OX5 .... 92 C1
Pettiwell OX44 .... 162 B4
Pevensey Ave RG4 .... 259 F3
Pheasant Wlk OX4 .... 142 A1
Phelps The OX5 .... 108 B4
Philcote St OX15 .... 33 F2
Phillimore Rd RG4 .... 259 E4
Phipps Rd OX4 .... 142 B2
Phoebe Ct OX2 .... 123 D3
Phyllis Ct Dr RG9 .... 244 C2
Pickett Ave OX3 .... 142 C4
Picklers Hill OX14 .... 160 A1
Picton Way RG4 .... 259 D2
Pieces The OX18 .... 134 C2
Pierces Hill RG31 .... 257 E1
Pigeon Farm Rd HP14 ..... 188 C3
Pigeon House La OX8 ...... 106 B3
Pigeonhouse La OX6 .... 95 F2
Piggotts Rd RG4 .... 259 E1
Piggy La OX6 .... 65 F1
Pike Terr OX1 .... 141 E4
Pikeshaw Way RG31 .... 257 E1
Pill La GL56 .... 26 C1
Pimpernel Cl OX4 .... 143 D1
Pine Cl Bicester OX6 .... 65 F3
Garsington OX44 .... 143 E1
Oxford OX4, OX44 .... 142 C2
Pine Woods Rd OX13 ...... 156 A1
Pinecroft OX18 .... 115 E1
Pines The SN7 .... 172 C2
Pinetree Ct OX4 .... 259 D3
Pinewood Dr RG4 .... 258 C3
Pingle Dr OX6 .... 80 C4
Pinhill Rd OX16 .... 16 A4
Pinkhill La OX8 .... 120 C3
Pinnocks Way OX2 .... 140 A4
Pinsley Rd OX8 .... 106 A4
Pioneer Rd Ambrosden OX6 . 81 D3
Faringdon SN7 .... 172 C1
Piper St OX3 .... 124 B1
Pipers Croft OX16 .... 16 A2
Pipit Cl OX4 .... 142 C1
Pipits Croft OX6 .... 81 D4
Pipkin Way OX4 .... 142 A3
Pitch The HP14 .... 189 E2
Pitreavie Ave OX18 .... 115 F2
Pitters Piece HP18 .... 129 D4
Pitts Rd OX3 .... 124 C2
Pixey Pl OX2 .... 122 C4
Pixton Cl OX11 .... 218 B4
Plain Rd The OX15 .... 14 A3
Plain The OX4 .... 141 F4
Plane Tree Way OX20 .... 91 E3
Plantation Rd
Chilton OX11 .... 234 C4
Oxford OX2 .... 123 D2
Plantation The OX17 .... 4 C1
Playfield Rd OX1 .... 160 C4
Playford Ct OX9 .... 147 F4
Playhatch Rd RG4 .... 260 A3
Playing Field Rd NN13 ...... 25 D2
Pleck La OX9 .... 167 F2
Plot Rd OX15 .... 14 A3
Plough Cl Cutteslowe OX2 . 109 D1
Warborough OX10 .... 203 D3
Plough Cnr OX9 .... 148 C1
Plough La RG9 .... 254 C1
Ploughley Cl Ardley OX6 .... 50 B2
Kidlington OX5 .... 108 B4
Ploughley Rd OX6 .... 81 E2
Plover Dr OX4 .... 142 C1
Plowden Park OX9 .... 167 F2
Plowden Way RG9 .... 254 C1
Plum La OX7 .... 85 E4
Plumbe Ct OX12 .... 214 B3
Pluto Rd OX11 .... 234 C4
Plym Dr OX11 .... 201 D1
Pochard Pl OX4 .... 142 C1
Pococks Cl OX18 .... 134 C2
Poffley End La OX8 .... 104 A1
Polecat End La OX33 .... 125 F2
Polstead Rd OX2 .... 123 D2
Polsted Rd RG31 .... 257 E1

Pond End Rd RG4 .... 253 D3
Pond Hill OX8 .... 89 E4
Pond La RG4 .... 257 F4
Ponds La OX3 .... 123 F3
Pony Rd OX4 .... 142 C3
Pool Close Cotts GL56 ...... 26 C1
Pooles La OX16 .... 16 A3
Poolside Cl OX16 .... 16 A3
Popes Acre HP17 .... 130 C3
Popes Piece OX8 .... 103 F1
Poplar Cl Banbury OX16 .... 16 C1
Garsington OX44 .... 143 E1
Kidlington OX5 .... 108 C4
Poplar Farm Cl OX7 .... 70 A1
Poplar Farm Rd OX44 ..... 184 B4
Poplar Gr OX4 .... 160 C4
Poplar Rd OX2 .... 122 B1
Poplars Rd OX17 .... 10 C2
Poplars The OX6 .... 66 B1
Port Hill RG9 .... 224 A1
Port Hill Rd OX10 .... 203 F3
Port Way
Crowmarsh G OX10 .... 221 F2
East Challow OX12 .... 214 A4
Kirtlington OX5 .... 78 A4
Lower Heyford OX6 .... 62 C3
Wantage OX12 .... 215 D3
Portal Dr OX6 .... 63 E4
Portal Dr N OX6 .... 63 E4
Portal Dr S OX6 .... 63 E4
Portland Pl OX7 .... 42 C2
Portland Rd
Cutteslowe OX2 .... 123 D4
Milcombe OX15 .... 21 D1
Portman Rd RG30 .... 258 B1
Portway Aynho OX17 .... 35 E4
Banbury OX16, OX17 .... 16 A4
Croughton NN13 .... 36 C4
Didcot OX11 .... 218 B4
Faringdon SN7 .... 172 C2
Wantage OX12 .... 214 B2
Portway Cres NN13 .... 36 C4
Portway Dr NN13 .... 36 B4
Portway Gdns OX17 .... 35 E4
Post Office La
Letcombe Bassett OX12 ..... 214 A1
Wantage OX12 .... 214 B2
Potenger Way OX14 .... 179 E3
Potkiln La RG8 .... 250 C4
Pott's Cl OX44 .... 145 D2
Pottery Piece OX4 .... 142 C1
Pottery Rd RG30 .... 257 F1
Pottle Cl OX2 .... 122 A1
Poultney Rd OX18 .... 115 E2
Poulton Pl OX4 .... 142 C2
Pound Cl
Ducklington OX8 .... 118 A2
Kirtlington OX5 .... 77 F2
Yarnton OX5 .... 108 A3
Pound Croft OX12 .... 214 B4
Pound Field OX3 .... 124 C3
Pound Hill OX7 .... 73 D2
Pound La Cassington OX8 . 107 E1
Cholsey OX10 .... 220 C1
Clanfield OX18 .... 133 F1
Sibford Gower OX15 .... 13 D1
Stanton St John OX33 ...... 125 E4
Upton OX11 .... 218 B1
Pound Piece SN6 .... 228 A4
Pound The Bloxham OX15 ... 21 F3
North Newington OX15 .... 15 D2
Wantage OX12 .... 215 D3
Pound Way OX4 .... 142 B3
Powell Cl OX33 .... 125 F2
Powys Gr OX16 .... 15 F4
Preachers La OX1 .... 141 E4
Prescott Ave OX16 .... 15 F3
Prescott Cl OX16 .... 16 A3
Preston Rd OX14 .... 179 F2
Prestwick Burn OX11 .... 200 C2
Prestwick Pl OX2 .... 122 C1
Prichard Rd OX3 .... 124 A2
Priest Cl RG9 .... 259 D1
Priest Hill RG4 .... 259 D2
Priest Hill La OX8 .... 103 F3
Primrose Cl RG8 .... 257 E3
Primrose La OX18 .... 134 C1
Primrose Pl 18 OX4 .... 142 C1
Prince Gr OX14 .... 160 A2
Prince William Dr RG31 ... 257 E1
Princes Ride OX20 .... 91 E3
Princes St OX4 .... 141 F4
Princess Gdns OX12 .... 214 B4
Princethorpe Dr OX16 ...... 16 C4
Prior's Forge OX2 .... 109 D1
Prior's La SN7 .... 155 F2
Priory Ave RG4 .... 259 D1
Priory Cl Bicester OX6 ...... 65 F1
Horton-cum-S OX33 .... 112 A3
Priory Copse RG4 .... 252 C3
Priory Cl OX6 .... 65 F1
Priory Green SN6 .... 190 A3
Priory La Bicester OX6 ...... 65 F1
Burford OX18 .... 100 C3
Lyneham OX7 .... 70 B3
Marcham OX13 .... 178 B3
Priory Mead SN7 .... 192 B1
Priory Mews OX10 .... 221 D1
Priory Orch OX12 .... 214 B3
Priory Rd Bicester OX6 ...... 65 F1
Lyneham OX7 .... 70 B3
Priory Vale Rd OX16 .... 16 C4
Pritchard Cl OX10 .... 182 B3
Promenade Rd RG4 .... 259 D1
Prospect Cl OX8 .... 89 E4

Prospect Pl OX9 .... 186 A1
Prospect Rd Banbury OX16 . 16 B3
Upton OX11 .... 218 B1
Prospect St RG4 .... 259 D1
Prunus Cl OX4 .... 142 C2
Puck La OX8 .... 104 A1
Puddleduck La SN7 .... 192 A4
Pudlicote La OX7 .... 71 F3
Pudsey Cl OX14 .... 179 F2
Pugsden La OX13 .... 199 D2
Pulker Cl OX4 .... 142 B2
Pullens Field OX3 .... 124 A1
Pullens La OX3 .... 124 A1
Pulling Cl SN7 .... 172 C2
Pumbro OX8 .... 89 E4
Purcell Rd OX3 .... 123 F2
Purfield Dr RG10 .... 255 F1
Purland Cl OX4 .... 142 B3
Purley La RG8 .... 257 E3
Purley Rise RG8 .... 256 C3
Purley Village RG8 .... 257 E3
Purley Way RG8 .... 256 C3
Purslane OX14 .... 180 A4
Pusey La OX1 .... 123 E1
Pusey St OX1 .... 123 E1
Putman Cl OX3 .... 148 A4
Putman Pl RG9 .... 244 C1
Pye St SN7 .... 173 D2
Pykes Cl OX1 .... 160 A1
Pym Wlk OX9 .... 129 F1
Pyrton La OX9 .... 186 A1
Pytenry Cl OX14 .... 160 A2
Pytt's La OX18 .... 100 C3

Quadrangle The
Bicester OX6 .... 65 F1
Woodstock OX20 .... 91 E4
Quadrant The OX14 .... 180 A4
Quaker La OX10 .... 203 D4
Quantock Ave RG4 .... 259 E3
Quantock View OX11 ...... 200 B1
Quarhill Cl OX7 .... 42 C3
Quarry Cl Bloxham OX15 .... 21 E2
Enstone OX7 .... 59 D3
Long Crendon HP18 .... 129 E4
Quarry End OX5 .... 108 A4
Quarry High St OX3 .... 124 C2
Quarry Hollow OX3 .... 124 C1
Quarry La OX7 .... 73 E2
Quarry Rd Chadlington OX7 . 57 D1
Oxford OX3 .... 124 C1
Sunningwell OX13 .... 159 F4
Witney OX8 .... 104 A2
Quarry School Pl OX3 ...... 124 C1
Quartermain Cl OX4 .... 142 A3
Quartermain Rd OX44 ..... 184 B3
Quebec Rd RG9 .... 254 C4
Queen Annes Gate RG4 .... 259 E2
Queen Cl RG9 .... 244 C1
Queen Elizabeth Cl OX11 .. 219 D4
Queen Emmas Dyke OX8 .. 117 F4
Queen St Abingdon OX14 .. 179 F4
Bampton OX18 .... 134 C2
Caversham RG4 .... 259 D2
Dorchester OX10 .... 182 B1
Eynsham OX8 .... 120 C4
Henley-on-T RG9 .... 244 C1
Hook Norton OX15 .... 30 A4
Middleton Cheney OX17 ...... 17 F4
Oxford OX1 .... 123 E1
Queen's Cl OX8 .... 120 C4
Queen's Cres
Clanfield OX18 .... 152 C4
Drayton (Banbury) OX15 ... 15 E4
Queen's La OX1 .... 123 E1
Queen's Rd Banbury OX16 . 16 A3
Carterton OX18 .... 115 F1
Thame OX9 .... 148 A4
Queens Ave Bicester OX6 .. 65 F1
Queens Ave Highworth SN6 . 190 A3
Kidlington OX5 .... 109 D4
Wallingford OX10 .... 203 D1
Queens Cl
Dorchester OX10 .... 182 B1
N Hinksey Vill OX2 .... 140 A4
Thame OX9 .... 129 F1
Queens Ct OX6 .... 65 F1
Queens La OX8 .... 120 C4
Queens Rd
Caversham RG4 .... 259 E1
Cholsey OX10 .... 220 C1
Queens Way OX11 .... 219 F4
Queens St OX15 .... 21 E4
Queensborough Dr RG4 ... 258 C3
Queensway Banbury OX16 . 16 A2
Caversham RG4 .... 259 E3
Didcot OX11 .... 218 C4
Quickset Cl OX7 .... 72 C4
Quintan Ave OX6 .... 81 E2

Rack End OX8 .... 137 E2
Radbone Hill OX7 .... 42 C3
Radcliffe Rd OX4 .... 141 F3
Radcliffe Sq OX1 .... 123 E1
Radcot Cl RG5 .... 260 C1
Radcot Rd SN7 .... 172 C3
Radford Cl OX4 .... 141 F2
Radley Rd OX14 .... 160 B1
Radnage Common Rd
HP14 .... 189 E3
Radnage La HP14 .... 169 E3
Radnor Rd RG9 .... 244 C1
Radnor Rd OX10 .... 221 D4
Raghouse La OX6 .... 49 F3
Raglan Gdns RG4 .... 259 E2

Ragley Mews RG4 .... 259 E3
Ragnall's La Beckley OX3 .... 111 F4
  Horton-cum-S OX33 .... 112 A3
Rahere Rd OX4 .... 142 B2
Railway La OX4 .... 142 A1
Railways Cotts RG8 .... 249 E3
Rainbow Way OX14 .... 160 A2
Raincliffe Cl OX17 .... 35 E4
Ralegh Cres OX8 .... 117 E4
Raleigh Park Rd OX2 .... 140 C4
Rampion Cl OX4 .... 143 D1
Ramsay Rd OX3 .... 124 C2
Ramsons Way OX14 .... 180 B4
Randall Rd GL54 .... 68 A2
Randolph Rd RG1 .... 259 D1
Randolph St OX4 .... 141 F4
Range Rd OX8 .... 103 E1
Rannal Dr OX9 .... 168 B3
Rattlecombe Rd OX15 ...... 6 B1
Rau Ct OX6 .... 66 A4
Raven Rd HP14 .... 188 C2
Ravencroft OX6 .... 81 D4
Ravensbourne Dr RG5 ...... 260 C1
Ravenscroft Rd RG9 .... 244 B3
Ravensmead Banbury OX16 .. 16 A2
  Chinnor OX9 .... 168 B3
Rawlings Gr OX14 .... 179 E4
Rawlins' Cl OX17 .... 23 D3
Rawlinson Cl OX7 .... 57 D1
Rawlinson Rd OX2 .... 123 D3
Rawson Cl OX2 .... 108 C1
Rawthey Ave OX11 .... 200 C2
Ray Ct OX11 .... 201 D1
Raymond Rd OX6 .... 65 E2
Raymund Rd OX3 .... 123 F3
Raynham Cl OX18 .... 115 F2
Reade Ave OX14 .... 180 A4
Reade Cl OX7 .... 70 A1
Reade's La RG4 .... 252 B2
Reading Rd Aldworth RG8 ... 248 A1
  East Hendred OX12 .... 216 A4
  Goring RG8 .... 249 F3
  Harwell OX11 .... 217 E3
  Henley-on-T RG9 .... 244 C1
  Kidmore End RG4 .... 252 A2
  Moulsford OX10 .... 239 D4
  Pangbourne RG8 .... 256 B3
  Streatley RG8 .... 249 D3
  Wallingford OX10 .... 221 E2
  Woodcote RG8 .... 240 C1
Recreation Rd
  Wargrave RG10 .... 255 F1
  Woodstock OX20 .... 91 E3
Rectory Cl
  Marsh Gibbon OX6 .... 67 F2
  Warmington OX17 .... 3 D2
  Wendlebury OX6 .... 80 A2
Rectory Cres OX7 .... 60 C4
Rectory Ct OX9 .... 187 D4
Rectory Farm Cl OX12 ..... 196 C4
Rectory Gdns OX15 .... 15 E4
Rectory Hill RG9 .... 206 A1
Rectory La Blewbury OX11 ... 237 F4
  Fringford OX6 .... 52 B3
  Kingston Bagpuize OX13 .. 176 B4
  Letcombe Bassett OX12 .. 231 F4
  Lewknor OX9 .... 166 C1
  Longworth OX13 .... 156 A2
  Middleton Cheney OX17 .. 10 C1
  Woodstock OX20 .... 91 D3
Rectory Meadow OX9 ...... 168 B4
Rectory Rd
  Caversham RG4 .... 259 D1
  Great Haseley OX44 ...... 164 C4
  Hook Norton OX15 .... 30 A4
  Oxford OX4, OX44 .... 141 F4
  Streatley RG8 .... 248 B4
Red Bridge Hollow OX1 .... 141 E2
Red Copse Rd OX1 .... 140 C1
Red Cross Rd RG8 .... 249 E3
Red Hill RG9 .... 253 F3
Red House Dr RG4 .... 253 D3
Red House Rd OX15 .... 22 C4
Red La Ewelme RG9 .... 206 B1
  Watlington OX9 .... 206 B1
  Woodcote RG8 .... 240 B2
Red Lion Dr HP14 .... 188 B3
Red Lion Sq OX1 .... 123 E1
Red Lion St Cropredy OX17 ... 4 C1
  Kings Sutton OX17 .... 23 F3
Red Poll Cl OX16 .... 16 A4
Redberry Cl RG4 .... 259 E3
Rede Ct OX3 .... 124 C1
Redland Rd OX3 .... 124 A3
Redmoor Cl OX4 .... 142 B1
Redmoor Ct OX6 .... 65 E2
Redwing Cl OX6 .... 66 A1
Redwood Cl
  Garsington OX4 .... 143 D1
  Kingston Bagpuize OX13 .. 156 C1
Redwood Way RG31 .... 257 E2
Reedmace Cl OX4 .... 143 D1
Regal Way SN7 .... 172 C2
Regency Hts RG4 .... 258 C2
Regent Gdns OX11 .... 219 D4
Regent Mall OX14 .... 214 B2
Regent Mews SN7 .... 172 C2
Regent St OX4 .... 141 F4
Regis Pl OX12 .... 214 A1
Reid Cl OX16 .... 16 A3
Reid Pl OX6 .... 63 D4
Remenham La RG9 .... 244 C2
Remus Gate NN13 .... 24 A3
Rest Harrow OX4 .... 142 C1
Retford Cl RG5 .... 260 C1

Retreat Gdns OX10 .... 221 F4
Retreat La HP14 .... 169 E1
Rewley Rd OX1 .... 123 D1
Reynolds Cl OX7 .... 70 B1
Reynolds Way
  Abingdon OX14 .... 179 F3
  East Challow OX12 .... 213 F3
Rhigos RG4 .... 258 C2
Richards La OX2 .... 123 D4
Richards Way OX3 .... 124 C1
Richens Dr OX18 .... 115 E1
Richfield Ave RG1 .... 258 C1
Richman Gdns OX16 ...... 15 F4
Richmere Rd OX11 .... 218 C4
Richmond Rd
  Caversham RG4 .... 258 C2
  Oxford OX1 .... 123 D1
Richmond St OX17 .... 23 F3
Rickyard The
  Ardington OX12 .... 215 E3
  Fulbrook OX18 .... 100 C3
Riddell Pl OX2 .... 109 D1
Ride The OX13 .... 158 A3
Riders Way OX9 .... 168 B3
Ridge Cl OX16 .... 16 B2
Ridge Hall Cl RG4 .... 258 C2
Ridge The RG8 .... 249 F1
Ridge Way OX12 .... 214 A4
Ridgefield Rd OX4 .... 142 A4
Ridgemont Cl OX2 .... 123 D4
Ridgemount Cl RG31 ..... 257 D1
Ridgeway Wargrave RG10 .. 255 F1
  Wootton (Oxford) OX1 ... 140 B1
Ridgeway Cl RG9 .... 223 D2
Ridgeway Rd Didcot OX11 .. 218 C4
  Oxford OX3 .... 124 C2
Ridgeway The
  Bloxham OX15 .... 21 F2
  Caversham RG4 .... 259 D2
  Nettlebed RG9 .... 224 B1
Riding La OX8 .... 103 E4
Riding The OX8 .... 86 C1
Ridings The
  Caversham RG4 .... 259 E4
  Kidlington OX5 .... 92 B1
  Oxford OX3 .... 142 C4
Ridley Rd OX4 .... 142 C3
Riely Cl OX8 .... 90 B1
Riley Cl OX14 .... 179 E3
Riley Dr OX16 .... 15 F4
Rimes Cl OX13 .... 156 C1
Ringwood Rd Oxford OX3 .. 125 D2
  Reading RG30 .... 258 A1
Ripley Rd RG30 .... 258 A1
Rippington Ct OX14 .... 179 D1
Rippington Dr OX3 .... 123 F2
Rise The Adderbury OX17 .. 23 D3
  Aston Rowant OX9 ..... 167 F2
  Caversham RG4 .... 259 D2
  Islip OX5 .... 93 F1
Rissington Cl RG31 .... 257 F2
Rissington Dr OX8 .... 117 F4
Rivacres RG8 .... 250 C2
River Cl OX14 .... 179 F3
River Gdns RG8 ...... 257 E3
River Rd RG4 .... 258 B2
River View Kennington OX1 .. 141 F1
  Sandford-on-T OX4 .... 161 D4
Rivermead Rd OX4 .... 141 F2
Riverside OX16 .... 16 C3
Riverside Gdns OX8 .. 104 A1
Riverside Rd OX2 .... 122 C1
Riverview Rd RG8 .... 256 B3
Rivy Cl OX14 .... 180 B4
Road Eight OX11 ..... 217 D1
Road Eighteen OX11 . 217 D1
Road Eleven OX11 ... 217 D1
Road Fifteen OX11 ... 217 D1
Road Five OX11 ..... 217 D1
Road Four OX11 .... 217 D1
Road Fourteen OX11 . 217 D1
Road Nine OX11 .... 217 D1
Road One OX11 ..... 217 D1
Road Six OX11 ...... 217 D1
Road Thirteen OX11 . 217 D1
Road Twelve OX11 .. 217 D1
Road Two OX11 .... 217 D1
Robert Robinson Ave
  OX4 .... 142 B1
Robert Sparrow Gdns
  OX10 .... 222 A3
Roberts Cl OX3 .... 125 D2
Robin Hill OX8 .... 90 A2
Robin Pl OX4 ...... 142 C1
Robins Cl
  Barford St M OX15 ... 32 C3
  Great Rollright OX7 .. 29 D2
Robins Platt OX9 .. 168 A3
Robins Way OX6 ... 81 D4
Robinson Cl OX18 . 115 E2
Robinswood OX16 . 16 A2
Robsart Pl OX2 ... 139 F2
Rochester Ave RG5 . 260 C1
Rochester Pl OX7 . 73 E2
Rochester Way OX17 . 23 D3
Rochford Gdns OX6 . 66 A2
Rock Cl OX18 .... 115 E2
Rock Edge OX3 .. 124 B1
Rock Farm La OX4 . 161 D4
Rock Hill OX7 ... 42 C2
Rock Rd OX18 ... 115 E2
Rock The OX15 .. 32 C4
Rockbourne Gdns RG30 . 258 A1
Rocky La RG9 ... 243 D2
Roding Way OX11 . 201 D1
Rodway Rd RG30 . 257 F1
Roebuck Ct OX11 . 219 D4
Roentgen Ave OX11 . 217 D1

Rofford La OX44 .... 164 A2
Rogers St OX2 .... 123 D4
Rokeby Dr RG4 .... 258 B4
Rolfe Pl OX4 .... 124 A2
Rolls Ct OX12 .... 214 B3
Roman Pl OX11 ...... 200 B1
Roman Rd OX33 .... 144 B4
Roman Way Beckley OX3 .. 111 D2
  Bicester OX6 .... 65 F1
  Brackley NN13 ...... 24 A4
  Lechlade GL7 .... 150 B3
  Oxford OX3, OX4 ... 142 C3
  Wantage OX12 ...... 214 B3
Romany Cl RG30 .... 258 A1
Romany La RG30 .... 258 A1
Romney Rd OX16 ... 8 C1
Romsey Rd RG30 ... 258 A1
Romulus Way NN13 . 24 A3
Rookery Cl
  Abingdon OX13 ..... 159 D1
  Bodicote OX15 ...... 22 C4
Rookery The OX5 ... 92 B1
Rookery Way OX6 .. 65 E2
Rooks La OX9 ...... 147 F4
Roosevelt Dr OX3 .. 124 B1
Roosevelt Rd OX8 . 106 A4
Rope Way OX15 ... 30 A3
Rope Wlk OX16 ... 16 B3
Roper Rd OX6 .... 63 E4
Rosamund Dr OX20 . 91 D4
Rosamund Rd OX2 . 122 C4
Rose Ave OX14 .... 159 F2
Rose Cl OX18 .... 115 E1
Rose Cnr HP14 ... 188 C3
Rose Ct OX4 ..... 142 A2
Rose Gdns OX2 ... 140 B4
Rose Hill OX4 .... 142 A2
Rose La OX1 .... 123 E1
Rose Pl OX1 .... 141 E4
Rosebay Cres OX12 . 214 B4
Rosebery Rd RG4 .. 258 B4
Rosedale Ave OX16 . 9 D1
Rosehill Park RG4 . 259 E4
Rosemary La OX18 . 134 C2
Rosemead Ave RG31 . 257 D2
Roses La OX7 .... 41 F3
Rosina Wlk OX16 . 9 D1
Ross Rd RG1 .... 259 D1
Rossendale Rd RG4 . 259 E2
Rotha Field Rd OX2 . 109 D1
Rother Garth OX11 . 201 D2
Rotherfield Rd RG9 . 254 C4
Rotherfield Way RG4 . 259 D2
Rothwell Gdns RG5 . 260 C1
Rothwell Wlk RG4 . 259 E1
Rothwells Cl OX10 . 221 D1
Rotten Row OX10 . 182 B1
Round Close Rd
  Adderbury OX17 .... 22 C2
  Hook Norton OX15 .. 30 A4
Roundham Cl OX5 .. 92 B1
Roundhead Dr OX9 . 129 F1
Roundhill Rd OX17 . 4 A2
Roundhills Mead SN6 . 190 A4
Roundtown OX17 ... 35 E4
Roundway The OX3 . 124 C2
Rouses La GL7 .... 132 A3
Rousham Rd OX5 .. 77 E4
Routh Rd OX3 .... 124 C2
Roves La SN6 .... 208 A4
Row La RG4 ...... 259 F4
Row The SN7 .... 155 F1
Rowallan Cl RG4 . 259 E3
Rowan Cl
  Carterton OX18 .... 115 E2
  Kidlington OX5 .... 108 A4
  Sonning Common RG4 . 252 C2
Rowan Gr OX4 .... 143 D1
Rowan Rd OX6 .... 65 F2
Rowel Dr OX5 .... 92 A1
Rowell Way OX7 .. 42 C2
Rowland Cl
  Cutteslowe OX2 .... 122 C4
  Wallingford OX10 .. 203 E1
Rowland Rd OX10 . 221 D1
Rowles Cl OX1 ... 141 F1
Rowney Pl OX4 .. 142 A2
Rowstock OX11 ... 217 D4
Roxburgh Dr OX11 . 200 B2
Royal Berkshire Ct OX11 .. 218 C4
Royal Mansions RG9 . 244 C1
Ruck Keene Cl OX6 . 65 E1
Rufus Isaacs Rd RG4 . 259 D1
Rumbolds Cl OX10 . 203 F3
Rumseys La OX11 . 237 D4
Rupert Cl RG9 .... 244 C2
Rupert House Sch RG9 . 244 C1
Rupert Rd Chalgrove OX44 . 184 B3
  Oxford OX4 .... 142 C3
Rupert Way OX9 .. 130 A1
Rupert's La RG9 .. 244 C2
Ruscote Ave OX16 . 16 A4
Ruscote Sq OX16 . 16 A4
Rushall Rd RG9 .. 130 A1
Rushmead Copse OX14 . 160 B1
Ruskin Ave OX14 . 179 F3
Ruskin Cl OX11 ... 219 D4
Ruskin Rd OX16 .. 16 B2
Ruskin Wlk OX6 .. 65 F2
Russell Jackson Cl OX10 . 182 B3
Russell Rd RG4 ... 258 B4
Russell St OX2 ... 123 D1
Russet Cl OX4 ... 143 D1
Russet Glade RG4 . 259 E4
Russet Rd OX6 .. 50 B2
Rutherfield Cl OX14 . 160 A1
Rutherford Ave OX11 . 217 D2
Rutherway OX2 ... 123 D2

Rutten La OX5 .... 108 A3
Rutters Cl OX5 ...... 108 B4
Rycote La OX9 ...... 146 B3
Rydal Ave RG30 .... 257 F1
Rydes Cl OX15 ..... 22 C4
Rydes The OX15 ... 22 C4
Ryc Cl OX16 ...... 8 C1
Rye Grass OX20 .. 91 E3
Ryecroft Cl
  Wargrave RG10 .... 255 F1
  Woodstock RG5 .... 260 C1
Rymans Cres OX11 . 219 D3
Rymers La OX4 .... 142 A3

Sackville Cl OX17 ... 8 C2
Sadler Wlk OX1 .... 141 D4
Sadlers Croft OX44 . 143 F1
Sadlers Ct OX14 ... 160 A2
Saffron Ct OX14 ... 180 A4
Sage Rd RG31 ..... 257 E2
Sage Wlk **3** OX4 ... 142 C1
St Alban's Ct OX10 . 221 E4
St Aldates OX1 .... 141 E4
St Amand Dr OX14 . 179 D3
St Andrew Ct OX9 . 147 F4
St Andrew's La OX3 . 124 B2
St Andrew's Rd
  Chinnor OX9 .... 168 B3
  Didcot OX11 .... 218 C4
  Oxford OX3 .... 124 B2
St Andrews Cl OX14 . 160 B1
St Andrews Ho OX9 . 168 B3
St Andrews Rd
  Caversham RG4 ... 258 C2
  Henley-on-T RG9 .. 254 B4
St Anne's Rd Banbury OX16 . 16 B2
  Oxford OX3 .... 124 B1
St Annes Cl OX6 .. 65 E2
St Annes Ct OX11 . 219 D4
St Annes Rd RG4 .. 259 D1
St Barnabas Rd RG4 . 259 D3
St Barnabas St OX2 . 123 D1
St Bernard's Rd OX2 . 123 D2
St Birinus Ct GL7 .. 150 B3
St Christopher's Pl OX4 . 142 B3
St Clement's St OX4 . 123 F1
St Cross Rd OX1 .. 123 E1
St Davids Cl RG4 .. 258 C3
St Denys Cl SN7 .. 194 C4
St Ebbes St OX1 .. 141 E4
St Edburg's Cl OX6 . 65 E1
St Edith's Way OX6 . 65 E1
St Edmund's La OX14 . 179 F3
St Edward's Ave OX2 . 123 D4
St Francis Rd HP14 . 189 E2
St George's Cres OX16 . 16 B2
St George's Pl OX1 . 123 E1
St George's Rd OX1 . 154 B1
St Georges Green OX10 . 203 E1
St Georges Rd OX10 . 221 E4
St Giles OX5 ..... 93 D4
St Giles' OX1 .... 123 E1
St Giles Cl OX6 .. 80 A2
St Helen's Ave OX10 . 203 F2
St Helen's Cres OX10 . 204 A2
St Helen's Ct OX14 . 179 F3
St Helen's Mews OX14 . 179 F3
St Helen's Pas OX1 . 123 E1
St Helen's Way OX10 . 203 F2
St Helen's Wharf OX14 . 179 F3
St Hilda's Cl OX6 . 65 F2
St Hildas Cl OX11 . 219 D4
St Hugh's Cl Bicester OX6 . 65 F2
  Stokenchurch HP14 . 188 C2
St Hugh's Pl HP14 . 188 C2
St Hughs Cl OX16 . 16 B2
St Hughs Rise OX11 . 219 D4
St Ives La OX11 .. 214 C4
St Ives Rd OX12 .. 214 C4
St James OX12 ... 214 B3
St James Cl RG8 . 256 B3
St James Ct OX8 . 89 E4
St James Rd OX14 . 160 C2
St James Terr OX14 . 160 C1
St James View OX12 . 197 D4
St John St OX1 .. 123 E1
St John's Cl Didcot OX11 . 219 D4
  Fyfield OX13 ...... 157 D1
St John's Green OX10 . 221 E3
St John's Rd
  Abingdon OX14 .... 180 A4
  Banbury OX16 ..... 16 B3
  Grove OX12 .... 196 C1
  Wallingford OX10 . 221 E4
St John's Row OX14 . 201 E4
St John's St Bicester OX6 . 65 F1
  Lechlade GL7 ..... 150 B2
St John's Way OX15 . 33 D2
St Johns Dr
  Carterton OX18 .... 115 F2
  Kidlington OX5 .... 92 C1
St Johns Rd
  Caversham RG4 ... 259 E1
  Tackley OX5 ...... 77 E3
St Katherines Rd RG9 . 254 B4
St Kenelm's Cl OX8 . 102 C1
St Lawrence Cl OX10 . 203 D1
St Lawrence Rd
  Lechlade GL7 ..... 150 B2
  South Hinksey OX1 . 141 D3
St Leonard's Cl OX16 . 16 C3
St Leonard's La OX14 . 221 E4
St Leonard's Rd OX3 . 124 B2
St Leonard's Sq OX11 . 221 E4
St Leonards Cl OX9 . 186 A1
St Lucian's La OX10 . 221 E3
St Luke's Rd OX4 . 142 C1

St Lukes Way RG4 ... 259 D2
St Margaret's Rd OX2 . 123 D2
St Marks Rd RG9 . 254 B4
St Martin's Rd OX4 . 142 A2
St Martin's St OX10 . 221 E4
St Mary's Av RG4 . 184 B3
St Mary's Cl Bicester OX6 . 65 E1
  Kidlington OX5 .... 92 C1
  Oxford OX4 .... 142 A1
St Mary's Ct OX8 . 118 A4
St Mary's Green OX14 . 159 F1
St Mary's La OX7 . 30 C2
St Mary's Mead OX8 . 118 A4
St Mary's Rd
  Adderbury OX17 .... 22 C1
  East Hendred OX12 . 216 C3
  Oxford OX4 .... 141 F4
St Mary's St OX10 . 221 E4
St Mary's Way OX12 . 214 B3
St Marys Ave RG8 . 257 E3
St Marys Cl
  Henley-on-T RG9 .. 254 A4
  Wheatley OX33 .... 144 A4
St Michael's Ave
  Abingdon OX14 .... 179 F4
  Highworth SN6 .... 190 A3
St Michael's Cl OX16 . 52 B3
St Michael's La OX5 . 107 F4
St Michael's St OX1 . 123 E1
St Michael's Way OX13 . 198 C2
St Michaels Cl OX7 . 85 E4
St Nicholas' Green OX14 . 159 F1
St Nicholas Rd Oxford OX4 . 142 B1
  Tackley OX5 ...... 77 E3
  Wallingford OX10 . 221 E4
St Omer Rd OX4 .. 142 B3
St Paul's Cres OX2 . 140 B4
St Peter's Cl
  Cassington OX8 .... 107 E1
  Stoke Lyne OX6 ... 51 D3
  Wootton (Oxford) OX13 . 159 D3
St Peter's Cres OX6 . 65 F2
St Peter's Pl OX10 . 221 E4
St Peter's Rd
  Abingdon OX14 .... 160 B1
  Brackley NN13 .... 24 A4
  Cutteslowe OX2 ... 122 C4
  Didcot OX11 ...... 218 C4
St Peter's St OX10 . 221 E4
St Peters Ave RG4 . 258 C2
St Peters Hill RG4 . 258 C2
St Peters Rd NN13 . 24 A4
St Ruald's Cl OX10 . 221 E4
St Rumbold's Rd OX10 . 221 E4
St Stephens Cl RG4 . 259 D1
St Swithun's Rd OX1 . 160 C4
St Thomas Dr OX15 . 33 F2
St Thomas' La OX1 . 123 D1
St Thomas's Cl SN7 . 155 F1
Salegate La OX4 .. 142 B3
Salesian Gdns OX4 . 142 B3
Salford Rd OX3 .. 123 F2
Salisbury Cres OX2 . 123 D4
Sallow Cl OX6 ... 65 F3
Salmon Cl OX15 . 21 F3
Salop Cl SN6 .... 209 D3
Salt La OX9 ..... 166 C1
Salter Cl OX1 ... 141 E4
Salters La HP18 . 98 B4
Salvia Cl OX9 ... 9 D1
Samian Way OX10 . 202 B4
Samor Way OX11 . 218 B4
Samphire Rd OX4 . 142 C1
Sand Hill SN6 ... 209 D4
Sand View SN7 .. 172 C1
Sandcroft Rd RG4 . 258 C3
Sandell Cl OX16 . 16 B3
Sanderling Wlk OX16 . 16 C2
Sandfield Rd OX3 . 124 A2
Sandfine Rd OX15 . 15 D1
Sandford Cl
  Abingdon OX14 .... 160 A1
  Woodcote RG8 .... 250 C4
Sandford Dr RG5 . 260 C1
Sandford Green OX16 . 15 F4
Sandford La OX1 . 160 C4
Sandford Park OX7 . 73 E2
Sandford Rd OX4 . 142 A1
Sandford Rise OX7 . 73 E2
Sandgate Ave RG30 . 257 F1
Sandhill Rd OX5 . 108 A4
Sandleigh Rd OX13 . 159 D4
Sandpiper Cl OX6 . 81 D4
Sandpit Hill MK18 . 39 F3
Sandringham Dr OX11 . 219 D4
Sandringham Rd OX17 . 23 F3
Sands Cl Bletchingdon OX5 . 93 D4
  Cumnor OX2 ...... 139 F3
Sands La OX15 ... 31 F4
Sands Rd OX11 .. 219 F3
Sands The Benson OX10 . 204 B3
  Ewelme OX10 ..... 204 B3
  Milton-u-W OX7 ... 70 A1
Sands Way OX10 . 203 F3
Sandy La Beckley OX3 . 111 D1
  Cholsey OX10 .... 220 C1
  Church Westcote GL54 . 68 A2
  Kingston Bagpuize OX13 . 156 C1
  Long Crendon HP18 . 129 D3
  Oxford OX4, OX33, OX4 . 142 C2
  Shrivenham SN6 ... 209 D3
  Stanford in the V SN7 . 174 B2
  Tiddington OX9 ... 145 F3
  Wootton (Oxford) OX1 . 140 B1
  Yarnton OX5 ...... 108 B4
Sandy La W OX4 . 142 B2
Sandy Lane Ct GL54 . 68 A2

Sarajac Ave OX12 .... 213 F2
Sarsden Cl OX7 .... 57 D1
Sarum Cl OX18 .... 115 F2
Satin La OX15 .... 33 F2
Satwell Cl RG9 .... 243 D2
Saunders Cl OX9 .... 186 A1
Saunders Ct RG8 .... 257 D3
Saunders Rd OX4 .... 142 A3
Saunders Wood Copse
HP14 .... 188 C2
Savile Rd OX1 .... 123 E1
Savile Way OX12 .... 196 B1
Saw Cl OX44 .... 184 B4
Sawpit Rd OX4 .... 142 C2
Sawpits La GL56 .... 40 A1
Saxel Cl OX18 .... 135 F2
Saxifrage Sq OX4 .... 142 C1
Saxon Cl OX10 .... 221 E4
Saxon Pl OX4 .... 214 A3
Saxon Way Oxford OX3 ... 124 A2
  Witney OX8 .... 118 A4
Saxons Heath OX14 .... 201 E4
Saxons Way OX11 .... 219 D4
Saxton Rd OX14 .... 179 F3
Sayers Orch OX11 .... 200 B1
Scafell Cl RG31 .... 257 E1
Scampton Cl OX6 .... 66 A2
Schilling St OX6 .... 63 D4
Schofield Ave OX4 .... 104 A2
Schofield Gdns OX8 ...... 104 A2
Schofields Way OX15 .... 21 F3
Scholar Pl OX2 .... 140 B4
Scholars Acre OX18 ...... 115 E2
Scholars Cl RG4 .... 258 C2
Schongau Cl OX14 .... 179 E2
School Cl Ickford HP18 ... 128 A2
  Long Compton CV36 ... 27 F3
  Longworth OX13 .... 156 B2
  Steventon OX13 .... 198 C2
School End OX17 .... 35 E4
School Hill
  Minster Lovell OX8 .... 102 C2
  Mollington OX17 .... 3 F2
  Wargrave RG10 .... 255 E1
School La
  Aston Rowant OX9 ..... 167 F2
  Banbury OX15, OX16, OX17 .... 16 B3
  Black Bourton OX18 ... 133 F3
  Caversham RG4 .... 259 D1
  Caversham, The Common
  RG4 .... 259 D3
  Chilson OX7 .... 71 F3
  Coleshill SN6 .... 191 D4
  Great Bourton OX17 ... 9 E4
  Harwell OX11 .... 217 F4
  Kingston Bagpuize OX13 ... 156 C1
  Middleton Stoney OX6 .... 64 A2
  Milton (Abingdon) OX14 ... 199 E3
  Milton (Abingdon) OX14 ... 199 E3
  Minster Lovell OX8 .... 102 C2
  North Newington OX15 ... 15 E2
  Shabbington HP18 ..... 128 B1
  Stoke Row RG9 .... 241 F2
  Sutton Courtenay OX14 ... 200 C4
  Upper Heyford OX6 .... 62 C4
  Wargrave RG10 .... 255 E1
  Warmington OX17 ...... 3 D2
School Paddock OX6 ..... 64 C4
School Pl OX1 .... 141 E3
School Rd
  Ardington OX12 .... 215 E3
  Finstock OX7 .... 88 B3
  Kidlington OX5 .... 92 C1
  West Hanney OX12 .... 196 C3
School View OX16 .... 16 C3
School Yd OX44 .... 163 E1
Schooler's La OX12 ...... 40 B2
Scotland End OX15 .... 30 A4
Scotsgrove Cotts HP17 ... 130 A2
Scott Cl Bicester OX6 ... 65 E2
  Caversham RG4 .... 259 D3
  Kidlington OX5 .... 108 B4
Scott Rd OX2 .... 123 D4
Scotts Cnr NN13 .... 25 D2
Scotts La OX6 .... 67 F1
Scours La RG30 .... 258 A1
Scruton Cl OX3 .... 124 C2
Seacourt Rd OX2 .... 122 B1
Sealham Rd OX8 .... 118 A2
Second Ave OX11 .... 200 B1
Second St Croughton NN13 ... 36 C3
  Harwell OX11 .... 217 E2
Sedgefield Cl RG4 .... 252 C3
Sedgemoor Dr OX9 ...... 130 A1
Sedgewell Rd RG4 .... 252 C3
Seelscheid Way OX6 .... 81 D4
Seeson Way OX12 .... 214 C2
Sefton Pl OX15 .... 22 C4
Sefton Rd OX3 .... 124 C2
Segsbury Rd OX12 .... 214 A3
Selborne Gdns RG30 .... 258 A1
Sellwood Dr OX18 .... 115 F2
Sellwood Rd OX14 .... 159 F1
Selwyn Cres OX14 .... 160 C1
Send Rd RG4 .... 259 E1
Sermon Cl OX3 .... 124 C1
Seven Acres
  Long Crendon HP18 ... 129 D4
  Thame OX9 .... 148 A4
Sevenfields SN6 .... 190 A4
Seventeenth St OX11 ... 217 D1
Seventh Ave OX33 .... 142 C4
Seventh St OX11 .... 217 D2
Severalls Cl OX10 .... 203 E1
Severn Cl OX6 .... 65 D2
Severn Rd Abingdon OX13 ... 159 E1
  Harwell OX11 .... 217 D1

Sewell Cl OX14 .... 160 B1
Sewell's La OX9 .... 167 F4
Shackleton Cl OX6 .... 66 A2
Shades The OX16 .... 16 B3
Shadwell Rd OX10 .... 182 B3
Shaftesbury Rd OX3 .... 124 C3
Shakespeare Cl RG4 .... 259 E3
Shakespeare Dr OX6 .... 65 E2
Shakespeare Rd OX8 ... 120 B4
Shannon Cl OX12 .... 196 C1
Shannon Rd OX6 .... 65 D1
Sharland Cl OX12 .... 214 C4
Sharman Beer Ct OX9 ... 147 F4
Shaw Cl OX6 .... 65 E2
Shaw's Copse OX14 ..... 160 C1
Sheards La SN7 .... 194 C4
Shearings The OX15 ..... 30 A4
Shearwater Dr OX6 ...... 81 D4
Sheen Cl OX2 .... 65 F3
Sheep St Bicester OX6 .. 65 F1
  Burford OX18 .... 100 C3
  Charlbury OX7 .... 73 C2
  Highworth SN6 .... 190 A3
Sheep Wlk RG4 .... 259 D2
Sheepwash La OX13 .... 199 D3
Sheepway Ct OX4 .... 142 A2
Sheepways La RG4 ...... 258 A3
Sheerstock HP17 .... 130 C3
Sheldon Rd HP18 .... 128 A2
Sheldon Way OX4 .... 142 B2
Shelford Pl OX3 .... 124 B1
Shelley Cl Abingdon OX14 ... 160 A1
  Banbury OX16 .... 16 A2
  Bicester OX6 .... 65 E2
  Oxford OX3 .... 124 C1
Shelley Rd OX4 .... 142 A3
Shepard Way OX7 .... 42 C2
Shepherd Gdns OX14 ... 179 E3
Shepherds Cl Grove OX12 ... 196 B1
  Weston-on-the-G OX6 .... 79 D1
Shepherds Hill
  Sandford-on-T OX4 .... 142 C1
  Woodstock RG5 .... 260 B1
Shepherds La RG4 .... 258 B3
Sheraton Dr RG31 .... 257 E1
Sherborne St GL7 .... 150 B2
Sherbourne Rd OX8 ..... 117 E4
Sheridan Ave RG4 .... 259 E3
Sheriff's Dr OX2 .... 122 C4
Sherwood Ave OX14 .... 180 A4
Sherwood Cl OX6 .... 66 B1
Sherwood Gdns RG9 .... 254 B4
Sherwood Pl RG8 .... 257 D2
Sherwood Rd OX11 ...... 218 B4
Sherwood Rise RG8 ..... 257 D2
Shifford La OX8 .... 137 E1
Shilbrook Manor OX18 ... 133 F2
Shillbrook Ave OX18 .... 115 E3
Shilldeane Dr OX18 ..... 115 E2
Shilton Rd Burford OX18 ... 100 C2
  Carterton OX18 .... 115 E2
Ship St OX1 .... 123 E1
Shiplake Bottom RG4 ... 252 C3
Shipston Rd CV36 .... 27 F4
Shipton Cl RG31 .... 257 E1
Shipton Rd Ascott-u-W OX7 ... 71 D1
  Shipton-u-W OX7 ...... 70 A1
  Woodstock OX20 .... 91 E3
Shirburn Rd OX9 .... 186 B1
Shirburn St OX9 .... 186 B1
Shirelake Cl OX1 .... 141 E4
Shires Rd NN13 .... 24 C3
Shirvell's Hill RG8 .... 250 C4
Shoe La
  East Hagbourne OX11 ... 218 C3
  Oxford OX1 .... 123 E1
Shooters Hill RG8 .... 256 A3
Short Furlong OX11 ..... 201 D1
Short St Caversham RG4 ... 259 D1
  Pangbourne RG8 .... 256 B3
  Watchfield SN6 .... 191 E1
Short The RG8 .... 257 E3
Shortlands Hill OX10 .... 238 B2
Shotover SN7 .... 211 E3
Shrieves Cl OX14 .... 160 A1
Shrivenham Hundred
SN6 .... 191 E1
Shrivenham Rd
  Highworth SN6 .... 190 A2
  Longcot SN7 .... 192 B1
Shute Ave SN6 .... 209 E4
Shutford Rd
  North Newington OX15 ... 15 D2
  Tadmarton OX15 .... 20 C4
Sibford Rd
  Hook Norton OX15 ..... 30 A4
  Shutford OX15 .... 13 F2
Sideleigh Rd OX15 .... 22 C4
Sidings Rd OX7 .... 55 F3
Sidney St OX4 .... 141 F4
Signet End OX18 .... 100 C2
Silkdale Cl OX4 .... 142 B3
Silver Birches OX33 ..... 125 F4
Silver La OX12 .... 213 E3
Silver Rd OX4 .... 142 A4
Silver St Bourton SN6 ... 209 D1
  Chacombe OX17 .... 10 C2
  Fernham SN7 .... 193 D2
  Tetsworth OX9 .... 166 A4
  Wroxton OX15 .... 15 D4
Silverdale Rd RG10 ..... 255 F1
Silvermead HP18 .... 127 E3
Silverthorne Dr RG4 .... 258 C3
Simmonds Wlk OX12 ... 214 B3
Simmons Rd RG9 .... 244 B2
Simmons Way OX9 ...... 129 F1
Simon's Cl OX33 .... 144 A4
Simons Cl RG31 .... 257 E2

Simons La OX7 .... 85 E4
Simpsons Way OX1 ...... 160 C4
Sinclair Ave OX16 .... 16 A4
Sinclair Dr OX16 .... 16 A4
Singer La RG9 .... 244 C1
Singers Cl RG9 .... 254 C4
Sinnels Field OX7 .... 85 F4
Sinodun Cl OX14 .... 201 E4
Sinodun Rd Didcot OX11 ... 218 C4
  Wallingford OX10 ...... 203 E1
Sinodun View OX10 ..... 203 D4
Sint Niklaas Cl OX14 .... 179 E2
Sir Georges La OX17 ... 23 D2
Siskin Rd GL54 .... 68 A3
Sixpenny La OX44 .... 184 C3
Sixteenth St OX11 ...... 217 D2
Sixth St Croughton NN13 ... 36 C4
  Harwell OX11 .... 217 D2
Skarries View RG4 .... 258 B4
Skene Cl OX3 .... 124 B1
Skerrit Way RG8 .... 257 E2
Skilton Rd RG31 .... 257 E2
Skimmingdish La OX6 ... 65 F3
Skimmingdish Rd OX6 ... 66 A2
Skinner Rd OX6 .... 66 B1
Skippett La OX7 .... 88 A2
Skippon Way OX9 .... 129 F1
Skittle Alley OX17 .... 35 E4
Slade Cl OX3 .... 124 B1
Slade End OX10 .... 203 D1
Slade End Rdbt OX10 ... 203 D1
Slade Rd Cholsey OX10 ... 221 D1
  Didcot OX11 .... 200 B1
  Stokenchurch HP14 ... 188 C2
Slade The Charlbury OX7 ... 73 E2
  Oxford OX3 .... 142 C4
Slave Hill HP17 .... 130 C3
Slaymaker Cl OX3 .... 124 C1
Sloan Ct RG8 .... 249 E3
Slopes The RG4 .... 259 E1
Small Ho OX15 .... 19 E4
Smith Barry Cres GL54 ... 68 A2
Smith Barry Rd GL54 ... 68 A2
Smith Cl RG4 .... 252 C3
Smith's Cl OX18 .... 135 F1
Smiths Farm La OX11 ... 200 B1
Smiths Hill OX12 .... 231 F3
Smiths Rickyard OX12 ... 216 B4
Snakehill La OX15 .... 33 D2
Snipe Rd GL54 .... 68 A2
Snowdon Mede OX3 ..... 124 A2
Snows La OX33 .... 125 E4
Snowshill Dr OX8 .... 103 E1
Snowsill Dr OX8 .... 117 E4
Snowswick La SN7 ..... 170 C3
Snuff La OX17 .... 8 B4
Snuggs La OX12 .... 197 D4
Soden Rd OX6 .... 63 E4
Solters Cl HP18 .... 129 E4
Somerton Rd Ardley OX6 ... 50 A2
  North Aston OX6 ...... 48 A4
  Upper Heyford OX6 ... 48 C1
Somerville OX11 .... 219 D4
Somerville Ct OX17 ..... 23 E2
Somerville Dr OX6 ...... 65 F2
Songers Cl OX2 .... 140 A4
Sonning La RG4 .... 260 B1
Sonning Meadows RG4 ... 260 B1
Soot La OX17 .... 3 D2
Sopwith Rd GL54 .... 68 A3
Sorrel Rd OX4 .... 143 D1
Sotwell St OX10 .... 202 C1
South Ave Abingdon OX14 ... 159 F1
  Henley-on-T RG9 ..... 254 C1
  Kidlington OX5 .... 108 C3
South Bar St OX16 ..... 16 B3
South Cl OX5 .... 108 C3
South Dr Harwell OX11 ... 217 E2
  Sonning RG4 .... 260 B1
South End
  Great Rollright OX7 ... 29 D2
  Haddenham HP17 ..... 130 C3
South Gate Ct GL54 .... 68 A2
South Hills HP18 .... 98 A1
South Leigh Rd OX8 .... 119 D4
South Mere OX18 .... 116 B2
South Newington Rd
  Barford St M OX15 .... 32 B3
  Bloxham OX15 .... 21 D1
South Par OX2 .... 123 D4
South Park Ave OX11 ... 218 B4
South Parks Rd OX1 ... 123 E1
South Rd RG9 .... 242 A1
South Row OX11 .... 235 E4
South Side OX6 .... 62 A4
South St Banbury OX16 ... 16 C4
  Blewbury OX11 .... 237 D4
  Caversham RG4 .... 259 D1
  Letcombe Bassett OX12 ... 214 A1
  Lower Heyford OX6 ... 63 D3
  Middle Barton OX7 ... 60 C4
  Oxford OX2 .... 141 D4
  Watchfield SN6 .... 191 E1
South Stoke Rd RG8 ... 240 A1
South View OX11 .... 9 E4
South View Ave RG4 ... 259 E1
South View Park RG4 ... 259 E1
Southam Rd
  Banbury OX16, OX17 ... 9 E2
  Cropredy OX17 .... 4 A2
  Great Bourton OX17 ... 9 E2
  Mollington OX17 .... 4 A2
Southampton St SN7 ... 172 C2
Southby Cl OX13 .... 158 A4
Southcroft OX3 .... 123 F3
Southdale Rd OX2 ...... 123 D4
Southdown Ct SN7 ..... 194 C4
Southdown Rd RG4 ..... 259 D3

Southend OX44 .... 162 C4
Southern By-pass Rd
  Kennington OX1 .... 141 E2
  N Hinksey Vill OX2 .... 140 C4
  Oxford OX1 .... 141 E2
  South Hinksey OX1 ... 141 D2
Southern Rd OX9 .... 147 F4
Southerndene Cl RG31 ... 257 E1
Southfield Dr OX14 ..... 199 F4
Southfield La OX6 .... 49 F4
Southfield Park OX4 .... 142 A4
Southfield Rd OX4 ...... 142 A4
Southlands OX18 .... 135 F1
Southlawn OX8 .... 117 F4
Southmoor Pl OX2 ...... 123 D2
Southmoor Rd OX2 ..... 123 D2
Southmoor Way OX14 ... 179 F4
Southrop OX15 .... 30 A3
Southwold OX6 .... 65 F3
Southwood Rd OX8 ..... 103 E1
Sovereign Cl OX11 ..... 219 D4
Spa Cl SN6 .... 190 A4
Span Hill RG4 .... 260 B4
Spareacre La OX8 ...... 120 C4
Sparrow Way OX4 ...... 142 C1
Sparsey Pl OX2 .... 109 D1
Sparsholt St OX12 ...... 212 C2
Spears The OX5 .... 108 A3
Speedwell St OX1 .... 141 E4
Spencer Ave OX5 .... 108 A3
Spencer Cres OX4 ...... 142 A2
Spencers Cl SN7 .... 194 B4
Spenlove Cl OX14 ...... 159 F1
Spenser Cl OX6 .... 65 E2
Spey Rd OX13 .... 159 E2
Speyside Cl OX18 .... 115 E3
Spier's La OX6 .... 67 F1
Spindleberry Cl OX4 ... 142 C1
Spindlers OX5 .... 92 C1
Spindleside OX6 .... 65 F3
Spinney Cl RG4 .... 259 D4
Spinney Dr OX16 .... 16 C2
Spinney Field OX4 ...... 142 C1
Spinney The
  Abingdon OX14 .... 159 E1
  Launton OX6 .... 66 B1
  Lechlade GL7 .... 150 B2
Spinneys Cl OX14 .... 160 C2
Spinneys The OX7 ...... 58 C3
Spitfire Cl OX6 .... 66 A2
Spooner Cl OX3 .... 124 C2
Sprigs Holly La HP14 ... 189 D4
Spring Cl OX8 .... 118 A4
Spring Copse OX1 ...... 141 E2
Spring Farm OX6 .... 47 E3
Spring Gdns OX14 ...... 179 E4
Spring Hill OX13 .... 176 B4
Spring Hill Rd OX5 ..... 107 F4
Spring La
  Aston Tirrold OX11 ... 237 D2
  Caversham RG4 .... 260 A3
  Great Bourton OX17 ... 9 E3
  Horspath OX33 .... 143 E4
  Idbury OX7 .... 69 D2
  Oxford OX3, OX33, OX4 ... 142 B1
  Oxford,Headington Quarry
  OX3, OX33, OX4 ...... 124 C1
  Watlington OX9 .... 186 B1
Spring Path OX9 .... 147 F4
Spring Pl OX7 .... 42 C1
Spring Rd OX14 .... 179 E4
Spring St OX7 .... 42 C2
Spring Wlk RG10 .... 255 E1
Springdale OX10 .... 221 E4
Springfield OX17 .... 8 C2
Springfield Ave OX16 ... 16 B2
Springfield Cl
  Shrivenham SN6 .... 209 D3
  Watlington OX9 .... 186 B1
Springfield Dr OX14 ... 179 F4
Springfield End RG8 ... 249 E4
Springfield Gdns OX9 ... 168 B4
Springfield Oval OX8 ... 103 F1
Springfield Park OX8 ... 103 F1
Springfield Rd
  Bicester OX6 .... 65 F4
  Kidlington OX5 .... 108 C4
  N Hinksey Vill OX2 ... 140 B4
  Stokenchurch HP14 ... 188 C2
  Wantage OX12 .... 214 C2
Springhill Rd RG8 ...... 249 E4
Springs The OX8 .... 118 A4
Springwell Hill OX5 .... 78 A3
Springwood La RG9 ... 253 D4
Spruce Dr OX6 .... 65 D2
Spruce Gdns OX4 ...... 161 F4
Spruce Rd OX5 .... 108 C4
Spur The RG10 .... 255 F2
Square Firs OX8 .... 90 A3
Square The
  Abingdon OX13, OX14 ... 179 E1
  Aston OX18 .... 135 F2
  Aynho OX17 .... 35 E4
  Ducklington OX8 ..... 118 A2
  Eynsham OX8 .... 120 C4
  Kings Sutton OX17 ... 23 E3
  Long Crendon HP18 ... 129 E3
  Longworth OX13 ..... 156 A2
  N Hinksey Vill OX2 ... 122 B1
  Pangbourne RG8 ..... 256 B3
  Swalcliffe OX15 ...... 19 E4
Squire's Wlk OX10 .... 221 E3
Squires Cl OX18 ...... 116 B2
Squires Rd SN6 .... 191 E1
Squitchey La OX2 .... 123 D4
Stable Cl MK18 .... 39 E4
Stable Rd OX6 .... 65 F2
Staddlestone Cl RG31 ... 257 E1

Stadhampton Rd
  Drayton St L OX10 ... 183 D3
  Little Milton OX44 ... 163 F3
Stadium Way RG30 .... 258 A1
Staffordshire Cl RG30 ... 257 F1
Stainer Pl OX3 .... 123 F2
Stainfield Rd OX3 ..... 124 A3
Stainswick La SN6 .... 209 E3
Stallpits Rd SN6 ...... 209 D4
Stanbridge Cl OX16 ... 16 A3
Standlake Rd
  Ducklington OX8 ..... 118 B2
  Northmoor OX8 .... 138 A1
Stanford Dr OX14 .... 179 F4
Stanford Rd SN7 ...... 173 D2
Stanier Pl OX16 ...... 16 C4
Stanley Cl OX2 .... 140 B4
Stanley Rd OX4 .... 141 F4
Stanmore Cres OX18 ... 115 F2
Stansfeld Pl OX3 ...... 124 C1
Stansfield Cl OX3 ..... 124 C1
Stanton Cl OX8 .... 117 F4
Stanton Harcourt Rd
  South Leigh OX8 ..... 119 E3
  Witney OX8 .... 118 B4
Stanton Rd
  Forest Hill OX33 ..... 125 F2
  N Hinksey Vill OX2 ... 140 C3
Stanville Rd OX2 ...... 140 A4
Stanway Cl OX8 .... 103 E1
Stanway Rd OX3 ...... 125 D2
Stanwell Cl OX17 ..... 11 D1
Stanwell Dr OX17 .... 11 D1
Stanwell Lea OX17 ... 11 D1
Stanwell Rd OX17 .... 9 E4
Stapleton Rd OX3 .... 124 B1
Star La SN6 .... 191 E1
Star Rd RG4 .... 259 E1
Starina Croft OX16 ... 9 D1
Starnham Rd OX8 .... 118 A2
Starwort Path OX4 ... 142 C1
Station App Bicester OX6 ... 65 F1
  Kidlington OX5 .... 92 B1
Station Field Ind Est OX5 ... 92 B1
Station La OX18 ...... 118 A3
Station Rd Ardley OX6 ... 50 B2
  Ashbury SN6 .... 228 A4
  Aynho OX17 .... 35 D3
  Bampton OX18 .... 134 C3
  Black Bourton OX18 ... 133 F3
  Blackthorn OX6 .... 82 A2
  Bletchingdon OX5 .... 93 D4
  Brize Norton OX18 ... 116 B2
  Chinnor OX9 .... 168 B3
  Chipping Norton OX7 ... 42 B1
  Cholsey OX10 .... 220 C1
  Churchill OX7 .... 54 C2
  Cropredy OX17 .... 4 C1
  Culham OX14 .... 180 C2
  Didcot OX11 .... 200 C1
  Eynsham OX8 .... 120 C4
  Faringdon SN7 .... 172 C2
  Goring RG8 .... 249 E3
  Grove OX12 .... 214 C4
  Haddenham HP17 ... 130 C3
  Henley on T RG9 .... 244 C1
  Highworth SN6 .... 190 A3
  Hook Norton OX15 ... 30 B4
  Kingham OX7 .... 54 C2
  Launton OX6 .... 66 C2
  Lechlade GL7 .... 150 B3
  Lower Heyford OX6 ... 62 B3
  Marsh Gibbon OX6 ... 67 F2
  Pangbourne RG8 ..... 256 B3
  Shiplake RG9 .... 255 D2
  Shipton-u-W OX7 ... 70 C1
  Shrivenham SN6 ..... 209 D3
  South Leigh OX8 .... 119 E3
  Uffington SN7 .... 211 E4
  Upton OX11 .... 218 B1
  Wallingford OX10 ... 221 E4
  Wargrave RG10 ...... 255 E1
  Wheatley OX33 ...... 144 A4
Station Yard Ind Est OX17 ... 23 D1
Station Yd Steventon OX13 ... 199 D2
  Thame OX9 .... 148 A4
Staunton Rd OX3 ..... 124 A2
Staverton Rd OX2 .... 123 D3
Steady's La OX8 ...... 138 A4
Steep Rise OX3 .... 124 B3
Steeple Cl OX15 ...... 21 F2
Steepness Hill OX15 ... 32 C2
Stenton Cl OX14 ..... 179 F3
Stephen Rd OX3 ...... 124 B2
Stephenson Rd OX12 ... 214 A4
Steptoe Cl OX12 ..... 196 B1
Sterling Cl Bicester OX6 ... 66 A2
  Kidlington OX5 .... 108 C4
Sterling Rd OX5 .... 108 C4
Sterling Road App OX5 ... 92 C1
Sterling Way RG30 ... 258 A1
Stert Rd OX9 .... 167 F2
Stert St OX14 .... 179 F4
Stevens La RG9 ...... 252 B4
Stevenson Cl OX6 ... 65 E2
Stevenson Dr OX14 ... 179 E4
Steventon Rd
  Drayton OX14 .... 199 D4
  East Hanney OX12 ... 197 F4
Stewart St OX1 ...... 141 E3
Stile Rd OX3 .... 124 B2
Stimpsons Cl OX2 ... 122 A1
Stirling Cl Carterton OX18 ... 115 E2
  Caversham RG4 ..... 259 E3
  Wantage OX12 .... 214 C3

Stirling Ct OX16 .... 15 F3
Stirlings Rd OX12 .... 214 B2
Stockey End OX14 .... 160 B1
Stockham Park OX12 ..... 214 B3
Stockham Way OX12 ...... 214 B3
Stocking La OX15 .... 6 B1
Stockleys Rd OX3 .... 124 A3
Stockmore St OX4 .... 141 F4
Stocks La OX13 .... 198 C2
Stocks Tree Cl OX5 .... 108 A3
Stoke Lyne Rd OX6 .... 52 B1
Stoke Pl OX3 .... 124 B2
Stoke Row Rd RG9 .... 252 C4
Stokes View RG8 .... 256 B3
Stone Cl OX2 .... 122 A1
Stone Ct OX7 .... 29 D2
Stone Hill OX15 .... 21 E2
Stone House Cl OX13 .... 156 C1
Stone Quarry La OX4 ..... 142 A2
Stone St Oxford OX4 ...... 142 A4
   Reading RG30 .... 258 A1
Stonebridge Rd OX13 .... 198 C3
Stoneburge Cres OX6 ..... 65 F2
Stonebury Cl OX12 .... 214 C3
Stonefield Dr SN6 .... 190 A2
Stonefield Way SN6 .... 209 E3
Stonefields Riding OX8 ... 89 E4
Stonehill OX14 .... 179 E2
Stonehill La OX13 .... 176 B4
Stonehill Wlk OX14 .... 179 F2
Stoneleigh Cl OX7 .... 57 D1
Stoneleigh Dr OX18 ...... 115 E3
Stonesfield OX11 .... 219 D4
Stonesfield La OX7 .... 73 E1
Stonesfield Rd OX8 .... 90 A3
Stonesfield Riding OX7 ... 74 B1
Stoney La OX9 .... 185 F4
Stonhouse Cres OX14 .... 160 C1
Stonor Cl OX11 .... 200 C1
Stonor Gn OX9 .... 186 A1
Stonor Ho RG9 .... 226 A4
Stonor Pl OX3 .... 124 A1
Stort Cl OX11 .... 200 C2
Stoutsfield Cl OX5 .... 108 A3
Stow Ave OX8 .... 117 E4
Stow Rd Bledington OX7 ... 54 B1
   Fifield OX7 .... 69 D1
Stowford Rd OX3 .... 124 C2
Stowhill OX12 .... 213 E2
Stowood Cl OX3 .... 124 C2
Strachey Cl RG8 .... 256 B1
Strafford Way OX9 .... 148 A4
Strainges Cl OX8 .... 118 A2
Stratfield Rd
   Cutteslowe OX2 .... 123 D3
   Kidlington OX5 .... 108 C3
Stratford Dr OX18 .... 120 B4
Stratford La OX20 .... 76 A1
Stratford Rd
   Drayton (Banbury) OX15 ... 15 F4
Stratford Rd continued
   Shenington OX15 .... 6 C3
   Wroxton OX15 .... 14 C4
Stratford St OX4 .... 141 F4
Strathmore Cl OX18 ...... 115 F3
Stratton Audley Rd
   Fringford OX6 .... 52 B3
   Stoke Lyne OX6 .... 51 D3
Stratton Way OX14 .... 179 F4
Strawberry Hill OX15 ...... 21 F3
Strawberry Path OX4 .... 142 C1
Strawberry Terr OX15 ..... 21 F3
Stream Rd OX11 .... 218 B1
Streatley & Goring Bridge
   RG8 .... 249 D3
Streatley Hill RG8 .... 248 C3
Street The
   Crowmarsh G OX10 ..... 221 F4
   Crowmarsh G, Ipsden OX10 ... 240 B4
   Crowmarsh G, N Stoke OX10 221 E1
   Moulsford OX10 .... 239 D3
   South Stoke RG8 .... 239 D2
   Stoke Lyne OX6 .... 51 D3
   Tidmarsh RG8 .... 256 B1
Stuart Cl OX4 .... 259 D3
Stuart Way OX9 .... 130 A1
Stubble Cl OX2 .... 140 A4
Stubbs Ave OX3 .... 142 C4
Studdridge Ct HP14 ...... 188 B2
Sturges Cl OX3 .... 124 C2
Sturt Cl OX7 .... 73 E1
Sturt Rd OX7 .... 73 E1
Styles Cl OX6 .... 67 F1
Styles The OX11 .... 217 E4
Sudbury Ct SN7 .... 173 D2
Sudbury La OX13 .... 156 B2
Suffolk Cl OX6 .... 67 F2
Suffolk Way OX14 .... 179 E3
Sugarswell La OX15 .... 6 A3
Sugworth Cres OX14 ..... 160 C3
Sugworth La OX14 .... 160 B3
Sulham La
   Pangbourne RG8 .... 256 C2
   Purley on T RG8 .... 256 C2
   Reading RG8 .... 256 C2
Summer Fields OX14 ..... 160 A2
Summer Ley OX15 .... 32 C3
Summerfield OX1 .... 141 E3
Summerfield Rd OX2 .... 123 D4
Summerfield Rise RG8 ... 249 E4
Summerhill Rd OX2 ...... 123 D4
Summers Cl OX17 .... 23 D3
Summerside Rd SN7 ..... 174 C4
Summerton Pl OX7 .... 42 C2

Summertown OX12 .... 197 D3
Summertown Ct OX2 .... 123 D4
Sunderland Ave OX2 ..... 109 D1
Sunderland Dr OX6 .... 66 A2
Sundew Cl OX4 .... 143 D1
Sunningwell Rd
   Oxford OX1 .... 141 E3
   Sunningwell OX13 .... 159 F2
Sunny Rise OX33 .... 143 E3
Sunnyside
   Benson OX10 .... 203 F3
   Oxford OX33, OX4 ...... 142 B3
   Wheatley OX33 .... 144 B4
Surley Row RG4 .... 259 D3
Sussex Dr OX16 .... 9 D1
Sutton Cl OX14 .... 179 F4
Sutton Courtenay Rd
   OX14 .... 199 F3
Sutton La OX8 .... 120 A1
Sutton Rd
   Milton (Abingdon) OX14 ... 199 F3
   Oxford OX3 .... 124 A3
Sutton Wick La OX14 .... 179 E1
Suzan Cres OX12 .... 214 C3
Swalcliffe Rd
   Swalcliffe OX15 .... 20 A4
Swale Dr OX11 .... 201 D1
Swallow Cl Bicester OX6 ... 81 D4
 12 Sandford-on-T OX4 ... 142 C1
   Lechlade GL7 .... 150 B2
   Middleton Cheney OX17 ... 17 F4
Swan Close Rd OX16 .... 16 B3
Swan Ct OX8 .... 118 A4
Swan Gdns OX9 .... 166 A4
Swan Ind Est OX16 .... 16 B3
Swan La Burford OX18 ... 100 C3
   Faringdon SN7 .... 172 C2
   Great Bourton OX17 .... 9 E4
   Long Hanborough OX8 ... 90 A1
Swan Lane La OX18 ...... 100 C3
Swan St Eynsham OX8 ... 120 C4
   Oxford OX2 .... 123 D1
Swan Wlk OX9 .... 147 F4
Swanhall La OX8 .... 104 A3
Swansea Rd RG1 .... 259 D1
Swansea Terr RG31 ...... 257 E1
Swansfield Bicester OX6 ... 81 D4
   Lechlade GL7 .... 150 B3
Swanston La RG8 .... 256 B4
Swarbourne Cl OX11 ..... 200 C2
Sweeps La OX18 .... 100 C3
Sweet Briar OX13 .... 178 B3
Sweetmans Rd OX2 ...... 140 B4
Swerford Rd OX15 .... 30 A3
Swift Cl Bicester OX6 ...... 65 E2
 17 Sandford-on-T OX4 ... 142 C1
Swift Way OX18 .... 204 B2
Swin La OX18 .... 101 F3
Swinbourne Rd OX4 ..... 142 A1
Swinbrook Cl RG31 .... 257 E2
Swinbrook Rd
   Carterton OX18 .... 115 E3
   Shipton-u-W OX7 .... 85 F3
Swinburne Rd
   Abingdon OX14 .... 180 A4
   Oxford OX4 .... 141 F3
Swindon Rd SN6 .... 190 A3
Swindon St SN6 .... 190 A3
Swingburn Pl OX8 .... 118 A4
Swinstead Ct OX44 .... 184 B3
Sworford La OX44 .... 144 C3
Sycamore Cl
   Abingdon OX13 .... 159 E1
   Long Crendon HP18 .... 129 E3
   Sibford Gower OX15 ..... 19 D4
   Watlington OX9 .... 186 A1
   Witney OX8 .... 104 B1
Sycamore Cres OX14 .... 160 C4
Sycamore Dr
   Banbury OX16 .... 16 B1
   Carterton OX18 .... 115 E2
   Thame OX9 .... 147 F4
Sycamore Gdns OX6 ...... 65 F2
Sycamore Rd
   Ambrosden OX6 .... 81 E2
   Launton OX6 .... 66 B1
   N Hinksey Vill OX2 ...... 140 B4
Sycamore Wlk OX12 ..... 196 B1
Sydenham Gr OX9 .... 167 F4
Sylvester Cl OX18 .... 100 C3
Sympson Ct OX4 .... 179 F3
Synderford Cl OX11 ...... 201 D1
Syringa Wlk OX16 .... 9 D1

Tackley Pl OX2 .... 123 D2
Tadmarton Rd
   Bloxham OX15 .... 21 D3
   Tadmarton OX15 .... 21 D3
Taggs Gate OX3 .... 124 C3
Tait Dr OX6 .... 63 D4
Talbot Cl Banbury OX16 ... 15 F4
   Caversham RG4 .... 259 E1
Talbot Fields OX18 .... 135 D2
Talbot Rd OX2 .... 109 D1
Talbot Way RG31 .... 257 E2
Talisman Rd OX6 .... 80 C4
Tamar Cres OX6 .... 65 D2
Tamar Way OX11 .... 201 D1
Tamarisk Gdns OX6 .... 65 F3
Tangmere Ave OX18 ..... 115 F2
Tangmere Cl OX6 .... 66 A2
Tanner's La OX18 .... 100 B3
Tanners Ct OX7 .... 73 D2
Tanners La
   Adderbury OX17 .... 22 C2
   Eynsham OX8 .... 120 C4
   Mapledurham RG4 ...... 258 C4

Tannery Cl OX18 .... 100 C3
Taphouse Ave OX8 .... 104 A1
Tarragon Dr OX4 .... 142 C1
Tarrant Ave OX8 .... 104 B1
Taston Rd OX7 .... 73 D4
Tatham Rd OX14 .... 159 F1
Tatlings Rd OX13 .... 198 C3
Taverner Pl OX3 .... 123 F2
Tavistock Ave OX11 ...... 218 B4
Tavy Cl OX11 .... 200 C2
Tawney St OX4 .... 142 A4
Taylor Cl OX16 .... 65 F2
Teal Cl Banbury OX16 ..... 16 C2
   Grove OX12 .... 196 B1
   Sandford-on-T OX4 ..... 142 C1
Teale Cl OX6 .... 96 C4
Teescroft OX11 .... 201 D2
Telford Cres RG5 .... 260 C1
Telford Rd OX6 .... 66 A2
Templar Rd OX2 .... 109 D1
Templars Cl OX33 .... 144 A4
Templars Sq OX4 .... 142 B2
Temple Cloisters OX4 .... 142 B3
Temple Rd OX4 .... 142 B3
Temple St Brill HP18 .... 98 A1
   Oxford OX4 .... 141 F4
Tenby Ave RG4 .... 259 E3
Tenlands OX17 .... 17 F4
Tennis The OX8 .... 107 E1
Tennyson Cl OX16 .... 16 A2
Tennyson Dr OX14 .... 179 E3
Tenpenny OX10 .... 202 B4
Tenth St OX11 .... 217 D2
Terrace The OX7 .... 70 A1
Terrington Cl OX14 .... 160 A1
Tessa Rd RG1 .... 258 C1
Tetbury Cl OX8 .... 103 E1
Tew La OX20 .... 75 F3
Tewer The OX8 .... 89 E4
Thackley End OX2 .... 123 D3
Thame La
   Clifton Hampden OX14 ... 181 D3
   Culham OX14 .... 180 B2
Thame Park Rd OX9 ..... 148 A3
Thame Rd Blackthorn OX6 ... 82 A2
   Chinnor OX9 .... 168 A4
   Great Haseley OX44 .... 164 C4
   Great Milton OX44 ...... 145 E1
   Haddenham HP17 .... 130 B3
   Little Milton OX44 ...... 164 A4
   Long Crendon HP18 .... 129 E2
   Piddington OX6 .... 97 E3
   Towersey OX9 .... 148 C3
   Warborough OX10 ...... 203 D4
Thames Ave Bicester OX6 ... 65 D2
   Pangbourne RG8 .... 256 B3
   Reading RG1 .... 259 D1
Thames Dr RG10 .... 260 C4
Thames Gdns OX7 .... 73 D2
Thames Mead OX10 ..... 221 F4
Thames Rd Goring RG8 ... 249 D3
   Harwell OX11 .... 217 D2
Thames Side
   Henley-on-T RG9 .... 244 C3
   Reading RG1 .... 259 D1
Thames Side Prom RG1 ... 259 D1
Thames St Abingdon OX14 ... 179 F3
   Charlbury OX7 .... 73 D2
   Eynsham OX8 .... 120 C4
   Lechlade GL7 .... 150 B2
   Oxford OX1 .... 141 E4
   Sonning RG4 .... 260 B2
   Wallingford OX10 ...... 221 E4
Thames View OX14 ...... 180 A4
Thames View Ind Park
   OX14 .... 180 A4
Thames View Rd OX4 ... 141 F2
Thatchers Cl OX15 .... 13 D3
Thenford Rd OX17 .... 11 E1
Theobald Dr RG31 .... 257 E2
Thesiger Rd OX4 .... 179 F4
Thetford Mews RG4 ..... 259 E3
Third Acre Rise OX2 ..... 140 A4
Third St Croughton NN13 ... 36 C3
   Harwell OX11 .... 217 D1
Thirlmere Ave RG30 ..... 257 F1
Thirteenth St OX11 ...... 217 D1
Thistle Dr OX4 .... 143 D1
Thistlecroft Cl OX14 ..... 160 A1
Thistledown RG31 .... 257 E1
Thompson Dr OX6 .... 65 F4
Thomson Ave OX11 ...... 217 D2
Thomson Terr OX4 .... 142 A1
Thornbury Rd OX8 .... 120 B4
Thorncliffe Rd OX2 ...... 123 D3
Thorne Cl OX5 .... 92 B1
Thorne La OX10 .... 202 B1
Thorney Leys OX8 .... 117 F4
Thornhill OX17 .... 10 C2
Thornhill OX12 .... 214 B3
Thornhill Wlk OX14 ...... 159 F1
Thorningdown OX11 ..... 235 E4
Thorpe Cl OX16 .... 16 C3
Thorpe Dr OX16 .... 16 C3
Thorpe La OX16 .... 16 C3
Thorpe Mead OX16 .... 16 C3
Thorpe Pl OX16 .... 16 C3
Thorpe Rd Chacombe OX17 ... 10 C2
   Wardington OX17 .... 10 C4
Thorpe St OX11 .... 219 F1
Thorpe Way OX16 .... 16 C3
Thorpes Field OX18 ..... 133 E3
Three Corners Rd OX4 ... 143 D1
Three Fields Rd OX3 .... 142 C4
Three Gables La RG8 .... 249 D4
Three Pigeons Cl OX12 ... 214 B2

Thrift Pl OX4 .... 142 C1
Thrupp La OX14 .... 160 B1
Thurne View OX11 .... 201 D1
Thurston Cl OX14 .... 179 F3
Tichborne OX12 .... 148 A4
Ticknell Piece Rd OX7 ... 73 E2
   Pangbourne RG8 .... 256 A1
   Tidmarsh RG8 .... 256 A1
Tidmarsh Rd
   Pangbourne RG8 .... 256 B2
   Tidmarsh RG8 .... 256 B2
Tidmarsh St RG30 .... 258 A1
Tidmore La RG8 .... 240 C1
Tilbury Cl RG4 .... 259 E2
Tilbury La OX2 .... 122 B1
Tilebarn Cl RG9 .... 244 B1
Tilehouse Cl OX3 .... 124 C2
Tilgarsley Rd OX8 .... 120 B4
Tilling Cl RG31 .... 257 D1
Tilsley Rd OX7 .... 42 B1
Timber Way OX9 .... 168 B3
Timbers La RG9 .... 223 E1
Timms Rd OX16 .... 16 B1
Timothy Way OX4 .... 142 C1
Tinker's La OX6 .... 65 F1
Tinkerbush La OX12 ..... 214 B3
Tinkers La OX14 .... 3 F2
Tippings HP14 .... 188 C3
Tippings La RG5 .... 260 C1
Tirrold Way OX12 .... 214 C3
Titchener Cl OX6 .... 65 E2
Tite La OX15 .... 30 A4
Tithe Ct OX16 .... 16 A3
Tithe La OX15 .... 34 B2
Tithings The OX15 .... 19 F4
Titup Hall La OX3 .... 124 C1
Tiverton Cl RG5 .... 260 C1
Tokers Green Rd RG4 ... 258 C4
Tokersgreen La
   Caversham RG4 .... 258 B3
   Mapledurham RG4 ...... 258 B3
Tollgate Rd OX14 .... 180 A2
Tollington Ct SN7 .... 172 C1
Tompkins La OX6 .... 67 F1
Toot Hill Butts OX3 ...... 124 C3
Top Station Rd NN13 ..... 24 A4
Torridge Dr OX11 .... 201 D1
Tothill OX7 .... 70 B1
Tower Cl
   Abingdon OX13, OX14 ... 179 E3
   Caversham RG4 .... 259 E4
   Marcham OX13 .... 178 B3
Tower Cres OX11 .... 123 E1
Tower Gdns OX11 .... 200 B1
Tower Hill OX8 .... 117 F4
Tower Rd OX10 .... 182 B3
Tower View SN7 .... 172 C1
Towersey Dr OX9 .... 148 A4
Towersey Rd OX9 .... 148 B4
Town Cl Finmere MK18 ... 39 E3
   Sutton Courtenay OX14 ... 200 A4
Town End Rd
   Bledlow Ridge HP14 .... 189 E4
   Faringdon SN7 .... 172 C1
Town Furlong
   Appleton OX13 .... 158 A4
   Bodicote OX15 .... 22 B4
Town Furze OX3 .... 142 B4
Town Pond La OX13 ..... 176 B4
Town Green The OX5 ..... 92 C1
Townhill OX15 .... 2 A2
Townsend
   Abingdon OX14 .... 179 F3
   Banbury OX15, OX16 ... 16 A3
   Barford St M OX15 .... 32 C3
   Harwell OX11 .... 217 F4
   Harwell, Chilton OX11 ... 217 E1
   Marsh Gibbon OX6 ...... 67 F1
Townsend La
   Marsh Gibbon OX6 ...... 67 F1
   Middleton Cheney OX17 ... 11 F3
Townsend Rd
   Aldworth RG8 .... 247 F2
   Shrivenham SN6 .... 209 D3
   Streatley RG8 .... 249 D4
Townsend Sq OX4 .... 141 F3
Townside HP17 .... 130 C3
Toy La OX7 .... 42 B1
Toynbee Cl OX2 .... 140 B4
Trafford Rd Oxford OX3 ... 124 C2
   Reading RG1 .... 258 C1
Traitor's Ford La OX15 ... 18 B2
Tramhill HP18 .... 98 A1
Tramway Rd OX16 .... 16 C3
Treadwells SN7 .... 194 C4
Tredegar Rd RG4 .... 259 C4
Tree La OX4 .... 142 A2
Treeground Pl OX5 ...... 108 C4
Trefoil Pl OX4 .... 143 D1
Treforgan RG4 .... 258 C3
Trelawney Dr RG31 ...... 257 E1
Trenchard Ave OX14 .... 199 E2
Trenchard Cl OX10 ...... 221 E4
Trenchard Cres OX6 ...... 49 E1
Trendell Pl OX14 .... 159 F1
Trent Cres OX6 .... 65 D2
Trent Rd OX11 .... 201 D1
Trenthams Cl RG8 .... 257 D3
Trevor Pl OX4 .... 142 A3
Trill Mill Ct OX1 .... 141 E4
Trinder Rd OX12 .... 214 C2
Tring Rd RG31 .... 257 E1
Trinity Cl Abingdon OX14 ... 160 A1
   Banbury OX16 .... 15 F4
   Bicester OX6 .... 65 F2
Trinity Pl OX4 .... 141 F3
Trinity Rd OX3 .... 124 C1

Trinity St OX1 .... 141 E4
Trinity Way OX17 .... 23 E2
Tristram Rd OX8 .... 118 A2
Troika OX16 .... 9 D1
Trot's La OX7 .... 85 E4
Troy La OX5 .... 77 F2
Truelocks Way OX12 .... 214 C3
Truemper Gr OX6 .... 65 F4
Trust Cnr RG9 .... 254 C4
Tubb Cl OX6 .... 65 E1
Tubbs Cl OX12 .... 214 B4
Tubbs La OX6 .... 80 A4
Tuck's La OX13 .... 156 A2
Tucker Rd OX4 .... 142 C2
Tuckers La SN6 .... 227 D2
Tuckers Rd SN7 .... 173 D2
Tudor Cl Banbury OX16 ... 16 B1
   Oxford OX4 .... 141 F2
Tudor Ct OX2 .... 140 A4
Tuer The OX8 .... 120 C4
Tullis Cl OX14 .... 199 F4
Tulwick La OX12 .... 197 D1
Tumbledown Hill OX2 ... 139 E3
Tuns La RG9 .... 244 C1
Turberville Cl OX14 ..... 179 F3
Turl St OX1 .... 123 E1
Turley La OX8 .... 104 A4
Turn Again La OX1 ...... 141 E4
Turnagain La OX14 ...... 179 F3
Turnberry Cl OX6 .... 66 A2
Turner Cl OX4 .... 142 B3
Turner Rd OX14 .... 179 E3
Turners Cl OX14 .... 160 C1
Turnfields HP18 .... 128 A2
Turnpike Rd
   Bicester OX6 .... 66 A4
   Cumnor OX2 .... 140 A3
   Highworth SN6 .... 190 A3
Turnstone Green OX6 ..... 81 D4
Tuscan Cl RG30 .... 257 F1
Tweed Cres OX11 .... 65 D2
Tweed Dr OX11 .... 200 C2
Twelth St OX11 .... 217 D2
Twelve Acre Dr OX14 ... 160 B2
Twentieth St OX11 ...... 216 C1
Twin Oaks RG4 .... 259 D3
Two Rivers Ind Est OX8 ... 118 A3
Two Tree Hill RG9 .... 254 C4
Twyford Ave OX17 .... 23 D3
Twyford Gdns OX17 ...... 23 D3
Twyford Gr OX17 .... 23 E4
Twynhams Rd OX5 .... 77 E3
Tyburn Glen OX11 .... 200 C1
Tyler Cl RG4 .... 258 C3
Tylorstown RG4 .... 258 C3
Tyndale Pl OX33 .... 144 B4
Tyndale Rd OX4 .... 141 F4
Tyne Ave OX11 .... 200 C1
Tyne Rd OX13 .... 159 E1
Tyrell Cl SN7 .... 194 B4
Tyrrell's Way OX14 ..... 199 F3
Tyrrells Cl OX11 .... 217 E3

Ulfgar Rd OX2 .... 122 C4
Ullswater Dr RG31 ...... 257 E2
Ulster Cl RG4 .... 259 E3
Underhill OX10 .... 239 D2
Underhill Circus OX3 ... 124 C2
Unicorn St OX15 .... 21 E2
Union St Banbury OX16 ... 16 A3
   Oxford OX4 .... 141 F4
   Woodstock OX20 .... 91 D4
Union Way OX8 .... 117 F4
Unity Cl RG4 .... 259 D3
Untons Pl SN7 .... 173 D2
Upavon Way OX18 ...... 115 E2
Upland Park Rd OX2 ... 123 D4
Upland Rise OX17 .... 9 E3
Uplands Rd RG4 .... 258 C3
Upper Barr OX4 .... 142 B2
Upper Brook Hill OX20 ... 91 D3
Upper Campsfield Rd
   OX20 .... 91 F3
Upper Comm La SN7 ... 211 E4
Upper Cres OX16 .... 16 A3
Upper Cres SN6 .... 102 C1
Upper Cross La OX11 ... 218 C3
Upper End OX18 .... 100 C4
Upper Fisher Row OX1 ... 123 D1
Upper Gn SN1 .... 194 C4
Upper High St OX9 ...... 147 F4
Upper Rd OX1 .... 141 F1
Upper Red Cross Rd ... 249 E3
Upper Warren Ave RG4 ... 258 B2
Upper Windsor St OX16 ... 16 B2
Upper Woodcote Rd RG4 ... 258 B3
Upperway Furlong OX11 ... 201 D1
Uppingham Dr RG5 ..... 260 C1
Uppingham Gdns RG4 ... 259 E3
Upthorpe Dr OX12 ...... 214 C3
Upton Cl Abingdon OX14 ... 160 A1
   Henley-on-T RG9 .... 244 C1
   Oxford OX4 .... 142 B1
Upway Rd OX3 .... 124 A3
Upwood Dr OX18 .... 115 F2
Urquhart La OX10 .... 241 D4
Usk Way OX11 .... 201 D2
Uxmore Rd RG9 .... 241 F2

Vale Ave OX12 .... 196 C1
Vale Cres RG30 .... 257 F1
Vale Rd Harwell OX11 ... 217 D2
   Witney OX8 .... 117 F4
Valence Cres OX18 ..... 103 F1
Valentia Cl OX5 .... 92 C4
Valentia Rd OX3 .... 124 B1
Valentine Cres RG4 ..... 259 C4

Valetta Way OX10 .... 204 B2
Valley Cl Brackley NN13 .... 24 A4
  Caversham RG4 .... 259 D2
  Goring RG8 .... 249 E3
Valley Cres NN13 .... 24 A4
Valley Rd Banbury OX16 .... 16 B2
  Brackley NN13 .... 24 A4
  Finmere MK18 .... 39 E3
  Henley-on-T RG9 .... 254 A4
  Horspath OX33 .... 143 F3
Valley Rise NN13 .... 24 A4
Valley View
  Great Bourton OX17 .... 9 E4
  Lower Heyford OX6 .... 62 C3
Van Dieman's SN7 .... 194 B4
Van Dieman's Rd OX9 .... 147 F4
Van Diemens Cl 168 B4
Van-Dieman's La OX4 .... 142 B2
Vanalloys Business Park
  RG9 .... 242 A2
Vanbrugh Cl OX20 .... 91 D4
Vane Rd OX9 .... 130 A1
Vanner Rd OX8 .... 104 B2
Vastern Rd OX6 .... 259 D1
Vauxhall Way OX11 .... 200 B1
Venables Cl OX2 .... 123 D2
Venetia Cl RG4 .... 259 E4
Venners Water OX11 .... 201 D2
Ventfield Cl OX33 .... 112 A3
Ventnor Rd RG31 .... 257 E1
Venvell Cl OX7 .... 58 C3
Verbena Way OX4 .... 142 C1
Verlam Gr OX11 .... 201 D1
Vermont Dr OX20 .... 91 D4
Vernon Ave OX2 .... 140 C3
Vestry Cl OX12 .... 196 B1
Vetch Pl OX4 .... 142 C1
Vicarage Cl Aston OX18 .. 135 E2
  Chalgrove OX44 .... 184 B4
  Grove OX12 .... 196 C1
  Oxford OX4, OX44 .... 142 A1
Vicarage Gdns OX17 .... 4 C1
Vicarage Hill OX12 .... 214 A2
Vicarage La
  Highworth SN6 .... 190 A3
  Long Compton CV36 .... 27 F3
  Oxford OX1 .... 141 E3
  Piddington OX6 .... 97 F3
  Shrivenham SN6 .... 209 E3
Vicarage Rd Didcot OX11 .. 218 C4
  Henley-on-T RG9 .... 254 C4
  Kidlington OX5 .... 92 C1
  Oxford OX1 .... 141 E3
  Steventon OX13 .... 198 C2
Vicarage Wood Way
  RG31 .... 257 D1
Vickers Rd GL54 .... 68 A3
Victor St OX2 .... 123 D1
Victoria Ct Bicester OX6 .... 65 F1
  Oxford OX1 .... 123 E1
Victoria Mead OX9 .... 148 A4
Victoria Pl Banbury OX16 .. 16 C3
  Chipping Norton OX7 .... 42 C2
Victoria Rd Abingdon OX14 .. 179 E4
  Bicester OX6 .... 65 F1
  Caversham RG4 .... 259 D2
  Cutteslowe OX2 .... 123 D4
  Reading RG31 .... 257 E1
  Wargrave RG10 .... 255 F1
Viking Dr OX11 .... 219 D4
Viking Terr OX10 .... 204 B2
Village Farm Ct OX6 .... 79 D1
Villeboys Cl OX14 .... 180 B4
Villiers La OX4 .... 142 A2
Villiers Rd OX6 .... 65 E1
Vine The HP18 .... 128 B2
Viner Cl OX8 .... 104 B1
Vinery The RG10 .... 255 E1
Vineyard OX14 .... 179 F4
Vineyard Cl 16 B4
Violet Way OX4 .... 161 F4
Virginia Gdns HP14 .... 189 F4
Virginia Way OX14 .... 179 E2
Vorda Rd SN6 .... 190 A4

Wadard's Meadow OX8 .... 118 B4
Wadham Cl OX6 .... 65 F2
Wainwrights HP18 .... 129 E3
Waites Cl OX18 .... 135 F1
Wales St OX17 .... 23 F3
Walk The OX5 .... 93 F1
Walker Dr OX9 .... 148 A4
Walker's Cl OX18 .... 101 F2
Walker's Ht OX7 .... 88 B3
Walkers Cl OX4 .... 106 A3
Wallace Cl OX14 .... 179 F3
Walled Gdn The RG10 .... 255 E1
Walled Gdns The OX6 ...... 65 F1
Waller Ct RG4 .... 259 D1
Waller Dr OX6 .... 16 A2
Wallingford Rd
  Cholsey OX10 .... 221 D2
  Crowmarsh G OX10 .... 221 F1
  Goring RG8 & OX10 .... 239 E3
  South Stoke RG8 & OX10 .. 239 E3
  Streatley RG8 .... 249 D4
  Warborough OX10 .... 203 D3
Wallingford St OX12 ...... 214 C2
Walls The SN6 .... 194 C4
Walmer Rd RG5 .... 260 C4
Walnut Cl Bicester OX6 .... 65 F3
  Deddington OX15 .... 34 C2
  Long Crendon HP18 ...... 129 E4
  Sonning Common RG4 .... 252 C3
  Wootton OX20 .... 75 F2
Walnut Ct SN7 .... 172 C2
Walnut Rise OX6 .... 48 C3

Walnut Tree Ct RG8 .... 249 E3
Walnut Trees Hill SN6 ... 228 A4
Walpole Cl OX6 .... 65 D2
Walterbush Rd OX7 .... 42 C1
Waltham Gdns OX16 .... 17 D3
Walton Ave
  Adderbury OX17 .... 23 D3
  Henley-on-T RG9 .... 254 C4
Walton Cl OX15 .... 22 C4
Walton Cres OX1 .... 123 D1
Walton La OX1 .... 123 D1
Walton St OX1, OX2 .... 123 D1
Walton Well Rd OX2 ...... 123 D2
Wanbourne La RG9 .... 224 B1
Wandhope Way RG31 ..... 257 E1
Wandle Beck OX11 .... 200 C2
Wansbeck Dr OX6 .... 65 D1
Wansbeck Wood OX11 ... 201 D2
Wantage Rd Didcot OX11 .. 218 B4
  Harwell OX11 .... 217 E3
  Streatley RG8 .... 248 C4
  Wallingford OX10 .... 203 D1
Wapping HP18 .... 129 E3
War Memorial Pl RG9 .... 254 C4
Warbler Wlk OX4 .... 142 C1
Warborough Rd
  Letcombe Bassett OX12 .. 232 A3
  Warborough OX10 .... 203 D3
Warbreck Dr RG31 .... 257 D2
Warburg Cres OX4 .... 142 C2
Ward Rd NN13 .... 24 A3
Wardington Rd OX17 .... 10 B3
Wardle Ave RG31 .... 257 E1
Wards Cres OX15 .... 22 C4
Wards Rd OX7 .... 42 C2
Ware Leys Cl OX6 .... 67 F2
Ware Rd SN7 .... 194 B4
Wargrave Hill RG10 .... 255 E1
  Cockpole Green RG9 ...... 255 D4
  Henley-on-T RG9 .... 244 C1
Warkworth Cl OX16 .... 15 F4
Warkworth Rd OX17 .... 17 F4
Warley Rise RG31 .... 257 E2
Warmans Cl OX12 .... 214 A3
Warnborough Rd OX2 .... 123 D2
Warneford La OX3 .... 124 A1
Warneford Rd OX4 .... 142 A4
Warner Cres OX11 .... 218 B4
Warren Cres OX3 .... 142 B4
Warren Hill OX44 .... 163 E1
Warren Rd RG5 .... 260 B1
Warren Row Rd RG10 .... 255 E2
Warren The Abingdon OX14 .. 180 A4
  Caversham RG4 .... 258 C2
Warwick Cl Abingdon OX14 .. 180 A4
  Carterton OX18 .... 115 E2
  Stanford in the V SN7 .... 194 C4
Warwick Ct OX6 .... 66 A2
Warwick Rd
  Banbury OX16, OX17 .... 8 C2
  Hanwell OX17 .... 8 C2
Warwick St OX4 .... 141 F3
Wasbrough Ave OX12 .... 214 B3
Washford Glen OX11 ...... 201 D1
Washington Rd RG4 .... 259 D1
Wastie's Orch OX8 .... 90 A1
Watcombe Rd OX9 .... 186 A1
Water Eaton La OX5 .... 109 D4
Water Eaton Rd OX2 ...... 123 E4
Water End Rd HP14 .... 189 E2
Water La Adderbury OX17 .. 23 D2
  Ardley OX6 .... 50 A2
  Bloxham OX15 .... 21 F3
  Brackley NN13 .... 24 A4
  Drayton St L OX10 .... 183 D3
  Little Tew OX7 .... 45 D3
  Steeple Aston OX6 .... 62 A4
Water St OX6 .... 48 C3
Waterloo Dr OX6 .... 16 C3
Watermans Pl RG1 .... 259 D1
Watermans Rd RG9 .... 254 C4
Watermans Way RG10 ... 255 E1
Watermead OX5 .... 109 D4
Watermill Way OX3 .... 125 D2
Waterperry Ct OX16 .... 16 C3
Waterperry Rd HP18 ...... 127 E3
Waters La OX17 .... 11 D1
Waterside Dr RG8 .... 257 E3
Waterslade Pens HP17 .. 130 C3
Watery La Brackley NN13 .. 24 A4
  Clifton Hampden OX14 ... 181 E2
  Hook Norton OX15 .... 30 A4
  Sparsholt OX12 .... 212 C2
Wates Way OX16 .... 16 C4
Watling La OX10 .... 182 B1
Watlington Ind Est OX9 .. 186 A1
Watlington Rd
  Benson OX10 .... 203 F2
  Garsington OX44 .... 162 B4
  Lewknor OX9 .... 186 C3
  Oxford OX4, OX44 .... 142 C2
Watlington St RG9 .... 224 C1
Watson Cres OX13 .... 159 D4
Watsons Cl OX18 .... 115 F1
Watts La OX11 .... 237 D4
Watts Way OX5 .... 92 C1
Waveney Cl Bicester OX6 .. 65 D1
  Didcot OX11 .... 201 D1
Waverley Ave OX5 .... 109 D4
Wavers Ground OX18 .... 115 F2
Waxes Cl OX14 .... 160 B1
Wayfaring Cl OX4 .... 161 F4
Wayfarings OX6 .... 65 F3
Wayland Ave OX12 .... 214 A4
Wayland Cres OX11 .... 217 E1
Wayland Rd OX12 .... 196 B1
Waynflete Rd OX3 .... 125 D2

Wayside Green RG8 .... 240 C1
Weald Rise RG30 .... 257 F1
Weald St OX18 .... 134 C1
Wealden Way RG30 .... 257 F1
Wear Rd OX6 .... 65 D1
Weaver Croft OX11 .... 201 D2
Weavers Cl OX8 .... 118 A4
Weavers Row OX15 .... 14 A3
Webb Cl OX16 .... 16 C4
Webb Cres OX7 .... 42 B1
Webb's Cl OX2 .... 122 B4
Webb's Way OX5 .... 92 C1
Webbs Cl OX7 .... 57 D1
Webster Cl OX9 .... 129 F1
Webster's Cl OX8 .... 106 A3
Wedgewood Way RG30 .. 257 F1
Wedgwood Rd OX6 .... 66 A2
Weedon Ct OX10 .... 221 E4
Weeping Cross OX15 .... 22 C4
Weighbridge Row RG1 ... 258 C1
Weir La OX6 .... 82 A2
Weirs La OX1 .... 141 E3
Welch Way OX8 .... 118 A4
Weldon Rd OX3 .... 123 F2
Weldon Way OX9 .... 148 A4
Welford Gdns OX14 .... 160 A1
Well Bank OX15 .... 30 A4
Well Hill OX7 .... 88 B3
Well La Curbridge OX8 ... 117 E3
  Stonesfield OX8 .... 89 E4
Well View RG9 .... 241 F2
Welland Ave OX11 .... 201 D1
Welland Cl Abingdon OX13 .. 159 E1
  Reading RG31 .... 257 E1
Welland Croft OX6 .... 65 D2
Wellbrook Cl OX10 .... 204 A4
Wellington Cl OX6 .... 66 A2
Wellington Pl OX1 .... 123 E1
  Watchfield SN6 .... 191 E1
Wellington Sq Oxford OX1 .. 123 E1
Wellington St Oxford OX2 .. 123 D1
  Thame OX9 .... 148 A4
Wellshead La OX11 .... 217 F3
Wellsprings OX10 .... 202 C1
Wenham Rd OX8 .... 117 F4
Wenlock Cl OX11 .... 200 B1
Wenman Rd OX9 .... 148 A3
Wenrisc Dr OX8 .... 102 C1
Wensum Cres OX6 .... 65 D2
Wensum Dr OX11 .... 201 D1
Wentworth Rd
  Cutteslowe OX2 .... 123 D4
  Thame OX9 .... 148 A4
Wesley Cl Bicester OX6 .... 65 E2
  Oxford OX4 .... 142 C2
Wesley Dr OX16 .... 16 A2
Wesley La OX6 .... 65 F1
Wesley Pl OX17 .... 10 C2
Wessex Cl SN7 .... 173 D2
Wessex Rd OX11 .... 218 C4
Wessex Way Grove OX12 .. 214 B4
  Highworth SN6 .... 190 A4
West Ave OX14 .... 160 A1
West Bar St OX16 .... 16 B3
West Chiltern RG8 .... 250 C4
West Cotts OX6 .... 52 B1
West Croft OX10 .... 182 B3
West Dr Harwell OX11 .... 217 D2
  Sonning RG4 .... 260 C1
West Edge OX6 .... 67 F1
West End
  Brightwell-cum-S OX10 .. 202 B1
  Chipping Norton OX7 ...... 42 C1
  Cholsey OX10 .... 220 C1
  Combe OX8 .... 90 A2
  Hornton OX15 .... 7 E3
  Kingham OX7 .... 54 C2
  Launton OX6 .... 66 B1
  Witney OX8 .... 104 A1
  Wootton OX20 .... 75 F2
West End Cl OX6 .... 66 B1
West End Ind Est OX8 ... 104 A1
West End La
  Bishopstone SN6 .... 227 E2
  Merton OX6 .... 95 E4
West Hawthorn Rd OX6 .. 81 E2
West Hill OX12 .... 214 B2
West Lockinge OX12 ...... 215 E2
West Oxon Ind Park OX18 .. 115 F2
West Rd RG9 .... 242 A1
West St Banbury OX15, OX16 .. 16 C4
  Bicester OX6 .... 65 E2
  Childrey OX12 .... 213 D2
  Chipping Norton OX7 ...... 42 C1
  Henley-on-T RG9 .... 244 B1
  Kingham OX7 .... 54 C2
  Oxford OX2 .... 123 D1
  Shutford OX15 .... 14 A3
  Sparsholt OX12 .... 212 C2
West St Helen St OX14 .. 179 F3
West View Oxford OX4 ... 142 A2
  Upper Heyford OX6 .... 49 D3
West Way Lechlade GL7 .. 150 B3
  N Hinksey Vill OX2 .... 122 B1
Westacott Rd OX6 .... 81 D3
Westbeech Ct OX16 .... 16 B3
Westbourne Ct OX15 .... 21 F2
Westbrook Faringdon SN7 .. 172 C2
  Grove OX12 .... 196 C1
Westbrook Green OX11 .. 236 C4
Westbrook Rd RG30 .... 258 B1
Westbrook St OX11 .... 236 C4
Westbury Cres OX4 .... 142 A2
Westby La RG8 .... 257 D3
Westcot La OX12 .... 212 C3
Westcote Cl OX8 .... 117 F4
Westdene Cres RG4 .... 258 C2

Western Ave
  Henley-on-T RG9 .... 254 C4
  Woodstock RG5 .... 260 C1
Western By-pass Rd
  Cutteslowe OX2 .... 108 C1
  Wytham OX2 .... 122 B3
Western Cres OX16 .... 16 C2
Western Oaks RG31 ...... 257 F1
Western Rd
  Henley-on-T RG9 .... 254 C4
  Oxford OX1 .... 141 E4
Westfield OX11 .... 217 E4
Westfield Cl Benson OX10 .. 204 A2
  Grove OX12 .... 214 B4
  Oxford OX4 .... 142 A3
Westfield Cres RG9 .... 255 D2
Westfield Rd Benson OX10 .. 204 A2
  Caversham RG4 .... 259 D1
  Cholsey OX10 .... 238 B4
  Long Wittenham OX14 ... 201 E4
  Wheatley OX33 .... 144 A4
  Witney OX8 .... 104 A1
Westfield Way OX12 ...... 215 D3
Westfields OX14 .... 179 E4
Westholm Ct OX6 .... 65 F1
Westland Rd SN7 .... 172 C1
Westland Way OX20 .... 91 D4
Westlands Ave OX6 .... 79 D1
Westlands Dr OX3 .... 124 A3
Westleigh Dr RG4 .... 252 C2
Westminster Cl NN13 ...... 24 A4
Westminster Cres NN13 .. 24 A4
Westminster Way
  Banbury OX16 .... 16 C3
  N Hinksey Vill OX2 .... 140 C4
Weston Cl CV36 .... 28 A3
Weston La OX9 .... 146 C4
Weston Rd OX9 .... 187 D4
Westonbirt Dr RG4 .... 258 C2
Westridge Ave RG8 .... 257 E3
Westrop SN6 .... 190 A3
Westrup Cl OX3 .... 123 F2
Westwater Way OX11 .... 201 D1
Westway RG8 .... 249 E4
Westwood Glen RG31 .... 257 E1
Westwood Rd
  Curbridge OX8 .... 103 E1
  Reading RG31 .... 257 E1
Westwood Row RG31 .... 257 E1
Wetherby Rd RG4 .... 259 E3
Wey Rd OX10 .... 182 B3
Weycroft OX11 .... 201 D2
Weyland Rd OX3 .... 124 C1
Whales La OX6 .... 67 F1
Wharf Cl OX14 .... 179 F3
Wharf La Henley-on-T RG9 .. 244 C1
  Lechlade GL7 .... 150 B2
  Souldern OX6 .... 35 D2
Wharf Rd OX10 .... 203 D3
Wharton Rd OX3 .... 124 B2
Whatleys Orch SN6 .... 227 E2
Wheatcroft Cl OX14 ...... 160 A1
Wheatfields OX11 .... 218 B4
Wheatley Campus
  (Brookes Univ) OX33 ... 126 B1
Wheatley Cl OX16 .... 16 C1
Wheatley Rd
  Garsington OX44 .... 143 F2
  Islip OX5 .... 109 F4
  Stanton St John OX33 ... 125 F2
Wheeler Ct RG31 .... 257 F1
Wheeler Rd OX9 .... 168 B3
Wheeler's Rise NN13 ...... 36 B4
Whimbrel Way OX16 .... 16 C2
Whimorel Cl OX16 .... 66 A1
Whirlwind Way OX10 ..... 204 B2
Whitamore Row RG9 ..... 254 C4
Whitby Green RG4 .... 259 E3
Whitchurch Rd RG8 .... 256 B3
White Cross OX13 .... 159 E2
White Hart HP18 .... 98 A4
White Hart Cl OX10 .... 203 F2
White Hart Wlk SN7 ...... 172 C2
White Hill
  Bishopstone SN6 .... 227 D1
  Burford OX18 .... 101 D2
  Henley-on-T RG9 .... 244 C1
  Shiplake RG9 .... 254 A3
White Hill La OX1 .... 140 A1
White Horse Cres OX12 .. 214 B4
White House Rd OX10 ... 239 F4
White La RG9 .... 243 F4
White Leys Cl OX11 ...... 200 C1
White Lion Wlk OX6 .... 16 B3
White Lodge Cl RG31 .... 257 D2
White Mews OX18 .... 100 C2
White Post Rd OX15 .... 16 C1
White Rd Chilton OX11 ... 235 E4
  East Hendred OX12 ...... 216 C4
  Oxford OX4 .... 142 C3
White Shoot OX11 .... 237 D3
White Way OX5 .... 108 C4
White's La OX14 .... 160 B2
Whitecross Rd HP17 ..... 130 C3
Whitehall Cl OX8 .... 102 B1
Whitehall La RG8 .... 241 D4
Whitehorn Way OX4 ...... 142 C1
Whitehorns Way OX14 .. 179 D1
Whitehouse Cl OX13 ..... 159 E1
Whitehouse La OX7 .... 42 C1
Whitehouse Rd
  Oxford RG8 .... 141 E4
  Woodcote RG8 .... 250 C4
Whitelock Rd OX14 .... 159 F1
Whitemoor La RG8 .... 249 D1
Whites Forge OX13 .... 158 A4
Whiteway OX17 .... 3 F2

Whitings La OX8 .... 104 A4
Whitley Cres OX6 .... 66 A2
Whitley Dr OX6 .... 63 E4
Whitley Rd OX10 .... 221 D1
Whitson Pl OX4 .... 142 A4
Whittall St OX17 .... 23 D3
Whittington Pl OX18 ..... 115 E1
Whittle Rd OX7 .... 148 A4
Whittons Cl OX15 .... 30 A4
Wick Cl Abingdon OX14 .. 160 B1
  Oxford OX3 .... 124 C2
Wick Green OX12 .... 196 B1
Wicks Cl OX18 .... 152 C4
Widmere La RG4 .... 253 D3
Widnell La OX6 .... 97 E4
Wigan's La HP14 .... 169 E3
Wigginton Rd OX15 .... 31 E4
Wigmore La RG30 .... 258 B1
Wigod Way OX10 .... 203 E1
Wilberforce St OX3 .... 124 B1
Wilcher Cl OX11 .... 218 C3
Wilcote La OX7 .... 88 A2
Wilcote Rd OX3 .... 124 C2
Wilcote Riding OX7 .... 88 B3
Wilcote View OX8 .... 105 E3
Wilcox Rd OX7 .... 42 C2
Wilder Ave RG8 .... 256 C3
Wilding Rd OX10 .... 203 E1
Wildmere Cl OX16 .... 16 C4
Wildmere Rd OX16 .... 9 F1
Wildmoor Gate OX14 .... 159 F1
Wilkins Rd OX4 .... 142 B3
Willes Cl SN7 .... 172 C2
William Bliss Ave OX7 .... 42 C1
William Cl OX16 .... 15 F4
William Kimber Cres OX3 .. 124 C2
William Orchard Cl OX3 .. 124 B2
William Smith Cl OX7 ...... 55 F2
William St OX3 .... 123 F2
Williamscot Hill OX17 .... 10 A3
Williamson Way OX4 ..... 142 A2
Willis Ct OX7 .... 70 B1
Willoughby Rd OX16 .... 16 B1
Willow Cl Garsington OX44 .. 143 E1
  Watlington OX9 .... 186 A1
  Yarnton OX5 .... 108 A3
Willow Court La OX10 .... 238 C3
Willow End GL56 .... 27 D1
Willow Gdns RG31 .... 257 D1
Willow La
  Milton (Abingdon) OX14 .. 199 E3
  Wantage OX12 .... 214 B2
  Wargrave RG10 .... 255 E2
Willow Mead OX44 .... 184 B3
Willow Rd Ambrosden OX6 .. 81 E2
  Banbury OX16 .... 16 B1
  Brackley NN13 .... 24 A3
  Chinnor OX9 .... 168 B3
  Thame OX9 .... 129 F1
Willow Tree Cl OX13 ..... 159 E1
Willow Way Begbroke OX5 .. 92 A1
  Kennington OX1 .... 160 C4
  Oxford OX4 .... 142 C1
Willow Wlk OX12 .... 214 B3
Willowbrook OX8 .... 137 F4
Willows Edge OX8 .... 120 B4
Willows The
  Caversham RG4 .... 259 D1
  Grove OX12 .... 214 B4
  Highworth SN6 .... 190 A3
  Witney OX8 .... 104 B1
  Wootton (Oxford) OX13 .. 159 D4
Willowside RG5 .... 260 C1
Wills Rd OX11 .... 200 B1
Wilmot Cl OX8 .... 117 F3
Wilmot Way OX12 .... 214 C3
Wilmots OX44 .... 162 A3
Wilsdon Way OX5 .... 92 B1
Wilsham Rd OX14 .... 179 F3
Wilson Ave RG9 .... 254 C4
Wilson Way OX6 .... 65 F4
Wilsons Cl OX14 .... 201 E4
Wilwyne Cl RG4 .... 259 E2
Wimble Straw Rd OX10 .. 182 B2
Wimblestraw Rd OX10 .. 182 B3
Wimborne Ave OX16 ...... 16 A3
Wimbourne Gdns RG30 .. 258 A1
Winaway OX11 .... 217 E3
Winchelsea Cl OX16 .... 8 C1
Winchester Cl OX16 .... 16 C4
Winchester Rd OX2 .... 123 D2
Winchester Way OX12 ... 214 B3
Wincroft Rd RG4 .... 258 C3
Windale Ave OX4 .... 142 C1
Windbush Mews OX11 ... 201 D2
Windle Gdns OX6 .... 65 E1
Windmill Ave OX6 .... 65 F2
Windmill Cl
  Banbury OX15, OX16 .... 16 B2
  Deddington OX15 .... 33 F2
  North Leigh OX8 .... 105 D3
  Towersey OX9 .... 148 C4
Windmill Heights OX8 ... 105 D3
Windmill La OX33 .... 144 A4
Windmill Pl OX12 .... 213 F2
Windmill Rd
  Haddenham HP17 .... 130 C3
  North Leigh OX8 .... 105 D3
  Oxford OX3 .... 124 B1
  Thame OX9 .... 130 C1
  Thame OX9 .... 147 F4
  Towersey OX9 .... 148 C4
Windmill St Brill HP18 .... 98 A1
  Deddington OX15 .... 33 F2
Windrush OX16 .... 16 A4

Windrush Cl Bicester OX6 ..... 65 E1
Burford OX18 .... 100 C2
Grove OX12 .... 196 B1
Witney OX8 .... 103 F1
Windrush Ct
Abingdon OX14 .... 179 E4
Burford OX18 .... 100 C2
Windrush Park Rd OX8 ...... 103 E1
Windrush Rd OX10 .... 182 B2
Windrush Valley Rd OX8 ... 103 F1
Windrush Way
Abingdon OX14 .... 160 A1
Standlake OX8 .... 137 E3
Windsor Cl Carterton OX18 .. 115 E1
Didcot OX11 .... 219 D4
Kings Sutton OX17 .... 23 F3
Windsor Cres
East Hagbourne OX11 .... 218 C3
Marston OX3 .... 123 F3
Windsor St Banbury OX16 ... 16 B3
Oxford OX3 .... 124 B1
Windsor Terr OX16 .... 16 B3
Windy Ridge SN7 .... 173 D2
Wingate Cl OX4 .... 142 C2
Wingfield Cl OX10 .... 204 C2
Winnyards The OX2 .... 139 F2
Winsmore La OX14 .... 179 F3
Winston Cl OX5 .... 108 C4
Winston Way RG8 .... 257 D3
Winter La OX12 .... 196 C4
Winter's Field UX10 .... 221 F4
Winterberry Way RG4 .... 258 C3
Winterborne Rd OX14 .... 179 E4
Winterbourne Cl OX6 .... 65 E1
Winterbrook OX10 .... 221 E3
Winterbrook La OX10 .... 221 E3
Wintergreen La OX10 .... 221 E3
Winters Way OX15 .... 21 E2
Wintringham Way RG8 .... 257 E3
Wise Ave OX5 .... 92 B1
Wise Cl OX15 .... 22 C4
Wise Cres OX6 .... 52 B3
Wisteria The OX16 .... 9 D1
Witan Way Wantage OX12 .. 214 B3
Witney OX8 .... 118 A4
Wither's Ct OX7 .... 42 C2
Withers Way OX7 .... 42 C1
Withington Ct OX14 .... 179 F4
Withington Rd OX6 .... 65 F1
Withycombe Dr OX16 .... 15 F3

Witney La OX8 .... 86 C2
Witney Rd
Brize Norton OX18 .... 116 B3
Crawley OX8 .... 103 F2
Ducklington OX8 .... 118 A3
Eynsham OX8 .... 120 B4
Finstock OX7 .... 88 A3
Leafield OX8 .... 87 D1
Long Hanborough OX8 ...... 90 A1
Standlake OX8 .... 137 D2
Witney St OX18 .... 100 C3
Wittenham Ave RG31 .... 257 D3
Wittenham Cl
Wallingford OX10 .... 203 E1
Woodcote RG8 .... 250 C4
Wittenham La OX10 .... 202 B4
Woburn Cl Banbury OX16 .... 16 C4
Caversham RG4 .... 258 C2
Wolseley Cl OX16 .... 16 A4
Wolsey Ct OX20 .... 91 F2
Wolsey Rd
Caversham RG4 .... 259 D1
Cutteslowe OX2 .... 109 D1
Wolvercote Green OX2 ..... 122 C4
Wolvercote Rdbt OX2 .... 108 C1
Wood End OX16 .... 16 C2
Wood Farm Rd OX3 .... 124 C1
Wood Gr RG8 .... 250 C4
Wood La Hailey OX8 .... 104 A4
Kidmore End RG4 .... 252 B2
Leafield OX8 .... 87 F1
Sonning Common RG4 ...... 252 C3
Woodcote RG8 .... 250 B4
Wood Lane Cl RG4 .... 252 C3
Wood St OX10 .... 221 E4
Wood's Farm Rd OX12 .... 216 B4
Woodberry Cl RG4 .... 259 D2
Woodbine Pl OX1 .... 123 D1
Woodbridge Cl OX18 .... 135 F1
Woodcote Rd Bicester OX6 ... 66 A4
Caversham RG4 .... 258 C2
South Stoke RG8 .... 239 F2
Woodcote Way
Abingdon OX14 .... 179 F2
Caversham RG4 .... 258 B3
Woodcroft OX1 .... 141 F1
Woodfield OX16 .... 16 A4
Woodfield Dr OX7 .... 73 E2
Woodfield Rd OX6 .... 65 F2
Woodford Cl
Caversham RG4 .... 258 C2
Enstone OX7 .... 58 C3
Woodgate Cl OX12 .... 196 B1

Woodgreen Ave OX16 .... 16 A3
Woodgreen Hill OX8 .... 104 B1
Woodhall Dr OX16 .... 16 C2
Woodhill Dr OX12 .... 214 B4
Woodhill La OX12 .... 214 A4
Woodhouse Way OX4 .... 142 A2
Woodland Rise OX8 .... 89 E4
Woodlands Freeland OX8 .... 106 A4
Kidlington OX5 .... 109 D4
Standlake OX8 .... 137 E2
Woodlands Cl
Milton-u-W OX7 .... 70 A1
Oxford OX3 .... 124 A2
Woodlands Gr RG4 .... 259 F2
Shiplake RG9 .... 254 C2
Sonning Common RG4 ...... 252 C3
Witney OX8 .... 104 B1
Woodlands The OX6 .... 79 F4
Woodley Cl OX14 .... 159 F2
Woodpecker Gn 11 OX4 .... 142 C1
Woodperry Rd OX3 .... 111 D1
Woodpiece Rd OX6 .... 96 C4
Woodruff Cl OX4 .... 142 C1
Woods Rd RG4 .... 259 F2
Woodside OX8 .... 105 E3
Woodside La RG4 .... 252 B3
Woodstock Cl OX2 .... 123 D4
Woodstock Rd
Begbroke OX5 .... 108 B2
Charlbury OX7 .... 73 E1
Cutteslowe OX2 .... 108 B2
Kidlington OX5 .... 91 F2
Oxford OX2 .... 123 D3
Stonesfield OX8 .... 89 E4
Witney OX8 .... 104 B1
Yarnton OX5 .... 108 B2
Woodview SN7 .... 172 C2
Woodview Rd RG8 .... 256 B3
Woodville OX9 .... 168 B3
Woodway Rd
Blewbury OX11 .... 237 D4
Middle Barton OX7 .... 60 C4
Sibford Ferris OX15 ...... 19 D4
Woolgate OX8 .... 118 A4
Woolstone Rd
Uffington SN7 .... 211 D3
Woolstone SN7 .... 211 D3
Wootten Dr OX4 .... 142 A2
Wootten End OX8 .... 89 E4
Wootton Rd
Abingdon OX13, OX14 ...... 159 F1
Henley-on-T RG9 .... 254 B4

Worcester Dr OX11 .... 219 D4
Worcester Pl OX1 .... 123 D1
Worcester Rd OX7 .... 42 B1
Worcester St OX1 .... 123 D1
Wordsworth Cl Bicester OX6 65 D2
Stanford in the V SN7 .... 194 B4
Wordsworth Ct RG4 .... 259 E4
Wordsworth Rd OX14 .... 179 E3
Workhouse La OX15 .... 21 E3
Wormald Rd OX10 .... 221 E3
Worminghall Rd HP18 .... 127 F2
Wormsley Cres HP14 .... 188 B2
Wortham Rd OX11 .... 200 B1
Worthington Way UX12 ...... 214 B3
Worton Rd OX7 .... 46 C1
Wotton End HP18 .... 98 B4
Wren Rd OX2 .... 109 E1
Wrenfield Dr RG4 .... 258 C3
Wright Cl GL54 .... 68 A3
Wright Rd GL54 .... 68 A3
Wrightson Cl OX33 .... 143 E3
Wroslyn Rd OX8 .... 106 A4
Wroxton Ct OX15 .... 15 D4
Wyatt Rd OX2 .... 109 D1
Wychcotes RG4 .... 258 C2
Wychwood Cl Benson OX10 .. 204 A2
Carterton OX18 .... 115 E3
Charlbury OX7 .... 73 E2
Milton-u-W OX7 .... 85 D4
Sonning Common RG4 ...... 252 C3
Witney OX8 .... 117 F4
Wychwood Dr OX7 .... 70 A1
Wychwood Gdns OX16 .... 16 A2
Wychwood La OX3 .... 125 D1
Wychwood Paddocks OX7 .. 73 D2
Wychwood View OX8 .... 102 C1
Wycombe Rd
Beacon's Bottom HP14 ..... 189 E2
Stokenchurch HP14 .... 189 E2
Wycombe Way OX18 .... 115 F1
Wye Cl OX6 .... 65 D2
Wyfold La RG9 .... 252 B4
Wyfold Rd RG4 .... 252 A3
Wykeham Cres OX4 .... 142 A2
Wykeham Gate HP17 .... 130 C3
Wykeham Park OX9 .... 148 A4
Wykeham Rise OX9 .... 168 B3
Wykeham Way HP17 .... 130 C3
Wykham Gdns OX16 .... 16 A2
Wykham La
Banbury OX15, OX16 .... 16 A1
Broughton OX15 .... 15 F1
Wykham Pl OX16 .... 16 A2

Wylie Cl OX3 .... 124 B3
Wynbush Rd OX4 .... 142 A2
Wyncies The SN6 .... 227 E2
Wyndale Cl RG9 .... 244 C1
Wyndham Cres RG5 .... 260 B1
Wyndham Gdns OX10 .... 221 B4
Wyndham Way OX2 .... 123 D3
Wyndyke Furlong OX14 ...... 179 E4
Wyre Ct RG31 .... 257 F2
Wysdom Way OX18 .... 100 C2
Wytham Cl OX8 .... 120 C4
Wytham St OX1 .... 141 F3
Wytham View OX8 .... 120 C4

Yare Ct OX11 .... 201 D3
Yarnell's Hill OX2 .... 140 B4
Yarnell's Rd OX2 .... 140 B4
Yarnton Cl RG4 .... 259 E3
Yarnton Ct OX5 .... 108 C4
Yarnton La OX5 .... 108 B3
Yarnton Rd Cassington OX8 . 107 E2
Kidlington OX5 .... 108 C4
Yarrow Cl OX4 .... 142 C1
Yatesbury Rd OX18 .... 115 F2
Yealm Cl OX11 .... 200 C2
Yeates Cl OX9 .... 129 F1
Yeats Cl OX4 .... 142 C3
Yeftly Dr OX4 .... 142 A1
Yeld Hall Rd OX14 .... 160 A1
Yeomans Cl NN13 .... 24 A3
Yew Cl Bicester OX6 .... 65 F3
Garsington OX4 .... 143 D3
Yew Tree Cl OX9 .... 166 B4
Yew Tree Ct RG8 .... 249 E3
Yew Tree Mews OX14 .... 179 F4
Yew Tree Rise NN13 .... 24 A3
Yolsum Cl HP17 .... 130 C3
York Ave OX3 .... 124 C1
York Cl OX6 .... 66 A2
York Pl OX4 .... 123 F1
York Rd Carterton OX18 .... 115 F2
Henley-on-T RG9 .... 244 B1
Oxford OX3 .... 124 C1
Reading RG1 .... 259 D1
West Hagbourne OX11 ...... 218 B2
Youghal Cl SN6 .... 209 D3
Ypres Way OX14 .... 159 E1

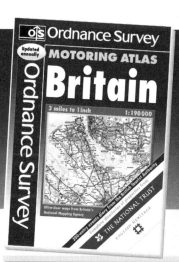

Ordnance Survey

STREET ATLASES ORDER FORM

The Street Atlases are available from all good bookshops or by mail order direct from the publisher. Orders can be made in the following ways. **By phone** Ring our special Credit Card Hotline on **01933 443863** during office hours (9am to 5pm) or leave a message on the answering machine, quoting your full credit card number plus expiry date and you full name and address. **By post or fax** Fill out the order form below (you may photocopy it) and post it to: **Philip's Direct, 27 Sanders Road, Wellingborough, Northants NN8 4NL** or fax it to: **01933 443849.** Before placing an order by post, by fax or on the answering machine, please telephone to check availability and prices.

COLOUR LOCAL ATLASES

PAPERBACK	Quantity @ £3.50 each	£ Total
CANNOCK, LICHFIELD, RUGELEY	☐ 0 540 07625 2 ➤	
DERBY AND BELPER	☐ 0 540 07608 2 ➤	
NORTHWICH, WINSFORD, MIDDLEWICH	☐ 0 540 07589 2 ➤	
PEAK DISTRICT TOWNS	☐ 0 540 07609 0 ➤	
STAFFORD, STONE, UTTOXETER	☐ 0 540 07626 0 ➤	
WARRINGTON, WIDNES, RUNCORN	☐ 0 540 07588 4 ➤	

COLOUR REGIONAL ATLASES

	HARDBACK	SPIRAL	POCKET	
	Quantity @ £10.99 each	Quantity @ £8.99 each	Quantity @ £4.99 each	£ Total
MERSEYSIDE	☐ 0 540 06480 7	☐ 0 540 06481 5	☐ 0 540 06482 3 ➤	
	Quantity @ £12.99 each	Quantity @ £8.99 each	Quantity @ £5.99 each	£ Total
BERKSHIRE	☐ 0 540 06170 0	☐ 0 540 06172 7	☐ 0 540 06173 5 ➤	
	Quantity @ £12.99 each	Quantity @ £9.99 each	Quantity @ £4.99 each	£ Total
DURHAM	☐ 0 540 06365 7	☐ 0 540 06366 5	☐ 0 540 06367 3 ➤	
	Quantity @ £12.99 each	Quantity @ £9.99 each	Quantity @ £5.50 each	£ Total
GREATER MANCHESTER	☐ 0 540 06485 8	☐ 0 540 06486 6	☐ 0 540 06487 4 ➤	
TYNE AND WEAR	☐ 0 540 06370 3	☐ 0 540 06371 1	☐ 0 540 06372 X ➤	
	Quantity @ £12.99 each	Quantity @ £9.99 each	Quantity @ £5.99 each	£ Total
BIRMINGHAM & WEST MIDLANDS	☐ 0 540 07603 1	☐ 0 540 07604 X	☐ 0 540 07605 8 ➤	
BUCKINGHAMSHIRE	☐ 0 540 07466 7	☐ 0 540 07467 5	☐ 0 540 07468 3 ➤	
CHESHIRE	☐ 0 540 07507 8	☐ 0 540 07508 6	☐ 0 540 07509 4 ➤	
DERBYSHIRE	☐ 0 540 07531 0	☐ 0 540 07532 9	☐ 0 540 07533 7 ➤	
EDINBURGH & East Central Scotland	☐ 0 540 07653 8	☐ 0 540 07654 6	☐ 0 540 07656 2 ➤	
NORTH ESSEX	☐ 0 540 07289 3	☐ 0 540 07290 7	☐ 0 540 07292 3 ➤	
SOUTH ESSEX	☐ 0 540 07294 X	☐ 0 540 07295 8	☐ 0 540 07297 4 ➤	
GLASGOW & West Central Scotland	☐ 0 540 07648 1	☐ 0 540 07649 X	☐ 0 540 07651 1 ➤	
NORTH HAMPSHIRE	☐ 0 540 07471 3	☐ 0 540 07472 1	☐ 0 540 07473 X ➤	

PHILIP'S

STREET ATLASES
ORDER FORM

COLOUR REGIONAL ATLASES

	HARDBACK Quantity @ £12.99 each	SPIRAL Quantity @ £9.99 each	POCKET Quantity @ £5.99 each	£ Total
SOUTH HAMPSHIRE	☐ 0 540 07476 4	☐ 0 540 07477 2	☐ 0 540 07478 0	➤ ☐
HERTFORDSHIRE	☐ 0 540 06174 3	☐ 0 540 06175 1	☐ 0 540 06176 X	➤ ☐
EAST KENT	☐ 0 540 07483 7	☐ 0 540 07276 1	☐ 0 540 07287 7	➤ ☐
WEST KENT	☐ 0 540 07366 0	☐ 0 540 07367 9	☐ 0 540 07369 5	➤ ☐
NORTHAMPTONSHIRE	☐ 0 540 07745 3	☐ 0 540 07746 1	☐ 0 540 07748 8	➤ ☐
OXFORDSHIRE	☐ 0 540 07512 4	☐ 0 540 07513 2	☐ 0 540 07514 0	➤ ☐
SURREY	☐ 0 540 06435 1	☐ 0 540 06436 X	☐ 0 540 06438 6	➤ ☐
EAST SUSSEX	☐ 0 540 07306 7	☐ 0 540 07307 5	☐ 0 540 07312 1	➤ ☐
WEST SUSSEX	☐ 0 540 07319 9	☐ 0 540 07323 7	☐ 0 540 07327 X	➤ ☐
WARWICKSHIRE	☐ 0 540 07560 4	☐ 0 540 07561 2	☐ 0 540 07562 0	➤ ☐
SOUTH YORKSHIRE	—	☐ 0 540 07667 8	☐ 0 540 07669 4	➤ ☐
WEST YORKSHIRE	☐ 0 540 07671 6	☐ 0 540 07672 4	☐ 0 540 07674 0	➤ ☐
	Quantity @ £14.99 each	Quantity @ £9.99 each	Quantity @ £5.99 each	£ Total
LANCASHIRE	☐ 0 540 06440 8	☐ 0 540 06441 6	☐ 0 540 06443 2	➤ ☐
NOTTINGHAMSHIRE	☐ 0 540 07541 8	☐ 0 540 07542 6	☐ 0 540 07543 4	➤ ☐
STAFFORDSHIRE	☐ 0 540 07549 3	☐ 0 540 07550 7	☐ 0 540 07551 5	➤ ☐

BLACK AND WHITE REGIONAL ATLASES

	HARDBACK Quantity @ £11.99 each	SOFTBACK Quantity @ £8.99 each	POCKET Quantity @ £3.99 each	£ Total
BRISTOL AND AVON	☐ 0 540 06140 9	☐ 0 540 06141 7	☐ 0 540 06142 5	➤ ☐
	Quantity @ £12.99 each	Quantity @ £9.99 each	Quantity @ £4.99 each	£ Total
CARDIFF, SWANSEA & GLAMORGAN	☐ 0 540 06186 7	☐ 0 540 06187 5	☐ 0 540 06207 3	➤ ☐

Name..

Address..

....

....

....

....Postcode.....................

◆ **Add £2 postage and packing per order**

◆ All available titles will normally be dispatched within 5 working days of receipt of order but please allow up to 28 days for delivery

☐ Please tick this box if you do not wish your name to be used by other carefully selected organisations that may wish to send you information about other products and services

Registered Office: 2-4 Heron Quays, London E14 4JP
Registered in England number: 3597451

Total price of order   £ ☐

(including postage and packing at £2 per order)

I enclose a cheque/postal order, for   £ ☐

made payable to *Octopus Publishing Group Ltd,*

or please debit my ☐ Mastercard ☐ American Express

☐ Visa   account by £ ☐

Account no

☐☐☐☐ ☐☐☐☐ ☐☐☐☐ ☐☐☐☐

Expiry date ☐☐ ☐☐

Signature...

Post to: Philip's Direct, 27 Sanders Road, Wellingborough, Northants NN8 4NL

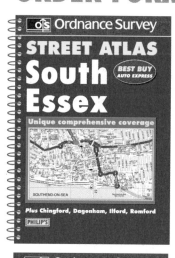

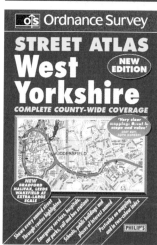

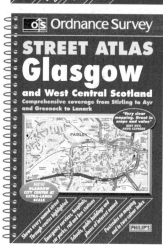